A Companion to American Immigration

BLACKWELL COMPANIONS TO AMERICAN HISTORY

This series provides essential and authoritative overviews of the scholarship that has shaped our present understanding of the American past. Edited by eminent historians, each volume tackles one of the major periods or themes of American history, with individual topics authored by key scholars who have spent considerable time in research on the questions and controversies that have sparked debate in their field of interest. The volumes are accessible for the non-specialist, while also engaging scholars seeking a reference to the historiography or future concerns.

Published:

A Companion to the American Revolution
Edited by Jack P. Greene and J. R. Pole

A Companion to 19th-Century America
Edited by William L. Barney

A Companion to the American South
Edited by John B. Boles

A Companion to American Indian History
Edited by Philip J. Deloria and Neal Salisbury

A Companion to American Women's History
Edited by Nancy Hewitt

A Companion to Post-1945 America
Edited by Jean-Christophe Agnew and
Roy Rosenzweig

A Companion to the Vietnam War
Edited by Marilyn Young and Robert Buzzanco

A Companion to Colonial America
Edited by Daniel Vickers

A Companion to 20th-Century America
Edited by Stephen J. Whitfield

A Companion to the American West
Edited by William Deverell

A Companion to American Foreign Relations
Edited by Robert Schulzinger

A Companion to the Civil War and Reconstruction
Edited by Lacy K. Ford

A Companion to American Technology
Edited by Carroll Pursell

A Companion to African-American History
Edited by Alton Hornsby

A Companion to American Immigration
Edited by Reed Ueda

A Companion to American Cultural History
Edited by Karen Halttunen

A Companion to California History
Edited by William Deverell and David Igler

A Companion to American Military History
Edited by James Bradford

A Companion Los Angeles
Edited by William Deverell and Greg Hise

A Companion to American Environmental History
Edited by Douglas Cazaux Sackman

In preparation:

A Companion to American Urban History
Edited by David Quigley

A Companion to Mexican History and Culture
Edited by William H. Beezley

A COMPANION
TO AMERICAN
IMMIGRATION

Edited by
Reed Ueda

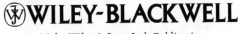

A John Wiley & Sons, Ltd., Publication

This paperback edition first published 2011
© 2011 Blackwell Publishing Ltd
except for editorial material and organization © 2011 by Reed Ueda

Edition history: Blackwell Publishing Ltd (hardback, 2006)

Blackwell Publishing was acquired by John Wiley & Sons in February 2007.
Blackwell's publishing program has been merged with Wiley's global Scientific,
Technical, and Medical business to form Wiley-Blackwell.

Registered Office
John Wiley & Sons Ltd, The Atrium, Southern Gate, Chichester, West Sussex, PO19 8SQ,
United Kingdom

Editorial Offices
350 Main Street, Malden, MA 02148-5020, USA
9600 Garsington Road, Oxford, OX4 2DQ, UK
The Atrium, Southern Gate, Chichester, West Sussex, PO19 8SQ, UK

For details of our global editorial offices, for customer services, and for information about how
to apply for permission to reuse the copyright material in this book please see our website at
www.wiley.com/wiley-blackwell.

The right of Reed Ueda to be identified as the author of the editorial material in this work has been
asserted in accordance with the UK Copyright, Designs and Patents Act 1988.

Library of Congress Cataloging-in-Publication Data

A companion to American immigration / edited by Reed Ueda.
    p. cm. — (Blackwell companions to American history ; 15)
  Includes bibliographical references and index.
  ISBN: 978-0-631-22843-1 (hardback : alk. paper)
  ISBN: 978-1-444-33883-6 (pbk. : alk. paper) 1. United States—Emigration and immigration.
I. Ueda, Reed. II. Series.
JV6465.C74 2006
304.8273—dc22

                                                                                          2005019818

A catalogue record for this book is available from the British Library.

Set in 10/12pt Galliard by Graphicraft Limited, Hong Kong

1 2011

Contents

Notes on Contributors

Tyler Anbinder is Professor of History at George Washington University. He received his PhD from Columbia University in 1990. His first book, *Nativism and Slavery* (1992), won the Avery Craven Prize from the Organization of American Historians. In 2001, he published *Five Points*, the history of a nineteenth-century immigrant enclave in New York City.

Irene Bloemraad is Associate Professor in Sociology at the University of California, Berkeley. Her research examines the intersection of immigration and politics, with emphasis on citizenship, immigrants' political and civic participation, and multiculturalism. Her work has appeared in journals such as *Journal for Interdisciplinary History*, *Social Forces*, *International Migration Review*, *Social Science Quarterly*, *Annual Review of Sociology*, *American Behavioral Scientist*, and the *Journal of Ethnic and Migration Studies*. Her books include *Civic Hopes and Political Realities: Immigrants, Community Organizations, and Political Engagement* (edited with Karthick Ramakrishnan, Russell Sage Foundation Press, 2008) and *Becoming a Citizen: Incorporating Immigrants and Refugees in the United States and Canada* (University of California Press, 2006), which won an honorable mention for the Thomas & Znaniecki Best Book Award from the American Sociological Association's International Migration section.

Nancy C. Carnevale is Assistant Professor of History at Montclair State University. Her publications include *No Italian Spoken for the Duration of the War: Language, Italian-American Identity, and Cultural Pluralism in the World War II Years*, which appeared in the *Journal of American Ethnic History* (Spring 2003). Her forthcoming book entitled *Living in Translation: Language and Italian Immigrants in the U.S., 1890–1945*, will be published by the University of Illinois Press. Her work has been supported by the International Migration Program of the Social Science Research Council with funds provided by the Andrew W. Mellon Foundation, the Rockefeller Foundation Humanities Institute sponsored by the Lower East Side Tenement Museum and UNITE!, and the National Endowment for the Humanities.

Barry R. Chiswick is UIC Distinguished Professor and Head of the Department of Economics at the University of Illinois at Chicago. He is also Program Director for Migration Studies at the Institute for the Study of Labor (IZA) in Bonn, Germany. He has published widely on issues related to the determinants of migration, the linguistic, geographic, consumption, and labor market adjustment of migrants, and the economic impact of migration on the host economy. His most recent book is *The Economics of Immigration* (Edward Elgar, 2005).

James J. Connolly is Associate Professor of History at Ball State University. His publications include *The Triumph of Ethnic Progressivism: Urban Political Culture in Boston, 1900–1925* (1998) and numerous articles and essays on American urban and ethnic politics. He is currently at work on a book entitled *Democratic Visions: The Urban Political Imagination in Industrializing America*.

Clara Cortina is a PhD candidate in Demography at the University Autonoma of

Barcelona and granted Researcher and Lecturer at the Centre d'Estudis Demogràfics. She has done work and research on nuptiality with a particular interest in patterns of assortative mating in contemporary Spain.

Albert Esteve is a Research Fellow at the Centre d'Estudis Demogràfics at the University Autonoma of Barcelona. He was a postdoctoral Research Associate at the Minnesota Population Center and the Institut National d'Études Démographiques, Paris. He specializes in integrating historical and contemporary census statistics and in international comparisons of assortative mating.

Paula S. Fass is the Margaret Byrne Professor of History at the University of California at Berkeley. Her books include *Outside In: Minorities and the Transformation of American Education* (1989); *The Damned and the Beautiful: American Youth in the 1920s* (1977); *Kidnapped: Child Abduction in America* (1997); and *Childhood in America* (2000, with Mary Ann Mason). Most recently, she was the editor-in-chief of the award-winning *Encyclopedia of Children and Childhood in History and Society* (2004) and is currently completing *Children of a New World*, a volume of essays that examine the history of childhood from social, cultural, and global perspectives.

Leon Fink is UIC Distinguished Professor of History and Director of the PhD concentration in the history of work, race, and gender in the urban world at the University of Illinois at Chicago. He also edits the journal *Labor: Studies in Working Class History of the Americas*. A specialist in labor and immigration history, he is the author or editor of seven books including *The Maya of Morganton: Work and Community in the Nuevo New South* (University of North Carolina Press, 2003), and the winner of the Thomas Wolfe Memorial Literary Award of the Western North Carolina Historical Association.

Donna R. Gabaccia holds the Rudolph J. Vecoli Chair in Immigration History and is Director of the Immigration History Research Center at the University of Minnesota. She has

written and edited many books and articles on immigrant life in the United States and Italian migration around the world. Her most recent works include: *Immigration and American Diversity: A Social and Cultural History* (Blackwell, 2003); *Emigranti: Le diaspore degli italiani dal Medioevo a oggi* (Einaudi, 2003); and, together with Vicki Ruiz, *American Dreaming, Global Realities: Rethinking U.S. Immigration History* (University of Illinois Press, forthcoming). She is also the author of *We Are What We Eat: Ethnic Food and the Making of Americans* (Harvard University Press, 1998).

David Gerber is Professor of History at the University of Buffalo (SUNY). As an immigration historian, his interests lie in social and personal identity and in American forms of social pluralism. His publications include *Black Ohio and the Color Line* (1976); *The Making of an American Pluralism: Buffalo, New York, 1825–1861* (1989); *Authors of Their Lives: The Personal Correspondence of British Immigrants to North America in the Nineteenth Century* (2005); and, as editor, *Anti-Semitism in American History* (1986) and *Disabled Veterans in History* (2000).

Marilyn Halter is Professor of History and Director of the American and New England Studies Program at Boston University. She is also a Research Associate at BU's Institute of Culture, Religion and World Affairs. Professor Halter's published works include: *Shopping for Identity: The Marketing of Ethnicity* (2000); *Between Race and Ethnicity: Cape Verdean American Immigrants, 1860–1965* (1993); *The Historical Dictionary of the Republic of Cape Verde*, with Richard Lobban (1988); and her edited volume, *New Migrants in the Marketplace: Boston's Ethnic Entrepreneurs* (1995). Her current research project is a national study of recent African immigrants and refugees to the United States.

James F. Hollifield is Ora Nixon Arnold Professor of International Political Economy, Director of International Studies, and Director of the John Goodwin Tower Center for Political Studies at Southern Methodist University. He is also member of the Council on Foreign

Relations. In addition to SMU, he has held faculty appointments at Duke, Brandeis, and Harvard. In 1992 he was Associate Director of Research at the CNRS and the Centre d'Etudes et de Recherches Internationales of the FNSP in Paris. From 1986 to 1992 he was a Research Associate at Harvard University's Minda de Gunzburg Center for European Studies, where he co-chaired the French study group, and in 1991–1992 he was an Associate at Harvard's Center for International Affairs.

Nian-Sheng Huang is Associate Professor and Chair of the History Program at California State University Channel Islands. He obtained his PhD in history from Cornell University in 1990. He has authored *Benjamin Franklin in American Thought and Culture* (1994) and *Franklin's Father Josiah* (2000), both published by the American Philosophical Society.

Guillermina Jasso is Silver Professor and Professor of Sociology at New York University. She earned her PhD at Johns Hopkins. Her main research interests are basic theory and international migration, topics on which she has published widely, including such articles as "How Much Injustice Is There in the World?"; "A New Unified Theory of Sociobehavioral Forces"; and "Estimating the Previous Illegal Experience of New Legal Immigrants." She served as Special Assistant to the Commissioner of the U.S. Immigration and Naturalization Service and as Director of Research for the U.S. Select Commission on Immigration and Refugee Policy, and currently is Co-Principal Investigator of The New Immigrant Survey. She was a Fellow at the Center for Advanced Study in the Behavioral Sciences and is an elected member/fellow of the Johns Hopkins Society of Scholars, the Sociological Research Association, and the American Association for the Advancement of Science.

Peter H. Koehn is Professor of Political Science at the University of Montana, Missoula. He is a member of the inaugural class of Fulbright New Century Scholars and recipient of the University of Montana's Distinguished Scholar award for 2005. He is co-editor of

The Expanding Roles of Chinese Americans in U.S.–China Relations: Transnational Networks and Trans-Pacific Interactions (M.E. Sharpe, 2002) and *Making Aid Work: Innovative Approaches for Africa at the Turn of the Century* (University Press of America, 1999). He is the author of *Refugees from Revolution: U.S. Policy and Third-World Migration* (Westview, 1991), and co-author of *Organizational Communication in Refugee-Camp Situations* (United Nations High Commission for Refugees, 2002), *Transnational Competence: Empowering Professional Curricula for Horizon-rising Challenges* (Paradigm Publishers, 2010), and *Transnational Competence in an Emergent Epoch*, a vision of international studies piece with James N. Rosenau, *International Studies Perspectives* 3 (May 2002: 105–27). He has taught at universities in Ethiopia, Nigeria, Namibia, China, and Hong Kong. His recent published work focuses on transnational competence in medical encounters and on sustainable development for climatic stabilization.

Alan M. Kraut is Professor of History at American University in Washington, DC and Chair of the Statue of Liberty–Ellis Island Foundation's History Advisory Committee. From 2000 to 2003 he served as President of the Immigration and Ethnic History Society. His research interests combine American immigration and ethnic history with the history of medicine and public health. He has authored or edited five books. His most recent volume, *Goldberger's War: The Life and Work of a Public Health Crusader* (2003), was awarded the 2004 Henry Adams Prize for the best book on the history of the federal government from the Society for History in the Federal Government, and the Arthur J. Viseltear Award for the best book on the history of public health from the American Public Health Association. A previous volume, *Silent Travelers: Germs, Genes and the "Immigrant Menace"* (1994), won the Theodore Saloutos Award from the Immigration and Ethnic History Society.

Erika Lee is Associate Professor of History and Asian American Studies at the University of Minnesota. Her publications include *Angel*

Island: Immigrant Gateway to America co-authored with Judy Yung (Oxford University Press, 2010) and *At America's Gates: Chinese Immigration During the Exclusion Era, 1882–1943* (University of North Carolina Press, 2003), which won the Theodore Saloutos Memorial Book Award in US immigration and ethnic history and the History Book Award from the Association for Asian American Studies. She is currently completing *Asian Americas: A Transnational History of Asian Migration to the Americas.*

Robert McCaa is Professor of History at the University of Minnesota. He specializes in population history, particularly of Latin America. Marriageways, including inter-ethnic marriage patterns, are a long-standing interest. His current research obsession is to preserve and harmonize the world's census microdata for the IPUMS-International project at the Minnesota Population Center.

John McClymer is Professor of History at Assumption College. He is the co-editor of *H-Ethnic.* His most recent book, *The Birth of Modern America, 1919–1939*, was published by Brandywine Press (2005). He has published extensively on immigrant, women's, and social history.

Jeffrey Melnick teaches American Studies at Babson College. He is also the editor-in-chief of the *Journal of Popular Music Studies.* His books include *A Right to Sing the Blues: African Americans, Jews, and American Popular Song* (Harvard University Press) and *American Popular Music: New Approaches to the Twentieth Century* (University of Massachusetts Press), a volume he co-edited with Rachel Rubin.

Paul W. Miller is Professor in the Department of Economics, School of Economics and Finance, Curtin University of Technology. His primary research interest is labor market performance, particularly as it relates to educational attainment, gender, ethnic, and racial origin. In 1997 he was elected as a Fellow of the Academy of the Social Sciences in Australia, and in 1994 and again in 2003, he was awarded the Economic Society of Australia's Best Paper Prize. Professor Miller has over 100 publications in refereed journals on labor market issues.

Michael R. Olneck is Professor of Educational Policy Studies and Sociology at the University of Wisconsin-Madison. He is particularly interested in the sociology and history of the responses of American schools to racial, ethnic, and linguistic diversity. His recent publications include "Immigrants and Education in the United States," in the *Handbook of Research on Multicultural Education*, 2nd edn., edited by J.A. Banks and C.A. McGee.

Mark Rosenzweig is the Frank Altschul Professor of International Economics and Director of The Economic Growth Center at Yale University. Prior to this position, he was a member of the faculty and Director of the Center for International Development at the John F. Kennedy School of Government at Harvard University and also taught in the economics departments at the University of Pennsylvania, where he was Departmental Chair for five years, and the University of Minnesota. In 1979–80 he was Director of Research for the U.S. Select Commission on Immigration and Refugee Policy and he is currently Co-Principal Investigator for the New Immigrant Survey, the first national longitudinal survey of immigrants in the United States.

Kenneth A. Scherzer is Professor of History at Middle Tennessee State University. He received his PhD at Harvard University and is the author of *The Unbounded Community: Neighborhood Life and Social Structure in New York City, 1830–1875* (1992) as well as articles on municipal finance and community structure. He is currently engaged in research for a study on the impact of seasons upon urban life.

Suzanne M. Sinke is Associate Professor of History at Florida State University. She is the author of *Dutch Immigrant Women in the United States, 1880–1920* as well as numerous articles on migration and gender. Her current research relates to marriage and international migration in the US context, from "bride ships" to matchmaking websites.

Daniel Soyer is Professor of History at Fordham University. He is author of *Jewish Immigrant Associations and American Identity in New York, 1880–1939*, editor of *A Coat of Many Colors: Immigration, Globalization and Reform in the New York City Garment Industry*, and co-editor of *"My Future Is in America": Autobiographies of Eastern European Jewish Immigrants*.

Michael S. Teitelbaum, a demographer, is Program Director at the Alfred P. Sloan Foundation in New York. He was educated at Reed College and at Oxford University. At Oxford, where he was a Rhodes Scholar, he earned the Oxford doctorate in demography. To date his career has spanned academe, government, and the non-profit sectors, including service as a faculty member at Princeton and Oxford Universities, as leader of a Congressional Committee and Vice Chair and Acting Chair of an influential bipartisan federal commission, as an officer of several scientific societies, and as a foundation executive. He has been elected Fellow of the American Association for the Advancement of Science, and a member of the Council on Foreign Relations. Dr. Teitelbaum's publications include 10 books and a large number of articles in scientific and popular journals.

Reed Ueda is Professor of History at Tufts University. He is the author of *Postwar Immigrant America: A Social History* (1994) and is co-editor of *Faces of Community: Immigrant Massachusetts, 1860–2000* (with Conrad Edick Wright, 2003). Professor Ueda is on the Steering Group of the Committee on International Migration at MIT and is a Research Associate at the Center for American Political Studies of Harvard University.

Xiao-huang Yin is Professor and Chair of the American Studies Program at Occidental College. He earned his PhD at Harvard University and is the author of *Chinese American Literature since the 1850s* (University of Illinois Press, 2000), co-editor (with Peter H. Koehn) of *The Expanding Roles of Chinese Americans in U.S.–China Relations: Transnational Networks and Trans-Pacific Interactions* (M.E. Sharpe, 2002), and contributor to more than a dozen books on Asian Americans. He is currently writing a book on Chinese American trans-Pacific migration and community networks.

Introduction

REED UEDA

This volume seeks to provide what has been called an "intellectual attention space," a meeting place of the mind where leading scholars, students, and informed citizens can encounter up-to-date interpretations (representative of the variety of academic disciplines) of one of the most pervasive and provocative issues in the United States, immigration. As the quintessential "land of immigrants," the United States had a special relationship to the events of worldwide history. From its colonial origins, the United States developed rapidly into the central destination point of both transoceanic and hemispheric currents of population movement. The origin points of immigration which first centered on Britain and western Europe until the late nineteenth century extended to nearly all regions of the world in the following 100 years. Likewise, the reception points for immigrants which were initially in seaports and nearby hinterlands in the United States during the industrial revolution have spread in the era of globalization to every corner of the country: thus small towns in Maine have become homes to East African immigrants and Minnesota towns have settlements of Indochinese refugees.

As a phenomenon of both global and local import, immigration requires an inquiry that embraces international, transnational, national, as well as ethnic-group levels of activity and experience. The topics investigated here reflect this range of subject matter. These issues have stimulated important scholarly research and have inspired lively debates in the political and public policy realm. The core of the volume consists of historically framed essays which analyze topics of continuing significance – such as immigration policy, education, family and gender, race relations, ethnic identity, politics, religion, social mobility, and assimilation – over the course of the mass immigrations from the nineteenth century to the present, and give treatment where relevant to the roots of these patterns in the colonial era. The essay topics are grouped under five broad areas – "Policy and Politics," "Ethnicity, Race, and Nation," "Population and Society," "Economy and Society," and "Culture and Community."

The comparative dimension is a defining feature of the intellectual approaches taken in this volume. These essays involve consideration of the differences and similarities between the immigrants of each era, and the differences and similarities between the conditions they faced; a conspectus of newcomers and their ethnic life in the nation "then and now." The authors have also considered what generalizations can be formed about immigrants of a particular historical period, as well as how specific groups can be compared within a shared time frame, in relation to central issues and themes of group history.

There is a broad outlook on continuity and change underlying these essays. Basically, interpretations are made by ranging across a succession of historical periods to follow the manifestations of a specific pattern – such as ethnic or racial identity, transnationalism, or citizenship – in the group life of immigrants and the total life of a pluralist nation. For example, how has the pattern of economic activity by immigrants evolved from colonization, to the industrial revolution, and to the post-industrial economy? To take another example, what conclusions can be drawn about how the United States as a host society worked or did not work to assimilate immigrants, over the whole span of national history?

The collection is primarily historical in approach, but many essays have been selected to exhibit the wide spectrum of conceptual and methodological approaches relevant to the historical study of American immigration. Several essays provide a social-science analysis of issues involving social mobility and the demographics of migration, while others use the perspective of literature and cultural studies: all of these offering potentially useful insights for the continuing development of historical research and interpretation. These essays are in keeping with this volume's theme of boundary-crossing intellectual encounter, engaging historiography with a host of interdisciplinary, multidisciplinary, and topical perspectives.

Each author has had the opportunity to go beyond a general summary to craft an original and overarching view with a fresh "take," to grapple with the key controversies underlying a topic, to describe why it has been a vital and stimulating subject of inquiry, and to assess how the scholarly field has approached it and should address it in future research. Taken all together, the essays provide a set of new interpretations that bridge disciplinary and chronological divides, thereby supplying a full, inclusive view much needed in a scholarly field so large that it is vulnerable to fragmentation. As a collective unit, these essays demonstrate the continuing vitality of the study of American immigration and point to future horizons of study that can serve as a new destination for intellectual discovery.

PART I

POLICY AND POLITICS

CHAPTER ONE

A Nation of Immigrants and a Gatekeeping Nation: American Immigration Law and Policy

ERIKA LEE

In March, 1882, US Congressman Edward K. Valentine rose before his colleagues in the House of Representatives and offered his opinion on the Chinese immigration restriction bill under consideration. Chinese immigrants, he and other supporters of the Chinese Exclusion Act argued, were a menace to American labor, society, and even its civilization. "The gate must be closed!" he urged (Gyory 1998, p. 238). When the act was passed in May of that year, the United States took on a new role as a gatekeeping nation, one which used immigration laws to exclude, restrict, and control allegedly dangerous foreigners, often on the basis of race, ethnicity, class, and sexuality. By the 1920s, most immigrants from Asia were barred from entering the country and the numbers of southern and eastern Europeans allowed to apply for admission had been greatly reduced under the discriminatory national origins quotas of the 1924 Immigration Act. Through the 1940s, immigration was viewed as a hindrance, rather than as a benefit, to the United States.

Eighty years after Valentine's impassioned speech, the national mood towards immigration had begun to shift. In 1958, President John F. Kennedy hailed the United States as a "nation of immigrants." Immigrants were no longer dangerous menaces, he explained, but rather the bedrock upon which the country had been built (J.F. Kennedy 1964, p. 85). In 1965, President Lyndon Baines Johnson answered Kennedy's call for immigration reform and signed into law the 1965 Immigration Act, which abolished the discriminatory system of regulation that had governed immigration for 40 years. The signing ceremony took place at the foot of the Statue of Liberty in the New York harbor and signaled a new era of immigration to the United States. Johnson proclaimed that with the new law, "the lamp of this grand old lady is brighter today – and the golden door that she guards gleams more brilliantly" (L.B. Johnson 1966, pp. 1037–40). Since 1965, the doors to the United States have been opened wider than at any other time since the late nineteenth century. Millions of people have been admitted into the country and immigration has transformed American society, economy, culture, and politics. The notion that the United States is indeed a nation of immigrants currently reflects reality more than at any other period in the country's history.

At the same time, however, Americans' ambivalence about immigration remains deeply ingrained in both public discourses and in immigration law. From the 1970s through the 1990s, an increase in illegal immigration, especially from Mexico, fueled fears of an "invasion" from the south and inspired what some observers describe as the militarization of the US–Mexico border (Andreas 2000; Dunn 1996). Following the terrorist attacks of September 11, 2001, new immigration control measures targeting suspected terrorists or those with links to terrorism were instituted, mostly by the US Justice Department and the Immigration and Naturalization Service. In the name of enhancing national security, immigration regulation was placed under the jurisdiction of the newly created Department of Homeland Security, prompting some critics to worry that all immigration would be equated with terrorism (Hing 2002).

Americans are thus once again forced to decide if immigration is good or bad for the country. Who should be allowed in and who should be kept out? How can immigration policy best serve the nation? How should the country control suspicious activities among foreigners already in the United States? And at what risk to immigrant communities and cost to our own civil liberties? Can the United States be both a nation of immigrants and a gatekeeping nation? Although contemporary events have propelled these questions to the forefront of domestic and international policy discussions, immigration law has been critically important to the formation of the United States since the end of the nineteenth century. Based on a complex intersection of economic interests, foreign policies, racial and ethnic biases, and other factors, immigration laws are the gates that allow some immigrants into the country while shutting others out. They control immigration patterns, shape immigrant lives in America, contribute to the formation of the American state, help define what it means to be an "American," and reflect and reinforce racial, ethnic, class, and gender relations. Historians have long chronicled the most important, landmark laws and studied the politics behind their passage (Divine 1957, p. vii; Bernard 1980; Seller 1984). But such a limited focus obscures the larger significance of immigration policy and its consequences for both immigrant and non-immigrant America.

Reflecting new interdisciplinary trends in scholarship on immigration, this essay analyzes a broad spectrum of local, national, and international immigration policies as well as their effects on both immigrant and non-immigrant communities from 1875 to the present. Considering the development and characterization of the United States as both a gatekeeping nation and a nation of immigrants, the history and contemporary state of US immigration law reflect a deep-rooted ambivalence about the role of immigration and immigrants in American society. Unrestricted or liberal immigration policies have acted as a force of progress, ushering in great waves of immigrants, while restrictive and exclusionary measures have legalized racism and other forms of discrimination in the name of national security. It has not been uncommon for these two divergent immigration goals to coexist at the same time. Understanding American immigration law is thus critically important not only to the study of international migration and immigrant communities, but also to the larger significance and consequences of immigration for the United States itself. The first section of this essay identifies the changing definitions of immigration law as well as major directions in new scholarship. I then explain the historical development of US immigration law and policy from 1875 to the present through three chronological sections: the origins of American gatekeeping (regulating for closure) from 1875 to 1924; immigration under the quota system, during depression, and World War II, from 1924 to 1965; and reform, "new" immigration, and transnational immigration regulation from 1965 to the present.

Definitions and Major Directions

Immigration law history is a relatively young sub-field. Primarily interested in migration patterns, community formation, and issues of assimilation, ethnicity, and identity, immigration historians have largely ignored the important role of immigration law and policy. Aristide Zolberg writes that social scientists studying incoming streams of migrants have "paid little or no attention to the fact that the streams were flowing through gates, and that these openings were surrounded by high walls" (Zolberg 1999a, p. 73). When they have focused on the laws and policies affecting immigrants, historians have traditionally focused on two areas: anti-immigrant nativism and the legislative history of immigration law. Studies of the former, building upon the foundation of John Higham's landmark 1955 study, *Strangers in the Land*, have sought to explain the motivations and social, intellectual, political, economic, racial, and ethnic factors behind nativist patterns in US history (Higham 1978, p. 4; Solomon 1989; Daniels 1962, 2004; De Leon 1983; Saxton 1971; Anbinder 1992; Kraut 1994). Other scholars have emphasized the congressional and presidential politics behind the passage of landmark immigration laws. Both bodies of scholarship employ the traditional definition of immigration law as "front gate immigration," the admission of foreigners who intend to become permanent residents of the United States (Fitzgerald 1996, pp. 17–18).

But immigration to the United States and immigrants already in the country are affected by a broad range of policies outside of those passed by Congress. These may include presidential executive orders, the administrative procedures and policies of the immigration service, and state- and local-based restrictions on social welfare benefits for foreigners, resident aliens, naturalized citizens, and native-born citizens. Studies that only focus on those who intend to become permanent residents unnecessarily limit scholarly inquiry. Foreigners arriving to and residing in the United States come as laborers, students, travelers, skilled professionals, refugees, asylum seekers, and relatives of citizens. Some are long-term residents, but do not become naturalized citizens. Others stay for only a short time and then return home. Some come illegally, either with no documents or with false ones, and are subjected to government harassment and perhaps arrest and deportation.

US immigration law thus has a far-reaching impact on a wide range of individuals in immigrant and ethnic communities. An interdisciplinary group of scholars, especially those involved in studying the relationship between law and society, have led an intellectual redefinition of immigration law to reflect this reality. A first group of writers has helped broaden our understanding of immigration law to include state and local laws; enforcement procedures by the courts, administrative agencies like the US Immigration and Naturalization Service, and consular officials abroad; and policies regulating the "back-door immigration" of undocumented immigrants and of refugees (Neuman 1993; Salyer 1995; Peffer 1999; Fitzgerald 1996, p. 18; E. Lee 2003; Ngai 2004; K. Johnson 2004). A broader perspective on immigration law has allowed us to better understand the historical development of immigration regulation and its expansion to a wider range of individuals. It also helps scholars re-examine the contests surrounding enforcement procedures, the place of immigration law in comparison to other aspects of US law, and the role that immigration law has played in the growth of the federal government's administrative power. Lucy Salyer's study of the enforcement of the immigration laws in the late nineteenth and early twentieth centuries, for example, demonstrates how federal immigration regulation moved out of the realm of federal courts and into newly created federal agencies, like the Bureau of Immigration (Salyer 1995). Many other scholars explore immigration law at its "bottom fringes," focusing on the ways in which policies have been interpreted and enforced by immigration officials, courts, government employees, and social workers and contested by immigrants themselves. The focus on enforcement, rather than solely on the legislation itself, has enabled scholars to address a number of larger issues, such as the role of government in American society, the social and economic goals of immigration policy, the rights of individuals, the construction and deployment of race, class, gender, and sexuality in immigration regulation, and the power of both immigrants and the state (Calavita 2000; E. Lee 2003; Schuck 1984; Zolberg 1999a; Hing 1993; Luibhéid 2002; Ngai 2004).

A third area of focus has been on the immigrants themselves, tracing the ways in which immigration laws have affected immigrant settlement patterns, identity construction, family relations, gender ratios, internal community dynamics and politics, social, economic, and political incorporation, and occupational opportunities (Hing 1993; Palumbo-Liu 1999; E. Lee 2003; Gutiérrez 1998; Ong 2003). These studies have fully demonstrated that immigrants have consistently and creatively challenged discrimination in immigration law and enforcement, through the judicial system, political action, and everyday acts of resistance and negotiation. A fourth group of scholars has paved the way in explaining how immigration policy is, as Kevin Johnson has described, a "magic mirror" reflecting and shaping attitudes about race, gender, class, sexuality, and national identity in the larger society (K. Johnson 1998, 2004; see also Lopez 1996; Ngai 2004; Jacobson 1998; Luibhéid 2002). Immigrants were targeted for immigration restriction on the basis of many factors, but race and ethnicity were especially important in determining which immigrants were considered to be the most threatening to the United States. Studies focusing on groups that were the greatest targets of immigration restriction – immigrants and refugees from Asia, Latin America, Africa, the Caribbean, and southern and eastern Europe – have contributed greatly to this area of scholarship. Donna Gabaccia and Eithne Luibhéid have also illustrated how immigration laws were used to control sexuality and women's admission into the United States (Gabaccia 1994; Luibhéid 2002).

While most studies on immigration law remain centered within the United States, a fifth new direction in the field has turned to the question of immigration policy as a transnational subject, one whose origins and impact may reach across national borders. Restrictions against Chinese immigrants, what Aristide Zolberg has called the world's "first immigration crisis," were implemented through North America, the Philippines, Australia, and New Zealand (Zolberg 1999b; Huttenback 1976; Price 1974; Markus 1979; E. Lee 2002b). Indeed, migration has dramatically increased across the world in the late twentieth and early twenty-first centuries, and as more nations grapple with its consequences, the importance of understanding immigration law becomes a question not only of local and national dimensions, but transnational and global ones as well (Cornelius, Martin, and Hollifield 1994).

Building America's Gates: 1875–1930s

Although the United States did not attempt to regulate foreign immigration on the federal level until the late nineteenth century, colonial and state governments played an important role in both encouraging and restricting immigrants prior to then. Western and southern states encouraged immigration to increase population in those regions. As Gerald Neuman has illustrated, state governments also attempted to prohibit the transportation of foreign criminals or paupers into their jurisdictions (Neuman 1993, pp. 1834, 1837–8). The federal government did set the terms for the naturalization of foreigners. At the same time extremely generous and highly restrictive, the 1790 Naturalization Act reflected the young nation's ambivalence about immigration and set important precedents for subsequent immigration and naturalization laws. The act allowed all "free white persons" who had been in the United States for as little as two years to be naturalized in any American court, thereby mirroring Congress's confidence in the ability of European immigrants to assimilate and become worthy American citizens. But the act also explicitly neglected to include non-whites under the naturalization statutes and thus encoded into law a racialized national identity that marked African Americans and American Indians (and later, immigrants from outside of Europe) as outsiders (Kettner 1978, pp. 108–10; Gerstle 2001, pp. 4–7; Schneider 2001).

The racial restrictions on naturalized citizenship allowed the federal government to assume gatekeeper functions and had long-lasting repercussions. When Asian immigrants tried to become naturalized citizens, they were consistently denied by the courts which ruled that they were not "white" as required by the Naturalization Act (Lopez 1996, pp. 79–110). Immigration laws also reaffirmed the ban on natur-alized citizenship for Asians (Chinese Exclusion Act, act of May 6, 1882 (22 Stat. 58); Immigration Act of 1924 (43 Stat. 153)). At the same time, the generous extension of naturalization to all whites allowed European immigrants to automatic-ally claim membership in the nation and foster a strong political presence. Although Italians, Greeks, Poles, Croats, and Slovenians were often considered or viewed as James Barrett and David Roediger have argued, "in-between people" in the larger American culture, the state still considered them "white" and consistently allowed them to be naturalized. As they explain, "the power of the national state [in the form of the country's immigration and naturalization laws] gave recent immigrants both their firmest claims to whiteness and their strongest leverage for enforcing those claims" (Barrett and Roediger 1997, pp. 9–10). Thomas Guglielmo has further argued that Italian immigrants were simply "white on arrival," and that this fact had profound implications in their ability to achieve socio-economic stability, start fam-ilies, and participate in local and national politics (Guglielmo 2003, pp. 6–7).

During the 1850s, immigration became a central political topic with the rise of the so-called Know-Nothings, an anti-Catholic political party which sought to decrease the political influence of new immigrants by extending the standard nat-uralization waiting period to 21 years. But immigrant labor had become central to the nation's industries, and the Know-Nothings never proposed restricting the flow of immigrants (Anbinder 1992, pp. 121–2). Just a few decades later, immigration restriction had become a political and legal reality in the United States. From 1880 to 1920, 23.5 million immigrants entered the United States, mostly from southern, central, and eastern Europe and from Asia (Barkan and LeMay 1999, p. xxxiv). These large-scale changes in the racial, ethnic, religious, and cultural composition of the immigrant population triggered an explosive xenophobic reaction based on racial and religious prejudice, fears of radicalism, and class conflict (Higham 1978). Combined with a new national identity that connected issues of immigration to sovereignty, the growth and expansion of the administrative capacities of the federal government that had begun during Reconstruction allowed it to exercise more control over immigration than ever before (Schuck 1984, p. 3).

The first immigrant group to be targeted for restriction were Chinese. From 1870 to 1880, a total of 138,941 Chinese immigrants entered the country, 4.3 percent of the total number of immigrants (3,199,394) who entered the country during the same decade. Their small numbers notwithstanding, Chinese immigrants were the targets of racial hostility, discriminatory laws, and violence. Opponents to Chinese immigration cited their use as cheap labor to support their argument that Chinese were a threat to white workingmen. Comparing Chinese immigration to the African American race "problem" in the south, anti-Chinese politicians warned that similar racial strife would beset the Pacific Coast states should Chinese immigration continue unabated. But class issues were inextricably tied to other race- and gender-based arguments that identified Chinese as too foreign and unassimilable. Chinese prostitution and what Americans believed to be aberrant gender relations among Chinese also fueled support for the restriction movement (E. Lee 2003, pp. 25–30; Wong 1998, p. 6; R. Lee 1999, p. 28; Leong 2000, pp. 131–48).

Politicians in Washington, DC responded to the California lobby and excluded Asian contract labor and women (mostly Chinese) suspected of entering the country for "lewd or immoral purposes" with the 1875 Page Act. As Tony Peffer has demonstrated, the law represented the country's first – albeit limited – regulation of immigration on the federal level, and served as an important step towards other immigration restriction, particularly the exclusion of Chinese immigrants (act of March 3, 1875 (18 Stat. 477); Peffer 1999, p. 28; Salyer 1995, p. 5). Seven years later, Congress passed the 1882 Chinese Exclusion Act, which prohibited the further immigration of Chinese laborers, allowed only a few select classes of Chinese immigrants to apply for admission, and affirmed the prohibition of naturalized citizenship on all Chinese immigrants (act of May 6, 1882, ch. 126 (22 Stat. 58)). The Chinese thus became the first immigrant group to be excluded from the United States on the basis of their race and class.

Early historians argued that the anti-Asian movements that targeted Chinese, and then all other Asian immigrants, were "historically tangential" to the main currents of American nativism. They identified debates over immigration and race in the 1920s – when a national origins quota system was established – as the most significant period of American immigration restriction (Higham 1978, preface, p. 167). More recent scholarship, however, argues that the Chinese Exclusion Act, together with the Page Law, transformed the nation into a gatekeeping nation. By affirming the right of sovereign states to control immigration and by legalizing restriction and exclusion based on race, the laws paved the way for subsequent immigration restriction policies. Equally important, the enforcement of the Chinese exclusion laws set in motion new bureaucracies, modes, and technologies of immigration regulation, such as federal immigration officials who inspected and processed newly arriving foreigners, government-issued identity and residence documents, such as US passports and "green cards," and further regulations such as illegal immigration and deportation policies (Daniels 1997, p. 3; Peffer 1999; Torpey 2000, pp. 97–100; E. Lee 2003, pp. 30–43).

Once the principle of immigration restriction had been established in law, Congress acted quickly to bar other allegedly dangerous aliens from the nation's shores on the basis of race, gender, class, physical and moral fitness, political beliefs, and sexuality, among other factors. In 1882, it passed an immigration law which barred criminals, prostitutes, paupers, lunatics, idiots, and those likely to become public charges (act of August 3, 1882, ch. 367 (22 Stat. 214)). Three years later, the Alien Contract Labor Law was passed on the grounds that such forms of immigrant labor were a detriment to white workers (The Foran Act (23 Stat. 332)). In 1891, Congress forbade the entry of polygamists and aliens convicted of a crime involving "moral turpitude" (Immigration Act of 1891 (26 Stat. 1084)). By 1907, another immigration law excluded anarchists and the moral exclusion clauses had been broadened (Immigration Act of 1903 (32 Stat. 1203, section 2); Immigration Act of 1907 (34 Stat. 898)). Many of the general immigration laws, such as the exclusions of immigrants who were "likely to become public charge" or who had committed a "crime involving moral turpitude," were gender-neutral, but as scholars have illustrated, immigrant women were disproportionately affected by them. As Donna Gabaccia explains, "any unaccompanied woman of any age, marital status, or background might be questioned" as a potential public charge, and sexual misdeeds such as adultery, fornication, and illegitimate pregnancy were all reasons for exclusion (Gabaccia 1994, p. 37).

Public concern about immigration in the early twentieth century revolved around a number of issues, but race played perhaps the largest role in determining which immigrant groups to admit or exclude. By the 1910s and 1920s, the arguments and lessons of Chinese exclusion were resurrected over and over again during the nativist debates over the "new" immigrants from Asia, Mexico, and southern and eastern Europe. Following the exclusion of Chinese, Americans on the West Coast became increasingly alarmed about new immigration from Asia, particularly from Japan, Korea, and India. Californians portrayed the new immigration as yet another "Oriental invasion," and San Francisco newspapers urged readers to "step to the front once more and battle to hold the Pacific Coast for the white race." In 1907, under pressure from Washington, DC, Japan signed a diplomatic accord, known as the "Gentlemen's Agreement," which effectively ended the immigration of Japanese and Korean laborers (E. Lee 2003, pp. 30–46).

On the East Coast, nativist groups such as Boston's Immigration Restriction League targeted the "new" waves of southern and eastern European immigrants settling and working in northeastern cities. Although these immigrants from Europe were considered legally white, many anti-immigrant leaders considered them racially different and inferior to Anglo-Saxons and northern and western European Americans. The sense of "absolute difference" that already divided white Americans from people of color was extended to certain European nationalities, and new "scientific" studies argued that immigrants from places like Austria-Hungary, Russia, Italy, Turkey, Lithuania, Rumania, and Greece were inferior compared to earlier immigrants from northern and western Europe. The US Immigration Commission's 1911 report gave credibility to such studies by announcing that new immigrants from southern and eastern Europe were highly unassimilable and that their presence caused social problems such as crime, prostitution, and labor problems (Higham 1978, pp. 132–3).

By the early twentieth century, the American public largely supported the call to "close the gates" to immigration in general. The Immigration Act of 1917 required a literacy test for all adult immigrants, tightened restrictions on suspected radicals, and as a concession to politicians on the West Coast, denied entry to aliens living within a newly conceived geographical area called the "Asiatic Barred Zone." With this zone in place, the United States effectively excluded all immigrants from India, Burma, Siam, the Malay States, Arabia, Afghanistan, part of Russia, and most of the Polynesian Islands (Immigration Act of 1917 (39 Stat. 874)). The Quota Act of 1921 limited annual admissions to 355,000 and restricted the number of aliens admitted annually to 3 percent of the foreign-born population of each nationality already residing in the United States in 1910. The act was designed to limit the immigration of southern and eastern European immigrants, whose populations had been much smaller in 1910. By the same token, the act was designed to favor the immigration of northern and western European immigrants who had as a group already been a large presence in the United States in 1910 (Quota Act of 1921 (42 Stat. 5, section 2)). Although the numbers of southern and eastern European immigrants decreased greatly after 1921, nativists pushed for even greater restrictions. The 1924 act thus reduced the total number of admissions to 165,000, changed the percentage admitted from 3 to 2, and moved the census date from 1910 to 1890, when southern and eastern European immigrants had yet to arrive in large numbers (Immigration Act of 1924 (43 Stat. 153); Higham 1978, pp. 308–24; Ueda 1994, p. 22). No restrictions were based on immigration from the Western Hemisphere, but the act closed the door on any further Asian immigration by denying admission to all aliens who were "ineligible for citizenship" (i.e. those to whom naturalization was denied) (Quota Act of 1921 (42 Stat. 5, section 2); Immigration Act of 1924 (43 Stat. 153); Higham 1978, pp. 308–24).

While historians had previously focused most of their attention on the nativist and legislative debates surrounding immigration law during this formative period, new studies are just beginning to concentrate on the consequences of the laws themselves and the ways in which they altered immigration patterns, labor markets, community and family formation, ethnic and racial identities and politics, the administrative state, and the very role of immigration in American life. First, immigration in general decreased dramatically, especially amongst those groups most affected by the new restrictions. While 23.5 million immigrants had entered the country from 1880 to 1920, fewer than 6 million entered from 1920 to 1965 (Barkan and LeMay 1999, p. xxxiv). In 1921, prior to establishment of the nationality quotas, 222,260 Italians entered the United States. From 1925 to 1930, the average number of Italians allowed into the country dropped to 14,969, about 7 percent of the 1921 entries (Zolberg 1999a, p. 75).

Moreover, due to the racial discrimination inherent in the laws themselves, late nineteenth- and early twentieth-century immigration debates and policies shaped new understandings and definitions of race and racial categories – a process that sociologists Michael Omi and Howard Winant have called "racial formation" (Omi and Winant 1994, p. 55). By the 1920s, a hierarchy of admissible and excludable immigrants had been codified into law, reinforcing ideas of "fitness" that were measured by an immigrant's race, ethnicity, class, and gender. As Mae Ngai has shown, the 1924 Immigration Act applied the invented category of "national origins" to Europeans – a classification that presumed a shared whiteness with white Americans and separated them from non-Europeans. The act thus established the legal foundations for European immigrants to become Americans, while "colored races . . . [were kept] outside the concept of nationality, and therefore, citizenship" (Ngai 2004, p. 27). Matthew Frye Jacobson further explains that immigration restriction, along with internal black migrations, "redrew the dominant racial configuration along the strict, binary line of white and black . . . creating Caucasians where before had been so many Celts, Hebrews, Teutons, Mediterraneans, and Slavs." By the 1960s, European immigrants and their descendants were well on their way to being accepted simply as Caucasians (Jacobson 1998, p. 14). Chinese, Japanese, Korean, Filipino and Asian Indian immigrants, on the other hand, were codified in the 1924 act as "aliens ineligible to citizenship," and as a result were further marginalized as outsiders within America (Ngai 1999, p. 70). Such debates about immigration and racial classifications directly affected African Americans, reinforcing and justifying their second-class citizenship and the Jim Crow laws of segregation during this period (King 2000, pp. 2, 138–65).

The great migrations of Asians, Europeans, and Mexicans in the late nineteenth and early twentieth centuries also coincided with and helped instigate a new level of expansion, centralization, and bureaucratization of the federal government. This "state-building" came in the form of regulating both foreigners arriving into the United States and foreigners and citizens already residing there (E. Lee 2003, pp. 21–2; Torpey 2000, p. 1; Palumbo-Liu 1999, p. 31; Fitzgerald 1996, pp. 96–144; Zolberg 1999a, pp. 71–93). The federal government increasingly gained full control over the regulation of immigration by creating a federal bureaucratic machinery with which to make and enforce immigration policy. The Immigration Act of 1891 gave to federal administrators the sole power to enforce immigration laws and established the Bureau of Immigration as part of the Treasury Department. By 1903, the Bureau had become a centralized and powerful agency and was transferred to its parent department, the newly created Department of Commerce and Labor (an act to establish the Department of Commerce and Labor (32 Stat. L., 825); Smith and Herring 1924, p. 10). In 1906, the Bureau of Immigration became the Bureau of Immigration and Naturalization, undertaking control over the naturalization of immigrants (act of June 29, 1906 (34 Stat. L., 596); Smith and Herring 1924, p. 12). By 1924, as political scientist Keith Fitzgerald has illustrated, a "national policy network for front-gate immigration policy had emerged." Standing congressional committees, national interest groups, federal bureaus and agencies all monitored immigration and shaped immigration policy (Fitzgerald 1996, p. 145).

Indeed, in the process of determining whom to let in and whom to keep out, the very definition of what it meant to be an "American" was constructed and reinforced. Excluded from the country and barred from naturalization, Asians were largely considered outside the circle of "we the people." Americans were more confident about the ability of immigrants from southern and eastern Europe to eventually acquire the necessary skills for responsible citizenship, but the drastic restrictions on new immigration were required, politicians argued, to allow the US to fully absorb the newcomers.

Half-Open Gates, 1924–65

Though traditionally overlooked by historians, the period of 1924 to 1965 has recently been the subject of renewed scholarly interest (Ueda 1994; Ngai 2004). Primarily seen as an era of limited immigration – due to the enactment of the national origins quotas with the 1921 and 1924 acts – this period is in fact significant on many levels. It represents an important intersection between the two periods of great migration, and both continuity with earlier periods and hints at reform characteristic of the post-1965 period are evident in the policy changes occurring during these years. World events such as the Great Depression, World War II, and the Cold War also impinged on immigration policies in ways that distinguished this era from other ones. Lastly, immigration to the United States did not cease despite the great effects of the restriction laws passed in the earlier period. Legal migration rose dramatically from specific regions of the world, not only shaping those immigrant communities in the United States, but also laying the foundation for subsequent immigration laws. More than 7 million immigrants and 4.7 million guest workers entered the United States from 1924 to 1954. Although these numbers reflect a great reduction in immigration prior to the quota acts, they do demonstrate that immigration was not completely halted. Many migrants during this period entered as "nonquota" immigrants, a new category created by the quota acts that gave preference to immigrants with occupational skills or who had spouses or parents already in the United States. From 1921 to 1924, professors, professionals, and domestic servants were among those with "preferred skills" allowed in under this category. After 1924, the class was redefined to include professors, students, and ministers only. Wives of US citizens and their unmarried children under 21 were also allowed to apply under this category after 1924. Such preferences were not completely new to immigration regulation. Reed Ueda points out that such selective measures (favoring occupational status and family relationship) were first instituted in the government's enforcement of the Chinese Exclusion laws and the Gentlemen's Agreement with Japan (Ueda 1994, pp. 24–5, 32). The largest number of immigrants during this period entered from the Western Hemisphere, which was exempted from quotas or ceilings. Migration from Canada and Mexico, in particular, rose dramatically in response to the labor shortages caused by the restrictions on Asian and European immigration. Over 1.4 million Canadians arrived in the United States from the 1920s to the 1950s. More than 5.5 million Mexicans came intending to settle or as temporary workers, of whom 840,000 intended to settle and 4.7 million were classified as temporary workers (Ueda 1994, p. 33). To regulate the dramatic increase of migration along the US–Mexico border, the US Border Patrol was created in 1925 (act of February 27, 1925: Relating to the Border Patrol (43 Stat. 1049–50)). Migration from the West Indies, Puerto Rico, and the Philippines also rose. From 1900 to 1930, more than 100,000 migrants from the West Indies entered the United States (Ueda 1994, p. 7). In 1920, there were just over 5,000 Filipinos on the mainland United States.

Ten years later, the number had jumped to 45,208 (Takaki 1989, p. 315). The Puerto Rican population in the United States experienced the most dramatic growth, fueled in part by the establishment of inexpensive air travel. From 1930 to 1950, the Puerto Rican population grew from 53,000 to almost a quarter of a million (Ueda 1994, p. 36). As US colonial subjects, both Puerto Ricans and Filipinos were exempted from the 1920s immigration restrictions that affected most other immigrant groups. Puerto Ricans entered the country as US citizens. Filipinos were considered "American nationals," a direct result of what Mae Ngai calls "imported colonialism" (Ngai 2004, pp. 13, 91–166).

Directly related to this increase in non-quota immigrants, temporary workers, American nationals and citizens was a significant increase in illegal immigration, which Ngai argues posed new legal and political problems. The illegal alien was a "new legal and political subject, whose inclusion within the nation was simultaneously a social reality and a legal impossibility – a subject barred from citizenship and without rights." The concept and practice of illegal immigration forced the federal government to respond in new, unprecedented ways and had a profound impact on notions of membership and belonging for both immigrants and native-born Americans (Ngai 2004, p. 27).

The economic depression of the 1930s sharply curtailed all migration and actually contributed to a large trend in return migration. Annual quotas for many nations were never filled from 1930 through the end of World War II, when less than 700,000 immigrants entered the country. The rate of return migration was greater during these years than new migration (Ueda 1994, p. 32). Nativists also renewed their calls for the restriction and deportation of immigrants during this decade, most notably Filipinos and Mexicans (Divine 1957, p. 60; Melendy 1976, pp. 115–16, 119–25). As the number of Mexicans applying for public relief increased with the economic downturn, local, state, and national officials launched aggressive deportation and repatriation programs during the 1930s. One recent estimate places the number of Mexicans, including American-born children who were returned to Mexico, at 1 million (Balderrama and Rodriguez 1995, p. 122). Furthermore, a 1929 law made it a felony for an alien to enter the country illegally and provided for more severe punishment for immigrants who returned after deportation (45 Stat. 1551).

The unrestricted immigration of Filipinos ended in 1934 when an unlikely coalition of nativists, anti-colonialists, and Filipino nationalists spearheaded the passage of the Tydings–McDuffie Act, which granted the Philippines independence and thus stripped Filipinos in the United States of their status as nationals. Now subject to the 1924 Immigration Act, Filipinos were reclassified as aliens and the Philippines were given an annual quota of 50 persons. Those already in the United States found themselves threatened with deportation and were ineligible for government assistance. The 1935 Repatriation Act – passed as part of the Philippine independence bill – sought to remove Filipinos from the United States by paying their transportation to the Philippines on the condition that they give up any right of re-entry back into the country (Divine 1957, pp. 68–76; Hing 1993, pp. 33, 36, 63; Takaki 1989, 331–4).

The crisis of world war during the 1940s had a tremendous impact on US immigration law. On the one hand, the door "opened a little," mostly in response to new wartime alliances and foreign policy agendas as well as the acute labor shortage (Reimers 1985, p. 11). On the other hand, immigration regulation reaffirmed the principle of restriction, even in the most dire cases of human need. The war with Japan necessitated the need for new and renewed alliances with Asian countries, but with the exclusion of Chinese immigrants still in place at the start of World War II, the United States faced the embarrassing situation of barring from immigration the citizens of an allied nation. Repeal of the Chinese Exclusion laws – framed mostly as a wartime measure to recognize China's new status as a war ally – thus attracted much public support and was passed in December of 1943. Historically important, repeal nevertheless had little practical effect on Chinese immigration, since the quota for Chinese was set at 105 persons per year (Reimers 1985, pp. 11–15; Riggs 1950). In 1946, Congress also granted quotas of 100 to India and the Philippines and allowed for the naturalization of immigrants from those countries as well. Both measures were approved out of concern to shore up support from Asian allies. In 1945 and in 1947, Congress continued to relax the country's immigration laws with the War Brides Acts, which allowed the spouses of American servicemen to enter the country (Divine 1957, pp. 152–4; Bennett 1963, pp. 63–4, 79–81, 86–7; Ueda 1994, p. 37). The gates were also allowed to be opened to an estimated 200,000 *braceros*, temporary farmworkers and other laborers from Mexico, who were admitted under the Bracero Program established by the US and Mexican governments. Working primarily in agriculture and in transportation, these migrants were officially classified as foreign laborers, rather than immigrants. Although the program was primarily seen as a wartime measure that would replenish the depleted workforce and increase wartime production in many industrial sectors, it remained in place until 1964. The peak year of *bracero* migration was 1959, when 450,000 Mexicans entered the country under the program (Ueda 1994, p. 34).

At the same time that immigration policy was liberalized in some areas, restriction remained the primary principle influencing others. First, national security was linked to immigration more explicitly during the 1940s. The Smith Act of 1940 granted American consuls the power to refuse visas to any individual they deemed a potential danger to "public safety." Under the act, the President could also deport any alien whose removal was "in the interest of the United States" (Ueda 1994, p. 42). Secondly, restrictionism became extended to refugee issues. During the crucial years of 1938, when pressure for Jews to leave Nazi Germany intensified, to 1941, when it became impossible for them to leave the country, the US Congress ignored a variety of bills directed at admitting Jewish refugees fleeing Nazism. Nativism, anti-Semitism, American isolationism, and the economic depression were all factors behind what scholars Norman and Naomi Zucker call the United States' "anti-refugee policy." The US State Department went so far as to erect what David Wyman has characterized as "paper walls" to prevent refugees from landing. The most notable case involved the US government's refusal to let the SS *St. Louis*, carrying 937 Jews, from docking in Miami, Florida. Not one passenger was granted a permit to land, and the ship was forced to return to Europe (Wyman 1968; Breitman and Kraut 1987; Zucker and Zucker 1996, p. 21). Within the United States, decades of anti-Japanese sentiment culminated following the Japanese attack on Pearl Harbor in December 1941. Within a span of a few short months, 120,000 Japanese immigrants and their American-born citizens were removed from their homes on the West Coast and interned behind barbed wire. Their incarceration reaffirmed their marginalization and represented an important continuity with earlier Asian exclusion policies that treated all Asians (even the second generation) as potential threats and perpetual aliens in the United States (Weglyn 1976; Daniels 1989, 1993; Irons 1993).

Foreign policy had always been a factor in determining immigration laws, but during the Cold War, the two became ever more intertwined (Zolberg 1995). The Internal Security Act of 1950 not only called for better tracking of "subversives" already within the United States; it also barred all aliens who had been Communist Party members and deported those already in the United States (Ueda 1994, p. 42). Refugee admissions were another area of immigration law that was directly influenced by American Cold War foreign policy agendas. Although the United States initially turned its back on refugees during World War II, subsequent refugee measures, primarily emanating from the executive branch, opened the gates a little, especially to those individuals fleeing Communist-held countries. In 1945, President Harry Truman signed an executive order allowing 40,000 refugees into the United States. In 1948, he signed the Displaced Persons Act, which issued 202,000 visas to refugees over a two-year period while still maintaining the quota system established in the 1920s. An amended version of the act in 1950 increased the annual admissions to 341,000, removed some of the discriminatory measures in the earlier law, and liberalized the admission and processing of refugee migration even more. The anti-Communist atmosphere in the United States inspired changes in the bill in 1953, 1957, and 1960 which allowed refugees from Communist-dominated countries or countries in the Middle East to enter the United States. These entries were "mortgaged" against their homelands' future quotas. The measure also favored refugees from Baltic states and discriminated against Jewish applicants. Such special refugee-related acts did not alter the national origins quota system established in the 1920s, but they did reflect a new trend in providing special admission provisions for various favored groups. It was in the arena of refugee policy that liberalization in immigration law, particularly in the weakening of quotas, also first began (LeMay 1987, p. 14; Ueda 1994, p. 37; Reimers 1985, pp. 22–4). Such measures not only provided a safe haven for refugees, but also reaffirmed the United States' image as a free, democratic nation in comparison to the Communist states the refugees had left behind.

One of the most important immigration laws passed during this period, the 1952 Walter–McCarran Act, clearly demonstrates both the continuity and change in relation to immigration law characterizing this era. It reinforced the tough restrictions of the 1920s by maintaining the national origins quotas, but it abolished the Asiatic Barred Zone, one of the most discriminatory aspects of previous immigration law. As a precursor to the 1965 act, it introduced a system of preference categories for skilled laborers and relatives of US citizens and permanent residents. It also removed all racial, gender, and nationality barriers to citizenship. Reflecting its Cold War era origins, the act strengthened the connection between immigration and national security by establishing strict security provisions designed to target suspected subversives. Liberals generally viewed the Walter–McCarran act as unduly harsh and racist because of it continuation of the national origins system. President Truman in fact vetoed it, but Congress overrode his veto (Reimers 1985, pp. 17–20).

Continuity and Change: Post-1965 Immigration Law

Motivated by Cold War politics and civil rights activism, the momentum for immigration reform increased by the 1960s. At a time when the United States emphasized its virtues of freedom and democracy over the totalitarianism of communism, the unequal treatment of immigrants based on race exposed the hypocrisy in American immigration regulation. Strong leadership came from the White House under President John F. Kennedy, whose 1958 book, *A Nation of Immigrants*, was an unabashed celebration of America's immigrant heritage and a call for immigration reform (J.F. Kennedy 1964, pp. ix–xi, 77–83). Following Kennedy's assassination, President Lyndon B. Johnson embraced the cause and declared that the national origins framework was "incompatible with our basic American tradition." Enacted as part of the Johnson administration's larger civil rights agenda, the 1965 Immigration and Nationality Act abolished the national origins quotas and created a new set of preference categories based on family reunification and professional skills (Immigration and Nationality Act (79 Stat. 911); King 2000, p. 243; Reimers 1985, p. 81). Cloaked in the rhetoric of liberal and civil rights reform, the 1965 act has been portrayed as representing a "high-water mark in a national consensus of egalitarianism" and a "reassertion and return to the nation's liberal tradition in immigration" (Daniels 1990, p. 338; Chin 1996, pp. 273, 277). Political opposition to the reforms was minimal (Stern 1974, pp. 248, 296). With such great public support behind them, lawmakers predicted that with the reforms, the United States – a "nation that was built by the immigrants of all lands" – would now be able to ask potential immigrants "What can you do for our country?" rather than "In what country were you born?" (L.B. Johnson 1965, p. 116).

The 1965 Immigration Act's assault on racism and the tremendous new immigration it has allowed into the country represent some of the most important changes in post-war American law and society. With the 1965 act, immigration policy grew beyond its original role of guarding against dangerous foreigners and sought to build upon earlier immigration, a legacy that was now seen as a strength to the nation. The abolition of the 1924 quota system flung open the gates to a multitude of peoples who had been excluded under the old regime, and the exponential growth in immigration has radically altered the racial composition of the United States. Prior to 1965, the peak decade for immigration was 1911–20, when 5,736,000 immigrants entered the country, mostly from Europe. During the 1980s, a record 7,338,000 immigrants came to the United States, followed by 6,943,000 from 1991 to 1997. The 2000 census figures reveal that the United States is accepting immigrants at a faster rate than at any other time since the 1850s (US Immigration and Naturalization Service 1999; Dinan 2002). Most new immigrants are from Asia and Latin America. In the 1980s, more than 80 percent of all immigrants came from either of these two geographic regions (Daniels 2001, p. 6). Between 1971 and 1996, 5.8 million Asians were admitted into the United States as legal immigrants, and over 1 million Asians have been admitted as refugees since 1975 (Zhou and Gatewood 2000, pp. 10–11). In the 1990s, immigrants born in Latin America made up more than half of all immigrants in the United States for the first time (Dinan 2002).

Despite such immense changes resulting from the new law, the act itself did not totally overturn all vestiges of the early gatekeeping system. Indeed, the conventional

focus on the transformation in immigration patterns after 1965 obscures the significant continuities that persisted in immigration regulation. Some of the most recent
scholarship in history, sociology, and legal studies indicates that immigration laws
continue to function in similar ways to their earlier predecessors. First and foremost,
the 1965 act may have opened up the gates to a wider number of immigrants, but
it never sought to dismantle the gates altogether or repudiate the principle of
gatekeeping. The United States has retained the right to use gates and gatekeepers
to control immigration and to document and keep track of immigrants already
within the United States. Secondly, restrictions based on race were formally rejected,
but the act still limited the number of immigrants allowed into the country each
year through new hemispheric and national quotas. Persons from the Eastern
Hemisphere were allotted 170,000 visas; persons from the Western Hemisphere
were allotted 120,000. No country in the Eastern Hemisphere could have more
than 20,000 visas. "Immediate" family members, such as spouses, minor children,
and parents of US citizens were exempt from the numerical limits. In 1976, the
Immigration and Nationality Act of 1965 was amended. The new provisions
extended to the Western Hemisphere the 20,000 per country limit and a slightly
modified version of the seven-category preference system. In 1978, immigration
legislation was passed to combine the separate hemispheric ceilings into a worldwide
ceiling of 290,000 with a single preference system (King 2000, p. 243; Reimers
1985, p. 81). Many of the barriers first established in the nineteenth century,
including the "likely to become a public charge" clause, physical and mental health
requirements, and ideological tests, also remained firmly in place (Daniels 1990,
pp. 340–1).

    Most notably, although the 1965 law's main intention was to end racial discrimina-
tion in immigration law, race played – and continues to play – a most important role
in the debates over immigration reform and in subsequent laws both during the
1960s and in our contemporary period. The 1965 act abolished the national origins
quotas, but lawmakers still expressed a desire to facilitate immigration from Europe
and to limit – or, at the very least, discourage – immigration from Asia, Latin
America, and Africa. Indeed, although a racial hierarchy was not explicitly written
into the new law as in 1924, it remained deeply imbedded in the 1965 act's design
and intent. European immigrants, the last group to be restricted in the pre-1924
period, were the first to be compensated for past discrimination. When Robert
Kennedy testified before Congress of the urgent need to eliminate discrimination in
immigration, the examples he cited pertained to European immigrants only (US
Congress 1964, pp. 410–12; Reimers 1985, p. 69). President Lyndon B. Johnson
stressed the bill's primary intent to redress the wrong done to those "from southern
and eastern Europe" (L.B. Johnson 1966, pp. 1037–40). And lawmakers predicted
that the main beneficiaries of the new law would be immigrants from Italy, Greece,
and Poland, countries which had the largest backlogs of persons awaiting visas.
No longer considered immigrant "menaces," these European immigrants came to
epitomize instead the nation's newfound celebration of its "immigrant heritage" by
the 1960s (Celler 1965, p. 21579; E. Kennedy 1965, p. 23352; Stern 1974, p. 160;
Reimers 1985, pp. 77–9). This emphasis on America's newfound identity as a "nation
of immigrants" was rooted in the European immigrant paradigm. It signaled the
total integration of pre-1924 European immigrants into the nation and became a

metaphor for the success of European immigrant assimilation and boot-strap upward mobility (Trucio-Haynes 1997, pp. 374, 387).

The 1965 act sought to encourage European immigration and maintain the racial and ethnic homogeneity achieved under the older 1924 quota system through the new family reunification preference category. A compromise measure between organized labor, which wanted continued limits on immigration, and those who wanted to abolish the national origins system, family reunification was supposed to privilege new immigration based on the existing (i.e. European American) population already in the United States. Critics who charged that the new law did not go far enough argued that such "reforms" were not reforms at all, but rather maintained the status quo, just under a different system and with the appearance of non-discrimination (Reimers 1985, p. 76).

At the same time that European immigrants were described in celebratory terms, concerns about an increase in immigration from Asian, Latin American, and African countries persisted, revealing continued anxiety about large increases in the admission of immigrants of color. The numerical caps placed on the Western Hemisphere in the 1965 act were designed to placate lawmakers wary of large-scale migration from Latin America. By counting immigrants from the Western Hemisphere against an annual quota for the first time, the number of Mexicans allowed to enter the country legally was dramatically reduced (Reimers 1985, pp. 84–5). This reduction has had long-standing consequences. The waiting list for applications of Mexican citizens who qualify for immigration as the brothers and sisters of adult citizens under the 1965 act was recently calculated as taking as long as nine years. Applications of those who filed their papers to come to the United States in March of 1989 were only being processed in March of 1998 (K. Johnson 1998, p. 1134). Lawmakers also dealt with Asian immigration very cautiously. The 1952 act had abolished the Asia–Pacific Triangle, which excluded all immigrants from this manufactured geographic region, but the action was viewed as a symbolic end to discrimination only. As the debates over the 1965 Immigration Act make clear, lawmakers were repeatedly assured that the number of non-European immigrants would not materially increase with the changes in the law. Representative Celler disputed charges that the bill would allow entry to "hordes" of Africans and Asians or that the bill would allow the United States to become the "dumping ground" for Latin America (Celler 1965, pp. 20781, 20950; Stern 1974, pp. 120–1; Reimers 1985, p. 81). Asian American Senator Hiram L. Fong from Hawaii declared in Congress that "racial barriers [were] bad for America," but he also assured his colleagues that only a small number of people from Asia would enter the United States under the 1965 act (King 2000, p. 244; US Congress 1965, pp. 23557–81; Stern 1974, pp. 162–3). As such cautious reforms guiding the 1965 act illustrate, the great new migrations from Asia and Latin America were largely unintentional. Congress desired to end the explicitly discriminatory national origins quota, but it did not want to totally abandon either immigration restriction in general or the racial and ethnic homogeneity that the earlier system had provided.

Given such motivations behind the act, it is thus significant that lawmakers did not attempt to rescind the laws or reinstate the older system when it became clear that the main immigrant groups to take advantage of the new law came from Asia and Latin America, rather than from Europe. The major provisions of the 1965 act remain largely intact, and both supporters and opponents of immigration characterize the post-1965 period as one of liberalized immigration in comparison with the earlier, pre-1924 period (Daniels 2001, pp. 46, 50, 58; Graham 2001, p. 157). Instead of an explicitly race-based hierarchy structuring immigration regulation, post-1965 policies give more weight to class and immigrant status in determining current immigration opportunities and treatment in the United States.

Gatekeeping ideologies, politics, and policies based on race, however, have not been totally abolished. Despite some observers' claims that the new nativism is not as racially based as the nativism of the pre-1924 period, the persistence of racialized understandings of which immigrants constitute a "threat" to the country demonstrate otherwise (Daniels 2001, pp. 46, 50, 58; Gotanda 1997, p. 253; Sanchez 1999, p. 373). The state's systematic efforts to regulate the entry of potentially dangerous foreigners applying for admission and to control those already residing in the country also remain central, even in the most humanitarian and liberal immigration policies. Gatekeeping does not function in the same way as it did in the earlier period. The immigrants, the gates, and the challenges are different, and immigration law and regulation reflect these important new contexts. Groups that had previously been targeted face less scrutiny from government officials. But other immigrants have taken their place, and the role of race in determining which immigrants are targeted follows patterns first established prior to 1924. The existence of a hierarchy of immigrant desirability and the increased importance of administrative, rather than legislative, regulations in immigration control also remain important continuities linking the two periods together. The cases of refugee resettlement following the Vietnam War, illegal immigration from Mexico, and the treatment of Muslim and Middle Eastern immigrants after September 11, 2001 are three important examples.

In its emphasis on egalitarianism and humanitarianism, the 1980 act, like its 1965 predecessor, to some extent reflects a distinct break from the explicitly discriminatory immigration laws of the early twentieth century. Scholars have described it as symbolic of "the avowed liberalization of American immigration law in the [late] twentieth century" and a "high water mark in the name of worldwide humanitarianism" (Daniels 2001, p. 44; Schuck 1998, pp. 18, 83, 291; Anker and Posner 1981, pp. 9, 12; Gee 2001, p. 577). Both a closer examination of the law itself and refugee resettlement programs, however, reveal that American gatekeeping and old and new domestic concerns about race (left over from earlier periods of nativism and produced by post-1965 immigration, civil rights era race relations, and the Vietnam War) conflicted with the humanitarian goals in refugee admissions and resettlement and became imbedded in the policies themselves.

Beginning in 1975, the United States' admission of the first waves of Vietnamese refugees was characterized as a necessary "rescue operation." As President Gerald Ford proclaimed, America's welcome to Vietnamese refugees was consistent with America's heritage of "opening its doors to immigrants of all countries." He also emphasized the middle- to upper-middle-class backgrounds of the first arrivals by stressing that the first-wave Vietnamese were "talented," "industrious," and would contribute to America. Attempting to connect the new migration of refugees to established analogies that celebrated immigration, Ford's remarks drew on the cultural pluralist notion that "all of us [Americans] are immigrants" (Loescher and Scanlan 1986, p. 113). Initially, the United States intended to evacuate only 17,600

American dependents and government employees from Vietnam. In the mass confusion following the fall of Saigon in April 1975, however, the small numbers of
evacuees had increased to a total of 130,400 Southeast Asian refugees by December
1975. By 1978, the annual admission of Southeast Asian refugees had increased
exponentially, most of them admitted under the Indochinese Parole Programs that
granted the attorney general *ad hoc* authority to "parole" into the United States any
alien on an emergency basis, with no real numerical limit or oversight from Congress. From 1978 to 1980, 267,800 refugees had been admitted into the United
States (Hing 1993, p. 126). The latter arrivals included second-wave Vietnamese
"boat people" who were primarily former political prisoners and ethnic Chinese
expelled from Vietnam, as well as a third and fourth wave of Cambodian refugees
fleeing the "killing fields" of Cambodia, and Laotian, Mien, and Hmong from Laos
who had fought the United States' "secret war" in Laos. With higher rates of
poverty and lower rates of education and transferable skills, these latter waves of
refugees arrived in the United States much less well prepared than the initial 1975
wave, and consequently faced more difficulty adapting to the challenges of their new
surroundings.

The dramatic increase in the number of Southeast Asian refugees following the
Vietnam War prompted large-scale debate about the nation's refugee policies. On
the one hand, groups like the Citizens' Commission on Indochinese Refugees
lobbied government officials to adopt a coherent and generous policy for the admission of Southeast Asian refugees. Highly publicized reports of refugees crowded into
unseaworthy boats in dangerous seas and cramped into makeshift refugee camps in
Southeast Asia led to growing pressure on Washington to take action. Lobbyists
argued that traditional restrictionist and anti-immigrant sentiment had no place in
the United States. Joseph Califano, Secretary of the Department of Health and
Human Services, stated that the refugee issue required the United States to "reveal
to the world – and more importantly to ourselves – whether we truly live by our
ideals or simply carve them on our monuments" (Gee 2001, pp. 640–1).

On the other hand, the initial welcome of refugees eventually led to debate,
negative reaction, and a return to restrictionism as both the numbers of new refugees
and the problems and cost of their resettlement grew. As early as April 1975, a
Harris poll found that 54 percent of Americans polled believed that Indochinese
should be excluded; while 36 percent believed they should be admitted. California
Congressman Burt Talcott recalled anti-Asian sentiment from the early twentieth
century and expressed American fears of another Asian invasion. "Damn it, we
[already] have too many Orientals," he is quoted as saying (Kelly 1977, p. 18).
Others connected the presence of Southeast Asian refugees in the United States with
the unwelcome reminder of America's divisive war in Vietnam. "I am sick, sick of
Vietnam, the boat people, and Southeast Asia," one letter writer claimed in the late
1970s. Interviews with Hmong refugees in Fresno, California revealed that such
sentiments were commonly made known to the new arrivals. "It seems that Americans
hate us," one informant simply told a resettlement worker (Palumbo-Liu 1999,
p. 245; Reder 1983, p. 15). In Washington, congressional debates during the Carter
administration repeatedly centered around the two themes of congressional authority
over refugee admissions and the need to prevent the opening of "numerical"
floodgates to Vietnamese refugees (Gee 2001, p. 639). By 1978, news and public

opinion polls revealed that the majority of those questioned opposed the relaxation of immigration laws to admit additional refugees. In the wake of the economic recession, a peak in American unemployment, and the continuing divisions surrounding the Vietnam War, the specter of large numbers of Southeast Asian refugees needing economic assistance and social welfare services prompted a strong backlash. In the Minneapolis and St. Paul areas, where a large concentration of Hmong refugees resettled in the early 1980s, rumors circulated that the government was granting higher welfare benefits, free apartments, and even tax-free income. Concerns that the new refugees would fail to assimilate and fears – especially among the nation's poor – that they would take away jobs were also prevalent (Reimers 1985, p. 178; Reder and Downing 1984, p. 9; Loescher and Scanlan 1986, p. 130). In short, Bill Ong Hing notes that "a major catalyst for the new refugee law was a disturbing anxiety felt by some members of Congress that thousands of Southeast Asians would destabilize many communities" (Hing 1993, p. 127).

Rhetoric surrounding the actual passage of the Refugee Act, however, largely ignored concerns that hinted at this unsavory restrictionist mood. Instead, the act was characterized by remarkable political consensus from both the left and the right in the United States. Co-sponsored by Senators Edward Kennedy and Strom Thurmond, the bill was hailed by lawmakers as further evidence of the nation's egalitarian and humanitarian policy towards immigrants and refugees. Congressman Peter Rodino defined the Refugee Act as "one of the most important pieces of humanitarian legislation ever enacted by a US Congress. . . . The United States once again [has] demonstrated its concern for the homeless, the defenseless, and the persecuted people who fall victim to tyrannical and oppressive government regimes" (Loescher and Scanlan, pp. 130–43). With its explicit welcome to refugees fleeing communist countries, the new law served America's Cold War politics, but Congress also hoped to set an example for other nations through its clear compliance with international standards in dealing with refugees. Overall, the act attempted to centralize refugee admissions by ending the executive branch's power to parole an unlimited number of refugees, and established an annual quota of 50,000 after a transition period. Presidents still retained some power to admit additional refugees as international events warranted. The act also incorporated the United Nations definition of "refugee" as a person who had a "well-founded fear of persecution" owing to race, religion, nationality, or membership in a social group or political movement. Finally, the act allowed for the admission of asylees – refugees who are already in the United States and are applying for entry and permanent residence (Hing 1993, p. 127; Parish 1992, pp. 923–4; Reimers 1985, p. 197).

Despite the humanitarian language surrounding the act, in practice, the Refugee Act resulted in a significant decline in the number of Southeast Asian refugees admitted. From 1975 to 1980, 432,676 refugees from Vietnam, Cambodia, and Laos arrived in the United States, with the peak year of immigration being 1980. By the early 1980s, an average of 50,000 refugees were admitted per year (Rumbaut 2000, p. 182). In light of such results, scholars have recently argued that the actual intent of the act was to limit, rather than facilitate, the admission of refugees from Southeast Asia. The emphasis on "humanitarianism," Bill Ong Hing suggests, clouds other political motivations such as the desire to limit refugee admissions. Kevin Johnson argues that the law's establishment of numerical limits on refugees was designed not only to restrict the power of the President in refugee admissions, but also to prevent future mass migrations. In fact, the number of Vietnamese refugees admitted fell so sharply that, in 1997, a number of Vietnamese citizens charged the US government with discrimination in visa processing under the Refugee Act (Hing 2002, p. 128; K. Johnson 1998, p. 1134; Gee 2001, p. 579).

An analysis of how refugee resettlement actually worked in practice demonstrates American gatekeeping at work and also supports the argument that the country's refugee policies were designed around racialized understandings of refugees as well as a desire to manage and monitor this particular population. Much like the intentions of earlier gatekeeping policies which sought to contain and control potential immigrant menaces, resettlement programs and philosophies drew from past and contemporary narratives of immigration and race that emphasized "transformation" in order to integrate these newcomers "without destabilizing [America's] social core." As Bill Ong Hing argues, the "same drive to control the work, the location, and even the families of Asian Americans" that originated during the Chinese exclusion era also informed admissions law and policy on Southeast Asian refugees (Hing 1993, pp. 122, 127, 129; Palumbo-Liu 1999, p. 239; Ong 2003). Thus, assimilation – shaped by deep-rooted doubts concerning the assimilability of Asians on the one hand and European immigrant models of "successful" integration on the other – became one major goal of refugee resettlement. David Palumbo-Liu points out that refugee resettlement policies "overlaid the 'classic' narrative of immigration upon the refugee crisis." Such approaches ignored the significant differences between European immigrants of the early twentieth century who came voluntarily and who enjoyed the privileges of whiteness, and post-Vietnam Southeast Asian refugees who not only experienced great wartime trauma and persecution, but who also entered a country adapting to unexpected new immigration and the divisions of the Vietnam War (Palumbo-Liu 1999, p. 242).

One of the US government's main intentions was to disperse the refugee population as widely as possible in order to facilitate assimilation and to minimize any potential negative social and economic impact on receiving communities. Initial proposals called for locating refugees on uninhabited islands or in "holding centers" for indefinite periods of time. Studies found that Southeast Asian refugees were "initially resettled in 813 separate zip code areas in every state, including Alaska, with about two-thirds settling in zip code areas that had fewer than 500 refugees. Only 8.5 percent settl[ed] in places with more than 3,000 refugees." In comparison with other immigrant or refugee populations, Southeast Asians were the most dispersely settled group (Palumbo-Liu 1999, p. 239; Rumbaut 2000, p. 183).

Self-sufficiency – informed by fears that refugees, like African Americans and other minorities, would become dependent upon welfare – became the other primary goal in refugee resettlement programs. Over the course of the 1980s, news reports of Southeast Asian refugees making "exemplary use of the welfare system," increased anxieties that they were failing to assimilate. In this way, the refugees' dependence on the welfare state became a measurement of assimilation (Palumbo-Liu 1999, p. 235). Refugee resettlement workers complained that it was "too easy" for Hmong refugees in Minnesota to receive cash assistance, and supported welfare cuts in order to "force" refugees into "work at making it here." As one government resettlement site report found, one worker suggested that "instead of just granting public assistance to the Hmong . . . welfare [should] be used as a tool to provide gentle pressure on the refugees" (Reder and Downing 1984, p. 38; Palumbo-Liu 1999, pp. 235–6, 240). Such resettlement program goals reveal how refugee policy was informed not only by domestic race relations of the 1970s and 1980s, but also by the American gatekeeping model first established in the pre-1924 period. As scholars of the refugee experience have been quick to observe, there exists a deeply-embedded "competition between compassion and restrictionism" in refugee policy in general. Norman and Naomi Zucker write that refugee policy "has become an exercise in alchemy: how to transform refugees into immigrants, immigrants who can be controlled, regulated, and above all, chosen" (Zucker and Zucker 1996, pp. 6–7).

The racial concerns both implicitly and explicitly encoded into the Refugee Act and its corresponding resettlement programs help explain the transition between immigration reform in the 1960s and the persistence of a racialized American gatekeeping in the late twentieth and early twenty-first centuries. By the 1970s, scholars have observed that "even liberals questioned refugee policy," as the "problems" associated with Southeast Asian resettlement were associated with growing concerns about the new immigration from Asia and Latin America (Palumbo-Liu 1999, p. 246; Loescher and Scanlan 1986, pp. 209–11).

American anxiety related to refugee resettlement first helped to fuel the political debate surrounding illegal immigration from Mexico. Caused in part by the Western Hemispheric caps in the 1965 act, illegal immigration from Mexico increased, beginning in the 1970s. Apprehensions of undocumented immigrants steadily rose from 500,000 in 1970 to nearly 1 million seven years later (Gutiérrez 1998, p. 188). In the midst of a deep national recession, alarmists talked of the "loss of control" over the country's borders, and their rhetoric reflected a larger anxiety and fear about the unprecedented demographic racial and ethnic changes brought on by the new post-1965 immigration. Racialized metaphors of war such as "invasion," "conquest," and "save our state" were commonly deployed to describe illegal immigration from Mexico, while illegal immigration from other countries was largely ignored. (A large percentage of the new Irish immigrants arriving in America in the 1980s had no proper documentation or overstayed their visas, and the high-profile cases of Chinese "smuggled" into the country by boat along the west and east coasts point to a dramatic increase of Chinese illegal immigration (Perea 1997, pp. 67, 73; Corcoran 1993, p. 144; Kwong 1997; K. Johnson 1998, p. 1137).) The US government's efforts to crack down on illegal Mexican immigrants have placed the entire Mexican American community under suspicion, making illegal immigrants, legal residents, and even native-born American citizens of Mexican descent vulnerable to scrutiny and government action (Garcia 1995; K. Johnson 2000).

The ways in which the US government has attempted to control illegal immigration offer additional evidence of the extension of pre-1924 gatekeeping practices, especially the centrality of administrative, rather than legislative, initiatives. As Lucy Salyer has demonstrated for the pre-1924 period, the Bureau of Immigration evolved into a highly powerful agency that enjoyed great administrative discretion and little interference from the courts in the enforcement of immigration laws (Salyer 1995, pp. 121–78). Beginning in the 1980s, the Bureau's successor, the Immigration and Naturalization Service (INS), has similarly relied upon its own administrative power and internal INS operations (with the sanction and increased budgets approved by

Congress) to control illegal immigration from Mexico. The Immigration Reform and Control Act of 1986 (IRCA) attempted to "get tough with" illegal immigrants and their employers, but lax enforcement and migrant adaptation have proven such provisions to be ineffectual (Daniels 2001, pp. 52–8). Instead, the US government has turned to border patrol initiatives with military codenames like "Operation Gatekeeper" in San Diego, California, "Operation Rio Grande" in Brownsville, Texas, "Operation Safeguard" in Nogales, Arizona, and "Operation Hold the Line" in El Paso, Texas. From 1993 to 1996, the US Congress increased funding for the Border Patrol by 102 percent (Peters 1996). The United States currently spends $2 billion a year to build walls and manage a 24-hour patrol over the border that includes the use of night scopes, motion sensors, communications equipment, jeeps, a 10-foot high steel wall, and 9,400 border agents (Schmitt 2002a). The US Border Patrol arrested approximately one million individuals along the US–Mexico border in the year 2000 alone. In contrast, only 11,000 people were arrested for illegally crossing the US–Canada border (*National Post*, November 7, 2001). With such efforts resulting in the militarization of the US–Mexico border, no other area of immigration control has so literally embodied American gatekeeping in the contemporary period.

In the wake of the terrorist attacks on America on September 11, 2001, the core components of American gatekeeping and immigration law were pushed to the very forefront of US and international policy. Political pundits and lawmakers argued that, in hindsight, American gatekeeping efforts did not work well enough. The Federal Bureau of Investigation failed to act upon internal reports of suspicious individuals who were later found to be among the hijackers who attacked the World Trade Center and the Pentagon. At least one September 11th hijacker entered the country on a student visa, while others studied at flight schools in the United States despite their lack of student visas (Lewis 2002). Several of the suspects spent time in Canada, where less stringent immigration laws allow immigrants and refugees to enter with false or no passports, apply for asylum, travel freely, and raise funds for political activities while their asylum applications are pending. Canada's open doors, critics have argued, increased the risk of America's own national security (*Chicago Tribune*, September 26, 2001; Crossette 2001; Bueckert 2001; *National Post*, October 4, 2001; Howe Verhovek 2001; *Seattle Times*, October 10, 2001).

Following the attacks, the identification of a new immigrant threat and the solutions that followed borrow from and extend earlier gatekeeping efforts. In the search for the perpetrators, entire Middle Eastern and Muslim immigrant communities were vulnerable to blanket racializations as "terrorists," "potential terrorists," or accomplices and sympathizers. Within days of the attacks, law enforcement officials had arrested more than 1,200 people, only a handful of whom were proven to have any links to terrorism. At the end of November, 2001, approximately 600 people were still in custody, held on unrelated immigration violations (Wilgoren 2001; Firestone and Drew 2001). Despite US government appeals to prevent racial scapegoating, hate crimes directed against Middle Eastern Americans and those who appear Middle Eastern rose throughout the nation, resulting in at least one murder, of a South Asian Sikh gas-station owner in Mesa, Arizona. Racialized as the latest immigrant menace, entire ethnic communities found themselves under suspicion (Goodstein and Niebuhr 2001; Goodstein and Lewin 2001; *The Detroit News*,

September 30, 2001). Newspapers reported on a "broad consensus" among both supporters of immigration and restrictionists on the need for additional immigration restriction as a matter of national security (Center for Immigration Studies 2001; *Miami Herald*, November 16, 2001).

In an effort to manage the new terrorist threat, drastic changes in immigration policy took effect in the few short months immediately following the attack. No formal legislation restricting the immigration from countries suspected of being breeding grounds for terrorists was passed, but other important controls on immigration, and, especially, immigrants already within the United States, were instituted as part of other laws. A section in the "Patriot Act" passed in the House of Representatives in October of 2001 allowed the long-term detention of non-citizens whom the attorney general "certified" as a terrorist threat (Toner and Lewis 2001). Similar to earlier gatekeeping efforts, internal, administrative decisions of the INS were also significantly altered to track, control, and detain immigrants suspected of terrorist activity or those deemed a potential threat to national security. Immigration officials quietly amended the INS's own administrative rules and procedures to grant them greater control over all foreigners. During November and December of 2001, US government agents targeted 200 college campuses nationwide to collect information on Middle Eastern students (Steinberg 2001). In November, the Justice Department expanded the power of its officers to detain foreigners even after a federal immigration judge had ordered their release for lack of evidence. The judicial order can be set aside if the immigration service believes that a foreigner is a "danger to the community or a flight risk." While immigration lawyers argued that the new law deprives the detainees of the fundamental right of bond hearings, supporters claimed that the change was necessary in the new war against terrorism. Still others noted that the agency appeared to be strategically using the new political climate to address long-standing concerns about the power of immigration courts (Firestone 2001).

In April of 2002, a Justice Department legal ruling set in motion the use of state police to enforce federal immigration laws. Under a proposed federal plan, local police officers were to become deputized as agents of the INS with the power to arrest immigrants for overstaying a visa or entering the country illegally (Schmitt 2002a). In June 2002 Attorney General John Ashcroft proposed new Justice Department regulations that would require Muslim men to be fingerprinted, photographed, and registered with the INS. Such a measure – so similar to the Geary Act of 1892, which required Chinese laborers to register with the federal government – is to provide a "vital line of defense" against terrorists, in the words of the attorney general (Schmitt 2002b). Critics claimed that such sweeping legal changes in immigration control institutionalized racial profiling and the suspension of liberties for immigrants, and government officials themselves have publicly questioned the merit of the program. Of the more than 83,000 immigrants considered suspect for ties to terrorism, only six were further investigated by the Department of Homeland Security. (Nearly 13,000 were found to be in the country illegally.) Furthermore, the September 11 Commission questioned these findings and reported that it had found little evidence supporting the Department's claim that these six individuals had any links to terrorism at all. Nevertheless, the Bush administration's proposals commanded strong public support, and as of early 2005, important vestiges of the original program remain in place. Most notably, immigrants from 25 countries are still required to register with immigration officials when they enter and leave the country (Purdy 2001; Swarns 2003).

Such drastic measures have been justified as part of America's new war against terrorism, and officials have been careful to assert that the new policies were put in place to target terrorists only. Nevertheless, the effects and consequences of these new policies have already been felt by all immigrants, and, indeed, all Americans. In 2002, Congress passed the Homeland Security Act of 2002, which, among many other things, abolished the Immigration and Naturalization Service and created two new divisions, the Bureau of Citizenship and Immigration Services and the Directorate of Border and Transportation Security (US Department of Homeland Security). The former deals primarily with naturalization, visa and work permits, and other services for new residents and citizens; the latter deals with border and immigration law enforcement. Placing both bureaus under the control of the new Homeland Security Department, immigrant advocates have argued, sends the message that all immigrants, not just those suspected of terrorism, are potential risks to national security (Hing 2002). Questions relating to the role of immigration in the United States, and America's identity as a nation of immigrants, let alone the serious questions of civil liberties and the effects that such a reorganization and paradigm shift will have on the millions of immigrants already in the country, remain to be answered.

Conclusion: A Global Era of Immigration Policy

One of the first changes in immigration regulation following the terrorist attacks in 2001 was the discussion of transnational immigration control, and cooperative efforts among the United States, Mexico, and especially Canada to enforce the northern and southern borders of the United States and to regularize immigration policies among the three countries. In late September of 2001, Paul Celluci, the US Ambassador to Canada, publicly called for Canada to "harmonize its [refugee] policies with those of the United States." President George W. Bush sketched out a vision of a "North American security perimeter" to which transnational immigration controls would be central. Discussions with Mexico have also secured that country's cooperation in improving security over the shared US–Mexico border (*National Post*, October 1, 2001). Such calls for transnational immigration regulation reflect the new global era of migration and migration policy that characterizes the early twenty-first century.

America's role as an immigrant-receiving nation is no longer unique in the world. Great Britain, France, Spain, Germany, Australia, and others have all begun to wrestle with the same types of questions and methods of immigration control that the United States has considered for over 125 years. European nations are currently grappling with the challenge of integrating the foreign laborers they had primarily perceived as temporary "guests" in their countries, but who have unexpectedly decided to stay and raise families. The need for labor in Japan has caused that country to increasingly rely upon foreign labor from Latin America (mostly ethnic Japanese), Korea, and other countries. In many ways, the United States has become a global example of a gatekeeping nation, and as immigration policies become more international, the nation – and indeed the world – enters a new era of immigration control. Wayne Cornelius, Philip Martin, and James Hollifield point out that the increasing mobility of migrants throughout the world has resulted in a new type of cooperation amongst nation-states to coordinate and harmonize migration policies, especially those concerning refugees. The economic interdependence and relaxation of internal borders that has accompanied the establishment of the European Union, in particular, has accelerated this shift. As a result, the authors posit that immigration policies are at a point of convergence. Among the United States, Canada, Britain, France, Germany, Belgium, Italy, Spain, and Japan, there is increasing similarity and cooperation in relation to the policy instruments used to control immigration, especially illegal immigration, and refugee admissions and to integrate those foreigners and their descendants already resident in each country. Public reaction to immigration in one country can directly affect public reaction in another as well (Cornelius, Martin, and Hollifield 1994, pp. 3, 6–7).

Such internationalization of immigration policy exemplifies the latest development in immigration law. For the United States, the contradictory impulses to both welcome and exclude immigrants have reflected and reinforced Americans' long-standing ambivalence towards immigration. Periods of reform and progress have been overshadowed by eras of restriction and exclusion. The history of immigration law is thus neither smooth nor predictable, but the laws themselves have always had long-lasting consequences (K. Johnson 2000, pp. 304–5). If, as historian Oscar Handlin wrote, "immigrants *are* American history," then immigration laws provide the crucial framework for understanding both immigrant and non-immigrant America (Handlin 1973, p. 3). Increasingly, migration and migration policy are essential to global history and global studies as well.

REFERENCES

Anbinder, Tyler (1992). *Nativism and Slavery: The Northern Know Nothings and the Politics of the 1850s.* New York: Oxford University Press.

Andreas, Peter (2000). *Border Games: Policing the U.S.–Mexico Divide.* Ithaca, NY: Cornell University Press.

Anker, Deborah E. and Michael H. Posner (1982). "The Forty Year Crisis: A Legislative History of the Refugee Act of 1980." *San Diego Law Review* 19(1): 1–89.

Balderrama, Francisco E. and Raymond Rodriguez (1995). *Decade of Betrayal: Mexican Repatriation in the 1930s.* Albuquerque: University of New Mexico Press.

Barkan, Elliott and Michael LeMay, eds. (1999). *U.S. Immigration and Naturalization Laws and Issues.* Westport, CT: Greenwood Press.

Barrett, James R. and David Roediger (1997). "Inbetween Peoples: Race, Nationality and the 'New Immigrant' Working Class." *Journal of American Ethnic History* 16(3): 3–44.

Bennett, Marion T. (1963). *American Immigration Policies: A History.* Washington, DC: Public Affairs Press.

Bernard, William S. (1950). *American Immigration Policy: A Reappraisal.* New York: Harper.

—— (1980). "Immigration: History of U.S. Policy." In Stephen Thernstrom, ed., *Harvard Encyclopedia of American Ethnic Groups.* Cambridge, MA: Harvard University Press, pp. 105–21.

Breitman, Richard and Alan M. Kraut (1987). *American Refugee Policy and European Jewry, 1933–1945.* Bloomington: Indiana University Press.

Bueckert, Dennis (2001). "Canadian Sovereignty Called into Question in Fight Against Terrorism." *Canadian Press Newswire*, October 3.

Calavita, Kitty (2000). "The Paradoxes of Race, Class, Identity, and 'Passing': Enforcing the Chinese Exclusion Acts, 1882–1910." *Law and Social Inquiry* 25(1): 1–40.

Celler, Emmanuel (1965). Testimony in US Congress, House, 89th Cong. 1st sess., August 24, 1965. *Congressional Record*. Washington, DC: Government Printing Office, p. 21579.

Center for Immigration Studies (2001). "Immigration and Terrorism." Panel Discussion and Transcript, November 6, 2001. http://www.cis.org/articles/2001/terrorpanel.html (February 1, 2003).

Chicago Tribune (2001). "Nation's Open Borders in Spotlight." September 26, p. 9.

Chin, Gabriel J. (1996). "The Civil Rights Revolution Comes to Immigration Law: A New Look at the Immigration and Nationality Act of 1965." *North Carolina Law Review* 75(1): 273–345.

Corcoran, Mary P. (1993). *Irish Illegals: Transients Between Two Societies*. Westport, CT: Greenwood Press.

Cornelius, Wayne A., Philip L. Martin, and James F. Hollifield, eds. (1994). *Controlling Immigration: A Global Perspective*. Stanford, CA: Stanford University Press.

Crossette, Barbara (2001). "A Nation Challenged: Neighbor; Support for U.S. Security Plans is Quietly Voiced across Canada." *New York Times*, October 1, p. B3.

Daniels, Roger (1962, 1977). *The Politics of Prejudice: The Anti-Japanese Movement in California and the Struggle for Japanese Exclusion*. Berkeley: University of California Press.

—— (1989). *American Concentration Camps: A Documentary History of the Relocation and Incarceration of Japanese Americans, 1942–1945*. New York: Garland.

—— (1990). *Coming to America: A History of Immigration and Ethnicity in American Life*. New York: HarperCollins.

—— (1993). *Prisoners Without Trial: Japanese Americans in World War II*. New York: Hill and Wang.

—— (2001). "Two Cheers for Immigration." In Roger Daniels and Otis Graham, eds., *Debating American Immigration, 1882–Present*. Lanham, MD: Rowman & Littlefield, pp. 5–72.

—— (2004). *Guarding the Golden Door: American Immigration Policy and Immigrants Since 1882*. New York: Hill and Wang.

De Leon, Arnoldo (1983). *They Called Them Greasers: Anglo American Attitudes Toward Mexicans in Texas, 1821–1900*. Austin: University of Texas Press.

The Detroit News (2001). "Lax U.S. Visa Laws Give Terrorists Easy Entry – Immigrants Difficult to Track as They Blend into Ethnic Communities." September 30.

Dinan, Stephen (2002). "Immigration Growth of '90s at Highest Rate in 150 years." *Washington Times*, June 5, p. A3.

Divine, Robert A. (1957). *American Immigration Policy, 1924–1952*. New York: Da Capo Press.

Dunn, Timothy J. (1996). *The Militarization of the U.S.–Mexico Border, 1978–1992: Low-Intensity Conflict Doctrine Comes Home*. Austin: University of Texas Press.

Fairchild, Amy (2003). *Science at the Borders: Immigrant Medical Inspection and the Shaping of the Modern Industrial Labor Force*. Baltimore: Johns Hopkins University Press.

Firestone, David (2001). "A Nation Challenged: The Immigrants; U.S. Makes it Easier to Detain Foreigners." *New York Times*, November 28, p. B7.

Firestone, David and Christopher Drew (2001). "A Nation Challenged: The Cases; Al Qaeda Link Seen in Only a Handful of 1,200 Detainees." *New York Times*, November 29, p. A1.

Fitzgerald, Keith (1996). *The Face of the Nation: Immigration, the State, and the National Identity*. Stanford, CA: Stanford University Press.

Gabaccia, Donna (1994). *From the Other Side: Women, Gender, and Immigration Life in the U.S., 1820–1990*. Bloomington: Indiana University Press.

Garcia, Ruben J. (1995). "Critical Race Theory and Proposition 187: The Racial Politics of Immigration Law." *Chicano-Latino Law Review* 17: 118–54.

Gardiner, Harvey C. (1981). *Pawns in a Triangle of Hate: The Peruvian Japanese and the United States*. Seattle: University of Washington Press.

Gee, Harvey (2001). "The Refugee Burden: A Closer Look at the Refugee Act of 1980." *North Carolina Journal of International Law and Commercial Regulation* 26: 559–651.

Gerstle, Gary (2001). *American Crucible: Race and Nation in the Twentieth Century*. Princeton, NJ: Princeton University Press.

Goodstein, Laurie and Tamar Lewin (2001). "A Nation Challenged: Violence and Harassment; Victims of Mistaken Identity, Sikhs Pay a Price for Turbans." *New York Times*, September 19, p. A1.

Goodstein, Laurie and Gustav Niebuhr (2001). "After the Attacks: Retaliation; Attacks and Harassment of Arab-Americans Increase." *New York Times*, September 14, p. A14.

Gotanda, Neil (1997). "Race, Citizenship, and the Search for Political Community Among 'We the People.'" *Oregon Law Review* 76: 233–58.

Graham, Otis (2001). "The Unfinished Reform: Regulating Immigration in the National Interest." In Roger Daniels and Otis Graham, eds., *Debating American Immigration, 1882–Present*. Lanham, MD: Rowman & Littlefield, pp. 89–185.

Guglielmo, Thomas (2003). *White on Arrival: Italians, Race, Color, and Power in Chicago, 1890–1945*. New York: Oxford University Press.

Gutiérrez, David (1998). *Walls and Mirrors: Mexican Americans, Mexican Immigrants, and the Politics of Ethnicity*. Berkeley: University of California Press.

Gyory, Andrew (1998). *Closing the Gate: Race, Politics, and the Chinese Exclusion Act*. Chapel Hill: University of North Carolina Press.

Hagihara, Ayako and Grace Shimizu (2002). "The Japanese Latin American Wartime and Redress Experience." *Amerasia* 28(2): 203–16.

Handlin, Oscar (1973). *The Uprooted: The Epic Story of the Great Migrations that Made the American People* [1951]. Boston: Little, Brown.

Higham, John (1978). *Strangers in the Land: Patterns of American Nativism, 1860–1925* [1955]. New York: Atheneum.

Hing, Bill Ong (1993). *Making and Remaking Asian America Through Immigration Policy, 1850–1990*. Stanford, CA: Stanford University Press.

—— (2002). "Testimony before the United States Senate Committee on the Judiciary Hearings on 'Immigration Reform and the Reorganization of Homeland Defense.'" June 26, 2002. http://www.ilw.com/lawyers/immigdaily/congress_news/2002,0702-senate-hing.shtm (February 1, 2003).

Howe Verhovek, Sam (2001). "A Nation Challenged: The Northern Border; Vast U.S.–Canada Border Suddenly Poses a Problem to Patrol Agents." *New York Times*, October 4, p. B1.

Huttenback, Robert A. (1976). *Racism and Empire: White Settlers and Colored Immigration in the British Self-Governing Colonies, 1830–1910*. Ithaca, NY: Cornell University Press.

Irons, Peter (1993). *Justice at War*. Berkeley: University of California Press.

Jacobson, Matthew Frye (1998). *Whiteness of a Different Color: European Immigrants and the Alchemy of Race*. Cambridge, MA: Harvard University Press.

Johnson, Kevin R. (1998). "Race, the Immigration Laws, and Domestic Race Relations: A 'Magic Mirror' into the Heart of Darkness." *Indiana Law Journal* 73: 1111–59.

—— (2000a). "Race and Immigration Law and Enforcement: A Response to Is There a Plenary Power Doctrine?" *Georgetown Immigration Law Journal* 14: 289–305.

—— (2000b). "Race Matters: Immigration Law and Policy Scholarship, Law in the Ivory Tower; and the Legal Indifference of the Race Critique." *University of Illinois Law Review* 525: 525–57.

—— (2004). *The "Huddled Masses" Myth: Immigration and Civil Rights*. Philadelphia: Temple University Press.

Johnson, Lyndon Baines (1965). "Annual Message to the Congress on the State of the Union." January 8, 1964. In Lyndon B. Johnson, *Public Papers of the Presidents of the United States, Lyndon B. Johnson: Containing the Public Messages, Speeches, and Statements of the President, 1963–1964, Book 1*. Washington, DC: Government Printing Office, pp. 112–18.

—— (1966). "Statement at the Signing of the 1965 Immigration and Nationality Bill." October 3, 1965. In Lyndon B. Johnson, *Public Papers of the Presidents of the United States, Lyndon B. Johnson: Containing the Public Messages, Speeches, and Statements of the President, 1963–1964, Book 2*. Washington, DC: Government Printing Office, pp. 1037–40.

Kelly, Gail Paradise (1977). *From Vietnam to America: A Chronicle of the Vietnamese Immigration to the United States*. Boulder, CO: Westview Press.

Kennedy, Edward (1965). Testimony in US Congress, Senate, 89th Cong., 1st sess., September 17, 1965. *Congressional Record*. Washington, DC: Government Printing Office, p. 23352.

Kennedy, John F. (1964). *A Nation of Immigrants*. New York: Harper and Row.

Kettner, James H. (1978). *The Development of American Citizenship, 1608–1870*. Chapel Hill: University of North Carolina Press.

King, Desmond (2000). *Making Americans: Immigration, Race, and the Origins of the Diverse Democracy*. Cambridge, MA: Harvard University Press.

Kraut, Alan (1994). *Silent Travelers: Germs, Genes, and the "Immigrant Menace."* Baltimore: Johns Hopkins University Press.

Kwong, Peter (1997). *Forbidden Workers: Illegal Chinese Immigrants and American Labor*. New York: New Press.

Lee, Erika (1999). "Immigration and Immigration Law: A State of the Field Assessment." *Journal of American Ethnic History* 18(4): 85–114.

—— (2002a). "Enforcing the Borders: Chinese Exclusion along the U.S. Borders with Canada and Mexico, 1882–1924." *Journal of American History* 89(1): 54–86.

—— (2002b). "The Example of Chinese Exclusion: Race, Immigration, and American Gatekeeping, 1882–1924." *Journal of American Ethnic History* 21(3): 36–62.

—— (2003). *At America's Gates: Chinese Immigration During the Exclusion Era, 1882–1943*. Chapel Hill: University of North Carolina Press.

Lee, Robert (1999). *Orientals: Asian Americans in Popular Culture*. Philadelphia: Temple University Press.

LeMay, Michael (1987). *From Open Door to Dutch Door: An Analysis of U.S. Immigration Policy Since 1820*. New York: Praeger.

Leong, Karen J. (2000). "'A Distant and Antagonistic Race': Constructions of Chinese Manhood in the Exclusionist Debates, 1869–1878." In Laura McCall, Matthew Basso, and Dee Garceau, eds., *Across the Great Divide: Cultures of Manhood in the American West*. New York: Routledge, pp. 131–48.

Lewis, Neil (2002). "Traces of Terror: The Overview: F.B.I. Chief Admits 9/11 Might Have Been Detectable." *New York Times*, May 30, p. A1.

Loescher, Gil and John Scanlan (1986). *Calculated Kindness: Refugees and America's Half Open Door, 1945 to the Present*. New York: Free Press.

Lopez, Ian F. Haney (1996). *White by Law: The Legal Construction of Race*. New York: New York University Press.

Luibhéid, Eithne (2002). *Entry Denied: Controlling Sexuality at the Border*. Minneapolis: University of Minnesota Press.

Markus, Andrew (1979). *Fear and Hatred: Purifying Australia and California, 1850–1901*. Sydney: Hale & Iremonger.

Melendy, H. Brett (1976). "The Filipinos in the United States." In Norris Hundley, ed., *The Asian-American: The Historical Experience*. Santa Barbara, CA: American Bibliography Center, CLIO Press, pp. 101–28.

Miami Herald (2001). "Immigration Scrutiny a 'Dramatic' Shift in Focus." November 16.

National Post (2001). "11,000 Arrested Last Year Trying to Sneak into the U.S." (Ontario, Can.), November 7.

National Post (2001). "Border Painted as Magnet for Terror: US Politicians Blame Canada but Their Officials Tell a Different Story." (Ontario, Can.), October 4, pp. A1, A15.

National Post (2001). "Bordering on Harmonization: Why Canada Faces Pressure." (Ontario, Can.), October 1, p. A10.

Neuman, Gerald L. (1993). "The Lost Century of American Immigration Law, 1776–1875." *Columbia Law Review* 93(8): 1833–901.

Ngai, Mae (1999). "The Architecture of Race in American Immigration Law: A Reexamination of the Immigration Act of 1924." *Journal of American History* 86(1): 67–92.

—— (2004). *Impossible Subjects: Illegal Aliens and the Making of Modern America*. Princeton, NJ: Princeton University Press.

Omi, Michael and Howard Winant (1994). *Racial Formation in the United States*. New York: Routledge.

Ong, Aihwa (2003). *Buddha is Hiding: Refugees, Citizenship, the New America*. Berkeley: University of California Press.

Palumbo-Liu, David (1999). *Asian/American: Historical Crossings of a Racial Frontier*. Stanford, CA: Stanford University Press.

Parish, T. David (1992). "Membership in a Particular Social Group under the Refugee Act of 1980: Social Identity and the Legal Concept of the Refugee." *Columbia Law Review* 92: 923–53.

Peffer, George Anthony (1999). *If They Don't Bring Their Women Here: Chinese Female Immigration Before Exclusion*. Urbana: University of Illinois Press.

Perea, Juan F., ed. (1997). *Immigrants Out! The New Nativism and the Anti-Immigrant Impulse in the United States*. New York: New York University Press.

Peters, Katherine McIntire (1996). "Up Against The Wall – Operation Gatekeeper." *Government Executive Magazine* http://www.govexec.com/archdoc/1096/1096s1.htm (January 3, 2001).

Price, Charles Archibald (1974). *The Great White Walls Are Built: Restrictive Immigration to North America and Australasia, 1836–1888*. Canberra: Australian Institute of International Affairs in association with Australian National University Press.

Purdy, Matthew (2001). "A Nation Challenged: The Law; Bush's New Rules to Fight Terror Transform the Legal Landscape." *New York Times*, November 25, p. A1.

Reder, Stephen M. (1983). "The Hmong Resettlement Study Site Report: Fresno, California." Washington, DC: US Dept. of Health and Human Services, Social Security Administration, Office of Refugee Resettlement.

Reder, Stephen M. and Bruce T. Downing (1984). "The Hmong Resettlement Study Site Report: Minneapolis-St. Paul, MN." Washington, DC: US Dept. of Health and Human Services, Social Security Administration, Office of Refugee Resettlement.

Reimers, David (1985). *Still the Golden Door: The Third World Comes to America*. New York: Columbia University Press.

—— (1998). *Unwelcome Strangers: American Identity and the Turn Against Immigration*. New York: Columbia University Press.

Riggs, Fred (1950). *Pressure on Congress: A Study of the Repeal of Chinese Exclusion*. New York: King's Crown Press.

Rumbaut, Rubén G. (2000). "Vietnamese, Laotian, and Cambodian Americans." In Min Zhou and James V. Gatewood, eds., *Contemporary Asian America: A Multidisciplinary Reader*. New York: New York University Press, pp. 175–206.

Salyer, Lucy (1995). *Laws Harsh as Tigers: Chinese Immigrants and the Shaping of Modern Immigration Law*. Chapel Hill: University of North Carolina Press.

Sanchez, George (1999). "Face the Nation: Race, Immigration, and the Rise of Nativism in Late Twentieth Century America." *International Migration Review* 31(4): 1009–30.

Saxton, Alexander (1971). *The Indispensable Enemy: Labor and the Anti-Chinese Movement in California*. Berkeley: University of California Press.

Schmitt, Eric (2001). "Ambivalence Prevails in Immigration Policy." *New York Times*, May 27, p. A14.

—— (2002a). "Ruling Clears Way to Use State Police in Immigration Duty." *New York Times*, April 4, p. A19.

—— (2002b). "Traces of Terror: Immigration; U.S. Will Seek To Fingerprint Visas' Holders." *New York Times*, June 5.

Schneider, Dorothy (2001). "Naturalization and United States Citizenship in Two Periods of Mass Migration: 1894–1930, 1965–2000." *Journal of American Ethnic History* 21(1): 50–82.

Schuck, Peter H. (1984). "The Transformation of Immigration Law." *Columbia Law Review* 84(1): 1–91.

—— (1998). *Citizens, Strangers, and in-Betweens: Essays on Immigration and Citizenship*. Boulder, CO: Westview.

Seattle Times (2001). "Bills Would Tighten U.S.–Canada Border." October 10, p. A1.

Seller, Maxine S. (1984). "Historical Perspectives on American Immigration Policy: Case Studies and Current Implications." In Richard R. Hofstetter, ed., *U.S. Immigration Policy*. Durham, NC: Duke Press Policy Studies, pp. 137–62.

Smith, Darrell Hevenor and H. Guy Herring (1924). *Bureau of Immigration: Its History, Activities, and Organization*. Baltimore: Institute of Government Research Monographs of the United States Government, No. 30.

Solomon, Barbara Miller (1989). *Ancestors and Immigrants: A Changing New England Tradition* [1955]. Cambridge, MA: Harvard University Press.

Steinberg, Jacques (2001). "A Nation Challenged: The Students; U.S. Has Covered 200 Campuses to Check Up on Mideast Students." *New York Times*, November 12, p. A1.

Stern, William (1974). "H.R. 2580, The Immigration and Nationality Amendments of 1965 – A Case Study." PhD diss., New York University.

Swarns, Rachel L. (2003). "Programs Value in Dispute as a Tool to Fight Terrorism." *New York Times*, December 21, p. A21.

Takaki, Ronald (1989). *Strangers from a Different Shore: A History of Asian Americans*. Boston: Little, Brown.

Tichnor, Daniel J. (2002). *Dividing Lines: The Politics of Immigration Control in America*. Princeton, NJ: Princeton University Press.

Toner, Robin and Neil Lewis (2001). "A Nation Challenged: Congress; House Passes Terrorism Bill Much Like Senate's, But With 5-Year Limit." *New York Times*, October 13, p. B6.

Torpey, John (2000). *The Invention of the Passport: Surveillance, Citizenship, and the State*. New York: Cambridge University Press.

Trucio-Haynes, Enid (1997). "The Legacy of Racially Restrictive Immigration Laws and Policies and the Construction of the American National Identity." *Oregon Law Review* 76(2): 369–425.

Ueda, Reed (1994). *Postwar Immigrant America: A Social History*. Boston: St. Martin's Press.

US Congress (1964). House. Subcommittee No. 1 of the Committee on the Judiciary. *Immigration*. Hearings, 89th Cong., 2nd sess. Washington, DC: Government Printing Office.

US Congress (1965). Senate Committee on the Judiciary, Subcommittee on Immigration and Naturalization. "Hearings on S. 500." 89th Cong., 1st sess., September 20, 1965, *Congressional Record*. Washington, DC: Government Printing Office, pp. 23557–81.

US Department of Homeland Security (2002). "The Homeland Security Act of 2002" (H.R. 5005–8). http://www.dhs.gov/dhspublic/display?theme=59&content=411 (February 1, 2003).

US Immigration and Naturalization Service (1999). *Statistical Yearbook of the Immigration and Naturalization Service, 1998*. Washington, DC: Government Printing Office. http://www.ins.usdoj.gov/graphics/aboutins/statistics/imm98list.htm (January 3, 2002).

Weglyn, Michi (1976). *Years of Infamy: The Untold Story of America's Concentration Camps*. New York: Morrow.

Wilgoren, Jodi (2001). "A Nation Challenged: The Detainees; Swept Up in a Dragnet, Hundreds Sit in Custody and Ask, 'Why?'" *New York Times*, November 25, p. B5.

Wong, K. Scott (1998). "Cultural Defenders and Brokers: Chinese Responses to the Anti-Chinese Movement." In Sucheng Chan and K. Scott Wong, eds., *Claiming America: Constructing Chinese American Identities During the Exclusion Era*. Philadelphia: Temple University Press.

Wyman, David S. (1968). *Paper Walls: America and the Refugee Crisis, 1938–1941*. New York: Pantheon Books.

Zhou, Min and James Gatewood (2000). "Introduction." In Min Zhou and James Gatewood, eds., *Contemporary Asian America: A Multidisciplinary Reader*. New York: New York University Press, pp. 1–48.

Zolberg, Aristide (1995). "From Invitation to Interdiction: U.S. Foreign Policy and Immigration since 1945." In Michael S. Teitelbaum and Myron Weiner, eds., *Threatened Peoples, Threatened Borders: World Migration and U.S. Policy*. New York: W.W. Norton, pp. 117–59.

—— (1999a). "Matters of State: Theorizing Immigration Policy." In Charles Hirschman, Philip Kasinitz, and Josh DeWind, eds., *The Handbook of International Migration: The American Experience*. New York: Russell Sage Foundation, pp. 71–93.

—— (1999b). "The Great Wall Against China: Responses to the First Immigration Crisis, 1885–1925." In Jan Lucassen and Leo Lucassen, eds., *Migration, Migration History, History: Old Paradigms and New Perspectives*. New York: Peter Lang, pp. 291–316.

Zucker, Norman L. and Naomi Flink Zucker (1987). *The Guarded Gate: The Reality of American Refugee Policy*. New York: Harcourt.

—— (1996). *Desperate Crossings: Seeking Refuge in America*. New York: M.E. Sharpe.

CHAPTER TWO

Naturalization and Nationality

IRENE BLOEMRAAD AND REED UEDA

Born in the caldron of revolution, being "American" must be understood as a product of political ideology, a manifestation of national identity and a pragmatic response to the demands of building a new country. Immigration played and continues to play a crucial role in defining Americans. Society and policy makers must decide whether to include outsiders and, if included, in what manner foreigners gain access to citizenship and nationality. Understanding such choices, and their fluctuation over time, illuminates the dynamics of immigrant incorporation and American nation-building.

In this chapter we examine naturalization and nationality. Through the process of naturalization, foreign-born individuals without direct kinship ties to the United States become American citizens. Because American citizenship knits together legal status with an affective identity, naturalization has provided immigrants with a path to national membership. Much of the early scholarship on nationality and citizenship, conducted by legal scholars or political scientists, focused on the laws and regulations by which foreigners became American. More recent research by historians and sociologists places policy decisions within a broader socio-cultural framework. We show how immigration and naturalization laws were used to create, restrict, and expand the boundaries of the nation. Although US naturalization laws are generous compared to many other countries, restrictions enacted at many points in American history denied citizenship to various groups.

We also analyze the factors that influence individuals' propensity to naturalize. How do those who naturalize differ from immigrants who fail to seek American citizenship? Interest in, and concern about, this question is long-standing. In the early twentieth century, negative judgments over southern Europeans' inclination and ability to become citizens fueled immigration restrictions. With the development of sophisticated statistical techniques and the availability of new historical naturalization data, we attempt to provide a more accurate analysis by looking at citizenship acquisition in the early twentieth century.

Finally, we consider some of the cultural understandings of immigrant-related diversity and citizenship in American history, a growing area of study. Cultural analysts examine views of citizenship held by the receiving society, or segments of that society, and students of immigration increasingly explore the ways that immigrants internalize citizenship ideals, even when they do not possess legal citizenship. We thus delve into legal history, cultural studies, and an investigation of naturalization statistics to provide a multi-layered look at naturalization and nationality in the United States.

Boundary Control: Naturalization Laws, Nationality and Becoming American

Among the grievances outlined in the US Declaration of Independence, the colonists charged that King George III "has endeavoured to prevent the Population of these States; for that Purpose obstructing the Laws for Naturalization of Foreigners. . . ." The right to naturalize, recognized in the US Constitution, represented a conscious repudiation of feudal subjectship. Under the feudal model individuals were indissolubly bound, without their express consent, to sovereign overlords and the states they ruled. Naturalization, as a manifestation of voluntary political allegiance and expatriation, was a corollary to Enlightenment theories of republican citizenship. The ideals of the American Revolution thus required that the boundaries of American nationality be cast broadly.

Initially, Article IV of the Articles of Confederation left citizenship to the individual states, but this arrangement proved unworkable. In the words of Madison, it was "a fault in our system . . . laying a foundation for intricate and delicate questions" (Hamilton, Madison, and Jay 1961, p. 269) because it was not clear that someone naturalized in one colony possessed reciprocal rights in another. The US Constitution of 1787 consequently empowered the federal government to "establish a uniform Rule of Naturalization" (Article 1, Section 8). This grant of authority was designed to produce a national standard that would be consistent with the Constitution's "comity clause," continuing the principle of reciprocal interstate citizenship. The federal government's power was construed as essentially negative, as the authority to set a rule for the removal of the disabilities of alienage or foreign birth.

The ideology of voluntarism expressed itself in the rhetoric of the oath of allegiance, required of all would-be adult citizens. The oath vigorously announced the naturalizing alien's free choice and power to establish political allegiances.[1] Through consensual allegiance, immigrants transferred to themselves the republican civic tradition, gaining possession of it and making it a part of their lives. Citizens, either by birthright or by naturalization, possessed the capacity to participate in public life through the exercise of free and rational will (Kettner 1978).

Yet American citizenship also contained important limits to its inclusive vision of universal voluntarism. In passing the first federal naturalization law in 1790, Congress specified that eligibility was restricted to any "free white person" who had resided for two years "within the limits and under the jurisdiction of the United States." American nationhood and citizenship brought together ideals of liberalism and republicanism, but they were also, according to Rogers Smith (1997), imbued with a strong belief in "ascriptive Americanism." Legal statutes, judicial decisions and legislative debates reveal "passionate beliefs that America was by rights a white nation, a Protestant nation, a nation in which true Americans were native-born men with Anglo-Saxon ancestors" (Smith 1997, p. 2). Slaves, indentured white servants, and non-whites born outside of the country could not gain political and national membership.

Even white migrants faced recurrent nativism. Nativist policy makers believed that collective cultures, especially as they were shaped by religion or race – the latter conceived to include racial divisions among whites – impaired the capacity of foreigners to adopt American nationality. Such doubts overlapped with cruder political maneuverings. Federalists, who feared immigrants' support of Jeffersonian Republicans, passed congressional legislation in 1798 that raised the residency requirement for naturalization to 14 years. A new law in 1802 restored the minimum wait period to five years, where it has remained to the present. The arrival of Catholic immigrants from Ireland and Germany in the decades before the Civil War caused native Protestants to reconsider the nation's capacity to assimilate newcomers. Anti-Catholic nativists, who organized the powerful Know Nothing Party of the early 1850s, promoted long residency requirements for naturalization – as much as 21 years – to discourage Catholic newcomers. The radical fringe of the Know Nothings even endorsed the repeal of all naturalization laws to make it impossible for any immigrant to become an American citizen (Anbinder 1992, pp. 121–2).

The original 1790 naturalization statute was amended several times over the next 35 years, but by the 1820s a legal consensus emerged that would define naturalization policy and procedure for the remainder of the nineteenth century. This consensus stipulated that applicants had to be free white persons and declare their intention to become citizens at least three years preceding the award of citizenship. They had to be resident in the United States for five years and one year in the state in which they applied, a residency requirement similar to that of many other settler countries of the nineteenth century.[2] Would-be citizens had to swear an oath to uphold the Constitution and renounce allegiance to any foreign sovereign. Applications for citizenship could be filed with "any common law court of record in any one of the states." In 1824, Congress shortened the minimum time between the application for citizenship (the "declaration of intention") and the final award of citizenship papers to two years; a person who had resided in the country as a minor for three years preceding his majority was allowed to take out both sets of papers at once. For a married male applicant, his wife and minor children (under 21 years) became citizens with his naturalization. America's simple and short naturalization process became a cornerstone of an immigration policy designed to recruit newcomers.

The arrival of large numbers of newcomers – a policy "success" in many regards – nevertheless reignited debates over membership. Nativism and ascriptive Americanism intensified in the period following the Civil War. The federal state sought to centralize and articulate a unified American national identity at a time when the number of immigrants arriving in the country continued to rise and, most importantly, diversify. By the standards of the early nineteenth century, the stream of newcomers entering after Reconstruction grew to flood proportions (Goldin 1993). In the 1880s, 5,200,000 immigrants entered a country that, according to the 1880 census, barely counted 50 million people. In the first decade of the twentieth century, almost 8,800,000 foreigners arrived in the United States (US Immigration and Naturalization Service 2002). As immigrants from southern and eastern Europe began to outnumber immigrants from northern and western Europe, it was believed that the foreign masses were becoming less assimilable (Higham 1988).

Policy-makers used two tools to shape the ethno-racial contours of the American nation: they progressively restricted immigration laws to control who could enter the country, and they passed exclusionary naturalization regulations to limit access to citizenship. The crucial naturalization measure adopted was the designation of Asian immigrants as "aliens ineligible for citizenship," disqualifying them from naturalization. This exclusion first appeared as a provision in the Chinese Exclusion Act of 1882 barring the entry of laborers from China. Through an intellectually inconsistent series of judicial decisions in local and federal courts that variously referenced the "scientific" classification of races, Congressional intent, the racial classification used by the "average man," and geographic origins, all other immigrants from East Asia and South Asia were excluded from naturalized citizenship on racial grounds (Gualtieri 2001; López 1996; Ngai 2004). Essentialist views of the cultural and racial qualifications of civic membership, and of the collective capabilities or disabilities of immigrants, led to an abandonment of the universalistic potential of republican citizenship by the end of the nineteenth century.

In contrast to Asian immigrants, judicial interpretations of the statutory requirement that an applicant be a "free white person" made aliens from southern and eastern Europe and the Middle East – including Jews, Armenians, Syrians, Palestinians, Turks, and Arabs – officially "white" with respect to naturalization policy, and thus equal to migrants from northern and western Europe (Hooglund 1987, p. 44). The sphere of homogenized white civic identity provided the rights, opportunities, and duties that opened access to processes of assimilation.

Ironically, illiberal provision within American citizenship – that is, those provisions that undermine the ideology of volitional adherence – served to protect the US-born children of immigrants from the more repressive features of American nativism. Volitional citizenship, as embodied in the Constitution and naturalization laws, coexists in US law with ascriptive and passive birthright citizenship (Schuck and Smith 1985). Originating in common law and feudal theory, birthright citizenship means that individuals are American merely due to birth within the territorial jurisdiction of the United States (the principle of *jus soli*) or from birth to parents who are already members of the national community (the principle of *jus sanguinis*), not because of their stated desire to be American. These provisions protected native-born Catholics and Asians against attempts to exclude them from the political and national community. In 1898, the United States Supreme Court decided in the case of U.S. v. Wong Kim Ark that a child of Chinese immigrants was entitled to American citizenship under the *jus soli* clause of the Fourteenth Amendment.[3] This decision set a crucial precedent (Schuck and Smith 1985, pp. 75–9). Even in Asian ethnic communities where the immigrant generation was deprived of citizenship, their descendants would be incorporated in the political community.

At the same time that Asians were being systematically excluded through immigration and naturalization policy, the sphere of American citizenship widened to include new ethno-racial groups, peoples absorbed in the course of territorial and national expansion. The treaty ending the Mexican War of 1846 incorporated the inhabitants of conquered Mexican territories as American citizens. In 1868 the Fourteenth Amendment provided that any person born in the United States, regardless of ancestral origin, became a citizen of the United States. In 1870, Congress extended the naturalization law to include "aliens of African nativity and to persons of African descent." Congress made Hawaiians eligible for citizenship in 1900, Puerto Ricans in 1917, American Indians in 1924, inhabitants of the Virgin Islands in 1927, and indigenous inhabitants of the Western Hemisphere in 1940. Asian exclusions began to fall during the rigors of war: Chinese immigrants gained access to citizenship in 1943, Filipinos and Asian Indians in 1946. In 1952, the McCarran–Walter Act established general eligibility for American citizenship and nationality for all, without regard to racial categorization.

Access to citizenship also varied by gender and marital status. Although white foreign-born women had access to US citizenship, those who were married progressively lost control over their status starting in 1855. By federal law, an immigrant woman automatically became a citizen upon her husband's naturalization, or, if he were a US citizen prior to marriage, upon their marriage, regardless of her wishes. The 1907 Expatriation Act extended the logic linking a woman's citizenship to her marital status and the status of her spouse. Under the act, a naturalized or US-born American citizen *lost* her US citizenship after marriage to an alien; she could regain it only if her husband naturalized. Only as women's suffrage appeared imminent – and concern built that thousands of immigrant women would have the right to vote without proving their suitability for citizenship – did politicians and the public push for a gender-neutral naturalization law. The 1922 Cable Act gave most women control of their nationality, ushering in the current practice that men and women must apply for citizenship independently, regardless of marital status (Sapiro 1984). Asian-born women remained legally barred from citizenship, and non-Asians who married foreign-born Asian men unable to naturalize continued to lose their US citizenship until 1931 (Bredbrenner 1998).

The early twentieth century also brought new regulations linking naturalization to immigrants' skills and knowledge: foreigners had to prove their worthiness for American citizenship. The Naturalization Act of 1906 sought to centralize administrative oversight of naturalization and standardize naturalization procedures, replacing the nineteenth-century tradition of lax local naturalization with a systematic national test for membership. The act initiated procedures for stricter verification of the five-year residency requirement. It also raised the qualifications for naturalization by demanding a rudimentary knowledge of American history and civics, a basic ability to speak and understand English, and proof of moral worth. An alien seeking naturalization had to appear before a judge with two witnesses who would vouchsafe his character for American citizenship.

The 1905 United States Commission on Naturalization, which served as a clearinghouse for the bill that became the Naturalization Act of 1906, provides a window onto some of the thinking underlying these changes. The Commission and the new law reaffirmed liberal, republican ideas that transference of allegiance should be based on individual qualification and voluntary initiative. The five-year minimum residency period worked, in the eyes of policy-makers, as an adequate probationary period for applicants to establish the civic knowledge and linguistic qualifications for naturalization, especially since so many were poorly educated, spoke a non-English mother tongue, and came from undemocratic states. The rationale behind the new English requirement stemmed, according to the Commission, from the belief that:

The child of foreign parents, born in the United States, is by our fundamental law a citizen of the United States from the moment of his birth. If he grows up in the United States it rarely happens that he remains ignorant of the English language, and he is in fact as well as in law, an American. But an immigrant is in a different case, and if he does not know our language he does in effect remain a foreigner, although he may be able to satisfy the naturalization laws sufficiently to serve our citizenship. . . . The Commission is aware that some aliens who can not learn our language make good citizens. They are, however, exceptions, and the proposition is incontrovertible that no man is a desirable citizen of the United States who does not know the English language. (Wise 1906, p. 7)

At the same time, citizenship would not be tied to class or religion and, with the exception of Asian aliens, would not depend on race or ethnicity. Naturalization policy undermined the dividing line between "old immigrants" and "new immigrants" that figured prominently in immigrant admissions policy.

Nativists worried about the effect of new immigration on American citizenship, but an emerging public consensus, led by progressive reformers, held that foreigners could be integrated into democratic life through guided naturalization, civic education, and participation in reformed popular politics. "Good" citizenship sprung from immigrants' personal commitment to the country, based on rational will and ideological attachment. Educators throughout the decades of the early twentieth century sought to prepare immigrants for naturalization by imbuing their teaching of English, civics, and history with veneration for the nation-state and its historic traditions. These Americanizers believed that they could transmit a formularized civic culture, a unifying code of ideals and values of citizenship. The result was an achieved form of nationality: an individual could incorporate him or herself democratically into American nationality through the voluntary internalization of the civic code and patriotic actions, reinforcing the image of civic loyalty and public equality between sub-groups.

This path stood out particularly in times of war. During World War I, many young aliens were conscripted into the armed forces. Federal officials saw their wartime military service as a vehicle of Americanization and sought to reward alien soldiers with the granting of American citizenship. In May 1918, Congress passed a law that waived the probationary period to naturalization and provided for the immediate naturalization of alien soldiers in the armed forces. Wartime service also stimulated a new effort to re-evaluate the racial citizenship bar faced by Asian immigrants. Judges in federal districts in Massachusetts and California decided that Filipino veterans should receive naturalized citizenship because their military service was more important than the racial test for citizenship (In re Mallari, 239 F. 416 (D. Mass. 1916); In re Bautista, 245 F. 765 (N.D. Cal. 1917)). In 1935, President Roosevelt signed the Nye–Lea Act, providing for the naturalization of all Asian veterans by exempting them from the racial bar applied to foreign-born Asians. Today citizenship continues to be used as a reward and recognition of military service. President George W. Bush declared the period since September 11, 2001 an "authorized period of conflict," permitting any lawful permanent resident who has served in this period to apply immediately for citizenship, regardless of residency period or physical presence in the United States.[4]

In the post-World War II period, despite ideological and cultural changes moving from Americanization to multiculturalism, the procedural requirements for naturalization have remained largely the same.[5] The 1952 McCarran–Walter Act added a further hurdle to citizenship by requiring applicants to be able to read and write basic English, not just speak and understand it. Conversely, by the 1980s would-be citizens no longer needed to provide two character witnesses during their hearing. Today, someone wishing to become a US citizen must prove five years of residence as a legal immigrant, pay a fee of $320, prove basic oral and written ability in English, and demonstrate knowledge of US government and history. A judge or the US Citizenship and Immigration Services (formerly the Immigration and Naturalization Service) can refuse to grant citizenship for a variety of reasons, including past criminal convictions, long visits outside the country, or a failure to demonstrate "good moral character." Immigrant children can derive citizenship when their parents naturalize, but all adults must apply for citizenship independently.[6]

Multiculturalism has also failed to significantly change the political and symbolic attachment to exclusive US citizenship, even though the legal status of single citizenship is questionable. US citizenship, and its attendant naturalization process, was originally conceived as an exclusive status; loyalties were indivisible. For this reason, when pledging the oath of allegiance during naturalization, aliens must disavow allegiance to their country of origin. Even when the US Citizenship and Immigration Service tried to update and modernize the oath of allegiance in 2003, it retained language renouncing prior national allegiances.[7] US courts, however, have been willing to accept multiple nationality and citizenship. Supreme Court decisions in the 1960s and 1970s allow US-born citizens to take up other citizenships without risk of losing their American status. The US State Department and US Citizenship and Immigration Service no longer monitor whether new Americans hold multiple passports, in part because they cannot control decisions by sending countries extending citizenship to nationals overseas. In 2001, 10 Latin American countries and 10 countries in the Caribbean basin allowed their citizens to hold dual nationality (Jones-Correa 2001). The United States does not have a specific law permitting dual citizenship, but in practice many naturalized immigrants can access multiple nationality.

Who Naturalizes? Understanding Immigrants' Acquisition of US Citizenship

Citizenship acquisition can be measured as a *level* or a *rate*. To determine naturalization levels, we identify an immigrant group or cohort and count how many possess US citizenship on a certain date. For example, the 1920 census reports that of the just under 14 million foreign-born individuals living in the United States, 6.5 million were citizens, a naturalization level of 49.5 percent. In comparison, the 2000 US Census suggests that out of a foreign-born population of over 31 million, just over 12.5 million, or 40 percent, hold US citizenship. The bars in Figure 2.1 show the dramatic changes in naturalization from 1890 to 2000. In the first half of the twentieth century, citizenship levels increased steadily, peaking at 79 percent in 1950. By 1980, citizenship acquisition fell back to 1920 levels, and in the 1990s, it declined further, hitting a low of 35 percent in 1997, before rising to 40 percent in 2000.

Aggregate levels are deceptive, however, since they vary greatly with migration flows and immigrants' length of residence. A more accurate statistic is a naturalization rate, which measures the time elapsed between moving to the United States and

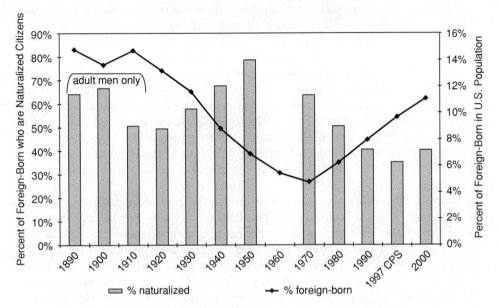

Figure 2.1 Percent of Foreign-born U.S. Residents Naturalized, 1890–2000

Source: Gibson and Lennon (1999); Schmidley and Gibson (1999), U.S. 2000 Census of Population and Housing

becoming a citizen. Census data from 1920 suggest that Irish immigrants were quicker to naturalize than French Canadians: on average, 9.7 years elapsed between migration and naturalization for adult Irish immigrants; French Canadians waited 13 years. The rate and level of naturalization are linked but not equivalent. An immigrant group that acquires citizenship slowly can have a high level of citizenship if the group has lived in the US for decades; a recent immigrant group might have a low level of citizenship, but be naturalizing quickly. Unfortunately, the census only recorded immigrants' year of naturalization in 1920 and the INS/USCIS release very little public data on naturalization levels.

The Impact of Length of Residence and Country of Origin

The difference between level and rate of naturalization is important because time spent in the United States is one of the strongest and most consistent predictors of naturalization. Federal law requires that immigrants meet a minimum residence requirement before applying for citizenship. The residence requirement affects aggregate naturalization levels most dramatically during sudden upswings in immigration. Figure 2.1 also includes a trend line tracking the percentage of the US population that is foreign-born at each census enumeration. During rapid influxes of immigrants, such as between 1880 and 1920 or since the mid-1960s, the aggregate naturalization level falls. New migrants increase the number of foreign-born individuals living in the United States – the denominator for calculations – but their presence drives down aggregate naturalization levels because they cannot become citizens immediately.

In addition, the more years an immigrant lives in his or her new home, the more likely he or she is to naturalize (Bernard 1936; Evans 1988; Liang 1994). Researchers debate why time is important: perhaps it reduces the costs of citizenship and makes the benefits more apparent (Jasso and Rosenzweig 1986; Yang 1994), or it may mark assimilation and growing attachment to the receiving society (Evans 1988; Liang 1994). Regardless of the reason, when few new immigrants arrive in the United States, naturalization levels rise as average length of residence increases. This trend is evident in the figures from 1920 to 1950. Immigration quotas introduced in 1921 and strengthened in 1924 cut off most migration to the United States. The doors only reopened in 1965. The striking difference in the trend of naturalization before and after 1965 arises in part from immigration policy, not migrants' desire for citizenship.

Failure to take into account length of residence can produce misleading analyses of immigrants' interest in citizenship. The 1907 Immigration (or Dillingham) Commission established clear differences in the naturalization of "new" immigrants from eastern and central Europe compared to "old" immigrants from western and northern Europe, bolstering the empirical case for immigration restrictions in the 1920s. Citizenship levels provided powerful proof that old immigrants assimilated better than the newer migrants: 92 percent of Swedes and 86 percent of Germans were American citizens, according to the report, compared to 30 percent of southern Italians and 28 percent of Russians. Immigration quotas subsequently made it difficult for "unassimilable" groups to enter the United States.

The statistics presented by the Dillingham Commission fail, however, to account adequately for length of residence. The Commission distinguishes between those with less than 10 years of residence and those with more, but as Gavit argues,

> those of the "older" races had been in the United States *considerably* longer than ten years, while those of the "newer" races had been here only *slightly* longer than ten years. . . . This means, of course, that the immigrants of the "older" races had had on average a much longer time than those of the "newer" to acquire "civic interest" and seek naturalization. (1922, pp. 209–10, emphasis in original)[8]

Such an omission makes it much easier to single out "bad" immigrant groups from the "good."

We can reanalyze the conclusions of the Dillingham Commission using microfile data from the 1900 census (Ruggles and Sobek 1997). At the aggregate level, we find clear variation. Among a sample of all foreign-born males 21 years and older, only 30 percent of Italians and 39 percent of Russians were naturalized citizens in 1900, while 84 percent of the Irish and 79 percent of German immigrants had become American citizens.[9] However, if we take into account how long these men had lived in the United States, we find much less variation. Figure 2.2 plots the level of naturalization for six cohorts of immigrants from seven countries of birth; it shows the percentage of those in each migrant cohort who are naturalized American citizens.[10] Most striking is the lack of a clear pattern of difference between the supposed culturally distant groups (i.e. the Italians or Russians) and the more culturally familiar ones. The Russian and Italian trend lines are slightly under those of most other groups, but not out-of-line with the general pattern. The Irish trend line

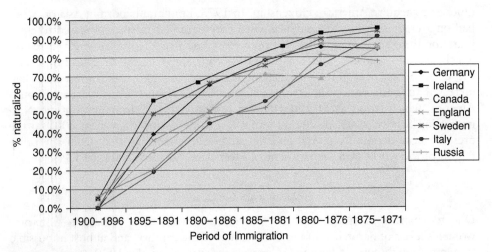

Figure 2.2 Naturalization Levels of Selected Birthplace Groups, by Migration Cohort, 1900 IPUMS Sample

is consistently above those of other groups, but not that far from the Swedes and Germans. Considering those with 10 to 14 years of residence in the United States at the time of the 1900 census, we find that 45 percent of Italians and 48 percent of Russians were American citizens, compared to 69 percent of Irish and 66 percent of Swedes. At 20 to 25 years of residence, the naturalization laggards become Canadians, of whom only 69 percent had become American, compared to 76 percent of Italians, 81 percent of Russians, 87 percent of those born in England, and 93 percent of Irish. The high Irish naturalization is not surprising given research on Irish immigrants' involvement in politics and urban machines (Clark 1975; Erie 1988), but more importantly the data clearly show that naturalization among *all* groups increased uniformly across migration cohorts, and that this increase tended to be quite rapid.

In the contemporary period, Latinos – and especially Mexicans – are frequently singled out as slow to naturalize and, by implication, to be lacking in civic spirit or loyalty to the United States. Yet public scrutiny is selective in identifying such groups. Data collected by the Immigration and Naturalization Service reveal that although some Latino groups do naturalize slowly, they are not the biggest laggards. Based on an immigrant cohort that entered the United States in 1977, INS figures show that by 1995 *all* 10 groups with the lowest naturalization levels came from developed industrial countries. On average, 46 percent of immigrants entering the United States in 1977 were citizens by 1995. Australian immigrants, at 9 percent, were least likely to be citizens, while the most rapid naturalizers came from Taiwan.[11] Ironically, the "assimilable" groups of 1907 are those with the lowest naturalization rates: only 14 percent of Swedes and 17 percent of Germans had taken out citizenship in 1995. Others in the "bottom 10" include immigrants from Norway, Denmark, Japan, Finland, Austria, Canada, and the Netherlands. Asians – those excluded from citizenship prior to World War II – tend to be among the quickest to acquire American citizenship. In 1975, immigrants born in Asia or Africa had on average six years of residence when they became citizens, compared to eight years for European immigrants and nine for those from North America, a region which includes Canada, Mexico, the Caribbean, and Central America. By 2000, the delay between acquiring permanent residence and citizenship for Asians had increased to eight years, but it was still less than for those from North or South America, which stood at 11 and 10 years respectively (US Immigration and Naturalization Service 2002, p. 201). From 1976 to 1995 and then from 2001 to the present, more people from Asia took up American citizenship than from any other region of the world (US Department of Homeland Security 2004, p. 134).

Gender and Citizenship

Due to changes in citizenship laws for married women, it is hard to interpret women's levels of naturalization in the first half of the century, and almost impossible to compare with current figures. At first glance, data from the 1920 census suggest that women were more eager to take out citizenship than men: 55 percent of foreign-born women held US citizenship compared to 49 percent of men. However, foreign-born women marrying Americans automatically became US citizens or they acquired citizenship when their immigrant husbands naturalized. If we take into account marital status – separating those never married from women married at least once – a different picture emerges. Only 27 percent of single women had naturalized, compared to 35 percent of single men.[12] The reverse is true for those married: 58 percent of women reported American citizenship compared to 50 percent of men.[13]

The largest gender differences occurred in 1940 and 1950. In 1940, 73 percent of immigrant men, but only 63 percent of immigrant women, reported US citizenship. One possible explanation of the gap is that women, now free – or forced – to naturalize on their own, were slower to do so than men. In addition, World War II most likely had an uneven effect on the sexes. While the United States had not entered the war in 1940, threat of imminent hostilities probably encouraged naturalization, or at least the reporting of American citizenship on the 1940 census. For example, the 1940 Smith Act required all aliens to be registered and fingerprinted, and it widened the grounds of deportation, something citizenship could prevent (Ueda 1996). Those who served in the US military – overwhelmingly men – were encouraged to become citizens and benefited from less stringent naturalization regulations.

Only slight gender differences appear in census data from 1970 to the present. Today researchers find that gender is either an insignificant predictor of naturalization or it correlates weakly with citizenship status (Liang 1994; Yang 1994). Whereas sex had a critical impact in the early 1900s due to naturalization laws, by the century's close it did not appear to affect naturalization greatly.

The Role of Residence on Naturalization

Even though the Constitution assigns jurisdiction over naturalization to the federal Congress, in the nineteenth and early twentieth centuries the process and benefits of naturalization varied widely by state. Most accounts of naturalization focus on length of residence or country of origin as the key factors determining immigrants' propensity to acquire US citizenship. Yet local considerations – driven by the relative costs or benefits of citizenship in any particular US state, variation in judges' attitudes toward applicants, or the presence of local urban machines – played an equally important role in naturalization outcomes.

After the War of Independence, the former colonies' practice of granting local citizenship persisted and states continued to regulate areas such as property rights, professional licenses, and suffrage based on diverse citizenship restrictions. Hoping to encourage settlement, some states granted aliens the franchise once an immigrant declared his intention to seek US citizenship (by filing "first papers") rather than upon the actual acquisition of citizenship. Other states adopted an anti-immigrant stance, reserving certain rights and benefits exclusively for citizens. Surprisingly, states that limited benefits to citizens often had lower levels of naturalization than states with more liberal statutes, suggesting that the "carrot" of a friendly environment might drive naturalization more than the "stick" of restrictive laws (Bloemraad 2000a).

The relative ease of naturalization also depended on locality. Federal or local courts could bestow citizenship, and judges enjoyed great latitude. After surveying 423 judges and examining more than 23,000 petitions for citizenship filed between July 1, 1913 and June 30, 1914, Gavit concludes:

> When we speak of the "personal equation" as an important factor in the adoption or rejection of an applicant for citizenship, we are likely to be thinking chiefly of the personality of the petitioner. . . . But this is only part. . . . For while it is true in one sense that the applicant does pass into the maw of a machine, constructed "of law rather than of men" . . . the fact is that there is hardly any other legal process in our governmental system in which personality – individual ideas, prejudices, idiosyncrasies – play so large a part. In no other activity of the courts is the individual petitioner so entirely at the mercy of the court, so completely without recourse in the event of a decision against him. (1922, p. 143)

In some cases, judges' antagonism toward newcomers made naturalization difficult. In others, judges facilitated citizenship acquisition, especially when they had a close relationship to local political party machines (Schneider 2001, pp. 53–5).

Progressives' concern over urban political machines largely fueled citizenship reform with the Naturalization Act of 1906. This act – which established the future INS – sought to standardize naturalization across the country. Progressives attacked machines' use of graft and corruption in courting and securing the immigrant vote. In its report to President Roosevelt, the Commission on Naturalization, charged with drafting a new citizenship law, argued for reform since:

> No motive to naturalization has been so productive of fraud as the desire to vote. . . . These aliens are sought out by unscrupulous political agents and are paid for the votes they are expected to cast, the payment being either in addition to the payment of the naturalization fees or the payment of the naturalization fees alone. In perpetrating this crime there are three conspirators – the political committee which employs the agent, the agent who bribes the alien, and the alien who accepts the bribe. The crime of bribery is always committed and the crime of false naturalization and perjury are often committed. . . . (US Commission on Naturalization 1905, p. 11)

According to Erie (1988), in 1844 the New York City machine known as Tammany Hall naturalized 11,000 foreigners, four years after opening its "Naturalization Bureau." By 1868, the system was perfected so that "Immigrants fresh off the boat were given red tickets, allowing them to get their citizenship papers free. Tammany paid the required court fees and provided false witnesses to testify that the immigrants had been in the country for the necessary five years" (Erie 1988, p. 51). Erie contends that by 1886, almost 80 percent of New York's Irish, German, and other western European immigrants had naturalized through the machine (1988, p. 53).

Yet machines' impact on aggregate US naturalization should not be exaggerated. The 1905 Commission on Naturalization took pains not to brand all politically interested immigrants as criminals:

> but not all of the naturalizations conferred immediately before an election are sought for unlawful or even improper reasons. When an important political contest is in progress many aliens who have not yet become citizens and are entitled to do so, having their interest aroused and desiring to have a voice in the election, apply for citizenship for praiseworthy reasons. . . . (US Commission on Naturalization 1905, p. 11)

In a similar vein, observer Hattie Williams found that despite the new, stricter citizenship law, local political actors mobilized immigrants in Nebraska to naturalize in 1908 and 1910 by highlighting the importance of the vote for defeating, among other issues, anti-alcohol initiatives (Williams 1912).

The idea that political participation encourages naturalization has strong roots in American history, as manifested in widespread alien suffrage laws (Keyssar). From the eighteenth century to 1926, many states allowed non-citizens the vote in state elections.[14] Since state electoral laws determined federal suffrage rights, immigrants in these states could also vote in federal elections.

Three distinct patterns of alien suffrage characterized nineteenth-century America. First, the constitutions of early Union members often granted suffrage to the "inhabitants" of the state. Local customs and legal decisions determined that in some cases (e.g. Ohio and Illinois) "inhabitants" included non-citizen immigrants, while in other states (e.g. Massachusetts) judges ruled that the term "inhabitants" was synonymous with US citizenship. Those allowing foreign male inhabitants to vote did so, as one Illinois judge put it, on the basis that

> to extend the right of suffrage to those who, having by habitation and residence identified their interests and feelings with the citizen, are upon the just principles of reciprocity between the governed and governing, entitled to a voice in the choice of the officers of the government, although they may be neither native nor adopted citizens. (Cited in Raskin 1993, p. 1405)

A second pattern characterized many midwestern states and territories, which granted suffrage to immigrants who had declared their intention to naturalize ("taken out first papers"). Starting with Wisconsin in 1848, lawmakers hoped that such overtures would entice newcomers to settle in their state. These rules were often enshrined in the state constitution, usually accompanied by an implicit assimilatory principle. By granting declarants the vote, "It now became, much more clearly, a pathway to citizenship rather than a possible substitute for it: *non*citizen voting became *pre*-citizen voting" (Raskin 1993, p. 1407, emphasis in original). A third wave of alien franchise followed Reconstruction as southern states' constitutions were rewritten. Since immigrants generally proved themselves staunch opponents of slavery, it was hoped that attracting more immigrants would change the demographic make-up of former members of the Confederacy (Rosberg 1977; Raskin 1993).

Although naturalization fraud did occur in the latter half of the nineteenth century, it generally involved only a few cities, benefited only a few immigrant groups, and did not begin to absorb the massive immigrant influx of 1880–1920. Erie (1988) convincingly argues that machines only encouraged naturalization in competitive two-party systems, and that they often failed to welcome new immigrants into politics. Because of limited resources, political machines could not provide benefits to an ever-expanding immigrant electoral base. Early immigrants, such as the Irish, benefited from machines' ability to effect rapid naturalization, but few later migrants received assistance.

Given local variation in the rights, benefits, and process of citizenship, we should expect to find interstate or regional differences in naturalization. Indeed, statistical modeling of individual-level census data shows that in 1900 an immigrant's place of residence influenced naturalization more than birthplace, ability to speak English, or literacy (Bloemraad 2000a). By 1920, however, interstate differences were decreasing, likely a function of the centralization and standardization attendant on the natural-ization reforms of 1906. By century's end, we find little difference in naturalization among states, once we hold constant variation in immigrants' country of origin, demographic characteristics, and socio-economic status (Bloemraad 2000b). Inter-state differences in the benefits associated with citizenship have become negligible (Plascencia, Freeman and Setzler 2003), alien suffrage is found in only a few excep-tional cases (Harper-Ho 2000), and the administration of naturalization is strongly centralized, formerly under the Immigration and Naturalization Service and, since March 1, 2003, under the US Citizenship and Immigration Services of the Depart-ment of Homeland Security.

Today, besides country of origin and length of residence, the strongest and most consistent predictors of naturalization are level of education and English ability. It is not surprising that those with greater English ability are more likely to be citizens since English skills are a requirement for US citizenship. Those with more education are generally also more likely to be US citizens, probably because the process of citizenship acquisition is less formidable to someone with more schooling. There is some indication, however, that at the very highest levels of education, beyond a college degree, immigrants are reluctant to acquire citizenship and are less likely to naturalize (Yang 1994). Other potential influences on citizenship, such as income or home ownership, appear, at best, to have only a marginal effect in increasing immigrants' inclination or ability to naturalize.

Diversity, Culture and American Nationhood

The assimilation of immigrants played and continues to play a critical role in state-building and the formation of American nationality. Indeed, despite periods of strong "ascriptive Americanism," it informs the very idea of American nationhood. At America's founding, various commentators announced that the nation's wellsprings lay in a multinational exodus. Although lawmakers used citizenship as a form of exclusion for some racialized populations, they also saw a popular naturalization process as a way to fuse immigrants into one nationality. Throughout the nineteenth and twentieth centuries, politicians, officials, and opinion makers continually referred to the United States as a polyglot republic of many peoples. This vision attracted celebrants like Booker T. Washington who hailed "a teeming nation of nations," and it repelled detractors like Henry Adams and Henry James who shuddered at a country of "multiplicity." Numerous presidents – among them, Abraham Lincoln, Theodore Roosevelt, Woodrow Wilson, Franklin D. Roosevelt, John F. Kennedy, and Ronald Reagan – invoked the United States as a nation of immigrants united by the twin enterprises of building democracy and rebuilding lives. Roosevelt perhaps spoke most succinctly for them all when he told a convention of the Daughters of the American Revolution, "Remember, remember always, that all of us, and you and I especially, are descended from immigrants and revolutionists."

Writers and opinion-makers spoke of immigrant elements transmuted by the social flux into a finer material, a process of metamorphosis often described in terms of alchemy. Crevecoeur (1981 [1782]) described how the average American gained a transformed social and familial life, "a new mode of living, a new social system," in which "individuals of all nations" were "melted" into "a new race of men." A half-century later, the transcendentalist philosopher Ralph Waldo Emerson predicted,

> As in the old burning of the Temple at Corinth, by the melting and intermixture of silver and gold and other metals a new compound more precious than any, called the Corinthian brass, was formed, so in this continent, – asylum of all nations – the energy of Irish, Germans, Swedes, Poles, and Cossacks, and all the European tribes – of the Africans and of the Polynesians will construct a new race, a new religion, a new state, a new literature. . . .

An English Jewish writer, Israel Zangwill, crafted the most memorable formulation of transmutation in his play of ethnic intermarriage in New York City, *The Melting Pot* (1908). The play's title became the evocative symbol of ethnic metamorphosis in the twentieth century. In the final scene of the play, the hero, David Quixano, exclaims, "East and West, and North and South, the palm and the pine, the pole and the equator, the crescent and the cross – how the great Alchemist melts and fuses them with his purging flame!" It was a grand vision of how immigrant diversity created a new nationality.

The conception of American nationality as ethnic transmutation was shaped not just by ideology but also by patterns of multiple ancestry in place well before the American Revolution. The first federal census of 1790 showed that more than two out of five whites in the United States were of non-English background and that the English were a minority population in all the colonies south of New England (McDonald and McDonald 1980). Colonial America did not possess a single culture, but an array of regional cultures transplanted from localities in Great Britain, Ireland, and various parts of the European continent (Fischer 1989). The archetypal formulation of ancestral mixing came in 1782 from a French immigrant and author, Hector St. Jean de Crevecoeur, who boasted, "I could point to you a family whose grandfather was an Englishman, whose wife was Dutch, whose son married a French woman, and whose present four sons have now four wives of different nations" (1981, pp. 69–70).

If America's colonial past suggested an immigrant nation, the practicality of nation-building required multi-ethnic inclusion. In the course of westward expansion and the industrial revolution, immigrants from a host of countries scattered across the nation's farming districts, small towns, and industrial cities. Each nineteenth-century decennial census became a referendum on the vitality of towns, cities, states, and territories; this vitality, usually measured by population growth, depended heavily on immigration (Anderson 1988). The image of ethnic eclecticism became omnipresent and highly colorful. When the historian Frederick Jackson Turner reminisced about his hometown of Portage, Wisconsin after the Civil War, he recalled,

> a mixture . . . of Irishmen . . . of Pomeranian immigrants . . . in old country garbs, of Scotch with Caledonia nearby; of Welsh with Cambria adjacent; of Germans some of them university trained . . . of Yankees . . . of Southerners . . . a few Negroes; many Norwegians and Swiss, some Englishmen, one or two Italians, who all got on together in this forming society. (Saveth 1948, p. 123)

Immigration turned the American social landscape into a vivid multi-ethnic tapestry.

In the twentieth century, nation-building, and especially American state-building, prompted even greater attention to the link between diversity and the American collective self-image. The New Deal promoted inclusion of ethnic and racial minorities in nationalist economic programs. The need for unity during war inspired public exhibitions demonstrating how a multitude of groups built the country, and therefore how the country belonged to all. Such projects initially borrowed from established metaphors of the melting pot and liberal citizenship, then in the post-World War II period moved to more explicit celebrations of multicultural diversity over cultural fusion.

American Counterpoint, a picture book by Alexander Alland published in 1943, vividly expressed some of these cultural impulses. Beginning with the declaration, "This is a family album . . . an album of the American family," *American Counterpoint* consisted of photo portraits of ordinary ethnic Americans. The pictured individuals represented over 50 different ethnic and national ancestries, illustrating America's fugue-like polyphony, the blending and coexistence of the numerous ethnic parts. In her introduction to the volume, Pearl S. Buck described this concept of harmonious group life, "America is not a nation, not a people, America is an idea." The essence of this idea was "that persons of many kinds can live together on a piece of the earth's surface, under a piece of the same sky," and through sharing a belief in "freedom" they can become "a united people." According to Buck, America was formed from "various races and nations" who came to "a land where they are free to be themselves." In other words, the "American Counterpoint" was made possible by the democratic principles of tolerance for diversity and coexistence.

Other wartime publications expressed similar sentiments. In *We Who Are America*, the Presbyterian missionary Kenneth D. Miller described American culture as a product of joint ethnic collaboration. "American Indians, Anglo-Saxon colonists, Negroes, German, Irish and Scandinavian immigrants, Orientals, newcomers from across the northern and southern borders, and later arrivals from Southeastern Europe," all played important parts in the grand saga of nation-building (1943, p. 7). Similarly, in *Nation of Nations* (1944), the Slovenian-American writer Louis

Adamic hailed the United States as a "new civilization" that owed its success not only to its Anglo-Saxon stock but to "a blend of cultures" that was "woven of threads from many corners of the world." Miller and Adamic presented the American public with a vision of America's diversity as reinforcing, rather than undermining, national unity, because it was based on shared and free participation in national life. All peoples were partners in a great national project, neither superior nor inferior. In essence, American liberty was the enabling condition for ethnic diversity and it was the glue that held the country together, rather than blood or ancestry.

Ironically, the integration of successive immigrant-origin generations – through social mobility, politics, education, and incorporation into modal patterns of national popular culture – led to the reawakening of ethnicity in the 1960s (Glazer and Moynihan 1963). The children and grandchildren of European immigrants worried that their ethnic heritage would disappear into the American melting pot. Assimilationist fears were further fed by a reaction to growing black nationalism and the cultural assertion of non-European groups, producing a cultural revival among many American ethnic communities. Intellectuals, opinion makers, and group leaders began to advocate cultural pluralism which, by the 1970s, they labeled "multiculturalism." The new model eschewed assimilation and revolved around a public ethos in which groups, often defined as distinctive quasi-subnationalities, sought to preserve their unique identities: "people of color," "Euro-Americans," "Latinos," "African Americans," "Native Americans," and "Asian-Pacific Americans."

Accelerating globalization makes it easier for immigrants to retain ties to the homeland, and thus to practice cultural retention. Cheap and easy transportation and communication make it possible as never before to remain in touch with family outside the United States and to be aware of developments in the sending country (Basch, Glick Schiller, and Szanton Blanc 1994; Levitt 2001; Portes, Guarnizo, and Landolt 1999). Yet this very internationalization – for some, transnationalism – also encourages cosmopolitan cultural selection. An individual can adopt practices from a variety of cultures and countries, and he or she can expect a certain acceptance of hybridity. Meanings of multiculturalism are thus open to interpretation. Early definitions implied a single and exclusive in-group cultural identity, combined with external integration into American economic and political institutions. Yet acculturation, mobility, and social integration – especially intermarriage – make exclusive cultural preservation difficult if not impossible, despite attempts to sensitize public institutions to multicultural realities (Alba and Nee 2003; Bean and Stevens 2003).[15] The dawn of the twenty-first century thus brings a new multiculturalism not only within the United States, but also relative to the rest of the world. American nationality has moved from an institution reflecting assimilation and homogenization in a single nation-state to one accommodating an unprecedented degree of internal group differentiation and external international ties. The broad and vociferous rebuttals to occasional calls for a return to Anglo-Protestant Americanization (Huntington 2004) merely underline how much American cultural conceptions of the nation have changed.

Conclusion

Citizenship is a legal status with attendant rights and, in countries such as the United States, it also carries a collective identity of "American" civic and social culture.

Understanding the dynamics of naturalization elucidates patterns of immigrant incorporation by showing how laws enable some to access citizenship while others are shut out, and by pointing to the factors that make certain individuals more or less likely to acquire citizenship. The study of naturalization also reveals the ebb and flow of national boundary maintenance as elites and ordinary people seek to expand, contract, or transmute conceptions of the American nation. Studying immigrants' inclusion and exclusion consequently provides a lens into the heart of American nation-building.

As this chapter should have made clear, the study of naturalization and nationality requires a diversity of evidence and methods, and even multiple conceptual approaches. Historians, social scientists, and political theorists have thus far privileged legal histories of naturalization and nationality, carefully examining laws, administrative regulations, and the ideologies that spawned such legal structures (Bredbrenner 1998; Schuck and Smith 1985; Smith 1997; Ueda 1982, 1996). Various political scientists and sociologists have more recently begun to probe patterns of naturalization through statistical analysis, but such endeavors center almost exclusively on contemporary migrant groups (Bloemraad 2002; DeSipio 2001; Jones-Correa 2001; Liang 1994; Yang 1994). As we have hinted here, much can be gained from using such techniques on historic data, including census files, naturalization petitions, and other local data sources.

The challenge for future scholars will be to link the insights gleaned from careful analysis of individual data, such as naturalization petitions, to larger societal or political dynamics. We would suggest that one important avenue for making such connections will be the investigation of organizations and institutions that mediated between the lives of ordinary immigrants and the wider socio-political system. The most obvious, and best studied, are the political machines. Yet it is probable that many immigrants had limited or sporadic contact with political parties. In comparison, religious institutions, unions, neighborhood organizations, and informal ethnic associations might have taught immigrants as much, if not more, about the meaning of citizenship, the process by which a foreigner could naturalize, and the immigrant's place in the American nation. Parallel institutions frequented by the native-born will have similarly transferred knowledge and beliefs about the newcomers arriving in the country, thereby shaping native Americans' attitudes about immigrants' place in their evolving society. Of particular interest are those institutions where the native-born and foreigners might have intermingled: schools and workplaces, churches, and neighborhood associations. Understanding how such organizations facilitated – or hindered – immigrants' entry to the American nation will add an important perspective to our understanding of citizenship and nationality, and it will help link the individual immigrant's decision to acquire citizenship with the evolution of American nationhood and democracy.

NOTES

1 Today the oath reads, "I hereby declare, on oath, that I absolutely and entirely renounce and abjure all allegiance and fidelity to any foreign prince, potentate, state, or sovereignty of whom or which I have heretofore been a subject or citizen; that I will support

and defend the Constitution and laws of the United States of America against all
enemies, foreign and domestic; that I will bear true faith and allegiance to the same; that
I will bear arms on behalf of the United States when required by the law; that I will
perform noncombatant service in the Armed Forces of the United States when required
by the law; that I will perform work of national importance under civilian direction when
required by the law; and that I take this obligation freely without any mental reservation
or purpose of evasion; so help me God."

2   The threshold in the United States equaled the probationary period for naturalization in
    New South Wales, Australia, but exceeded the requirement in countries such as Canada,
    South Africa, Mexico, Argentina, and Brazil which stood at two or three years (US
    Congress 1905, p. 10; Flournoy and Hudson 1929). See also Cockburn (1869) for
    concise comparisons of naturalization laws in various countries.

3   U.S. v. Wong Kim Ark, 169 US 649 (1898).

4   In addition, as of October 1, 2004 all naturalization filing fees are waived for those in
    service or who have served since September 11, 2001.

5   Other societies that have eschewed redefining themselves as "immigration countries"
    maintain laws and regulations that are far more restrictive. In Japan, Korean migrants have
    retained their status as non-nationals and non-citizens over the course of three generations.
    Up to 2000, German citizenship law was similarly restrictive. These countries embrace
    the *jus sanguinis* tradition of citizenship – citizenship by ancestry – and reject the *jus soli*
    principle of gaining citizenship through territorial birth (Brubaker 1992).

6   A number of special provisions can modify these requirements. The most important are
    a reduced three-year residency requirement for the spouses of US citizens and provisions
    that allow long-time elderly residents to prove knowledge of US laws and history in
    their own language. The fee is current as of January 1, 2005 and does not include a
    $70 charge for biometrics.

7   In late summer of 2003 USCIS was set to announce a new oath of allegiance, effective
    from September 17 of that year. The bureau came under heavy criticism, however, for
    failing to allow adequate public debate over the proposed changes and, according to
    some, diluting the language by which new citizens swear to defend the United States.
    Importantly, the proposed new language kept the spirit of exclusivity characterizing the
    old oath, by asking would-be citizens to "Solemnly, freely, and without any mental
    reservation . . . renounce under oath all allegiances to any foreign state."

8   See also Bernard (1936).

9   We exclude those under the age of 21, since the law only allowed adults 21 years of age
    and older to naturalize independently, and women, since many had no independent
    control over their naturalization. The enumerator instructions for the 1900 census
    explicitly tell census-takers, "The question of naturalization (column 18) applies only
    to foreign-born males 21 years of age and over" (Graham 1980, p. 22). The resultant
    sample contains 6,798 cases.

10 The graph does not include immigrants who came to the United States in 1870 and
    earlier because there are too few Russian and Italian cases. Naturalization levels for these
    long-time residents tend to be over 90 percent.

11 The statistics on the 1977 cohort come from the 1995 INS Fact Sheet. Last accessed
    September 20, 2001 at http://www.ins.usdoj.gov/graphics/aboutins/statistics/299.htm

12 These numbers are calculated from the IPUMS 1920 Census sample microfiles.

13 Examining citizenship rates rather than levels, we find virtually no gender gap for those
    married at least once: men have an average wait time of 20.9 years and a median of
    20 years between arrival and naturalization, while for women the numbers were
    19.6 years and 19 years respectively. Among those never married, a category comprising
    only 10 percent of all adult women, women took longer than men to acquire citizenship:

on average they waited 16.1 years (a median of 12 years) compared to 12.8 for men (a median of 9 years).

14   Aylsworth (1931) reports that in the nineteenth century, at least 22 states and territories granted alien suffrage; our own count puts the number higher, at 28.

15   Space limitations prevent a discussion of the character of immigrant assimilation. Historically, commentators and academics assumed that immigrants would – and should – integrate into the white American middle class. Today, various researchers identify multiple integration trajectories that depend on race and socio-economic class (Gans 1992; Portes and Zhou 1993; Waters 1999; Zhou and Bankston III 1998).

REFERENCES

Adamic, Louis (1944). *Nation of Nations.* New York: Harper and Brothers.

Alba, Richard and Victor Nee (2003). *Remaking the American Mainstream: Assimilation and Contemporary Immigration.* Cambridge, MA: Harvard University Press.

Alland, Alexander (1943). *American Counterpoint.* New York: John Day Company.

Anbinder, Tyler Gregory (1992). *Nativism and Slavery: The Northern Know Nothings and the Politics of the 1850s.* New York: Oxford University Press.

Anderson, Margo (1988). *The American Census: A Social History.* New Haven, CT: Yale University Press.

Aylsworth, Leon E. (1931). "The Passing of Alien Suffrage." *American Political Science Review* 25(1): 114–16.

Basch, Linda, Nina Glick Schiller, and Cristina Szanton Blanc (1994). *Nations Unbound: Transnational Projects, Postcolonial Predicaments and Deterritorialized Nation-States.* Langhorne, PA: Gordon and Breach.

Bean, Frank D. and Gillian Stevens (2003). *America's Newcomers and the Dynamics of Diversity.* New York: Russell Sage Foundation.

Bernard, William S. (1936). "Cultural Determinants of Naturalization." *American Sociological Review* 1: 943–53.

Bloemraad, Irene (2000a). "American Citizenship and Naturalization in the Early 20th Century." Social Science History Association. Pittsburgh, PA.

—— (2000b). "U.S. Naturalization in Historic Perspective: What Can the Past Tell Us About the Present?" American Sociological Association. Washington, DC.

—— (2002). "The North American Naturalization Gap: An Institutional Approach to Citizenship Acquisition in the United States and Canada." *International Migration Review* 36(1): 193–228.

Bredbrenner, Candice Lewis (1998). *A Nationality of Her Own: Women, Marriage, and the Law of Citizenship.* Berkeley: University of California Press.

Brubaker, William Rogers (1992). *Citizenship and Nationhood in France and Germany.* Cambridge, MA: Harvard University Press.

Clark, Terry Nichols (1975). "The Irish Ethic and the Spirit of Patronage." *Ethnicity* 2(4): 305–59.

Cockburn, Sir Alexander James Edmund (1869). *Nationality: Or, The Law Relating to Subjects and Aliens, Considered with a View to Future Legislation.* London: W. Ridgway.

Crevecoeur, J. Hector St. Jean de (1981). *Letters From an American Farmer* [1782]. New York: Penguin.

DeSipio, Louis (2001). "Building America, One Person at a Time: Naturalization and the Political Behavior of the Naturalized in Contemporary American Politics." In Gary Gerstle and John Mollenkopf, eds., *E Pluribus Unum? Contemporary and Historical Perspectives on Immigrant Political Incorporation.* New York: Russell Sage, pp. 67–106.

Erie, Steven P. (1988). *Rainbow's End: Irish-Americans and the Dilemmas of Urban Machine Politics, 1840–1985*. Berkeley: University of California Press.

Evans, M.D.R. (1988). "Choosing to Be a Citizen: The Time-Path of Citizenship in Australia." *International Migration Review* 22(2): 243–64.

Fischer, David Hackett (1989). *Albion's Seed: Four British Folkways in America*. New York: Oxford University Press.

Flournoy, Richard W., Jr. and Manley O. Hudson (1929). *A Collection of Nationality Laws of Various Countries as Contained in Constitutions, Statutes and Treaties*. New York: Oxford University Press.

Gans, Herbert (1992). "Second-Generation Decline: Scenarios for the Economic and Ethnic Futures of the Post-1965 American Immigrants." *Ethnic and Racial Studies* 15(2): 173–90.

Gavit, John Palmer (1922). *Americans by Choice*. New York: Harper and Brothers.

Glazer, Nathan and Daniel Patrick Moynihan (1963). *Beyond the Melting Pot*. Cambridge, MA: MIT Press.

Goldin, Claudia (1993). "The Political Economy of Immigration Restriction in the United States, 1890 to 1921." Working Paper No. 4345. Cambridge, MA: National Bureau of Economic Research.

Graham, Stephen N. (1980). *1900 Public Use Sample, User's Handbook*. Seattle, WA: Center for Studies in Demography and Ecology, University of Washington.

Gualtieri, Sarah (2001). "Becoming 'White': Race, Religion and the Foundations of Syrian/ Lebanese Ethnicity in the United States." *Journal of American Ethnic History* 20: 29–58.

Hamilton, Alexander, James Madison, and John Jay (1961). *The Federalist Papers*, ed. Clinton Rossiter. New York: Penguin.

Harper-Ho, Virginia (2000). "Noncitizen Voting Rights: The History, the Law and Current Prospects for Change." *Law and Inequality Journal* 18: 271–322.

Higham, John (1988). *Strangers in the Land: Patterns of American Nativism, 1860–1925*, 2nd edn. New Brunswick, NJ: Rutgers University Press.

Hooglund, Eric J., ed. (1987). *Crossing the Waters: Arabic-Speaking Immigrants to the United States Before 1940*. Washington, DC: Smithsonian Institution Press.

Huntington, Samuel P. (2004). *Who Are We? The Challenges to America's National Identity*. New York: Simon & Schuster.

Jasso, Guillermina and Mark R. Rosenzweig (1986). "Family Reunification and the Immigrant Multiplier: U.S. Immigration Law, Origin-Country Conditions, and the Reproduction of Immigrants." *Demography* 23(3): 291–311.

Jones-Correa, Michael (2001). "Under Two Flags: Dual Nationality in Latin America and Its Consequences for Naturalization in the United States." *International Migration Review* 35(4): 997–1029.

Kettner, James H. (1978). *The Development of American Citizenship*. Chapel Hill: University of North Carolina Press.

Keyssar, Alexander (2000). *The Right to Vote: The Contested History of Democracy in the United States*. New York: Basic Books.

Levitt, Peggy (2001). *The Transnational Villagers*. Berkeley: University of California Press.

Liang, Zai (1994). "Social Contact, Social Capital, and the Naturalization Process: Evidence from Six Immigrant Groups." *Social Science Research* 23: 407–37.

López, Ian F. Haney (1996). *White by Law: The Legal Construction of Race*. New York: New York University Press.

McDonald, Forrest and Ellen McDonald (1980). "The Ethnic Origins of the American People, 1790." *William and Mary Quarterly Review* 37 (April): 179–99.

Miller, Kenneth D. (1943). *We Who Are America*. New York: Friendship Press.

Ngai, Mae (2004). *Impossible Subjects: Illegal Aliens and the Making of Modern America*. Princeton, NJ: Princeton University Press.

Plascencia, Luis F.B., Gary P. Freeman, and Mark Setzler (2003). "The Decline of Barriers to Immigrant Economic and Political Rights in the American States, 1977–2001." *International Migration Review* 37(1): 5–23.

Portes, Alejandro and Min Zhou (1993). "The New Second Generation: Segmented Assimilation and Its Variants." *Annals of the American Academy of Political and Social Science* 530: 74–96.

Portes, Alejandro, Luis Eduardo Guarnizo, and Patricia Landolt (1999). "Introduction: Pitfalls and Promise of an Emergent Research Field." *Ethnic and Racial Studies* 22(2): 217–37.

Raskin, Jamin B. (1993). "Legal Aliens, Local Citizens: The Historical, Constitutional and Theoretical Meanings of Alien Suffrage." *University of Pennsylvania Law Review* 141: 1391–470.

Rosberg, Gerald M. (1977). "Aliens and Equal Protection: Why Not the Right to Vote?" *Michigan Law Review* 75: 1092–136.

Ruggles, Steven and Matthew Sobek (1997). "Integrated Public Use Microdata Series: Version 2.0." Minneapolis: Historical Census Projects, University of Minnesota. www.ipums.org

Sapiro, Virginia (1984). "Women, Citizenship and Nationality: Immigration and Naturalization Policies in the United States." *Politics and Society* 13: 1–26.

Saveth, Edward N. (1948). *American Historians and European Immigrants*. New York: Columbia University Press.

Schneider, Dorothee (2001). "Naturalization and United States Citizenship in Two Periods of Mass Migration: 1894–1930, 1965–2000." *Journal of American Ethnic History* 21(1): 50–82.

Schuck, Peter H. and Rogers M. Smith (1985). *Citizenship Without Consent: Illegal Aliens in the American Polity*. New Haven, CT: Yale University Press.

Smith, Rogers M. (1997). *Civic Ideals: Conflicting Visions of Citizenship in U.S. History*. New Haven, CT: Yale University Press.

Ueda, Reed (1982). "Naturalization and Citizenship." In Richard A. Easterlin, David Ward, William S. Bernard, and Reed Ueda, eds., *Immigration*. Cambridge, MA: Belknap Press, pp. 106–54.

—— (1996). "The Changing Path to Citizenship: Ethnicity and Naturalization During World War II." In Lewis A. Erenberg and Susan E. Hirsch, eds., *The War in American Culture: Society and Consciousness During World War II*. Chicago: University of Chicago Press, pp. 202–16.

US Commission on Naturalization (1905). Report to the President. Washington DC: Government Printing Office.

US Congress. House of Representatives (1905). Report to the President of the Commission on Naturalization, Document No. 46. Washington, DC: US Government Printing Office.

US Department of Homeland Security (2004). *Yearbook of Immigration Statistics, 2003*. Washington, DC: US Government Printing Office.

US Immigration and Naturalization Service (2002). *Statistical Yearbook of the Immigration and Naturalization Service, 2000*. Washington, DC: US Government Printing Office.

Waters, Mary C. (1999). *Black Identities: West Indian Immigrant Dreams and American Realities*. Cambridge, MA: Harvard University Press.

Williams, Hattie Plum (1912). "The Road to Citizenship." *Political Science Quarterly* 27(3): 399–427.

Wise, John S. (1906). *A Treatise on Citizenship*. Northport, NY: Edward Thompson Co.

Yang, Philip Q. (1994). "Explaining Immigrant Naturalization." *International Migration Review* 28(3): 449–77.

Zhou, Min and Carl L. Bankston III (1998). *Growing Up American: How Vietnamese Children Adapt to Life in the United States*. New York: Russell Sage Foundation.

CHAPTER THREE

Immigration and Ethnic Politics

JAMES J. CONNOLLY

Ethnicity has long mattered in American politics. How it has mattered and how historians have understood the relationship between ethnicity and politics in the United States has changed significantly over the past quarter-century. Before the 1980s, most scholars looked to social categories such as ethnicity to explain political behavior. More recently they have recognized that group identities are not fixed attributes and that politics itself is a creative force that has had a powerful impact on the experiences and self-understandings of immigrants and their progeny. The civic environment the famine Irish entered differed from that encountered by early twentieth-century Italians and differed sharply from that which Latino migrants found as they arrived during the 1990s. As a result, for reasons quite apart from their distinctive cultural inheritances, these and other groups have perceived their relationship with the wider society in significantly different ways.

Two broad theoretical transformations fueled this shift in the scholarly approach to ethnic politics. The first involved a move away from primordial understandings of ethnicity and toward an approach highlighting the invention and reinvention of group identities. The declining authority of socially driven models of political development and the emergence of interpretations stressing the socially creative role of public culture constituted the second important intellectual development. Together they opened the way for a more dynamic historical approach to the relationship between ethnicity and politics, one in which civic culture and political institutions played a central role in shaping group identities.

The most important of these changes is the rethinking of ethnicity itself. An older "primordialist" approach stressed shared ancestry and inherited culture as the markers of largely static group identities. During the 1960s Nathan Glazer and Daniel Moynihan (1963) challenged this interpretation, presenting ethnicity as a basis for interest group action and arguing that its political persistence stemmed largely from its utility as a vehicle for collective mobilization. By the end of the decade, Frederick Barth and other scholars insisted that the social boundaries that separated ethnicities were more vague and more permeable than once imagined (Barth 1969). More recently, postmodern theory has fueled a thorough rethinking of the meaning and character of ethnicity in several disciplines. Literary and cultural theorists have been particularly influential. They emphatically reject the primordialist view and argue that ethnicity is better seen as an invention, a "collective fiction" designed (and frequently redesigned) "to substantiate politically motivated feelings of peoplehood" (Sollors 1989, pp. xii–xiii). Most historians of ethnicity in America have accepted a modified version of the latter approach, one that stresses time and place and limits the range of possible inventions. Insisting on the importance of historical context for understanding the development of ethnic groups, they have nevertheless accepted the basic notion that ethnicity is a cultural construction rather than a fixed category (Conzen et al. 1992).

As ideas about ethnicity grew more fluid, so too did approaches to the relationship between politics and society. For several generations, historians approached politics as the expression of conflicts generated in a separate realm. Interpretations within this paradigm changed: the progressive and Marxist emphasis on class conflict as the driving force of public life gave way to "ethno-cultural" explanations that used statistical analysis to document a relationship between ethnic and religious group membership and voting behavior. Group explanations have shaped urban political historiography as well. Scholars writing after World War II depicted city politics as a clash between immigrant-based party machines and native-born, middle-class reformers. Revisionists ultimately expanded the list of reformers to include workers, women, and even some immigrants, but they never discarded the notion that political action should be conceived in terms of groups and that groups took shape outside politics.

A new generation of historians and social scientists has successfully challenged socially driven approaches to politics. Some emphasize the necessity of understanding politics on its own terms, as a sphere of activity that operates independently of changes in society. Others note the importance of institutions, especially the state, in shaping social identity. The configuration and shape of the government, as Theda Skocpol has argued, "encourage some kinds of group formation and political action, but not others" (1985, p. 20). Analysts of political culture have explored the ways in which political language and culture supply meanings for collective action and help define the relationship between individuals or groups and the wider community and society. These new avenues of research highlight the role of politics as a formative force in the creation of social groups.

These changes in political and ethnic history have moved the study of ethnic politics – civic action on the basis of a perceived cultural or national identity – in new directions. The cultural baggage immigrant groups carried with them had a profound impact on their experiences and identities in the United States. But developments in the host society mattered as well, and the evolution of American political institutions and culture constituted a key dimension of those changes. To fully grasp the process of ethnic group formation requires careful consideration of the civic contexts immigrants encountered as they entered the United States and became politically active.

Each of the three major waves of immigrants to the United States during the nineteenth and twentieth centuries encountered a distinctive political environment. Irish and German immigrants arriving during the middle of the nineteenth century joined a polity where universal manhood suffrage had only recently been established. Parties had just emerged as the principal means of mobilizing electoral majorities, and the new arrivals, especially the Irish, were swept into these novel organizations. The rapid embrace of the party machine provided them with a sharp partisan identity and credentials as bona fide Americans, paving the way for the development of an ethnic-American identity predicated on a culturally plural vision of American society.

The southern and eastern Europeans who came to the United States in large numbers between 1880 and the 1920s entered a changing public sphere. Urban machines proved less likely to mobilize them as they had the Irish and Germans a half-century earlier. A scarce supply of patronage and a firm grip on power meant that most party organizations had little reason to encourage electoral participation among Italians, East European Jews, and other newcomers. Since these new arrivals did not speak English and had less experience with political activism than their Irish predecessors, it took them longer to develop a politicized group consciousness. When they did, unsympathetic machines often forced them to find alternative avenues of political expression outside the regular party organizations, although this process differed depending on the circumstances on the ground in each setting. Faced with this resistance, they developed a sharp sense of ethnic distinctiveness and articulated a fuller and more forcefully expressed vision of ethnic pluralism. That vision faced a sharp challenge from intolerant Americanizers during the 1920s but ultimately American political life proved open enough to accommodate them.

The latest wave of immigrants to the United States, originating largely from Latin America and Asia, has experienced a substantially different political culture. The power of parties has diminished sharply, alternative forms of political action inspired by the civil rights movement have increased dramatically, and government welfare programs, some geared toward specific racial and ethnic groups, have expanded significantly. The possibility of maintaining a transnational identity has also increased substantially. The result is a political culture that places a premium on group identity, often conceived in racialized categories such as Hispanic and Asian. The politicization of recently arrived Dominicans, Guatemalans, Vietnamese, and Arabs has occurred in these terms rather than as partisans, and their sense of opposition to mainstream American society has been especially sharp. From this context, a multicultural politics has arisen, one that stresses the conflict between ethnic groups and American society as a whole. Whether it can sustain itself against the assimilative force of American mass culture remains an open question.

A history of ethnic politics that emphasizes the influence of politics on ethnicity represents a departure from the perspective that prevailed a generation ago. One measure of this difference comes from an examination of Edward Kantowicz's essay on "Politics" in the once-standard *Harvard Encyclopedia of American Ethnic Groups*, published in 1980. Neatly capturing the period's scholarship, the essay featured a summary of ethno-cultural voting patterns, a description of machine politics, and group-by-group sketches of political behavior and experience. Questions of group formation are absent from the analysis. Instead, it asserted that "ethnicity formed the basis of party politics through much of American history [and] it was most visible in the realm of big-city boss politics" (Kantowicz 1980, p. 806). In this formulation the meaning and character of ethnicity went unquestioned and public life was imagined as a clash of groups that had formed outside of the political realm. Machine politics represented the classic example of this process and the machine model was assumed to fit almost every city. Although not wholly static in its treatment of ethnic political experience, the essay placed little emphasis on the broad institutional and cultural shifts that have defined American political development. Such limitations are not testimony to its failures but to the shape of the field at that moment and, read now, to the historiographic changes of the last three decades that have made a more dynamic account of American ethnic politics possible.

The Party Period

Although the American colonies featured a substantial degree of cultural diversity, the mobilization of voters on the basis of ethnicity intensified substantially after 1830. At that point a large stream of immigrants from Ireland and Germany began flowing into the young nation. Other groups – most notably Scandinavians and French Canadians – came as well, but the Irish and Germans were the largest groups and had the most significant political impact. Numbers alone did not create a distinctly ethnic politics. The institutional arrangements necessary to incorporate them into American civic life had taken shape as well. The emergence of a full-fledged mass party politics by 1840 fostered the rapid inclusion of immigrants in the electorate. Even as nativist hostility intensified, the structure and ideology of American politics provided immigrants with opportunities to respond politically and to demonstrate loyalty to their new nation. And while both Irish and German immigrants brought from the old country characteristics that shaped their political thought and action, the institutional and cultural milieu of mid-nineteenth-century American public life had a decisive effect on the identities they created for themselves in the new nation.

The influx of Irish and German migrants laid the groundwork for the American republic's first politics of ethnicity. More than 2.5 million Irish immigrants arrived in the United States between 1840 and 1880 (Daniels 1990, p. 129). Most were Catholic and most settled in cities along the eastern seaboard. Peasants fleeing political oppression and economic devastation, they lacked skills and money. But they did bring the political experience of mobilizing against British power, which provided both a sense of national identity and familiarity with political organization, qualities that would help them acclimatize to democratic politics in the United States. They also spoke English, which made political participation easier.

Close to 2.9 million Germans entered the country during the same period (Daniels 1990, p. 146). They did not speak English and they were divided by religious and regional differences, obstacles to effective political action in the United States. But most brought with them sufficient skills and wealth to migrate beyond the east coast and to create a substantial institutional and cultural network in middle America, a base from which they could make their political presence felt.

The civic incorporation of the Irish and Germans did not proceed without resistance. Anti-Catholicism, pervasive in the colonial period, remained a powerful source of nativism during the nineteenth century. The close association between Protestantism and national identity meant that the initial arrival of Irish Catholics during the 1820s and 1830s prompted expressions of alarm. Anti-Catholic tracts such as Samuel Morse's (1835) warning about the "imminent dangers" presented by immigrant newcomers, and violent incidents such as the burning of an Ursuline convent in Charlestown, Massachusetts reflected the increasing threat many perceived in the growing Irish presence in the United States. The rush of famine migrants and

German Catholics during the 1840s and 1850s only intensified these concerns, which received fullest expression in the explosive growth and electoral success of the American ("Know Nothing") Party during the early 1850s.

Despite nativist antagonism, the mobilization of Irish and German immigrants occurred remarkably quickly because of the character of American politics at mid-century. These newcomers arrived *en masse* just as the second party system took shape. Changes in the economic, social, and political order of mid-nineteenth-century America fueled a transformation in the nation's political culture. Industrialization created a large body of wageworkers for whom traditional political distinctions between merchant and mechanic carried little weight. The elimination of property restrictions gave most white men the vote, undercutting the politics of deference that had prevailed in the early republic. Faced with these altered circumstances, party leaders devised new ways of organizing and mobilizing the expanding electorate, particularly in cities. Although the Whig Party would fade and the Republican Party emerge as the second party system gave way to the third, the partisan character of American public life would persist through the remainder of the nineteenth century.

The machine style of party politics taking shape in cities encouraged the political incorporation of immigrants. Urban Democratic organizations aggressively sought to mobilize recently arrived immigrants, often overlooking the five-year residency requirement dictated by naturalization law. In 1840s Buffalo, courts produced as many as 200 new citizens per week in the run-up to spring and fall elections, almost all Democrats (Gerber 1989, p. 339). New York City's Tammany Hall machine transformed newcomers into American citizens at an incredible rate during these years – 9,207 per year between 1856 and 1867, most of them Irish. It produced another 41,112 in 1868 alone in order to win a key state election (Erie 1988, p. 51).

As the party of the workingman and the "Democracy" – the party of the people – Democrats attracted nearly all the Irish and many Germans. More comfortable than their Whig counterparts with the idea of partisanship and its concomitant vision of a plural, conflict-ridden society, Democratic leaders readily developed group-oriented appeals. Attacks on nativism, critiques of temperance, defenses of the Catholic Church, celebrations of ethnic holidays, and scathing indictments of British policy in Ireland became key elements of the rhetorical stock in trade of Democratic politicians during the 1840s and 1850s. Recognition also came in the form of public offices, patronage, and policy decisions. Not only did these gestures cement the loyalty of immigrants to the Democratic Party and to the state, they reinforced their sense of collective identity by distributing the benefits on a group basis.

But partisanship was more than a proxy for ethnicity. Membership in a party constituted an identity unto itself, sustained through a range of popular rituals such as parades, rallies, and summer outings, as well as a plethora of speeches and pamphlets. It was as partisans that immigrants became more directly engaged in civic life, particularly at the local level. As Michael McGerr (1986) has noted, parties, not group identities, were "the basic principle of public life" in the northern United States until late in the nineteenth century. The Democratic Party, political home to most immigrants, helped teach its rank and file how to be Americans, an identity it defined in egalitarian and racialized terms (Baker 1983). After the Civil War, public displays such as Tammany Hall's elaborate Fourth of July celebration reaffirmed the party's loyalty to the nation and its members' patriotism. Joining the Democracy thus not only reinforced and ratified a sense of ethnic group membership; it provided evidence of immigrants' Americanization in the face of nativist attacks.

By providing a means through which immigrants could express group identity and loyalty to America simultaneously, parties encouraged a pluralistic sense of national identity. As Lawrence Fuchs (1990, pp. 19–23, 35–53) has argued, the political incorporation of nineteenth-century Irish and German immigrants through party organizations fueled the growth of "voluntary pluralism," the idea that being American required a commitment to republican institutions rather than a common ancestry or cultural identity. David Gerber's (1989) study of antebellum Buffalo demonstrated how the rise of the second party system played a key role in forging a plural conception of American society. Though the ideal of a multi-ethnic society would not receive systematic philosophical treatments until the twentieth century, it became an article of faith in ethnic circles by the middle of the nineteenth century. Party politics was hardly the sole source of this development, but as the principal form of civic action it helped create the perception that ethnic loyalty and American identity were compatible.

There were limits to the nineteenth-century pluralist vision. Most notable were its racial dimensions. Scholars such as David Roediger (1991), Noel Ignatiev (1995), and Matthew Jacobson (1998) have argued that the inclusion of European immigrants in definitions of mainstream American identity rested in part on their classification as whites. The highly fluid concept of whiteness provided a means by which these groups distinguished themselves as suitable republican citizens in relation to African Americans. Democratic Party culture, with its emphasis on minstrelsy and racist ideology, underscored the whiteness of its immigrant adherents, especially the Irish. In similar fashion, campaigns against Asian immigrants were spearheaded by west coast politicians such as Dennis Kearney, a process that bolstered Irish claims to whiteness and by extension to full citizenship (Jacobson 1998, p. 159).

Partisanship was not the only basis for immigrant activism during the nineteenth century. Nonpartisan reform movements occasionally attracted ethnic support. German Americans were a key element in the anti-Tammany coalition that formed in New York during the Tweed Ring scandal. In Worcester, Massachusetts during the 1880s Irish Democrats and some Yankee Republicans joined in support of Citizen's tickets to carry a series of municipal elections (Meagher 2001, pp. 146–7). More often, immigrants turned to labor activism as an alternative means of political action, especially after the Civil War. Labor parties and organizations, most notably the Knights of Labor, attracted substantial ethnic followings. Henry George's 1886 mayoral campaign in New York City earned the support of many Irish workers (Burrows and Wallace 1999, pp. 1100–8). In Chicago, labor groups earned broad support from immigrant workers, sufficient enough to push the Democratic Party toward a new agenda that foreshadowed the social welfare liberalism of the twentieth century (Schneirov 1998).

But partisanship generally eclipsed efforts to mobilize German and Irish immigrants as citizens and workers. Most nonpartisan citizens' movements were transient during the Gilded Age, rarely lasting more than a few years. Labor insurgencies attracted substantial support in ethnic communities but lacked the staying power of party machines. When George's mayoral run threatened to draw large numbers of

Irish out of the ranks of Tammany, the machine responded with a fierce effort to return them to the party fold, in part by accommodating working-class styles (Shefter 1978). While labor made inroads within the Democratic Party in Gilded Age Chicago, it was as Democrats rather than as members of workers' organizations that ethnics most often cast their votes. The identities they carried with them to the polls cannot be simply reduced to ethnicity, class, or any other single category. But the pervasiveness of partisanship in nineteenth-century American politics – both in institutional and in cultural terms – meant that it usually overlay other solidarities in a manner that underscored their compatibility with an American identity.

The Rise of Interest Group Politics

The next major wave of immigrants, arriving primarily from southern and eastern Europe between 1880 and 1924, encountered a different polity. Parties remained powerful but lost their monopoly on electoral office, especially at the local level. Interest group action, whether in the form of a civic organization, a union, or less formal agitation, became an increasingly effective means of exercising power. Urban machines, straining to accommodate the demands of their existing supporters, were less receptive to newcomers than they had been a half-century earlier. As a result, newly arrived Italians, Slavs, and East European Jews frequently engaged in different kinds of politics, acting as interest groups rather than partisans. In the short run, this alternative form of mobilization sharpened ethnic conflict. But American national identity and the civic life of this era ultimately proved capacious enough to incorporate them without forcing them to abandon their ethnic identity.

The surge of immigration to the United States commencing around 1880 brought newcomers who were less well equipped to enter American politics than their Irish and German predecessors. During the peak decade (from 1901 to 1910), more than 2.1 million people came to the United States from the Austro-Hungarian Empire, more than 2 million from Italy, and almost 1.6 million from Russia (Daniels 1990, p. 188). These broad categories belie the ethnic and religious complexity of this European influx, which included Jews, Poles, Hungarians, Slavs, and Italians with many provincial loyalties. Most did not speak or read English, few had useful skills, and many Americans regarded them as so culturally alien or racially unfit that they were incapable of functioning in a democracy. Large portions of some groups, such as Italians, did not intend to stay permanently in the United States and so never pursued naturalization or sought to participate in civic life. Immigrants from Japan and China – there were approximately 70,000 of each in the United States in 1910 according to the federal census – were legally barred from becoming citizens (Daniels 1990, pp. 240, 250).

Those who could and did engage in political activity confronted a changing political environment. The "party period" gave way during the 1890s to what political scientists call the "System of 1896." A process of long-term party decline began at the end of the nineteenth century, triggered by diminished partisan competition in most regions following the 1896 partisan realignment, the structural reforms of the Progressive era, and shifts in political culture. The state grew larger and more active and interest group activism became a more effective and prominent feature of American public life. The "spectacular" grassroots politics of the party era faded, replaced by a more bureaucratic "advertised" politics that made voters consumers instead of participants (McGerr 1986). Party culture did not disintegrate entirely, especially in urban settings, but the opportunities for political involvement within party structures diminished while other avenues of action opened.

Urban machines persisted through these changes in many instances, often growing more powerful as an expansive state created new resources for them. But they also faced significant constraints. By the late nineteenth century, the specter of middle-class tax revolts bred fiscal conservatism among most urban party organizations. Unwilling to spend too much and provoke reform campaigns, bosses grew stingy with patronage and less interested in mobilizing new groups into party coalitions. Immigrants arriving after 1880 thus found Irish-dominated machines such as Tammany Hall reluctant to spend scarce resources on mobilizing and rewarding Italians and Jews. New York's rapid naturalization rates of the 1850s and 1860s had slowed considerably by the 1880s and remained slow thereafter, despite massive immigration (Erie 1988, pp. 91–100). Similar patterns developed in Boston, San Francisco, and other cities where Irish politicians were entrenched. Boston ward boss Martin Lomasney, famous for controlling his multi-ethnic district with an iron hand from the 1880s to the 1930s, proved far less receptive to the newer groups that arrived after 1900 than he was to the Irish during the nineteenth century (Connolly 2003). When they did seek to reward other ethnic groups, machine politicians used symbolic gestures or social legislation that would benefit immigrants collectively rather than individually.

There were substantial local variations to this pattern. In Chicago, where two-party competition remained strong and where structural reform failed, both parties recruited new immigrants aggressively through the 1920s. Harold Gosnell (1937) found in 1928 that 70 percent of the city's Democratic precinct captains had assisted immigrants in the naturalization process. The Democratic Party's ultimate consolidation of power in the form of the Cook County machine resulted in large part from its ability to create a political "House for All Peoples" (Allswang 1971). But Chicago was an exception to the rule. For the most part, urban party organizations proved far less responsive to groups arriving after 1880 than they had been to those that had established a presence in the United States by the middle of the nineteenth century.

Denied spoils, turn-of-the-century newcomers sought alternative paths to power. Labor organization offered one route, though it was often closed to recent immigrants. The more inclusive style of pan-ethnic unionism practiced by the Knights of Labor had largely faded by the Progressive era, although the IWW persisted in advancing a comparable vision. The American Federation of Labor's conservative style of trade unionism proved more durable and provided some ethnics with access to power. Though recent scholarship has suggested that the American Federation of Labor was politically active despite its apolitical rhetoric, it primarily served the interests of skilled workers, few of whom were recent arrivals from southern and eastern Europe or Asia (Greene 1998; Mink 1986). There were efforts by radicals at the local level to create cross-ethnic class-based politics. But efforts to mobilize immigrants on the basis of class bore only limited fruit and were largely undercut by the anti-radical hysteria triggered by World War I.

Progressive reform provided other means of mobilizing the immigrants cut out of machine coalitions. The political reforms of the early twentieth century not only weakened parties, they also encouraged alternative forms of civic action. A distinctive version of this process unfolded at the grassroots, particularly in neighborhood settings where ethnic leaders – or those claiming such roles – were able to use the rhetoric and style of this new politics to exercise political power on behalf of immigrant communities. Although older immigrant groups had at times employed extrapartisan civic action throughout the nineteenth century, it became an especially important political method during the early twentieth century. This activity took several shapes, including nonpartisan civic groups, public protests, and, as Evelyn Sterne (2004) has demonstrated, organizational efforts rooted in Catholic parish life.

Progressivism itself provided a political style allowing ethnic leaders to circumvent party organizations. Pitting "the people" against selfish interests, it proved a remarkably flexible rhetorical tool for framing nonpartisan civic action. In Boston, Jews and Italians repeatedly organized reform insurgencies against Irish Democrat Martin Lomasney's machine between 1900 and the early 1930s, with increasing effectiveness (Connolly 2003). Chicago's ethnics, including Bohemians, Poles, Italians, and other recently arrived groups, organized the United Societies for Local Self Government (USLSG), a federation of more than 350 ethnic organizations that agitated for a range of policy issues, most notably home rule for the city and local control of liquor policy. The USLSG portrayed itself in Progressive terms, as a representative of the people resisting the "arrogant demands of private interests and political bosses," and remained a force in Chicago politics into the 1930s (Flanagan 1987, p. 140). Even members of non-European ethnic groups such as Mexicans and Chinese found in the Progressive style a means for taking political action when partisan means were unavailable, both before and after World War I (Johnson 2000; Sanchez 1993, pp. 108–25; Yung 1995, pp. 101–5).

In the short run, ethnic interest group politics fueled cultural tensions. Entering political life in explicitly ethnic terms and without partisan cover made these groups more visible and left them open to the charge that they held dual loyalties. During World War I, ethnic leaders spearheaded liberty loan campaigns designed to demonstrate the patriotism of their groups. While they did just that, they also drew attention to themselves as groups that were less purely American and helped feed the nativist hostility that peaked during the 1920s. The cultural controversies of that decade, particularly immigration restriction, prohibition, and the rise of the Ku-Klux-Klan, created issues around which ethnic notables could organize political action and contributed to the conflicts that defined that turbulent decade. In urban settings tensions between immigrant groups over power and recognition also sharpened as they became more politically active during the 1920s and 1930s.

The tribalism of the 1920s faded quickly, in part because American political culture remained inclusive, at least for European ethnics. There were to be sure other sources of the shift. The Great Depression forced cultural issues to the background, while the virtual cessation of mass immigration engineered through the Johnson Act of 1924 reduced fears that alien newcomers would overwhelm the nation. But the capacity of American civic life to accommodate newcomers without requiring complete assimilation remained high as well, assuring that the prevailing definition of American identity remained largely open despite the racially based nativism that peaked in the 1920s.

In institutional terms, the party system ultimately proved capacious enough to absorb recent immigrant groups into its coalitions. Although urban party organizations often remained uninterested in, and even hostile to, the mobilization of new immigrants, the national parties, especially the Democrats, attracted their support. The Democratic Party's nomination of Al Smith fueled a process that attracted most of these new voters, whose allegiances were cemented by the policies of the New Deal and the persona of Franklin Roosevelt. This process often unfolded outside the purview of the urban machine rather than within it. The Smith campaign circumvented many local organizations, reaching out to eastern and southern European immigrants as groups through its Naturalized Citizens Division, which issued foreign-language literature directed at Carpetho-Ruthanians, Danes, Croats, Armenians, Czechs, Slovaks, Hungarians, Franco-Americans, Greeks, Lithuanians, Puerto Ricans, Norwegians, Serbs, Rumanians, Slovenians, Spaniards, Swedes, and Syrians (Slayton 2001, p. 278). In Boston, five organizations worked separately on behalf of Smith during the 1928 campaign, including a "Smith Italian League of Massachusetts" headed by an anti-machine politician from the city's North End (Connolly 1998, p. 192). New Deal supporter Fiorello LaGuardia was able to defeat Tammany Hall and become Mayor of New York through an independent campaign and direct appeals to Italian and Jewish voters.

New Deal welfare policies also wedded ethnics to the Democratic Party. The creation of the WPA and other federal programs deepened the pool of available patronage. In Chicago, Pittsburgh, and a few other cities, local party organizations gained control of WPA job programs and other benefits and used them to mobilize recent immigrants. Though not every machine controlled the distribution of these benefits, those that did were able to solidify multi-ethnic coalitions. By the mid-1930s, southern and eastern European ethnics – along with the Irish – had become the backbone of the Democratic Party's New Deal coalition and would remain so into the 1960s.

Partisan mobilization worked differently during the 1930s than it had during the nineteenth century, but with similar results. Irish and Germans had entered politics in large part to defend a shared communal life from culturally hostile challenges. Most of these threats were local; national party loyalty was to a large degree a byproduct of neighborhood concerns. In the New Deal era, as Lizabeth Cohen (1990, pp. 255–8) has shown, working-class ethnics came to view Roosevelt, the national Democratic Party, and the federal government as a direct source of assistance and the direct object of their loyalty. These benefits were distributed without explicit reference to groups. By making claims on national institutions in this fashion ethnics reinforced their sense of American citizenship.

Beyond the institutional links that fostered a sense of national identity, the broader civic culture allowed immigrants and their heirs to be both ethnic and American. To a substantial degree immigrants themselves had forged that pluralist vision. Al Smith's presidential campaign, the insistence of ethnics that they were loyal Americans, the writings of Horace Kallen and others, and ethnic participation in two world wars all challenged more exclusionary conceptions of the nation and its people. And as Lawrence Fuchs (1990) has argued, there was a longer civic tradition that insisted national identity was a matter of commitment to civic principles rather than membership in a particular racial or ancestral group. Though this tradition was honored in the breach as often as not, it remained a powerful force for inclusivity well into the twentieth century, and was particularly salient during the 1930s and 1940s as the United States mobilized against and fought explicitly racialist enemies.

As in the nineteenth century, whiteness remained an essential component of the pluralist vision. Blacks became an important segment of the New Deal coalition and became junior partners in Democratic machines in Chicago and elsewhere. But they were never accorded full legitimacy by white ethnics and their spokesmen. As large numbers of African Americans migrated to northern cities during and after both world wars, they faced fierce and often violent discrimination in the workplace and in residential settings. Urban machines proved unresponsive to the needs and concerns of these newcomers and often explicitly supported the exclusionary actions of their white constituents. Several scholars have suggested that this resistance to black inclusion was part of a process by which ethnics established their whiteness (Jacobson 1998, pp. 91–135; Sugrue 1996, p. 234; Luconi 2001), while others see it as part of a racist tradition that is every bit as fundamental to American civic culture as Fuchs's voluntary pluralism (Smith 1997; King 2000). At the very least it underscores the racial limits of the pluralist politics practiced by mid-twentieth-century ethnics, limits that ultimately drove African Americans to seek political power by new means after World War II and fueled a new kind of ethnic politics in the closing decades of the century.

The Multicultural Era

Recent immigrants have encountered a political culture that has encouraged them to think and act as outsiders. Unlike earlier eras, when politics helped create and legitimate mutually compatible ethnic and American identities, the political developments of the last decades of the twentieth century have fostered a sense of antagonism between minority groups and mainstream American society. The further decline of parties, the growth of state policies geared toward group interests and lobbying organizations devoted to obtaining government benefits for racial groups, and especially the remaking of American political culture spurred by the evolution of the civil rights movement have all contributed to this transformation. Although some observers point to the apparently vast racial and cultural differences between recent arrivals, most of whom are from Asia and Latin America, and earlier European immigrants, they often underestimate the impact of the nation's political culture on identity formation and intergroup relations in late twentieth-century America.

The passage of the Hart–Celler Act in 1965 inaugurated an era of mass immigration that has continued into the early twenty-first century. Although the authors of the law did not expect significant changes in the rate of immigration to the United States, the elimination of the quota system combined with Cold War exigencies and economic globalization triggered a huge influx of immigrants. Immigration rates increased steadily after 1970 and more immigrants came to the United States during the 1990s – 9,095,417 – than in any decade in the nation's history, surpassing the previous high during the 1980s of 8,795,386. Most of these newcomers came from Latin America and Asia rather than Europe. As a result, the 2000 census reported, 11.1 percent of the American population was foreign-born, the highest proportion since the implementation of the Johnson Act in 1924 (and up from 4.7 percent in

1970). More than half (51.7 percent) were from Latin America and the Caribbean and more than a quarter (26.4 percent) were from Asia (Castro 2002).

The different origins of the late twentieth-century wave raised fears in some quarters that the newest immigrants could not be absorbed. Unlike earlier influxes of Europeans, some observers worried, the racial and cultural differences between Hispanic and Asian arrivals and white Americans were so pronounced that they would make it much more difficult, if not impossible, to weave the newcomers into the national fabric. Conservative observers such as Peter Brimelow (1995, p. 264) called for a reduction in immigration in order to preserve the "racial balance" of the United States. Such a step was necessary because "race is destiny in American politics," he added, noting such a claim was especially valid in the wake of the political and policy changes triggered by the civil rights movement.

Brimelow's fears reflected a shaky grasp of the history of race in the United States. Racial categories have never been fixed and Americans have in the past made racial distinctions among groups currently classified as white. Nineteenth-century Irish immigrants and southern and eastern European immigrants arriving during the early twentieth century often found themselves classified as separate races with inborn characteristics that many believed would prevent them from becoming Americans. Over time these groups came to be classified as whites. The racial barriers to their acceptance as legitimate Americans were just as high as those that Asians and Hispanics faced at the end of the twentieth century.

What did change was politics. Public life since the 1960s has done more to encourage recent immigrants to embrace non-white racial identities and done less to encourage them to think of themselves as American than in any previous era. Changes in both the structure and culture of American politics fueled this shift. Both the means by which Americans of all backgrounds pursued political ends and the character of the political identities that ethnics assumed changed substantially during the final decades of the twentieth century.

Numerous political scientists and historians have noted sharp changes in the American polity since the end of World War II. The power of parties, declining since the Progressive era, diminished steadily during the second half of the twentieth century. Although parties remained significant factors in policy making, their ability to organize the electorate and to shape the political identities of ordinary citizens dropped sharply after 1950. Fewer Americans voted and those who did were less likely to identify themselves as a member of either major party and more likely to vote a split ticket. By the late twentieth century, politics in the United States entered what Benjamin Ginsberg and Martin Shefter (1990) called a "postelectoral era," in which the exercise of power at the national level is most likely to take the form of investigations, media revelations, or judicial proceedings. Intensive lobbying and symbolic protest politics became a common means of civic action at both the national and local levels. An expanding welfare state that kept close track of group membership and distributed benefits on the basis of group grievances, though reined in somewhat after 1980, has also created incentives for collective mobilization and extra-electoral action by ethnic and racial groups.

Structural encouragement for what Ginsberg and Shefter called "politics by other means" meshed with the political and cultural effects of the civil rights movement. It is difficult to underestimate the impact of the African American campaign for full citizenship during the 1950s and 1960s on the civic life of the United States. Not only did it achieve legislative successes, it effectively challenged the legitimacy of existing institutions and created a model of non-electoral political action that many groups have since employed. Although Martin Luther King, the Southern Christian Leadership Conference, and the Student Nonviolent Coordinating Committee (SNCC) did not invent the civil disobedience and protest tactics that the movement used, they demonstrated their efficacy and established their validity in dramatic fashion. These methods highlighted and frequently provoked immoral, often violent resistance from the constituted authorities in southern states. The rejection of delegates from the Mississippi Freedom Democratic Party at the 1964 Democratic National Convention and the lack of federal support for civil rights activists in the south underscored the intransigence of established institutions and political processes. As Philip Gleason (2001) has argued, these events undercut the moral legitimacy of American politics and government in the eyes of many and encouraged alternative means of pursuing group ends.

The growing militancy of African American civil rights protesters during the 1960s intensified this perspective. As Malcolm X drew increased attention, as the SNCC became more radical, and as the Black Panthers emerged as a force in urban settings, the vision of the United States as a fundamentally racist and oppressive society gained currency. Urban riots and racially charged clashes between the police and African Americans in various cities further sharpened the perception that America was a fundamentally hostile place for racial minorities. Even Martin Luther King's foray into Chicago met ferocious white resistance, demonstrating for many the depth and pervasiveness of racism in the United States. Other protest movements, including the anti-Vietnam War campaign and the activism of aggrieved ethnic groups, borrowed both the tactics and the mentality of the civil rights movement.

It was in this context that the ethnic politics of the final decades of the twentieth century unfolded. Traditional means of immigrant incorporation, such as party politics and union activism, lost much of their authority. Interest group lobbying grew in importance, but remained a route open only to those with sufficient financial resources and organizational capacity. Mass protest appeared to be the only means available for those otherwise disenfranchised. Immigrants from Latin America and Asia, and even more established European groups organized in ethnic terms, increasingly adopted the civil rights style, a process that fueled the creation of collective identities marked by a pronounced hostility toward what they saw as mainstream white America.

This remaking of American civic culture most directly and immediately influenced Mexicans. Unlike other Hispanic groups, Mexicans had been a substantial presence in the United States since the nineteenth century. Owing to the proximity of their homeland and the fierce discrimination they faced, the Mexican embrace of American identity had always been more tentative and varied than that of their European counterparts. Benjamin Heber Johnson's (2000) examination of Mexican American politics in south Texas during the early twentieth century reveals three responses to the social and economic upheavals of the era: participation in party politics, Progressive-style independent political action, and militant, violent resistance to white power inspired in part by the Mexican Revolution. When radical action failed, a middle-class program based on a combined Mexican American identity emerged in the form of the League of United Latin American Citizens (LULAC). Stressing patriotism, a pluralist vision of American society, and civil rights for Mexican Americans, LULAC remained a powerful and moderate force in Mexican American politics through the mid-twentieth century (Marquez 1993). But a steady flow of Mexican migrants, legal and illegal, into the United States sustained a sense of allegiance to Mexico and a rejection of American identity for many members of the group and fueled tensions within it (Gutiérrez 1995).

The civil rights revolution fueled a transition in Mexican American politics during the 1960s. Cesar Chavez and the United Farm Workers drew directly on civil rights methods and ideals to promote the interests of Mexican farm workers and Mexican Americans more generally. Inspired partly by the rise of black nationalism, the Chicano movement went even further, celebrating a "bronze" race and envisioning a pan-Mexican identity that not only cut across class lines but also linked Mexican Americans with non-citizens in the United States and with Mexicans residing south of the border. It portrayed those living in the United States as an alien group victimized by more than a century of white oppression. The vocabulary of the movement underscored this ideal. The term "Chicano," originally a reference to working-class Mexican newcomers, came to represent all those of Mexican descent (and later all Latin Americans). The vision of "Atz'lan," a mythical territory encompassing both Mexico and the United States, offered a geographic basis for this sense of racial unity. Choosing "La Raza Unida" – a phrase drawn from the era of the Mexican Revolution – as the name of their militant political party highlighted the belief of Mexican radicals that they represented a racially and culturally distinct group that stood apart from mainstream American life. Even more moderate organizations such as LULAC and the Mexican American Political Association increasingly sought to speak to and for all people of Mexican descent living in the United States, regardless of their citizenship status or national allegiance (Gutiérrez 1995).

Descendants of southern and eastern Europeans also attempted to borrow the civil rights model, though it never fit comfortably. Michael Novak's *The Rise of the Unmeltable Ethnics* (1972) argued that PIGS – Poles, Italians, Greeks, and Slavs – had sustained a sense of group identity and deserved to be seen as victims of oppression at the hands of mainstream America, and a revival of ethnicity among these and other European groups developed during the early 1970s. But greater access to political power through traditional channels, including the remnants of party machines operating in some cities, along with the absence of group-based benefits such as affirmative action, meant that such claims rarely provided the basis for sustained political organization and action. The legacy of the civil rights movement was also two-edged in the case of white ethnics. It offered them a model for minority group action but it also made racial divisions – particularly the black–white divide – central to understanding American society. More often than not, members of these groups came to place themselves on the white side of that boundary, particularly when it came to political action, or at least grew increasingly hostile to a liberalism devoted to the redressing of minority grievances. Their ethnicity mattered in private and communal settings, but grew less relevant to political life in this context.

Though the militancy that characterized ethnic politics during the 1960s and early 1970s eventually diminished, the legacies of the era's upheavals continued to shape American ethnic politics. Some ethnic activists continued to draw on civil rights movement models to shape their activism while others sought to create minority coalitions based on shared racial grievances among Asians, Latinos, and African Americans (Kochiyama 1994; Marable 1994). Many observers located the persistence of 1960s activism in the growth of multiculturalism during the 1980s and 1990s. Some commentators envisioned a "soft" multiculturalism that allowed significant diversity inside the umbrella of nationhood, an ideal consistent with older notions of cultural pluralism. Others, drawing on the ideas of black nationalists, promoted a "hard" multiculturalism that presented America as an oppressive state and encouraged racial and ethnic groups to position themselves against the dominant society in both cultural and political terms. They rejected identification with American nationality as either impossible or highly undesirable for racially excluded groups (Gerstle 2001, pp. 349–52). One arena where both varieties of multiculturalism made headway was the classroom, where civic education increasingly focused on group differences and on the history of racism and discrimination minorities faced.

Another development that has discouraged the inclusion of recent immigrants in American politics has been a growing transnationalism. Though long a part of the immigrant experience for some groups, the globalization of the economy and improvements in transportation and communication have made it possible for many more newcomers to keep alive their connections to the old country (Guarnizo 2001). Some nations have allowed immigrants to maintain their status as citizens and voters in their country of origin even while residing permanently in the United States. These dual loyalties have discouraged many new immigrants, particularly Latin Americans, from firmly committing themselves to American civic life. They also prevent the formation of multi-group coalitions similar to those formed in cities by eastern and southern European groups during the New Deal era. In some cases, the connection to homeland politics has hindered coalition building because groups fleeing communist rule, such as Cubans or Nicaraguans, have aligned themselves with the Republican Party while other minority groups have tended to support the Democrats (Henry 1994).

Public policies also reinforced the tendency to imagine group identity in racial terms. The development of affirmative action and other group-oriented governmental policies designed to redress past discrimination encouraged the politicization of broad racial identities such as Hispanic and Asian American. These classifications encompass extraordinary cultural variety but serve as a convenient means to mobilize individuals and pursue collective benefits. Mexican Americans, a long-established group, increasingly identified themselves as Hispanics for political purposes (Gutiérrez 1995, p. 217 n. 1). Similarly, immigrants from places as different as Vietnam, Korea, and the Philippines began to act politically in pan-Asian terms during the late twentieth century. In some respects, the creation of these broad categories may represent a step toward the creation of hyphenated identities such as "Asian-American," much as the transition from provincial to "Italian-American" marked an increased sense of connection to the United States (Luconi 2001).

Institutional arrangements that had once fostered the creation of ethnic-American identities lost much of their capacity to do so by the end of the twentieth century. Firm identification with parties, and by extension with the state and nation, grew less common. Labor unions, another source of political access for some immigrants, lost much of their clout as well. Other non-electoral forms of action served the interests of organized middle- and upper-class activists but rarely provided opportunities for civic participation to recent immigrants (DeSipio 2001). Local government, traditionally the most accessible level of the state for new immigrants, also declined in importance compared to federal authority. Few of the institutions that helped immigrants gain a political foothold in, and a sense of identification with, America mattered as much as they once did.

The nationalist impulses of the late twentieth century have also worked against the creation of mutually compatible ethnic and American identities. Demands for Americanization during the 1980s and 1990s came from the right and were too often reminiscent of earlier waves of nativism. Criticism of illegal immigration, bilingual education, and social services to the immigrant poor often accompanied conservative calls for greater immigrant loyalty, making them far less likely to win a sympathetic hearing from most ethnics. On the left, the Democratic Party proved more comfortable with a multicultural vision, especially its softer variant, but remained committed to affirmative action and other group-oriented policies and appeals that muted assimilating forces. Neither the two major parties nor a coterie of ideologically driven commentators from both ends of the political spectrum were able to formulate an effective call for greater ethnic inclusiveness in American public life as the century closed.

There were a handful of voices, especially in academia, seeking to develop a nationalism that could accommodate group differences as the twenty-first century arrived. David Hollinger's (1995) *Postethnic America* called for a cultural environment in which Americans were free to define their identities with as much or as little reference to their ethnic or racial ancestries as they chose, without risking their status as Americans. Todd Gitlin (1995) sought an alternative to the culture wars and identity politics of the era that recognized diversity but also cultivated a common cultural ground as a basis for pursuit of a common good. Gary Gerstle (2001) argued for a revival of civic nationalism that abandoned older racialist notions of American identity, although he was not optimistic about the prospects of such a project. Commentators on the right as well as the left, including Jim Sleeper (1990), Arthur Schlesinger (1992), Michael Lind (1995), Alan Wolfe (1996), and Peter Schuck (2003), pursued similar ends.

The sense of crisis following the terrorist attacks on the United States in September 2001 may amplify the calls for an inclusive nationalism. There was an immediate backlash against Arabs and Muslims in the United States and the federal government moved to tighten control of the nation's borders and make it more difficult to enter the country. President Bush even backed away from a historic agreement to loosen border restrictions between the United States and Mexico. But the campaign against terrorism also provided opportunities for immigrant groups to demonstrate their loyalty to the nation. More significantly it presented an enemy seeking to impose its culture on the rest of the world, much as the United States faced in World War II. Such a context may help Americans define themselves once again in pluralistic and democratic terms, an effort that could create an opportunity to revive the more flexible definitions of nationhood and American identity that prevailed in earlier eras.

It is uncertain whether such attempts to remake the civic culture can succeed. The absence of the integrative political institutions of the past, particularly party organizations active at the local level, makes the challenge more difficult. Yet the continued assimilative power of American mass culture and the material opportunities available to immigrants give us some reason for optimism. As second-generation immigrants establish themselves economically and socially, they will also be better positioned to take advantage of current civic arrangements. And American identity has proven to be extraordinarily flexible in the past and is likely to remain so. But as Wendy Cho's (1999) examination of political socialization of recent immigrants shows, a process of civic education is essential to the process of political inclusion. If advocates of a more inclusive nationalism can begin to shape school curricula and popular portrayals of American civic life, perhaps some headway can be made. If political leaders and civic activists can begin to craft new institutions that draw a range of participants and that can provide a sense of connection to the community and the nation, such as the volunteer programs developed by the Clinton administration and by private groups, the prospects for an inclusive civic revival increase. But for such efforts to succeed they will have to counter the political and cultural trends of the final four decades of the twentieth century.

REFERENCES

Allswang, J.M. (1971). *A House for All Peoples: Ethnic Politics in Chicago, 1890–1936.* Lexington: University of Kentucky Press.

Baker, J.H. (1983). *Affairs of Party: The Political Culture of Northern Democrats in the Mid-Nineteenth Century.* Ithaca, NY: Cornell University Press.

Barth, F., ed. (1969). *Ethnic Groups and Boundaries. The Social Organization of Culture Difference.* Boston: Little, Brown.

Brimelow, P. (1995). *Alien Nation: Common Sense About America's Immigration Disaster.* New York: HarperCollins.

Burrows, E.G. and M.L. Wallace (1999). *Gotham: A History of New York City to 1898.* New York: Oxford University Press.

Castro, M.J. (2002). "Migration by the Numbers." North-South Center Update. www.miami.edu/nsc/publications/newsupdates/Update54.html (June 10, 2002).

Cho, W.K.T. (1999). "Naturalization, Socialization, Participation: Immigrants and (Non)-Voting." *Journal of Politics* 61: 1140–55.

Cohen, L. (1990). *Making a New Deal: Industrial Workers in Chicago, 1919–1939.* Cambridge: Cambridge University Press.

Connolly, J.J. (1998). *The Triumph of Ethnic Progressivism: Urban Political Culture in Boston, 1900–1925.* Cambridge, MA: Harvard University Press.

—— (2003). "Beyond the Machine: Martin Lomasney and Ethnic Politics." In R. Ueda and C.E. Wright, eds., *Faces of Community: Immigrant Massachusetts, 1860–2000.* Boston: Northeastern University Press.

Conzen, K.N., David, A. Gerber, Ewa Morawska, George F. Pozetta and Rudolf Vecoli (1992). "The Invention of Ethnicity: A Perspective from the U.S.A." *Journal of American Ethnic History* 12: 3–42.

Daniels, R. (1990). *Coming to America: A History of Immigration and Ethnicity in American Life.* New York: HarperCollins.

DeSipio, L. (2001). "Building America, One Person at a Time: Naturalization and Political Behavior of the Naturalized in Contemporary American Politics." In G. Gerstle and J. Mollenkopf, eds., *E Pluribus Unum? Contemporary and Historical Perspectives on Immigrant Political Incorporation.* New York: Russell Sage Foundation, pp. 67–107.

Erie, S.P. (1988). *Rainbow's End: Irish-Americans and the Dilemmas of Urban Machine Politics, 1840–1985.* Berkeley: University of California Press.

Flanagan, M.A. (1987). *Charter Reform in Chicago*. Carbondale: Southern Illinois University Press.

Fuchs, L.H. (1990). *The American Kaleidoscope: Race, Ethnicity, and the Civic Culture*. Hanover, NH: Wesleyan University Press.

Gerber, D.A. (1989). *The Making of an American Pluralism: Buffalo, New York, 1825–60*. Urbana: University of Illinois Press.

Gerstle, G. (2001). *American Crucible: Race and Nation in the Twentieth Century*. Princeton, NJ: Princeton University Press.

Ginsberg, B. and M. Shefter (1990). *Politics By Other Means: The Declining Importance of Elections in America*. New York: Basic Books.

Gitlin, T. (1995). *The Twilight of Common Dreams: Why America is Wracked by the Culture Wars*. New York: Henry Holt.

Glazer, N. and D.P. Moynihan (1963). *Beyond the Melting Pot: The Negroes, Puerto Ricans, Jews, Italians, and Irish of New York City*. Cambridge: MIT Press.

Gleason, P. (2001). "Sea Change in the Civic Culture in the 1960s." In G. Gerstle and J. Mollenkopf, eds., *E Pluribus Unum? Contemporary and Historical Perspectives on Immigrant Political Incorporation*. New York: Russell Sage Foundation, pp. 109–42.

Gosnell, H.F. (1937). *Machine Politics: Chicago Model*. Chicago: University of Chicago Press.

Greene, J. (1998). *Pure and Simple Politics: The American Federation of Labor and Political Activism, 1881–1917*. New York: Cambridge University Press.

Guarnizo, L.E. (2001). "On the Political Participation of Transnational Migrants: Old Practices and New Trends." In G. Gerstle and J. Mollenkopf, eds., *E Pluribus Unum? Contemporary and Historical Perspectives on Immigrant Political Incorporation*. New York: Russell Sage Foundation.

Gutiérrez, D.G. (1995). *Walls and Mirrors: Mexican Americans, Mexican Immigrants, and the Politics of Ethnicity*. Berkeley: University of California Press.

Henry, C.P. (1994). "Urban Politics and Incorporation: The Case of Blacks, Latinos, and Asians in Three Cities." In J. Jennings, ed., *Blacks, Latinos and Asians in Urban America: Status and Prospects for Activism*. Westport, CT: Praeger, pp. 17–28.

Hollinger, D.A. (1995). *Postethnic America: Beyond Multiculturalism*. New York: Basic Books.

Ignatiev, N. (1995). *How the Irish Became White*. New York: Routledge.

Jacobson, M.F. (1998). *Whiteness of a Different Color: European Immigrants and the Alchemy of Race*. Cambridge, MA: Harvard University Press.

Johnson, B.H. (2000). "Sedition and Citizenship in South Texas, 1900–1930." PhD thesis, Yale University.

Kantowicz, E.R. (1980). "Politics." In A. Thernstrom, A. Orlov, and O. Handlin, eds., *Harvard Encyclopedia of American Ethnic Groups*. Cambridge, MA: Harvard University Press, pp. 803–13.

King, D. (2000). "Making Americans: Immigration Meets Race." In G. Gerstle and J. Mollenkopf, eds., *E Pluribus Unum? Contemporary and Historical Perspectives on Immigrant Political Incorporation*. New York: Russell Sage Foundation, pp. 143–72.

Kochiyama, Y. (1994). "The Impact of Malcolm X on Asian-American Politics and Activism." In J. Jennings, ed., *Blacks, Latinos and Asians in Urban America: Status and Prospects for Activism*. Westport, CT: Praeger, pp. 129–42.

Lind, M. (1995). *The Next American Nation: The New Nationalism and the Fourth American Revolution*. New York: Free Press.

Luconi, S. (2001). *From Paesani to White Ethnics: The Italian Experience in Philadelphia*. Albany: State University of New York Press.

McGerr, M.E. (1986). *The Decline of Popular Politics: The American North, 1865–1928*. New York: Oxford.

Marable, M. (1994). "Building Coalitions Among Communities of Color: Beyond Racial Identity Politics." In J. Jennings, ed., *Blacks, Latinos and Asians in Urban America: Status and Prospects for Activism*. Westport, CT: Praeger, pp. 29–44.

Marquez, B. (1993). *LULAC: The Evolution of a Mexican American Political Organization*. Austin: University of Texas Press.

Meagher, T.J. (2001). *Inventing Irish America: Generation, Class, and Ethnic Identity in a New England City, 1880–1928*. Notre Dame, IN: University of Notre Dame Press.

Mink, G. (1986). *Old Labor and New Immigrants in American Political Development: Union, Party, and State, 1875–1920*. Ithaca, NY: Cornell University Press.

Morse, S.F.B. (1835). *Imminent Dangers to the Free Institutions of the United States Through Foreign Immigration and the Present State of Naturalization Laws*. New York.

Novak, M. (1972). *The Rise of the Unmeltable Ethnics: Politics and Culture in the Seventies*. New York: Macmillan.

Roediger, D.R. (1991). *The Wages of Whiteness: Race and the Making of the American Working Class*. London: Verso.

Sanchez, G.J. (1993). *Becoming Mexican-American: Ethnicity, Culture and Identity in Chicano Los Angeles, 1900–1945*. New York and Oxford: Oxford University Press.

Schlesinger, A.M., Jr. (1992). *The Disuniting of America*. New York: Norton.

Schneirov, R. (1998). *Labor and Urban Politics: Class Conflict and the Origins of Modern Liberalism in Chicago, 1864–97*. Urbana: University of Illinois Press.

Schuck, P.R. (2003). *Diversity in American: Keeping Government at a Safe Distance*. Cambridge, MA: Harvard University Press.

Shefter, M. (1978). "The Electoral Foundations of City Machines: New York City, 1884–1897." In J. Silbey, A. Bogue, and W. Flanigan, eds., *The History of American Electoral Behavior*. Princeton, NJ: Princeton University Press, pp. 263–298.

Skocpol, T. (1985). "Bringing the State Back In: Strategies of Analysis in Current Research." In P.B. Evans, D. Reuschemeyer, and T. Skocpol, eds., *Bringing the State Back In*. New York: Cambridge University Press, pp. 3–37.

Slayton, R.A. (2001). *Empire Statesman: The Rise and Redemption of Al Smith*. New York: Free Press.

Sleeper, J. (1990). *The Closest of Strangers: Liberalism and the Politics of Race in New York City*. New York: Norton.

Smith, R.M. (1997). *Civic Ideals: Conflicting Visions of Citizenship in U.S. History*. New Haven: Yale University Press.

Sollors, W. (1989). "Introduction: The Invention of Ethnicity." In W. Sollors, ed., *The Invention of Ethnicity*. New York: Oxford University Press, pp. iii–xiv.

Sterne, E.S. (2004). *Ballots and Bibles: Ethnic Politics and the Catholic Church in Providence*. Ithaca, NY: Cornell University Press.

Sugrue, T.J. (1996). *The Origins of the Urban Crisis: Race and Inequality in Postwar Detroit*. Princeton, NJ: Princeton University Press.

Wolfe, A. (1996). *Marginalized in the Middle*. Chicago: University of Chicago Press.

Yung, J. (1995). *Unbound Feet: A Social History of Chinese Women in San Francisco*. Berkeley: University of California Press.

CHAPTER FOUR

Immigrant Transnationals and US Foreign Relations

XIAO-HUANG YIN AND PETER H. KOEHN

Scholars typically approach the relationship of population movements and foreign relations in terms of immigration, ethnic group lobbies, and state policies and actions. However, our era of unprecedented transmigration requires a multiplayer framework for appreciating the construction and impact of foreign relations. The new framework must incorporate the role of transnationally competent and influential individuals with multilocal experiences and multiple identifications, diasporic communities, and nonstate collectivities and networks. In this chapter, therefore, we highlight the dynamic and interactive cross-border ways in which transmigration has shaped and continues to affect the formulation and execution of foreign relations involving the United States.

Immigrant transnationals "are integrated, to varying degrees, into the countries that receive them, at the same time that they remain connected to the countries they leave behind" (Levitt 2001, p. 5). To illustrate the interaction of foreign-policy-relevant domestic and cross-border forces, we have chosen three of the top five nationalities admitted to the United States in the 1990s (Mexicans, Dominicans, and Chinese) plus one additional reference group of predominantly political migrants from the Global South (Eritreans). Among these communities, transnationalism constitutes a selective adaptive response that "co-exists with other, more traditional forms" of migration (Portes 2001, p. 183).

Foreign policy is "the channel by which external action and responsibilities have to be addressed . . ." (Hill 2003, p. 23). Although they are still important, analysts recognize that states no longer dominate the foreign policy arena. Increasingly, the responsibility of relating policies and projects to outsiders involves multiple and competing actors and principles (see Hill 2003, p. 23), including international law and organizations, nongovernmental allies, transmigrants, diasporic communities, international NGOs, humanitarian and human rights considerations, historical claims, and global health, international security, and sustainable development needs.

Although Nathan Glazer and Daniel Moynihan's 1975 contention that immigration constitutes "the single most important determinant of American foreign policy" (pp. 23–4) can still be contested, ethnic identity groups have expanded the scope and sophistication of their formal involvements over the past three decades (see, for instance, Huntington 1997). Even though their members continue to be under-represented in the "highest councils of government," the pluralistic and deeply special-interest-penetrated US political system allows ethnic lobbies to influence foreign policy making in the same ways practiced by other interest groups (Smith 2000, pp. 9, 87–9, 93–5; see also Palmer 2000, pp. 246–9; Rendon 1981, p. 189; Ambrosio 2002a, pp. 143, 147, 2002b, p. 2). Ethnic identity groups typically are committed to an active US role in international affairs (T. Smith 2000, pp. 64, 77, 157) – particularly when they identify a "commonality of circumstance" (Scott and Osman 2002, pp. 72, 77, 87). At times, they apply their formidable lobbying power regarding parts of the world they are intimately concerned with in ways that complicate the articulation of efficient (i.e. "coherent and consistent") foreign policy approaches (T. Smith 2000, pp. 3, 78). In *Foreign Attachments: The Power of Ethnic Groups in the Making of American Foreign Policy*, Tony Smith (2000, pp. 2, 45, 132–5, 165) suggests that, historically as well as theoretically, the dominance of highly organized and singularly self-interested ethnic lobbies can result in serious negative consequences for the US national interest (see also Huntington 1997). Smith's claim is undermined, however, by recognition that US government policy positions cannot be equated with the national interest (Aleinikoff and Klusmeyer 2002, p. 32). Indeed, the prospect of reaching consensus on a single, unambiguous national interest (or on the process and standards to utilize in determining such) becomes increasingly elusive as the multicultural nature of US society and politics advances as a consequence of globalization and sustained infusions of relatives and others from diverse homelands (Clough 1994, p. 2; Levitt 2001, pp. 18–19; Vidal 1997). Moreover, internal divisions within diasporic communities along with the checks and balances inherent in the US political system and fears of offending dominant perceptions and positions (see Koehn and Yin 2002b, p. xxxi) limit and modify the efforts of migrants to affect foreign relations by influencing US government actions and policies regarding the country of origin or its leaders.

In any event, ours is an era of circular migration (Duany 2002) and durable multi-level transnational connectivities (Sheffer 2003, pp. 79, 83, 130–1; Thomas-Hope 2002; Levitt 2001, pp. 8, 19), of dual nationality, dual citizenship, and individual "postnational" rights and entitlements that are universal rather than dependent on full membership or residence in a nation-state (Aleinikoff and Klusmeyer 2002, pp. 22–3, 27, 39; Soysal 1994, pp. 3, 131–2, 136–7, 142, 145–8, 164; Levitt 2001, p. 5), of growing acceptance by the body politic of multiple identities and ethnic identity group influence (Ambrosio 2002b, pp. 3, 8; Shain 1999, p. xi; T. Smith 2000, p. 65; Levitt, DeWind, and Vertovec 2003; C. Gutierrez 1999, p. 559; Baubock 2003, pp. 704, 713), and of the transfer of "social remittances" ("ideas, behavior, and social capital") from receiving to sending communities (Levitt 2001, p. 11). By maintaining close contacts in the sending society – what Appadurai (1996, p. 22) refers to as initiating "new conversations between those who move and those who stay" – transmigrants are able to sustain valuable transnational analytic, emotional, creative, communicative, and functional skills (Koehn and Rosenau 2002, p. 117).

While recognizing the continued importance of ethnic interest groups as a force in US politics, the focus of this chapter is on immigrant transnationals as *direct particip-ants* in overseas affairs. In this context, transnational actors include unorganized individuals and diasporic groups that transcend, and link interests across, the borders of nation-states (Neack 2003, p. 10; Baubock 2003, p. 705) without necessarily traveling back and forth (Ostergaard-Nielsen 2003, p. 761). Transnationals "do not need governments in order to conduct international relations" (Hill 2003, p. 189). Grassroots transnational actors who engage in regular or occasional cross-border contacts possess an impressive capacity for political action and exerting influence over foreign relations from below (Levitt 2001, pp. 63–4) that is independent of receiving- and sending-state governments. Immigrant transnationals are plugged into elaborate social networks built upon interpersonal bonds of trust across borders with kin, colleagues, and friends. They possess access to the same political resources available to domestic bilateral activists in the country of origin by virtue of "process expertise" – understanding of local political culture and terrain, bureaucratic rules, the history of conflicts and coalitions, likely sources of support and resistance. In addition, transnationals possess considerable political acumen in translating and "fitting" insights garnered abroad to windows of opportunity in ways that are compelling domestically (Steinberg 2001, pp. 16–17, 143–9). Although frequently unnoticed or ignored by the host society, the influence of political transnationalism has transformed foreign relations into a "three-level game" in which countries of origin and receiving states interact with ethnic identity groups that cross state boundaries (Shain and Wittes 2002, pp. 170–2, 175, 190; see also Ambrosio 2002b, p. 15). In a particularly striking example, Iranian American groups, including the Iranian Muslim Association of North America and the Iranian Professionals Association of South Florida, raised and directly distributed more than $1 million within a week to earthquake victims in a country labeled as part of an "axis of evil" by US President George W. Bush (*Missoulian*, January 4, 2004, p. A7).

Indeed, to the extent that foreign policy today is about "mediating between community and cosmopolis," between nationalism and globalization, and about acting on cross-binding responsibilities toward outsiders (Hill 2003, p. 304), transmigrants and diasporic communities are more interesting players than nation-states that are preoccupied with the strategic accumulation of power and with military responses to perceived security threats. As Rosenau (2003, pp. 24–5) observes, "both singly and collectively . . . individuals have become increasingly central to the course of events." Portes (2003, p. 877) adds that "the onset of transnational activities in all fields has been due to the initiatives of the immigrants themselves, who have mobilized for this purpose their long-distance networks."

Although transnationalism signals the empowerment of ethnic identity groups from the Global South in international affairs, the independent, informal, and multilevel ways in which diasporic nonstate actors directly undertake initiatives within the country of origin and shape sending- and receiving-state positions and institutions typically have been neglected in international relations and foreign policy scholarship (Shain and Wittes 2002, p. 190; Baubock 2003, p. 702; Adamson 2002, pp. 155–6). Furthermore, these contributions have not yet been fully enumerated. In our conceptualization, immigrant transnationals access a variety of strategies in their efforts to influence developments in the ancestral homeland. The potentially powerful strategic arsenal available for mobilizing pressures from above and below for change or for reinforcing the status quo include:

- alliances with (local and multinational) NGOs and GONGOs (Ostergaard-Nielsen 2003, p. 772; Adamson 2002, pp. 156, 160, 162), international organizations (Evans 2004, p. 15), social movements engaged in confrontational activities (Ostergaard-Nielsen 2003, p. 769), and third states;

- investing and transferring funds, technology, expertise, and other resources that can alter local and international power relations (Adamson 2002, p. 160);
- participation in sustainable development projects (Koehn 2004b);
- voting and serving as an elected representative in the country of origin (Portes 1999, p. 467);
- personal appeals to political leaders; that is, acting as "citizen diplomats" (Sharp 2001).
- efforts to sway mass public opinion in ways that reinforce or undermine official discourse (Shain and Wittes 2002, pp. 171, 190; Sheffer 2003, pp. 226, 236–7; Adamson 2002, p. 156);
- e-mail and internet communications (Ostergaard-Nielsen 2003, p. 769);
- the assumption of policy level and civil service positions in the sending country (Aleinikoff and Klusmeyer 2002, p. 41).

As we shall discover in the case studies that follow, one finds persons and groups situated within the sending or receiving state, as well as circular migrants, engaged in these capacities as they work the "transnational political fields that stretch between and therefore tie together the political environments of home and host states" (Adamson 2002, p. 156). As transnational networks become more deeply involved in decision making, two dimensions of transmigration assume increasing import-ance. First, transnational competence comes into play as a key factor determining behavioral outcomes (e.g. see Koehn 2004a and 2004b). Second, "the very concept of exclusive political loyalty becomes more problematic" (Aleinikoff and Klusmeyer 2002, p. 30).

Critics such as Samuel Huntington (1997) and Tony Smith (2000, pp. 8, 134, 165–6) paint independent transnational communal politics as captive to the demands of foreign governments or movements and/or as a potent source of disunity for the receiving society. The implication of their critique is that "the Anglo-American establishment of the cold war years should be restored to its former glory and left to work out its foreign policy positions undisturbed by other influences" (Shain 1999, p. 207). In our contrasting view, transmigrants can possess collapsed (Duany 2002, p. 167; Shain 1999, p. 208), expanded (Aleinikoff and Klusmeyer 2002, p. 30), emancipated (Matsuoka and Sorenson 2001, p. 4; Portes 1999, pp. 467–8), globally and state-constrained (Matsuoka and Sorenson 2001, p. 8), transnationally permeated (Thomas-Hope 2002, p. 200), and at times conflicted (see T. Smith 2000, p. 24) loyalties, but one cannot assume, as Smith (2000, pp. 44, 155) suggests, that they ("implicitly") privilege the agendas of the sending place over those of the United States (see also Shain 1999, p. 200) or insist, as he does (2000, pp. 142–3, 164), that a "reasonable construction" of the US national interest should "take precedence over cosmopolitan or ethnic loyalties" when the two conflict. In today's world, *individuals* determine the priority they place or choose not to place on (multi)ethnic, (trans)national, diasporic/virtual nation (Cheung 2004, p. 675), and other subnational (e.g. family, business, religious, gender (D. Gutierrez 1999, p. 514)) loyalties and obligations (see also Aleinikoff and Klusmeyer 2002, p. 32). Moreover, diasporic com-munities are divided (see Shain 1999, pp. 201–2; Koehn and Yin 2002a, pp. 285–6; Watanabe 2002, pp. 137, 139) and, frequently, ambivalent, skeptical, and/or cynical toward the latest government of sending states (D. Gutierrez 1999, p. 517; Portes 1999, p. 468). To avoid attempts at co-optation and manipulation that threaten to compromise the viability of their cross-boundary initiatives and their position in the United States, immigrant transnationals manage to distance themselves from the official enticements of sending-state governments (Portes 2003, p. 877; Shain 1999, p. 207).

As Gabriel Sheffer (2003, p. 245) insightfully observes, "state-linked diasporas have the potential to generate unpleasant conflictual situations in their relations with homelands and host countries, but when weighing such dangers against their positive contributions, the latter win out." Thus, while we do not deny the possibility that diasporic communities will act in ways that conflict with perceived official US interests and can even endanger public interests (for examples, see Shain and Wittes 2002, pp. 174, 180, 182, 190; Sheffer 2003, pp. 234–5; T. Smith 2000, pp. 79, 160–1, 165), we elect to concentrate here on their extensive positive and promising connections and actions, on their roles as "mediators and bridge-builders" (Sheffer 2003, pp. 201, 83). This focus is important for at least two reasons. First, the multiplicity of positive, often small-scale and unreported, direct contributions made by transmigrants to common US and diasporic objectives are underestimated and undervalued by scholars and the receiving public at large. Second, calling attention to the positive contributions and opportunities promises to affirm their value among ethnic and nonethnic identity groups and to underscore their future potential for mutually beneficial sending- and receiving-society outcomes.

Case Studies

Mexican Immigrant Transnationals

Immigrants from Mexico constitute nearly 30 percent of the total foreign-born population of the United States. More than one-third of the 20 million persons of Mexican descent currently living in the United States were born in Mexico (C. Gutierrez 1999, p. 545; Jones-Correa 2002, pp. 116, 126n.). Surveys indicate that roughly half of the population of Mexico are related to someone living in the United States (D. Gutierrez 1999, p. 513n.). Annual remittances from Mexican Americans to relatives living in the country of origin exceed $14 billion (Thompson 2005, p. 48; Jones-Correa 2002, p. 120; M. Smith 2003, p. 473). Total migrant remittances are estimated to equal national income from agricultural exports and to constitute 80 percent of foreign direct investment (Guarnizo 2003, p. 686). Zacatecas State secures "more money in remittances than it does from the federal government of Mexico" (Jones-Correa 2002, p. 127n.). In Ticuani *municipo*, 51 percent of the residents "live in households that depend for 90 percent of their income on remittances from New York" (R. Smith 1998, p. 206).

In Mexico, many migrant remittances, or "migradollars," have been channeled into productive investments in small-scale enterprises in the community of origin (Guarnizo 2003, p. 672; M. Smith 2003, p. 481). Durand, Parrado, and Massey (1996, p. 441) show that the massive return flow of migradollars directly and indirectly through the multiplier effect results in substantially higher "levels of employment, investment, and income within specific communities and the nation as a whole." Since "virtually all" of these benefits are realized by the poorest segments of Mexico's population, they conclude (p. 441) that "Mexico–US migration must be regarded as one of the most important agents of social change in contemporary Mexico and a powerful catalyst of economic development." Through a host of habitual interpersonal interactions in "transnational social space," moreover, transmigrants are involved in the "constant transformation of Mexican national identity, as shown by the patterns of life imported from the United States into the high-emigration regions in Mexico" (C. Gutierrez 1999, pp. 558–9; D. Gutierrez 1999, p. 513; Shain 1999, p. 195).

In the past, immigrant transnationals have been wary of associations with Mexican authorities that might raise questions about their loyalty. The Mexican government's legalization of dual nationality in 1996 (Shain 1999, p. 194) opened the door to dramatic changes in immigrant transnational involvement in Mexico. Community leaders have been in the forefront of efforts to increase understanding among Mexican government officials regarding "the diaspora's interests as citizens of the United States" and appreciation for the "Mexican-American agenda" (Shain 1999, pp. 176, 184; T. Smith 2000, p. 156). In addition, although many deem themselves capable of full participation at all levels in Mexico's political system (M. Smith 2003, p. 495), Mexican Americans' "deep distrust of Mexico's political system and its corrupt bureaucracy has inhibited their relations with official Mexico" (Shain 1999, p. 176; M. Smith 2003, p. 495). Given the scale of migrant remittances and their potential voting power under the terms of Mexico's dual-nationality provisions, "all three major parties now seek to forge links with transnational migrants . . ." (M. Smith 2003, p. 498). In 2004, Andres Bermudez, "a migrant-turned-millionaire who shuttles between California and the town of Jerez [Zacatecas], won the mayorship . . . [and] Martin Carvajal, a furniture factory owner from Fort Worth, Tex., won as mayor of his hometown of Apulco . . ." (*New York Times*, July 6, 2004, p. A6). In June 2005, Mexico's Congress passed a law that allowed ten million Mexicans living in the United States (about 14 percent of the total electorate) to cast mailed absentee ballots for the first time in the 2006 presidential election (McKinley 2005, p. A4).

Mexican American immigrant transnationals have "used their increased political [and economic] power to work toward achieving a greater say inside Mexico" (Shain 1999, p. 184) and to "create an alternative hierarchy of power in relation to Mexican authority" (Roberts, Frank, and Lozano-Ascencio 1999, p. 251; Thompson 2005, p. A8). The ability of immigrant transnationals to influence Mexican policy is evident in the establishment of the Paisano program, which aims "to improve the treatment that returning migrants receive at the hands of Mexican officials by reducing corruption and abuse," as well as in the decision to recognize dual nationality (Jones-Correa 2002, pp. 120, 122). The manifestations of political transnationalism by Mexican Americans range from partnership and support to resistance and opposition (M. Smith 2003, pp. 498–9). For instance, Mexican consular officials lamented to Portes (1999, p. 475) that "Oaxacan Indian demands had to be given greater attention when made in California than in Oaxaca."

David Gutierrez (1999, p. 513) provides a revealing reference to some of the additional ways in which transmigrants informally are involved in influencing foreign relations. He reports that Mexican American health professionals, environmental experts, and labor organizers are acting "in ways that transcend the old arbitrary boundaries of the nation-state by experimenting in building transnational public health coalitions, developing environmental impact statements, and forming new multinational forms of labor organization and strike support committees." Mexican transmigrants also raise funds for local infrastructure projects, educational campaigns, and scholarships in their communities of origin (C. Gutierrez 1999, p. 559; Guarnizo 2003, p. 672). Professional associations, such as the Association of Mexican Professionals of Silicon Valley (MEXPRO), undertake economic development projects in Mexico, and Mexican-origin entrepreneurs have developed small-scale niche markets in cross-border trade (Roberts, Frank, and Lozano-Ascencio 1999, p. 247).

By 1995, more than 150 Mexican hometown and 10 state-level associations operated in the Los Angeles metropolitan area alone (Roberts, Frank, and Lozano-Ascencio 1999, p. 249). Some hometown civic associations participate in schemes that partner their contributions to local development projects with national or subnational government funds (Jones-Correa 2002, p. 121; Guarnizo 2003, p. 674; Roberts, Frank, and Lozano-Ascencio 1999, p. 249). Designated partner projects include the provision of transportation and communication infrastructure, electrification, water supply, sewage disposal, and new housing (M. Smith 2003, pp. 477, 487). Project selection is a two-way process. In the process of determining which public initiatives merit external support, "migrants compel authorities to take their wishes and priorities into account" (Guarnizo 2003, p. 676; M. Smith 2003, p. 480).

At the regional level, Guanajuato, under the leadership of Partido Accion Nacional (PAN) elites that at one time included former governor Vicente Fox, has engaged in special efforts to mobilize transmigrant Guanajuatenese living in California in support of local and regional development projects in their communities of origin (M. Smith 2003, pp. 468–70, 473–4). Mexico's sub-regional authorities have been the most involved with immigrant transnationals and their associations (R. Smith 1998, p. 203). The Ticuani Solidarity Committee of New York provides an excellent example. The Committee has contributed to the construction of two schools, a series of small projects, and a large-scale potable-water scheme in Ticuani, a *municipo* of less than 2,500 inhabitants in southern Mexico (R. Smith 1998, pp. 196, 207). In the midst of the water-pipe project, Committee members at times boarded a Friday afternoon flight from JFK airport to Mexico City, from whence they traveled overland for five hours to Ticuani, "consulted with the municipal authorities and contractors, and returned by Monday to their [full-time] jobs in New York" (R. Smith 1998, p. 196). At other times, they conducted business "collectively by phone" without leaving New York (R. Smith 1998, p. 214). The impoverished population of Ticuani benefits more from the resources contributed and local projects successfully executed by this civil society association of immigrant transnationals than from *municipo* activities (R. Smith 1998, pp. 206, 215).

Mexican immigrant transnationals have also been politically attentive to US policies affecting transmigration. Although employer resistance and the outbreak of World War II ensured that its efforts did not come to fruition, the Congress of Spanish-speaking peoples set the stage for contemporary multi-ethnic and transnational politics by insisting on Pan-American coalitions and demanding relaxation of US immigration, naturalization, and citizenship requirements in light of the growing *de facto* integration of the border region (D. Gutierrez 1999, p. 499). Mexican American leaders have been deeply involved in opposition to "extreme measures of migratory control that directly or indirectly encourage xenophobic or discriminatory attitudes toward people of Mexican origin . . ." (C. Gutierrez 1999, p. 552; T. Smith 2000, p. 75). Since the mid-1980s, they have been active in shaping acts of the US Congress that have facilitated accelerated migration from Mexico to the United

States (T. Smith 2000, p. 75). At the state level, hometown associations linked to Zacatecas State and allied with the AFL-CIO supported a California bill allowing the issuance of driver's licenses to undocumented migrants (M. Smith 2003, p. 494).

Dominican Immigrant Transnationals

Like Mexico, the Dominican Republic is a country of substantial population out-migration (Portes 2001, p. 190). It is the ancestral homeland of some 600,000 professionals and former rural laborers residing primarily in the northeastern United States who migrated in search of economic opportunity (Jones-Correa 2002, p. 116; Portes, Guarnizo, and Haller 2002, p. 284). Their annual remittances to the Dominican Republic exceed $1.5 billion – over 70 percent of the value of the country's exports (Jones-Correa 2002, p. 120). Current and projected family remittances are used by the government as "collateral for the solicitation of international loans" and as a key indicator of the country's creditworthiness (Portes 2003, p. 876).

Strong connections exist between Dominicans in New York City and successful small business entrepreneurs in the Dominican Republic. Many enterprise owners in the sending country are "returned or transnational migrants who acquired skills abroad, have clients in New York, and have used remittances to start or maintain their businesses" (Guarnizo 2003, p. 673). By carrying goods back and forth for sale or as gifts, moreover, Dominican transmigrants make available consumer items that low-income relatives and other nonmigrants could not afford on the local market, and, thereby, contribute to raising the standard of living in the homeland (Itzigsohn et al. 1999, pp. 324–5).

The ability of immigrant transnationals to exert influence over sending-country policies is clearly illustrated by the case of Dominicans residing in New York City. Aspiring Dominican office holders "routinely make trips to the city to hold fund raisers and emphasize the ties between the two communities" (Jones-Correa 2002, p. 121; see also Shain 1999, p. 172). Dominicans living abroad contribute an estimated 15 percent of the total amount expended on general elections in the Dominican Republic (Jones-Correa 2002, p. 121). The legitimacy, desirability, and policy responsiveness afforded campaign contributions from Dominican transnationals stand in stark contrast to the reaction that would greet similar initiatives by the Central Intelligence Agency or other arms of the US foreign policy establishment.

In the interest of sustained transnational mobility, Dominicans in the United States were eager to retain their Dominican citizenship upon naturalization in the receiving land (Itzigsohn et al. 1999, p. 327). As in the Mexican case, the Dominican Republic's official recognition of dual nationality in 1994 and the ability of transmigrants to retain land-ownership rights have largely been "due to the fact that immigrants in the United States used their financial clout – reflected in remittances and campaign contributions" to shape political party and legislative decisions (Jones-Correa 2002, pp. 122–3; see also Shain 1999, pp. 172, 194; Itzigsohn et al. 1999, p. 327). In response to extensive pressure applied by Dominicans resident in the USA, authorities granted naturalized US citizens of Dominican descent the right to vote and hold office on the island (Itzigsohn 2000, p. 1129; Levitt 2001, pp. 19, 141). Several US-based Dominicans have secured places on party lists and have served in the Dominican Congress (Levitt 2001, p. 142). Levitt (2001, p. 138) found that Partido Revolucionario Dominicano (PRD) leaders in Boston continue to shape party affairs and political outcomes on the island. Other immigrant transnationals have served in high-level bureaucratic positions in the Dominican Republic (Itzigsohn et al. 1999, p. 327). Dominicans abroad have also pressed for the creation of an overseas congressional electoral district (Itzigsohn et al. 1999, p. 328; Levitt, 2001, p. 142). In May of 2004, Dominicans voted overwhelmingly to return Leonel Fernandez, who spent much of his early life in New York, to the presidency (*Missoulian*, August 17, 2004, p. A3).

One study estimates that 15 percent of all Dominicans living in the United States are "regular cross-border political activists" (Portes 2003, p. 879). This group includes those who belong to a political party in the Dominican Republic (13 percent), contribute money to a sending-country political party (11 percent), and take part in home-country political campaigns (12 percent). Another 23 percent occasionally become involved as a political party member and an additional 16 percent contribute money to a party on occasion. Longer US residence increases regular transnational political involvement in the ancestral homeland, and the most deeply involved are "solid family men – educated, well-connected and firmly established" in the United States, rather than the "recently arrived and downwardly mobile" (Portes 2003, pp. 880–1). Politicians in the Dominican Republic believe that the "opinions of Dominican transmigrants are important in influencing the voting decisions of Dominicans on the island" (Itzigsohn et al. 1999, p. 326; see also Levitt 2001, p. 157). In most cases, immigrant transnationals have been catalysts for political reform in the sending country (Levitt 2001, pp. 153–5).

In addition, an estimated 27 to 30 percent of the Dominicans living in the United States are regular or occasional members of a hometown civic association or charity and donate money to community projects in the country of origin (Portes 2003, pp. 883–4). Levitt (2001, pp. 180–1, 186–90) documents how members of the Boston Miraflores Development Committee (MDC) have contributed to community development in Miraflores. In the early 1990s, the Boston MDC raised and transferred more than $70,000 for an aqueduct that provided Miraflorenos with a reliable water supply, and funded land purchases, renovations to the village school, health clinic, and community center, physician salaries, and medical supplies. Its sister chapter on the island primarily shoulders project implementation responsibilities. The two groups "communicate regularly by phone to update one another about their progress, exchange village news, and resolve disputes." On at least one occasion when a disagreement arose, the two chapters "conducted a transnational town meeting via conference call during which they discussed their concerns and agreed on a project-implementation plan" (p. 180). Members of Dominican religious groups in the United States also raise funds in support of school construction in the Dominican Republic (Itzigsohn et al. 1999, p. 329). In these transnational development undertakings, immigrant transnationals often hold the upper hand. According to Levitt (2001, pp. 181, 191–5), for instance, "since migrants funded so much of the MDC's work, their vision for Mirafloreno community development often took precedence over the needs and goals of those still residing there." Coincidentally, the efforts of the MDC enhanced the ability of villagers to negotiate with public agencies and to place successful demands on the Dominican state.

Immigrant transnationals from the Dominican Republic have also demonstrated concern for migration-related issues. In the 1990s, US- and foreign-born Dominicans joined with Latino advocacy groups and other allies in the successful effort to extend temporary protected status for Central Americans residing in the United States (Jones-Correa 2002, pp. 125–6).

Chinese Immigrant Transnationals

At more than 3 million persons, Chinese Americans constitute the largest Asian American community. They also stand out for their extensive involvement in transnational activities throughout history. Their strong interest in events in China offers one compelling reason why immigrant transnationals, as individuals and as a community, have participated in and exerted influence over US relations with their former countries. The fact that Chinese in America have strengthened rather than weakened ties with their native land during the migration process constitutes a remarkable divergence from the traditional assimilation model, demonstrating a distinctive complexity that existing immigration theories are unable to explain fully (H. Liu 2004, pp. 135–53).

Although Chinese have settled in America in significant numbers since the 1850s, they remain a predominantly first-generation community. Except for a short span of 20 years – between 1940 and 1960 – immigrants have always outnumbered the native-born in Chinese America. About 90 percent of the current immigrant community has arrived within the past 30 years from the Chinese world – countries and regions in Asia that are populated by the Chinese – and more than 60 percent of all Chinese Americans were born overseas (IPUMS 2000, 5 percent Data). According to US census reports, among immigrants from the People's Republic of China (PRC), nearly 78 percent came to the United States after 1980, with 48.5 percent arriving only in the 1990s (IPUMS 2000, 5 percent Data). This phenomenon is of particular significance for understanding Chinese American interests in China because PRC immigrants have become the largest subgroup. Totaling 1,011,805 in 2000, they represent 65.1 percent of Chinese immigrants in the United States. Those from Hong Kong and Taiwan account for 13.3 percent and 21.6 percent, respectively. Given the fact that the Chinese American community is constantly replenished with substantial numbers of newcomers and that its status has always been affected by bilateral relations, it is not surprising that Chinese immigrant transnationals have consistently maintained close ties with their place of origin, cared about US policy toward China, and focused on immigration issues (Yin and Lan 1997, pp. 35–57).

Chinese immigrants first came to the United States to work as unskilled laborers in the mid-nineteenth century. As peasants from rural regions in Guangdong (Canton) in South China, they possessed strong loyalty to their native land and maintained attachment because of the "sojourner mentality" in traditional Chinese culture. Such a mentality can be summarized in a dictum: "Luoye guigen" ("Falling leaves return to their roots" – meaning a man who resides away from his birthplace should eventually return to his ancestral land). Thus, many dreamed of returning home once they were able to make some money in the new country. When they gained little support from the ruling Manchu court in China in their struggle for survival in a strange land, they attributed the hardships, especially the racial discrimination they encountered in US society, to the weakness of their homeland. Consequently, modern Chinese nationalism had a unique appeal to Chinese in the United States and early Chinese immigrants widely shared the view that a strong China could help them win acceptance in the United States.

From the very beginning, therefore, Chinese American involvement in transnational activities had a sharp political edge – "to save the motherland, to save ourselves." As a Chinese community leader argued emotionally in an interview with reporters in New York in 1901: "Why can't you be fair? Would you talk like that if mine was not a weak nation?" (McKee 1977, p. 51). Even poor Chinese laundrymen would identify China's fortunes with their own and hold the belief that a powerful home-land would benefit and protect them in the United States. This explains why, when asked by Chinese leaders for donations to help China, Chinese immigrants would respond enthusiastically even though many of them lived in poverty. In this sense, the involvement of early Chinese immigrants in transnational affairs reflected a strong desire to improve their status in the new country (A Ying 1960, pp. 1–26).

The early Chinese immigrants included a few intellectuals. Although they only accounted for a tiny fraction of the Chinese American community, they made an impact on transnational relations. Among them, Yung Wing (1828–1912) was a prominent figure. Brought to America by missionaries in 1847, he graduated from Yale College in 1854. He later became a friend of President Ulysses S. Grant and writer Mark Twain and made an important contribution to the development of early US–China relations during his service as co-commissioner of the Chinese Educational Mission to America in the 1870s. Yung also set up a record for Chinese transnational philanthropic giving to China when he donated 500 taels of silver (around $500) to build a western-style school in his hometown in Zhongshan (Xiangshan) County in Guangdong in 1871. Named "Zhenxian" (Truly Benevolent), the school was the first public project financed by immigrant transnationals in modern Chinese history. In fact, Chinese Americans funded the establishment of most of the elite missionary schools in Guangdong in the late nineteenth century, such as Peiying High School (1882), Lingnan University (1888), Peidao Women's School (1888), and Peizheng High School (1889) (Zhuang 2001, p. 238; Li et al. 1996, p. 319; Yin 2000, pp. 69–84).

The transnational interests of Chinese Americans were reinforced with the rise of Chinese nationalism during the anti-Manchu revolution at the turn of the twentieth century. This is evidenced in their many politically motivated donations to China. Between June and December of 1911, for instance, Zhigong Tong, a popular semi-secret society with branches all over Chinatowns in North America, collected more than $400,000 in donations to support the anti-Manchu uprising in China at the critical moment (Mei and Zhang 2001, p. 225). Financial contributions from Chinese Americans have played pivotal roles in China's social and political development since the late nineteenth century. It was the generosity and enthusiasm of Chinese immig-rants abroad, including those in the United States, in giving to the struggle to topple the Manchu court that led Dr. Sun Yat-sen, founding father of the Republic of China, to make the famous eulogy: "Overseas Chinese are the mother of the Chinese revolution" (Feng 1993, p. 137).

Chinese American participation in transnational activities was further developed during the World War II era. Since China was an ally, Chinese Americans were able to play a prominent role in the US wartime policy regarding China. A dispropor-tionately large number of Chinese Americans served as liaison officers or interpreters in the US military or in diplomatic missions in China. Chinese American donations to China's war efforts grew dramatically. In October 1938, for example, San Fran-cisco's Chinese community gave more than $530,000 to the Chinese government for purchasing planes during the war with Japan. Between 1937 and 1945, Chinese Americans donated more than $25 million to help China's war against Japan (Chen and Hong 2003, pp. 161–3; Li et al. 1996, p. 291; Lai 1992, pp. 296–302).

Following the defeat of Japan in 1945 and the emergence of the People's Republic of China in 1949, divisions among Chinese Americans increased. The existence of two rival governments and Washington's anxiety about Communism influenced the character and politics of the Chinese American community. In the decades of the Cold War era, the prevailing anti-Communist disposition allowed Chinese American supporters of the Nationalist Party (KMT) in Taiwan to exert powerful leverage on China-related events. They shaped US–China relations by helping the KMT establish a favored position in the China policy arena and by persuading Washington to maintain close ties with Taiwan (Zhao 2002, pp. 152–84).

However, once mainstream politicians decided that a change in China policy would serve US interests, even the influential group of Chinese Americans who strongly opposed the PRC could not reverse the trend. When President Richard Nixon began to explore the normalization of relations with Beijing in the early 1970s, the opinions expressed by Chinese Americans, orchestrated by Taiwan supporters, were overwhelmingly critical of the new policy. Nevertheless, the Nixon administration continued its new China policy, and the pro-PRC forces in the Chinese American community gained visibility in transnational activities. With the normalization of relations, moreover, Chinese Americans, drawing on their ethnic and cultural identification with China, became actively involved in further developing ties. For example, throughout the 1970s and 1980s, the PRC government welcomed many Chines American scholars as distinguished guests. They played an active role not only in establishing academic exchange programs between the two nations, but also in promoting dialogue and understanding across the Pacific (Yin and Lan 1997, pp. 35–57).

The participation of Chinese immigrants in transnational activities has entered a distinctively new phase in recent years as an outcome of cultural, political, and socio-economic forces that have profoundly changed the makeup and dynamics of the Chinese American community. If, in the past, Chinese immigrants were motivated by the belief that a strong motherland would help improve their fate in the United States, their new interest in transnational events results from improved socio-economic status, growing ethnic consciousness, the ability to maintain close ties with the Chinese world, and openings in domestic politics and intercultural appreciation in both countries. Among the multiple factors that have enhanced Chinese American participation in transnational activities, four stand out: (1) the presence of an unprecedented number of highly educated immigrants who possess knowledge and expertise in areas that are central to transnational affairs; (2) the rapid development and solidification of extensive trans-Pacific Chinese economic and communication networks that allow immigrants concomitantly to stay in touch with both societies; (3) the increased flexibility in receiving-society responses to newcomers; and (4) changes in US foreign policy orientations and reactions in Asia in the post-Cold War era.

Today's Chinese immigrants are highly educated. Statistics show that about 47 percent of the immigrants from the PRC, 52 percent from Hong Kong, and 68 percent from Taiwan possess a bachelor's degree or higher. In comparison, less than 25 percent of the US population have completed a college education (IPUMS 2000, 5 percent Data). The arrival of large numbers of well-educated immigrants has deeply impacted Chinese America. Although there were Chinese students and scholars in the United States in the early years, Chinese student immigration did not gain momentum until the late 1940s. The Communist victory in China in 1949 led to an influx of Chinese intellectuals to the United States, including some 5,000 students and scholars. They came for advanced training, but they were stranded in the United States because of the sudden change of government in their homeland. Most of these "stranded students" later settled in the country and many have distinguished themselves in academia. Between 1950 and the mid-1980s, nearly 150,000 students from Taiwan came to the United States for advanced education; a large majority of them stayed on after graduation (Yin 2000, pp. 157–83). The last two decades of the twentieth century also saw approximately 250,000 students and scholars from the PRC studying in US institutions of higher learning. Most of them eventually settled in the United States, including more than 80,000 who adjusted their status under President George H.W. Bush's Executive Order #12711 and "Act 106 *Students-at-Large*" passed subsequently by Congress in 1990. Known as the "Chinese Student Protection Act," Act 106 granted permission to stay to PRC citizens who entered the United States "after June 4, 1989 and before April 11, 1990" (Li 2002, pp. 20–35). With their strong educational credentials, these Chinese intellectuals have integrated into mainstream US society, succeeded in their careers, and produced a disproportionately large number of America's top scientists and scholars, including six Nobel laureates – five in physics and one in chemistry.

The presence of so many well-educated immigrants and deeply integrated immigrants enhanced the involvement of Chinese Americans in transnational activities. Regardless of differences in their backgrounds and personal opinions, immigrant scholars have displayed interest in transnational events. Knowing how to seek out political allies in mainstream society, and being sought out by the mainstream mass media, they frequently appear in the spotlight on issues related to China. Their knowledge of China provides the general public with insight into the complexities of transnational events. In this way, immigrant scholars have expanded the Chinese American role in US–China relations and encouraged other Chinese Americans to participate in transnational activities.

The familiarity and identification of immigrant scholars with traditional Chinese culture has also helped moderate concern in China about the political and cultural values that have accompanied globalization. This moderation, in turn, has allowed overseas scholars to influence China's policies toward the United States. Whereas Chinese leaders tend to question the motives of US politicians and diplomats, they are open to listening to Chinese immigrant scholars, who share discursive proximity in the high-context culture of China (Shen 2002, pp. 97–107). The role of T.D. Lee (Tsung Dao Lee, or Li Zhengdao), a Chinese American Nobel laureate in physics, as an informal messenger between Washington and Beijing in the Tiananmen crisis is a case in point. When the Bush administration imposed economic sanctions on China after the Tiananmen incident in June 1989, straining US–China relations, Lee flew to Beijing to meet with Chinese leader Deng Xiaoping. Upon his return, he briefed then-President George H.W. Bush on what Deng had told him. In spite of the tension between the two countries, China wanted to maintain close ties with the United States. Lee thus served as a crucial bridge between the two sides at a time of crisis. By acting as intermediaries and consultants for both the US and Chinese governments, the work of Lee and other immigrant scholars highlights the increasing role that Chinese immigrant transnationals are playing in the evolution and development of transnational relations (Wang 2002, pp. 207–34; Yin 2002, p. M3).

In addition, the rapid emergence and development of trans-Pacific migration and business networks have turned Chinese America into an increasingly transnational community. The powerful trends of economic globalization have coincided with China's opening up to the outside world in the post-Mao era. The quickly developing economy and social stability in China have provided opportunities for Chinese Americans to work in their country of origin. Two parallel and interconnected developments have critically affected the growth of transnational linkages in Chinese America. One is the tremendous increase in trade, finance, and other business activities between China and the United States, which has spun a rich and complex web of networking between Chinese Americans, especially new immigrants, and their family members and friends across the Pacific. The other is the reverse flow of large numbers of Chinese Americans, both immigrant transnationals and US-born, who return to their native land to establish offices and production outlets or are hired to manage existing large-scale multinational enterprises and corporations in China. One study shows that among those who run foreign businesses in Beijing, 50 percent are overseas Chinese (Zhuang 2001, p. 360). Many of them are Chinese Americans. As Ping K. Ko, a former professor of microelectronics at UC Berkeley who now runs a high-tech venture capital company in China, sums up: "It used to be that if you went to the US, it was 'By-by, see you when you're 65.' But opportunity now is worldwide. [Working in China] is no different than working in California and looking for job opportunities in Texas" (*Los Angeles Times*, November 25, 2002, B6).

The complex and expanding web of economic contacts among Chinese immigrants with their relatives and friends across the Pacific has led to massive increases in trade and financial services involving the PRC, Taiwan, Hong Kong, and the United States. One result is a huge influx of Chinese capital into North America. Stories about the average Chinese immigrant family bringing assets of $200,000 to the United States are obviously exaggerated. However, there is little doubt that the inflow of Chinese capital to North America from the economically prosperous Chinese world in Asia is astounding. It has varied from several billion dollars to over $10 billion a year since the 1970s. According to a well-documented source, $1.5 billion of Taiwan's capital wound up in the Los Angeles area alone each year between 1985 and 1990 (Yin and Lan 1997, pp. 35–57). In just one week in July 1995, several billion dollars of capital flowed from Taiwan into southern California because of the tension across the Taiwan Strait. Another study reveals that while the Chinese population in Los Angeles County grew 6 times between 1970 and 1990, Chinese-owned businesses increased more than 15 times, from 1,100 to over 16,600 (Chan 2002, p. 145). The majority of these businesses were set up with Chinese capital from Asia.

While Chinese investors throughout the Chinese world pump increasing amounts of capital into US business ventures and real estate, Chinese Americans are making massive investments in their country of origin. Profit-driven Chinese American entrepreneurs have demonstrated enormous enthusiasm in the China market. They see that China's stunning transformation from a centrally planned economy into a free market provides extraordinary investment opportunities and they believe that they can take advantage of their Chinese heritage to reap huge profits from such a rapidly growing economy. At the same time, attracting overseas Chinese investment and honoring contributors identified through personal connections constitutes an integral part of the economic development strategy pursued by provincial units of the PRC government (Cheung and Tang 2001, pp. 108–9). Of the $336 billion foreign direct investment in China between 1980 and 2000, more than 50 percent came from Chinese overseas. Chinese American capital ranks fourth largest among overseas investments in China – after that from Hong Kong, Taiwan, and Southeast Asia (Geithner 2003, p. 3). Chinese immigrant transnationals have carried with them a network of connections that enhances the flow of capital, entrepreneurial talent, and professional activities between the two countries. These developments cast a fresh, multidimensional light on how contemporary Chinese Americans influence transnational economic development at a time when economic power in the PRC is "migrating" from government to society (Lampton 2001, p. 20).

The enduring transnational routes and linkages that early Chinese Americans built become even more prominent when they coincide with networks established by recent immigrants along functional lines and in response to perceived common identities. Many new types of transnational community organizations have emerged in Chinese America over the past two decades. They include various kinds of fraternity-style transnational associations formed by recent immigrants and based on their hometown origins in China. *Beijing Tongxianghui* (Beijingers Association), *Nanjing Tongxianghui* (Nanjingers Society), *Shanghai Tongxianghui* (Shanghainese Association), and *Daxinan Tongxianghui* (Southwestern Association of China) in southern California are a few notable examples. These new transnational societies are based on voluntary participation and transient membership (Yin 2005). Registered as nonprofit organizations in the United States, they are highly successful in sponsoring transnational activities such as organizing academic and professional conferences on China, holding Chinese cultural events or US–China trade fairs, and arranging business as well as other service-related tours to the Chinese world.

It is noteworthy that most of the newly established immigrant transnational organizations are actively engaged in philanthropic activities in China. In general, their giving aims to support public welfare programs, disaster relief, or a particular project in their hometowns in China. When the earthquake hit the Nijiang region in Southwest China in 1996, for example, Zhong Meng, then President of the Southwestern Association of China, initiated a fund-raising campaign among the Chinese community in southern California and succeeded in collecting $1.5 million for disaster relief (Fu and Wang 2000, p. 218). The activities of immigrant transnational organizations and cultural leaders have also created multiple reference points and transmitted new values, practices, and approaches with the potential to transform China from the diaspora (see, for instance, Qian 2002, pp. 37–8). These transnational Chinese American networks represent emerging trends in immigrant life in the age of globalization. While remaining largely unknown to the general public, they enjoy enormous popularity among recent immigrants, and they have contributed, in one way or another, to social, economic, and political development in China. These extensive new networks have become powerful and effective vehicles for recent Chinese immigrants to develop and maintain close ties with their "old home" in Asia.

Communications advances have also stimulated the interest of Chinese transnationals in sending-country issues in recent years. Breakthroughs in information technology have transplanted the Chinese world into the living rooms of the Chinese American community. As a result, Chinese Americans today are well informed regarding developments across the Pacific. The daily activities of Beijing's leaders, Taiwan's parliamentary debates, and the gyrations of the Hong Kong stock market are common fare for discussion in America's Chinatowns (Yin 2000, pp. 157–83). Extensive and prompt coverage of China-related news from a "perspective different from mainstream American news outlets" (Freedman 2000, p. 143) reinforces the interest of Chinese Americans in transboundary activities. As ethnic studies scholars generally agree, it makes immigrants feel much more involved if their homeland is "just on the other side of the border."

Chinese Americans have also become more concerned with transnational developments, especially those influenced by Washington's China policies, because, as an immigrant community, they remain vulnerable to the ups and downs of US–China relations in the post-Cold War era. The increasing prominence of international affairs in domestic politics, in general, and volatile US–China relations, in particular, has compelled Chinese Americans to become involved in the bilateral relationship, sometimes out of self-defense. When a US Navy spy plane collided with a Chinese fighter and was forced to land at a Chinese military airport in April 2001, for example, some callers to radio talkshows in mainstream society demanded that Chinese Americans be sent to internment camps (Yin 2002, p. M3). Many Chinese American activists who used to focus on domestic issues now realize that they can no longer remain on the sidelines of US relations with China. They have been transformed from bystanders to participants in transnational activities.

These changing attitudes are further manifest in the large numbers of American-born Chinese majoring in China studies at US colleges and universities in recent decades and by their growing involvement in transnational affairs that are "changing political economic conditions in states such as California, Washington, and Hawaii . . ." (Nakanishi 2001, p. 120). The highly publicized trip to China in October 1997 by Gary Locke, Governor of Washington State, offers a good example. Locke, an American-born Chinese, made his trip to China, which included a visit to his grandparents' village in Guangdong, less than a year after his election as governor. His expressed goal was to strengthen links across the Pacific (Hu-DeHart 1999, pp. 1–28; Yin 2002, p. M3).

Although highly diverse in ideological views, cultural identities, and socio-economic interests, Chinese Americans have expanded their involvement in transnational affairs. One survey conducted by a Chinese American newspaper in New York during the 1996 US presidential election, for instance, showed that 78 percent of Chinese American voters regarded candidates' positions on US policy toward China as an important consideration in deciding whom to vote for. In comparison, only 19 percent considered the personal character of a candidate to be important in their decision (Yin 1999, pp. 331–49). Further, while many are new arrivals, nearly 51 percent of Chinese immigrants had become naturalized US citizens as of 2000, while the figure for Mexican immigrants was 22 percent (IPUMS 2000, 5 percent Data). With their growing voting power, Chinese Americans are poised to become a new force that must be reckoned with in US foreign policy making. Although they are missing from high-level posts in the foreign policy establishment, the extensive presence of Chinese Americans in the vital cultural, social, economic, and political interstices that cement transnational affairs offers ample opportunities to influence relations with and within the Chinese world through personal connections (see

Freedman 2000, p. 142). Most of these connections are invisible to the media and the wider public. One notable exception is the New York-based Committee of 100 (C-100). The prominent, well-connected, and bicultural members of C-100 work openly and assiduously to enhance relations between the United States and the Chinese world (see Wheeler 2002, pp. 191–4).

While Chinese Americans are increasingly involved in transnational activities, they also hold diversified attitudes toward China. Multiple interest groups speak out on controversial issues and different segments of the Chinese American community have adopted opposing stances on China-related issues. The attitudes and views of Chinese immigrant transnationals partly reflect their professional interests and personal stakes in the development of transnational relations. For example, those who actively participated in China's dissident movement support a confrontational policy toward China in order to quickly bring down the Beijing regime. Others – Chinese American entrepreneurs, members of the influential C-100 organization, foundation and NGO personnel, and those who work in China-related professions – prefer a more constructive US–China relationship and seek to improve political, environmental, and/or economic conditions in the sending country. Speaking with more than one voice may weaken the influence of immigrant transnationals on official US foreign policy making, but such diversity allows Chinese Americans to adapt to changing domestic political circumstances in both sending and receiving societies and to take advantage of informal opportunities to influence cultural and economic developments in China.

Eritrean Immigrant Transnationals

The vast majority of first-generation Eritreans living in the United States migrated primarily for political and not economic reasons. Most fled from persecution at the hands of the government of Ethiopia during the 1970s or 1980s or to escape life-threatening violence associated with the three-decade armed struggle for independence (Koehn 1991, pp. 121–2; Koser 2002, p. 140). Today, perhaps 100,000 Eritrean men, women, and children reside in the USA (Hepner 2003, p. 289).

The deep links that exist between Eritreans in the diaspora and in Eritrea can be traced to the long period of struggle for independence from Ethiopia. The organization and operations of the Eritrean Relief Association (ERA) illustrate how immigrant transnationals can shape foreign relations in ways that extend beyond the reach of US government agencies. Skilled Eritrean professionals who had fled war and/or political persecution formed the Association in 1975. Some returned to initiate development projects among rural people living in remote and rugged parts of Eritrea that were outside the control of the Ethiopian military (Sorenson 1994, p. 70, 79–83). For instance, "ERA and the Eritrean Medical Association (formed among Eritrean doctors living in Europe and North America) contributed to the development of the Eritrean Public Health Care Programme" – which included staffing and operation of a sophisticated underground hospital, establishment of 8 health centers and 50 health stations, and installation of a pharmaceutical production laboratory (Sorenson 1994, pp. 82–3). Working in tandem with religious NGOs and other donors, the ERA transported relief supplies across the border from Sudan and throughout Eritrea until the end of the war. Its operations, which reached more than one million people, helped prevent further massive outflows of refugees and famine victims (Sorenson 1994, pp. 70–1, 76).

The global network of mass organizations of Eritreans in the diaspora cultivated by the Eritrean People's Liberation Front (EPLF) helped to pay for the eventually successful liberation effort and to raise awareness regarding the Eritrean cause among host-country political leaders (Koser 2002, p. 145). Most prominently, the auto-nomous Eritreans for Liberation in North America (EFLNA) contributed "today's equivalent of over 1 million dollars per year . . . [to the] EPLF and communicated intensively with the front's leadership concerning all aspects of the revolution" (Hepner 2003, pp. 274–5, 290). However, conflicts in the diaspora among former Eritrean Liberation Front (ELF) and EPLF supporters prevented the formation of unified community associations. In most cases, refugees living in the United States preferred to engage in humanitarian efforts in Eritrea through nonpartisan organ-izations and "resisted all attempts by EPLF and its supporters to control diaspora activities . . ." (Hepner 2003, p. 276).

In a study conducted in the mid-1980s among Eritreans living in the Washington, DC metropolitan area, the principal considerations affecting repatriation decision making were: (1) realization of the goals of national liberation; (2) regime change in Ethiopia; and (3) an end of armed conflict and improved personal security (Koehn 1991, pp. 368, 372). With the termination of armed hostilities and the overthrow of Mengistu Haile Mariam's regime at the end of that decade and the arrival of independence for Eritrea in 1993, these obstacles to repatriation no longer existed (see also Bascom 1994, p. 237). Although few repatriated, an estimated 40,000 Eritrean transmigrants residing in Europe and North America returned for short intervals each year through the end of the 1990s (Koser 2002, pp. 141, 143; see also Tekle 1998, p. 104). Instead of repatriating, most Eritrean transmigrants have elected to advance their position in the receiving country while retaining close links to family and community members in Eritrea (Koser 2002, p. 138; Koehn 1991, p. 359). Among those living in the United States, a number of drawbacks, including lack of adequate housing, educational opportunities for children (Koehn 1991, p. 359), adequate health-care, and employment opportunities, have influenced the decision not to return permanently (see also Koser 2002, pp. 141, 150). Moreover, rather than encourage massive and immediate repatriation, the new state's political leader-ship opted to pursue a far-sighted approach that balanced the need for contacts with and support from immigrant transnationals living and learning in the north against pressing demands for returnees who possessed skills in short supply in Eritrea (Koehn 1995, p. 349; see also Van Hear 2003, p. 15). In addition, the relatively secure immigration status most Eritreans hold by virtue of initial admission as refugees has encouraged a transnational response (see also Koser 2002, pp. 142–3). The Eritrean case illustrates a transnational response in which refugee communities in the diaspora participate in post-conflict reconstruction in the sending country without necessarily physically returning.

Historically, remittances from Eritrean immigrant transnationals living in the north have exerted a substantial impact on the capital- and resource-deprived sending country. In "normal" times, the government of Eritrea maintains that Eritreans overseas remit about $300 million annually (cited in Koser 2002, p. 144). Nearly every Eritrean household in the diaspora sends money to relatives living in the homeland (Al-Ali, Black, and Koser 2001, p. 619). Matsuoka and Sorenson (2001, p. 107) note that "while Eritreans in the diaspora avoid conspicuous displays of material wealth, relatives in Eritrea expect them to achieve success and support families at home." Remittances from relatives abroad serve as an important safety net during periods of economic shortfall and, at times, underwrite family contributions to community development projects (Al-Ali, Black, and Koser 2001, p. 619).

Eritrea's three-decade struggle for independence and its post-independence border conflict with Ethiopia (Shain and Wittes 2002, p. 173), as well as the government's post-war reconstruction efforts, have been supported by an extraordinary flow of contributions from the diasporic community. Since 1999, moreover, Eritreans in the United States have spent millions of dollars on the purchase of bonds issued by the government of Eritrea (Al-Ali, Black, and Koser 2001, p. 620). The government expects all Eritreans abroad to contribute 2 percent of their monthly income directly to its coffers. Until recently, most Eritrean migrants have felt obliged to forward these payments (Al-Ali, Black, and Koser 2001, p. 620). Tricia Hepner (2003, p. 290) reports that the experience of the Chicago Eritrean community "shows that failure to contribute creates obstacles for participation in local Eritrean society (buying or selling property, for example), and is also held up as a measure of one's national commitment." During the armed struggle with Ethiopia that began in 1998, the government asked Eritreans living overseas to increase their "voluntary" contributions in order to help finance the war effort and emergency assistance for those displaced by the conflict (Al-Ali, Black, and Koser 2001, p. 620; Koser 2002, p. 147). Eritreans in North America pledged to raise $100 million for emergency relief, reconstruction, resettlement, and economic development purposes following the devastating war with Ethiopia. The Eritrean diaspora as a whole responded with contributions that totaled between $400 and $600 million (Matsuoka and Sorenson 2001, p. 78).

US-based Eritreans have also been collectively and personally involved in activities aimed at advancing Eritrea's development in the post-independence era. In North America, collective activity has been organized by the Association of Eritrean Professionals and Academics for Development (AEPAD) – a group consisting of several hundred engineers, accountants, computer scientists, physicians, and business and public administration practitioners. To cite just one instance of individual initiative over the course of a decade, an Eritrean refugee employed by the state of Nevada organized development project training sessions for high-level government officials, advised several government agencies interested in revamping cumbersome position classification schemes, and participated in a consultancy project aimed at improving the capacity of local governments to deliver health and education services. The Eritrean government's preference for self-reliance and contributions from committed members of the diasporic community over dependence on foreign assistance (Koser 2002, p. 147) has enhanced the role of immigrant transnationals relative to external donors in shaping development outcomes in Eritrea.

The Eritrean state continues to count all Eritreans living abroad as part of the total population of the nation and recognizes persons born outside the country to one (or two) Eritrean parents as citizens. Citizenship rights include voting in national elections and buying, selling, and inheriting property (Hepner 2003, p. 290). In terms of political participation in the country of origin, at least 90 percent of the Eritreans living in the diaspora are estimated to have voted in the 1993 worldwide referendum on independence (Al-Ali, Black, and Koser 2001, p. 620). Eritrean immigrant transnationals also participated in the drafting and 1997 ratification of the homeland constitution. Al-Ali, Black, and Koser (2001, p. 620) report that "elected representatives of the diaspora [6 out of 50] served on the Executive Assembly of the Constitutional Commission" (see also Koser 2002, p. 145). Feedback received on three externally and internally circulated drafts from Eritreans in the diaspora reportedly contributed "to the final wording of several parts of the Constitution" (Koser 2002, p. 145).

In the years following independence, some immigrant transnationals insisted upon "greater direct representation in Eritrean affairs in exchange for their continued financial support" (Al-Ali, Black, and Koser 2001, p. 628). However, internal fragmentation, community divisions, and resistance to the government of Eritrea's efforts to coordinate diasporic activities through local chapters of the People's Front for Democracy and Justice (PFDJ) party (successor to the EPLF) have weakened secular associations across the United States (Hepner 2003, pp. 277–9). Eritrean church congregations linked to counterparts in the country of origin have provided a nonpartisan alternative vehicle for Orthodox, Catholic, and Pentecostal Eritreans to participate in transnational civil society activity that encompasses humanitarian and cultural redefinition initiatives (Hepner 2003, pp. 277, 279, 285–6).

Many Eritrean immigrant transnationals have been disheartened by recent government decisions and the heavy-handed treatment of critics of Issaias Afeworki's rule. In 2001, the PFDJ responded forcefully to internet- and locally-initiated criticism and debate over issues of democracy and the rule of law for Eritrea. The regime banned the formation of alternative political parties at home or abroad and arrested prominent veterans of the EPLF and other critics (Hepner 2003, pp. 284, 290). These and subsequent actions have provoked widespread resistance and calls for political change in the diaspora. Across the United States, "indigenous human rights groups, political parties, and 'democratic coalitions' [have] formed and demonstrated . . . against the ruling regime's increasing repression" (Hepner 2003, p. 284).

Conclusions

States no longer monopolize foreign policy making. The expanding roles of transnational nonstate actors must also be taken into account. Although levels of immigrant transnational involvement vary widely (Portes 2003, p. 882), persons born outside the United States, especially recent arrivals who actively participate in diasporic and host communities and maintain close ties with the sending country, are increasingly influential in the unfolding of foreign relations initiatives. The June 2004 decision of the Bush administration to limit Cuban Americans to one trip to Cuba every three years and to restrict legal cash and gift transfers to the sending country (Goodnough and Aguayo 2004) provides revealing evidence that even the US government recognizes that the personal contacts of immigrant transnationals can undermine official foreign policy objectives.

The mostly unheralded personal and collective projects pursued by immigrant transnationals typically are neither inspired, sanctioned, nor effectively regulated by the US foreign policy establishment or the sending-country government (Portes 1999, p. 467). In the aggregate, however, activist US immigrant transnationals from a diverse set of countries of origin are expanding their social networks through circular migration (Thomas-Hope 2002, p. 194; H. Liu 2004, pp. 135–53) and "modifying the fortunes and cultures" of their sending localities and nation-states (Portes 2003, p. 876). The cases reviewed here also reveal that all immigrant transnationals need not leave the United States in order to qualify as foreign relations activists. For instance, some Dominicans expend considerable time, effort, and funds in support of the activities of a political party in the Dominican Republic without traveling regularly to the sending country (Itzigsohn et al. 1999, p. 327).

The illustrations of expanding involvement on the part of transmigrants holding multiple loyalties presented in this chapter suggest profound implications for official foreign policy processes as well as for the actors involved. First, immigrant transnationals bring fresh perspectives and different interpretations of national interests into the practice of US foreign policy. Based on experience in both sending and receiving societies, many hold alternative outlooks on interstate (especially North–South) relations and interdependence challenges (Koehn 2007). To the extent that ongoing participation in transnational networks liberates transmigrants from mainstream foreign policy perspectives and from preoccupation with attempting to influence or implement hegemonic US government policies, they offer interpersonal opportunities for resisting what Shain (1999, pp. x, 8) perceives to be powerful official and social pressures to export American values abroad. We found support for Schiller, Basch, and Blanc-Szanton's (1999, p. 26) suggestion that "by maintaining many different racial, national, and ethnic identities, transmigrants are able to express their resistance [in small, everyday ways] to the global political and economic situations that engulf them. . . ." Nevertheless, diasporic communities are socially stratified and politically differentiated (Adamson 2002, pp. 158–9; Levitt 2001, pp. 13–14). Moreover, some members of the second and later generations are destined to become "roots tourists" rather than active participants in transnational activities (Kasinitz 2004, pp. 284–5; E. Liu 1998, pp. 115–44). The extent to which individual transmigrants express resistance to hegemonic foreign policy initiatives depends upon the nature of their sending- and receiving-country experiences (Portes 2003, p. 881), the level of receiving-state tolerance for dissident views and behavior, access to social-class and political resources, sustained interactions with a continuous flow of immigrants and visitors (Itzigsohn 2000, p. 1137), the degree of individual and community sensitivity to the interests of the global commons, and the level of civic support received in host and sending societies. It is not surprising to discover, therefore, that the political activities of immigrant transnationals include "both opposition to and support for the current political regime and its foreign policy goals" (Ostergaard-Nielsen 2003, p. 762).

The cases explored in this chapter confirm that sending governments, in the interest of advancing the reach of the globally peripheral state, are now inclined to encourage emigrants to incorporate and prosper in the North rather than to return to the place of origin (see also Portes 1999, p. 467). However, immigrant transnationals increasingly are "involved in national-ethnic, panethnic, and transnational political activities at the same time" (Itzigsohn 2004, p. 201). Ironically, "the experience of living under a democratic system . . . socializes immigrants into a new political outlook" and increases both "opposition to entrenched structures of privilege" and expectations for change in the sending country (Portes 1999, pp. 474–5). Among all of the diasporic communities considered here, we encountered evidence that immigrant transnationals who "are offered integration on fair terms" and gain "shared experience of democratic incorporation in the receiving state" are more likely "to export democracy to their countries of origin rather than to import authoritarian political ideologies from there" (Baubock 2003, pp. 706, 710; see also Ostergaard-Nielsen 2003, p. 773). They push to open local politics to new actors and aim to realign political power without radical transformation of the existing social structure (see Itzigsohn 2000, p. 1137). Concomitantly, the development of multicultural/multinational identity and transnational competence, selective host-country incorporation (Levitt, DeWind, and Vertovec 2003), disillusionment with homeland economic and political conditions, and/or the experience of persecution/expulsion incline most transmigrants to resist pressures to act as a disloyal or subversive force within the United States (see Sheffer 2003, p. 82; Shain and Wittes 2002, p. 183; Adamson 2002, p. 155).

The cases analyzed here suggest that independent immigrant transnationals who engage in translocal politics at the grassroots level are both advancing and modifying official US foreign policy objectives in at least two critical ways. First, they are directly empowering local community members, expanding civil society, and inspiring the introduction of democratic practices in sending countries (Ostergaard-Nielsen 2003, pp. 763, 773). Such activities are facilitated by the recent opening of sending-country political systems through dual-citizenship/nationality provisions and by expanded opportunities for transnationals to give greater voice to their own objectives (Portes 1999, p. 475; Wang 2002, pp. 207–34). In most of the countries considered in this chapter, immigrant transnationals are directly involved in national and/or local politics by virtue of grants of voting rights and/or the right to hold elective office. Second, they are making decisive contributions to the local and regional development of the sending country – through direct investments of capital and human ingenuity and by pressuring national and subnational governments to participate in specific projects (see also Baubock 2003, p. 708; Portes, Guarnizo, and Haller 2002). In both cases, the activities of immigrant transnationals generate different, deeper, and more sustainable outcomes than many of the efforts of the US Department of State, the US Agency for International Development, or international organizations such as the International Monetary Fund and the World Bank. In quantitative terms, for instance, migrants' annual remittances have exceeded official development assistance by approximately 20 percent in recent years (Guarnizo 2003, p. 670) – although the potential of remittances to transform or reconstruct societies plagued by poverty and/or conflict has not been realized (Van Hear 2002, pp. 222–3). Moreover, migrant desires for transnational living result in demands for goods and services that "generate a complex array of backward and forward economic linkages" that enlarge national markets and enable entrepreneurs in sending countries and in the United States to "transnationalize their operations" (Guarnizo 2003, pp. 676–7). Migrant initiatives have become critical, then, for current and future national economic growth and for local prosperity and poverty reduction in sending countries (Guarnizo 2003, p. 682).

While ethno-nationalist interests and particular sending-country challenges and opportunities provide one focus of transmigrant attention, sustaining and advancing transnational mobility opportunities and identities also constitutes a common and potentially unifying priority (e.g. see Gustafson 2002, p. 465; Jones-Correa 2002, p. 126). Immigrant transnationals are prone to perceive immigration and emigration policy as paramount foreign policy issues (Jones-Correa 2002, p. 126; Ostergaard-Nielsen 2003, p. 762). Their demonstrated concerns include:

- ease of movement (additional and circular migration, family migration) (Baubock 2003, p. 713; Goodnough and Aguayo 2004);
- ease of transnational financial transactions (remittances; money transfers within the diaspora and with the homeland);
- ease of transnational business transactions and tax exemptions (Ostergaard-Nielsen 2003, p. 762; Chan 2002, pp. 145–61);
- ease of cross-cultural contact and family sustenance (Lam, Yeoh, and Law 2002);
- ease of opportunity to participate in politics in the sending country (Ostergaard-Nielsen 2003, p. 762).

Creating promising new relationship opportunities and/or removing obstacles to mobility and network interactions are objectives that are advanced by official foreign policies that promote generally friendly relations between the United States and the sending state(s). Transnationalism is much harder to sustain in the face of hostile state-to-state relations. Gabriel Sheffer (2003, p. 226) notes that "as long as relations between their homelands and host countries are friendly, or at least cordial, most diasporans will not face major difficulties in determining the balance between their loyalties and maintaining the pattern of [dual] loyalties they have forged." Moreover, an ethnic identity group's status, daily life, and policy effectiveness in the receiving country can be adversely affected by sending-government or terrorist actions that violate host-culture norms or harm host-country nationals (Shain and Wittes 2002, pp. 188–9) as well as by bilateral confrontations. These considerations compel diasporic communities and individual immigrant transnationals to become involved in the formal foreign policy process. In particular, they seek to mitigate conflicts and enhance understanding between the United States government and the government and citizens of their country of origin. The cases we examined suggest that immigrant transnationals in the United States have achieved limited success in these efforts. The largest groups (persons of Mexican and Chinese heritage) and those able to link with powerful business interests have managed to influence official US relations with the country of origin (see, for instance, M. Smith 2003, p. 494). In contrast, Eritreans have been less successful in championing the sending country's cause among US policy makers or the US public (Koser 2002, p. 149).

Although the interests of their ethnic kin remain paramount, under certain circumstances transmigrants can be mobilized to pursue transnational projects that serve the global commons (Henry 2000, p. 11; Koehn 2001, 2004b) even when these concerns are not high on the official agenda in the country of origin. Such circumstances include the compelling nature of the shared concern and the strength of the appeal to sending-society interests (Scott and Osman 2002, p. 87; Wang 2002, pp. 207–34). Immigrant transnationals occupy particularly critical global civil society roles under conditions of state-to-state stalemate (Koehn 2004b).

In conclusion, this review suggests that immigration continues to be related to US foreign relations in fundamental and, at times, decisive ways. The new twist in this complex and enduring relationship is the increased capacity of immigrant transnationals to shape outcomes in their country of origin directly, informally, and even more powerfully than can official agents of the US foreign policy establishment. The opportunity to engage in actions that affect relations with the sending country has been advanced by technological developments that facilitate mobility, political mobilization, and cross-boundary participation (Portes, Guarnizo, and Haller 2002, p. 281; Vertovec 2001, p. 574), by strengthened organizational and interpersonal ties, by the spread of dual nationality/citizenship and transnational competence, and by expanded tolerance for sustained country-of-origin identification among the increasingly multicultural US public. To comprehend foreign relations fully in an age of transmigration, one needs to take into account the variable, reinforcing and conflicting, and contested ways in which immigrant transnationals operating independently and skillfully through their own transnational networks reinforce and/or undercut concurrent state policies and overtures. Increasingly, whether one likes it or not, immigrant transnationals holding dual/multiple identities and loyalties "speak for the United States" abroad.

REFERENCES

A Ying [Qian Xingcun] (1960). *Fanmei huagong jinyue wenxueji* [*Anthology of Chinese Literature against the American Exclusion of Chinese Laborers*]. Shanghai: Zhonghua.
Adamson, Fiona B. (2002). "Mobilizing for the Transformation of Home: Politicized Identities and Transnational Practices." In Nadje Al-Ali and Khalid Koser, eds., *New Approaches to Migration? Transnational Communities and the Transformation of Home*. London: Routledge, pp. 155–68.
Al-Ali, Nadje, Richard Black, and Khalid Koser (2001). "Refugees and Transnationalism: The Experience of Bosnians and Eritreans in Europe." *Journal of Ethnic and Migration Studies* 27(4): 615–34.
Aleinikoff, T. Alexander and Douglas Klusmeyer (2002). *Citizenship Policies for an Age of Migration*. Washington, DC: Carnegie Endowment for International Peace.
Ambrosio, Thomas (2002a). "Entangling Alliances: The Turkish–Israeli Lobbying Partnership and its Unintended Consequences." In Thomas Ambrosio, ed., *Ethnic Identity Groups and U.S. Foreign Policy*. Westport: Praeger, pp. 143–67.
—— (2002b). "Ethnic Identity Groups and U.S. Foreign Policy." In Thomas Ambrosio, ed., *Ethnic Identity Groups and U.S. Foreign Policy*. Westport: Praeger, pp. 1–19.
Appadurai, A. (1996). *Modernity at Large: Cultural Dimensions of Globalization*. Minneapolis: University of Minnesota Press.
Bascom, Johnathan (1994). "The Dynamics of Refugee Repatriation: The Case of Eritreans in Eastern Sudan." In W.T.S. Gould and A.M. Findlay, eds., *Population Migration and the Changing World Order*. Chichester: Wiley, pp. 225–47.
Baubock, Rainer (2003). "Towards a Theory of Migrant Transnationalism." *International Migration Review* 37(3): 700–23.
Chan, Wellington K.K. (2002). "Chinese American Business Networks and Trans-Pacific Economic Relations since the 1970s." In Peter H. Koehn and Xiao-huang Yin, eds., *The Expanding Roles of Chinese Americans in U.S.–China Relations: Transnational Networks and Trans-Pacific Interactions*. Armonk, NY: M.E. Sharpe, pp. 20–35.
Chen, Gongchun and Yonghong Hong (2003). *Chen Jiagen xingchun* [*A New Biography of Tan Kah Kee*]. Singapore: Tan Kah Kee International Society and Global Publishing Co.

Chen, Yong (2000). *Chinese San Francisco: A Trans-Pacific Community, 1850–1943*. Stanford: Stanford University Press.

Cheung, Gordon C.K. (2004). "Chinese Diaspora as a Virtual Nation: Interactive Roles between Economic and Social Capital." *Political Studies* 52: 664–84.

Cheung, Peter T.Y. and James T.H. Tang (2001). "The External Relations of China's Provinces." In David M. Lampton, ed., *The Making of Chinese Foreign and Security Policy in the Era of Reform, 1978–2000*. Stanford: Stanford University Press, pp. 91–120.

Chin, Ko-lin (1999). *Smuggled Chinese: Clandestine Immigration to the United States*. Philadelphia: Temple University Press.

Clough, Michael (1994). "Grass-roots Policymaking." *Foreign Affairs* 73(1): 2–7.

Duany, Jorge (2002). "*Irse pa' fuera*: The Mobile Livelihoods of Circular Migrants between Puerto Rico and the United States." In Ninna N. Sorensen and Karen F. Olwig, eds., *Work and Migration: Life and Livelihoods in a Globalizing World*. London: Routledge, pp. 161–83.

Durand, Jorge, Emilio A. Parrado, and Douglas S. Massey (1996). "Migradollars and Development: A Reconsideration of the Mexican Case." *International Migration Review* 30(2): 423–44.

Evans, Leslie (2004). "African Union Representative Explains New Continent Wide Organization." *UCLA African Studies Center Newsletter* Fall: 3, 6–7, 11, 15.

Feng, Ziping (1993). *Haiwai chunqiu* [*History of Overseas Chinese*]. Shanghai: Shangwu.

Freedman, Amy L. (2000). *Political Participation and Ethnic Minorities: Chinese Overseas in Malaysia, Indonesia, and the United States*. New York: Routledge.

Fu, Teyuan and Xiaoqin Wang (2000). *Chuangyi Meiguo* [*Successful Careers of New Chinese Immigrants in America*]. Baoding: Hebei University Press.

Geithner, Peter F. (2003). "Background note." Diaspora Philanthropy: Comparative Analysis of China and India Diaspora Philanthropy Workshop, Asia Center, Harvard University. Unpublished manuscript.

Glazer, Nathan and Daniel P. Moynihan (1975). "Introduction." In Nathan Glazer and Daniel P. Moynihan, eds., *Ethnicity: Theory and Experience*. Cambridge, MA: Harvard University Press, pp. 1–30.

Goodnough, Abby and Terry Aguayo (2004). "Limits on Trips to Cuba Cause Split in Florida." *New York Times*, June 24, pp. A1, A18.

Guarnizo, Luis E. (2003). "The Economics of Transnational Living." *International Migration Review* 37(3): 666–99.

Gustafson, Per (2002). "Globalisation, Multiculturalism and Individualism: The Swedish Debate on Dual Citizenship." *Journal of Ethnic and Migration Studies* 28(3): 463–81.

Gutierrez, Carlos G. (1999). "Fostering Identities: Mexico's Relations with its diaspora." *Journal of American History* 86(2): 545–67.

Gutierrez, David G. (1999). "Migration, Emergent Ethnicity, and the 'Third Space': The Shifting Politics of Nationalism in Greater Mexico." *Journal of American History* 86(2): 481–517.

Henry, Charles P. (2000). "Black Global Politics in a Post-Cold War World." In Charles P. Henry, ed., *Foreign Policy and the Black (Inter)National Interest*. Albany: State University of New York Press, pp. 1–13.

Hepner, Tricia R. (2003). "Religion, Nationalism, and Transnational Civil Society in the Eritrean Diaspora." *Identities: Global Studies in Culture and Power* 10: 269–93.

Hill, Christopher (2003). *The Changing Politics of Foreign Policy*. London: Palgrave Macmillan.

Hsu, Madeline (2000). *Dreaming of Gold, Dream of Home: Transnationalism and Migration Between the United States and South China, 1882–1942*. Stanford: Stanford University Press.

Hu-DeHart, Evelyn, ed. (1999). *Across the Pacific: Asian Americans and Globalization*. Philadelphia: Temple University Press.

Huntington, Samuel P. (1997). "The Erosion of American National Interests." *Foreign Affairs* 76(5): 28–49.

Itzigsohn, Jose (2000). "Immigration and the Boundaries of Citizenship: The Institutions of Immigrants' Political Transformation." *International Migration Review* 34(4): 1126–53.

—— (2004). "The Formation of Latino and Latina Panethnic Identities." In Nancy Foner and George M. Fredrickson, eds., *Not Just Black and White: Historical and Contemporary Perspectives on Immigration, Race, and Ethnicity in the United States.* New York: Russell Sage Foundation, pp. 197–216.

Itzigsohn, Jose, Carlos D. Cabral, Esther H. Medina, and Obed Vazquez (1999). "Mapping Dominican Transnationalism: Narrow and Broad Transnational Practices." *Ethnic and Racial Studies* 22(2): 316–39.

Jones-Correa, Michael (2002). "Latinos and Latin America: A Unified Agenda?" In Thomas Ambrosio, ed., *Ethnic Identity Groups and U.S. Foreign Policy.* Westport: Praeger, pp. 115–30.

Kasinitz, Philip (2004). "Race, Assimilation, and 'Second Generations,' Past and Present." In Nancy Foner and George M. Fredrickson, eds., *Not Just Black and White: Historical and Contemporary Perspectives on Immigration, Race, and Ethnicity in the United States.* New York: Russell Sage Foundation, pp. 278–98.

Koehn, Peter H. (1991). *Refugees from Revolution: U.S. Policy and Third-World Migration.* Boulder: Westview Press.

—— (1995). "Repatriation of African Exiles: The Decision to Return." In Robin Cohen, ed., *The Cambridge Survey of World Migration.* Cambridge: Cambridge University Press, pp. 347–52.

—— (2001). "Cross-National Competence and U.S.–Asia Interdependence: The Explosion of Trans-Pacific Civil-Society Networks." In Julian Weiss, ed., *Tiger's Roar: Asia's Recovery and Its Impact.* Armonk: M.E. Sharpe, pp. 227–35.

—— (2007). "Global Climatic Stabilization: Challenges for Public Administration in China and the United States." In Ali Farazmand and Jack Pinkowski, eds., *Handbook of Globalization, Governance, and Public Administration.* Boca Raton: CRC Press, pp. 1045–1073.

—— (2004a). "Global Politics and Multinational Health-Care Encounters: Assessing the Role of Transnational Competence." *EcoHealth* 1(1): 69–85.

—— (2004b). "Sustainable Development Frontiers and Divides: Transnational Actors and U.S./China Greenhouse-Gas Emissions." *International Journal of Sustainable Development and World Ecology* 11(4): 380–96.

Koehn, Peter H. and James N. Rosenau (2002). "Transnational Competence in an Emergent Epoch." *International Studies Perspectives* 3(May): 105–27.

Koehn, Peter H. and Xiao-huang Yin (2002a). "Chinese American Transnationalism and U.S.–China Relations: Presence and Promise for the Trans-Pacific Century." In Peter H. Koehn and Xiao-huang Yin, eds., *The Expanding Roles of Chinese Americans in U.S.–China Relations: Transnational Networks and Trans-Pacific Interactions.* Armonk: M.E. Sharpe, pp. xi–xl.

—— (2002b). "Transnationalism, Diversity, and the Future of U.S.–China Relations." In Peter H. Koehn and Xiao-huang Yin, eds., *The Expanding Roles of Chinese Americans in U.S.–China Relations: Transnational Networks and Trans-Pacific Interactions.* Armonk: M.E. Sharpe, pp. 284–90.

Koser, Khalid (2002). "From Refugees to Transnational Communities?" In Nadje Al-Ali and Khalid Koser, eds., *New Approaches to Migration? Transnational Communities and the Transformation of Home.* London: Routledge, pp. 138–52.

Lai, Him Mark (1992). *Cong huaqiao dao huaren* [*From Overseas Chinese to Chinese Americans*]. Hong Kong: Joint.

Lam, Theodora, Brenda S.A. Yeoh, and L. Law (2002). "Sustaining Families Transnationally: Chinese-Malaysians in Singapore." *Asian and Pacific Migration Journal* 11(1): 117–43.

Lampton, David M. (2001). "China's Foreign and National Security Policy-Making Process: Is it Changing, and Does it Matter?" In David M. Lampton, ed., *The Making of Chinese Foreign and Security Policy in the Era of Reform, 1978–2000*. Stanford, CA: Stanford University Press, pp. 1–36.

Levitt, Peggy (2001). *The Transnational Villagers*. Berkeley: University of California Press.

Levitt, Peggy, Josh DeWind, and Steven Vertovec (2003). "International Perspectives on Transnational Migration: An Introduction." *International Migration Review* 37(3): 565–75.

Li, Hongyi et al., eds. (1996). *Guangdongshen zhi: Huaqiao zhi* [*A History of Guangdong Province: Overseas Chinese Volume*]. Guangzhou: Guangdong renmin.

Li, Sufei (2002). "Navigating U.S. China Waters: The Experience of Chinese Students and Professionals in Science, Technology and Business." In Peter H. Koehn and Xiao-huang Yin, eds., *The Expanding Roles of Chinese Americans in U.S.–China Relations: Transnational Networks and Trans-Pacific Interactions*. Armonk, NY: M.E. Sharpe, pp. 20–35.

Liu, Eric (1998). *The Accidental Asian: Notes of a Native Speaker*. New York: Random House.

Liu, Haiming (2004). "Transnational Historiography: Chinese American Studies Reconsidered." *Journal of History of Ideas* 65(1): 135–53.

—— (2005). *The Transnational History of a Chinese Family: Immigrant Letters, Family Business, and Reverse Migration*. New Brunswick: Rutgers University Press.

McKee, Delber L. (1977). *Chinese Exclusion versus the Open Door Policy, 1900–1906*. Detroit: Wayne State University Press.

Matsuoka, Atsuko and John Sorenson (2001). *Ghosts and Shadows: Construction of Identity and Community in an African Diaspora*. Toronto: University of Toronto Press.

Mei, Weiqian and Guoxong Zhang (2001). *Wuye huaqiao huarenshi* [*A History of Overseas Chinese from Five Counties in Guangdong*]. Guangzhou: Guangdong Higher Education Press.

Nakanishi, Don T. (2001). "Beyond Electoral Politics: Renewing a Search for a Paradigm of Asian Pacific American Politics." In Gordon H. Chang, ed., *Asian Americans and Politics: Perspectives, Experiences, Prospects*. Washington, DC: Woodrow Wilson Center Press, pp. 102–29.

Neack, Laura (2003). *The New Foreign Policy: U.S. and Comparative Foreign Policy in the 21st Century*. Lanham: Rowman & Littlefield.

Ong, Aihwa and Donald M. Nonini, eds. (1997). *Ungrounded Empires: The Cultural Politics of Modern Chinese Transnationalism*. New York: Routledge.

Ostergaard-Nielsen, Eva (2003). "The Politics of Migrants' Transnational Political Practices." *International Migration Review* 37(3): 760–86.

Palmer, Ronald D. (2000). "A Personal Road to Diplomacy." In Charles P. Henry, ed., *Foreign Policy and the Black (Inter)National Interest*. Albany: State University of New York Press, pp. 239–50.

Pan, Lynn (1994). *Sons of the Yellow Emperor: A History of the Chinese Diaspora*. New York: Kodansha International.

Portes, Alejandro (1999). "Conclusion: Towards a New World – the Origins and Effects of Transnational Activities." *Ethnic and Racial Studies* 22(2): 463–77.

—— (2001). "Introduction: The Debates and Significance of Immigrant Transnationalism." *Global Networks* 1(3): 181–93.

—— (2003). "Conclusion: Theoretical Convergencies and Empirical Evidence in the Study of Immigrant Transnationalism." *International Migration Review* 37(3): 874–92.

Portes, Alejandro, Luis E. Guarnizo, and William J. Haller (2002). "Transnational Entrepreneurs: An Alternative Form of Immigrant Economic Adaptation." *American Sociological Review* 67 (April): 278–98.

Qian, Suoqiao (2002). "Transnational Sensibilities in Chinese American Diasporic Literature." In Peter H. Koehn and Xiao-huang Yin, eds., *The Expanding Roles of Chinese Americans in U.S.–China Relations: Transnational Networks and Trans-Pacific Interactions.* Armonk: M.E. Sharpe, pp. 36–55.

Rendon, Armando B. (1981). "Latinos: Breaking the Cycle of Survival to Tackle Global Affairs." In Abdul A. Said, ed., *Ethnicity and U.S. Foreign Policy.* New York: Praeger, pp. 183–200.

Roberts, Bryan R., Reanne Frank, and Fernando Lozano-Ascencio (1999). "Transnational Migrant Communities and Mexican Migration to the US." *Ethnic and Racial Studies* 22(2): 238–66.

Rosenau, James N. (2003). *Distant Proximities: Dynamics beyond Globalization.* Princeton: Princeton University Press.

Schiller, Nina G., Linda Basch, and Cristina Blanc-Szanton (1999). "Transnationalism: A New Analytic Framework for Understanding Migration." In Stephen Vertovec and Robin Cohen, eds., *Migration, Diasporas and Transnationalism.* Cheltenham: Edward Elgar, pp. 26–49.

Scott, Fran and Abdulah Osman (2002). "Identity, African-Americans, and U.S. Foreign Policy: Differing Reactions to South African Apartheid and the Rwandan Genocide." In Thomas Ambrosio, ed., *Ethnic Identity Groups and U.S. Foreign Policy.* Westport: Praeger, pp. 71–91.

Shain, Yossi (1999). *Marketing the American Creed Abroad: Diasporas in the U.S. and their Homelands.* Cambridge, Eng.: Cambridge University Press.

Shain, Yossi and Tamara C. Wittes (2002). "Peace as a Three-Level Game: The Role of Diasporas in Conflict Resolution." In Thomas Ambrosio, ed., *Ethnic Identity Groups and U.S. Foreign Policy.* Westport: Praeger, pp. 169–97.

Sharp, Peter (2001). "Making Sense of Citizen Diplomats: The People of Duluth, Minnesota, as International Actors." *International Studies Perspectives* 2(2): 131–50.

Sheffer, Gabriel (2003). *Diaspora Politics: At Home Abroad.* Cambridge: Cambridge University Press.

Shen, James Jingguo (2002). "Communicating Through Conflict, Compromise, and Cooperation: The Strategic Role of Chinese American Scholars in the U.S.–China Relationship." In Peter H. Koehn and Xiao-huang Yin, eds., *The Expanding Roles of Chinese Americans in U.S.–China Relations: Transnational Networks and Trans-Pacific Interactions.* Armonk: M.E. Sharpe, pp. 97–107.

Smith, Michael P. (2003). "Transnationalism, the State, and the Extraterritorial Citizen." *Politics and Society* 31(4): 467–502.

Smith, Robert C. (1998). "Transnational Localities: Community, Technology and the Politics of Membership within the Context of Mexico and U.S. Migration." In Michael P. Smith and Luis E. Guarnizo, eds., *Transnationalism from Below.* New Brunswick: Transaction Publishers, pp. 196–238.

Smith, Tony (2000). *Foreign Attachments: The Power of Ethnic Groups in the Making of American Foreign Policy.* Cambridge, MA: Harvard University Press.

Sorenson, John (1994). "Refugees, Relief and Rehabilitation in the Horn of Africa: The Eritrean Relief Association." In Howard Adelman and John Sorenson, eds., *African Refugees: Development Aid and Repatriation.* Boulder: Westview, pp. 69–93.

Soysal, Yasemin N. (1994). *Limits of Citizenship: Migrants and Postnational Membership in Europe.* Chicago: University of Chicago Press.

Steinberg, Paul F. (2001). *Environmental Leadership in Developing Countries: Transnational Relations and Biodiversity Policy in Costa Rica and Bolivia.* Cambridge, MA: MIT Press.

Tekle, Woldemikael (1998). "Eritrean and Ethiopian Refugees in the United States." *Eritrean Studies Review* 2(2): 89–109.

Thomas-Hope, Elizabeth (2002). "Transnational Livelihoods and Identities in Return Migration to the Caribbean: The Case of Skilled Returnees to Jamaica." In Ninna N. Sorensen and Karen F. Olwig, eds., *Work and Migration: Life and Livelihoods in a Globalizing World.* London: Routledge, pp. 187–201.

Thompson, Ginger (2005). "Mexico's Migrants Profit from Dollars Sent Home." *New York Times,* February 23, p. A8.

Tu, Wei-ming, ed. (1994). *The Living Tree, the Changing Meaning of Being Chinese Today.* Stanford, CA: Stanford University Press.

Van Hear, Nicholas (2002). "Sustaining Societies Under Strain: Remittances as a Form of Transnational Exchange in Sri Lanka and Ghana." In Nadje Al-Ali and Khalid Koser, eds., *New Approaches to Migration? Transnational Communities and the Transformation of Home.* London: Routledge, pp. 202–23.

—— (2003). *From Durable Solutions to Transnational Relations: Home and Exile among Refugee Diasporas.* Geneva: UNHCR, Evaluation and Policy Analysis Unit.

Vertovec, Steven (2001). "Transnationalism and Identity." *Journal of Ethnic and Minority Studies* 27(4): 573–82.

Vidal, David J. (1997). *Defining the National Interest: Minorities and U.S. Foreign Policy in the 21st Century.* New York: Council on Foreign Relations.

Wang, Zuoyue (2002). "Chinese American Scientists and U.S.–China Scientific Relations: From Richard Nixon to Wen Ho Lee." In Peter H. Koehn and Xiao-huang Yin, eds., *The Expanding Roles of Chinese Americans in U.S.–China Relations: Transnational Networks and Trans-Pacific Interactions.* Armonk: M.E. Sharpe, pp. 207–34.

Watanabe, Paul Y. (2002). "Asian-Americans and U.S.–Asia Relations." In Thomas Ambrosio, ed., *Ethnic Identity Groups and U.S. Foreign Policy.* Westport: Praeger, pp. 131–42.

Wheeler, Norton (2002). "Improving Mainland Society and U.S.–China Relations." In Peter H. Koehn and Xiao-huang Yin, eds., *The Expanding Roles of Chinese Americans in U.S.–China Relations: Transnational Networks and Trans-Pacific Interactions.* Armonk: M.E. Sharpe, pp. 185–206.

Wu, Frank H. and Francey L. Youngberg (2001). "People from China Crossing the River: Asian American Political Empowerment and Foreign Influence." In Gordon H. Chang, ed., *Asian Americans and Politics: Perspectives, Experiences, Prospects.* Washington, DC: Woodrow Wilson Center Press, pp. 311–53.

Yin, Xiao-huang (1999). "The Growing Influence of Chinese Americans on U.S.–China Relations." In Peter Koehn and Joseph Y.S. Cheng, eds., *The Outlook for U.S.–China Relations Following the 1997–1998 Summits: Chinese and American Perspectives on Security, Trade, and Cultural Exchange.* Hong Kong: Chinese University Press, pp. 331–49.

—— (2000). *Chinese American Literature since the 1850s.* Urbana: University of Illinois Press.

—— (2002). "Chinese Americans: A Diverse People Build Bridges that Span the Pacific." *Los Angeles Times,* October 27, p. M3.

—— (2005). "Continuity and Changes in Chinese American Philanthropy to China: A Case Study of Chinese American Transnationalism." *American Studies* 45(2): 65–99.

Yin, Xiao-huang and Zhiyong Lan (1997). "Chinese Americans: A Rising Factor in U.S.–China Relations." *Journal of American–East Asian Relations* 6(1): 35–57.

Yu, Renqiu (1992). *To Save China, to Save Ourselves: The Chinese Hand Laundry Alliance of New York.* Philadelphia: Temple University Press.

Zhao, Xiaojian (2002). *Remaking Chinese America: Immigration, Family, and Commmunity, 1940–1965.* New Brunswick: Rutgers University Press.

Zhuang, Guotu (2001). *Huaqiao huaren yu zhongguo di guangxi* [*The Relationship between Overseas Chinese and China*]. Guangzhou: Guangdong gaoden jiaoyu.

CHAPTER FIVE

Bodies from Abroad: Immigration, Health, and Disease

ALAN M. KRAUT

Commenting on the relationship of international migration to the spread of infectious disease in the last decade of the twentieth century, United States Surgeon General, Dr. Antonia C. Novello remarked, "Viruses and bacteria don't ask for a green card" (*Washington Post*, April 24, 1993). The SARS (Sudden Acute Respiratory Syndrome) epidemic and the threat of avian flu coming from the other side of the globe to menace residents of western countries in the first years of the twenty-first century confirms Novello's point and is a reminder that the threat of newly emerging infectious disease from abroad has been heightened, not diminished. The same rapid transportation – the planes, and ships and trucks – that make the world a smaller place, and a place more prosperous for some, as commerce and migrants move across one border and then another, allows pathogens to travel the same routes and at the same speed (Markel 2004, p. 9).

All too often immigration historians have paid little attention to disease, health, and health-care as integral parts of the larger migration narrative to which they attend. They say too little about the fear of infectious disease in shaping immigration policy. Nor do they address the issue of immigrant policy – what happens after migration as newcomers seek to integrate into their adopted societies. Migration scholars have also fail to sufficiently explicate the roles of individuals and institutions in the field of health that shape this cultural negotiation between migrants and the host society. Immigration scholars neglect the physician and his or her concerns. Healers are not viewed as the cultural mediators they have been historically. Nor do historians adequately plumb the culture of medicine, especially institutions such as medical inspection facilities, hospitals, dispensaries, and other places where newcomers turned for cure and care. Scholars must conscientiously patrol the border between the culture of health and well-being as understood by migrants and the host society's culture of medicine. Such an understanding is crucial to a broader comprehension of how newcomers are or are not integrated into host societies. A narrative of migration to America with special concern for matters of health and disease can initiate the quest for a history of American migration that integrates the insights of migration scholars and historians of medicine. It can highlight those areas and topics that most need scholarly attention.

The relationship of health, disease, and migration is as old as human history and as contemporary as the latest flight landing at LAX or Kennedy International Airport in New York.

Epidemics of infectious disease have shaped the fates of societies. For centuries, the only means that communities had at their disposal for avoiding infectious disease from afar was quarantine. In July 1377, the municipal council of Ragusa on the Dalmatian coast mandated a 30-day period of isolation for those coming from places known to have experienced bubonic plague – the Black Death. Eventually the period was extended to 40 days, hence the term quarantine, derived from *quarantenaria* (Rosen 1958, p. 69). Quarantine remains even now an important aspect of disease prevention, although scholars have rarely linked it to the ebb and flow of migration and commerce.

Fourteenth-century Europeans were not alone in fearing disease from afar and understanding the importance of isolating those who might be sick from those who are not. Native Americans exercised quarantine when they isolated menstruating women or fled villages when smallpox erupted. Smallpox and other diseases such as measles and chicken pox brought to the New World by European explorers devastated Native American tribes after initial contact in the late fifteenth century. Because Native Americans lacked acquired immunities to the diseases that were endemic in the European countries from which the Europeans sailed, the deadly illnesses that ensued are often called "virgin soil epidemics" (Crosby 1976, pp. 293–4). Sometimes referred to as the Columbian Exchange, the initial contact between Europeans and the native population cost Native American peoples hundreds of thousands of lives.

Both Native Americans and Europeans interpreted the cataclysm of the Columbian Exchange in theological terms. Tribes that trapped animals believed that the sickness they suffered was a conspiracy against them by the souls of the game animals they hunted (Martin 1978, *passim*). The Cherokee in South Carolina, struck by smallpox, blamed it on the wrath of divine spirits angered by the sexual promiscuity of tribal youth (S. Williams 1966, pp. 244–5).

European arrivals also comprehended the illnesses that befell Native Americans in terms divine. It seemed to European Christians, especially to English settlers, that God was clearing the way for his "chosen flock." Puritan minister Cotton Mather, observing the horrors of the 1616–17 epidemic, thought the pestilence of smallpox divinely mandated to rid the land of Indians, whom he described as "those pernicious creatures," and to "make room for better growth" (Mather 1855, p. 55). Later, awed by the smallpox that ravaged local tribes, Governor William Bradford of Plymouth recounted in his history of the colony the Indians' "lamentable condition as they lie on their hard mats, the pox breaking and mattering and running into one another." Bradford proudly recounted how Englishmen braved the risk of infection and unselfishly cared for these non-Christians. Without an understanding of the workings of immunity, Bradford concluded that his neighbors did not get sick from contact with the Indians because of their religious beliefs (Bradford 1981, pp. 302–3). However, variolation, the inoculation of healthy individuals with matter from those infected with smallpox to prevent the disease, was already known in western Europe. The English colonists may have relied on more than just faith to fend off the dreaded disease.

While some thought the felling of Native Americans divinely determined, most Europeans and Americans of European background attributed disease to vapors arising from decaying organic matter, or miasmas. The miasmatic theory of disease causation derived from the observation that malaria was frequently contracted by individuals who lived in swampy, low-lying areas. Similarly foul-smelling effluviums, as they were sometimes also called, seemed to emanate from the parts of towns and villages where the poor resided. Some suggested that the poor would be less vulnerable to disease if the miasmas could be banished. However, not until the mid-nineteenth century did American public health advocates and sanitarians endeavor to banish disease through water purification, efficient waste disposal, ventilation of congested housing, and ensuring the wholesome freshness of milk, bread, and other foods. They believed that cleanliness alone might prevent disease. Others thought that specific contagia were the exclusive causes of infections and epidemic diseases. But precisely how the contagia spread and how to prevent infection remained unknown until the discovery of germ theory at the end of the nineteenth century. A third notion synthesized miasmatic and contagion theories. Some historians of medicine dubbed it "contingent contagionism." This view explained disease as the result of contagia, whether specific or nonspecific. However, contingent contagionists additionally believed that contagia could not cause disease unless certain conditions prevailed that nourished the contagia or facilitated their transmission. Thus, a specific virus might cause a specific disease, but the virus was not harmful unless climatic conditions were such that the virus could breed. And where might such breeding occur? Some thought sewers and filthy basements were ideal places (Rosen 1958, pp. 288–9).

Because many eighteenth-century European colonists associated the presence of harmful contagia with those who lived in unhealthy surroundings where such contagia might flourish, community leaders sought to take precautions. Many associated the worst conditions with the impoverished foreign-born who were arriving in the colonies. Colonial laws suggest how colonists hoped to deal with the menace from abroad. In 1700, Massachusetts Colony passed an immigration law including a provision for the exclusion of the sick or physically disabled. According to the law, "No lame, impotent, or infirm persons, incapable of maintaining themselves, should be received without first giving security that the town in which they settled would not be charged with their support." Should new arrivals in fact be unable to support themselves, the master of the ship upon which they arrived was responsible for returning the passengers to the port of embarkation. After much debate and revision, a 1756 law expressly prohibited admission to sick or infirm persons "from foreign ports or other colonies," without the approval of a town's selectmen and security posted by the captain of the ship upon which the newcomers had arrived (*Massachusetts Colony Acts and Resolves*, quoted in Proper 1967, pp. 29–30).

After the American Revolution, colonial legislation was often recast as state law to reflect the reservations that many Americans had about the arrival of immigrants. Neither the federal government nor the state governments initially had systematic procedures for inspecting and excluding newcomers because they were deemed physically or mentally unfit. As it had since the Middle Ages, quarantine remained the first line of defense against disease from abroad.

Crowded, unhealthy conditions aboard most immigrant ships in the late eighteenth and early nineteenth centuries left many dead. Shipboard epidemics of typhus, cholera, and smallpox stirred Congressional intervention. The Act of March 2, 1819 limited the number of passengers a ship might carry and initiated the collection of vital data on the foreign-born. Now masters of arriving ships had to furnish port authorities with a manifest of all passengers on board. Each passenger's and crew member's name and national origin must be listed. Later passenger acts improved the health of ship passengers by specifying the amount of space per passenger that must be permitted and the ventilation, privy facilities, and cooking accommodations that must be provided. The Act of March 3, 1855 (10 Stat. 715) included a 19-provision code governing the treatment and processing of migrants, but left enforcement up to individual states (Solis-Cohen 1947, p. 33; Hutchinson 1981, pp. 21–2).

Specific epidemics were often attributed to the foreign-born and stimulated change in how communities provided for the public health. A devastating yellow fever epidemic that struck Philadelphia in 1793 caused the city to strengthen its quarantine capabilities (Powell 1949, *passim*). State laws in 1806 and 1818 created a Board of Health for Philadelphia and gave the governor of Pennsylvania authority to appoint board members and staff. The fear of disease from abroad outweighed the fear of government involvement in the lives of its citizens. Among the actions taken by this new board was the creation of a quarantine station, the Lazaretto, located on the Delaware River, about 10 miles south of Philadelphia. When epidemics seemed impending, especially during the summer months, the Lazaretto physician examined passengers and seamen on all incoming vessels. The port's quarantine master inspected each ship and its cargo for signs that the ship might pose a health risk for Philadelphia. If there was a sign of sickness, health officers would detain the ship and transfer the sick to a port hospital. Only then could the ship be certified and allowed to pull into the dock. During the rest of the year a port physician was responsible for detaining, inspecting, and certifying arriving ships. Early nineteenth-century American cities regarded such quarantine procedures as a routine defense against diseases brought from other ports on the bodies of newcomers or in a ship's cargo (Morman 1984, *passim*).

As immigration to the United States from northern and western Europe escalated in the 1840s and 1850s, there was an increasing need for regulation to ensure the health and safety of newcomers and natives alike. Between 1840 and 1860, approximately 4.5 million immigrants arrived in the United States. Over 1.8 million of these newcomers were impoverished Irish fleeing the southern provinces. The flow from Ireland heightened during the Great Hunger of the 1840s. The busy port of New York converted Castle Garden into the New York State Emigration Depot in 1855. At Castle Garden and similar state-operated depots, state officers interrogated newcomers and recorded vital information. An insufficient number of health officers caused states such as New York to rely on the voluntarism of private physicians whose sense of civic duty encouraged them to donate some of their time during peak immigration months to inspecting newcomers to ensure that infectious diseases did not endanger the city's population. Physicians were also careful to exclude those whose poor health or physical impairments might prevent them from supporting themselves, leaving them dependent upon the care of strangers and the charity of others.

In 1832 a severe cholera epidemic swept across the Atlantic and devastated New York and several other cities. Caused by the bacterium *Vibrio cholerae*, cholera is an acute infection with symptoms of diarrhea, vomiting, muscular cramps, dehydration, and collapse. It is contracted by drinking water or eating foods contaminated by the excretion of infected persons. The incubation period is 72 hours, with a crisis several days after the initial symptoms appear. Death can result if the dehydration and chemical imbalances are not treated. In 1832, little was understood about cholera. The epidemic that year had originated in Asia. Quarantines and other precautions had proven inadequate. In cities along the east coast large numbers of immigrants got sick and perished. Especially hard hit were the poorest newcomers which included the Irish. In an era well before germ theory, some Americans saw a link between two unwelcome arrivals – cholera and the Irish (Rosenberg 1987, *passim*).

The Irish were the target of suspicion and stigmatized as responsible for the 1832 epidemic for a variety of reasons. Many Americans of Protestant English ancestry despised the Irish for their Catholicism and regarded their faith as evidence of their backwardness. Irish ignorance was believed by some native-born Protestants to be the cause of Irish vice and poverty, the root causes of their vulnerability to disease. However, in congested urban areas there was always the risk that the diseases to which the debauched Irish were vulnerable might be spread to those who did not deserve such retribution at the hands of the divine. Many Americans regarded the "low Irish" as vulnerable because of their intemperance and lack of cleanliness. Anti-Irish nativists were only too willing to believe that bars and political clubhouses frequented by the Irish were the breeding grounds for cholera and that the disease was disproportionately visited upon the Irish as divine punishment for their sinful ways.

Although the Irish were hardly the only victims of cholera, neither native-born victims nor those of other groups, such as the Germans, were regarded as the cause of their own disease as frequently as were the Irish. Cooler temperatures in the autumn of 1832 ended the epidemic. However, it was not the last cholera epidemic to menace the eastern seaboard in the early and mid-nineteenth century. There were severe epidemics in 1849 and 1866. According to data compiled by historian of medicine Charles Rosenberg, hospital statistics for six cities (Cincinnati, New York, Buffalo, Brooklyn, Boston, and New Orleans) indicate that 4,309 of 5,301 patients at the peak of the 1849 cholera epidemic were listed in the census as foreign-born (Rosenberg 1987, p. 135 n. 5). By 1849, fewer native-born Americans saw cholera among the Irish as evidence of God's retribution against sinful and spiritually unworthy Irish Catholics. More saw the priority as cleaning up streets and living quarters that nurtured contagia, and recasting municipal government so that it might more effectively cope with public health challenges. However, not until 1866 did New York City form a Metropolitan Board of Health. In New York and elsewhere, future epidemics would be battled with permanent public health agencies that could marshal data and expertise.

The arrival of millions of newcomers created the need not only to improve public health, but also to create institutions that could meet the needs of sick or disabled newcomers for care and cure. While the native-born were often kept at home to battle diseases of the body and mind, the poor and especially newcomers required institutionalization in almshouses and asylums. Data on rates of insanity among pre-Civil War immigrant groups such as the Irish suggest disproportionate rates of such illness. From 1849 to 1859, three-quarters of the admissions to New York City's lunatic asylum on Blackwell's Island were immigrants. Two-thirds of these were

Irish (Ernst 1965, p. 54). As historian Gerry Grob has noted, definitions of mental illness were highly protean in this era and there seems little doubt that many new-comers suffered more from the stresses of the journey, unfamiliar surroundings, and grinding poverty than anything else. However, the data and descriptions of Irish patients, especially female patients, as noisy and disruptive only served to reinforce negative stereotypes of the Irish among native-born Americans. Opponents of immi-gration depicted the Irish as abnormal in behavior and appearance (Grob 1973, p. 238). An 1851 *Harper's Magazine* article described the "Celtic physiognomy" as "distinctly marked – the small and some what upturned nose, the black tint of the skin; the eyes now looking gray, now black; the freckled cheek, and sandy hair. Beard and whiskers covered half the face, and short, square-shouldered bodies were bent forward with eager impatience" (*Harper's Monthly*, p. 833).

Aware that the mass migration of Irish Catholics to the United States had aroused nativist hatreds and social pressures, the Roman Catholic Church acted to protect its flock with a new institution. Churchmen such as New York's Bishop John Dubois and Bishop John Hughes encouraged the construction of Catholic hospitals so that impoverished newcomers might not be a burden on the community where they settled and contribute to anti-Catholic feelings. However, an even more important rationale for hospitals such as St. Vincent's in New York or St. Joseph's in Philadelphia for the Irish, and Philadelphia's St. Mary's Hospital for the Germans, was to ensure that poor Catholics could take strength from their faith as they sought to heal their bodies. In Catholic hospitals, patients could have ready access to priests who would administer the sacraments, and dietary restrictions such as meatless Fridays were observed. Most importantly from the Church's perspective, in Catholic hospitals, patients were protected from evangelical Protestant clergy who often attempted deathbed conversions in other institutions (Kraut 1994, pp. 44–7).

Catholics were not the only ones concerned about supporting their flock during times of illness. German Jews in Cincinnati opened the first Jewish hospital in the United States in 1850 to care for the many immigrant peddlers who used the city as a hub. Here and later at New York's Jews' Hospital (eventually renamed Mount Sinai), Jewish patients could eat kosher food, attend service, and have the ministrations of a rabbi. In a Jewish hospital they would not suffer the derisive and disrespectful glances of anti-Semitic fellow patients or physicians (Kraut 1994, p. 208). There are few studies of Catholic and Jewish hospitals and much work remains to be done by scholars to fully understand their role in fostering integration.

Nativists who claimed that immigrants posed a threat to the public's health and a potential financial burden to communities if they could not work hard and support themselves persisted in their arguments well beyond the first wave of immigration in the 1840–1860 era. After the Civil War, most newcomers continued to come from northern and western Europe, especially the British Isles and the German states. However, beginning in the last two decades of the nineteenth century, the flow of migration shifted. An increasing number of newcomers were arriving from southern and eastern Europe, as well as China, Japan, and parts of Latin America. Between 1880 and the early 1920s, 23.5 million newcomers arrived. The United States was hardly the only destination. Canada, Australia, Argentina, and Brazil also attracted migrants, but the United States attracted the greatest number (Kraut 2001, p. 17). The presence of millions of migrants from countries that had not previously been donor nations to the United States aroused greater fears than ever before. The fear that newcomers breed might bring disease and genes of an inferior sort encouraged Congressional reassessment of America's immigration policies and challenged states and cities to revise their public health policies to cope with the flood of new arrivals.

State quarantine laws and haphazard inspection by state officers no longer seemed adequate protection against potential health menaces from abroad. As early as the 1870s fears of yellow fever garnered support in Congress for a national board of health that would administer national quarantine policy. Others preferred keeping the federal government distant from state affairs. The compromise was short-lived and weak. The National Board of Health (1879–83) was designed merely to support state and local efforts. It had little power except to take over state quarantine powers in those states proven to be not up to the task. However, by the time its funding expired in 1883, the National Board was unable to impose a national quarantine. State rights, localism, and jurisdictional rivalries with the US Marine Hospital Service (later renamed the US Public Health Service) had scuttled its efforts (Kraut 1994, p. 51).

Less than a decade after the National Board of Health's failure, the federal government took decisive action to ensure that the bodies of arriving immigrants did not become vehicles for contagia. Congress passed the Act of March 3, 1891 (26 Stat. 1084) which mandated that migrants headed for the United States must stand health inspections before departure and after arrival in the United States.

Now federal law required steamship companies, which were growing rich on the immigrant trade, to assist in preventing the spread of disease from the Old World to the New. The companies were required to vaccinate, disinfect, and medically examine migrants to certify their health prior to departure. Ship companies were liable for the cost of housing and feeding passengers detained by American authorities for reasons of ill health. Those newcomers who could not be admitted were returned to their ports of embarkation and their costs paid by the steamship companies.

The task of inspecting and interrogating emigrants was great during peak periods of migration. Wealthy transportation companies such as the Hamburg-Amerika Line constructed villages to house migrants prior to departure and where they might undergo a physician's examination as part of the pre-boarding routine. Because such examinations tended to be cursory as ship companies sought to maximize their trade, the federal government determined to improve the quality of the inspection after newcomers crossed the ocean.

Facing the greatest administrative task since organizing the society for civil war in the 1860s, the federal government established immigration depots where federal officers could inspect and interrogate newcomers. Until the Civil War the federal government hardly touched the lives of most citizens. Most Americans had contact with the government in Washington only when they were interrogated by a census taker or when they picked up their mail at the post office. In what historian Robert Wiebe called a "search for order," the federal government was expanding its role. The need to protect the public health was forcing that expansion. The health examination of newcomers seemed to many fulfillment of the federal government's responsibility to protect the safety of its citizens (Wiebe 1967, *passim*).

The great migration of the late nineteenth and early twentieth centuries occurred at the same time as other crucial changes were transforming understanding of human well-being. Germ theory, derived from the research of Robert Koch of Germany and

Louis Pasteur of France, changed the way that physicians thought about disease causality. Now physicians sought microorganisms that intruded upon human bodies. Specific germs caused specific diseases. Diagnosis and therapy would never be the same. By the 1890s protecting the public's health from disease brought by newcomers became a hunt for those carrying harmful pathogens on their bodies or belongings. Federal physicians endeavored to intercept newcomers carrying infectious diseases before they spread those diseases to their unwitting hosts. Physicians as well as immigration officers manned newly constructed depots at America's ports of entry.

The flagship of immigration depots was the one constructed on Ellis Island in the busy port of New York. On January 1, 1892, Annie Moore, a 15-year-old from Ireland, became the first immigrant to enter the United States through Ellis Island. Approximately 14 million followed until Ellis closed its doors in 1954. Quarantine procedures were gradually transferred to federal jurisdiction, but remained in the hands of state officials in some states such as New York until the 1920s. However, once state quarantine inspectors determined whether there was a need to quarantine any passengers or everyone on a ship because of an outbreak of infectious disease, the inspection of individual immigrants was in the hands of federal authorities. First and second class ship passengers were given perfunctory examinations in their cabins, but those traveling third class or steerage stood the line inspection in immigration depots. Immigrants on Ellis Island, for example, were lined up and passed under the gaze of uniformed US Marine Hospital Service physicians who would determine their fitness for admission to the United States. (For a full description of the Ellis Island inspection, see Kraut 1994, pp. 53–77 and Fairchild 2003, pp. 83–115.)

After carrying hand luggage to the top of the stairs leading to Ellis Island's Great Hall, where the inspection was to begin, immigrants' hands, eyes, and throats were examined to check the effect on them of mild physical stress. As medical technology improved over the years, so did the diagnostic abilities of physicians. However, the best instrument was always the experienced clinical gaze of the physicians who scrutinized newcomers. Throughout the peak era of migration, the test that most intimidated new arrivals was the eversion of their eyelids to look for the tell-tale lesions of trachoma, a disease that if left untreated could render its victims blind. Immigrants' scalps were probed for evidence of favus, a highly contagious dermatological disease. Physicians turned the heads of immigrants to better examine facial expressions. Medical experts believed that certain facial expressions were indicative of mental illness or insufficiency. Examining physicians made chalk marks on the clothing of newcomers whom they wished to subject to further inspection. Each letter marked on a newcomer's clothing stood for a suspected disability: K for hernia, G for goiter, X for mental illness, and so on. Those individual examinations were conducted with attention to modesty and respect. Officials segregated the sexes and made certain that women physicians and nurses examined female immigrants.

Some detainees who required treatment were assigned to one of the two hospitals on Ellis Island. A general hospital with full surgical capabilities handled cases of non-contagious illness or injury. Contagious diseases were treated in a separate facility on the island constructed on the pavilion style so that patients with different infectious diseases could be isolated from one another – patients in measles wards isolated from tuberculosis patients, etc. Physicians could re-gown and re-glove as they left one ward and entered another. Because the immigrants were not yet American citizens, or even legally admitted aliens, while they were on Ellis Island, they could not refuse medical attention, including detention. Any protest could result in exclusion and a return journey.

No diagnosis disturbed immigration officers and physicians as much as those of mental deficiency and insanity. The Immigration Act of 1882 had excluded "any convict, lunatic, idiot or person unable to take care of himself or herself without becoming a public charge." However, there were no easily administered tests to determine mental fitness. Drs. Henry Knox and E.H. Mullan developed block tests to use with immigrants to weed out mental defectives. Immigrants had to place wooden blocks back in the right-sized places in a specified amount of time. Failure to do so was taken as evidence of mental incapability (Kraut 1994, p. 74).

Although fewer than 3 percent of those inspected on Ellis Island were denied admission, an increasing percentage of those excluded were denied admission for medical reasons, whether deficiency of physical or mental health. From less than 2 percent in 1898, the percentage increased to 57 percent in 1913 and 69 percent by 1916. One reason for the increase was improved diagnostic techniques. When Ellis Island first opened in 1892, the Public Health Service physicians diagnosed tuberculosis (TB) by auscultation, studying with a stethoscope the character of the sounds that cavities in diseased lung tissue produced. By 1910, the use of X-ray technology for such diagnoses was routine, as was analysis of residue from patients' lungs. Only a slide showing the tubercle bacillus in an immigrant's sputum was sufficient evidence to bar a newcomer for TB. Similarly, the Wassermann test markedly improved rates of syphilis diagnosis over observation and examination (Kraut 1994, pp. 66–7). The physicians of the Public Health Service insisted that their job was diagnosis only and refused to sit on boards of review that decided whether a particular migrant would be admitted or rejected. However, improved medical technology vastly improved the chances of diagnosing an excludable condition (Kraut 1994, pp. 68–9).

Late nineteenth- and early twentieth-century immigrants' first encounter with the culture of American medicine was at immigration depots such as New York's Ellis Island. There is no evidence that immigrants' physical condition, of such great concern to policy makers, engendered an epidemic or other specific health crisis in the United States. Of course, neither congressmen nor administrators in Washington had any way of knowing in advance how little menace the newcomers would pose to Americans' health. The inspection reflected their apprehensions.

What, then, is the broader significance of the immigration inspection mandated by the federal government for the first time in the 1890s? Historian Amy Fairchild has argued that it was an initiation into the life of the American working class. Fairchild cites the low rates of rejection at Ellis Island and other ports of entry as evidence that the government's goal was to admit robust workers who would lend their productivity to the growing industrial strength of the United States. The inspection was a means of introducing these newcomers from so many different societies to the norms and discipline of American industrial life, to ready them for the shop floor (Fairchild 2003, *passim*). Others, such as Howard Markel, suggest that how the quarantine and inspection procedures were applied reflected efforts to scientifically justify ethnic preferences (Markel 1997, *passim*). Whatever ensemble of subtexts existed, most officers of the US Public Health Service attempted to be fair and professional in their protection of the public health (Kraut 1994, pp. 64–73).

The encounter between the physicians and immigrants might be viewed as a negotiation between the biological and the social, as physicians made diagnoses that would have a profound effect on each immigrant's future and the larger peopling of the United States. However, it would be too easy to dismiss the close scrutiny to which Public Health Service physicians subjected newcomers as mere ethnocentricity or a pragmatic initiation into industrial life. Federal physicians were engaged in their own personal negotiations between the demands of their medical oath to minister unto the individual and their statutory responsibility to guard the public's health. Their decisions to pass or detain particular newcomers transformed Ellis Island into a kind of Progressive fortress designed to protect the United States and its people from potentially dangerous infections and the possibility that newcomers might endanger rather than enhance the country's productivity.

When newly arrived immigrants left Ellis Island in the port of New York or Angel Island in the port of San Francisco, where most Chinese and many Japanese were processed, the federal government ceased being responsible for their health and well-being. The United States has never had an official immigrant policy designed to shape the integration of newcomers. Migrants joined the masses of native-born Americans in the cities and countryside of the United States. There the negotiation continued over matters of health and disease. Now, however, that negotiation was not about admission or exclusion from the country, but about the integration, or assimilation, of newcomers into the society and culture of the United States. While scholars have paid considerable attention to negotiations between newcomers and native-born in matters of politics, religion, music, food, and social behaviors of various kinds, insufficient attention has been paid to the ongoing conversation between aliens and Americans over matters of the body, especially health, disease, and therapy after arrival.

The two largest groups of arrivals in the late nineteenth and early twentieth centuries were the southern Italians and the East European Jews. Their experiences illustrate the complexities of reconciling Old World and New World perceptions of disease causality and health.

As did the Irish in an earlier era, the southern Italians arrived in large numbers seeking opportunities to escape the grinding poverty of the southern provinces. Between 1880 and 1921, 4.5 million arrived, more than any other group. The number of Italian migrants will always be imprecise because most were migrant laborers, "birds of passage" as they were dubbed by American immigration officers. And as were the Irish of an earlier era, the southern Italians were regarded by some Americans as especially unclean and unhealthy. One Columbia University professor of political economy offered his view of the Italian immigrants he had observed in New York tenements: "Huddled together in miserable apartments in filth and rags, without the slightest regard to decency or health, they present a picture of squalid existence degrading to any civilization and a menace to the health of the whole community" (Mayo-Smith 1890, p. 133). It was this perspective on the Italians which caused them to be stigmatized as disease carriers when certain east coast cities suffered a polio epidemic in 1916.

In addition to descriptions of the filth attributed to Italian unsanitary habits and poor personal hygiene, cultural differences between the Italians and native-born Americans account for the accusations that the Italians were responsible for spreading polio during the 1916 epidemic. One public health nurse specifically mentioned the Italian custom of kissing the dead as perpetuating the epidemic. The custom was a ritualized expression of sadness and respect for the deceased (Vecoli 1977, p. 33). However, in the eyes of public health nurse Ida May Shevlin, the practice epitomized disrespect for the living and a flaunting of the insights of medical science regarding how disease is spread through a population. Most often, though, nurses commented upon how suspicious and fearful Italian newcomers were of American nurses and physicians. When a child was stricken with polio, frightened immigrant mothers and fathers barred their doors to public health nurses and, at times, even sought to physically intimidate the nurses. These Italian newcomers saw the nurses as intruders who despised them and their ways (Kraut 1994, p. 111).

In fact southern Italian arrivals and their American hosts did have very different ideas about disease causality and therapy. Definitions of illness and remedy were derived from a blend of religion and folk beliefs that were not the same in every region of Italy. Christianity came to the cities before the countryside, where pagan deities prevailed and pagan customs marked life passages. North of Rome, Italian Roman Catholicism was similar to the faith practiced by the rest of northern Europe, but south of Rome, Catholicism was amalgamated with pre-Christian traditions and customs. There was a lack of uniformity in the South because in some places, such as Campania and Sicily, a Greco-Roman tradition prevailed, while coastal areas echoed a Hellenistic medical tradition inherited from Greek physicians. In still more isolated regions, superstition and magic unrelated to any tradition held on in the hearts and minds of residents (P. Williams 1938, p. 135).

Within the Italian Catholic tradition, there were common practices that transcended regional divides. Prayers for continued health or recovery from illness were addressed to particular saints and the object of the prayers was often the relic of a particular saint. Saint Rocco who protected devotees against illness and Saint Lucy who guarded their eyesight are not found in the Bible or other Christian writings, but were substitutes for old Greek or Roman gods and spirits of the forests or rivers. Prayers to local Madonnas often had the flavor of pre-Christian ritual. Rather than risk marginalization, Catholic missionaries had often permitted the blending of folk customs and traditions into Catholic worship (P. Williams 1938, pp. 136–7).

Southern Italians harbored beliefs about illness and remedy common to many peasant cultures. Illness was attributed to the ill will of others. Those who practiced *jettatura* (sorcery) used the *mal'occhio* (evil eye). With a glance, jealous men or women who possessed the evil eye could cause physical injury, sickness, or even death. Amulets and ritual incantations might be used to ward off the evil eye. Popular amulets were often made of a precious metal, coral, or lava and often represented the horns, claws, or teeth of an animal. Amulets could be placed over a doorpost or on a bedroom wall or on a chain around the neck (P. Williams 1938, pp. 143–4).

Southern Italians relied on folk remedies when illness struck, relying on witches, barbers, midwives, and herbalists. There were few physicians and many residents did not trust physicians, regarding them as intruders whose affluence and education marked them as outsiders and perhaps allied with the landed classes of the north that so oppressed southern Italian *contadini* (townspeople). Folk healers' diagnoses often associated physiological characteristics with particular patterns of personality or disease, such as "He who has long ears will live long." People with long necks were considered especially susceptible to tuberculosis, while those with hooked noses or livid faces were likely to possess the evil eye (P. Williams 1938, p. 162).

The diseases that folk healers and physicians confronted in southern Italy were often accompanied by high fevers, including malaria, typhoid, and rheumatic fever. In the warm southern climate, respiratory diseases such as bronchitis, pneumonia, and tuberculosis were relatively rare. Tuberculosis was especially feared because often diagnosis could not be made until the disease was in its last stages. A tuberculosis diagnosis meant almost certain death.

The mass migration of southern Italians to the United States did not mean automatic abandonment of traditional ideas of disease causation and remedies. As anthropologist Robert Orsi has explained, prayer to a Madonna, such as the Madonna of 115th Street in East Harlem, was one important response to disease (Orsi 1985, pp. 181–2, 193–5, 209–10). Beyond prayer, *contadini* (townspeople) who migrated to New York, Chicago, or Philadelphia continued to attribute disease to the ill will of others and to prefer consulting with folk healers who prescribed folk remedies. Physicians, though often more readily available in the United States than in Italy, remained suspect because they were perceived to be the allies of the rich and powerful who had oppressed southern Italians in their homelands.

If new arrivals hesitated to consult a physician for their ailments, Italian physicians often took the initiative and advocated the cause of the newcomers, offering low-cost care and acting as cultural mediators between the immigrant and American society. One such was Dr. Antonio Stella. Although from the southern provinces, Stella was the well-educated son of an attorney. He received his medical degree from the Royal University in 1893 and migrated to the United States, becoming a citizen in 1909. Stella was devoted to the poor. An internist, Stella was also a prolific author, with a special interest in tuberculosis (often called consumption) (Kraut 1994, p. 123). He gathered statistics and in one book argued that the health problems encountered by Italian newcomers were often acquired on this side of the Atlantic. He attributed the markedly low rates of tuberculosis among the Italians to poor reporting and the fact that, once diagnosed, many Italians returned home to be cared for by family and often died in Italy rather than where they had contracted the disease (Stella 1975, pp. 66–8). Stella rejected notions that the Italians were responsible for their own ill health because they were unclean or inferior physically. Instead he demonstrated that congested housing and dark, unventilated sweatshops weakened the otherwise robust bodies of Italian men and women who had come to work in the United States. He explained that poor environmental conditions could curb the body's ability to fight infection. He wrote,

> We know now-a-days that the penetration of a pathogenic germ into our system is not sufficient to cause a disease. It must find our body in a state of temporary paralysis of all its natural defenses, to be able to give rise to certain morbid processes, the evolution of which constitutes a disease. (Stella 1904, pp. 486–9)

Antonio Stella's view of what was making the Italian migrants sick was confirmed by Italian immigration officials who watched as their "birds of passage" flocked home ill and dying.

Because physicians were also cultural mediators, the clearest calls for change in the way Italian immigrants lived and their view of allopathic medicine came from physicians of their own group. Dr. Rocco Brindisi put it directly albeit sympathetically, "The Italians, like all peoples with ancient habits and traditions, cling to many prejudices and superstitions, which often hamper those who work with them." Brindisi believed that education and "the missionary work of the physicians" would bring hygiene and modern views of disease and therapy into Italian homes in the United States (Brindisi 1904, p. 486).

What Drs. Stella and Brindisi, among many others, did for southern Italian immigrants, Dr. Maurice Fishberg did for East European Jewish newcomers in the same era. Of the 23.5 million newcomers between 1880 and 1921, over 2.25 million were East European Jews. Fishberg, medical examiner for the United Hebrew Charities, shared Antonio Stella's interest in tuberculosis. Not only was TB a killer of poor Jews as it was of poor Italians, but nativists often referred to consumption as the "Jewish disease" or the "Tailor's disease," stigmatizing Jews as disproportionately prone to contract the disease and perhaps spread it among their non-Jewish American hosts.

Fishberg marshalled statistical data demonstrating that Jews were less prone, not more prone, to contracting TB than members of New York's other poor immigrant populations. Fishberg believed that East European Jews' willingness to consult with physicians coupled with their habits of nutrition and hygiene grounded in religious beliefs, including *kashruth*, accounted for low rates of Jewish mortality and resistance to particular diseases, rather than innate racial characteristics. Fishberg also addressed Jewish immigrants, urging them to practice habits of health and hygiene that would sustain them in the United States (Fishberg 1902, pp. 75–6).

As cultural mediators, Drs. Antonio Stella and Maurice Fishberg sought to explain their respective groups' experiences to Americans. However, they also sought to advise members of their groups in habits of health and hygiene that would make them healthy productive members of American society, even if the price was abandonment of traditional beliefs about the origins of disease and definitions of therapy. Studies of individual physicians in various immigrant communities must further explore their roles as cultural mediators.

Health-care facilities as well as physicians could be important in the cultural mediation between natives and newcomers. Fearing the charge that Jewish immigrants who contracted TB represented a burden to the broader American community, Jewish philanthropists and community members founded their own health-care facilities in the late nineteenth and early twentieth centuries. The National Jewish Hospital in Denver, the Jewish Consumptive Relief Society in the same city, the Montefiore Home and Hospital in New York, and many others were TB sanatoria, founded to care for Jewish consumptives, although they were open to those of all faiths and creeds. Opened in 1884, the Montefiore Sanatorium thrived as philanthropists such as the Lewisohn family contributed to the building of a new pavilion expanding the number of beds. In Denver, the National Jewish Hospital was founded by assimilationist German Jews, many of whom practiced Reform Judaism. Under the leadership of Rabbi William Friedman, a committee of Denverites pledged $3,000 and incorporated the Jewish Hospital Association. However, some Jewish tuberculosis victims, especially among the East European Jews, were orthodox in religious outlook and insisted upon a level of ritual observance beyond that which the National Jewish Hospital provided. Humble Jewish tradesmen – tailors, cigarmakers, house painters – pooled their modest funds to begin the Jewish Consumptive Relief Society under the leadership of Dr. Charles Spivak (né Chaim Dovid Spivakovski), a physician who had begun life as a radical hunted by the Russian secret police before emigrating to the United States. The clashes between the two hospitals reflect cultural tensions between the more affluent, assimilated Germans and their poorer, more orthodox, politically radical co-religionists. The options for care and cure in particular groups were thus often shaped by conflicts that had little to do with the body and much to do with ethnic and class divisions (Kraut 1994, 159–63).

Non-Europeans also founded their own institutions to provide medical care in culturally familiar surroundings to members of their group. In 1900, the Chinese Benevolent Association, an influential fraternal society grounded in the regional origins of its immigrant members, built their own medical facility in the Chinese community of San Francisco. The Tung Wah Dispensary in San Francisco's Chinatown served the immigrant community. In 1925, the facility was incorporated into the Chinese Hospital. It sought to reconcile patient preferences and assimilationist pressures by hiring both western-trained physicians and Chinese herbalists (Kraut 1994, p. 198).

Groups as different as the southern Italians, East European Jews, and Chinese came to the United States for improved economic opportunities. At a moment when the United States was industrializing and beginning to realize its massive economic potential in both manufacturing and agriculture, the plentiful, low-cost labor offered by migrants was critical to the development of the American economy. The migrants and the country needed each other, but conditions in the American workplace often threatened the health and safety of workers – newcomers and native workers alike – and threatened to limit the productivity of the American workforce.

Even as most physicians in the United States and the other industrializing societies of western Europe were pursuing the pathogens that caused particular diseases, some were noting that how one lived determined the diseases to which one was most vulnerable. The hazards of industrial urban life and the industrial workplace menaced the lives of some immigrant workers. However, those who settled in the countryside were not necessarily healthier. Occupational disease and disability among various immigrant groups is a rich and largely unexplored terrain in immigration history.

Although the health hazards of the workplace affected all regardless of their immigration status, an increasing percentage of the American workforce were foreign-born. A 1911 United States Immigration Commission report, directed by Senator William Paul Dillingham, included a 21-industry survey which found that 57.9 percent of all employees were foreign-born (US Immigration Commission, 1911b, p. 297). If the immigrant worker was so crucial to American economic prosperity, why was the workplace increasingly a public health nightmare haunted by the ghosts of immigrant women and men whose health was shattered by disease and disability? Those who have studied America's cities between the 1880s and the 1920s have seen the visual record that Jacob Riis, Lewis Hine, and other photographers of the era left behind. The poor health of many immigrant workers is readily apparent as historians look at the pictures of overworked, emaciated Slavic or Irish miners dragging their exhausted bodies from mines, perspiring Bohemian cigarmakers in stifling tenement apartments, stoop-shouldered Russian Jews bent over their sewing machines, or sore-fingered Italians crouching over the crops they were picking in the fields of northeastern or midwestern states. Jobs and salaries higher than those that could be earned in their home countries were the prizes. However, the opportunity came at a cost. Disease and disaster were the ever-present companions on the journey to a new life.

Because immigrants often took hazardous, low-paying jobs that American workers shunned, injury and illness rates were higher among immigrant workers than among the native-born. The Pittsburgh Survey sponsored by the Russell Sage Foundation treated work accidents and found that between July 1, 1906 and June 30, 1907, 526 workers in Pittsburgh were killed performing duties related to their jobs; 293 of them were immigrants, almost 56 percent (Eastman 1969, p. 14).

Often the illnesses suffered by immigrant workers were the result of the substances with which they worked. Highly toxic substances such as lead caused great suffering. The research of reformer Dr. Alice Hamilton exposed the terrible toll that lead took on the health of workers. One report described the fate of one immigrant suffering from lead poisoning: "A Polish laborer worked only three weeks in a very dusty white-lead plant at an unusually dusty emergency job, at the end of which he was sent to the hospital with severe lead colic and palsy of both wrists" (Hamilton 1943, pp. 123–4). While some Americans reacted to this suffering with compassion, others turned it into an additional justification for nativism and blamed the victims for their ailments. One 1913 critic said of Slavic workers, "This class of eastern European peasant lacks the intelligence and initiative either to avoid the ordinary dangers of rough labor or to keep in efficient health; and their employers have to pay the bills for teaching them" (Dosch 1913, p. 699).

Different trades affected different parts of a worker's body, but all took their toll on workers' lives. Some laborers got sick and recovered, but many found their general condition compromised by industrial illness. They were less able to resist infection. Many suffered the rest of their lives with disabling handicaps. In addition to lead, phosphorous poisoning was the bane of workers in American parlor match manufacturing. The match industry was important in an era before electric lighting and before gas or electric stoves became standard appliances in American homes. Heads of parlor matches were made by dipping one end of a small wooden stick into a paste that included highly toxic white or yellow phosphorous. Workers exposed to the phosphorous in any way were at risk, especially in environments where the ventilation was inadequate. Poisoned workers suffered anemia, declined vitality, and possibly "phossy jaw." This last condition, more properly called phosphorous necrosis, was a disease caused by absorption through cavities in the teeth. Infection soon extended along the length of the jaw, teeth fell out, and the jaw decomposed. Later the infection spread throughout the body (Kraut 1994, p. 171).

Dusts of various kinds swirled in the mines, factories, and stone quarries where many immigrants worked. The danger of the "dusty trades" was not only that inhaled dust might contain poisonous particles but that even nonpoisonous dust could "impair the lungs and the delicate membranes of the air passages." Dusts of all kinds were major health hazards for industrial workers. Historians David Rosner and Gerald Markowitz have done groundbreaking research on dust diseases such as silicosis, a disease of the lung resulting from the inhalation of fine particles of silica dust. Extended exposure to silica destroys the lung's capacity to function, much as black lung in miners. Italian quarry workers in Barre, Vermont often became ill from silicosis. Often workers whose lungs had been compromised by silicosis fell vulnerable to tuberculosis (Rosner and Markowitz 1991, *passim*).

Home work was no guarantee of better health. In cramped, ill-ventilated apartments where male immigrant workers rolled cigars and female immigrant workers made ladies' hats and artificial flowers, tuberculosis spread easily (Boris and Daniels 1989, *passim*). There were also health hazards common in particular trades such as "cigarmaker's neurosis," a neuropathy from repetitive motion in rolling cigars (Dickerman 1918, pp. 62–3).

Although labor unions recruited immigrant workers and negotiated for better working conditions, not all newcomers belonged to labor unions. Unionization progressed slowly and unevenly. Many newcomers could not afford union dues, needing every cent to support their families. Others shunned union membership because they did not expect to remain in the United States long enough to reap its benefits. Unionization in the garment trades was spurred by the danger to the health and safety of male and female workers. The United Brotherhood of Cloakmakers, formed in 1900, grew slowly. By 1906 it had organized only 2,500 of the 42,500 cloakmakers. Partially favorable settlements in the shirtwaist-makers' strike of 1909 and the cloakmakers strike of 1910 with its famous Protocol of Peace were hopeful signs. However it was a single industrial disaster, the Triangle Shirtwaist fire, that alerted the world to the dangers of industrial life to the health and well-being of workers, especially those employed in the nation's garment shops.

The Triangle Shirtwaist fire swept the upper floors of a 10-story building in lower Manhattan. There 700 employees were at work over sewing machines or hoisting bolts of cloth. The doors were locked from the outside to keep the young workers from leaving the work area before the end of the workday. By the end of that day, 146 men and women had lost their lives. Almost a third died when they jumped from windows to escape the flames. Reports of the industrial tragedy spread, reaching the villages of Russia from which some of the workers and their families had come. Why so many deaths? An inadequate fire escape that consisted of a single ladder running down to a rear narrow court, and a single narrow door giving access to the ladder, contributed to the death toll. So, too, did the inadequacy of the fire equipment at the scene. Ladders reaching to only the seventh floor could not save those who had fled to the roof (Von Drehle 2003, *passim*).

Perhaps no one better described the perils of industrialization for the immigrants and their children who worked in America's factories and mines than Rose Schneiderman, the organizer for the International Ladies Garment Workers and the Women's Trade Union League, who spoke at a memorial meeting for the Triangle workers on April 2, 1911. Schneiderman told attendees,

> The old Inquisition had its rack and its thumbscrews and its instruments of torture with iron teeth. We know what these things are today; the iron teeth are our necessities, the thumbscrews are the high powered and swift machinery close to which we must work, and the rack is here in the firetrap structures that will destroy us the minute they catch fire. (Schneiderman 1911, pp. 81–7)

The subsequent lawsuit did little for the Triangle victims' families. Settlements averaged $75 per lost life. The lives of young immigrant workers were not deemed to be worth much.

Episodes such as the Triangle Shirtwaist fire have become part of the mainstream narrative of American immigration history, labor history, urban history, and history of medicine. Television documentaries, such as the episode of Ric Burns's *New York* that treated the fire, and popular volumes on the disaster, such as the one by *Washington Post* journalist David Von Drehle, have periodically reminded the general public of the occupational hazards that workers, especially the foreign-born, faced as they experienced urban industrial life. However, less attention has been paid to those immigrants whose lives were at risk in the countryside.

Rural workers and their health problems have often been obscured by the diffuse distribution and migratory patterns of the agricultural workforce, especially the foreign-born. Hard for labor organizers to reach, rural immigrant workers' illnesses often went undetected and unrelieved in the early twentieth century. An exception occurred when American growers violated the laws against peonage and foreign governments protested to Washington.

After the Civil War many foreign-born workers labored in the south replacing the recently emancipated black slaves (Brandfon 1967, pp. 144–5, 147–8). However, by 1873 the number was dwindling, as immigrants were replaced by native-born share-croppers and tenant farmers. Only a decade or two later, though, the southern textile industry required additional workers and once again the foreign-born were in demand. Now Italian *padrones*, labor brokers, coaxed new arrivals from the cities of the north to the fields and mills of the south (Kraut 1994, pp. 192–6).

The health hazards that Italian laborers faced in the south were quite different from those in the north. While few contracted tuberculosis in the south's sunny fields, malaria was a very real threat. In the low-lying swampy fields of the Mississippi Delta and in other places where cotton production was high, so was the probability of being bitten by the female *Anopheles* mosquito. Those bitten suffered paroxysms of chills, fever, sweating, anemia, and an enlarged spleen. Malaria was chronic, relapsing, and could be fatal, if left untreated.

The 1911 report of the United States Immigration Commission found 4,142 Italian families engaged in rural pursuits. Although the agricultural lifestyle seemed by and large salutary, there were many cases of malaria in delta communities. In a familiar pattern the report laid blame on the victims: "The Italians are very careless about their health; they will not boil their drinking water, nor take the necessary care of themselves during the damp weather. The women are so busy that they give the children very little attention, leaving them to their own resources" (US Immigration Commission 1911c, p. 44). What the report mentioned little was the economic deprivation that was rampant and made communities vulnerable to malaria and other diseases. The labor system in which many of these newcomers were trapped, peonage, was at the root of the problem.

It was peonage, or debt servitude, that supplanted slavery as an oppressive labor system after the Civil War in many parts of the south. As farmers fell deeper and deeper into debt to landowners, they found themselves tied to the land they farmed, forced to pay off their debts in back-breaking labor. Only a federal investigation of peonage launched during Theodore Roosevelt's administration, led by Mary Grace

Quackenbos, the first woman US attorney, fully described the health hazards faced by the Italians in the Mississippi Delta. Italian peons stricken with malaria on Mississippi plantations such as Leroy Percy's Sunnyside did not even have access to physicians who spoke Italian and could understand their medical complaints. Quackenbos argued for inexpensive visits to physicians' offices, a ready supply of quinine, the drug of choice in battling malaria, and even some support for two Catholic nuns, Sisters of Mercy, who agreed to care for the sick and teach English. The Italian consul in New Orleans agreed to supply free quinine to immigrants in need of it. While Quackenbos gained some concessions from Percy and other owners, none acknowledged any responsibility for easing the suffering of foreign-born workers, and Percy, who became a US Senator in 1911, helped quash any further peonage investigations (Daniel 1972, pp. 102, 107).

The health menaces that immigrants faced in the workplace remain a fertile field for scholarship. The health hazards faced by non-European groups in the workplace have been largely neglected. While there have been studies of groups such as the Chinese (Chan 1986, *passim*) and Mexicans (Foley 1998, *passim*) in rural America, the treatment of health conditions among rural immigrant populations awaits scholarly exploration.

Cultural negotiations between native-born and newcomers over health and well-being often occurred in institutional arenas outside of the workplace. Faith-based health-care in Catholic and Jewish hospitals or health-care provided by ethnic institutions such as the Tung Wah Dispensary brought such negotiations to the very bedside of sick immigrant patients. However, hospitals and dispensaries were not the only venues where such encounters occurred. At times, the negotiation occurred in the very homes of newcomers. Agencies providing nursing care for the poor sprang up in various parts of the United States, but especially in those cities of the northeast and midwest with high concentrations of immigrants. The women of the visiting nurse services were expected to bring medical care into the homes of the ill, but beyond that they educated the poor and foreign-born in good health habits and proper hygiene even as they themselves served as models of moral rectitude (Kraut 1994, pp. 211–17).

The needs of the urban poor for health-care were greater than most cities could handle even with the assistance of denominational hospital funding. And while hospital costs were on the rise, visiting nurses provided health-care at bargain prices. Often a settlement house or insurance company, such as the Metropolitan Life Company in New York, subsidized a visiting nurse service. Visiting nurses, many of whom were highly idealistic and motivated by a strong sense of social duty, worked 8 to 10 hours a day, six days or more a week. Visiting 8 to 12 patients per day, they confronted a wide variety of illnesses, often infectious and highly contagious diseases, almost always compounded by poverty and the newcomers' lack of facility with the language and culture of their new home.

Although visiting nurses often had to rely upon a neighbor or child in the household as interpreter, they were quite popular among immigrant patients. A visiting nurse often received a plant or some knitted lace or an invitation to a christening party as a show of appreciation. However, at times the nurses' desire to hasten immigrants' assimilation caused them to be judgmental and condescending. Nurses and their supervisors worked long days to save lives and battle disease among immigrants.

Still, it was not uncommon to hold in contempt the very individuals they labored to make healthy. For example, visiting nurses often tried to teach immigrant mothers the value of cleanliness in the home, hygiene, and techniques of childcare and preferred means of assisting in childbirth. Some of the nurses seemed insensitive to the reality that the women they sought to instruct were in taking excellent care of their families, as their economic circumstances allowed, and understood the fundamentals of childbirth, having learned through experience.

In addition to the cultural dialogue over health and well-being between visiting nurses and their patients, such negotiation also took place in settlement houses and public schools. Jane Addams's Hull House, which addressed the problems of the surrounding Italian immigrant community, and Lillian Wald's Henry Street Settlement in the heart of New York's Jewish Lower East Side were institutions created to offer newcomers health education and assistance in maintaining health in the American environment. In addition to the visiting nurse service that Wald began at the Henry Street Settlement, eventually taken over by the Metropolitan Life Insurance Company, the settlement house itself became a locus for the distribution of classes and health information. At the Henry Street Settlement, founders Lillian Wald and Mary Brewster were joined by other dedicated nurses and social workers. They held cooking classes, baby-care classes, English language classes, and many others. Always, Wald said, she was aware that her nurses and other settlement workers had class prejudices and cultural biases to overcome. Wald hoped they would endeavor to be sensitive to those they served and perhaps reverse the patterns of authority (Wald 1915, *passim*).

Wald worked with local physicians to assist immigrant families. The ethnic lodges and fraternal organizations to which many immigrants belonged often offered the services of a physician. Immigrants were frequently critical of these physicians who ensured themselves a trade by contracting with one or more of the many mutual benefit societies serving immigrant communities. Though many of the physicians employed by East European Jewish lodges, or *landsmannschftn*, were attentive and sympathetic to their patients, others grew so tired of climbing tenement stairs that they would call up to a sick patient, make the diagnosis, and suggest a prescription from the bottom of the stairs. Their patient fees, often tossed to them from an upper-story window, were low because they were receiving most of their compensation from the lodge. Ironically, newcomers often had greater access to low-cost health-care than the native-born. While immigrants sometimes referred to such physicians in a derisive tone, they called upon them in moments of crisis. Unlike some of the settlement house workers, the lodge doctors spoke their language and understood, even if they did not share, their patients' perspectives on health and disease (Kraut 1994, pp. 151–2).

Settlement houses were supported with the charitable dollars of philanthropists, often individuals from the ethnic groups they were seeking to help. In an era before significant government involvement in the health of individual citizens, there were no government budgets at state or federal levels to care for any Americans, and certainly no public funding to assist immigrants in matters of health, hygiene, or anything else. However, in the early twentieth century the public school played a larger role in encouraging health and hygiene than is true in the early twenty-first century.

Young immigrants and the American-born children of newcomers were part of the educational system's captive audience. According to the 1911 United States Immigration Commission's report on 37 cities across the country, almost 58 percent of all public school pupils in a sample of 1,048,490 had foreign-born fathers. The proportion was even greater in cities such as New York (71.5 percent), Boston (63.5 percent), Chicago, and Cleveland (59.6 percent). These were the young who would become either tomorrow's robust Americans or part of the enfeebled and eventually disaffected mass (US Immigration Commission 1911a, p. 17). In a 1909 "Report on National Vitality, Its Wastes and Conservation," Yale's Professor Irving Fisher observed that the schools were essential to "conserving national efficiency" which "increases economic productivity." Others thought the public school important because, "It is the melting pot which converts the children of immigrants of all races and languages into sturdy, independent American citizens" (Fisher 1909, p. 1).

The role of the public school in the health of students was contested turf. Embattled urban school administrators, teachers, and school health-care personnel felt more reviled than revered by immigrant parents. A minefield of misunderstandings often seemed to separate them from the immigrant families whose children they sought to help become healthy, productive citizens. One reason for the misunderstandings was the responsibilities which school officials of necessity undertook in providing assistance.

At times, schools were turned into medical facilities to aid children. Parents, though informed by the schools prior to any treatment, often misunderstood what was being done to their youngsters. A riot ensued on New York's Lower East Side in June 1906 when physicians, conducting minor surgery in a school building, removed the swollen adenoids of students suffering from blockage in the nose above the throat which caused the youngsters to breathe through their mouths, a practice that physicians of the day believed could lead to insufficient oxygen reaching the brain. Although the parents had signed forms giving their consent to the surgery, many did not realize what they were approving, and the rumors of blood being shed on the day of the surgery led some parents to believe that their children were being harmed rather than undergoing a routine surgical procedure (Kraut 1994, pp. 228–32).

Public schools were also venues for vaccination against smallpox, diphtheria, and later other diseases. Because millions of immigrant children were arriving from a diversity of cultures and health environments, the annual inspection of students and health education were expanded. While school buildings were becoming important in the sanitary codes passed by legislatures, Americans were increasingly following the example of Europeans in believing that the health of the school child was a community responsibility. In addition to being examined to detect contagious disease, children in some cities were required to read the eye chart during the fall semester. Those who strained and squinted received a note to their parent or guardian briefly citing the defect. Arranging for further examinations and the purchase of glasses was left to the guardian, although many schools took up collections so that the poorest children could be provided for. At times, there were tensions between local physicians and the schools. The former feared that their patient pool was being diminished by the performance of medical examinations and treatment by school physicians and nurses. However, there is little doubt that the schools were performing important functions. School records of children being excluded from classes on health grounds suggest the dimension of the problem, especially in poor urban areas where so many immigrant children lived. It was not unusual for children to suffer with lice, trachoma, scabies, and ringworm all at the same time. (Baker 1939, p. 236). Inspections identified cases of even more serious conditions, including measles, diphtheria, scarlet fever, whooping cough, and mumps.

In addition to school examinations by volunteer physicians, school nurses were being hired in some cities in response to the need. Some saw the school nurses as agents of assimilation as well as care providers. One advocate of school nurses wrote, "Among foreign populations she [the school nurse] is a very potent force for Americanization" (Gulick and Ayres 1910, p. 80). School officials and nurses often found the cultural divide between themselves and the children they treated to be wide. Dr. Jacob Sobel, borough chief of the New York Health Department's Bureau of Child Hygiene described the complexities. He said the best efforts of health professionals in the schools were often met with a "fusillade of prejudice, tradition, and superstition, ignorance, distrust, apprehension, indifference, irresponsibility, poverty and antagonism" (Sobel 1913, pp. 78–88). Still, the medical examinations by physicians and the watchfulness of teachers and school nurses resulted in healthier children, ready to learn and to take advantage of the opportunities that life in the United States could offer.

Scholars still have much to do if they are to fully explore the role that schools played in the health and well-being of immigrant children in the early twentieth century. Today's scholars and physicians concerned with the health of children in recently arrived immigrant groups have begun to re-examine with great interest the potential of public schools to improve the health and well-being of contemporary immigrant children and their families. Increasingly during the late twentieth century school systems took less and less responsibility for seeing that children got the health-care they required. In 1998 the National Research Council issued a report, *From Generation to Generation: The Health and Well-Being of Children in Immigrant Families*, the product of a two-year study. Physicians, psychologists, sociologists, anthropologists, and a historian (the author) examined the health and well-being of children among today's migrants to the United States and made recommendations for improvement. One recommendation was revisiting the public school classroom as a venue for bringing health-care and health education to immigrant children (Hernandez and Charney 1998, pp. 122–3).

The United States is again experiencing a peak period of immigration. Today, immigrants and their children number over 60 million individuals, or one-fifth of the entire population. Migrants from Ireland, Germany, Tsarist Russia, and Italy have been replaced at the country's ports of entry by Mexicans, Filipinos, Vietnamese, Indians, and Pakistanis. If current birth rates persist, by the year 2050, one-third of all Americans will be either Asian or Latino. And, as in the past, matters of health and disease are crucial and intimately linked to matters of cultural integration. In cities with large populations of Southeast Asian migrants, shamans and their amulets are often preferred to physicians with their syringes and sophisticated technology. In immigrant communities such as the Hmong community of St. Paul, Minnesota, physicians have learned that the most expeditious way of getting a patient's permission for invasive procedures such as blood tests is to establish collaborative relationships with shamans. Both stand at the patient's bedside and support each other's efforts

(Deinard and Dunigan 1987, p. 862). This collaborative cultural approach is a far cry from the competition of physicians with traditional healers that occurred in earlier generations.

When cultural misunderstandings do occur in matters of health, the results can be disastrous. In May 2002, Omaha Nebraska police suspected that several Hmong families were engaged in child abuse. The evidence was coin-shaped scars that appeared on the youngsters' bodies. Police investigators did not recognize the scars as evidence of coining therapy or *cao gio* (Olson 2002). The therapy involves rubbing warm oils or gels across a person's skin with a coin, spoon, or other flat object. It leaves bright red marks or bruises, but many Asian families believe the marks signify that bad blood is exiting the body, allowing better circulation and healing. Arrests for coining no longer happen in St. Paul because the Hmong Cultural Center there has educated the community about the practice (Goode 1993, pp. 74–6). Elsewhere the cultural negotiation has also proceeded smoothly because of a willingness of American medical personnel to engage in cultural sensitivity. In Nashville, the Vanderbilt University Medical Center includes an image on its website of the long red bruises created by coining so that physicians can distinguish the practice from child abuse.

Mental disorders among migrants continue to be as difficult to diagnose and treat today, as they were in the early twentieth century. As in the past, difficulty in adjusting to a new environment remains a central cause of emotional distress. Early in the twentieth century, Dr. Maurice Fishberg encountered a newcomer who was requesting funds to return home from the United Hebrew Charities. The reason he gave was that the air in the United States was "too strong" for him (Fishberg 1903, p. 5). Khmer refugees from war-torn Cambodia in the 1990s spoke of being *bebotchit*. In a culture that has no western concept of depression, *bebotchit* is defined in Khmer as "a deep sadness inside oneself" caused by a specific set of circumstances (Mollica, Donelan, Tor, Lavelle, Elias, Frankel, Bennett, and Blendon 1990, p. 46).

Today's physicians often understand that effective therapy relies on a nuanced cultural negotiation because some mental illnesses are culture-bound. Examples of such illnesses include: *pa feng*, a phobic fear of wind and cold among Chinese; *hwa byung*, a suppressed anger syndrome suffered by Koreans; and *latah*, a Malaysian and Indonesian psychosis that leads to uncontrolled mimicking of other people (Kershaw 2003). Although precise cultural equivalents are difficult to establish with certainty, some symptoms appear to be related to what western psychiatry calls post-traumatic stress disorder (PTSD). Some experts speak of PTSD as a "form of cultural bereavement related to the loss of homeland, culture, tradition, and national identity" (Mollica, Donelan, Tor, Lavelle, Elias, Frankel, Bennett, and Blendon 1990, p. 50). Sometimes victims of trauma related to the migration experience engage in dissociation. They distance themselves from trauma by depersonalizing and detaching from the world. Dissociation can lead to psychosomatic illness. Some Khmer arrivals who survived Cambodia's killing fields suffered psychosomatic blindness after seeing loved ones killed (Cooke 1991, pp. 24–5, 45–8). Only culturally sensitive therapy offers hope to such victims.

The experience of today's migrants with illness and injury in the workplace also echoes experiences of an earlier era. Today's Latino workers tend to accept dangerous, low-paying jobs unacceptable to other Americans, much as Poles and Italians and Jews did in the early twentieth century. In February 1992 the *New York Times* reported that studies conducted in Illinois, California, and New Jersey showed that Latino workers – regardless of whether they were legal or undocumented – had injury rates two or three times higher than non-Latino Caucasian Americans who held the same jobs. African American workers suffer higher rates than Caucasians, too, but lower rates than Latino workers.

As in earlier eras, one reason for the higher injury rates is language. Latino workers suffer greatly. Job training is often not in Spanish. Workers operating dangerous machines or handling toxic substances are at greater risk if they cannot understand or read instructions. A second issue is that Latino workers often do not understand their rights in the workplace, and undocumented workers are reluctant to complain, fearing deportation. Finally, data is uneven because no organization collects information on the ethnic origins of workers who get sick or sustain injury. Rarely is there a collective response in the name of workers of particular groups, although some groups are affected disproportionately by harmful conditions. Likewise, there are many health risks endemic to farm work, such as skin cancers from overexposure to the sun and the effects of chemical pesticides, leukemia, lymph node cancer, and multiple myeloma (Wilk 1990, pp. 3–4). Fearing job loss, migrant workers, especially undocumented workers, generally avoid taking time off work to seek medical attention. Language and cultural barriers, as well as the mobility of the migrant labor force, render health education and care problematical and incline Latino migrant workers to obtain the ministrations of *curanderos* (healers) and *bujas* (witches) (Meister 1991, pp. 503–18).

In the early twenty-first century, issues of migration, health, and disease are intertwined. In a nation of immigrants all aspects of the culture, including the culture of medicine and public health, are affected by the arrival of newcomers, their needs and their perspectives. In a global age of rapid transportation and instant communication, it is imperative that historians alert those responsible for the preservation of the public's health, to the role of migration and ethnicity in shaping perceptions of disease and definitions of therapy (Markel 2004, *passim*). In 2003 SARS was identified in China and within days of that identification it was threatening lives in Virginia, New Jersey, and Toronto (Brookes 2005, pp. 185–92). Some Americans reacted constructively and compassionately. Others stigmatized those of Asian background, just as the Irish, the Italians, and the East European Jews had been stigmatized in an earlier era. Social humiliation and economic loss were the consequences. It was a startling reminder of the need to learn from the past so that earlier cultural insensitivity to the foreign-born is not repeated in an age when illness more than ever before is a transnational experience.

REFERENCES

Baker, S. Josephine (1939). *Fighting for Life*. New York: Macmillan.

Boris, Eileen and Cynthia R. Daniels, eds. (1989). *Homework: Historical and Contemporary Perspectives on Paid Labor at Home*. Urbana: University of Illinois Press.

Brandfon, Robert L. (1967). *Cotton Kingdom of the New South, a History of the Yazoo Mississippi Delta from Reconstruction to the Twentieth Century*. Cambridge, MA: Harvard University Press.

Bradford, William (1981). *Of Plymouth Plantation, 1620–1647* [1856]. New York: Random House.

Brindisi, Rocco (1904). "The Italian and Public Health." *Charities* 12: 483–6.

Brookes, Tim (2005). *Behind the Mask, How the World Survived SARS, the First Epidemic of the Twenty-first Century*. Washington, DC: American Public Health Association.

Chan, Sucheng (1986). *This Bitter-Sweet Soil: The Chinese in California Agriculture, 1860–1910*. Berkeley: University of California Press.

Cooke, Patrick (1991). "They Cried Until They Could Not See." *The New York Times Magazine*, June 23.

Crosby, Alfred (1976). "Virgin Soil Epidemics as a Factor in the Aboriginal Depopulation in America." *William and Mary Quarterly*, 3rd series, 33: 289–99.

Daniel, Pete (1972). *The Shadow of Slavery: Peonage in the South, 1901–1969*. New York: Oxford University Press.

Deinard, Amos S. and Timothy Dunigan (1987). "Hmong Healthcare – Reflections on a Six-Year Experience." *International Migration Review* 21: 857–65.

Dickerman, Charles (1918). "Cigar Makers' Neurosis." *National Eclectic Medical Association Quarterly* 10: 62–3.

Dosch, Arno (1913). "Our Expensive Cheap Labor." *The World's Work* 26: 699–703.

Eastman, Crystal (1969). *Work Accidents and the Law*. Vol. 2 of Paul Underwood Kellogg, ed., *The Pittsburgh Survey, Findings in Six Volumes* [1910]. New York: Arno.

Ernst, Robert (1965). *Immigrant Life in New York City, 1825–1863* [1949]. New York: Ira J. Friedman.

Fairchild, Amy L. (2003). *Science at the Borders: Immigrant Medical Inspection and the Shaping of the Modern Industrial Labor Force*. Baltimore: Johns Hopkins University Press.

Fishberg, Maurice (1902). "Health and Sanitation of the Immigrant Jewish Population." *The Menorah* 33: 37–179.

—— (1903). "Health Problems of the Jewish Poor." A paper read before the Jewish Chatauqua Assembly on Monday, July 27, 1903, at Atlantic City, New Jersey; later a pamphlet reprinted from *The American Hebrew*. New York: Press of Philip Cowan.

Fisher, Irving (1909). "Report on National Vitality, Its Wastes and Conservation." Bulletin 30 of the Committee of One Hundred on National Health. Washington, DC: Government Printing Office.

Foley, Neil (1998). *The White Scourge: Mexicans, Blacks and Poor Whites in Texas Cotton Culture*. Berkeley: University of California Press.

Goode, Erica (1993). "The Culture of Illness." *US News and World Report* 15: 74–6.

Grob, Gerald (1973). *Mental Institutions in America, Social Policy to 1875*. New York: Free Press.

Gulick, Luther Halsy and Leonard P. Ayres (1910). *Medical Inspection of Schools*. New York: Charities Publication Committee.

Hamilton, Alice (1934). *Industrial Toxicology*. New York: Harpers Brothers.

—— (1943). *Exploring the Dangerous Trades: The Autobiography of Alice Hamilton, M.D.* Boston: Little, Brown.

Harper's Monthly (1851). "A Scene from Irish Life". 3: 833.

Hernandez, Donald J. and Evan Charney, eds. (1998). *From Generation to Generation: The Health and Well-Being of Children in Immigrant Families*. A published report by the Committee on the Health and Adjustment of Immigrant Children and Families, a committee convened by the Board on Children, Youth, and Families and the Institute of Medicine of the National Research Council. Washington, DC: National Research Council.

Hutchinson, E.P. (1981). *Legislative History of American Immigration Policy, 1798–1965*. Philadelphia: University of Pennsylvania Press.

Kershaw, Sarah (2003). "Freud Meets Buddha: Therapy for Immigrants." *New York Times*, January 18.

Kraut, Alan M. (1994). *Silent Travelers: Germs, Genes, and the "Immigrant Menace."* New York: Basic Books.

—— (2001). *The Huddled Masses: The Immigrant in American Society, 1880–1921.* Wheeling, IL: Harlan Davidson.

Markel, Howard (1997). *Quarantine! East European Jewish Immigrants and the New York City Epidemics of 1892.* Baltimore: Johns Hopkins University Press.

—— (2004). *When Germs Travel: Six Major Epidemics That Have Invaded America Since 1900 and the Fears They Have Unleashed.* New York: Pantheon Books.

Martin, Calvin (1978). *Keepers of the Game: Indian–Animal Relationships and the Fur Trade.* Berkeley: University of California Press.

Mather, Cotton (1855). *Magnalia Christi Americana,* Vol. 1. Hartford: Andrus and Son.

Mayo-Smith, Richmond (1890). *Emigration and Immigration: A Study in Social Science.* New York: Scribner's.

Meister, Joel (1991). "The Health of Migrant Farm Workers." *Occupational Medicine* 6: 503–18.

Mollica, Richard F., Karen Donelan, Svong Tor, James Lavelle, Christopher Elias, Martin Frankel, Douglas Bennett, and Robert J. Blendon (1990). "Repatriation and Disability: A Community Study of Health, Mental Health and Social Functioning of the Khmer Residents of Site Two." Working Document, Harvard Program in Refugee Trauma, vol. 1, "Khmer Adults." Cambridge, MA: Harvard School of Public Health and the World Federation for Mental Health.

Morman, Edward T. (1984). "Guarding Against Alien Impurities: The Philadelphia Lazaretto, 1854–1893." *Philadelphia Magazine of History* 107: 131–52.

Olson, Jeremy (2002). "Asian Remedy Raises Few Alarms Elsewhere. People in Cities with Closer Ties to Hmong Culture Say the Issue No Longer is a Concern." *Omaha World Herald,* May 3. http://hmongunivers.angelcities.com/news20020503b.html

Orsi, Robert Anthony (1985). *The Madonna of 115th Street: Faith and Community in Italian Harlem, 1880–1950.* New Haven: Yale University Press.

Powell, J.H. (1949). *Bring Out Your Dead: The Great Plague of Yellow Fever in Philadelphia in 1793.* Philadelphia: University of Pennsylvania Press.

Proper, Edward Emberson, ed. (1967). *Colonial Immigration Laws: A Study of the Regulations of Immigration by the English Colonies in America.* New York: AMS Press.

Rosen, George (1958). *A History of Public Health.* New York: MD Publications.

Rosenberg, Charles E. (1987). *The Cholera Years: The United States in 1832, 1849, and 1866* [1962]. Chicago: University of Chicago Press.

Rosner, David and Gerald Markowitz (1991). *Deadly Dust, Silicosis and the Politics of Occupational Disease in Twentieth Century America.* Princeton: Princeton University Press.

Schneiderman, Rose (1911). Speech at memorial meeting for Triangle Shirtwaist victims, April 2, 1911, *The Survey* 26 (April 8): 81–7.

Sobel, Jacob (1913). "Prejudices and Superstitions Met With in Medical Inspection of School Children." In Thomas A. Storey, ed., *Transactions of the Fourth International Congress on School Hygiene, Buffalo, New York, USA, August 25–30, 1913.* Buffalo, NY: Courier Company of Buffalo.

Solis-Cohen, Rosebud T. (1947). "The Exclusion of Aliens from the United States for Physical Defects." *Bulletin of the History of Medicine* 21: 33–50.

Stella, Antonio (1904). "Tuberculosis and the Italians in the United States." *Charities* 12: 486–9.

—— (1975). *Some Aspects of Italian Migration to the United States: Statistical Data and General Consideration Based Chiefly Upon the United States Census and Other Official Publications* [1924]. New York: Arno Press.

United States Immigration Commission (1911a). *Abstracts of Reports of the Immigration Commission*, 61st Cong., 3rd sess., 1910, S. Doc. 747. Washington, DC: Government Printing Office.

United States Immigration Commission (1911b). *Immigrants in Industries.* Washington, DC: Government Printing Office.

United States Immigration Commission (1911c). "Recent Immigrants in Agriculture." In *Immigrants in Industries.* Washington, DC: Government Printing Office.

Vecoli, Rudolph J. (1977). "Cult and Occult in Italian-American Culture." In Randall M. Miller and Thomas D. Marzik, eds., *Immigrants and Religion in Urban America.* Philadelphia: Temple University Press.

Von Drehle, David (2003). *Triangle: The Fire That Changed America.* New York: Atlantic Monthly.

Wald, Lillian (1915). *The House on Henry Street.* New York: Henry Holt and Company.

Wiebe, Robert (1967). *The Search For Order, 1877–1920.* New York: Hill and Wang.

Wilk, Valerie A. (1990). "Farmworkers and the Health Risks of Pesticides." *Farmworker Justice* 4: 3–4.

Williams, Phyllis H. (1938). *South Italian Folkways in Europe and America: A Handbook for Social Workers, Visiting Nurses, School Teachers and Physicians.* New Haven: Yale University Press.

Williams, Samuel Cole, ed. (1966). *[James] Adair's History of the American Indians (1775).* New York: Argonaut Press.

FURTHER READING

Fairchild, Amy L. (2003). *Science at the Borders: Immigrant Medical Inspection and the Shaping of the Modern Industrial Labor Force.* Baltimore: Johns Hopkins University Press.

Kraut, Alan M. (1994). *Silent Travelers: Germs, Genes, and the "Immigrant Menace."* New York: Basic Books.

—— (2001). *The Huddled Masses: The Immigrant in American Society, 1880–1921.* Wheeling, IL: Harlan Davidson.

Markel, Howard (1997). *Quarantine! East European Jewish Immigrants and the New York City Epidemics of 1892.* Baltimore: Johns Hopkins University Press.

—— (2004). *When Germs Travel, Six Major Epidemics That Have Invaded America Since 1900 and the Fears They Have Unleashed.* New York: Pantheon Books.

Rosen, George (1958). *A History of Public Health.* New York: MD Publications.

Rosenberg, Charles E. (1987). *The Cholera Years: The United States in 1832, 1849, and 1866* [1962]. Chicago: University of Chicago Press.

CHAPTER SIX

The Politics of Immigration and the Rise of the Migration State: Comparative and Historical Perspectives

JAMES F. HOLLIFIELD

Introduction

The movement of individuals across national boundaries challenges many of the basic assumptions that social scientists make about human behavior – for example, that individuals tend to be risk averse, that they are always in need of community, or as Aristotle put it, "man is a social animal." If individuals move over long distances, leaving their families and communities behind and crossing national, ethnic, or cultural boundaries, then there must be some extraordinary forces compelling them to do this. Hence, in the study of immigration we should begin by pointing out that the vast majority of the world's population is in fact sedentary. At the turn of the twenty-first century only 175 million people live outside of their country of origin. So emigration is the exception rather than the rule. Why then should we bother to study it, if most people are born, live and die in the same geographic area, if not in the same village?

The answer to the "so what" question is not straightforward. It is clear, however, that immigration provokes a sense of political crisis (Schlesinger 1992; Weiner 1995; Huntington 2004). Immigration has been steadily increasing in the industrial democracies of Europe, North America, Asia, and Australia as a result of social and economic forces that seem to be beyond the control of states and communities (Sassen 1996; Massey 1998). An anthropologist or sociologist might argue that this sense of crisis stems from a fear of the other, of the unknown, and of those who are different (Lévi-Strauss 1952; Barth 1969; Schnapper 1998). In this sense, xenophobia could be considered a basic human instinct. An economist or a demographer might argue that immigration places a strain on resources. It can cause a hemorrhage of scarce human capital – a brain drain – from the sending society, if the brightest and most talented people leave their home countries (Bhagwati 1976). If, however, those leaving are the most destitute, least educated and with low levels of human and social capital, then they may pose a threat for the receiving society. Many economists and demographers have argued in Malthusian terms, that even the wealthiest societies have a limited amount of space (land) and capital, which should be preserved for the national or indigenous population. Overpopulation and overcrowding can strain urban infrastructures and cause environmental damage, while saturated urban labor markets can drive down wages, hurting those who are at the bottom of the social ladder (Bouvier 1992).

In those receiving societies with highly developed welfare states, there is a fear that immigrants will become public charges, placing an unfair burden on the public purse (Borjas 1990). Then there is the fear of loss of national identity and purpose, voiced most strongly by Samuel Huntington in a book provocatively entitled, *Who Are We?* (2004). Of course, the same arguments can be made in reverse: migration poses no threat to either the sending or receiving society and it is in fact a boon, providing remittances for the sending society and an influx of human capital and entrepreneurial talent for the receiving society (Russell 1986; Simon 1989; Chiswick 1982). In either case, the focus is on the abundance or scarcity of resources, the social or human capital of migrants and how well they can integrate into the receiving society. The overriding concern is for "the national interest" and how states can design a grand strategy that allows them to reap the maximum economic benefits from immigration (or emigration), without upsetting the political or social order (Rudolph 2003).

The Political Aspect of Immigration

At its most basic level politics involves "control, influence, power, or authority." If we add to this definition Weber's concerns about legitimacy and the importance of controlling territory, together with Aristotle's more normative focus on issues of participation, citizenship, and justice, we have a fairly complete picture of what Robert Dahl (1991) calls the political aspect. We can see immediately how migration touches on each of these dimensions of politics: the procedural or distributional dimension – who gets what, when and how; the legal or statist dimension, involving issues of sovereignty and legitimacy; and the ethical or normative dimension, which revolves around questions of citizenship, justice, and participation. Choosing policies to control migration leads us to ask who is making those decisions and in whose interest? Are policies being made in the interest of migrants, workers, employers, or some other group? Are these policies contributing to the national interest of the state and are they just? Does migration weaken or strengthen the institutions of sovereignty and citizenship? At what point should migrants become full members of society, with all the rights, duties, and responsibilities of a citizen? Should they be allowed to retain the nationality of their country of origin, or have multiple nationalities and citizenships?

As in other social sciences, but especially economics, the key concept here is one of interest – of the individual, the community, and the state. But, unlike economics, where the emphasis is on scarcity and efficiency, in the study of politics the primary emphasis is on power, influence, and authority, with very strong ethical and normative overtones, concerning justice, membership, and citizenship (Walzer 1983; Carens 1989; Schuck 1998). In a free market, the allocation of scarce goods and resources takes place according to the logic of the marketplace – the interaction of supply and demand. The exercise of power, however, takes place in the ideational, legal, and institutional confines of states. These range from the most autocratic (e.g. North Korea) – where decisions are made by a single individual, surrounded by a small clique of military or party officials – to the most democratic (e.g. Switzerland) – where decisions are made by "the people" according to elaborate constitutional arrangements and with safeguards often built into the system to protect individuals and minorities from the "tyranny of the majority." Obviously migration is less of a problem in North Korea than in Switzerland. Almost by definition, the more liberal and democratic a state is, the greater the likelihood that immigration control will be an issue; and that there will be some level of "unwanted migration" (Hollifield 1992a; Martin 1994; Joppke 1998b).

Not surprisingly, therefore, almost all the literature on the politics of control is focused on the receiving countries, many but not all of which are liberal democracies. Very little has been written about the politics of control from the standpoint of the sending countries. As the world has become more open and democratic, since the end of World War II and especially since the end of the Cold War (Hollifield and Jillson 1999), from a political standpoint, entry rather than exit is more problematic. Aristide Zolberg (1981) pointed out the hypocrisy of liberal democracies, which, throughout the period of the Cold War, worked to create a right to exit, but without a concomitant right to entry. With the steady increase in immigration in the advanced industrial democracies in the postwar period (OECD 2001; IOM 2000; Castles and Miller 1998), many states began to search for ways to stop or slow the influx, and immigration has been injected into the politics of these countries. In states like the United States, Canada, or Australia, which I shall call "nations of immigrants," immigration has long been a national political issue; whereas for many of the states of western Europe, which I call "countries of immigration," immigration and the ethnic diversity that it entails are relatively new phenomena that have taken many politicians and the public by surprise. How have these different states managed immigration? What difference does it make to be a *nation* as opposed to a *country* of immigration? Has there been a convergence of policy responses to the rise in immigration, or is each state pursuing different control policies? These are some of the questions addressed in this chapter.

As we survey the politics of immigration, a central puzzle emerges. Since the 1970s, almost all of the receiving states have been trying to reassert control over migration flows, often using similar policies and in response to public opinion, which has been increasingly hostile to high levels of immigration. Yet immigration has persisted and there is a growing gap between the goals of immigration policies – defined as outputs – and the results or outcomes of these policies (Hollifield 1986, 1990, 1992a). This argument has since come to be known as the *gap hypothesis* (Cornelius, Martin, and Hollifield; Cornelius, Tsuda, Martin, and Hollifield 1994, 2004). Moreover, if control of borders is the *sine qua non* of sovereignty and if states are unable to control immigration, does it not follow that the institutions of sovereignty and citizenship are threatened (Soysal 1994; Sassen 1996; Schuck 1998; Castles and Davidson 1998; Shanks 2000; Hollifield 2005).

With this puzzle and the gap hypothesis in mind and armed with a panoply of theories, political scientists set off in search of answers. Some, like Aristide Zolberg, Anthony Messina, and to a lesser extent Gary Freeman, questioned the empirical premise of the argument. Zolberg (1999) argues that liberal states never lost control of immigration and that the migration crisis itself is much exaggerated. Messina (1996) and Freeman (1994) pointed to Great Britain as a major outlier – a liberal democracy that has been very efficient at controlling its borders. Yet Freeman (1998b, p. 2) concedes that

> the goal of a theory of immigration politics must be to account for the similarities and differences in the politics of immigration receiving states and to explain the persistent gaps between the goals and effects of policies as well as the related but not identical gap between public sentiment and the content of public policy.

The challenge, therefore, for political scientists is to develop some generalizable or unifying hypotheses to account for variation in (1) the demand for and the supply of immigration policy – whether greater restriction or more liberal admission policies – and (2) the outcomes or results of those policies, as measured in terms of increasing or decreasing flows and stocks. Looking at immigration from the standpoint of the politics of control, these are, in effect, two separate dependent variables; and they in no way address the problems of integration or incorporation, which Thomas Hammar (1985) analyzes under the rubric of immigrant, as opposed to immigration, policy, and which Patrick Ireland (1994) refers to as the "challenge of ethnic diversity."

As in any social science discipline, the choice of dependent and independent variables is driven largely by theoretical considerations and the hypotheses which flow from them. This brings us back to our definition of politics (above) and raises the broader question of how political explanations for immigration are related to economic or sociological explanations. If politics is defined primarily in terms of process and the struggle for "influence, power, and authority," it is a relatively straightforward exercise to develop a theoretical framework for explaining the demand for and supply of immigration policy, as well as the gap between policy outputs and outcomes. This is the approach taken by Gary Freeman, who, following the work of James Q. Wilson on *The Politics of Regulation* (1980), argues that the demand for immigration policy – like any public policy in a democracy – is heavily dependent on the play of organized interests. To understand the politics of immigration control, we must be able to define the distribution of costs and benefits, which will then enable us to separate winners from losers in the policy-making process. Depending on the scarcity or abundance of productive factors (land, labor, and capital), as well as the substitutability of immigrant for native labor, the costs and benefits of immigration will be either concentrated or diffuse. From this simple factor-cost logic, we can deduce what position powerful interest groups, like organized labor and agricultural or business lobbies, are likely to take in debates over immigration policy. Again following Wilson, Freeman (1995, 1998b) associates different cost-benefit distributions with specific "modes of politics" – interest group, clientelist, entrepreneurial, or majoritarian.

Using this essentially microeconomic framework, Freeman predicts that when – as is often the case with immigration policy – benefits are concentrated and costs are diffuse, a clientelist politics will develop. The state will then be captured by powerful organized interests, who stand to benefit handsomely from expansive immigration policies – like fruit and vegetable growers in the southern and southwestern United States, the software and computer industry in the northwest, or perhaps the construction or health-care industries in Germany or Japan. This would seem to explain why many states persist with admissionist or guest-worker policies, even during recessionary periods when the economic conjuncture (and high levels of unemployment) would seem to dictate greater restriction. If we combine Freeman's "modes of politics" approach with the work of Alan Kessler (1998) – who argues in a similar vein that the demand for immigration policy is heavily dependent on the relative rates of return to factors and the substitutability or complementarity of immigrant and native factors – we have a fairly complete theory of the politics of immigration control, albeit one that is heavily indebted to microeconomics and may be (like the old push-pull arguments) economically overdetermined.

The reason for this is not hard to see. If we start with a definition of politics which reduces the political process to an economic calculus, we have in effect defined away some of the more interesting and difficult questions associated with immigration politics. In this formulation, the role of the state is particularly problematic, since the state is merely a reflection of societal interests. By focusing so exclusively on process, we lose sight of the importance of institutional and ideological variation within and among states. Both Freeman and Kessler concede that the supply of immigration policy does not always match demand. Policy outputs are heavily contingent on ideational, cultural, and institutional factors, which often distort the market interests of different groups, to such an extent that some groups (organized labor, for example) may end up pursuing policies that would seem to be irrational, or somehow at odds with their economic interests (Haus 1995, 1999). Likewise, many employers in western Europe were initially skeptical of the need to import guest workers (Hollifield 1992a). As Freeman (1998b: 17) puts it, the drawback of these economic models of politics "is their extreme parsimony. They leave us with generalizations about labor, landowners and capitalists; useful abstractions, surely, but probably too crude for the satisfactory analysis of immigration politics in particular countries, especially highly developed ones." So where does this leave us with respect to our ability to advance generalizable and testable hypotheses about the politics of immigration control?

Freeman offers several solutions. One obvious way to get around the limitations of factor-endowment or factor-cost models is to disaggregate or break factors down into their sectoral components, which would lead us into an industry-by-industry analysis of immigration politics. We also would want to distinguish between the political positions of skilled labor (e.g. software engineers or mathematicians) and unskilled workers (e.g. in the construction trades or service sectors). In the end, Freeman seems to retreat to a position that is a bit more *ad hoc*, from a theoretical and empirical standpoint. He argues that there is not that much uniformity in immigration policies among the western democracies. He also draws a sharp distinction between the settler societies (nations of immigrants) – such as the United States, Canada, or Australia – which continue to have more expansionist immigration policies, and the newer countries of immigration in western Europe. For example, Britain, France, Germany, Switzerland and The Netherlands are still struggling to cope with the fallout from post-colonial and guest-worker migrations (Thränhardt 1996; Freeman 1998a; Joppke 1998b).

An alternative to Freeman's interest-based approach to the politics of immigration control can be found in my own work, which one reviewer aptly described as the "liberal state" thesis (Schmitter-Heisler 1993). Rather than focusing on politics defined as process, which leads us inexorably into a factor-cost logic, where productive factors in the guise of interest groups are the units of analysis, my work takes the state as the unit of analysis (Hollifield 1992a, 1997a). The dependent variable also differs from that of Freeman and many other political scientists (e.g. Money 1999), who are more interested in explaining policy outputs – the demand for and the supply of immigration or immigrant policy – than in explaining policy outcomes – flows and stocks of immigrants across time and space, or policies for integrating the newcomers. From a political and theoretical standpoint, it is admittedly more difficult to explain outcomes than it is to explain outputs, because we are compelled to look at a broader range of independent variables. If we want to know why individuals move across national boundaries and if we want to explain variation in those movements over time, or if we want to explain political or social integration, it will not be enough just to look at policy outputs and the political process. As I pointed out above, theories of international migration have been propounded primarily by economists and sociologists. Economists have sought to explain population movements in terms of a basic push-pull and cost-benefit logic, whereas sociologists have stressed the importance of transnationalism and social networks. What is missing from these accounts is a theory of the state and the way in which it influences population movements (Massey 1999).

The types of push and pull factors identified by scholars may vary, but the logic of looking at individual migrants as preeminently rational, utility maximizing agents remains the same (e.g. Stark 1991). Some economists, like George Borjas or Julian Simon, have injected important political or policy considerations into their analysis. Borjas in particular has argued that the welfare state can act as a powerful pull factor, which may change the calculation of potential migrants. In his formulation, before the rise of the welfare state, individuals chose to emigrate on the basis of their chances of finding gainful employment. However, after the advent of generous social policies in the principal receiving countries, like the United States, even migrants with low levels of human capital were willing to risk the move, confident in the fact that they would be cared for by the host society (Borjas 1990, 1999). Gary Freeman (1986) also argues that the logic of the modern welfare state is one of closure and that large-scale immigration may ruin public finances, bankrupt social services, and undermine the legitimacy of the welfare state. But none of these works has really elevated policy outputs and the state to the status of independent variables.

Many sociologists and anthropologists have built upon the factor-cost logic of push-pull, often setting up their work in direct opposition to economists, in order to inject more sociological reasoning into theories of immigration. A pioneer in this regard is Douglas Massey, who was one of the first sociologists to point out the importance of social networks in linking sending and receiving societies (Massey 1987, 1998). In the same vein, Alejandro Portes has developed the notion of transnational communities to explain international migration. Portes and his collaborators have done extensive empirical research on the human and social capital of different immigrant groups in the United States. They seek to explain not only why individuals emigrate, but patterns of immigrant incorporation as well (Portes and Bach 1985; Portes and Rumbaut 1996). Both network and social capital theory help to explain the difficulty that states may encounter in their efforts to control immigration.

Kinship, informational networks, and transnational communities are in effect a form of social capital. As they develop, they can substantially reduce the risks that individual migrants must take in moving from one country to another, thereby stimulating immigration. States must then find a way to intervene in or break up the networks, in order to reduce an individual's propensity to migrate.

Still, by their own admission, sociologists have been unable to incorporate political variables into their analysis of international migration. In recent articles, both Massey and Portes lament the absence of a political theory of international migration. Massey (1999, p. 303) writes that "until recently, theories of international migration have paid short shrift to the nation-state as an agent influencing the volume and composition of international migration." Portes (1997, p. 817) argues along the same lines that "detailed accounts of the process leading to major legislation . . . have not been transformed into a systematic theoretical analysis of both the external pressures impinging on the state and the internal dynamics of the legislative and administrative bodies dealing with immigration."

The Rise of Rights-Based Politics

In response to this challenge, the liberal state thesis draws our attention to a third independent variable, namely *rights*, which are heavily contingent upon legal and institutional developments. Rights must be considered in any theory of international migration. Thus, in my formulation, international migration can be seen as a function of (1) economic forces (demand-pull and supply-push), (2) networks, and (3) rights (Hollifield 1992a; Hollifield 2005; Cornelius, Martin, and Hollifield 1994; Cornelius, Tsuda, Martin, and Hollifield 2004). Much of the variation in immigration over time can be explained in economic terms. In the post-World War II period, south–north labor migration started largely in response to demand-pull forces. We should not, however, underestimate the role that colonization and decolonization played in creating family and kinship networks between sending and receiving societies. The politics of post-colonial and refugee migrations are admittedly different from the politics of labor migration (see Zolberg, Suhrke, and Aguayo 1989; Joppke 1998a; Gibney 2004). The major industrial democracies suffered labor shortages, from the 1940s through the 1960s; and foreign workers were brought in to meet the increasing demand for labor. In the United States, these shortages, especially in agriculture, were met in part through the *bracero* program; whereas in western Europe, *Gastarbeiter* programs were put in place to recruit immigrant and guest workers, thus placing the imprimatur of the liberal state on certain types of (presumably temporary) emigration. But when demand for immigrant and foreign labor began to decline in the 1970s, in the wake of the first oil shock in 1973, powerful supply-push factors came into play. The population of the sending countries (for example, Algeria, Turkey, and Mexico) was increasing rapidly, at the same time that the economies of these developing states were reeling from the first truly global recession of the postwar period. Networks helped to sustain immigration, even in countries that attempted to stop all forms of immigration, including family and refugee migration. These economic and sociological factors were the *necessary* conditions for continued migration; but the *sufficient* conditions were political and legal. In the last three decades of the twentieth century, a principal factor which has sustained immigration (both south–north and to a lesser extent east–west) is the accretion of rights for foreigners in the liberal democracies, or what I have called the rise of "rights-based liberalism" (Cornelius, Martin, and Hollifield 1994, pp. 9–11).

Politics affects migration, like many other social and economic phenomena, at the margins. But this does *not* mean that politics (like culture) is simply a residual variable. In any social process, it is often what happens at the margins that is of greatest importance and also the most difficult to incorporate into our analysis. To use a familiar Weberian metaphor, if the speeding train of international migration is fueled by economic and sociological forces, it is the state which acts as a switching mechanism, which can change the course of the train, or derail it altogether. In the oft-quoted words of the Swiss novelist Max Frisch, who was speaking of the guest-worker program in Switzerland: "we asked for workers but instead human beings came. . . ."

But where do rights come from, how are they institutionalized, and how do they affect the ability of states to control immigration? Much of the remainder of this chapter will be devoted to answering these questions, through comparative and historical analysis. Unlike recent works in sociology, which see rights flowing from international organizations (like the UN or the EU) and from human rights law – a kind of post-national or transnational citizenship (Soysal 1994; Jacobson 1996; Bauböck 1994) – I argue that rights still derive primarily from the laws and institutions of the liberal state and they fall into the three categories described by the sociologist T.H. Marshall: namely civil, political, and social rights (Marshall 1964; Schmitter 1979; Castles and Davidson 1998). My interpretation of "rights-based liberalism" differs from Marshall's in the sense that I do not espouse the same linear and evolutionary sequence, which Marshall first identified in Great Britain. Rather, I argue that rights vary considerably, both cross-nationally and over time; moreover, the integration of immigrants does not follow a smooth linear process; and it too will vary from community to community, and from generation to generation. For example, Portes and Rumbaut (1996) and Alba and Nee (2003) argue that linear conceptions of assimilation have given way to multiculturalism and an increasingly uneven or segmented incorporation, whereby large segments of the second generation, particularly among the unskilled and uneducated, experienced significant downward mobility (see also Hollifield 1997b). Therefore, the empirical and theoretical challenge for migration scholars is to find a way to incorporate rights, as an institutional and legal variable, into our analyses of immigration and integration.

I have done this in three ways. First, by measuring the impact of specific policy changes (either expanding or contracting rights for immigrants and foreigners) on immigration flows, while controlling for changes in the business cycle (Hollifield 1990, 1992a; Hollifield and Zuk 1998; Hollifield 2005). Secondly, I have looked specifically at how rights act, primarily through independent judiciaries, to limit the capacity of liberal states to control immigration (Hollifield 1999a, 1999b). Finally, in a study of immigrant incorporation in the Dallas–Fort Worth Metroplex, I examine the role of rights in the incorporation of five immigrant communities (Brettell, Cordell, and Hollifield 1999). With the exception of the local study, which is based on survey and ethnographic research, the level and unit of analysis is the state; and the method is statistical, comparative, and historical. The best way to think about how rights act to limit the capacity of states to control immigration is to envision a time-series curve of immigration flows. The United States is currently well into the fourth great wave of immigration in its history. What is driving this immigration wave? To what extent is it driven by economic or political factors? To answer these questions, Valerie Hunt, Daniel Tichenor, and I used time-series analysis to look at the effect of business cycles on immigration flows from 1890 to 1996. We were able statistically to demonstrate the impact of major policy shifts on flows during this time period, net of the effects of the economic conjuncture. The most striking result of our analysis is the gradual weakening of the effect of business cycles on flows after 1945, but especially from the 1960s to the late 2000s. The impact of legislation passed after the Civil Rights Act of 1964 was so expansive that it negates the effect of business cycles, in stark contrast to the period before 1945, when flows were much more responsive to economic cycles. Thus, to explain the politics of control in western democracies, it is crucial to take account of changes in the legal and institutional environment. It is not sufficient simply to look at winners and losers, or focus on politics defined narrowly in terms of process and interest.

From the works of Zolberg, Freeman, myself, and others, we are starting to get a better picture of how politics matters in driving and channeling international migration. Two theories and their attendant hypotheses have been advanced: (1) the interest-based argument of Freeman, that states are subject to capture by powerful organized interests. These groups have pushed liberal democracies towards more expansive immigration policies, even when the economic conjuncture and public opinion would argue for restriction; and (2) the more comparative, historical, and institutional analysis – which I have summarized as the liberal state thesis – that, irrespective of economic cycles, the play of interests, and shifts in public opinion, immigrants and foreigners have acquired rights; therefore the capacity of liberal states to control immigration is constrained by laws and institutions. This is not meant to imply that rights, once extended to foreigners, can never be revoked. Laws and institutions can and do change. Like any social, economic, or political variable, rights vary, cross-nationally and over time; and we have seen evidence in the past 10 to 15 years that many liberal states have indeed tried to roll back immigrant rights (Hollifield 1999a). But, rights in liberal democracies have a long half-life. Once extended, it is difficult to roll them back, which may explain why many liberal states, especially in western Europe, are so reluctant to make even small or incremental changes in immigration and refugee law. Governments fear that any move to expand the rights of foreigners could open up the floodgates; and that such change (like amnesties or wholesale naturalizations) would send the wrong message to others wanting to emigrate.

Both the more procedural (and mildly rational choice) theory of Freeman, as well as my own more institutional and state-centric theory look at policy outputs as well as outcomes. But Freeman tends to focus more on the demand for and supply of immigration policy, whereas my work is more focused on outcomes, that is, immigration flows. To this point, my review has barely touched on the core issues of sovereignty and citizenship. If we turn our attention from the politics of control to international relations and the politics of national security (Weiner 1993; Teitelbaum and Weiner 1995), we can add a third hypothesis (3) concerning the capacity of states to control migration. This is what I call the globalization thesis, which, in its original formulation, was developed by sociologists, although some political scientists have contributed to its elaboration and testing (Sassen 1996; Cornelius 1998; Koslowski 2000; Levitt 2001). Simply put, there is a process of economic globalization at work in the late twentieth century, buttressed by social networks and transnational communities. Globalization has led to a structural demand for foreign labor (at the high and low ends of the labor market) and a loss of control of borders, to the point that sovereignty and even citizenship itself may be redundant (Bauböck 1994; Soysal 1994; Castles and Davidson 1998).

The Rise of the Migration State

The nineteenth and twentieth centuries saw the rise of what Richard Rosecrance (1986) has labeled the *trading state*. The latter half of the twentieth century has given rise to the *migration state*. In fact, from a strategic, economic, and demographic standpoint, trade and migration go hand in hand, because the wealth, power, and stability of the state are now more than ever dependent on its willingness to risk both trade *and* migration (Lusztig 1996; Hollifield 1998). By opening their societies to higher levels of immigration, Europeans are (reluctantly) following the American and Canadian examples in order to enhance their material power and wealth.

For centuries states have been in the business of organizing mass migrations for the purposes of colonization, economic development, and to gain a competitive edge in a globalizing economy. Once an international market for labor has been created, it may be difficult to manage or regulate. Migration can quickly become self-perpetuating because of chain migration and social networks (Massey 1987, 1998). Word begins to spread from one family and one village to another about the possibilities for gainful employment – or even striking it rich. At the same time, the individual risks and costs associated with migration are reduced by these kinship networks, which can grow into transnational communities and constitute a form of social capital (Morawska 1990; Portes 1996, 1997). As international migration accelerates, states are forced to respond by developing new policies, to cope with newcomers and their families (in the host country) or to deal with an exodus and potential return migration (in the sending country). Looking at the eighteenth and nineteenth centuries – a period of relatively free migration – many states with open frontiers, like the United States and Russia, were happy to receive immigrants; whereas overpopulated societies, with a growing rural exodus and burgeoning cities, were happy to be rid of masses of unskilled and often illiterate peasants and workers (Thomas 1973; Bade 1992; Nugent 1992). Inequalities and disequilibria in the international political economy, as well as land/labor/capital ratios have played an important role in the history of international migration, just as they have in the history of trade (Rogowski 1989). But, as I pointed out in my critique of Freeman's argument (above), this type of straightforward political economy or coalitional approach only tells part of the story.

By the end of the nineteenth and beginning of the twentieth century, the sending societies in Europe were well into the industrial revolution and entering a demographic transition, with falling birth rates and more stable populations. Nationalism was on the rise (Hobsbawm 1990) and it was increasingly important, in terms of military security, for states to be able to identify their citizens and to construct new demographic regimes (Koslowski 2000). The need to regulate national populations, for purposes of taxation and conscription, led to passport and visa systems, and the concomitant development of immigration and naturalization policies (Torpey 1998). Every individual was expected to have one and only one nationality; and nationality, as a legal institution, would provide the individual with a measure of protection in a hostile and anarchic world of nation-states (Shaw 1997). Countries of emigration, like Germany, tended to opt for nationality laws based upon *jus sanguinis* (blood, kinship, or ethnicity), whereas nations of immigrants and countries of immigration, like the United States and France, developed a more expansive political citizenship based upon *jus soli* (soil or birthplace). The German nationality law of 1913 had a strong ethnic component, and it was designed specifically to accommodate return migration; whereas birthright citizenship in the United States, as codified in the Fourteenth Amendment to the Constitution, was more inclusive (Brubaker 1989, 1992; Schuck 1998). It is important to remember, however, that the Fourteenth Amendment was adopted in the aftermath of the Civil War, and its primary purpose was to grant immediate and automatic citizenship to former slaves (Kettner 1978). Moreover, American immigration policy in the late nineteenth and early twentieth centuries evolved along racial lines, culminating in the Chinese Exclusion Act of 1882 and the national origins quota system, enacted in 1924 (Smith 1997; King 2000; Hollifield 2000c).

Until 1914, international migration was driven primarily by the dynamics of colonization and the push and pull of economic and demographic forces (Hatton and Williamson 1998), even though many receiving states were struggling to put in place national regulatory schemes to manage the growing international market for labor. Illegal or unauthorized immigration was not recognized as a major policy issue, and there were virtually no provisions for political migration, that is, refugees and asylum seekers. To a large extent, efforts to regulate international migration would be rendered moot by the outbreak in 1914 of war in Europe, which stopped economic migration in its tracks. However, war and decolonization fostered the rise of intense and virulent forms of nationalism – often with a strong ethnic dimension.

War sparked irredentism, and the redrawing of national boundaries in Europe, which in turn fostered new kinds of migration. Millions of displaced persons, refugees, and asylum seekers would cross national boundaries in the twentieth century to "escape from violence" (Zolberg, Suhrke, and Aguayo 1989). Thus, World War I marked a crucial turning point in the history of migration and international relations. States would never return to the relatively open migration regimes of the eighteenth and nineteenth centuries, when market forces (supply-push and demand-pull) were driving international migration (Thomas 1973). Instead, the twentieth century world became increasingly closed, and travel would require elaborate documentation. World War I also marked the beginning of the end of imperialism, with struggles for independence and decolonization in Asia and Africa – movements that would eventually result in the displacement of more millions of people.

In the interwar years, the *Westphalian system* of nation-states hardened and became further institutionalized in the core countries of the Euro-Atlantic region, and it continued to spread around the globe with the creation of new states (or the re-emergence of old ones) in Asia, Africa, and the Middle East. Old and new states guarded their sovereignty jealously and peoples in every region gained a stronger sense of citizenship and national identity. Because of these developments, international migration took on more of a political character, with diaspora and exile politics coming to the fore (Shain 1989). Henceforth, crossing borders had the potential of being a political, as well as an economic, act, and states reasserted their authority with a vengeance. The rise of anti-state revolutionary movements, such as anarchism and communism, provoked harsh crackdowns on immigration, and the roll back of civil rights and liberties, in the name of national security and national identity (Reimers 1998; Smith 1997; King 2000).

The interwar period was also marked by intense protectionism and nativism (Eichengreen 1989; King 2000). States enacted draconian laws to protect their markets and their populations. The international community was not prepared to deal with new forms of political migration. Under international law, states are not required to admit aliens. But, if they do, they are obliged to treat them in a humane and civilized manner. This concern for the rights of aliens was clearly enunciated in Articles 22 and 23 of the Covenant of the League of Nations, which created a kind of rudimentary human rights law, aimed at protecting peoples in former colonies (Shaw 1997).

The events of the 1930s and 1940s in Europe radically changed legal norms governing international migration. The Holocaust and World War II led to the creation of the United Nations and a new body of refugee and human rights law. Although states retained sovereign control over their territory, and the principle of non-interference in the internal affairs of others still holds, the postwar international order created new legal spaces (i.e. rights) for individuals and groups. The 1951 Geneva Convention Relating to the Status of Refugees established the principle of asylum, whereby an individual with a "well-founded fear of persecution," once admitted to the territory of a safe state, cannot be arbitrarily expelled or sent back to the state of his or her nationality. Under international law, the individual is entitled to a legal hearing; but it is important to remember that no state is compelled to admit an asylum seeker (Goodwin-Gill 1996; Gibney 2004). If, however, the state is a signatory of the Convention, it cannot legally send an individual back to his or her country of origin, if he or she is threatened with persecution and violence. This is the principle of *non-refoulement*.

The United Nations Charter as well as the Universal Declaration of Human Rights, which was adopted by the UN General Assembly in December 1948, reinforced the principle of the rights of individuals "across borders" (Jacobson 1996). Likewise, as a direct response to the Holocaust and other crimes against humanity, the international community in 1948 adopted and signed the Convention on the Prevention and Punishment of the Crime of Genocide. Alongside these developments in international law, we can see a growing "rights-based liberalism" in the politics and jurisprudence of the most powerful liberal states in Europe and North America (Cornelius, Tsuda, Martin, and Hollifield 2004). These liberal developments in international and municipal law feed off of one another, creating new rights (legal spaces) for aliens at both the international and domestic level. An intense debate has erupted among migration scholars over the source of migrant rights. Do they arise primarily from domestic-legal sources (Joppke 2001), or do they find their origins in international or regional human rights laws (Soysal 1994; Jacobson 1996; Hollifield 2005). Obviously, both domestic and international law/institutions play a role, but from the standpoint of international law, states are still the primary source of protection for their nationals (Shaw 1997), and human rights still depend heavily on the willingness of the most powerful liberal states to promote and enforce them.

Why are these legal developments so important? Unlike trade and financial flows, which can be promoted and regulated through international institutions like the WTO and the IMF, the movement of individuals across borders requires a qualitatively different set of regulatory regimes – ones based squarely on the notion of civil and human rights. It is almost a truism to point out that individuals, unlike goods, services, or capital, have a will of their own and can become subjects of the law and members of the societies in which they reside (Hollifield 1992a; Weiner 1995). They can also become citizens of the polity (Koslowski 2000). The question, of course, is how far are states willing to go in establishing an international regime for the orderly (legal) movement of people (Ghosh 2000), and to what extent would such a regime rely upon municipal as opposed to international law (Hollifield 2000a)?

The last half of the twentieth century has marked an important new chapter in the history of globalization. With advances in travel and communications technology, migration has accelerated, reaching levels not seen since the end of the nineteenth century. At the beginning of the twenty-first century, roughly 175 million people are living outside of their country of birth or citizenship. The trend in immigration has been steadily upward since the end of World Ward II (IOM 1996, 2000). Even though this figure constitutes a mere 3 percent of the world's population, the perception is that international migration is rising at an exponential rate, and that it is a permanent feature of the global economy. It seems that economic forces compelling people to move are intensifying. With more than half the world's migrant population in the less developed countries (LDCs), especially those rich in natural resources, such as oil, gold, or diamonds, the biggest regulatory challenge confronts states like South Africa or the United States, which share land borders with over-populated and underdeveloped states. Supply-push forces remain strong, while the ease of communication and travel has reinforced migrant networks, making it easier than ever before for potential migrants to gather the information that they need in order to make a decision about whether or not to move.

To some extent supply-push forces are constant or rising and have been for many decades. What is variable, however, is demand-pull forces, both in the OECD world and in the wealthier LDCs, many of which suffer from a shortage of skilled and unskilled labor. The oil sheikdoms of the Persian Gulf are perhaps the best examples, but increasingly we have seen labor shortages in the newly industrialized countries (NICs) of East and Southeast Asia as well (Fields 1994). Singapore, Malaysia, Hong Kong, and Taiwan, for example, have become major importers of cheap labor from other LDCs in Southeast Asia, particularly the Philippines and Thailand. Taiwan has also experienced rising levels of illegal migration from mainland China – which poses a security threat for the island country.

With very few exceptions, however, these LDCs have not evolved elaborate laws or policies for governing migration. Wealthier third world states have put in place contract or guest-worker schemes, negotiated with the sending countries, and with no provisions for settlement or family reunification. These types of pure manpower policies leave migrants with few if any rights, making them vulnerable to human rights abuses and arbitrary expulsion. The only protections they have are those afforded by the negotiating power of their home countries, which may choose to protest the treatment of their nationals. But, more often than not, the sending countries are unwilling to provoke a conflict with a neighboring state over individual cases of abuse, for fear of losing access to remittances, which are one of the largest sources of foreign exchange for many LDCs (Russell 1986). Hence, economics and demography (forces of supply-push and demand-pull) continue to govern much of international migration in the developing world; and the liberal paradox is less acute, because there are fewer legal or institutional constraints on the behavior of states *vis-à-vis* foreign nationals. Summary deportations and mass expulsions are viable options for controlling immigration in non-liberal states.

In the advanced industrial democracies, immigration has been trending upward for most of the post-World War II period, to the point that well over 40 percent of the world's migrant population resides in Europe and America, where roughly 10 percent of the population is foreign-born (IOM 2000; OECD 2001). Postwar migration to the core industrial states of Europe and North America has gone through several distinct phases, which make these population movements quite different from the transatlantic migration of the nineteenth century or economic migrations in the third world today. As pointed out above, the first wave of migration in the aftermath of World War II was intensely political, especially in Europe, where large populations were displaced as a result of the redrawing of national boundaries, irredentism, and ethnic cleansing. Much of the remaining Jewish population in central Europe fled to the United States or Israel, whereas large ethnic German populations in eastern central Europe flooded into the newly created Federal Republic of Germany. The partition of Germany, the Cold War, and the division of Europe contributed to the exodus of ethnic populations, seeking refuge in the democratic west. Until the construction of the Berlin Wall in 1961, 12 million German refugees arrived in West Germany.

Once this initial wave of refugee migration had exhausted itself and Europe began to settle into an uneasy peace that split the continent between the superpowers – thus cutting (West) Germany and other industrial states in western Europe off from their traditional supplies of surplus labor in eastern central Europe – new economic forms of migration began to emerge. The massive effort to reconstruct the war-ravaged economies of western Europe in the 1950s quickly exhausted indigenous supplies of labor, especially in Germany and France. Like the United States, which launched a guest-worker (*bracero*) program (1942–64) during World War II to recruit Mexican agricultural workers (Calavita 1992), the industrial states of north-west Europe concluded bilateral agreements with labor-rich countries in southern Europe and Turkey, which allowed them to recruit millions of guest workers during the 1950s and 1960s (Miller and Martin 1982).

However, from the beginning of the guest-worker phase, we could see an important distinction between those European states, like France, which had a legal immigration policy that allowed for the settlement of immigrant workers and their families, and those states, like Germany or Switzerland, which attempted to maintain strict rotation policies with a minimum of settlement and family reunification (Rogers 1985; Hollifield 1992a; Cornelius, Tsuda, Martin, and Hollifield 2004). Britain was some-thing of a special case in that its economy was growing at a slower pace and it had continuous access to Irish labor to fill any gaps in the British labor market. Moreover, the struggle to regulate post-colonial migrations began earlier in Britain than in the former imperial powers on the continent (e.g. France and Holland), thus injecting a bias towards restriction into British policy (Layton-Henry 1992; Joppke 1998c; Hansen 2000).

The guest-worker phase ended in the United States with the winding down of the *bracero* program in the 1950s, whereas in Europe it continued until the first signs of economic slowdown in 1966. However, the big shift in migration policy in western Europe came in 1973–4, following the first major oil shock and recession, which rapidly spread around the globe. European governments abruptly suspended all foreign-/guest-worker recruitment and took steps to encourage foreigners to return home. Policies were put in place to discourage or wherever possible prevent settlement and family reunification. The prevailing sentiment was that guest-worker migrations were primarily economic in nature, and that these workers constituted a kind of economic shock absorber (*Konjunkturpuffer*). They were brought into the labor market during periods of high growth and low unemployment, and they should be sent home during periods of recession (Miller and Martin 1982; Rogers 1985; cf. also Castles and Kosack 1973). Moreover, during the recessions of the 1970s, the hardest hit sectors in the West European economies were heavy industry and manufacturing, both big users of cheap, unskilled foreign labor. In these circumstances of recession and rising unemployment, it seemed logical that guest workers should behave, like all commodities, according to the laws of supply and demand.

The governments of western Europe had succeeded in creating an international labor market, in response to a high demand for unskilled or semi-skilled foreign labor. Yet just when this labor was no longer needed, powerful supply-push forces and networks came into play to sustain it at high levels, even after the official suspension of recruitment programs in 1973–4. Turkish migration to Germany and North African migration to France continued well into the 1980s, taking the form of family rather than worker migration. What made the family reunification phase of postwar migration possible was the intervention of courts, extending rights of residence to guest workers and their families (Hollifield 1992a, 2000b). Executive and administrative authorities were hampered by legal/constitutional constraints in their quest to reverse the migration flows. States with universalistic, republican traditions (like the United States, France, and to a lesser extent Germany), along with elements of separation of powers, including a strong and independent judiciary, had much greater difficulty in cutting immigration flows (Weil 1991; Hollifield 1994, 1999b; Joppke 1998b, 2001). Again, Britain, with its system of parliamentary supremacy, unitary government, and the absence of a universalistic, republican tradition, constitutes something of an exception among the industrial democracies – one theorist refers to Britain as the "deviant case" (Freeman 1994; cf. also Messina 1996 and Hansen 2000).

The difficulty of using guest workers for managing labor markets in western Europe is a perfect illustration of the liberal paradox. Importing labor to sustain high levels of non-inflationary growth during the 1950s and 1960s was a logical move for states and employers. This move was in keeping with the growing trend towards internationalization of markets for capital, goods, services, and labor; and it was encouraged by international economic organizations, particularly the OECD (Hollifield 1992a). Unlike goods or capital, migrants (*qua* human beings) can and do acquire rights, particularly under the aegis of the laws and constitutions of liberal states, which afford migrants a measure of due process and equal protection. When it became clear that the guests had "come to stay" (Rogers 1985), the initial reaction of most governments was to stop further recruitment of foreign workers, try to induce those residing in the country to return, and prevent family reunification. When this proved not to be possible, these liberal states had to accept the fact that large numbers of guest workers and their family members would become permanent settlers, leading most governments to redouble their efforts to stop any future immigration.

The settlement of large foreign populations transformed the politics of western Europe, giving rise to new social movements and political parties demanding a halt to immigration (Betz 1994; Kitschelt 1995). Public opinion was by and large hostile to immigration, and governments were at a loss how to manage ethnic diversity (Freeman 1979; Ireland 1994; Fetzer 2000; Bleich 2003). Problems of integration began to dominate the public discourse, amid perceptions that Muslim immigrants in particular posed a threat to civil society and to the secular (republican) state. The fear was (and is) that dispossessed and disillusioned youth of the second generation would turn to radical Islam, rather than following the conventional, secular, and republican path to assimilation (Kepel 1988; Kastoryano 1997). European societies looked increasingly like the United States where older, linear conceptions of assimilation had given way to multiculturalism and an increasingly uneven or segmented incorporation, whereby large segments of the second generation, particularly among the unskilled and uneducated, experienced significant downward mobility (Hollifield 1997b; Portes and Rumbaut 1996; Alba and Nee 2003).

In part because of the (perceived) crisis of integration and the threat it posed, pressures for greater control of immigration intensified, not only in western Europe, but in the United States and Australia as well. However, in the face of these political pressures, it is important to note the pervasive and equally powerful rights-dynamic in the liberal democracies. Rights for minorities and foreigners were deeply embedded in the jurisprudence and the political culture of these societies, helping to blunt the impact of nativist and xenophobic movements. The more draconian laws, like the 1986 and 1995 Pasqua Laws in France, Proposition 187 in California, or the 1996 Illegal Immigration Reform and Immigrant Responsibility Act in the United States, were either struck down by the courts or substantially modified to conform with liberal, constitutional principles (Hollifield 1997a, 1999b, 2000b; Schuck 1998; Tichenor 2002). Even though all states have the right to expel unauthorized migrants, deportation is not a very attractive policy instrument, and it is used sparingly and largely for its symbolic and deterrent effect (Ellermann 2005). Mass expulsions (like Operation Wetback in the United States in the 1950s) are not politically or legally viable, even in the aftermath of the September 11th attacks.

In spite of the enormous pressures on the asylum process that were building in the last two decades of the twentieth century, European democracies maintained a relatively strong commitment to the 1951 Convention and the international refugee and human rights regime. In the 1980s and 1990s, asylum seeking became the principal avenue for entry into western Europe, in the absence of full-fledged legal immigration policies and in the face of growing fears that large numbers of asylum seekers would undermine the refugee regime and destabilize European welfare states (Freeman 1986).

In this atmosphere of crisis, control policies shifted in the 1990s to stepped-up external (border) control – Operations Gatekeeper and Hold the Line on the US–Mexican border, and the Schengen system in western Europe to allow states to turn away asylum seekers, if they had transited a "safe third country" – internal regulation of labor markets (through employer sanctions and the like), and integrating large, established foreign populations (Brochmann and Hammar 1999; Cornelius, Tsuda, Martin, and Hollifield 2004). International migration had entered a new phase in the 1980s and 1990s, with refugee migration and asylum seeking reaching levels not seen since the period just after World War II. The situation in Europe was further complicated by a resurgence of ethnic nationalism (Brubaker 1996), by war in the Balkans, and by a dramatic increase in the number of refugees from almost every region of the globe. By the mid-1990s there were over 16 million refugees in the world, with two-thirds of them in Africa and the Middle East. The UN system for managing refugee migration, which had been created during the Cold War primarily to accommodate those fleeing persecution under communist rule, suddenly came under enormous pressure (Teitelbaum 1980, 1984). The United Nations High Commission for Refugees (UNHCR) was transformed virtually overnight into one of the most important international institutions. The UNHCR was thrust into the role of managing the new migration crisis, as the western democracies struggled to contain a wave of asylum seeking. The claims of the vast majority of those seeking asylum in western Europe and the United States would be rejected, leading western governments (and their publics) to the conclusion that most asylum seekers are in fact economic refugees (Fetzer 2000). By the same token, many human rights advocates feared that genuine refugees would be submerged in a tide of false asylum seeking.

Whatever conclusion one draws from the high rate of rejection of asylum claims, the fact is that refugee migration surged in the last two decades of the twentieth century, creating a new set of dilemmas for liberal states (Teitelbaum 1980; Gibney 2004). A large percentage of those whose asylum claims were refused would remain in the host countries either legally – pending appeal of their cases – or illegally, simply going underground. With most of the European democracies attempting to slow or stop all forms of *legal* immigration, the number of *illegal* immigrants – many of whom are individuals who entered the country legally and overstayed their visas – has increased steadily. Closing off avenues for legal immigration in western Europe led to a surge in illegal migration. But with the perception among western publics that immigration is raging out of control and with the rise of right-wing and xenophobic political parties and movements, especially in western Europe, governments are extremely reluctant to create new programs for legal immigration, or to expand existing quotas.

Instead, the thrust of policy change in western Europe and the United States has been in the direction of further restriction. To give a few examples, Germany in 1993 amended its constitution in order to eliminate the blanket right of asylum that was enshrined in Article 16 of the old Basic Law. France in 1995–6 enacted a series of laws (the Pasqua and Debré Laws) that were designed to roll back the rights of foreign residents and make it more difficult for immigrants to naturalize (Brochmann and Hammar 1999). Also in 1996, in the United States the Republican Congress enacted the Illegal Immigration Reform and Immigrant Responsibility Act, which curtailed social or welfare rights for all immigrants (legal as well as illegal), and severely limited the due process rights of illegal immigrants and asylum seekers.

Yet, at the same time that the US Congress was acting to limit immigrant rights, it took steps to expand legal immigration, especially for certain categories of highly skilled immigrants. The H-1B program, which gives American businesses the right to recruit foreigners with skills that are in short supply among native workers, was expanded in the 1990s. In France in 1997 and in Germany in 1999, laws were passed by left-wing governments to liberalize naturalization and citizenship policy (Hollifield 1999b, 2000b, 2000c). Most European governments recognize that they now preside over multicultural/immigrant societies, and attempts to ostracize settled foreign populations only feed the flames of xenophobia and racism. Moreover, with stagnant or declining populations and a shortage of highly skilled workers, European governments are now turning to new recruitment programs, seeking to emulate some aspects of American and Canadian immigration policy and make their economies more competitive in a rapidly globalizing world.

How can we make sense of these seemingly contradictory trends? Have states found ways of escaping the dilemma of immigration control, or are they still caught between economic forces that propel them toward greater openness (to maximize material wealth and economic security) and political forces that seek a higher degree of closure (to protect the *demos*, maintain the integrity of the community, and preserve the social contract)? This is already a daunting task – for states to find the appropriate "equilibrium" between openness and closure – but they also face the very real threat of terrorism. The attacks of September 11, 2001 on the United States served as a reminder that the first responsibility of the state is to provide for the security of its territory and population.

Although liberal states have a range of policy instruments available to them, all things being equal, they will opt for external strategies of control, placing the most stress on border control, or control of territory. The reason for this is simple: territorial closure and sovereignty are essential to the maintenance of the social contract and the rule of law, and this cannot be questioned without questioning the authority and legitimacy of the state itself. Moreover, a show of force at the border, especially during periods of heightened threat, has great symbolic importance – a way of quickly demonstrating the government's resolve to protect the populace, even if the efficiency of such policies is questionable. If a liberal state has the capacity for extraterritorial control, it will opt for further externalization of control, extending its authority to the high seas, to the territory of neighboring states, or to the territory of the sending states themselves. The Schengen Agreement (see above and Geddes 2003) is a classic example of extraterritorial control. It has helped to create buffer states, and to shift some of the burdens and dilemmas of control outside the jurisdiction of the liberal states of western Europe. If control cannot be externalized, then a series of internal control policies will come into play, raising questions about how far liberal states can go in restricting the civil liberties of individuals (citizens as well as foreigners) and rolling back rights. The limits of control are imposed by ideas, institutions, and culture, as well as certain segments of civil society, which may resist encroachments by the state on negative and/or positive freedoms.

Conclusion

International migration is likely to increase in coming decades, unless there is some cataclysmic international event, like war or economic depression. Even after the 9/11 terrorist attack on the United States, the liberal democracies have remained relatively open to international migration. Global economic inequalities mean that supply-push forces remain strong, while at the same time demand-pull forces are intensifying (Martin and Widgren 1996). The growing demand for highly skilled workers and the demographic decline in the industrial democracies create economic opportunities for migrants in the industrial democracies. Transnational networks have become more dense and efficient, linking the sending and receiving societies. These networks help to lower the costs and the risks of migration, making it easier for people to move across borders and over long distances. Moreover, when legal migration is not an option, migrants have increasingly turned to professional smugglers, and a global industry of migrant smuggling – often with the involvement of organized crime – has sprung up, especially in the last decade of the twentieth century. Hardly a week passes without some news of a tragic loss of life associated with migrant smuggling (Kyle and Koslowski 2001).

But migration, like any type of transnational economic activity (such as trade and foreign investment), cannot and does not take place in a legal or institutional void. As we have seen, states have been and still are deeply involved in organizing and regulating migration, and the extension of rights to non-nationals has been an extremely important part of the story of international migration in the post-World War II period. For the most part, rights that accrue to migrants come from the legal and constitutional protections guaranteed to all "members" of society (Hollifield 1992a, 1999a). Thus if an individual migrant is able to establish some claim to residence on the territory of a liberal state, his or her chances of being able to remain and settle will increase. At the same time, developments in international human rights law have helped to solidify the position of individuals *vis-à-vis* the nation-state, to the point that individuals (and certain groups) have acquired a sort of international legal personality, leading some analysts to speculate that we are entering a post-national era, characterized by "universal personhood" (Soysal 1994), the expansion of "rights across borders" (Jacobson 1996), and even "transnational citizenship" (Bauböck 1994).

Others have argued that migrants have become transnational, because so many no longer reside exclusively on the territory of one state (Glick-Schiller 1999; Levitt 2001), opting to shuttle between a place of origin and destination. This line of argument gives priority to agency as a defining feature of contemporary migrations; but it ignores the extent to which state policies have shaped the choices that migrants make. The migration state is almost by definition a liberal state, inasmuch as it creates a legal and regulatory environment in which migrants can pursue individual strategies of accumulation.

But, regulating international migration requires states to answer the questions of whom and how many to admit. And what status (or statuses) should be accorded to migrants. States which have developed such policies are by definition migration states. But liberal states in particular must be attentive to the (human or civil) rights of migrants; if migrant rights are ignored or trampled upon, then the *liberal* state risks undermining its own legitimacy and *raison d'être* (Hollifield 1999a). As international migration increases, pressures build upon states to find new and creative ways to cooperate, to manage flows. The definition of the national interest and *raison d'état* must take this reality into account; and, as rights become more and more a central feature of domestic and international politics, states will be under increasing pressure to accord basic human rights to migrants. New international regimes will be necessary if states are to risk more openness, and rights-based (international) politics will be the order of the day (Hollifield 1992b, 2005, 2000b; Cornelius, Martin, and Hollifield 2004; Ghosh 2000).

Some politicians and policy makers, as well as international organizations, continue to hope for market-based/economic solutions to the problem of regulating international migration. Trade and foreign direct investment – bringing capital and jobs to people, either through private investment or official development assistance – it is hoped, will substitute for migration, alleviating both supply-push and demand-pull factors (Bhagwati 1983; Martin and Widgren 1996). Even though trade can lead to factor–price equalization in the long term, as we have seen in the case of the European Union (Stolper and Samuelson 1941; Mundell 1957; Tapinos 1974; Straubhaar 1988), in the short and medium term exposing LDCs to market forces often results in increased (rather than decreased) migration, as is evident with NAFTA and the US–Mexican relationship (Martin 1993; Massey, Durand, and Malone 2002). Likewise, trade in services can stimulate more "high end" migration, because these types of products often cannot be produced or sold without the movement of the individuals who make and market them (Bhagwati 1998; Ghosh 1997).

In short, the global integration of markets for goods, services, and capital entails higher levels of international migration; therefore, if states want to promote freer trade and investment, they must be prepared to manage higher levels of migration. Many states (like Canada and Germany) are willing, if not eager, to sponsor high-end migration, because the numbers are manageable, and there is likely to be less political resistance to the importation of highly skilled individuals. However, mass migration of unskilled and less educated workers is likely to meet with greater political resistance, even in situations and in sectors, like construction or health-care, where there is high demand for this type of labor. In these instances, the tendency is for governments to go back to the old guest-worker models, in hopes of bringing in just enough temporary workers to fill gaps in the labor market, but with strict contracts between foreign workers and their employers that limit the length of stay and prohibit settlement or family reunification (Miller and Martin 1982). The alternative is illegal immigration and a growing black market for labor – a Hobson's choice.

At the time of writing (in March 2005), the United States and Mexico are edging closer to a new migration agreement, which may involve the creation of a new guest-worker program and some type of legalization (amnesty) for the millions of undocumented Mexicans living in the United States. Negotiations were derailed by the 9/11 attack, which brought military (homeland) security considerations surging to the fore. But in 2003, the rights of Mexican foreign workers were again on the table for negotiation.

Now more than ever, international security and stability are dependent on the capacity of states to manage migration. It is extremely difficult, if not impossible, for states to manage or control migration either unilaterally or bilaterally. Some type of multilateral/regional regime is required, similar to what the EU has constructed for nationals of the member states. The EU model, as it has evolved from Rome to Maastricht to Amsterdam and beyond, points the way to future migration regimes, because it is not based purely on *homo economicus*, but incorporates rights for individual migrants and even a rudimentary citizenship, which continues to evolve (Kostakopolou 2001). The problem, of course, in this type of regional migration regime is how to deal with third country nationals (TCNs). As the EU expands and borders are relaxed, the issue of TCNs, immigrants, and ethnic minorities becomes ever more pressing, and new institutions, laws, and regulations must be created to deal with them (Geddes 1995, 2003; Guiraudon 1998).

In the end, the EU, by creating a regional migration regime and a kind of supranational authority to deal with migration and refugee issues, allows the member states to finesse, if not escape, the liberal paradox (Geddes 2000, 2003). Playing the good cop/bad cop routine and using symbolic politics and policies to maintain the illusion of border control helps governments fend off the forces of closure, at least in the short run (Rudolph 2003). In the end, however, it is the nature of the liberal state itself and the degree to which openness is institutionalized and (constitutionally) protected from the "majority of the moment," that will determine whether states will continue to risk trade and migration (Hollifield 2000d).

REFERENCES

Alba, Richard and Victor Nee (2003). *Remaking the American Mainstream: Assimilation and Contemporary Immigration*. Cambridge, Mass: Harvard University Press.

Bade, Klaus J., ed. (1992). *Deutsche im Ausland – Fremde in Deutschland: Migration in Geschichte und Gegenwart*. Munich.

Barth, Fredrik (1969). *Ethnic Groups and Boundaries: The Social Organization of Culture Difference*. Boston: Little Brown.

Bauböck, Rainer (1994). *Transnational Citizenship: Membership and Rights in International Migration*. Aldershot: Edward Elgar.

Betz, Hans Georg (1994). *Radical Right-wing Populism in Western Europe*. New York: St. Martin's Press.

Bhagwati, Jagdish (1976). *The Brain Drain and Taxation: Theory and Empirical Analysis*. New York: American Elsevier.

Bleich, Erik (2003). *Race Politics in Britain and France*. New York: Cambridge University Press.

Borjas, George J. (1990). *Friends or Strangers: The Impact of Immigrants on the U.S. Economy*. New York: Basic Books.

—— (1999). *Heaven's Door: Immigration Policy and the American Economy*. Princeton: Princeton University Press.

Bouvier, Leon F. (1992). *Peaceful Invasions: Immigration and Changing America*. Lanham, MD: University Press of America.

Brettell, Caroline, Dennis Cordell, and James Hollifield (1999). "City and State as Context: A Research Model for Immigrant Incorporation in the United States." *Demographie aktuelle: Vortrage-Aufsatze-Forschungsberichte* 14: 26–44.

Brochmann, Grete and Tomas Hammar, eds. (1999). *Mechanisms of Immigration Control: A Comparative Analysis of European Regulation Policies*. Oxford: Berg.

Brubaker, Rogers, ed. (1989). *Immigration and the Politics of Citizenship in Europe and North America*. Lanham, MD: University Press of America.

—— (1992). *Citizenship and Nationhood in France and Germany*. Cambridge, MA: Harvard University Press.

—— (1996). *Nationalism Reframed. Nationhood and the National Question in the New Europe*. Cambridge: Cambridge University Press.

Calavita, Kitty (1992). *Inside the State: The Bracero Program, Immigration and the INS*. New York: Routledge.

Carens, Joseph H. (1989). "Membership and Morality: Admission to Citizenship in Liberal Democratic States." In Rogers Brubaker, ed., *Immigration and the Politics of Citizenship in Europe and North America*. Lanham, MD: University Press of America.

Castles, Stephen and Alastair Davidson (1998). *Citizenship in the Age of Migration: Globalisation and the Politics of Belonging*. London: Macmillan.

Castles, Stephen and Godula Kosack (1973). *Immigrant Workers and Class Structure in Western Europe*. London: Oxford University Press.

Castles, Stephen and Mark Miller (1998). *The Age of Migration: International Population Movements in the Modern World*. New York: Guilford.

Chiswick, Barry R., ed. (1982). *The Gateway: U.S. Immigration Issues and Policies*. Washington, DC: American Enterprise Institute.

Cornelius, Wayne A. (1998). "The Structural Embeddedness of Demand for Mexican Immigrant Labor: New Evidence from California." In Marcelo M. Suárez-Orozco, ed., *Crossings: Mexican Immigration in Interdisciplinary Perspectives*. Cambridge, MA: Harvard University Press.

Cornelius, Wayne A., Philip L. Martin, and James F. Hollifield, eds. (1994). *Controlling Immigration: A Global Perspective*. Stanford, CA: Stanford University Press.

Cornelius, Wayne A., Takeyuki Tsuda, Philip L. Martin, and James F. Hollifield, eds. (2004). *Controlling Immigration: A Global Perspective*. Stanford: Stanford University Press.

Dahl, Robert A. (1991). *Modern Political Analysis*. Englewood Cliffs, NJ: Prentice-Hall.

Eichengreen, Barry (1989). "The Political Economy of the Smoot-Hawley Tariff." *Research in Economic History* 12: 1–43.

Ellermann, Antje (2005). "Deportation and State Capacity: The Problem of Public Ambivalence." Unpublished Manuscript.

Fields, G. (1994). "The Migration Transition in Asia." *Asian and Pacific Migration Journal* 3(1): 7–30.

Fetzer, J.S. (2000). *Public Attitude towards Immigration in the United States, France, and Germany*. Cambridge, Eng.: Cambridge University Press.

Freeman, Gary P. (1979). *Immigrant Labor and Racial Conflict in Industrial Societies: The French and British Experiences*. Princeton, NJ: Princeton University Press.

—— (1986). "Migration and the Political Economy of the Welfare State." *The Annals* 485 (May): 51–63.

—— (1994). "Britain, the Deviant Case." In Wayne A. Cornelius, Philip L. Martin, and James F. Hollifield, eds., *Controlling Immigration: A Global Perspective*. Stanford, CA: Stanford University Press.

—— (1995). "Modes of Immigration Politics in Liberal Democratic States." *International Migration Review* 19(4): 881–902.

—— (1998a). "The Decline of Sovereignty? Politics and Immigration Restriction in Liberal States." In Christian Joppke, ed., *Challenge to the Nation-State*. Oxford: Oxford University Press.

—— (1998b). "Toward a Theory of the Domestic Politics of International Migration in Western Nations." South Bend, IN: The Nanovic Insititute, University of Notre Dame.

Geddes, Andrew (1995). "Immigrant and Ethnic Minorities and the EC's Democratic Deficit." *Journal of Common Market Studies* 33(2): 197–217.

—— (2000). *Immigration and European Integration: Towards Fortress Europe?* Manchester: Manchester University Press.

—— (2003). *The Politics of Migration and Immigration in Europe.* London: Sage.

Ghosh, Bimal (1997). *Gains from Global Linkages: Trade in Services and Movement of Persons.* London: Macmillan.

—— ed. (2000). *Managing Migration: The Need for a New International Regime.* Oxford: Oxford University Press.

Gibney, Matthew J. (2004). *The Ethics and Politics of Asylum: Liberal Democracy and the Response to Refugees.* Cambridge: Cambridge University Press.

Glick-Schiller, Nina (1999). "Transmigrants and Nation-States: Something Old and Something New in the U.S. Immigrant Experience." In Charles Hirschman, Philip Kasinitz, and Josh DeWind, eds., *The Handbook of International Migration: The American Experience.* New York: Russell Sage, pp. 94–119.

Goodwin-Gill, Guy S. (1996). *The Refugee in International Law.* Oxford: Clarendon.

Guiraudon, Virginie (1998). "Third Country Nationals and European Law: Obstacles to Rights' Expansion." *Journal of Ethnic Studies* 24(4): 657–74.

Hailbronner, Kay (1984). *Ausländerrecht.* Heidelberg: C.F. Müller.

Hammar, Tomas, ed. (1985). *European Immigration Policy: A Comparative Study.* New York: Cambridge University Press.

—— (1990). *Democracy and the Nation-State: Aliens, Denizens and Citizens in a World of International Migration.* Aldershot: Avebury.

Hansen, Randall (2000). *Immigration and Citizenship in Postwar Britain.* Oxford: Oxford University Press.

Hatton, T.J. and J.G. Williamson (1998). *The Age of Mass Migration: Causes and Economic Impact.* New York: Oxford University Press.

Haus, Leah (1995). "Openings in the Wall: Transnational Migrants, Labor Unions and U.S. Immigration Policy." *International Organization* 49(2): 285–313.

—— (1999). "Labor Unions and Immigration Policy in France." *International Migration Review* 33(3): 683–716.

Hobsbawm, Eric (1990). *Nations and Nationalism since 1780.* Cambridge: Cambridge University Press.

Hollifield, James F. (1986). "Immigration Policy in France and Germany: Outputs vs. Outcomes." *The Annals* 485 (May): 113–28.

—— (1990). "Immigration and the French State." *Comparative Political Studies* 23 (April): 56–79.

—— (1992a). *Immigrants, Markets and States: The Political Economy of Postwar Europe.* Cambridge, MA: Harvard University Press.

—— (1992b). "Migration and International Relations: Cooperation and Control in the European Community." *International Migration Review* 26(2): 568–95.

—— (1994). "Immigration and Republicanism in France: The Hidden Consensus." In Wayne A. Cornelius, Philip L. Martin, and James F. Hollifield, eds., *Controlling Immigration: A Global Perspective.* Stanford, CA: Stanford University Press.

—— (1997a). *L'Immigration et L'Etat-Nation à La Recherche d'un Modèle National.* Paris: L'Harmattan.

—— (1997b). "Immigration and Integration in Western Europe: A Comparative Analysis." In Emek M. Uçarer and Donald J. Puchala, eds., *Immigration Into Western Societies: Problems and Policies.* London: Pinter.

—— (1998). "Migration, Trade and the Nation-State: The Myth of Globalization." *UCLA Journal of International Law and Foreign Affairs* 3(2): 595–636.

—— (1999a). "Ideas, Institutions and Civil Society: On the Limits of Immigration Control in Liberal Democracies." *IMIS-Beiträge* 10 (January): 57–90.

—— (1999b). "On the Limits of Immigration Control in France." In Grete Brochmann and Tomas Hammar, eds., *Mechanisms of Immigration Control*. Oxford: Berg.

—— (2000a). "Migration and the 'New' International Order: The Missing Regime." In Bimal Ghosh, ed., *Managing Migration: The Need for a New International Regime*. Oxford: Oxford University Press.

—— (2000b). "Immigration and the Politics of Rights." In Michael Bommes and Andrew Geddes, eds., *Migration and the Welfare State in Contemporary Europe*. London: Routledge.

—— (2000c). "Immigration in Two Liberal Republics." *German Politics and Society* 18(1): 76–104.

—— (2000d). "The Politics of International Migration: How Can We Bring the State Back In?" In C. Brettell and J. Hollifield, eds., *Migration Theory: Talking Across Disciplines*. New York: Routledge.

—— (2005). "Sovereignty and Migration." In Matthew J. Gibney and Randall Housen, eds., *Immigration and Asylum*. Santa Barbara, CA: ABC Clio.

Hollifield, James F. and Calvin Jillson, eds. (1999). *Pathways to Democracy: The Political Economy of Democratic Transitions*. New York: Routledge.

Hollifield, James F. and David L. Martin (1996). "Strange Bedfellows? Immigration and Class Voting on Prop 187 in California." Paper prepared for the American Political Science Association. San Francisco, CA.

Hollifield, James F., Valerie Hunt, and Daniel Tichenor (forthcoming). "Immigrants, Markets, and the American State: The Political Economy of US Immigration." In Marco Giugni and Florence Passy, eds., *Explaining Immigration Policy*. New York: Pearson.

Huntington, Samuel P. (2004). *Who Are We? The Challenges to America's National Identity*. New York: Simon & Schuster.

IOM (1996). *Foreign Direct Investment, Trade, Aid and Migration*. Geneva: International Organization for Migration.

—— (2000). *World Migration Report 2000*. Geneva: International Organization for Migration.

Ireland, Patrick (1994). *The Policy Challenge of Ethnic Diversity: Immigrant Politics in France and Switzerland*. Cambridge, MA: Harvard University Press.

Jacobson, David (1996). *Rights Across Borders: Immigration and the Decline of Citizenship*. Baltimore, MD: Johns Hopkins University Press.

Joppke, Christian, ed. (1998a). *Challenge to the Nation-State: Immigration in Western Europe and the United States*. Oxford: Oxford University Press.

—— (1998b). "Why Liberal States Accept Unwanted Migration." *World Politics* 50(2): 266–93.

—— (1998c). *Immigration and the Nation-State*. Oxford: Oxford University Press.

—— (2001). "The Legal-Domestic Sources of Immigrant Rights: The United States, Germany and the European Union." *Comparative Political Studies* 34(4): 339–66.

Kastoryano, Riva (1997). *La France, l'Allemagne et leurs immigrés: négocier l'identité*. Paris: Armand Colin.

Kepel, G. (1988). *Les Banlieus de l'Islam*. Paris: Seuil.

Kessler, Alan E. (1998). "Distributional Coalitions, Trade and the Politics of Postwar American Immigration." Paper prepared for the American Political Science Association. Boston, MA.

Kettner, James (1978). *The Development of American Citizenship, 1608–1870*. Chapel Hill, N.C.: University of North Carolina Press.

King, Desmond (2000). *Making Americans: Immigration, Race and the Diverse Democracy*. Cambridge, MA: Harvard University Press.

Kitschelt, Herbert (1995). *The Radical Right in Western Europe*. Ann Arbor: University of Michigan Press.

Koslowski, Rey (2000). *Migration and Citizenship in World Politics: From Nation-States to European Polity*. Ithaca, NY: Cornell University Press.

Kostakopolou, T. (2001). *Citizenship, Identity and Immigration in the European Union*. Manchester: Manchester University Press.

Kyle, D. and R. Koslowski (2001). *Global Human Smuggling: Comparative Perspectives*. Baltimore, MD: Johns Hopkins University Press.

Layton-Henry, Zig (1992). *The Politics of Race: Immigration, "Race" and "Race" Relations in Post-war Britain*. Oxford: Blackwell.

Lévi-Strauss, Claude (1952). *Race and History*. Paris: UNESCO.

Levitt, Peggy (2001). *The Transnational Villagers*. Berkeley: University of California Press.

Lusztig, Michael (1996). *Risking Free Trade: The Politics of Trade in Britain, Canada, Mexico and the United States*. Pittsburgh: University of Pittsburgh Press.

Marshall, T.H. (1964). *Class, Citizenship and Social Development*. Garden City, NY: Doubleday.

Martin, Philip L. (1993). *Trade and Migration: NAFTA and Agriculture*. Washington, DC: Institute for International Economics.

Martin P.L. and J. Widgren (1996). "International Migration: A Global Challenge." *Population Bulletin* 51(1): 1–48.

Massey, Douglas S. (1987). *Return to Aztlan: The Social Processes of International Migration from Western Mexico*. Berkeley: University of California Press.

—— (1998). *Worlds in Motion: Understanding International Migration at the End of the Millennium*. Oxford: Oxford University Press.

—— (1999). "International Migration at the Dawn of the Twenty-First Century: The Role of the State." *Population and Development Review* 25(2): 303–22.

Massey, Douglas S. et al. (1993). "Theories of International Migration." *Population and Development Review* 19(3): 431–66.

Messina, Anthony (1996). "The Not So Silent Revolution: Postwar Migration to Western Europe." *World Politics* 49(1): 130–54.

Miller, Mark J. and Philip L. Martin (1982). *Administering Foreign Worker Programs*. Lexington, MA: D.C. Heath.

Money, Jeannette (1999). *Fences and Neighbors: The Geography of Immigration Control*. Ithaca, NY: Cornell University Press.

Morawska, E. (1990). "The Sociology and Historiography of Immigration." In V. Yans-McLaughlin, ed., *Immigration Reconsidered. History, Sociology, and Politics*. New York: Oxford University Press.

Mundell, Robert A. (1957). "International Trade and Factor Mobility." *American Economic Review* 47: 321–35.

Nugent, W. (1992). *Crossings: The Great Transatlantic Migrations, 1870–1914*. Bloomington, IN: Indiana University Press.

OECD (2001). *Trends in International Migration*. Paris: Organization for Economic Cooperation and Development.

Portes, Alejandro (1996). "Transnational Communities: Their Emergence and Significance in the Contemporary World-System." In R.P. Korzeniewidcz and W.C. Smith, eds., *Latin America in the World Economy*. Westport, CT: Greenwood.

—— (1997). "Immigration Theory for a New Century." *International Migration Review* 31(4): 799–825.

Portes, Alejandro and Robert L. Bach (1985). *Latin Journey: Cuban and Mexican Immigrants to the United States*. Berkeley: University of California Press.

Portes, Alejandro and Ruben Rumbaut (1996). *Immigrant America: A Portrait*. Berkeley: University of California Press.

Reimers, D.M. (1998). *Unwelcome Strangers: American Identity and the Turn Against Immigration*. New York: Columbia University Press.

Rogers, Rosemarie, ed. (1985). *Guests Come to Stay: The Effects of European Labor Migration on Sending and Receiving Countries*. Boulder, CO: Westview.

Rogowski, Ronald (1989). *Commerce and Coalitions: How Trade Affects Domestic Political Alignments*. Princeton, NJ: Princeton University Press.

Rosecrance, Richard (1986). *The Rise of the Trading State*. New York: Basic Books.

Rudolf, Christopher (2003). "Security and the Political Economy of International Migration." *American Political Science Review* 97(4): 603–20.

Russell, Sharon Stanton (1986). "Remittances from International Migration. A Review in Perspective." *World Development* 41(6): 677–96.

Sassen, Saskia (1996). *Losing Control? Sovereignty in an Age of Globalization*. New York: Columbia University Press.

Schlesinger, Arthur, Jr. (1992). *The Disuniting of America*. New York: Norton.

Schmitter, Barbara E. (1979). "Immigration and Citizenship in West Germany and Switzerland." PhD dissertation, University of Chicago.

Schmitter-Heisler, Barbara (1986). "Immigrant Settlement and the Structure of Emergent Immigrant Communities in Western Europe." *The Annals* 485: 76–86.

—— (1993). "Review of Hollifield, *Immigrants, Markets and States*." *Work and Occupations* 20(4): 479–80.

Schnapper, Dominique (1998). *La Relation à l'autre*. Paris: Gallimard.

Schuck, Peter H. (1998). *Citizens, Strangers and In-Betweens: Essays on Immigration and Citizenship*. Boulder, CO: Westview.

Shain, Yossi (1989). *The Frontier of Loyalty: Political Exiles in the Age of the Nation-State*. Middletown, CT: Wesleyan University Press.

Shanks, Cheryl (2000). *Immigration and the Politics of American Sovereignty, 1890–1990*. Ann Arbor, MI: University of Michigan Press.

Shaw, Malcolm N. (1997). *International Law*. Cambridge: Cambridge University Press.

Simon, Julian (1989). *The Economic Consequences of Immigration*. Oxford: Blackwell.

Smith, Rogers (1997). *Civic Ideals: Conflicting Visions of Citizenship in U.S. History*. New Haven: Yale University Press.

Soysal, Yasemin N. (1994). *Limits of Citizenship: Migrants and Postnational Membership in Europe*. Chicago: University of Chicago Press.

Stark, Oded (1991). *The Migration of Labor*. Cambridge, MA: Basil Blackwell.

Stolper, Wolfgang Friedrich and Paul A. Samuelson (1941). "Protection and Real Wages." *Review of Economic Studies* 9: 58–73.

Straubhaar, Thomas (1988). *On the Economics of International Labor Migration*. Bern: Haupt.

Tapinos, Georges (1974). *L'Economie des migrations internationales*. Paris: Colin.

Teitelbaum, Michael S. (1980). "Right Versus Right: Immigration and Refugee Policy in the United States." *Foreign Affairs* 59(1): 21–59.

—— (1984). "Immigration, Refugees and Foreign Policy." *International Organization* 38(3): 429–50.

Teitelbaum, Michael S. and Myron Weiner (1995). *Threatened Peoples, Threatened Borders*. New York: Norton.

Thomas, Brinley (1973). *Migration and Economic Growth*. Cambridge: Cambridge University Press.

Thränhardt, Dietrich, ed. (1996). *Europe: A New Immigration Continent*. Münster: Lit verlag.

Tichenor, Daniel J. (2002). *Dividing Lines: The Politics of Immigration Control in America*. Princeton, NJ: Princeton University Press.

Torpey, John (1998). "Coming and Going: On the State's Monopolization of the Legitimate 'Means of Movement.'" *Sociological Theory* 16(3): 239–59.

Walzer, Michael (1983). *Spheres of Justice: A Defense of Pluralism and Equality.* New York: Basic Books.

Weber, Max (1947). *The Theory of Social and Economic Organization.* New York: Oxford University Press.

Weil, Patrick (1991). *La France et ses étrangers: L'aventure d'une politique de l'immigration 1938–1991.* Paris: Calmann-Lévy.

Weiner, Myron ed. (1993). *International Migration and Security.* Boulder, CO: Westview.

—— (1995). *The Global Migration Crisis: Challenge to States and to Human Rights.* New York: HarperCollins.

Wilson, James Q., ed. (1980). *The Politics of Regulation.* New York: Harper.

Zolberg, Aristide R. (1981). "International Migration in Political Perspective." In Mary M. Kritz, Charles B. Keely, and Silvano M. Tomasi, eds., *Global Trends in Migration: Theory and Research in International Population Movements.* New York: Center for Migration Studies.

—— (1999). "Matters of State: Theorizing Immigration Policy." In Douglas Massey, ed., *Becoming American, American Becoming.* New York: Russell Sage.

Zolberg, Aristide R., Astri Suhrke, and Sergio Aguayo (1989). *Escape from Violence: Conflict and the Refugee Crisis in the Developing World.* New York: Oxford University Press.

Part II

Ethnicity, Race, and Nation

CHAPTER SEVEN

Ethnic and Racial Identity

MARILYN HALTER

The study of ethnic and racial identity in tandem as a subfield of American immigration history is a relatively recent development. Prior to the late 1970s, with few exceptions, immigration scholarship was synonymous with research concerning voluntary arrivals from Europe and, within that framework, European newcomers were thought to have ethnic identities. Issues of racial identity, however, belonged exclusively to the domain of African American history, a field that in its early stages focused on the population created by the forced migrations of hundreds of thousands of Africans in the slave trade lasting into the first decade of the nineteenth century. Just as immigration scholars overlooked race and the coerced migrations of African Americans in the past, African American scholars concentrating on the slave trade ignored migration; somehow the migration experience and the scholarship related to it were not considered to be a part of the relocations of slavery. Thus, the two disciplines, immigration history and African American history, followed two separate trajectories, with ethnicity the province of immigration studies and race the subject of African American history. This was a black and white world, where Asians, Latinos, and Caribbeans rarely appeared on the scholarly radar. Furthermore, on both sides of this divide, questions of identity itself were peripheral. Among immigration historians, ethnicity figured much more prominently within discussions of assimilation or nativism than in analysis of distinctive cultural practices and the performance of ethnic identities, while scholars of African America were preoccupied with the subjects of slavery, prejudice, and discrimination, not the nuances of race and culture, topics that did not begin to receive serious attention until the late 1980s.

The mass migrations of people from Asia, Latin America, the Caribbean and Africa in the last decades of the twentieth century and still ongoing, however, have radically reshaped the ethno-racial landscape of the United States and along with this far-reaching transformation, the false dichotomy between immigrants and racial minorities has been upended. Inclusion of the booming multiracial population of recent years, both immigrant and second generation, further confounds questions of racial and ethnic identity, mandating not only fresh perspectives on contemporary demographics but also a re-examination of how these populations were categorized, classified, and labeled in the past.

When it comes to the study of ethnicity, immigration historians owe a great debt to scholars in other disciplines. The adjective "ethnic" was first used in 1906 by a social scientist, William Graham Sumner, in his *Folkways*, while the term "ethnicity" appeared several decades later during the early 1940s when the Chicago School anthropologist W. Lloyd Warner was conducting his classic community studies and introduced the concept as a tool to help distinguish the various cultural groups in his research. Moreover, key theoretical perspectives widely used in research on ethnicity today come from fields other than history, including the notion of symbolic ethnicity (sociology: Herbert Gans 1979), the invention of ethnicity (literature: Werner Sollors 1988), and optional ethnicity (sociology: Mary Waters 1990). The two thematic essays on the subject of ethnicity included in the *Harvard Encyclopedia of American Ethnic Groups* (1980), "Concepts of Ethnicity" and "Literature and Ethnicity," were written by a sociologist and a literature scholar respectively. One exception to this extensive cross-disciplinary borrowing has been the evolution of whiteness studies in which historians such as David Roediger and Matthew Jacobson have played pioneering roles.

Coming from differing disciplinary perspectives, scholars have had trouble agreeing on a precise definition of ethnicity. Indeed, it has been so elusive a term that a 1974 survey of its usage found that the great majority of those who wrote on the subject avoided defining it altogether (Isajiw 1974, p. 111). At the very least, however, almost all definitions incorporate the features of a shared culture and a real or putative common ancestry. Moreover, contemporary understandings encompass a recognition that individuals can self-identify or be identified by others as belonging to the same ethnic group. Whereas earlier notions of ethnicity saw it as an ascribed phenomenon, today its socially constructed nature is emphasized. Thus, ethnicity is not a primordial human characteristic but rather ethnic groups are involved in a continual process of reinvention in response to changing historical circumstances and shifting realities both internal and external to the group itself. Furthermore, such conceptions of ethnic identity formation give immigrants historical agency as they actively negotiate, make, and remake the dimensions of collective identity structures in the process of ethnicization (Conzen, Gerber, Morawska, Pozetta and Vecoli 1992).

Definitions of race are even thornier. Most genetic authorities are now in agreement that there are no longer (and may never have been) pure and fixed racial entities or categories based on biological definitions of race. Race, like ethnicity, is socially constructed, not a physical fact, but instead an ever-changing set of notions subject to shifting socio-political realities and power structures. Thus, race is most useful if understood as a term that refers to "a way in which one group designates itself as 'insider' and other groups as 'outsiders' to reinforce or enforce its wishes and/or ideas in social, economic, and political realms" (Rohrl 1996, p. 96). Indeed, race and its cognates have been so discredited as viable social scientific categories that some scholars refuse to use the terms at all unless bracketed in quotes. Nonetheless, even if the conceptual terminology is admittedly tenuous and the categories widely acknowledged as weak and unstable, the potent realities of race persist as powerful constants in the dynamics of everyday life in the United States. Race unquestionably still matters, shaping perceptions and influencing behaviors at all levels of society. As David Hollinger has succinctly stated, "Racism is real, races are not" (1995, p. 39). In addition, whether certain immigrant populations are classified as a race or as an ethnic group has also been subject to shifting historical circumstances, further evidence of the elasticity of these categories. For example, at the turn of the last century Italians in the United States were typically categorized as a race whereas today they are considered an ethnic group.

Another common pattern has been for new immigrants to identify initially with their particular geographic region or island of origin, rather than arriving with a strong national identity, particularly if the home country itself was in a state of flux at the time of their migration. This was the case for much of the first wave of German-speaking migrants in the nineteenth century since the nation-state of Germany was not formed until 1871. Furthermore the German influx represented differing religious traditions of devout Lutherans, Catholics, and Jews that further countered any quick shift to a unifying German-American consciousness. Likewise, the Italian newcomers who followed them into the early twentieth century also maintained strong provincial identities and residential patterns, seeing themselves first as Sicilians, Calabrians, or Neapolitans, and so on, and as part of the adaptation process then became Italians and ultimately Italian-Americans. Similarly recent arrivals from the British Caribbean may initially think of themselves as Jamaicans or Trinidadians or Panamanians but as they settle in the United States they are likely to take on the designation of West Indian.

The relationship of "ethnic" or "ethnicity" to "racial" and "race" is complex and contested. "Ethnic" originally was utilized as a substitute for the much older category of race and it further gained popularity as an identity apart from that of social class. Since the beginning of its widespread use in public discourse and scholarly writing, the word "ethnic" has usually been meant to signify the descendants of European immigrants only. Those of non-European background fell under racial designations or were subsumed under the broader category of "minorities." Thus, a serious limitation of the traditional ethnicity paradigm is the assumption that those of European heritage in the United States have an ethnic identity but those of African descent do not. In other words, if you are "white" – whether Anglo-Saxon, Polish, or Greek – you are defined by ethnicity, but if you are "black" you are defined by race alone. Yet there are a multitude of ethno-cultural differences among the non-white population, especially as increasing numbers of immigrants are arriving in the United States with multiracial backgrounds. If you identify as "black," you could also define yourself as Haitian, Jamaican, or Ethiopian, and so on, depending on your cultural origins.

A more recent concurrent trend has been the conflation of ethnicity and race to represent the broadest spectrum of cultural groupings. The term "ethnicity" with its more benign connotations and associations is used to refer to all nationalities, no matter what their purported racial composition. Within this interpretive framework, for example, African Americans, who in the past almost never were referred to as "ethnics," are today commonly construed as simply another ethnic group. Similarly, university Ethnic Studies programs typically encompass curricula related to Asian Americans, Latinos, American Indians, and African Americans, populations that traditionally were designated as racial minorities, not ethnics. In some arenas then, the usage of "ethnic" and its variants has become increasingly diluted to carry the most inclusive meaning possible, while in other instances it has simply become a substitute for "race." While acknowledging that she is oversimplifying, the research that Susan Greenbaum conducted covering over a century of Afro-Cuban presence in Tampa,

Florida led her to sum up the difference in the two categories in this way: "Race is a uniform you wear, and ethnicity is a team on which you play. We all have both race and ethnicity, a color-coded phenotypic identity and membership in some historically defined natal community" (2002, p. 9).

As for the term "identity," usage in the social sciences is relatively recent, especially given how intrinsic the concept has become to scholarship dealing with ethnicity or, for that matter, the subject of immigration. Only in the 1950s do we begin to see "identity" coming into significant use in such pivotal works as Will Herberg's *Protestant, Catholic and Jew* (1955) or C. Vann Woodward's 1958 essay "The Search for Southern Identity." However, it was social psychologist Erik Erikson who really put the idea on the map in the early 1960s, and America's love affair with questions of identity has been going strong ever since. Erickson, particularly in his elucidation of the notion of the "identity crisis," conceptualized identity in relation to the individual, but since the late 1960s, the term has also had salience at the level of the group, especially with regard to identity politics, and in relation to the process of belonging. As with notions of race and ethnicity, personal identity contains a subjective component since the idea is based on how we see ourselves as well as how others see us. Discussions of identity, typically emphasizing its fluidity, have become so pervasive in the literature that some scholars, critical of what they see as the tendency toward ambiguous or oversimplified interpretations, have called into question its very efficacy as an analytic category (Brubaker and Cooper 2000).

Changing systems of official ethnic and racial classifications further reflect historical shifts in both self-identification and outside perceptions, sometimes triggering considerable controversy. For instance, the term "Hispanic," meaning the Spanish-language peoples of the Americas, and including Mexicans, Cubans, Puerto Ricans, Dominicans, and other South and Central Americans, first came into widespread use in 1970 as an official catch-all term for the purposes of US census tallies. It was a category foisted upon those with Spanish-speaking backgrounds, not a self-identifying label, but over the last 35 years, more and more Spanish-speaking Americans identify themselves as "Hispanics," a label now used interchangeably with "Latinos."

In general, despite the incongruities, the economy and convenience of panethnic terminology such as "Latino" or "Asian" have made it preferable at the institutional level and in the marketplace, but most individuals find these umbrella categories imprecise, artificial, and without personal meaning. Take the case of Brazilians. Usually they are subsumed under the social category of Latino or Hispanic. Originating from a Latin American country, the former term does apply, but since Brazil is a Portuguese-rather than Spanish-speaking country, lumping them under the identity of Hispanic is simply inaccurate and many Brazilian immigrants chafe at the extra burden of always having to correct and explain the difference. Their resentment may go beyond having to play the role of educator, however, since resistance to the Hispanic label is also related to a desire to dissociate themselves from a population that is perceived to be non-white and of lower status. Many Brazilian immigrants come from more middle-class backgrounds, identify as white, and tout their higher levels of educational attainment and, thus, want to be recognized as distinctive and to downplay any connection to the Hispanic population.

Even when Hispanic is used correctly in reference to Spanish-speaking populations, it still only signifies people who share a common language and does not account for the great diversity of cultures within its rubric. Yet, at least the term connotes the element of linguistic unity; in the case of Asian American collective identity, the various populations that constitute this category do not even share language in common. Furthermore, some of those grouped under this label, such as Japanese- and Korean-Americans, come from cultures and societies that for much of their history considered themselves enemies because of a legacy of protracted political and military conflict.

Another serious limitation of these blanket terms is the tendency to equate Latinos, Asians, and Caribbeans with the racial status of non-whites. Yet the people who fall under these classifications exhibit enormous variation in skin color and phenotype, spanning the spectrum of physical characteristics. These are populations, sometimes referred to as representatives of the "browning" of America, whose identities cross-cut entrenched notions of black and white and whose very presence challenges the oversimplified terminology and its assumptions about racial designations. With the diversity of cultures represented by the burgeoning population of non-European immigrants in recent decades, the inadequacies and ambiguities of these tags and labels have become increasingly more apparent, but problems with ethnoracial classi-fication in relation to non-European groups have a long history.

As a byproduct of a society that had been organized on the basis of an even more rigid binary racial structure in the nineteenth and twentieth centuries than it is today, official government records such as those compiled by the US census or the Bureau of Immigration were hopelessly deficient regarding immigrants of African descent. For example, entrenched standards of "black" and "white" formed the basis of classification when the Afro-Portuguese immigrants from the Cape Verde Islands, located off the west coast of Senegal, began to arrive during the latter part of the nineteenth century. Routinely grouped under other broader categories, those look-ing phenotypically most European or "white" were listed as "Portuguese" while the remainder were haphazardly labeled "African Portuguese," "Black Portuguese," and "Atlantic Islanders." Similarly, while British West Indians were distinguished from Puerto Ricans and Cubans, they were not differentiated from French or Dutch West Indians. Moreover, the US Immigration and Naturalization Service collected demo-graphic information only on those who were perceived to be mulatto under the designation "West Indian Race"; those appearing to be darker-skinned were simply grouped under the generalized label of "African Race," and no effort was made to gather data concerning the social characteristics of this population. Finally, information on Jamaicans was not compiled separately until 1953. Rather they were consolidated under "British West Indians" and then further subsumed under the classification of "Other Caribbean." As for arrivals from the continent of Africa, it was not until the 1960s that US immigration records listed them separately by country of origin. The confusion in such official categorization has not only meant that reasonable popula-tion estimates and accurate demographic profiles of these groups have been almost impossible to determine, but, more importantly, it only furthered the sense of invisibility that permeated their experience of migration to the United States.

The consequences of official racial designations were even graver when the issue was the legal definition of whiteness. Because federal law passed in 1790 required that immigrants had to be white in order to be naturalized as US citizens, such determinations were of critical importance to the incorporation of racial minorities into American society, especially for Asian immigrants since, as part of Reconstruction, legislation was passed in 1870 to at least nominally exempt immigrants of African descent from the ban. The 1790 law triggered numerous court cases over the years culminating in a flurry of litigation during the early twentieth century revolving around the question of who is legally considered to be Caucasian. The late nineteenth century saw the rise of rabid anti-Chinese sentiment and the law was invoked as part of a host of economic, legal, and governmental measures implemented to keep the Chinese from full participation in the civic culture of American society. The first litigants were Chinese but they were followed with legal cases brought by Japanese, Korean, Burmese, Hawaiian, and Filipino representatives where time and again, on the basis of the putative scientific theory of race – a nativist ideology at its height in this period which ordered human beings on a hierarchical scale of intelligence and competence – it was judged that they belonged to the inferior "Mongolian" rather than the desired "Caucasian" race. Such pseudo-scientific arguments became even more slippery when claims of whiteness were brought by Asian Indians, Armenians, and Syrians, however. For example, in the United States v. Thind case (1923), when a native of India argued that he was eligible for citizenship because Asian Indians were classified as Caucasian and previous judgments had clearly established that Caucasian equaled white racial status, the court suddenly retreated from weighty scientific rationales and argued instead for the validity of common perceptions about who is white. Under these criteria, Asian Indians simply did not qualify because they did not look white. The Supreme Court proceeded to strike down earlier determinations in the case, stripping Bhagat Thind of his naturalized citizenship along with dozens of other Asian Indians (Lopez 1996).

For the most part, immigrants and ethnics would much rather be recognized on the basis of a more specific cultural identity such as Cuban or Dominican, Cambodian or Vietnamese. Other times, particular populations may assert claims on an identifying label that springs from the grassroots, such as the term Chicano to name Americans of Mexican descent. Even the use of the hyphen in the labeling of ethnic Americans, as in "Chinese-American" versus "Chinese American or "Irish-American" versus "Irish American," has been a matter of debate. Despite these concerns, however, it is fairly commonplace in contemporary rhetoric to use the general phrase "hyphenated Americans" to refer to immigrants and ethnics. Moreover, the very language of hyphenated identities is quite particular to the United States. By contrast, for example, consider that despite the significant Turkish presence in Germany, they are never called "Turkish-Germans."

Although in recent years the landscape of race and ethnicity has become somewhat more elastic and the boundaries more porous, for much of the nineteenth and twentieth centuries, immigrants were arriving on the shores of a society organized around a bipolar racial structure in which the population was divided into black or white. For immigrants of African descent, such a rigid color line made the adaptation process particularly challenging. Until very recently, scholarship that treated the black immigrant experience in America was exceedingly sparse. The first and only book-length overview to date on the subject is Ira Reid's 1939 monograph *The Negro Immigrant: His Background, Characteristics and Social Adjustment, 1899–1937*. Up to this point, the vast majority of black immigrants to the United States, who established the most long-standing communities, were Haitians, Cape Verdeans, and British West

Indians. In the post-1960s era, increasing numbers of newcomers from other countries in Africa and the Caribbean began to arrive, as well as people of African descent emigrating from nations where the dominant population is not black, for example Afro-Cubans. Furthermore, varying proportions of other Spanish-speaking multiracial societies in Latin America who migrate may be classified as black in the United States, further swelling the percentages of those of African descent.

Because American blacks are often seen solely in racial terms, their distinctive cultural identities go unrecognized. The range of cultural and linguistic backgrounds that the migrants bring with them has become increasingly more diverse. How they identified themselves was often constrained by how they were viewed by both whites and native-born blacks. Would they be recognized as members of an immigrant group or just simply as black? Over 30 years after the publication of *The Negro Immigrant*, Roy Bryce-LaPorte addressed these issues in a pivotal *Journal of Black Studies* article in which he put forward the notion of double invisibility as applied to immigrants of African descent. He argued that as blacks and as black foreigners they suffered more inequality and greater levels of pressure concerning questions of identity than either native-born blacks or European immigrants (Bryce-LaPorte 1972).

Indeed, feeling invisible is a recurrent theme in the personal narratives of members of all such immigrant groups that do not readily fit the traditional binary racial scheme of American society, a sector that comprises the vast majority of recent newcomers including Latinos, Asians, and Caribbeans, and which is represented by significant earlier flows as well, not to mention those with biracial identities. The absence of an identity is precisely how one journalist titled his commentary on Cape Verdean immigrants – "A People without a Race." Also unable to readily classify this population, another referred to them as "the green people," taking literally the translation of Cape Verde (quoted in Halter 1993, p. 14). Similarly Afro-Hispanics have been termed "los excluidos" (the excluded ones), while one scholar of Afro-Cuban migration simply titled his study, "Who Ever Heard of a Black Cuban?" (Dixon 1982). At both the institutional and interpersonal levels, as they adjust to their new circumstances, many are unprepared for the rude discovery that a sweeping gulf exists between their own clearly defined identities and how they are perceived by the wider society. Often, the newcomers find that in their interactions with Americans their cultural uniqueness goes unrecognized and in the process their identities get erased. Koreans are mistaken for Japanese, Cubans for Puerto Ricans, and Nigerians for Ethiopians – if it even registers that there are diverse nationalities on the continent of Africa or elsewhere – or something of the reverse occurs, such as those of Chinese descent who have been Americans for generations routinely being treated as foreigners in their own country.

The history of the relationship between native and foreign-born blacks in the United States has often been an uneasy one filled with ambivalence on both sides. In addition to the distinguishing cultural features represented by immigrants of African descent, the crucible of voluntary versus involuntary migration has been a factor to rationalize the separation of immigrants from the native-born. Dissociation from American-born blacks, whether by Haitians, Cape Verdeans, West Indians, Dominicans, or any of the many nationalities represented by recent migrants from Africa, has rested on the experience of having made the United States their home of their own volition as opposed to being a descendant of those forced and brought to the country in chains.

At times the realities of race have drawn the two populations together, particularly when outside discrimination has triggered a reactive solidarity. More often, however, cultural differences have superseded alliances based on color. Immigrants typically attempt to assert their cultural distinctiveness, foster ethnic solidarity, and resist identification with what has been the most subordinated sector of American society, while African Americans may exhibit resentment at the perceived preferential treatment accorded the foreigners, regarding them as a competitive threat in an economy where resources available to racial minorities are scarce.

With the arrival of significant numbers of immigrants and refugees from sub-Saharan Africa especially since the 1990s, issues of ethnic and racial identity continue to percolate particularly in relation to the native-born black population. Will these African migrants who come from some 30 different nations and who represent a wide range of ethnic, cultural, religious, and language backgrounds become the newest African Americans? Will they identify as black? Or will this diverse assortment of cultural groups come together to form a panethnic African identity? Initial trends suggest that African adaptation patterns resemble those of other foreign-born blacks such as West Indians, whereby the immigrant generation attempts to emphasize distinctive cultural traditions and resists being grouped with African Americans, while the second generation is much more likely than their parents to associate and identify with native-born minorities. Alternatively, research on Dominican youth in Providence, Rhode Island has led one scholar to argue that post-1965 immigrants and especially the second generation are transforming entrenched notions of black/white racial categorization altogether. The young people in the study privileged their ethno-linguistic and cultural background as their racial designation whether as Dominican, Spanish, or Hispanic rather than identifying in terms of black or white (Bailey 2001).

Perhaps the most dynamic recent development in scholarship related to the history of immigrant racial and ethnic identity has been the evolution of whiteness studies. Even once a widespread scholarly consensus on the social constructiveness of race had been reached, studying race was still understood to be synonymous with research on the experience of African Americans and other racial minorities, reinforcing the familiar cleavage of race equaling "black" and ethnicity meaning "white." Yet whiteness is also a variant of racial identity so that the initial contribution that scholars of the subject made was to expand the meaning of race to include interrogations of the classifications of so-called white or Caucasian populations alongside those of non-whites. With the path-breaking publication of his *Wages of Whiteness: Race and the Making of the American Working Class* in 1991, a volume that explores white racial formation among Irish immigrants of the nineteenth century, David Roediger is typically credited with founding the field, although labor historian David Brody (2001) has pointed out that the first book to introduce the notion of whiteness as an analytic category, Alexander Saxton's *The Rise and Fall of the White Republic: Class Politics and Mass Culture in Nineteenth-Century America*, actually appeared a year before Roediger's.

The basic premise of this scholarship holds that European immigrant and ethnic groups, populations that have long been unquestionably thought of as white, did not, in fact, automatically belong to the white race but instead went through a process by which the status of whiteness had to be claimed. Moreover, achieving whiteness was always predicated on the systematic racial exclusion of others, and viewing these dynamics from such a perspective helps our understanding of the vicissitudes of working-class racism. Certainly, immigrant groups such as the Irish and later the newcomers from southern and eastern Europe were often treated as inferior races, victims of nativist policies and discriminatory practices, and charged with polluting and degrading the purity of Anglo-Saxon stock, but what has raised so much controversy in this assessment is that, notwithstanding their ambiguous racial status, these are still populations that were deemed white under the law, eligible for citizenship with all the privileges and benefits that come with legal membership in American society. This is precisely the position that Thomas Guglielmo takes in *White on Arrival* (2003), his study of early twentieth-century Italian immigrants' encounters with race and color in Chicago. The author explores issues of racial identity and categorization finding that while the new Italian arrivals were widely treated as racially inferior, the prejudice was framed within an assumed white racial status. That is, they were clearly accepted as white at all levels of the institutional structure of American society, even if they exhibited what was viewed as a substandard and undesirable brand of whiteness.

Such studies of the relationship of whiteness to immigrant identity formation and the process by which formerly racialized groups become white led Nancy Foner, in her study of New York's immigrants, past and present, to raise the provocative issue of the future status of Asians in this schema, noting that, "Asians have become the 'whitest' of the non-white groups" and "with more intermarriage and intermingling, the category 'white' may eventually be expanded to include Asians as well as lighter-skinned Hispanics, although a more pessimistic view holds that persistent discrimination will prevent Asians from ever being accepted as belonging to white America" (2000, p. 167).

If nothing else, whiteness studies scholarship reinforces yet one more time the striking deficiencies of seeing the world in black and white. Indeed, the complex gradations of whiteness – as with the variegated contours of blackness – that characterize so many ethnoracial populations, past and present, have prompted and challenged scholars to search for new terms and categories that might better denote the intricacies of such identities. Karen Brodkin refers to Jews as "racially not-quite-white" in her study *How Jews Became White Folks* (1998), while James Barrett and David Roediger (1997) coined the phrases "inbetween peoples" and "inbetween Americans" in their examination of immigrant workers from southern and eastern Europe. Matthew Jacobson prefers the term "probationary whites" to signify this same cohort of migrants in his *Whiteness of a Different Color* (1998). In writing about Asian American identities, Yen Le Espiritu captures the ironies of racial notions when she describes the perception and treatment of Asians during the nineteenth and most of the twentieth century as "almost blacks but not blacks," and then points out that in more recent years, especially in the way that Asians have been cast as the model minority, they inhabit a similarly ambiguous racial status, but with a twist. Now they are "almost whites, but not whites" (Espiritu 1997). Taking her cue from Cuban nationalist José Marti's proclamation that Cubans are "more than white, more than black," Susan Greenbaum titled her study of the settlement patterns of the Afro-Cuban sector, *More Than Black* (2002). *In Puerto Ricans: Born in the USA* (1989), Clara Rodriguez calls her chapter on race "The Rainbow People" and speaks of dialectical distance, the phenomenon of Puerto Ricans straddling two polarities, while Haitians have been characterized as a "minority within a minority" (Stafford 1987).

Similarly, individuals caught "between race and ethnicity" (Halter 1993) have come up with their own self-designations, such as Latinos who see themselves as "not white, not black" (Lopez 1996), or more directly as simply "Brown," the title and subject of noted writer Richard Rodriguez's latest memoir (2002). As a youngster, golf phenomenon Tiger Woods came up with his own original name for his ethnic identity, "Cablinasian," to account for his mixed Caucasian, black, Indian, and Asian ancestries; now he refers to himself more generically as an "ethnically global person." In Hawai'i, the offspring of mixed-race parents are called "hapa-haole," the pidgin phrase for half-white ("hapa" means "half" and "haole" is slang for the white settler population on the islands, a term that is usually used pejoratively, though, interestingly, its derivative, "hapa-haole," does not normally carry negative connotations). Yet another label invented to name Americans with parents of differing racial identities is "Amerasian."

Whatever the signifying labels, the importance of ethnicity in constructing both personal and group identities has persisted down to the present. Once again taking advantage of interdisciplinary perspectives, especially that of cultural anthropology, immigration historians have focused on ethnic festivals and celebrations as key markers of evolving ethnic identities in the United States. In her study of nineteenth-century German-American festive culture, Kathleen Conzen (1989) spells out the ways in which parades and festivals not only encoded a distinctive immigrant cultural identity unifying a fractious and heterogeneous community divided by religion, social class, and politics, but in the German case, the rituals, symbols, and values exhibited through such pageantry eventually influenced already established modes of public festivity celebrated by the American-born population. April Schultz (1994) takes this approach one step further by selecting just one such public spectacle celebrated by Norwegian settlers in Minnesota, the 1925 Norwegian-American Immigration Centennial, to organize a book-length study of the dynamics of ethnic identity, highlighting the ways in which even commonplace cultural activities can signify the invention of identities and in the process carry meanings much broader than the events themselves. To explore questions of assimilation, bicultural identity, and the development of Japanese-American ethnicity, Lon Kurashige (2002) traced the history of Nisei Week in Los Angeles from the 1930s to the 1990s. The largest Japanese public celebration in the United States became the lens through which Kurashige interrogated issues of community and conflict, racial status, and social class as the Japanese population negotiated the internal complexities of their local neighborhoods as well as the wider, often hostile, American social milieu.

Ethnic festivals have been the optimal sites for displaying identifying features of immigrant cultures, as was the case in Lindsborg, Kansas in 1941, when the Swedish community held its first Swedish Pioneer Festival and introduced the smorgasbord as the centerpiece of its celebration. But such events are not a thing of the past. On the contrary, as one of the primary manifestations of the late twentieth-century ethnic revival, ethnic festivals have become even more prevalent in recent years. Typically the outcome of a combination of commercial, civic, and cultural resources, they have become paradigmatic occasions to celebrate cultural diversity and are the primary venues for cultural performance and entertainment, including beauty pageants, fashion and talent shows, in which traditional and invented foods, music, dance, costume, art and artifacts are showcased. In some instances, long-standing celebrations have been remade and as they evolve have become increasingly more elaborate. This has been the case with the Tulip Festival in Holland, Michigan, which began in 1929 to celebrate the Dutch heritage of the community's original settlers and today is still a flourishing event drawing upwards of 500,000 visitors annually. Because Tulip Time has become so essential to the local economy over the years, town shopkeepers have gone so far as to renovate their storefronts in keeping with the design of a traditional Dutch village, to appeal to the tourists who flock to the festival seeking an authentic Dutch experience (Sinke 1992).

But especially since the 1970s, wholly new happenings have sprung up all across the country from national multicultural extravaganzas like the Smithsonian-sponsored Festival of American Folklife in Washington, DC, to neighborhood events that highlight several different heritages at once such as New York's Lower East Side Festival, to even more localized festivities organized around a single group or region, such as Chicago's Rizal Day (named for the Filipino nationalist hero José Rizal), the Armenian Cultural Festival and Block Party in Watertown, Massachusetts, or the West Indian Carnival in Brooklyn. Indeed, some of the most incisive analysis of the politics of Caribbean ethnic identity formation and the rituals of meaning-making derives from research on West Indian Carnival, a celebration that gets more and more elaborate every year (Kasinitz 1992; Buff 2001). Similarly Carnival Miami, a raucous and hugely popular gathering, held along Calle Ocho, the most famous street in Little Havana, has stretched into a week-long whirlwind of celebration with daily parades and an array of concerts, sporting events, and cooking contests.

Although the reigning models to explain the assimilation of European newcomers at the turn of the last century, Anglo-conformity and the melting pot thesis, both assumed the disappearance of the original cultures of the immigrants – in the case of the former, eclipsed by the dominant Anglo-Saxon way of life, while in the latter, diverse heritages would melt away into a new unifying American culture – a third theory from this era, articulated in the 1920s by philosopher Horace Kallen, conveyed, instead, the idea that immigrant groups would retain their distinctive ethnic features, including language, foods, religious beliefs, customs, and history, to create an American society characterized by cultural pluralism. Indeed, as the arrivals from southern and eastern Europe began to settle primarily in the metropolitan cities of the northeast and midwest, a parallel process of assimilation and ethnicization began to take place.

Earlier generations of ethnic Americans typically may have wished to assimilate into the mainstream as rapidly as possible, but found that they were defining themselves and being defined by the larger society according to their compatriot community affiliations and the constraints of ghetto life. Definitive and distinguishing ethnic group markers, most notably language, but also the still vibrant cuisines, music, literature, and religious practices of their native lands, surrounded them. They felt tied to neighborhoods, parishes, local politics, and an active network of voluntary organizations. Among the immigrant generation, ethnic particularities persisted and continued to have import. In the 1920s, when restrictive legislation shut the doors to an open immigration policy, the ongoing cultural infusions that new arrivals brought to established ethnic enclaves were closed out as well, expediting the Americanization process for those already in the United States over the next several decades. By the mid-twentieth century, the institutional structures of America's traditional ethnic communities experienced significant erosion.

When most people think about the social unrest on the home front of the United States during the 1960s, they have in mind the civil rights movement, anti-war protests, the blossoming counterculture, maybe Women's Liberation, but in the annals of American immigration history, the most transformative event of all in that quintessential decade of upheaval was the quiet passage of the Immigration Reform bill in 1965 ending the preferential quotas for Europeans which had been in place since the 1920s. Here was legislation that, in the years since its approval, has led to kaleidoscopic demographic change and to so complete a shake-up of the country's racial and ethnic composition that by 2050, when today's pre-schoolers will have reached middle-age, experts predict there will be no white majority; every American will belong to a minority group.

The other significant legacies of the 1960s related to the contours of American ethnic identities today were the movements by traditionally oppressed groups for recognition and self-determination within the wider culture, spearheaded by black nationalism and quickly followed by the American Indian movement and the stirrings of a new Chicano militancy. These largely political initiatives were embellished by momentous cultural transformations that included unearthing buried roots and occluded histories as well as celebrating distinctive heritages. Moreover, the worldview of the 1960s counterculture and of its New Left politics legitimized cultural hybridity, since much of it was based on rebellion against the previous decade's penchant for humdrum conformity. The colorless "organization man" gave way to the colorful non-conformist whose individuality could readily be expressed in ethnic terms. Indeed, sixties radical, Tom Hayden, founding member of Students for a Democratic Society and author of the organization's Port Huron Statement, a visionary document articulating the connections between the personal life of individuals and the politics of nations, went on to become not only a California state senator but also a pro-ponent of Irish pride, who today lectures widely on the history and psychology of the culture that is his heritage.

By the mid-1970s, initially driven by a backlash against minority group movements for racial power, white descendants of immigrants who had arrived primarily from southern and eastern Europe during the sweeping second wave in the late nineteenth and early twentieth centuries and who had also faced discrimination from the native population at the time, began to assert their own brand of ethnic pride. At first con-strued largely as a defense against the perceived threats of black power and the encroachment of African Americans into white ethnic neighborhoods, the ethnic resurgence ultimately went beyond such narrow aims to encompass a cultural alter-native to assimilation and a political alternative to individualism for both black and white ethnics.

Thus, in addition to all the newcomers from other lands streaming in today, these early, often reactive impulses to reclaim roots had evolved by the century's end into a full-blown and multifaceted ethnic revival across a broad spectrum of the popula-tion that carries a much more benign rhetoric of rainbows and salad bowls to explain the dynamics of American pluralism. After decades in which assimilation was the accepted standard for the incorporation of diverse populations, cultural pluralism re-emerged to take its place as the leading model. When Congress passed the Ethnic

Heritage Act in 1974 to support the funding of initiatives that promote the distinctive cultures and histories of the nation's ethnic populations, it was clear that this philosophy had taken hold at even the highest levels of government. The so-called roots phenomenon accounts for the flourishing of ethnic celebrations, a passion for genealogy, increased travel to ancestral homelands, special programs in universities, museums dedicated to the preservation and interpretation of ethnic history and culture, and a general escalation of interest in ethnic artifacts, cuisine, music, literature, and, of course, language.

Much has changed in the 30 years since Margaret Mead pronounced, "Being American is a matter of abstention from foreign ways, foreign food, foreign ideas, foreign accents" (1975, p. 189). Although cultivating a foreign accent may not yet be a sign of true Americanness, relearning one's ancestral tongue, eating ethnic cuisine, displaying ethnic artifacts, fostering a hyphenated identity, even reverse name-changes (back to the old-country original) have become the American way. What some scholars viewed as a passing fad of the 1970s has only intensified. This renaissance is a form of voluntary ethnicity that has made any conflict between identifying oneself as American and affirming one's foreign heritage disappear. Indeed, as sociologist Robert Wood has pointed out, "In an age that celebrates diversity and multiculturalism, it has become almost a civic duty to have an ethnicity as well as to appreciate that of others" (1998, p. 230). Because hyphenated identities are so valued in contemporary American society, post-1965 immigrants have felt much less pressure to give up their distinctive cultural practices than did earlier generations of newcomers, making the possibilities for becoming Americans without losing the specificity of their ethnic identities much more attainable.

The pivotal role of immigration in shaping American society has made it commonplace to refer to the United States as a nation of nations. Contemporary Americans, however, are also a nation of roots-seeking Americans as evidenced by the astounding response to the Ellis Island website made its debut in 2001, digitizing their immigration records. The Foundation was completely taken by surprise by the magnitude of traffic seeking immigration information. It averaged more than 25,000 hits per *second*. And this with less than half of the current population who actually have relatives who passed through that particular gateway to the United States. Perhaps nothing better illustrates the extent to which the ethnic revival has permeated American culture than hearing the renowned baby and child care expert, Dr. T. Barry Brazelton, proclaim: "Every baby should get to know their heritage." In the fundamentals of twenty-first-century American child-rearing, roots training comes even before potty training.

Not surprisingly, the magnitude and diversity of new immigrant arrivals of the last two decades coupled with the emphasis on hyphenated identities and an explosion of interest in reclaiming roots has quickly captured the attention of the commercial sector. Advertising trends demonstrate that ethnicity is highly combustible, fueling free enterprise and molding our consumer patterns. The marketing of ethnic identity has resulted in US companies spending well over $2 billion a year on promotions designed to win the attention of new immigrants and capture the loyalty of minority customers, whose buying power is estimated at more than $1 trillion annually and who are eager to acquire the markers of their cultural heritage. And while identifying with a specific ethnic group used to be associated with lower-class standing, recent

174   MARILYN HALTER

studies show that getting back to one's roots and getting ahead financially go hand in hand (Halter 2000).

The shift from "being" to "becoming" reflected in recent titles in immigration and ethnic studies, such as *Becoming Mexican American* (Sanchez 1993), *How the Irish Became White* (Ignatiev 1995), or *Becoming Asian American* (Kibria 2002), signifies a monumental reorientation in how identity is constructed and expressed. In traditional societies, ethnicity had an ascriptive status in which cultural affinities were an imperative, but with the evolution of modernity, what characterizes ethnicity is its optionality and malleability. Individuals can decide for themselves not only the degree to which they identify with their cultural group but even if they want to identify at all. Most do. They pick and choose the when and how of ethnic expression, creating highly individualized and multidimensional variations of cultural formations. We also live in a time and a cultural milieu that magnifies ethnicity and ancestry as markers of identity. Thus, any identity is better than none. This type of ethnicity is so flexible and sporadic that it is possible to switch from one cultural form to another and then back again with ease. Not only does this mean ethnicity by choice but it also means that people's ethnic identities are often only one part of a configuration of several identity choices available to them.

Yet it must be pointed out that the notion of voluntary or part-time ethnicity has been relevant primarily to hyphenated Euro-American groups. Whites simply have had more options to identify with one group or another, whether as Irish, Swedish, or Italian, or to choose to ignore their ethnic heritage altogether. Historically, non-whites, including African Americans, Asians, Hispanics, and Native Americans, have been much more bound to their particular ethnoracial group, while the social and political liabilities of such identities have been much greater. Racial difference, even when ambiguous, still is more readily identifiable and less easily a matter of choice in contemporary America.

REFERENCES

Bailey, B. (2001). "Dominican-American Ethnic/Racial Identities and United States Social Categories." *International Migration Review* 35(3): 677–708.
Barrett, J.R. and D. Roediger (1997). "Inbetween Peoples: Race, Nationality and the 'New Immigrant' Working Class." *Journal of American Ethnic History* 16(3): 3–44.
Brodkin, K. (1998). *How Jews Became White Folks and What That Says About Race in America.* New Brunswick, NJ: Rutgers University Press.
Brody, D. (2001). "Charismatic History: Pros and Cons." *International Labor and Working-Class History* 60: 43–7.
Brubaker, R. and F. Cooper (2000). "Beyond Identity." *Theory and Society* 29: 1–47.
Bryce-LaPorte, R.S. (1972). "Black Immigrants: The Experience of Invisibility and Inequality." *Journal of Black Studies* 3: 29–56.
Buff, R. (2001). *Immigration and the Political Economy of Home: West Indian Brooklyn and American Indian Minneapolis, 1945–1992.* Berkeley and Los Angeles: University of California Press.
Conzen, K.N. (1989). "Ethnicity as Festive Culture: Nineteenth-century German America on Parade." In W. Sollors, ed., *The Invention of Ethnicity.* New York: Oxford University Press, pp. 44–76.

Conzen, K.N. and D. Gerber, E. Morawska, G. Pozetta, and R. Vecoli (1992). "The Invention of Ethnicity: A Perspective from the U.S.A." *Journal of American Ethnic History* 12: 3–42.

Dixon, H. (1982). "Who Ever Heard of a Black Cuban?" *Afro-Hispanic Review* 1: 3–10.

Espiritu, Y.L. (1997). *Asian American Women and Men*. Thousand Oaks, CA: Sage.

Foner, N. (2000). *From Ellis Island to JFK: New York's Two Great Waves of Immigration*. New Haven, CT: Yale University Press.

Gans, H. (1979)."Symbolic Ethnicity: The Future of Ethnic Groups and Cultures in America." *Ethnic and Racial Studies* 2(1): 1–20.

Greenbaum, S.D. (2002). *More Than Black: Afro-Cubans in Tampa*. Gainesville: University Press of Florida.

Guglielmo, T. (2003). *White on Arrival: Italians, Race, Color, and Power in Chicago, 1890–1945*. New York: Oxford University Press.

Halter, M. (1993). *Between Race and Ethnicity: Cape Verdean American Immigrants, 1860–1965*. Urbana: University of Illinois Press.

—— (2000). *Shopping for Identity: The Marketing of Ethnicity*. New York: Schocken Books.

Herberg, W. (1955). *Protestant, Catholic and Jew*. New York: Doubleday.

Hollinger, D.A. (1995). *Postethnic America*. New York: Basic Books.

Ignatiev, N. (1995). *How the Irish Became White*. New York: Routledge.

Isajiw, W. (1974). "Definitions of Ethnicity." *Ethnicity* 1: 111–24.

Jacobson, M. (1998). *Whiteness of a Different Color: European Immigrants and the Alchemy of Race*. Cambridge, MA: Harvard University Press.

Kasinitz, P. (1992). *Caribbean New York: Black Immigrants and the Politics of Race*. Ithaca, NY: Cornell University Press.

Kibria, N. (2002). *Becoming Asian American: Second Generation Chinese and Korean American Identities*. Baltimore, MD: Johns Hopkins University Press.

Kurashige, L. (2002). *Japanese American Celebration and Conflict: A History of Ethnic Identity and Festival in Los Angeles, 1934–1990*. Berkeley and Los Angeles: University of California Press.

Lopez, I.H. (1996). *White by Law: the Legal Construction of Race*. New York: New York University Press.

Mead, M. (1975). "Ethnicity and Anthropology in America." In G. DeVos and L. Romanucci-Ross, eds., *Ethnic Identity: Cultural Continuities and Change*. Palo Alto, CA: Mayfield, pp. 173–97.

Reid, I.A. (1970). *The Negro Immigrant: His Background, Characteristics and Social Adjustment, 1899–1937* [1939]. New York: AMS Press.

Rodriguez, C.E. (1989). *Puerto Ricans: Born in the USA*. Boston: Unwin Hyman.

Rodriguez, R. (2002). *Brown: The Last Discovery of America*. New York: Viking Press.

Roediger, D.R. (1991). *Wages of Whiteness: Race and the Making of the American Working Class*. New York: Verso.

Rohrl, V.J. (1996). "The Anthropology of Race: A Study of Looking at Race." *Race, Gender, and Class* 2(2): 85–97.

Sanchez, G.J. (1993). *Becoming Mexican American: Ethnicity, Culture and Identity in Chicano Los Angeles, 1900–1945*. New York: Oxford University Press.

Saxton, A. (1990). *The Rise and Fall of the White Republic: Class Politics and Mass Culture in Nineteenth-Century America*. New York: Verso.

Schultz, A.R. (1994). *Ethnicity on Parade: Inventing the Norwegian American Through Celebration*. Amherst: University of Massachusetts Press.

Sinke, S. (1992). "Tulips are Blooming in Holland, Michigan: Analysis of a Dutch-American Festival." In M. D'Innocenzo and J. Sirefman, eds., *Immigration and Ethnicity: American Society – "Melting Pot" or "Salad Bowl"*? Westport, CT: Greenwood Press, pp. 3–14.

Sollors, W., ed. (1989). *The Invention of Ethnicity*. New York: Oxford University Press.

Stafford, S.B. (1987). "The Haitians: The Cultural Meaning of Race and Ethnicity." In
    N. Foner, ed., *New Immigrants in New York*. New York: Columbia University Press,
    pp. 131–58.
Thernstrom, S., ed. (1980). *Harvard Encyclopedia of American Ethnic Groups*. Cambridge,
    MA: Harvard University Press.
Waters, M.C. (1990). *Ethnic Options: Choosing Identities in America*. Berkeley and Los
    Angeles: University of California Press.
Wood, R. (1998). "Tourist Ethnicity: A Brief Itinerary." *Ethnic and Racial Studies* 21(2):
    218–42.
Woodward, C.V. (1958). "The Search for Southern Identity." *Virginia Quarterly Review* 34:
    321–38.

CHAPTER EIGHT

Nativism and Prejudice Against Immigrants

TYLER ANBINDER

Just as interest in immigration history has increased tremendously over the past 20 years, so too has interest in the history of anti-immigrant sentiment, or "nativism." Once rarely used outside of academia, the term "nativism" became a staple of editorials and op-ed columns in the 1990s, its use increasing nearly 10 times from the previous decade according to the LexisNexis Academic newspaper database. Scholars also devote far more attention to nativism than they did in the past, when they focused primarily upon the physical, psychological, and economic adjustments made by those who immigrated. Some recent interest in anti-immigrant sentiment has undoubtedly resulted from the perception that contemporary nativism is on the rise, but the study of nativism has increased primarily because of a heightened awareness that anti-immigrant prejudice has for centuries played an important role in shaping the experiences of the American immigrant and the history of the United States.

Because the term "nativism" has only recently entered the popular vocabulary, there is no consensus as to the precise meaning of the term. Some use the word to describe the movement to restrict the flow of immigrants into the United States. But this definition is inadequate, especially for the period before 1880, when even the most die-hard nativists opposed limiting the flow of newcomers to the relatively underpopulated North American continent. Other scholars focus on mindset rather than policy goals when defining nativism, describing it as an ethnocentric ideology that seeks to maintain the racial, religious, and political status quo of the nation. I believe that both worldview and a desire to roll back the impact of immigrants are essential components of nativism. In this chapter, therefore, the term "nativist" will be used to describe someone who fears and resents immigrants and their impact on the Untied States, and who wants to take some action against them, be it through violence, immigration restriction, or placing limits on the rights of newcomers already in the United States. "Nativism" describes the movement to bring the goals of nativists to fruition.

Nativism has been a factor in American life since the early 1600s. Almost as soon as the English, Dutch, French, and Spanish began settling North America, their colonists began trying to deter other religious and ethnic groups from joining them. The scholarly study of nativism, on the other hand, dates back only to the beginning

of the twentieth century. The first book on the subject resulted from a political
science dissertation written at Columbia University by Louis Dow Scisco. Published
in 1901 as *Political Nativism in New York State*, the monograph chronicled anti-
immigrant sentiment in New York in the first half of the nineteenth century, focusing
primarily on the rise and decline of the Know Nothing Party of the 1850s. Yet the
appearance of Scisco's book did not motivate other historians to study nativism.
No other significant work on the subject would appear for another 25 years. Interest
in nativism did not die altogether, but it became the province of amateur historians
writing in county historical journals (G. Schneider 1900; Shenk 1906–9; Hensel
1915). Scisco himself abandoned the study of nativism, devoting the rest of his life
to documenting the history of colonial Maryland.

The first sustained scholarly interest in nativism began in the 1920s, when historian
Richard J. Purcell's graduate students at Catholic University in Washington, DC began
to write dissertations on antebellum nativism. Just as Columbia's William Dunning
stimulated the study of Reconstruction, Purcell sparked interest in nativism, and by
the late 1930s his students had produced theses examining anti-immigrant sentiment
(primarily anti-Irish and anti-Catholic feeling) in virtually every state (see, for example,
M. McConville 1928; McGrath 1930; Thomas 1936; Noonan 1938; Gohmann 1938;
Fell 1941; McGann 1944). The content of the studies produced under Purcell's
tutelage rarely varied. His students described the history of anti-Catholicism in a
particular state, recounted the Know Nothing Party's success or failure in various
elections, and applauded the movement's quick demise. These monographs also
focused particular attention on controversies involving public funding of Catholic
schools (something Catholics wanted and Protestants vehemently opposed), the
use of the Bible in public schools (something Protestants wanted but Catholics
vehemently opposed), and the anti-Catholic legislation that nativists advocated.

Although the studies conducted at Catholic University assembled a good deal of
factual information, they suffered from several limitations. In most cases, Purcell's
students relied too heavily on the testimony of Know Nothing opponents when
gathering evidence for their indictments of the nativist party, and as a result their
depictions of the Know Nothings are one-dimensional and often unconvincing.
Furthermore, because their primary goal was to document the history of American
anti-Catholicism, Purcell's students rarely acknowledged that factors other than
religious animosity might have contributed to the Know Nothings' remarkable success. That the authors of these theses were almost invariably women indicates that,
despite Purcell's efforts, the profession still considered nativism a subject of only
marginal interest.

The lack of respect given to studies of nativism began to change in the late 1930s.
At Harvard, historian Arthur Meier Schlesinger had been encouraging his students
to study immigration, until then a subject of little interest to scholars at the United
States' elite universities. One result of Schlesinger's prodding was the publication in
1941 of Oscar Handlin's path-breaking book, *Boston's Immigrants.* Another was
the release in 1938 of Ray Allen Billington's *The Protestant Crusade, 1800–1860:
A Study of the Origins of American Nativism.*

The Protestant Crusade is an exceedingly thorough account of anti-immigrant
sentiment in the United States from 1820 to 1860, with an overwhelming focus on
anti-Catholicism as the source of antebellum nativism. Every riot, every convent

burning, and every nativist fraternal order, both major and minor, seems to be recounted. But *The Protestant Crusade* differs in several important ways from the earlier studies of nativism. First, Billington considers the nativists on their own terms, making far more use of the nativists' own writings than had previous chroniclers of anti-immigrant sentiment. He was also far less judgmental than Purcell's students. He admits that antebellum nativists were "overzealous," yet for the most part he lets readers draw their own conclusions about the merits of the nativists' agenda (Billington 1938, p. 430).

Billington's most important contribution to the historiography of nativism was his focus on the intellectual history of the movement. About half of the book's 500 pages are devoted to an analysis of the voluminous writings of pre-Civil War nativists. Anti-Catholic publications by Samuel F.B. Morse, Lyman Beecher, "Maria Monk," and others only became familiar to professional historians outside of Catholic circles due to Billington's efforts. Billington also brought the story of nativism to a significant number of non-academics, as his book was published by a trade press, Macmillan, and was reissued 14 years later by another trade publisher. Yet nativism was still not a topic to build a career upon. Like Scisco, Billington never wrote about nativism again, though he did enjoy a long and distinguished career as a historian of the American West, teaching at Smith College and Northwestern University, winning the Bancroft Prize (for his biography of Frederick Jackson Turner), and serving as president of the Organization of American Historians (Billington 1949, 1956, 1971, 1973).

With the anti-Catholic roots of antebellum nativism having been thoroughly chronicled both by Purcell's students and by Billington, it was perhaps inevitable that subsequent writers would begin to question the overwhelming emphasis on religious hatred found in their studies. This skepticism first manifested itself in writings about the Know Nothings, still by mid-century the most popular subject for those examining American nativism. The American Party (as the Know Nothings eventually renamed themselves) captured a dozen governorships, more than 100 Congressional races, and at least 1,000 legislative seats in 1854 and 1855. No other nativist party before or after came close to matching the Know Nothings' electoral success, so it seemed reasonable to wonder if factors other than anti-Catholicism might have contributed to their popularity. A number of political historians soon published studies suggesting that the Know Nothings' anti-Catholic harangues were largely insincere diversions meant to deflect attention from the slavery issue then polarizing the nation. Noting that the Know Nothings' own presidential candidate, Millard Fillmore, had sent his daughters to Catholic schools, these historians argued that the Know Nothings' unprecedented success was due largely to Americans' desire to save the Union, rather than persecute Catholics (Carman and Luthin 1940, pp. 217–18; Nevins 1947, p. 401).

After World War II, Congress began to reconsider American immigration laws, in part because the manifest biases in these statutes (such as the near total ban on Asians and the severe restrictions on southern and eastern Europeans) were an embarrassment in the propaganda battles of the early Cold War. In the 1920s when these statutes had been enacted, a number of academics had argued in favor of these restrictions on the grounds that the southern and eastern Europeans being barred from the United States were innately inferior to immigrants of Anglo-Saxon origin. But when a presidential commission was organized after World War II to study the issue further, Handlin submitted a report to the commission condemning the nativist underpinnings of the immigration quotas put in place in the 1920s. Although the revisions enacted by Congress in 1952 made only token changes to the discriminatory quota system, Handlin's role in the hearings indicated that academics could no longer be counted upon to legitimize the racism that lay at the heart of American immigration policy (President's Commission on Immigration and Naturalization 1952, pp. 327–33, 1839–63).

The most influential studies of nativism, however, were still being written by intellectual historians, and the publication in 1955 of two landmark works of American history, Richard Hofstadter's *Age of Reform* and John Higham's *Strangers in the Land,* marked the long overdue emergence of nativism from the fringes of historical study. In some ways, *Strangers in the Land* is a sequel to *The Protestant Crusade.* Higham's work begins at exactly the point where Billington's concluded and, like Billington's work, Higham's is encyclopedic and based on a remarkably thorough reading of the writings of nativists, both prominent and obscure. Higham's thesis, like Billington's, is also relatively straightforward and unremarkable. Higham asserts that nativism from 1860 to 1925 arose from both fundamental cultural differences between natives and newcomers and specific events and movements of the period that enflamed these cultural differences. Higham emphasizes the economic causes of nativism in the half of the book that addresses the late nineteenth century; while the second half of the book focuses upon the protection of the American "race" as the most important motivator of early twentieth-century nativists.

Yet *Strangers in the Land* is a far more sophisticated and erudite book than any short summary of its main thesis can convey. Whereas Billington merely documented the long cavalcade of authors and events that inspired the rise of antebellum nativism, Higham explained nativism as a complex ideology, examining the intertwined threads of nationalism, anti-Catholicism, anti-radicalism, and racism that were woven together to form the fabric of twentieth-century nativism. Two other facets of the book make it especially impressive. First, as Billington himself noted in the *Saturday Review, Strangers in the Land* abounds in "the sparkling prose of a gifted writer." In addition, while Higham was just 34 when he published the book, it is chock-full of what Billington aptly called "the sweeping generalizations of a seasoned scholar" (Billington 1955, p. 18). The book contains thoroughly convincing thumbnail sketches of an extremely diverse group of protagonists: from blue-blooded ministers to sleazy politicos, from Social Gospel reformers to battle-hardened labor leaders, and from haughty Harvard dons to charismatic Klan leaders. Higham read so widely, described so many interesting events, and wrote such insightful profiles of so many important movements and people that readers inevitably find themselves awed by the remarkable sweep of Higham's study.

Higham's work is not without its faults. The manner in which he makes sweeping characterizations of entire decades in his chapter titles ("The Nationalist Nineties," "The Tribal Twenties," etc.) strikes the reader as simplistic and thus detracts from the overall sophistication of the study. Higham also devotes no effort to identifying what kinds of Americans joined the nativist movements that he describes. One wonders exactly *who* composed the nativist rank and file. Higham's book about anti-immigrant sentiment also has remarkably few immigrants in it – the reader often yearns to know how the newcomers reacted when faced with such hatred. Finally,

Higham depicts nativism as a movement directed exclusively by white, native-born Protestants, ignoring the many instances of inter-ethnic conflict that wracked the United States in the post-Civil War years. Even Billington had recognized the significant contributions that immigrants (albeit mostly Protestant immigrants) had made to the antebellum nativist cause. Nativism to Higham was above all an intellectual phenomenon, not something experienced firsthand in the streets or in the workplace. He does describe a few particularly violent episodes, such as the lynching of Leo Frank, the anti-Italian riot in New Orleans in 1891, and some brutally suppressed strikes, but to Higham nativism was something that was preached rather than practiced. One might argue in Higham's defense that in an era before social history became popular, one could not expect scholars to consider such subjects. But historians had addressed such topics before. Syracuse University historian Robert J. Ernst had published an account of workplace nativism in New York City in 1948, while the first systematic study of a nativist political party's membership had been published by George H. Haynes, a historian at the Worcester Polytechnic Institute, as early as 1896 (Ernst 1948; Haynes 1896). Nonetheless, *Strangers in the Land* is a brilliant piece of intellectual history, a work of remarkable breadth and insight that has become the benchmark against which all other studies of nativism are inevitably judged.

While *Strangers in the Land* has had a lasting influence on American historiography, and especially immigration history, the book did not make a big splash initially, in part because it was published by a small and relatively insignificant university press (Rutgers), and in part because the subject was not one likely to attract a large audience in 1955. But Richard Hofstadter's *The Age of Reform: From Bryan to F.D.R.*, which like *Strangers in the Land* was released in the autumn of 1955, suffered from neither of these problems. Published by a distinguished trade press, Alfred A. Knopf, *The Age of Reform* garnered immediate and widespread attention and praise in the popular media, became a best-seller, won the Pulitzer Prize in history, and quickly sparked intense debates about its depictions of nativism within American reform movements.

The *Age of Reform* is typically cited as a prime example of "consensus history," a purported trend during the early years of the Cold War in which historians discounted the possibility that sharp ideological conflict had ever divided the American people. Consensus history is sometimes said to have been characterized by an excessively celebratory tone, as these works usually focus upon how and why the United States became the freest, richest, and "greatest" nation on earth. Higham, in fact, was the first to identify and condemn "consensus" as a trend in historical writing of the period, complaining in 1957 that a compulsion to downplay "divisive forces in American history" had, for example, driven Handlin to underestimate the extent of American anti-Semitism before 1890 (Higham 1957, p. 561). In one of his many articles on the subject, Higham named Hofstadter first when listing the most important "consensus historians" (Higham 1974, p. 5).

Why Higham became obsessed with "consensus history" is not clear. Perhaps he felt that the trend explained why his own work on nativism and anti-Semitism (the subject to which he turned after *Strangers in the Land* was published) was not given the attention he believed it deserved. He certainly thought that he had recognized a pattern in historical writing and undoubtedly felt it his duty as an intellectual historian to draw attention to it and consider its consequences. But although historians still cling to consensus as the defining trend in historical writing in the years after World War II, I would argue that the idea of a consensus school of history in this period is a myth (or if not a myth then terribly exaggerated). There is far more conflict present in the works of consensus historians such as Hofstadter than Higham was willing to admit. *Class* conflict may not have been a popular subject for historians in the 1950s, but a scholar of nativism and bigotry such as Higham ought to have recognized, especially in the wake of the Holocaust, that religious, ethnic, and racial bigotry could be just as divisive and deadly as class conflict.

That Hofstadter should be caricatured by Higham as a consensus historian is especially surprising inasmuch as Hofstadter found nativist conflict in places that even Higham had not noticed it, and Hofstadter's emphasis on anti-immigrant sentiment in the Populist and Progressive movements became one of the most controversial aspects of *The Age of Reform*. "Populism and Progressivism were in considerable part colored by the reaction to this immigrant stream among the native elements of the population," Hofstadter wrote in the book's introduction. Higham had virtually ignored the Populists in *Strangers in the Land*, noting the anti-Semitism of one of their leaders, Ignatius Donnelly, while at the same time describing the Minnesotans' opposition to the restrictionist efforts of the American Protective Association. But Hofstadter found nativism to be a defining aspect of Populism, emphasizing its presence in its campaign platforms and in the writings of its leaders such as Donnelly, Tom Watson, and Mary Elizabeth Lease. Hofstadter argued that the Progressives were likewise motivated not merely by a desire to repair the societal ills brought on by industrialization and robber barons, but by a wish to roll back the influence of the immigrants who worked in the magnates' factories as well. The Progressive impulse, he concluded, "was strongly tainted with nativism" (Hofstadter 1955, pp. 9, 61–93, 178; Higham 1955, pp. 82, 94, 116–22).

While *The Age of Reform* received overwhelmingly favorable reviews, it created a firestorm of controversy within academic circles, especially among midwesterners who did not endorse a characterization of their Populist ancestors as bigoted reactionaries. These critics insisted that *all* native-born Americans harbored nativist and anti-Semitic views in the late nineteenth century (these were the true "consensus historians"!), and that nativism was therefore irrelevant to the Populists' story. Hofstadter's emphasis on the Populists' "status anxiety," rather than their real economic grievances, said these critics, made the Populists seem like irrational fools rather than admirable resisters of economic oppression (Pollack 1960, 1962; Woodward 1960; Nugent 1963). A few historians who had chronicled the depths of American nativism and anti-Semitism came to Hofstadter's defense (most notably Handlin 1965), but Hofstadter's interpretation of Populism did not win many converts. Hofstadter himself later admitted that he had erred in not emphasizing that some of the Populists' economic grievances were legitimate and that nativism and anti-Semitism were widespread outside of Populist and Progressive circles (Collins 1989, pp. 156–7). Yet by pointing out in *The Age of Reform* that nativism suffused huge swaths of the mainstream electorate, Hofstadter's book played a vital role in insuring that Americans would no longer view nativism as a fringe movement that had little impact on the major currents of their history.

The influence of *The Age of Reform* went well beyond its historical content, for although Hofstadter's analysis of the Populists and Progressives had many critics, historians did find the concept of status anxiety fascinating. Soon the idea began cropping up in American historical works in all fields. Status anxiety neatly explained why relatively wealthy and comfortable colonists would foment the American Revolution. Others used the concept to account for the prominence of once-conservative ministers in the abolition and temperance movements, and to explain why southerners would secede despite Republican promises not to interfere with slavery where it already existed. Historians of nativism became enamored of status anxiety as well. In 1958, in the first of many essays in which he attempted to refine his original analysis of nativism in *Strangers in the Land*, Higham placed much more stress on "status rivalries" as a cause of nativist outbreaks than he had in his book. Other historians subsequently made the same argument (Higham 1958, p. 151; Berthoff 1960, pp. 504–5; Curran 1963; Higham 2000).

The Age of Reform influenced the study of nativism in other ways as well. Implicit in Hofstadter's book was the contention that Americans obsessed with supposed "conspiratorial force[s]" threatening the nation too often launched into "psychic sprees that purport to be moral crusades" (Hofstadter 1955, p. 17). Hofstadter made this argument more explicit in an influential essay published in 1966 called "The Paranoid Style in American Politics" (a shorter version had appeared in *Harper's Magazine* in November 1964). American politicians, observed Hofstadter, often fed on voters' paranoia and susceptibility to conspiracy theories to whip Americans into a frenzy of hatred and bigotry. He cited nativist movements as one of the prime examples of this paranoid "frame of mind" (Hofstadter 1966, pp. 19–23).

Many writers subsequently interpreted the history of American nativism as an example of the paranoid style. Social scientists equated nativism explicitly with McCarthyism and other examples of twentieth-century "right-wing extremism" (Mandelbaum 1964; Lipset and Raab 1970). Others took a less histrionic approach but came to similar conclusions (Renshaw 1968). David Brion Davis, like Higham and Hofstadter an intellectual historian, produced one of the most sophisticated studies in this vein. Davis argued persuasively that the many similarities in the conspiracy theories espoused by anti-Masonic, anti-Mormon, and anti-Catholic writers in the antebellum years indicated that these apparently dissimilar movements must have all sprung from the same "fears, prejudices, hopes, and perhaps even unconscious desires." Given that these three groups often appealed to widely divergent constituencies, Davis posited, historians such as Higham were wrong to seek the roots of nativism in ethnic animosities or status rivalries between specific social groups. Instead, Davis contended, such movements must instead reflect more "fundamental tensions within a culture," in this case the "rootless environment" of the pre-Civil War years. "Shaken by bewildering social change," he concluded, "the nativist found unity and meaning by conspiring against imaginary conspiracies." Davis did not state, however, exactly which social changes might have inspired antebellum nativists (Davis 1960, pp. 205, 224). In fact, one might well ask when in the past Americans have *not* been subject to bewildering social change. A few years after Davis's article appeared, Stanley Coben made a similar argument to explain the nativism rife in the Red Scare of 1919–20 (Coben 1964).

The historian who best explained how social transformations might encourage nativism was Michael F. Holt. In "The Politics of Impatience," published in the *Journal of American History* in 1973, Holt ascribed the Know Nothings' success to "a general popular malaise and sense of dislocation caused by rapid social and economic change in those years." He argued that the Know Nothings drew most of their support from workingmen, both artisans and unskilled laborers, whose liveli-hoods were threatened by workplace mechanization and cheap immigrant labor. In the years of the Know Nothings' greatest success, Holt insisted,

> workers and many from the huge floating population – men who appeared one year in a town's city directory and were gone the next, probably because they had left in search of a job – voted for the first time. Because these men suffered most from the traumatic economic changes of the decade, they became most susceptible to the cries of Catholic conspiracy raised at that time. (Holt 1973, pp. 313, 329–30)

Holt could muster no evidence for his claim that the Know Nothings were particularly popular among workingmen (after all, manual workers supplied the majority of votes to *all* parties in urban areas). Subsequent discoveries of Know Nothing lodge minute books, in fact, indicate that members in Massachusetts and New York were no more likely to be manual workers than the general population (Anbinder 1992, pp. 34–6). Nor could Holt prove that the Know Nothings attracted huge numbers of first-time voters. Holt's interpretation nonetheless be-came widely accepted. In 1989, economic historian Robert W. Fogel propounded the same explanation for the Know Nothings' popularity in his far-ranging book *Without Consent or Contract: The Rise and Fall of American Slavery*.

That Holt, an unabashed historian of parties and party systems, should have devoted so much attention to nativism reflected the influence of one of Hofstadter's former Columbia colleagues, Lee Benson. Whereas Hofstadter had hoped to make historical writing more literary with *The Age of Reform*, Benson was convinced that history should move in the other direction, toward the empirical rigor of the social sciences. Benson believed that historians too often based their assessments of voting behavior on the biased testimony of the candidates themselves. Scholars typically assumed, Benson noted, that if one candidate defeated another, voters must have found the campaign propaganda of the winner more appealing than that of the loser. Benson argued that only an analysis of more objective sources, such as voting records and census data that could establish the socio-economic background of the voters, would allow historians to divine the true motivations of the American electorate (Benson 1961, p. 81).

Benson decided to evaluate his theories by examining the politics of the Jacksonian era, whose leading parties (according to the historical orthodoxy of the day) had been the plebian Jacksonian Democrats and the more well-to-do Whigs. Using New York State as a test case, Benson found that wealth did not differentiate Democrats from Whigs. Leaders of both parties, he found, were relatively prosperous, and the counties that tended to vote Whig were no wealthier than those that overwhelmingly supported the Democrats. To formulate an alternate explanation of Jacksonian-era voting behavior, Benson turned to the work of sociologist Robert K. Merton, who had found, in Benson's words, that the "actions, attitudes, and values" of one societal group were often chosen because they contradicted the actions, attitudes, and values of the group "to which it stands in opposition" (Benson 1961, p. 27). Benson argued that "ethnic and religious pressures" were the characteristics that voters used to define themselves and their enemies. Areas with large Catholic concentrations tended to vote Democratic in the Jacksonian era, he found, while counties with certain types of Protestants voted primarily Whig. A voter's ethnic background, concluded Benson, predicted voting behavior far better than income or occupation (Benson 1961, p. 163).

Benson's thesis, though provocative and original, had its weaknesses. He railed against the use of impressionistic sources, but used precisely such sources as the basis for many of his conclusions. A huge portion of his argument rested on an analysis of the election results of 1844, a year in which religious strife between Catholics and Protestants reached unprecedented levels. Had he relied upon data from the depression-era contests of 1837 and 1838, he might have been forced to re-evaluate his conclusions. Nonetheless, Benson's work inspired many historians to change the way they looked at both elections and political behavior. And by emphasizing the importance of "ethno-cultural" issues such as temperance and public funding for parochial schools, subjects whose debates were often tinged with nativism, Benson legitimized the study of anti-immigrant sentiment for subsequent generations of political historians (Benson 1961, pp. 196–7, 201–5, 216–69).

Benson's influence was far reaching. Scholars calling themselves "new political historians" began hunting for nativism and other indications of ethno-cultural conflict throughout American political history. Building on Benson's work, Joel Silbey and Ronald P. Formisano found that nativism abounded in the Jacksonian period. Paul Kleppner compiled evidence of anti-immigrant sentiment in the politics of the post-Civil War years. But such scholars focused most intently on the 1850s, because the unprecedented success of the Know Nothings seemed to indicate that the pre-Civil War decade constituted the high-water mark of nineteenth-century nativism. Holt, Silbey, Formisano, and William E. Gienapp wrote books and articles in which they insisted that ethno-cultural issues were even more important than slavery during the first half of the 1850s, when the party system pitting Whigs against Democrats was still in place. Breaking with the traditional interpretation of the period, these scholars argued that nativism and the political issues that grew out of it – rather than slavery – destroyed the Whig Party and with it the "Second Party System" of Whigs and Democrats. Only later, they concluded, in late 1855 or early 1856, did slavery manage to overtake nativism and become the dominant political issue in the nation, though even by that point, they insisted, nativism remained a potent part of the Republicans' appeal (Kleppner 1970; Silbey 1973; Formisano 1971, 1983, 1994; Holt 1969, 1978, 1999; Gienapp 1985, 1987).

Nativism had once been portrayed as a movement led by cranks and fanatics. Hofstadter then recast the nativist impulse as a major undercurrent of two of the more respectable and well-known third-party movements in American history. By the 1970s, the new political historians were arguing that nativism was a central part of the ideologies of the mainstream Whig and Republican parties. The place of nativism in the American historical imagination had certainly come a long way.

Yet political historians were not the only ones who discovered nativism in the 1960s and 1970s. Other scholars began to insist that the histories of common men and women were just as important as those of the political, social, and intellectual elite. Their demand that history be written "from the bottom up" revolutionized the discipline and prompted unprecedented interest in social history. The increasing popularity of social history, in turn, often led historians to focus their attention on nativism.

The emergence of African American history from the fringes of the profession, for example, prompted more interest in the Ku Klux Klan, which during its revival in the 1920s was as much a nativist as a racist organization (Alexander 1965; Chalmers 1965; Jackson 1967). Another subfield that blossomed during this period was labor history. Once primarily interested in the study of unions and their organizers, labor historians in the 1970s began to devote far more attention to the workers themselves. Scholars looking to discover why unions were so weak in the pre-Civil War years and why socialism never became very popular in the post-bellum era often concluded that inter-ethnic conflict between workers made the unification of the American working class impossible. These historians wrote some of the most sophisticated studies of nativism produced up to that point. When Herbert Gutman published a landmark essay on American attitudes toward work, he likewise found it imperative to discuss nativism (Dubofsky 1961; Montgomery 1972; Gutman 1973; Gitelman 1973; Wilentz 1984).

These new social and political historians ended the intellectual historians' domination of the study of nativism. In sharp contrast to scholars such as Higham, social historians *did* want to know how nativism was experienced in the streets and in the workplace. Anti-immigrant violence, as well as the nativism inspired by immigrant rioting, thus became topics of intense interest (Foner 1969; Feldberg 1975; Renner 1976; Rorabaugh 1976; Adelman 1976). The social and cultural histories of nativism began to intrigue historians as well. Even the artistic manifestations of nativism were fair game, especially the art of German immigrant Thomas Nast, whose anti-Catholic images in *Harper's Weekly* are still the best-known visual expressions of nineteenth-century American nativism (Keller 1968; Curtis 1971).

But it was in one particular subfield of social history – immigration history – that discussions of nativism became especially common. Ever since historians had begun to write about immigrants, community studies such as Handlin's *Boston's Immigrants* and Robert J. Ernst's *Immigrant Life in New York City* had dominated this portion of the discipline. And such works invariably included short discussions of the discrimination immigrants faced. The most important immigration histories published as part of the social history boom of the 1970s, such as Jay Dolan's *The Immigrant Church*, Kathleen Conzen's *Immigrant Milwaukee*, Irving Howe's *World of Our Fathers*, and Virginia Yans-McLaughlin's *Family and Community*, all addressed nativism. These works continued to shift the study of nativism away from the perspective of the nativist and toward the viewpoint of the immigrants, as nativism became a standard feature in analyses of immigrants' adjustment to life in America (Handlin 1941; Ernst 1949; Dolan 1975; Conzen 1976; Howe 1976; Yans-McLaughlin 1977).

For certain immigrant groups, nativism has played an especially central role in their experiences in the United States. Asian immigrants, for example, have been persecuted in one form or another almost from the day they began arriving in the United States in significant numbers. The nativism directed at them has been especially persistent and deep-rooted, unlike that focused upon European immigrants, which has tended to ebb and flow with the tides of immigration and with changes in the domestic political situation. Anti-Chinese rioting in the post-Civil War west, for instance, persisted and even increased in the late 1880s, years *after* Chinese immigration had been severely curtailed by the Exclusion Act of 1882. Historians of the Asian American experience have thoroughly documented this violence as well as the legal discrimination suffered by Asian Americans (Daniels 1962; Miller 1969; Saxton 1971; Daniels 1978; Takaki 1989; Wunder 1992; McClain 1994; Salyer 1995).

The study of nativism directed at Asian immigrants was long overdue, as earlier generations of nativism experts such as Higham had virtually ignored anti-Asian legislation and violence. But anti-Asian nativism has remained something of a field apart. Those who examine the subject tend to focus solely on the Chinese or the Japanese, and they rarely compare discrimination against Asian immigrants to that perpetrated against European or even Latino newcomers. While these scholars may be attempting to emphasize that Asian immigrants have been treated differently from other newcomers, their studies do not typically make any effort to substantiate this point. We might learn something by juxtaposing the discrimination faced by Asian immigrants with that of European immigrants (or even native-born African Americans). The study of anti-Asian nativism has also been dominated for too long by works that merely chronicle court cases or list riots, though some more innovative works published at the turn of the twenty-first century indicate that the scholarship in this field is finally beginning to mature (Gyory 1998; Chan 2000; E. Lee 2003; Aarim-Heriot 2003).

It is noteworthy that at the same time that the study of anti-Asian sentiment was blossoming, interest in anti-Semitism, another facet of nativism, was waning. American anti-Semitism had been the subject of countless books and articles even before the social history revolution of the 1960s and 1970s had made nativism a more popular subject among academics. But those who wrote about the subject before the 1980s, like those who studied anti-Asian sentiment, usually discussed anti-Semitism without much reference to other forms of American nativism. These scholars tended to focus on the relationship of American anti-Semitism to anti-Jewish sentiment worldwide. Only occasionally, such as during the debate sparked by Hofstadter's depiction of Populist anti-Semitism, did anti-Semitism enter mainstream American history debates. But in the 1980s, the historical study of anti-Semitism did revive, and scholars by that point usually did place the phenomenon within the wider nativist context (Ribuffo 1983; Mayo 1988; Rausch 1993; Dinnerstein 1994; Jaher 1994).

A further boost to the study of nativism came with the rise of "multiculturalism." In the first three-quarters of the twentieth century, Americans generally believed that immigrants should assimilate as quickly and as completely as possible. By the late 1970s, however, many began to challenge this supposed responsibility to bury one's ethnic origins. The phenomenal popularity of Alex Haley's *Roots* (1976) contributed to this trend, as did the success of movements to fight discrimination against Mexican and Asian Americans. The last two decades of the twentieth century thus witnessed an unprecedented outpouring of ethnic pride.

With Americans increasingly willing to celebrate their multicultural heritages, scholars began to rewrite the history of the United States with an increased emphasis on the country's ethnic and racial heterogeneity, and authors made discussions of nativism a staple of these works. Even books devoted entirely to the history of American prejudice began to proliferate, and these authors devoted more attention to anti-immigrant sentiment than previous histories of American bigotry (Lipset and Raab

1970; Leonard and Parmet 1971; Curran 1975; Greeley 1977; Bennett 1988; Perlmutter 1992). But many of these writers seemed more determined to chronicle famous instances of discrimination rather than thoroughly understand them. Given that most northern Know Nothings were ardent supporters of the anti-slavery movement, for example, it made little sense for authors such as David Bennett to characterize the Know Nothings as part of the "far right" in American politics (Bennett 1988; Anbinder 1992, pp. 99–101, 145–57). Far more disturbing was the tendency of some of these surveys to insinuate that ethnic and racial minorities were only the victims of prejudice and never the perpetrators. Ronald Takaki's *A Different Mirror*, for instance, chronicles countless examples of prejudice and persecution perpetrated against immigrants and their offspring, but because he includes no examples of the immigrants' own prejudices, the reader is left with the implausible impression that they do not harbor any (Takaki 1993).

Had Takaki wanted to devote more attention to immigrants' animosity towards other immigrants, his efforts would have been hampered by the terrible paucity of work on the subject. One might have imagined that Nathan Glazer and Daniel Patrick Moynihan's *Beyond the Melting Pot*, which addressed inter-ethnic and racial tensions in New York, would have inspired more work in this area. But historians have virtually ignored the subject. Even social scientists, who have examined the issue far more extensively, consider "ethnic conflict" a topic pertinent primarily in other parts of the world. While it may be true that inter-ethnic clashes in the United States have been less prevalent and deadly than elsewhere, ethnic antagonisms often played a major role in shaping immigrants' experiences. Only the ethnic tensions within the American Catholic church have received sustained attention. Remaining aspects of ethnic conflict in America are in need of further study (Glazer and Moynihan 1963; Bayor 1978; Stack 1979; Kuzniewski 1980; Otzak 1987, 1989; J. Lee 2002).

One reason so little has been published on inter-ethnic conflict is that so much of American immigration history has followed what one might call the "We Came, We Suffered, We Persevered, We Succeeded" paradigm. Such works, which dominated the field until recently, usually examine a single immigrant group in a particular city and are usually written by a member of the ethnic group in question. These studies document the arrival of the immigrants and the difficult living and working conditions they encountered. They describe the discrimination the immigrants faced at the hands of the natives and the strategies the newcomers used to combat such intolerance. And such works typically conclude with the immigrants assimilating (though not *too* thoroughly) and becoming "Americans." As long as so much immigration history clung to this paradigm, there was little chance that such authors would consider that their ancestors might have been as bigoted as the natives who persecuted them. Now that immigration history has grown more sophisticated, its practitioners need to devote more attention to the role of inter-ethnic (and even intra-ethnic) hostility in the shaping of American immigrant life.

While some scholars are beginning to recognize that immigrants can harbor as much prejudice as natives, others in recent years have suggested that the extent of American nativism has been exaggerated or that nativists too often are unfairly condemned without carefully considering the merits of their arguments. Richard Jensen, for example, has argued persuasively that the purported ubiquity of "No Irish

Need Apply" signs in the Civil War era is largely a myth. Robert Zeidel has suggested that nativism played a far smaller role in shaping the immigration restriction
laws of the 1920s than most historians have imagined. Other recent studies have
highlighted the Know Nothings' "progressive" views on slavery, workers' rights,
public education, and political reform. Peter Brimelow, a conservative columnist
(and immigrant from England) who advocates steep cuts in American immigration, has
made an even more provocative assertion, arguing that nativism is a healthy part of
the American political psyche, allowing Americans to protect their national character
and standard of living. While some may question this view, his assertion that not
everyone who wants to reduce America's immigration rate should be branded a nativist
is certainly true. Some without Brimelow's self-avowed policy agenda are coming to
similar conclusions. Echoing Holt and Davis, Michael Katerberg contends in an
article in the *American Quarterly* that the "parochial identities" that foster nativism
"offer a sense of rootedness that bureaucratic, consumerist societies probably cannot
provide." Nativism and the feelings that inspire it, he contends, are more "ironic"
than "tragic. . . . For good reasons, people are unable to live without them." These
provocative studies indicate that, at the start of the twenty-first century, histories of
nativism have reached a welcome new level of sophistication and complexity (Jensen
2002; Zeidel 2004; Taylor 2000; Voss-Hubbard 2002; Brimelow 1995; Katerberg
1995, p. 513).

The study of nativism in the new century is also more wide ranging than it has
ever been before; work in the field has moved in a variety of directions. One current
trend is a focus on the role of nativism in the shaping and enforcement of American
immigration restrictions, an issue that, until recently, had received little more than
passing attention (Gyory 1998; Hirobe 2001; E. Lee 2002; Luibhéid 2002; Tichenor
2002; Allerfeldt 2003; Doty 2003; Ngai 2003, 2004; Daniels 2004; Zeidel 2004).
Another trend in recent studies of nativism has been an increasingly nuanced depiction
of the role of nativism in nineteenth-century politics. Ward McAfee has recently
published a thorough and insightful study of the debate over public funding of
parochial schools in the 1870s and the anti-Catholicism and nativism that underlay
that debate. Bruce Levine has likewise written a thought-provoking article linking
the origins of the Know Nothing Party to "Whiggish bourgeois conservatives" who
were willing to limit the political rights of immigrants and others in order "to promote the development of [a] capitalist economy." Although Levine offers important
insight into the men who founded the Know Nothing Party, he never fully explains
why the Know Nothings attracted hundreds of thousands more members than did
previous nativist fraternal orders that were founded by the same men on the same
conservative, bourgeois basis (McAfee 1998; Levine 2001, pp. 486–8). Historians
have even begun to study contemporary nativism, something they almost never did
in the past, though most studies of that subject are still written by sociologists and
other social scientists (Sánchez 1997; Perea 1997; Reimers 1998; Barkan 2003).

Another recent historiographic trend is the increasing importance of nativism in
literary studies. One of the most influential works of literary criticism of the 1990s
was Walter Benn Michaels's *Our America: Nativism, Modernism, and Pluralism*, in
which Michaels argues that understanding American nativism is the key to appreciating the meanings of the modernist American literature of the 1920s. Nativism
and anti-Catholicism have also become far more prominent in recent studies of

nineteenth-century American literature, though these critics have noted that some American literary figures had an ambivalent and sometimes even sympathetic attitude towards Catholicism and its immigrant practitioners (Franchot 1994; Michaels 1995; Von Hallberg 1996; Adeeko 1998; Goluboff 2000).

The most influential historical subfield shaped in recent years by the study of nativism, however, is that of "whiteness" studies, whose seminal work is David R. Roediger's *The Wages of Whiteness* (1991). In the portion of his wide-ranging book pertinent to this chapter, Roediger argues that the prejudice faced by Irish immigrants in antebellum America was so intense that their very status as whites was thrown into question. Irish Americans' persecution of blacks in the workplace and in various riots was in large part a response to such nativism and represented the immigrants' attempt to prove their whiteness and establish their status as true Americans. Noel Ignatiev expanded upon Roediger's argument in his widely-read book *How the Irish Became White* (1995).

A much more nuanced study of immigrants and their perceived racial status is Matthew Frye Jacobson's *Whiteness of a Different Color* (1998). Jacobson contends that in the early days of the republic, Americans looked at people as either black or white. By the Civil War, however, after Irish and German immigrants had been pouring into the country at unprecedented rates for more than a decade, Jacobson finds that native-born Americans had adopted a notion of "variegated whiteness." These immigrants might still be white in the legal sense, but they were less white and therefore less desirable than "Anglo-Saxons." Jacobson sees this era of racial fluidity lasting until the immigration restrictions of the 1920s, when "Caucasian unity" triumphed over "Anglo-Saxonist exclusivity" (Jacobson 1998, pp. 41–3, 91–2).

Whiteness studies such as these have become hugely popular. Hundreds of articles and books have appeared on the subject in little more than a decade, and many of them focus on nativism as the cause of an immigrant group's less than fully white status. But by 2004, the inevitable backlash against the depiction of immigrants as non-white was already well under way. Several major historiographical review essays chided the best-known whiteness studies scholars for "sloppy methodology" and a dearth of evidence supporting their theories of how Americans perceived immigrants' racial status. Thomas Guglielmo's recent *White on Arrival* (which argues that Italian immigrants, at least, were never perceived as anything but white) has received several major awards, perhaps suggesting that many historians sympathize with his critique of Roediger and Jacobson (Arnesen 2001; Kolchin 2002; Guglielmo 2003).

There is good reason to read the whiteness literature with a healthy dose of skepticism. For example, to date, not a single piece of evidence has been presented indicating that the Irish adopted their stance on slavery in America in order to win the approval of native-born whites. By the eve of the Civil War, most whites in the north (where most Irish immigrants lived) opposed slavery or its extension, so Irish Catholics' decision to align themselves with a Democratic party dominated by southerners was hardly a logical means by which to ingratiate themselves with their new neighbors. The "ethno-cultural" argument – that the Irish adopted the slavery stance of urban Democrats because the Whig Party was home to the most ardent anti-Catholic nativists – is a far more compelling explanation for the political behavior of Irish immigrants, and one which the Irish often cited when explaining their stance on slavery. Another weakness of the Roediger/Ignatiev/Jacobson argument is that so much of it rests on the weight of a few quotations to the effect that if too many more immigrants arrive in the United States, there will be no work left for "white men" (e.g. Jacobson 1998, p. 47). A careful reading of these quotations in their original context suggests that these speakers and writers were using "white men" as shorthand for "White Anglo-Saxon Protestants" in an era before the term "WASP" had been coined. There is ample evidence that nineteenth-century native-born Americans considered immigrants inferior, but little support for the argument that natives ever really considered the race of the European newcomers anything but white.

With studies of nativism appearing these days in every subfield of American history, one might surmise that little significant work on the subject remained to be done. Yet numerous aspects of American nativism still need further study. For example, published studies of nativism have focused overwhelmingly on two periods – the antebellum years (when the Know Nothings skyrocketed to power) and the early twentieth century (as the nation began adopting increasingly restrictive immigration laws). As a result, other periods of American nativism have received scant attention. We especially need studies of nativism in the seventeenth and eighteenth centuries; the few existing works in this field are badly outdated (Ray 1936; Smith 1956; Brown 1972). Brendan McConville's insightful study of Pope Day illustrates how fruitful modern reexaminations of colonial nativism can be (McConville 2000; see also Cogliano 1995). Another period that has been largely ignored is the Gilded Age, especially the years from 1880 to 1900. Many writers undoubtedly believe that Higham's work on the period is still authoritative, yet there are dozens of topics touched upon briefly in his book that desperately require more detailed analysis. Only a few such studies have appeared to date (Anbinder 1997; Kennedy 2000; Summers 2000; Webb 2002). The most neglected period of all, however, is the period since 1924. The nativism that purportedly brought about passage of the immigration restrictions of the 1920s could hardly have disappeared overnight once these laws were enacted. The lack of work on nativism in this period probably relates to the lack of attention immigration historians have devoted to the post-1924 period overall. Although the twentieth century has probably received more attention than any other era of American history in recent years, immigration historians have done only a tiny portion of this work. The nativism often apparent in the New Deal political battles of the 1930s, the Red Scare of the late 1940s and early 1950s, and the debates over immigration, guest-worker, and refugee policy in the same period especially cry out for further study (though many intellectual histories of this period do address nativism in their assessments of the "radical right"). A recent article by geographer Colin Flint examining the political geography of nativism in twentieth-century Pennsylvania reflects the untapped potential for studies of modern nativism (Flint 2001).

Another aspect of nativism that has been almost wholly ignored to date is the role of women in the movement. In recent years, historians have finally begun to appreciate the significant power that women have always exerted in American politics, even before they won the right to vote in the early twentieth century. A number of sophisticated studies have appeared documenting women's use of reform organizations, petition campaigns, household lobbying, and other means to influence elections and shape legislation. But other than a fine work on women in the twentieth-century Ku Klux Klan (Blee 1991), the world of the female nativist remains largely unexplored. It is doubtful that such studies will reveal anything dramatically new about American nativism, but such work will help add nuance and depth to our understanding of nativist political activism.

The scarcity of work on female nativists can be attributed in part to a lack of sources, but no such excuse can be made for the dearth of studies of anti-Mexican nativism. The lack of attention to this subject may result from the general paucity of nativism studies concerning the period since 1924, when most of the animus towards Mexican immigrants has appeared, and also from the relatively nascent state of Mexican American historiography. Still, the absence of work on anti-Mexican nativism is shocking; the hostility aimed at no other major American immigrant group has received as little consideration. Other than two relatively narrow monographs covering the 1850s and the 1930s, the subject has been virtually ignored. This fact is especially surprising given that so many studies have been written about discrimination against Asian immigrants, who like Mexicans have generally concentrated in the west (Hoffman 1974; Peterson 1975).

While there are many histories of anti-Asian sentiment in the west, studies of anti-Asian nativism outside of that region are badly needed, for almost all the published work on nativism aimed at Asians focuses upon the Pacific coast. The significant Asian populations of the east and midwest must have suffered from discrimination as well, yet because non-western Asian communities were small and economically isolated, one imagines that the nativism focused upon them might have been less intense and less concerned with their economic impact. Natives in the east seemed especially concerned with the social impact of Chinese immigrants; and the efforts made by Euro-Americans to keep Asians from buying or renting housing in their neighborhoods badly needs study, as does the role of the "opium den" in anti-Chinese nativism. Why Asians in the east were able to find judges willing to naturalize them, long after western judges had stopped making Chinese immigrants into American citizens, and why these eastern judges eventually reversed their policy, also deserves further study. That Chinese Americans in the east made the most important court challenges to the 1890s legislation requiring Chinese immigrants to carry photo-identification (at the time making them the only Americans required to carry identification) also indicates the importance of studying discrimination against Asian immigrants outside of the west.

Another grossly understudied aspect of American nativism is the makeup of the movement's rank and file. While the membership of the twentieth-century Ku Klux Klan has been relatively well documented (Moore 1991; MacLean 1994), we still know frustratingly little about who joined the nineteenth-century nativist organizations. Historians need to continue scouring local historical society libraries for the minute books of nativist fraternal orders. Although such archival finds are rare, newspapers (especially those that endorsed the nativist cause) can be culled for lists of the movement's supporters, whose socio-economic status can now be easily tabulated thanks to census and city directory records that can be searched on-line. It was through the perusal of such lists that historians discovered that New York political "Boss" William M. Tweed, renowned in his own day and since as a friend of the immigrant, actually headed a New York nativist fraternal order at the outset of his political career (Anbinder 1995). Even more significantly, such studies could help settle the debate concerning which members of society found nineteenth-century nativism most attractive. Though many historians have speculated that nativist groups must have been especially popular with those whose economic status was insecure and who felt threatened by immigrant employment competition, I suspect that additional discoveries documenting membership in antebellum nativist organizations will corroborate the evidence found to date, which suggests nativists in that era were just as well off as other native-born Americans. Nineteenth-century nativists saw immigrants as more of a threat to their political than their economic status, and worried more about the threat immigrants posed to their children's schools than to their pocketbooks. But only the discovery of more nativist membership data will allow us to make such assessments with assurance.

Because so much nineteenth-century nativist animus was directed at Catholics and their religious leaders, historians have for decades characterized the movement as a "Protestant Crusade." Yet despite the hundreds of studies of nativism that have been written since Ray Billington coined this phrase in 1938, we know scarcely more about the relationship between American Protestant leaders and the nativist movement than we did in Billington's day. Billington and Higham based their limited analyses of Protestant leaders' roles in the nativist movement almost entirely on an assessment of their sermons, pamphlets, and books. But we need to unearth the correspondence of these ministers in order to develop a more thorough understanding of the role of Protestant leaders in fomenting the nativism of this period. Richard Carwardine has published an impressive book on evangelicals and politics that touches upon the subject, but much more work on this topic is needed (Carwardine 1993). We especially need to know the extent to which ministers attempted to influence the votes of their parishioners and the stances that politicians took on political issues that mattered to nativists. My own very limited investigations suggest that Protestant leaders may have been less directly involved in spearheading the nativist movement than one might imagine. For example, the antebellum Methodist leaders whose manuscript collections are housed at Drew University appear to have busied themselves much more with intra-denominational politics than Know-Nothing politics. Whether or not these Protestant leaders were typical remains to be seen. But with so much of their correspondence now available, historians must continue to reassess the role of the nineteenth-century Protestant leaders in the spreading of anti-Catholic nativism.

Given the vital role that Protestant anti-Catholicism played in fomenting eighteenth- and nineteenth-century American nativism, we also need more research on the links between American and British anti-Catholicism. John Wolffe, a professor of religion in the United Kingdom, has noted that "during the middle third of the nineteenth century, anti-Catholicism was, on both sides of the Atlantic, very much the essence of evangelicalism" (Wolffe 1994, p. 179; see also Carwardine 1978). Wolffe's brief article on the subject points out the many similarities between evangelical anti-Catholic organizations in the two countries, but scholars still need to discover the precise nature of the relationship between the two groups. We know, for example, that certain itinerant ministers lectured to large crowds in both nations, and that anti-Catholic publicists in the United States often borrowed liberally from the writings of their English counterparts. But a thorough investigation of the links between the organized exponents of anti-Catholic sentiment in the two nations is badly needed, as is a comparative study of anti-Irish sentiment in Great Britain and North America.

Finally, historians need to conduct more research on the nativism harbored by immigrants themselves. We know that Protestant Irish and even anti-clerical Italian Catholic immigrants sometimes heartily endorsed the Know Nothings, and that Irish immigrants from diverse backgrounds often directed the assaults on Chinese immigrant miners in the west. Labor leaders who were themselves mostly immigrants likewise led the immigration restriction movement in the late nineteenth and early twentieth centuries. More recently, clashes between Jewish and African immigrants in Crown Heights, Brooklyn in 1991, and looting by Mexican immigrants that targeted Korean American store-owners in the Los Angeles riots of 1992, demonstrate the continuing importance of inter-ethnic conflict in immigrant life. Sociologists are devoting significant attention to contemporary inter-ethnic conflict, though typically they concentrate only on animosity between immigrants and native-born African Americans (Abelman and Lie 1995; Weitzer 1997; J. Lee 2002). Historians need to follow their lead. A 2001 dissertation by Grace Delgado documenting anti-Chinese sentiment among Mexican Americans in the Arizona/Sonora borderlands highlights the fascinating insights that can be gleaned from innovative research in inter-ethnic relations (Delgado 2001). African American nativism, the subject to date of only a few brief articles, also merits further study (Rubin 1978; Fuchs 1990; Jo 1991).

A decade or so ago, it appeared that nativism would once again become an important factor in American civic life. California voters had recently adopted Proposition 187, severely limiting the dispensing of state assistance to immigrants. Conservative commentator Patrick J. Buchanan made complaints about the economic and cultural impact of immigrants one of the cornerstones of his surprisingly popular bid for the Republican presidential nomination in 1992. California governor Pete Wilson, another Republican, made immigration restriction the centerpiece of his 1996 presidential campaign. The media forecast the dawning of a new age of American nativism. Yet the expected anti-immigrant backlash never materialized. Voters refused to follow Buchanan into battle to wage his "cultural war," and Wilson's calls for immigration restriction failed to resonate with voters. Even when a bipartisan commission headed by former Congresswoman Barbara Jordan called in 1995 for a reduction in the number of immigrants legally admitted to the country each year, and President Bill Clinton endorsed the commission's recommendations, the public was apathetic, and the immigration bill that resulted from the commission's work died quietly in committee. Few mourned its demise.

These events reflect a fundamental rejection of nativism by the overwhelming majority of modern-day Americans. Only in a few parts of the United States, such as southern California and Miami (where non-English-speaking immigrants seem to outnumber natives), is there widespread resentment of legal immigration. It has been three-quarters of a century since restricting the flow or the rights of immigrants has formed the basis of a significant social or political movement. Even in California, the courts and legislature have restored most of the services that Proposition 187 denied to illegal immigrants. The press clearly senses the national mood; in the first three years of the twenty-first century, the term "nativism" has appeared in major newspapers at barely half the rate that it did in the 1990s (LexisNexis Academic Database). Americans, like most people, are still leery of those who are different from themselves, but they rarely seek to alter the immigration laws as a means to allay those fears. Although some of the more draconian features of the "Patriot Act" of 2001 are eerily reminiscent of the Alien and Sedition Acts of 1798, the new law does not seem to portend any widespread revival of nativism. Nonetheless, as long as scholarly studies of anti-immigrant sentiment continue to branch out in new and exciting directions, it appears that nativism will remain an important facet of American cultural, social, and immigration history for many years to come.

REFERENCES

Aarim-Heriot, Najia (2003). *Chinese Immigrants, African Americans, and Racial Anxiety in the United States, 1848–82.* Urbana: University of Illinois Press.

Abelman, Nancy and John Lie (1995). *Blue Dreams: Korean Americans and the Los Angeles Riots.* Cambridge, MA: Harvard University Press.

Adeeko, Adeleke (1998). *Proverbs, Textuality, and Nativism in African Literature.* Gainesville: University of Florida Press.

Adelman, William (1976). *Haymarket Revisited: A Tour Guide of Labor History Sites and Ethnic Neighborhoods Connected with the Haymarket Affair.* Chicago: Illinois Labor History Society.

Alexander, Charles C. (1965). *The Ku Klux Klan in the Southwest.* Lexington: University Press of Kentucky.

Allerfeldt, Kristofer (2003). *Race, Radicalism, Religion, and Restriction: Immigration in the Pacific Northwest, 1890–1924.* Westport, CT: Praeger.

Anbinder, Tyler (1992). *Nativism and Slavery: The Northern Know Nothings and the Politics of the 1850s.* New York: Oxford University Press.

—— (1995). "'Boss' Tweed: Nativist." *Journal of the Early Republic* 15: 109–16.

—— (1997). "Ulysses S. Grant, Nativist." *Civil War History* 43: 119–40.

Arnesen, Eric (2001). "Whiteness and the Historian's Imagination." *International Labor and Working-Class History* 60: 3–32.

Bachin, Robin F. (2003). "At the Nexus of Labor and Leisure: Baseball, Nativism, and the 1919 Black Sox Scandal." *Journal of Social History* 36: 941–62.

Barkan, Elliott R. (2003). "Return of the Nativists? California Public Opinion and Immigration in the 1980s and 1990s." *Social Science History* 27: 229–83.

Bayor, Ronald H. (1978). *Neighbors in Conflict: The Irish, Germans, Jews, and Italians of New York City, 1929–1941.* Baltimore, MD: Johns Hopkins University Press.

Bennett, David H. (1988). *The Party of Fear: The American Far Right from Nativism to the Militia Movement.* Chapel Hill: University of North Carolina Press.

Benson, Lee (1961). *The Concept of Jacksonian Democracy: New York as a Test Case.* Princeton, NJ: Princeton University Press.

Berquist, James M. (1986). "The Concept of Nativism in Historical Study Since *Strangers in the Land*." *American Jewish History* 76: 125–41.

Berthoff, Rowland (1960). "The American Social Order: A Conservative Hypothesis." *American Historical Review* 65: 495–514.

Billington, Ray Allen (1938). *The Protestant Crusade, 1800–1860: A Study of the Origins of American Nativism.* New York: Macmillan.

—— (1949). *Westward Expansion: A History of the American Frontier.* New York: Macmillan.

—— (1955). Review of *Strangers in the Land*. *Saturday Review* 38 (December 31): 18.

—— (1956). *The Far Western Frontier, 1830–1860.* New York: Harper & Row.

—— (1971). *The Genesis of the Frontier Thesis: A Study in Historical Creativity.* San Marino, CA: Huntington Library.

—— (1973). *Frederick Jackson Turner: Historian, Scholar, Teacher.* New York: Oxford University Press.

Blee, Kathleen M. (1991). *Women of the Klan: Racism and Gender in the 1920s*. Berkeley: University of California Press.

Brimelow, Peter (1995). *Alien Nation: Common Sense About America's Immigration Disaster*. New York: Random House.

Brown, Thomas M. (1972). "The Image of the Beast: Anti-Papal Rhetoric in Colonial America." In Richard O. Curry and Thomas M. Brown, eds., *Conspiracy: The Fear of Subversion in American History*. New York: Holt, Rinehart, and Winston.

Carman, Harry J. and Reinhard H. Luthin (1940). "Some Aspects of the Know-Nothing Movement Reconsidered." *South Atlantic Quarterly* 39: 213–34.

Carwardine, Richard J. (1978). *Transatlantic Revivalism: Popular Evangelicalism in Britain and America, 1790–1865*. Westport, CT: Greenwood Press.

—— (1993). *Evangelicals and Politics in Antebellum America*. New Haven, CT: Yale University Press.

Chalmers, David M. (1965). *Hooded Americanism: The First Century of the Ku Klux Klan, 1865–1965*. Garden City, NY: Doubleday.

Chan, Sucheng (2000). "A People of Exceptional Character: Ethnic Diversity, Nativism, and Racism in the California Gold Rush." *California History* 79: 44–85.

Coben, Stanley (1964). "A Study in Nativism: The American Red Scare of 1919–20." *Political Science Quarterly* 79: 52–75.

Cogliano, Francis D. (1995). *No King, No Popery: Anti-Catholicism in Revolutionary New England*. Westport, CT: Greenwood Press.

Collins, Robert M. (1989). "The Originality Trap: Richard Hofstadter on Populism." *Journal of American History* 76: 150–67.

Conzen, Kathleen (1976). *Immigrant Milwaukee, 1836–1860: Accommodation and Community in a Frontier City*. Cambridge, MA: Harvard University Press.

Curran, Thomas J. (1963). "The Know Nothings of New York." PhD diss., Columbia University.

—— (1975). *Xenophobia and Immigration, 1820–1930*. Boston: Twayne Publishers.

Curtis, L. Perry, Jr. (1971). *Apes and Angels: The Irishman in Victorian Caricature*. Washington, DC: Smithsonian Institution Press.

Daniels, Roger (1962). *The Politics of Prejudice: The Anti-Japanese Movement in California and the Struggle for Japanese Exclusion*. Berkeley: University of California Press.

—— ed. (1978). *Anti-Chinese Violence in North America*. New York: Arno Press.

—— (2004). *Guarding the Golden Door: American Immigration Policy and Immigrants Since 1882*. New York: Hill and Wang.

Davis, David Brion (1960). "Some Themes of Counter-Subversion: An Analysis of Anti-Masonic, Anti-Catholic, and Anti-Mormon Literature." *Mississippi Valley Historical Review* 47: 205–24.

Delgado, Grace Peña (2001). "In the Age of Exclusion: Race, Religion, and Chinese Identity in the Making of the Arizona-Sonora Borderlands, 1863–1943." PhD diss., University of California, Los Angeles.

Dinnerstein, Leonard (1994). *Antisemitism in America*. New York: Oxford University Press.

Dolan, Jay P. (1975). *The Immigrant Church: New York's Irish and German Catholics, 1815–1865*. Baltimore, MD: Johns Hopkins University Press.

Doty, Roxanne Lynn (2003). *Anti-Immigrantism in Western Democracies: Statecraft, Desire, and the Politics of Exclusion*. New York: Routledge.

Dubofsky, Melvin (1961). "Organized Labor and the Immigrant in New York City, 1900–1918." *Labor History* 2: 182–201.

Ernst, Robert J. (1948). "Economic Nativism in New York City during the 1840s." *New York History* 29: 170–86.

—— (1949). *Immigrant Life in New York City, 1825–1860*. New York: King's Crown Press.

Feldberg, Michael (1975). *The Philadelphia Riots of 1844: A Study of Ethnic Conflict*. Westport, CT: Greenwood Press.

Fell, Sister Marie Leonore (1941). *The Foundations of Nativism in American Textbooks, 1783–1860*. Washington, DC: Catholic University of America Press.

Flint, Colin (2001). "Right-Wing Resistance to the Process of American Hegemony: The Changing Political Geography of Nativism in Pennsylvania, 1920–1998." *Political Geography* 20: 763–86.

Fogel, Robert W. (1989). *Without Consent or Contract: The Rise and Fall of American Slavery*. New York: W.W. Norton.

Foner, Philip S., ed. (1969). *The Autobiographies of the Haymarket Martyrs*. New York: Humanities Press.

Formisano, Ronald P. (1971). *The Birth of Mass Political Parties: Michigan, 1827–1861*. Princeton, NJ: Princeton University Press.

—— (1983). *The Transformation of Political Culture: Massachusetts Parties, 1790s–1840s*. New York: Oxford University Press.

—— (1994). "The Invention of the Ethnocultural Interpretation." *American Historical Review* 99: 453–77.

Franchot, Jenny (1994). *Roads to Rome: The Antebellum Protestant Encounter with Catholicism*. Berkeley: University of California Press.

Fuchs, Lawrence H. (1990). "The Reactions of Black Americans to Immigration." In Virginia Yans-McLaughlin, ed., *Immigration Reconsidered: History, Sociology, and Politics*. New York: Oxford University Press, pp. 293–314.

Gienapp, William E. (1985). "Nativism and the Creation of a Republican Majority in the North before the Civil War." *Journal of American History* 72: 529–59.

—— (1987). *The Origins of the Republican Party, 1852–1856*. New York: Oxford University Press.

Gitelman, H.M. (1973). "No Irish Need Apply: Patterns of and Responses to Ethnic Discrimination in the Labor Market." *Labor History* 14: 56–68.

Glazer, Nathan, and Daniel Patrick Moynihan (1963). *Beyond the Melting Pot: The Negroes, Puerto Ricans, Jews, Italians, and Irish of New York City*. Cambridge, MA: Harvard University Press.

Gohmann, Mary de Lourdes (1938). *Political Nativism in Tennessee to 1860*. Washington, DC: Catholic University of America Press.

Goluboff, Benjamin (2000). "'If Madonna Be': Emily Dickinson and Roman Catholicism." *New England Quarterly* 73: 355–85.

Gorn, Elliott J. (1987). "'Good-Bye Boys, I Die a True American': Homicide, Nativism, and Working-Class Culture in Antebellum New York City." *Journal of American History* 74: 388–410.

Greeley, Andrew M. (1977). *An Ugly Little Secret: Anti-Catholicism in North America*. Kansas City: Sheed, Andrews, and McMeel.

Guglielmo, Thomas A. (2003). *White on Arrival: Italians, Race, Color, and Power in Chicago, 1890–1945*. New York: Oxford University Press.

Gutman, Herbert (1973). "Work, Culture, and Society in Industrializing America, 1815–1919." *American Historical Review* 78: 531–88.

Gyory, Andrew (1998). *Closing the Gate: Race, Politics, and the Chinese Exclusion Act*. Chapel Hill: University of North Carolina Press.

Handlin, Oscar (1941). *Boston's Immigrants: A Study in Acculturation, 1790–1880*. Cambridge, MA: Harvard University Press.

—— (1957). *Race and Nationality in American Life*. Boston: Little, Brown.

—— (1965). "Reconsidering the Populists." *Agriculture History* 39: 68–74.

Haynes, George H. (1896). "A Chapter from the Local History of Know Nothingism." *New England Magazine* 21: 82–96.

Hensel, W.V. (1915). "A Withered Twig: Dark Lantern Glimpses into the Operation of Know Nothingism in Lancaster Sixty Years Ago." *Journal of the Lancaster County [Pennsylvania] Historical Society* 19: 174–81.

Higham, John (1952). "Beyond Consensus: The Historian as Moral Critic." *American Historical Review* 67: 609–25.

—— (1955). *Strangers in the Land: Patterns of American Nativism, 1860–1925.* New Brunswick, NJ: Rutgers University Press.

—— (1957). "Anti-Semitism in the Gilded Age: A Reinterpretation." *Mississippi Valley Historical Review* 43: 559–578.

—— (1958). "Another Look at Nativism." *Catholic Historical Review* 44: 147–58.

—— (1959). "The Cult of the 'American Consensus': Homogenizing our History." *Commentary* 27 (February): 93–100.

—— (1974). "Hanging Together: Divergent Unities in American History." *Journal of American History* 61: 5–28.

—— (2000). "Instead of a Sequel, or How I Lost My Subject." *Reviews in American History* 28: 327–39.

Hirobe, Izumi (2001). *Japanese Pride, American Prejudice: Modifying the Exclusion Clause of the 1924 Immigration Act.* Stanford, CA: Stanford University Press.

Hoffman, Abraham (1974). *Unwanted Mexican Americans in the Great Depression.* Tucson: University of Arizona Press.

Hofstadter, Richard (1955). *The Age of Reform: From Bryan to F.D.R.* New York: Alfred A. Knopf.

—— (1966). *The Paranoid Style in American Politics and Other Essays.* New York: Alfred A. Knopf.

Holt, Michael F. (1969). *Forging a Majority: The Formation of the Republican Party in Pittsburgh, 1848–1860.* New Haven, CT: Yale University Press.

—— (1973). "The Politics of Impatience: The Origins of Know Nothingism." *Journal of American History* 60: 309–31.

—— (1978). *The Political Crisis of the 1850s.* New York: Wiley.

—— (1999). *The Rise and Fall of the American Whig Party: Jacksonian Politics and the Onset of the Civil War.* New York: Oxford University Press.

Howe, Irving (1976). *World of Our Fathers: The Journey of the East European Jews to America and the Life They Found and Made.* New York: Simon & Schuster.

Ignatiev, Noel (1995). *How the Irish Became White.* New York: Routledge.

Jackson, Kenneth T. (1967). *The Ku Klux Klan in the City, 1915–1930.* New York: Oxford University Press.

Jacobson, Matthew Frye (1998). *Whiteness of a Different Color: European Immigrants and the Alchemy of Race.* Cambridge, MA: Harvard University Press.

Jaher, Frederic C. (1994). *A Scapegoat in the New Wilderness: The Origins and Rise of Anti-Semitism in America.* Cambridge, MA: Harvard University Press.

Jensen, Richard (2002). "'No Irish Need Apply': A Myth of Victimization." *Journal of Social History* 36: 405–29.

Jo, Moon H. (1991). "Korean Merchants in the Black Community: Prejudice Among the Victims of Prejudice." *Ethnic and Racial Studies* 15: 395–410.

Katerberg, William H. (1995). "The Irony of Identity: An Essay on Nativism, Liberal Democracy, and Parochial Identities in Canada and the United States." *American Quarterly* 47: 493–524.

Keller, Morton (1968). *The Art and Politics of Thomas Nast.* New York: Oxford University Press.

Kennedy, Lawrence W. (2000). "Pulpits and Politics: Anti-Catholicism in Boston in the 1880s and 1890s." *Historical Journal of Massachusetts* 28: 56–75.

Kleppner, Paul (1970). *The Cross of Culture: A Social Analysis of Midwestern Politics, 1850–1900*. New York: Free Press.

Kolchin, Peter (2002). "Whiteness Studies: The New History of Race in America." *Journal of American History* 89: 154–73.

Kuzniewski, Anthony J. (1980). *Faith and Fatherland: The Polish Church War in Wisconsin, 1896–1918*. Notre Dame, IN: University of Notre Dame Press.

Lee, Erika (2002). "Enforcing the Borders: Chinese Exclusion along the U.S. Borders with Canada and Mexico, 1882–1924." *Journal of American History* 89: 54–86.

—— (2003). *At America's Gates: Chinese Immigration During the Exclusion Era, 1882–1943*. Chapel Hill: University of North Carolina Press.

Lee, Jennifer (2002). *Civility in the City: Blacks, Jews, and Koreans in Urban America*. Cambridge, MA: Harvard University Press.

Leonard, Ira and Robert Parmet (1971). *American Nativism, 1830–1860*. New York: Van Nostrand Reinhold.

Levine, Bruce (2001). "Conservatism, Nativism, and Slavery: Thomas R. Whitney and the Origins of the Know-Nothing Party." *Journal of American History* 88: 455–88.

Lipset, Seymour Martin and Earl Raab (1970). *The Politics of Unreason: Right Wing Extremism in America*. New York: Harper & Row.

Luibhéid, Eithne (2002). *Entry Denied: Controlling Sexuality at the Border*. Minneapolis: University of Minnesota Press.

McAfee, Ward (1998). *Religion, Race, and Reconstruction: The Public School in the Politics of the 1870s*. Albany: State University of New York Press.

McClain, Charles J. (1994). *In Search of Equality: The Chinese Struggle Against Discrimination in Nineteenth-Century America*. Berkeley: University of California Press.

McConville, Brendan (2000). "Pope Day Revisited, 'Popular' Culture Reconsidered." *Explorations in Early American Culture* 4: 258–80.

McConville, Sister Mary St. Patrick (1928). *Political Nativism in the State of Maryland, 1830–1860*. Washington, DC: Catholic University of America Press.

McGann, A.G. (1944). *Nativism in Kentucky to 1860*. Washington, DC: Catholic University of America Press.

McGrath, Sister Paul-of-the-Cross (1930). *Political Nativism in Texas, 1825–1860*. Washington, DC: Catholic University of America Press.

MacLean, Nancy (1994). *Behind the Mask of Chivalry: The Making of the Second Ku Klux Klan*. New York: Oxford University Press.

Mandelbaum, Seymour J. (1964). *The Social Setting of Intolerance: The Know-Nothings, the Red Scare, and McCarthyism*. Chicago: Scott, Foresman.

Mayo, Louise A. (1988). *The Ambivalent Image: Nineteenth-Century America's Perception of the Jew*. Rutherford, NJ: Fairleigh Dickinson University Press.

Michaels, Walter Benn (1995). *Our America: Nativism, Modernism, and Pluralism*. Durham, NC: Duke University Press.

Miller, Stuart C. (1969). *The Unwelcome Immigrant: The American Image of the Chinese, 1785–1882*. Berkeley: University of California Press.

Montgomery, David (1972). "The Shuttle and the Cross: Weavers and Artisans in the Kensington Riots of 1844." *Journal of Social History* 5: 411–46.

Moore, Leonard (1991). *Citizen Klansmen: The Ku Klux Klan in Indiana, 1921–1928*. Chapel Hill: University of North Carolina Press.

Nevins, Allan (1947). *Ordeal of the Union: A House Dividing, 1852–1857*. New York: Scribner.

Ngai, Mae M. (2003). "The Strange Career of the Illegal Alien: Immigration Restriction and Deportation Policy in the United States, 1921–1965." *Law and History Review* 21: 69–107.

—— (2004). *Impossible Subjects: Illegal Aliens and the Making of Modern America*. Princeton, NJ: Princeton University Press.

Noonan, C.J. (1938). *Nativism in Connecticut*. Washington, DC: Catholic University of America Press.

Nugent, Walter (1963). *The Tolerant Populists: Kansas, Populism, and Nativism*. Chicago: University of Chicago Press.

Otzak, Susan (1987). "Causes of Ethnic Conflict and Protest in Urban America, 1877–1889." *Social Science Research* 16: 185–210.

—— (1989). "Labor Unrest, Immigration, and Ethnic Conflict in Urban America, 1880–1914." *American Journal of Sociology* 94: 1303–33.

Perea, Juan F., ed. (1997). *Immigrants Out: The New Nativism and the Anti-Immigrant Impulse in the United States*. New York: New York University Press.

Perlmutter, Philip (1992). *Divided We Fall: A History of Ethnic, Religious, and Racial Prejudice in America*. Ames: Iowa State University Press.

Peterson, Richard H. (1975). *Manifest Destiny in the Mines: A Cultural Interpretation of Anti-Mexican Nativism in California, 1848–1853*. Saratoga, CA: R and E Publishers.

Pollack, Norman (1960). "Hofstadter on Populism." *Journal of Southern History* 26: 478–500.

—— (1962). "The Myth of Populist Anti-Semitism." *American Historical Review* 68: 76–80.

President's Commission on Immigration and Naturalization (1952). *Hearings before the President's Commission on Immigration and Naturalization*. Washington, DC: Government Printing Office.

Rausch, David A. (1993). *Fundamentalist-Evangelicals and Anti-Semitism*. Valley Forge, PA: Trinity Press International.

Ray, Sister Mary Augustina (1936). *American Opinion of Roman Catholicism in the Eighteenth Century*. New York: Columbia University Press.

Reimers, David M. (1998). *Unwelcome Strangers: American Identity and the Turn Against Immigration*. New York: Columbia University Press.

Renner, Richard W. (1976). "In a Perfect Ferment: Chicago, the Know-Nothings, and the Riot for Lager Beer." *Chicago History* 5: 161–9.

Renshaw, Patrick (1968). "The IWW and the Red Scare." *Journal of Contemporary History* 3: 63–72.

Ribuffo, Leo P. (1983). *The Old Christian Right: The Protestant Far Right from the Great Depression to the Cold War*. Philadelphia: Temple University Press.

Roediger, David R. (1991). *The Wages of Whiteness: Race and the Making of the American Working Class*. New York: Verso.

Rorabaugh, W.J. (1976). "Rising Democratic Spirits: Immigrants, Temperance, and Tammany Hall, 1854–1860." *Civil War History* 22: 138–57.

Rubin, Jay (1978). "Black Nativism: The European Immigrant in Negro Thought, 1830–1860." *Phylon* 39: 193–202.

Salyer, Lucy E. (1995). *Laws Harsh as Tigers: Chinese Immigrants and the Shaping of Modern Immigration Law*. Chapel Hill: University of North Carolina Press.

Sánchez, George J. (1997). "Face the Nation: Race, Immigration, and the Rise of Nativism in Late Twentieth Century America." *International Migration Review* 31: 1009–30.

Saxton, Alexander (1971). *The Indispensable Enemy: Labor and the Anti-Chinese Movement in California*. Berkeley: University of California Press.

Schneider, Dorothee (1998). "'I Know All About Emma Lazarus:' Nationalism and its Contradictions in Congressional Rhetoric of Immigration Restriction." *Cultural Anthropology* 13: 82–99.

Schneider, George (1900). "Lincoln and the Anti-Know Nothing Resolutions." *McLean County [Illinois] Historical Society Transactions* 3: 87–91.

Scisco, Louis D. (1901). *Political Nativism in New York State.* New York: Columbia University Press.

Shenk, Hiram H. (1906–9). "The Know Nothing Party in Lebanon County." *Lebanon County [Pennsylvania] Historical Society Papers* 4: 54–74.

Silbey, Joel (1973). *Political Ideology and Voting Behavior.* Englewood Cliffs, NJ: Prentice-Hall.

Smith, James M. (1956). *Freedom's Fetters: The Alien and Sedition Laws and American Civil Liberties.* Ithaca, NY: Cornell University Press.

Stack, John F., Jr. (1979). *International Conflict in an American City: Boston's Irish, Italians, and Jews, 1935–1944.* Westport, CT: Greenwood.

Summers, Mark W. (2000). *Rum, Romanism, and Rebellion: The Making of a President, 1884.* Chapel Hill: University of North Carolina Press.

Takaki, Ronald (1989). *Strangers from a Different Shore: A History of Asian Americans.* Boston: Little, Brown.

—— (1993). *A Different Mirror: A History Of Multicultural America.* Boston: Little, Brown.

Taylor, Steven (2000). "Progressive Nativism: The Know-Nothing Party in Massachusetts." *Historical Journal of Massachusetts* 28: 167–85.

Thomas, Sister M. Evangeline (1936). *Nativism in the Old Northwest, 1850–1860.* Washington, DC: Catholic University of America Press.

Tichenor, Daniel J. (2002). *Dividing Lines: The Politics of Immigration Control in America.* Princeton, NJ: Princeton University Press.

Von Hallberg, Robert, ed. (1996). *"Our America* and Nativist Modernism: A Panel." *Modernism/Modernity* 3: 99–126.

Voss-Hubbard, Mark (2002). *Beyond Party: Cultures of Antipartisanship in Northern Politics Before the Civil War.* Baltimore, MD: Johns Hopkins University Press.

Wang, Fang (1998). "Nativism in the 1990s." PhD diss., California Institute of Technology.

Webb, Clive (2002). "The Lynching of Sicilian Immigrants in the American South, 1886–1910." *American Nineteenth Century History* 3: 45–76.

Weitzer, Ronald (1997). "Racial Prejudice Among Korean Merchants in African American Neighborhoods." *Sociological Quarterly* 38: 587–606.

Wilentz, Sean (1984). *Chants Democratic: New York City and the Rise of the American Working Class, 1788–1850.* New York: Oxford University Press.

Wolffe, John (1994). "Anti-Catholicism and Evangelical Identity in Britain and the United States, 1830–1860." In Mark A. Noll, David W. Bebbington, and George A. Rawlyk, eds., *Evangelicalism: Comparative Studies of Popular Protestantism in North America, the British Isles, and Beyond, 1700–1990.* New York: Oxford University Press, pp. 179–97.

Woodward, C. Vann (1960). "The Populist Heritage and the Intellectual." In *The Burden of Southern History.* Baton Rouge: Louisiana State University Press.

Wunder, John R. (1992). "Anti-Chinese Violence in the American West, 1850–1910." In John McLaren, Hamar Foster, and Chet Orloff, eds., *Law for the Elephant, Law for the Beaver: Essays in the Legal History of the North American West.* Pasadena, CA: Ninth Judicial Circuit Historical Society.

Yans-McLaughlin, Virginia (1977). *Family and Community: Italian Immigrants in Buffalo, 1880–1930.* Ithaca, NY: Cornell University Press.

Zeidel, Robert F. (2004). *Immigrants, Progressives, and Exclusion Politics: The Dillingham Commission, 1900–1927.* DeKalb: Northern Illinois University Press.

Chapter Nine

Assimilation and American National Identity

Michael R. Olneck

The Relationship Between National Identity and Assimilation

A nation is an "imagined community" (B. Anderson 1991) whose members conceive of themselves as compatriots sharing a common history and future, inhabiting a specific territory, owing obligations to one another by virtue of being co-nationals, having a particular "public culture" concerning how life is to be lived together, and possessing a collective will that is ideally realized through a sovereign state (D. Miller 1995). The problem of assimilation is a subset of the generic problem of the cultural and political reproduction of any nation, and arises particularly in those nations which accept immigrants. While assimilation pertains to what individuals or groups must learn, do, and become if they are to be accepted as members of the nation, it also pertains to the articulation of the nature of the entity to which they must assimilate. The question of assimilation, therefore, inherently entails the articulation of national identity, and fundamentally concerns the preservation of the sense of continuity and wholeness of a nation in the face of a potentially rupturing process of receiving new and dissimilar elements into its population.

National identity expresses a nation's consciousness of itself (Huntington 2004). Through its national identity a nation represents its specificity, uniqueness, and distinctiveness from other nations. Among the most significant aspects of national identity are language, myths, symbols and rituals, a common history, and a shared vernacular culture (D. Miller 1995). Language is of particular significance for the problem of immigrant assimilation since linguistic diversity is, as Ronald Schmidt Sr. has observed, "often expressed as a corruption of the nation that must be repressed or eradicated as expeditiously as possible" (Schmidt 2000, p. 44).

Nations, however, do not exhaust the communities to which individuals belong, so the degree of autonomy of other identities – for example, religious, ethnic, regional, linguistic, racial – from national identity is a potentially open question. The degree of exclusivity claimed for the national identity, the manner and degree of subordinacy of sub-national identities to the national identity, and the nature and degree of diversity among sub-national identities, are potentially problematic and open to contestation. Since immigrants arrive with distinctive identities formed outside the national community, the question of sub-national identities may be particularly salient for them, and thus assimilation must address not merely the content of identity, but the permissibility of, and relationships among, multiple identities.

National identities may be distinguished on several dimensions. The most important of these include the construction of the constituent unit of the polity as individuals or groups, the degree of cultural and identity diversity or homogeneity expected of members of the nation, voluntaristic versus ascriptive criteria of membership in the nation, and the role of ideological principles in the construction of national identity. Struggles among groups adhering to one or another of distinct models of national identity have been central to the prominence of assimilation in our national debates and conflicts, and the influence of distinct models of national identity on social policies and practices has shaped the sociological nature of assimilation on the ground.

What is Assimilation?

"Assimilation" is a symbolically and normatively loaded word that has been part of Americans' "vocabularies of public life" (Wuthnow 1992) since the nineteenth century. Its meanings, salience, and uses have been contested and have varied by historical context. But at all times it has referred to the terms upon which newcomers were to be included, and has been part of how Americans have *ordered*, *perceived*, and *judged* population diversity. It is, like the idea of a "nation" itself, fundamentally a "category of practice" that has been adopted as a "category of analysis" (Brubaker 1996).

Robert Park and his colleagues and students at the University of Chicago during the 1920s and 1930s provided the first elaborated theory of immigrant assimilation in the United States. Park, and his co-author, Ernest Burgess, in their 1921 introductory sociology text, *Introduction to the Science of Sociology*, defined assimilation as "a process of interpenetration and fusion in which persons and groups acquire the memories, sentiments, and attitudes of other persons or groups, and, by sharing their experience and history, are incorporated with them in a common cultural life" (cited in Alba and Nee 2003, p. 19). In Richard Alba and Victor Nee's view, Park was writing in opposition to prevailing views of Americanization, and his "definition of assimilation envisioned a diverse mainstream society in which people of different ethnic/racial origins and cultural heritages evolve a common culture that enables them to sustain a common national existence" (Alba and Nee 2003, p. 10). This does not require the erasure of all signs of ethnic origins, but, rather, emphasizes the changes that bring ethnic minorities into the mainstream, while leaving ample room for persistence of ethnic elements within a common national frame. But, according to Alba and Nee (2003), because Park also defined assimilation not merely as a process, but as the end point in his famous "race relations cycle," he has been associated with a conventionally strong model of assimilation, in which cultural homogeneity is the result, and his more flexible conception of assimilation was lost in much subsequent scholarship.

Some scholars have recognized that not only may assimilation permit the persistence of ethnicity, but the emergence of ethnic groups is, itself, a product of assimilation. This view recognizes that immigrants from various locales may not initially recognize themselves as co-ethnics, but that under the experience of immigration may come to recognize their commonalities, especially as they are categorized more broadly by natives than they classified themselves prior to immigration, and as they pursue their common interests. Thus, immigrants assimilate to one another as ethnics, and are assimilated into an identity scheme organized around the designation of ethnic groups (Fuchs 1990).

Milton Gordon, in his 1964 classic, *Assimilation in American Life*, contributed a complex analysis that recognized related and interacting dimensions of assimilation whose contingencies could not be fully predicted. In particular, Gordon distinguished "cultural" or "behavioral" assimilation, pertaining broadly to acculturation to society's core patterns of values, beliefs, and behaviors, from "structural assimilation," pertaining to the acceptance of ethnic group members into the institutions and primary associations of the majority. Gordon regarded cultural assimilation as proceeding apace, with structural assimilation an uncertain later outcome (Kazal 1995).

Alba and Nee, themselves, define assimilation as "the decline, and at its endpoint the disappearance of an ethnic/racial distinction and the cultural and social differences that express it" (Alba and Nee 1997, p. 863). Assimilation, in Alba and Nee's view, can be accomplished by changes in all groups involved. They stress the incremental, largely intergenerational, and even unintended, assimilative consequences of the pragmatic choices and decisions that immigrants make in the workaday world, as they strive to accomplish their goals within the context created by the behavioral assumptions, incentives, opportunities, rewards, and penalties that characterize American institutions.

It is not only individuals or groups that assimilate, or are assimilated to one another. Cultures, too, may assimilate or blend. While we may imagine assimilation as immigrants and their offspring entering the "mainstream," what Kathleen Conzen (1991) has called the "localization of culture" may occur, in which aspects of immigrant culture are incorporated into the mainstream, and lose their ethnic marking. The result is that what is "American" and what it means to be an "American" may change (Kazal 1995). In the view of the sociologist Ruben Rumbaut,

> The ultimate paradox of assimilation American-style may well be that, in the process, what is being assimilated metamorphoses into something quite dissimilar from what any of the protagonists ever imagined or intended, and the core itself is ineluctably transmuted, even as it keeps its continental name [i.e. America]. (Rumbaut 1997, p. 954)

The Relationship Between the Problematic Nature of American National Identity and Assimilation

All nations' identities are symbolic and discursive construction (Wodak, De Cillia, Reisigl, and Liebhart 1999), and, so, are inherently problematic in that they can be contested and changed. But national identities are problematic in historically specific ways that reflect nations' origins, composition, and historical experience. National identity in the United States has been an endemic, even intrinsic problem. The United States is not a *patria* (fatherland or motherland), nor an ancient "homeland" in which national identity can be anchored (Walzer 1996). Having been newly established, the durability of the nation could not be assumed since the political and cultural terms of its construction could (and would be) contested. A feeling from the start that the United States could fall apart was keen, and, as the War Between the States was to prove, prescient. Anxiety about holding together is, then, a founding element in American political culture.

Additionally, the United States was from its origins diverse in composition, and over the next two centuries would almost continuously become increasingly diverse in ways that would challenge representation of the national ethnos. Further, creedal principles, which have been central to the expression of American national identity, fail, in and of themselves, to provide for thick bonds to link diverse Americans to one another (Lind 1995; Huntington 2004). One can wonder, as well, if individualism, a central social principle of the American Creed (Arieli 1961), and its correlate, a strong distinction between private and public realms, militate against a strongly salient national identity. John Hall and Charles Lindholm (1999) contend that Americans' cultural assumptions about individualism cause them to fail to recognize what they share, and make them particularly anxious about national cohesion

America's creedal principles have interacted in contradictory ways with the nation's diversity in establishing American national identity. On the one hand, the Creed has provided rhetorical, ideological, and moral resources and guidance to those battling against the founding exclusions and oppressions associated with race and gender. And it undergirds conceptions of America as open to immigrants, and, in some conceptions, as hospitable to cultural diversity among individuals. On the other hand, the idea of a creed, whose principles and implied ways of living must be comprehended and adhered to, has, on occasion, served as a reference point against which to suspect dissimilar others of willfully violating the creed's precepts, or of lacking the necessary capacities for comprehension of, and adherence to, the creed's demands, thus legitimating their exclusion or extending their periods of probation (Wiebe 1975; Fuchs 1990).

Finally, what John Higham (1999) has called the "preeminent myth of national identity," namely the epic of migration, in which immigrants are central, is inherently contradictory. On the one hand, it provides an archetype of experience with which most Americans can identify. On the other hand, it is a myth expressing permanent flux, loss as well as fulfillment, repeated encounters with strangers, and unsettledness.

For these reasons, then, the meaning of American national identity is a persistent and unresolvable problem that in varying degrees historically has generated unease and anxiety, and has prompted quests for a "whole America" (Wiebe 1975, p. 90), of which insistence on assimilation is one example. The expectation of and insistence upon assimilation derives as well from the central American myth of progress and willed emancipation (Rumbaut 1997; Gerstle 1997). Immigrant assimilation recapitulates the American saga embodied in the very founding of the nation of exodus, rejection of a backward past, and transformation.

One institution above all others has been the site of debates, contests, policies, and practices concerning the relationship between assimilation and national identity in the United States. This is the school. The growth of the nineteenth-century common school was accelerated by the desire to expose largely Irish, and later German, immigrants to Americanizing influences, while the Protestant ethos of the common schools was an impetus to Catholics to establish parochial schools (Kaestle 1983). In the early twentieth century, especially during World War I, the schools were used to infuse immigrant children with American principles, loyalties, personae, and identities, and to teach them English as rapidly as possible. In doing so, the schools vivified and symbolized the meaning of being American for immigrants and natives alike (Olneck 1989). During the 1930s and 1940s, the schools were the site of efforts by "interculturalists" to advance a mildly pluralistic model of American identity that promoted a common core culture, while permitting some expression of distinctive identities (Olneck 1990). Between the late-1960s and the present, the schools have been the focus of debate on the role of languages other than English in American life, culminating, at least for the present, in the recent ban on bilingual education in a number of states, and the replacement of the Bilingual Education Act of 1968 with the English Language Acquisition, Language Enhancement, and Academic Achievement Act of 2001 (San Miguel 2004). Within schools an intensified emphasis on rapid acquisition of English has led some to speak of a new Americanization project (Olsen 1997).

American History, Models of National Identity, and Insistence Upon Assimilation

Americans have consistently expected that immigrants would assimilate, and sometimes have demanded and coerced them to do so, though what assimilation means has varied historically, and according to distinct models of national identity. Whether American national identity is conceived of in ethno-racial, creedal, ethno-cultural, pluralistic-individualistic, or multicultural terms has had important consequences for the meanings of assimilation.

Ethno-racial criteria were, until the mid-1960s, constitutive of the American community (Smith 1987; King 2000, 2001). Gary Gerstle has identified this strain of American identity as "racial nationalism," which conceives of Americans "as a people held together by common blood and skin color and by an inherited fitness for self-government" (Gerstle 2001, p. 4). Enshrined in early documents, like the Constitution, and the Naturalization Law of 1790, which was not repealed until 1952, racial nationalism presumed that people of color did not belong in the republic nor could they be accepted as full-fledged members, but, rather, must be expelled, segregated, or subordinated. Such racial nationalism clearly predominated during the 1789–1861 period that Michael Lind (1995) has named the "Anglo-American Republic." While (white) immigrants were permitted to enter the United States during this period, there is no sense in which their presence was incorporated into national self-representation, and suspicion abided among some native Americans that the Irish, especially, were inimical to the nation's well-being. Yet, for the Irish, racial nationalism provided a resource for assimilation. As Ronald Takaki has pointed out, "a powerful way to transform their own identity from 'Irish' to 'American' was to attack blacks. Thus, blacks as the 'other' served to facilitate the assimilation of the Irish foreigners" (Takaki 1993, p. 151).

Racial nationalism had contradictory effects in the post-Civil War through World War II period. In the late nineteenth century, American Anglo-Saxons reasserted their claim to cultural preeminence (Wiebe 2002). A new racialism, of the kind previously applied exclusively to people of color, took hold in the early twentieth century, in which a sense of "absolute difference" between European immigrants, now largely eastern and southern Europeans, and native Americans was propounded (Higham 1970). This view claimed victory in the 1921 and 1924 enactment of immigration restriction based on national origins, which sought to steer the nation's population composition to its pre-1900 patterns. This was not, however, a revival of antebellum Anglo-American nativism; rather, it reflected enlargement of the definition of "whiteness" from Anglo-Saxon to Germano-Celtic (Lind 1995).

While racial nationalism was deployed to halt unwanted immigration from southern and eastern Europe, later it combined with more inclusive notions of American identity, to produce and legitimate the celebrated (white) American "melting pot" that is so powerfully symbolized by the Statue of Liberty, images of Ellis Island, and the "one of each" platoon in World War II movies (Lind 1995; Gerstle 2001). In the years after 1930, non-Anglo-Saxon-Germano-Celtic Americans "became white" (Jacobson 1998), and gained acceptance into the mainstream. The acceptance of the second generation of those immigrants whose presence had so agitated World War I era restrictionists reflected the immigrants' offspring's progressive assimilation, and the influences of creedal, ethno-cultural, and mildly individualistic-pluralistic elements in American national identity, as well as the imperatives of unity during World War II. During the war, President Roosevelt reminded Americans that their troops included "the Murphys and the Kellys, the Smiths and the Jones, the Cohens, the Carusos, the Kowalskis, the Schultzes, the Olsens, the Swobodas, and – right in with all the rest of them – the Cabots and the Lowells," telling them that "All these and others like them are the life blood of America" (Parks and Parks 1965, cited in Fuchs 1990).

Expression of American national identity, while tacitly rooted in racialist assumptions about who could be an American, was, in its earliest formulations, and subsequently, explicitly ideological. Commitment to republican principles of liberty, equality, and government by consent of the governed became equated to what being American meant (Mann 1979; Gleason 1980). Beyond these ideological dimensions framed by the Founders, little else was specified (Jacoby 2004c). The basic tie uniting Americans was to be "civic belief" (Mann 1979). Citizenship, not ethnicity, would be the touchstone of American nationality, and the American Creed (Myrdal 1944) would serve as an "instrument of civic homogenization" (Mann 1979, p. 95). It would provide an otherwise scattered people with a sense of unity as a "free people in a free society" (Wiebe 2002, p. 70), as well as serve as a "surrogate for mutual trust" that might more naturally flow from cultural homogeneity (Wiebe 1975, p. 146). Through to the present, what Martin Marty (1997) has called the "constitutional myth" has been an important source of common identity and shared discourse, albeit with often conflicting interpretations among the nation's subgroups. Adherence to the universalistic principles of the American Creed remains an important part of what Americans believe is required to be a "true American" (Citrin, Reingold, and Green 1990).

The implications of a creedal definition of American identity for the significance of assimilation have been contradictory. On the one hand, the universalistic principles of the American Creed warrant an open and inclusive policy toward immigration, and limit the criteria of admission to profession of belief in the principles of the Republic (Mann 1979). Principles of liberty and individual rights militate against coercing cultural conformity, and provide a defense for asserting cultural distinctiveness. Belief in the power of a society organized according to the Creed to transform social life provides reassurance that minimal efforts need be made to acculturate immigrants, which was the approach taken through most of the nineteenth century (Jacoby 2004c). On the other hand, the very fact of relatively open immigration makes the question of immigrant assimilation more salient, particularly in periods of large-scale entrance of groups perceived as culturally different. Moreover, the assumptions of personal and social transformation associated with promulgation of republican principles, and with the American experiment as a rejection of the Old World, create expectations that immigrants will demonstrably change from their prior selves into Americans. The expression of cultural distinctiveness is expected to be confined to non-public spheres, while the public square is to express what is held in common (Jacoby 2004c). Finally, the principles of the American Creed are not merely matters of propositional belief, but have entailed within them a template for a particular way of life to which immigrants are expected to conform (Arieli 1961; Karst 1989). At the heart of that way of life has been individualism (Arieli 1961), which has not only provided a standard against which to measure the values and behavior of Americans, but has undermined the authority of collective attachments, and promoted assimilation, not least through high rates of ethnic intermarriage (Salins 1997).

While many recognize the importance of the creedal component in American national identity, some (e.g. Gleason 1980) also recognize that the United States does possess a vernacular culture that, while related to the precepts of the American Creed, cannot be reduced to that. They advance a model of ethno-cultural American identity. As Michael Lind has observed "a real nation is a concrete historical community, defined primarily by a common language, common folkways, and a common vernacular culture" (Lind 1995, p. 5), and such, Lind contends, America has been for hundreds of years. In Lind's assessment, as well as those of some others (e.g. Conzen 1991; Alba and Nee 2003), America's common culture is syncretic, uniquely blending elements from diverse sources, and yielding a culture in which, speaking metaphorically, "the colors are smeared and blended together on the palette, beyond any hope of reconstitution in their original hues" (Lind 1995, p. 269). Lind, nevertheless, concedes that the incorporation of diverse cultural elements has been selective, and that a basic "grammar of Americanness" has been sustained, rooted in what he says has been the most fertile soil of American culture, "four centuries of Protestant preachers irrigating the continent, week after week, with sermons and prayers" (Lind 1995, p. 217).

Samuel P. Huntington (2004) is not as generous as Lind in his assessment of the cultural contours of the United States, and insists upon the virtually exclusive centrality of the Anglo-Protestant culture of the founding settlers to American national identity, language, beliefs, social, political, and moral values, and institutions. To some degree, the American public complements its incorporation of the American Creed into conceptions of American national identity with cultural imperatives, with a very large majority regarding speaking English as a prerequisite for being a "true American," and a modest majority requiring belief in God as a signal of that status (Citrin, Reingold, and Green 1990). Ethno-cultural conceptions of American national identity have been responsible for two major campaigns for immigrant assimilation, the Americanization movement of the first quarter of the twentieth century, and the Official English campaigns of the last 20 years or so.

During the 1930s the term "pluralism" came into vogue for describing the American social order. The term did not refer to the cultural federation of nationalities that

Horace Kallen had celebrated a decade earlier, nor did it refer to the politics of recognition that was to arise in the late 1960s. Rather, it referred to the idea that America comprised culturally diverse individuals, whose differences warranted our respectful tolerance, even as the expression of those differences was to be circumscribed within the private or civil sphere (Glazer 1975, 1998). This is the model of national identity that I call "individualistic-pluralistic." During World War II, celebration of diversity, with an "Americans All!" theme, emerged as a means of promoting war-time unity (Gerstle 2001). Adherents of this view differed among themselves as to how long cultural differences or identities rooted in national origins might persist, but they generally anticipated eventual assimilation to a common American mold in which religious affiliations would provide the main enduring axis of difference (see Herberg 1955). Though not grappling with complex questions about black culture or black identity, and their relationships to American identity, many of these pluralists advocated racial tolerance and integration along with acceptance of religious and ethnic diversity.

While signifying a milestone shift that expanded conceptions of who belonged within the American national community, pluralism of the 1930s-to-mid-1960s variety was not antithetical to assimilation. Indeed, it was a *form* of assimilation (Fuchs 1990; Gleason 1992). Acceptance of cultural diversity was contingent on behavioral or value differences being minor or kept out of view, and was predicated on acceptance of the core American value system, though whether ethnic Americans during the mid-third of the twentieth century did share an understanding of a core American value system may be questioned. Robert Wiebe (1975) argues that contrary to elite assumptions, no one combination of cultural values constituted *the* true American core. However, the appearance of consensus could be conveyed by a "carefully designed scheme of hyphenations" which, in Wiebe's assessment, "provided by far the best glossary for America's culturally fragmented society" (1975, p. 70).

In Michael Walzer's view, the hyphen remains the image that best captures the nature of identity in an America that holds the "twinned American values of a singular citizenship and a radically pluralist civil society" (Walzer 1996, p. 17). Walzer claims that there is, indeed, a recognizable American national culture, but that it is distinctively "nonexclusive" (p. 42). The hyphen functions as a "plus sign," and life can be lived on either side of the hyphen, because full commitment to citizenship does not require "a full commitment to American (or to any other) nationality" (p. 45). The image of the hyphen may not, however, do justice to the sociological and psychological complexities of participating and living through multiple identities. It works only if there are clear distinctions between the domains in which one acts and experiences oneself as simply "American," and those in which one acts as and feels oneself to be only ethnic.

Lawrence Fuchs (1990) has characterized the model of American diversity as "voluntary pluralism," in which elements of ethno-cultural, creedal, and individualistic-pluralistic models are synthesized. Fuchs assigns central importance to a "civic culture," based on the founding principles of liberty and self-government. America's civic culture, according to Fuchs, provides integrative opportunities for political participation in the exercise of civil rights, while at the same time it "permits and protects expressions of ethnic and religious diversity based on individual rights and . . . also inhibits and ameliorates conflict among religious, ethnic, and racial groups" (Fuchs

1990, p. xv). The civic culture, by virtue of its principles of separation of church and state, and rights of free speech and assembly, both "facilitate[s] and protect[s] the expression of ancestral cultural values and sensibilities" (Fuchs 1990, p. 23), and establishes opportunities for immigrant groups to mobilize in pursuit of their economic and political interests. In Fuchs's view, immigrants have in the past, and continue to, become attached to America by developing ethnic group identities, pursuing their interests in the political sphere, and developing emotional attachment to the symbols and rituals of patriotism rooted in the creedal expression of American identity. Paradoxically, it is through their pursuit of particularistic interests in the political sphere that immigrant groups become integrated into American society, reinforcing the civic culture as the basis of national unity. The model of "voluntary pluralism," which Fuchs likens to John Higham's (1975) model of "pluralistic integration," and which can be likened, as well, to aspects of Nathan Glazer's (1975) "American ethnic pattern," permits individuals to choose to be as ethnic or non-ethnic as they wish, and results in an ethnic "kaleidoscope" which is "complex and varied, changing form, pattern, color . . . continually shifting from one set of relations to another; rapidly changing" (Fuchs 1990, p. 276).

If we are to believe the litany of jeremiads of the last 30 years, none of the models of American national identity discussed above any longer prevail. Rather, because of mis-turns taken by those protesting racial and ethnic exclusion and oppression, we now live in an America characterized by "ethnic federalism" (Salins 1997), "anti-assimilationism" (Salins 1997), and "a new particularism" (Higham 1975). It is an America in which we "no longer imagine . . . that [we] belong . . . to the same national community or that [we] share . . . a common set of ideals" (Gerstle 2001, p. 345). Rather, we are told, America is now viewed by intellectual, academic, and political elites, as well as by ethnic activists, as a "complex patchwork of distinctive communities" (Hollinger 1995, p. 65), or as "a federation of nationalities or cultures sharing little or nothing but a common government" (Lind 1995, p. 1), each of which must be equally recognized, subsidized, and enabled to maintain its identity and have its needs met. This view, it is alleged, while not that of the population at large, guides policy in education, politics, culture, and labor markets. Bilingual and multicultural education, multilingual ballots, "majority minority" Congressional districts, and affirmative action are prominent examples of such policies. Michael Lind sums up, declaring that multiculturalism is the "de facto orthodoxy of the present American regime: Multicultural America" (Lind 1995, p. 97).

The erosion of common identity that multiculturalism is said to have effected holds particular salience for immigrants and their assimilation. Immigrants are alleged to make collective demands upon the resources of the state based on multiculturalist rationales, and to have rejected the "immigrant bargain" in which welcome and opportunity are extended in return for immigrants taking the assimilationist path (see, for example, Hanson 2003; Huntington 2004). I consider this argument below. Here it is important to point out that multiculturalism of any strong separatist variety is far from triumphant. As the critics point out, multiculturalism has gained little legitimacy with the larger public (Citrin, Reingold, and Green 1990). More significantly, what passes for multicultural education in the schools is usually far from the kinds of multiculturalism to which critics so vociferously object. Rather, contemporary educational practices are consistent with, at most, a program of mild multicultural inclusion and integration, not separatism (Olneck 1990, 2001; Wills, Lintz, and Mehan 2004). Bilingual education, the *bête noire* of many critics, has never been practiced on nearly as expansive a scale as many believe; the privileged position it held in federal policy ended in the early 1980s; and, as noted above, the Bilingual Education Act itself has been replaced by the English Language Acquisition Act of 2001. College enrollment and graduation data and employment data do not suggest that the reach of affirmative action has been wide or deep (US Department of Education, National Center for Education Statistics 2001). Moreover, affirmative action, as Michael Walzer (1980), has pointed out, provides mobility for individuals; it does not provide voice for a group. Furthermore, affirmative action has been rolled back or circumscribed by state initiatives and legislation, and by decisions of federal courts (C. Anderson 1999; P. Schmidt 2003).

We *do* live in a society far more accepting of diversity among individuals than in the past, and officially more committed to racial equality than in the past, but we do not live in Michael Lind's (1995) or others' fantasy "Multicultural America." More accurate are John Hall and Charles Lindholm's conclusion that "such differences as do exist in America, though passionately embraced, are objectively relatively small: while ideologically 'all are different,' Americans in fact are remarkably 'all the same'" (Hall and Lindholm 1999, p. 146), and Claude Fischer's conclusion that "contemporary patterns of assimilation do not seem qualitatively different from those of earlier eras. . . . What may be new and substantially different is that an ideology of diversity, of multiculturalism exists today that did not exist before" (Fischer 1999, p. 218).

"Is Assimilation Dead?" Perception and Reality

In 1993, Nathan Glazer asked "Is Assimilation Dead?" Glazer's own answer, then, and in a subsequent version of the same piece (Glazer 1998) has been "no." However, numerous recent observers claim that contemporary immigrants are, in presumed contrast to previous waves of immigrants, failing to assimilate to American life (see, for example, J. Miller 1998; Hanson 2003; Huntington 2004; Salins 2004). These claims repeat those heard in the late 1970s and early to mid-1980s, which, upon scrutiny, were found to be exaggerated (Fuchs 1990). The failure to assimilate is, in the view of some, both a result of, and a further cause of, the erosion of American national identity (Huntington 2004). These observers perceive contemporary immigrants as clustering, perhaps permanently, in immigrant enclaves, failing to learn or use English, maintaining dual citizenship and dual loyalties, and failing to experience social mobility. They attribute lagging assimilation to the ongoing flow of immigration, with no interruption in sight, the proximity of the Mexican and US borders, the ease of travel and communication between immigrant destinations and homelands, deep differences between immigrants' and natives' cultural values and practices, and policies and institutional practices of "multiculturalism."

Of particular relevance to questions of national identity are claims like those of Huntington (2004) that the cultures of contemporary immigrants, especially that of Mexicans, differ from American culture much more sharply than in the past, thus endangering the prospects of successful assimilation and integration. It is ironic to read arguments that early twentieth-century immigrants were more similar to Americans of the time because they were "European." Certainly, native Americans of that period failed to recognize their kinship with those who were then being labeled the "new" immigrants, to distinguish them from the "old" immigrants from Germany, Ireland, and Scandinavia, now remembered as more assimilable than the masses of Jewish, Italian, and Polish immigrants. And, of course, in the nineteenth century, the assimilability of the now "old" immigrants had, itself, been often questioned.

Historically, native Americans have failed to recognize and appreciate the ways in which, and the extent to which, immigrants have, in fact, integrated into American society. What historians and sociologists have later recognized as transitional experiences, practices, and institutions, have seemed to natives of the times to portend permanent "alien" communities and ways. For example, immigrant settlement areas that early twentieth-century observers saw as examples of "clannishness" proved to be way-stations to immigrant dispersion, albeit in stages. The replenishment of communities with new immigrants gave an illusory appearance of linguistic, residential, and cultural persistence. The immigrant press and theater loomed large in its time, but persisted beyond the first generation in only attenuated form. Ethnic political organization that struck some as separatist and un-American proved incorporative and integrative. Examination of current data suggests, unsurprisingly, that fears that today's immigrants are rejecting assimilation are unwarranted. Indices bearing most directly on the relationship between national identity and assimilation concern language, attitudes and values, self-identification, and citizenship.

Today's immigrants recognize the imperative to learn English, and a substantial majority agree that learning English should be obligatory (Farkas, Duffett, and Johnson 2003). Among immigrant youth, becoming or being American is equated with being able to speak English (Olsen 1997; Valenzuela 1999). Today's immigrant parents, like those of the past, are encountering the refusal of their children to use their native language, and many report that their children speak primarily English among their friends (*Washington Post*/Kaiser 1999; Farkas, Duffett, and Johnson 2003). In the 1999 *Washington Post*/Kaiser survey, for example, close to 60 percent of Latinos with children 18 and under reported that their children "usually" spoke English with their friends, and 36 percent reported that their children spoke only English with their friends (*Washington Post*/Kaiser 1999). In the Children of Immigrants Longitudinal Sample (CILS), even among Mexican second-generation respondents, who are sometimes characterized as resisting the acquisition of English, the preference for using English rises from 45 percent in eighth or ninth grade (Portes and Hao 1998, p. 273) to 70 percent in twelfth grade (Portes and Rumbaut 2001, Table 6.3, p. 122). Even among Cuban respondents attending bilingual schools in the heart of Miami's ethnic enclave, students overwhelmingly prefer to communicate in English, leading Portes and Schauffler to conclude that "contrary to nativist fears, what is at risk is the preservation of the languages spoken by immigrant parents [not the absence of English proficiency and use among immigrants]" (1996, p. 28).

Intergenerational patterns of language use show pronounced trends away from sole reliance on languages other than English, even within the home, to the point that among third-generation Latinos in the 1999 *Washinton Post*/Kaiser national survey of Latinos, only a minuscule 1 percent spoke only Spanish or more Spanish than English in the home, only 21 percent spoke both Spanish and English equally, while 78 percent spoke only English (Goldstein and Suro 2000). It is true that because of lower levels of exogamy, higher than average enclave employment, higher proximity to other Spanish speakers, and higher population concentrations in states in which Spanish-speakers reside, Mexican Americans are slower than contemporary Asian American immigrants or Euro-American immigrants of the past to shift to the sole use of English (Alba, Logan, Lutz, and Stults 2002), and it is uncertain if patterns of bilingualism among Mexican Americans might portend the emergence of a degree of stable bilingualism (Lopez and Stanton-Salazar 2001; Bean and Stevens 2003). Nevertheless, even an unusually stable retention of Spanish may reflect only "limited bilingualism" in which English is dominant, and knowledge of Spanish is residual and rudimentary (Portes and Rumbaut 2001). Moreover, there is no evidence that knowledge, and even use, of a language other than English is necessarily indicative of a lack of facility with English. There is no reason to believe that retention of Spanish impedes the acquisition of English (Rodriguez 2004). Further, the availability of Spanish-language media, often identified by critics as an impediment to linguistic assimilation, apparently does not stem the shift to English among immigrant populations. Across generations, individuals watch less and less Spanish-language television; moreover, among even first-generation Latinos, only 31 percent watch all or the majority of their television viewing in Spanish (Goldstein and Suro 2000).

Critics fear that bilingual education diminishes the incentive to learn English quickly, and conveys the message that learning English is of minor importance. Immigrant parents clearly do not want anything to stand in the way of their children learning English, and somewhat over 60 percent of them join the general American public in favoring the exclusive use of English as the language of instruction in schools. Over 70 percent believe that "public schools should teach new immigrants English as quickly as possible even if this means they fall behind," as against agreeing that the schools should teach new immigrant kids "other subjects in their native language even if this means it takes them longer to learn English" (Farkas, Duffett, and Johnson 2003, p. 25). While Mexican immigrants are more favorable toward bilingual education than other immigrants or the general American public, still a slight majority favor an all-English pedagogy, and two-thirds of them agree that the schools should teach English as quickly as possible, even at the cost of their children falling behind in some subjects (Farkas, Duffett, and Johnson 2003, p. 53).

Those concerned that contemporary immigrants are so culturally different from Americans that they will not acquire or hold the attitudes, beliefs, and values that promote successful integration into American society receive very little support for their views from systematic data. Optimism that the United States offers far greater opportunities to their children for a better life than does their home country is pervasive among immigrants (*Washington Post*/Kaiser 1999; Farkas, Duffett, and Johnson 2003). Immigrants widely recognize and appreciate the democratic character of government and society, and are overwhelmingly positive about the decision to emigrate to the United States, praising the United States as superior to their home countries in guaranteeing rights, having a government that could be trusted, providing for a good education, and, despite recognizing discrimination, being a society which values respect for diverse kinds of people (Farkas, Duffett, and Johnson 2003).

Immigrants appreciate the need for cultivating commonality among diverse groups. For example, somewhat over three-quarters of Latino immigrants in the 1999

Washington Post/Kaiser survey reported that it was important that different racial and ethnic groups "change so that they blend into the larger society as in the idea of the melting pot" (*Washington Post*/Kaiser 1999, p. 12). Nevertheless, they believe strongly that it is also important to "maintain their distinct cultures" (p. 13). The combination of blending in and maintaining their distinct cultures is entirely consistent with the widespread expression of "symbolic ethnicity" among Americans (Gans 1979). Where immigrants do express criticism of American values and norms, it is in the direction of favoring socially conservative values and norms that would strengthen and enhance respect for family life.

Some groups of immigrants are more skeptical than white Americans that hard work offers a guarantee of success. For example, while two-thirds of Anglos disagree that hard work offers little guarantee of success, just a majority of Latino immigrants do so (*Washington Post*/Kaiser 1999, pp. 19, 20), and 37 percent of Latinos agree that "it doesn't do any good to plan for the future because you don't have control over it," as compared with 18 percent of Anglos (pp. 19, 20). Given the extremely hard working lives that many immigrants experience, without substantial income gains or mobility, this should not be surprising. Nevertheless, contrary to the views of some, immigrants overwhelmingly regard providing for oneself, and staying off welfare, as a cardinal virtue (Farkas, Duffett, and Johnson 2003). Furthermore, expression of "fatalism," as represented in the statement concerning the value of planning for the future, attenuates markedly over immigrant generations (Pew/Kaiser 2004b) and as immigrants or their children acquire English (Pew/Kaiser 2004a).

Significantly, views on a range of social issues, for example gender roles within the family, intra-familial obligations, and abortion, also show the same marked pattern of converging across generations toward the views of other Americans, as well as converging as individuals acquire knowledge of English. Interestingly, in the Pew/Kaiser survey data, holding constant language dominance, there are no significant effects of generation on the social attitudes assessed. This means that generational status alone, without the acquisition and use of English, does not cultivate social attitudes more congruent with those of the American "mainstream." This finding accords with the claims of both proponents of English monolingualism and proponents of bilingualism that cultural dispositions and language are intimately entwined (Pew/Kaiser 2004a).

From these data, there is no reason to suppose that contemporary immigrants and their offspring are less likely than immigrants of the past to concur with the American Creed or the American way of life. There is, Amitai Etzioni has rightly concluded, "ample evidence" that "Americans of all racial and ethnic backgrounds hold their most important beliefs in common" (Etzioni 2004, p. 213), and that while considerable diversity of beliefs may be found within groups, there is considerable similarity across racial and ethnic groups.

Critics worry that immigrants and their offspring are not establishing the attachments to American society that would make them authentic Americans, and are not adopting American identities. Their concern arises, in part, because, when asked, immigrants often identify themselves with labels that refer to their native countries or to ethnic affiliations, and do not exclusively or unambiguously identify themselves as "Americans." The patterns of these reports by generation and linguistic dominance, however, show a pronounced trend toward affirming the identity label "American"

(Pew/Kaiser 2004b). Moreover, other survey results suggest a greater identification with America among first-generation immigrants than is reflected above. In the 2002 Public Agenda survey of immigrant adults, over half the respondents reported that they "mostly think of themselves as Americans"; 22 percent say they "mostly think of themselves in terms of the country where they were born" and 23 percent say they mostly think of themselves in terms of America and home country about equally (Farkas, Duffett, and Johnson 2003).

While the intergenerational data seem unambiguous in revealing a trend toward identification as "Americans," they obscure shifts in identity attribution that individuals may experience. Immigrant high school youth, apparently, to some extent, relinquish identifying as hyphenated Americans (e.g. Chinese American) or as American, and adopt pan-ethnic labels (e.g. Latino, Asian), or the name of their parents' country of origin (Portes and Rumbaut 2001). These shifts are not evidence of closer attachments to their parents' identities, and occur despite evident shifts toward more Americanized behavior. They are expressions of "reactive ethnicity" that develops in the context of living in the United States, and reflects increasing awareness among second-generation individuals of their status as racialized minorities within the scheme of available American identities (Portes and Rumbaut 2001; Stepick, Stepick, Eugene, Teed, and Labissiere 2001; Fernandez-Kelly and Curran 2001; Portes 2004).

There is no question that today's immigrants are able to maintain closer ties to their homelands than were immigrants in the past. For Latino immigrants, proximity to the United States is an important factor. For all immigrants, modern and affordable communications technology permits phone calls and e-mailing, and relatively inexpensive airfares permit occasional trips even for those whose homelands are a great distance from the United States. These kinds of ties, however, weaken considerably as immigrants are in the United States longer. Moreover, some ties remain primarily symbolic. The proportion of Latino immigrants who are dual citizens, for example, is in the order of 80 percent, but the proportion who have voted in elections in their home countries after arriving in the United States is only about one-quarter (*Washington Post*/Kaiser 1999, p. 35).

Lower rates of naturalization than in the past have disturbed some critics, leading them to question whether today's immigrants are wholeheartedly transferring their allegiance to the United States. However, numerous non-citizens have not been in the United States long enough to apply for citizenship, are in the process of pursuing citizenship, or are planning to, and only about 10 percent report not planning to seek citizenship (*Washington Post*/Kaiser 1999). While lagging in actual attainment of citizenship, more Mexican than other immigrants say becoming a citizen is extremely important (Farkas, Duffett, and Johnson 2003), and an overwhelming 80 percent of Mexican immigrants in the 2002 Public Agenda survey say that the United States will be their permanent home, a figure higher than for all but European immigrants, and considerably higher than among Caribbean immigrants (Farkas, Duffett, and Johnson 2003). Moreover, those who are deeply anxious over large concentrations of Mexican immigrants maintaining historically unprecedented close attachments to their homeland – what John Higham has referred to as "an indelible foreignness" (1999, p. 56), what Victor Hanson (2003) imagines as the dystopia of "Mexifornia," and Samuel P. Huntington (2004) refers to ominously as the "challenge of Hispanicization" – fail to appreciate the salient distinctions of identity and boundaries with which Mexican immigrants differentiate themselves from those remaining in Mexico and those merely sojourning in America (Vila 2000).

Forecasting the future of assimilation is, to be sure, an uncertain endeavor. Astute and careful scholars like Richard Alba and Victor Nee (2003) anticipate a society in which boundary "blurring" will prove to be a central dynamic to increased assimilation. By boundary blurring, Alba and Nee mean that "the social profile of a boundary has become less distinct, and the clarity of the social distinction involved has become clouded" (2003, p. 61). They acknowledge, however, the possibility of a scenario in which this process leaves African Americans, and some immigrants more readily classified as "black," within strongly racialized boundaries. This is a possibility that underlies the forecasts of some that contemporary immigrant groups may well experience "segmented assimilation," under which some groups will enjoy upward mobility and integration, and others will be consigned to socio-economic stagnation and racialized isolation (see, for example, Portes and Rumbaut 1996, 2001). Alba and Nee, however, emphasize the potential fluidity of even racial boundaries, and the impact that an increasingly composite mainstream culture, that itself values individual diversity, may have on those boundaries. In their judgment, their version of an assimilation model "offers the best way to understand and describe the integration into the mainstream experienced across generations by many individuals and ethnic groups, even if it cannot be regarded as a universal outcome of American life" (Alba and Nee 1997, p. 827), and they are confident that "assimilation remains a pattern of major importance for immigrant groups entering the United States, and it is likely to reshape the future ethnic contours of American society, as it did those of the past" (Alba and Nee 2003, p. 270).

If Alba and Nee are correct, we may anticipate that symbolic representation of American national identity in the foreseeable future will be primarily both ethno-cultural, emphasizing a shared culture, albeit one that is considerably more diverse in its origins, and more permeable, than in the past, and what I have called pluralistic-individualistic, representing the nation as a shared community of highly diverse individuals. Lest this be interpreted in an overly optimistic fashion, it is important to recognize that an inclusive symbolic representation of national identity need not be accompanied by diminished racial and class inequality. It is, however, very possible that an inclusive symbolic representation of national identity is a minimum prerequisite for greater equality (Gitlin 1995; D. Miller 2004).

Conclusion

Immigrant assimilation and American national identity, to be sure, exist in tension. It is, however, perhaps useful to conclude by observing that however severe the challenges to American national identity posed by the question of immigrant assimilation, they are less severe than they are in several western European nations which have experienced large-scale immigration in recent decades. Comparison with these countries may help to deepen our understanding of the relationship between American national identity and assimilation, and to put the points made above into a comparative perspective.

Immigration is central to American historical experience, and while particular episodes of immigration, including the most recent, may prompt nativist reactions, immigration does not challenge the nation's fundamental conception of itself as it does in countries, such as Germany, whose identities have, until recently, been expressed in strictly ethno-national terms, and for which large-scale immigration is a novel and unexpected development. Immigration is part of America's "national narrative" (De Cillia, Reisigl, and Wodak 1999). "America's concept of nationhood is uniquely resilient," Christian Joppke has observed, "because it is politically, rather than ethnically constituted. . . . From this it follows that the ethnic recomposition of American society in the era of Third-World immigration is not per se a threat to American nationhood" (Joppke 1996, p. 463). Joppke continues, ". . . the bonds of the American 'new nation,' are recreated by every single immigrant who is turned into a citizen" (p. 490).

Nor has the United States experienced, as has postwar Britain, any recent fundamental challenge to its conception of national boundaries and membership. At the end of Empire, British *national* identity was not well defined, as membership in the Empire and, then, the Commonwealth were emphasized. In response to Commonwealth immigration, particularly from the West Indies and South Asia, Britain narrowed its conception of membership, indirectly, but obviously, on racial grounds (Grillo 1998). The "immigrant" became the site for the reconstruction of British identity (Doty 1996), in which "the devolution of empire meant adjusting an over-inclusive nationality to an exclusive identity based on 'blood and culture'" (Joppke 1999, p. 223). In contrast, American national identity as ethnically, if not racially, inclusive was solidified during the World War II period, and movement toward racial inclusivity arose, in part, from the war experience (Gerstle 2001).

Neither has recent immigration in the United States posed a challenge to deeply held principles of political organization associated with national identity as it has in France, where fundamental tenets of republican citizenship, such as public secularism, are perceived to have been challenged by seemingly non-assimilative, non-individualistic North African Muslims (Favell 2001a, 2001b; Kastoryano 2002). Ethnicity as a basis for political participation in American society has, since the nineteenth century, been a familiar phenomenon.

Furthermore, the United States is not pressured by threats of sub-national separatisms, like those represented by Bretons, Catalonians, or Scots, nor by the demands of supra-national integration like those of the European Union. While unauthorized immigration from Mexico may prompt some to exaggerated anxieties over indirect irredentism and re-annexation, no seriously plausible movement exists among Mexican Americans for secession. While the future of the nation-state may be perceived as uncertain in Europe, thereby exacerbating anxieties over immigration and assimilation, no such dynamic is at play in the United States.

The construction of national identity, like the construction of any identity, is inherently contrastive (Triandafyllidou 2001). The "nation" is differentiated from an "Other," which may be external to the borders of the nation, or may be internal, such as immigrants. Differentiation from the "Other" may be implicit or it may be explicit; and it may shift historically. Such differentiation is accomplished by greater or lesser degrees of specificity about the Other (what we are *not*) and about "ourselves" (what we *are like*). While some scholars have claimed that Spanish in the United States is, like Islam in Europe, representative of the "Other," and that both "are metonyms for the dangers that those most opposed to immigration perceive as looming ahead: loss of cultural identity, accompanied by disintegrative separatism and communal conflict," each representing "equally dramatic" instances of cultural conflict (Zolberg and Woon 1999, p. 5), I believe that there are significant differences between the two cases that point to the greater compatibility between immigration and national identity in the United States than in Europe.

There is no doubt that many English-speaking non-Latino Americans resent and fear the "intrusion" of Spanish into "their" public spaces (Crawford 1992; R. Schmidt 2000), and recent campaigns against bilingual education have been largely successful (San Miguel 2004). However, those campaigns have not been conducted on the basis of repelling the demands of Spanish-speakers, but, rather, on the grounds of providing "English for the Children," which, while unquestionably valorizing linguistic homogeneity, conveys an "assimilative invitation" (Gusfield 1963). Proposals to make English "official," while enjoying popularity, have had only uneven success and, at least up until now, limited practical consequences (Crawford 2004).

In Europe, particularly in France, the "problem" of Islam is more vexatious than that of Spanish in the United States. Symbolized by successive public controversies over Muslim girls wearing religiously significant headscarves (*les foulards*) in schools, the French have as yet been unable to provide the means for mutually compatible self-identification as French and Muslim (Favell 2001b). On the one hand, insistence on wearing headscarves violates deeply held, repeatedly affirmed republican tenets of excluding religious expression within official public spheres (Moruzzi 1994; Kastoryano 2004). On the other, Islam, rather than national origin, is evolving as the basis of organized ethnicity in France, and elsewhere, seeking recognition through institutionalized channels heretofore defined as strictly religious (Kastoryano 2004). In Britain, Muslims pose difficult problems of recognition in that they have become a racialized minority but are not acknowledged in Britain's institutionalized structure of anti-discrimination and race relations measures (Favell 2001b). "What is at stake," Riva Kastoryano has observed, "is the contemporary acceptance of Islam as part of Europe's historical continuity" (Kastoryano 2004). American debates over language policies and practices do not rise to the same levels of intensity or significance as European debates about the integration of Islam into the fabric of national identity and citizenship.

To be sure, neo-nativist campaigns, like that for California's Proposition 187, passed in 1994, which attempted to deny public benefits to unauthorized immigrants, are characterized by ugly, racist rhetoric. The public rhetoric favoring Proposition 187 referred most prominently to immigration as "dangerous water," with phrases like "awash under a brown tide," "overwhelming flood," and "relentless flow," evoking threats of inundation, engulfment, and dispossession (Santa Ana 2002). Other metaphors depicted immigration as an invasion, disease, or burden (Santa Ana 2002; Ono and Sloop 2002). Some supporters of Proposition 187 argued that Americans needed to "take back" their country (Chavez 1997). Certainly, this rhetoric constructs dichotomies of "we"/"they," "us"/"them," "ours"/"theirs" (Santa Ana 2002), and reasserts a "narrow nationalist construction of the nation" (Chavez 1997, p. 73). Nevertheless, this rhetoric does not name or depict *particular* "Others" to be excluded or refashioned, as did the more strident and explicit rhetoric of early twentieth-century Americanization campaigns (Carlson 1987). Moreover, the rhetoric of Proposition 187 proponents was addressed, however much for pragmatic reasons, to the "problem" of "illegal" immigration, and did not fundamentally question the place of immigrants in the American national community (Barkan 2003). In the years subsequent to passage of Proposition 187, the conjunction of conditions which produced passage of the measure dissipated, and, rather than a stable nativist consensus having emerged, divisions and tensions entailing a "residual nativist temperament" and a "concurrent vein of toleration for the expanding ethnic diversity" persisted (Barkan 2003, p. 267). Claims that "racial nativism," evident in attacks on Latinos and Koreans during the 1992 Los Angeles riots, in tracts like Peter Brimelow's *Alien Nation: Common Sense About America's Immigration Disaster*, and in the campaign for Proposition 187, "point to a resurgence of a nativism unparalleled in this country since the 1920s," and claims that "today's nativism is as virulent as any that has gone before" (Sanchez 1997, p. 1013) are over-generalized. Nonetheless, while over 60 percent of native-born Americans agree that the United States *is* a "country made up of many cultures and values that change as new people come here," a similar proportion agree that the United States *should be* a "country with a basic American culture and values that immigrants take on when they come here." Among immigrants, however, approximately 60 percent believe that the United States both is *and* should be a "country made up of many cultures and values that change as new people come here" (NPR/Kaiser/Kennedy School 2004, p. 2). This suggests that while a European observer's conclusion that there is no "fermentation of national identit[y]" in the United States, redrawing boundaries in relation to a symbolic immigrant Other, as there may be in European countries (Triandafyllidou 2001), immigrant assimilation, as policy, discourse, political conflict, and experience, will remain part of the ongoing construction of American national identity.

REFERENCES

Alba, Richard and Victor Nee (1997). "Rethinking Assimilation Theory for a New Era of Immigration." *International Migration Review* 31(4): 826–74.

—— (2003). *Remaking the American Mainstream: Assimilation and Contemporary Immigration*. Cambridge, MA: Harvard University Press.

Alba, Richard, John Logan, Amy Lutz, and Brian Stults (2002). "Only English by the Third Generation? Loss and Preservation of the Mother Tongue among the Grandchildren of Contemporary Immigrants." *Demography* 39(3): 467–84.

Anderson, Benedict (1991). *Imagined Communities: Reflections on the Origin and Spread of Nationalism*. London: Verso.

Anderson, Corinne E. (1999). "Comment: A Current Perspective: The Erosion of Affirmative Action in University Admissions." *Akron Law Review* 32: 181–32.

Arieli, Yehoshua (1961). "Individualism and National Consciousness in the United States." *Scripta Hierosolymitana* 7: 296–337.

Barkan, Elliott R. (2003). "Return of the Nativists? California Public Opinion and Immigration in the 1980s and 1990s." *Social Science History* 27(2): 229–83.

Bean, Frank D. and Gillian Stevens (2003). *America's Newcomers and the Dynamics of Diversity*. New York: Russell Sage Foundation.

Brubaker, Rogers (1996). *Nationalism Reframed: Nationhood and the National Question in the New Europe*. New York: Cambridge University Press.

Carlson, Robert A. (1987). *The Americanization Syndrome: A Quest for Conformity*. London: Croom Helm.

220 MICHAEL R. OLNECK

Chavez, Leo R. (1997). "Immigration Reform and Nativism: The Nationalist Response to the Transnationalist Challenge." In Juan F. Perea, ed., *Immigrants Out! The New Nativism and the Anti-Immigrant Impulse in the United States*. New York: New York University Press, pp. 61–77.

Citrin, Jack, Beth Reingold, and Donald Philip Green (1990). "American Identity and the Politics of Ethnic Change." *Journal of Politics* 52: 1124–54.

Conzen, Kathleen N. (1991). "Mainstreams and Side Channels: The Localization of Immigrant Cultures." *Journal of American Ethnic History* 11(1): 5–20.

Crawford, James (1992). *Hold Your Tongue: Bilingualism and the Politics of "English Only."* Reading, MA: Addison-Wesley.

—— (2004). "Language Legislation in the U.S.A." http://ourworld.compuserve.com/homepages/JWCRAWFORD/langleg.htm#stateleg

De Cillia, Rudolf, Martin Reisigl, and Ruth Wodak (1999). "The Discursive Construction of National Identities." *Discourse and Society* 10(2): 149–73.

Doty, Roxanne Lynn (1996). "Immigration and National Identity: Constructing the Nation." *Review of International Studies* 22: 235–55.

Etzioni, Amitai (2004). "Assimilation to the American Creed." In Tamar Jacoby, ed., *Reinventing the Melting Pot: The New Immigrants and What it Means to be American*. New York: Basic Books, pp. 211–20.

Farkas, Steve, Ann Duffett, and Jean Johnson, with Leslie Moye and Jackie Vine (2003). *Now That I'm Here: What America's Immigrants Have to Say About Life in the U.S. Today*. New York: Public Agenda.

Favell, Adrian (2001a). "Multicultural Nation-Building: 'Integration as Public Philosophy and Research Paradigm in Western Europe.'" *Swiss Political Science Review* 7(2): 116–24.

—— (2001b). *Philosophies of Integration: Immigration and the Idea of Citizenship in France and Britain*. Basingstoke: Palgrave.

Fernandez-Kelly, Patricia and Sara Curran (2001). "Nicaraguans: Voices Lost, Voices Found." In Rubin Rumbaut and Alejandra Portes, eds., *Ethnicities: Children of Immigration in America*. Berkeley: University of California Press.

Fischer, Claude (1999). "Uncommon Values, Diversity, and Conflict in City Life." In Neil J. Smelser and Jeffrey C. Alexander, eds., *Diversity and Its Discontents: Cultural Conflict and Common Ground in Contemporary American Society*. Princeton, NJ: Princeton University Press, pp. 213–27.

Fuchs, Lawrence (1990). *The American Kaleidoscope: Race, Ethnicity, and the Civic Culture*. Hanover, NH: University Press of New England.

Gans, Herbert J. (1979). "Symbolic Ethnicity: The Future of Ethnic Groups and Cultures in America." *Ethnic and Racial Studies* 2: 1–20.

—— (2004). "The American Kaleidoscope, Then and Now." In Tamar Jacoby, ed., *Reinventing the Melting Pot: The New Immigrants and What it Means to be American*. New York: Basic Books, pp. 33–45.

Gerstle, Gary (1997). "Liberty, Coercion, and the Making of Americans." *Journal of American History* 84: 524–58.

—— (2001). *American Crucible: Race and Nation in the Twentieth Century*. Princeton, NJ: Princeton University Press.

Gitlin, Todd (1995). *The Twilight of Common Dreams: Why America is Wracked by Culture Wars*. New York: Metropolitan Books.

Glazer, Nathan (1975). *Affirmative Discrimination*. New York: Basic Books.

—— (1993). "Is Assimilation Dead?" *The Annals* 530: 122–36.

—— (1998). "Is Assimilation Dead?" In Arthur M. Melzer, Jerry Weinberger, and M. Richard Zinman, eds., *Multiculturalism and American Democracy*. Lawrence: University of Kansas Press, pp. 15–36.

—— (2004). "Assimilation Today: Is One Identity Enough?" In Tamar Jacoby, ed., *Reinventing the Melting Pot: The New Immigrants and What it Means to be American*. New York: Basic Books, pp. 61–73.

Gleason, Philip (1980). "American Identity and Americanization." In S. Thernstrom, ed., *The Harvard Encyclopedia of American Ethnic Groups*. Cambridge, MA: Belknap Press, pp. 31–58.

—— (1992). *Speaking of Diversity: Language and Ethnicity in Twentieth-Century America*. Baltimore: Johns Hopkins University Press.

Goldstein, Amy and Roberto Suro (2000). "A Journey in Stages; Assimilation's Pull is Still Strong, but its Pace Varies," *Washington Post*, January 16, p. A01.

Grillo, R.D. (1998). *Pluralism and the Politics of Difference: State, Culture, and Ethnicity in Comparative Perspective*. Oxford: Clarendon Press.

Gusfield, Joseph R. (1963). *Symbolic Crusade: Status Politics and the American Temperance Movement*. Urbana: University of Illinois Press.

Hall, John A. and Charles Lindholm (1999). *Is America Breaking Apart?* Princeton, NJ: Princeton University Press.

Hanson, Victor Davis (2003). *Mexifornia: A State of Becoming*. San Francisco: Encounter Books.

Herberg, Will (1955). *Protestant, Catholic, Jew: An Essay in American Religious Sociology*. Garden City, NY: Doubleday.

Higham, John (1970). *Strangers in the Land: Patterns of American Nativism, 1860–1925*. New York: Atheneum.

—— (1975). *Send These to Me: Jews and Other Immigrants in Urban America*. New York: Atheneum.

—— (1999). "Cultural Responses to Immigration." In Neil J. Smelser and Jeffrey C. Alexander, eds., *Diversity and Its Discontents: Cultural Conflict and Common Ground in Contemporary American Society*. Princeton, NJ: Princeton University Press, pp. 39–61.

Hollinger, David A. (1995). *Postethnic America: Beyond Multiculturalism*. New York: Basic Books.

Huntington, Samuel P. (2004). *Who Are We? The Challenges to America's National Identity*. New York: Simon and Schuster.

Jacobson, Matthew Frye (1998). *Whiteness of a Different Color: European Immigrants and the Alchemy of Race*. Cambridge, MA: Harvard University Press.

Jacoby, Tamar (2004a). "Defining Assimilation for the 21st Century." In Tamar Jacoby, ed., *Reinventing the Melting Pot: The New Immigrants and What it Means to be American*. New York: Basic Books, pp. 3–16.

—— (2004b). "The New Immigrants: A Progress Report." In Tamar Jacoby, ed., *Reinventing the Melting Pot: The New Immigrants and What it Means to be American*. New York: Basic Books, pp. 17–29.

—— (2004c). "What it Means to Be American in the 21st Century." In Tamar Jacoby, ed., *Reinventing the Melting Pot: The New Immigrants and What it Means to be American*. New York: Basic Books, pp. 293–314.

Joppke, Christian (1996). "Multiculturalism and Immigration: A Comparison of the United States, Germany, and Great Britain." *Theory and Society* 25(4): 449–500.

—— (1999). *Immigration and the Nation-State: The United States, Germany, and Great Britain*. Oxford: Oxford University Press.

Kaestle, Carl F. (1983). *Pillars of the Republic: Common Schools and American Society, 1780–1860*. New York: Hill and Wang.

Karst, Kenneth L. (1989). *Belonging to America: Equal Citizenship and the Constitution*. New Haven, CT: Yale University Press.

Kastoryano, Riva (2002). *Negotiating Identities: States and Immigrants in France and Germany*. Princeton, NJ: Princeton University Press.

—— (2004). "Religion and Incorporation: Islam in France and Germany." *International Migration Review* 38(3): 1234–55.

Kazal, Russell A. (1995). "Revisiting Assimilation: The Rise, Fall, and Reappraisal of a Concept in American Ethnic History." *American Historical Review* 100(2): 437–71.

King, Desmond (2000). *Making Americans: Immigration, Race, and the Origins of the Diverse Democracy.* Cambridge, MA: Harvard University Press.

—— (2001). "Making Americans: Immigration Meets Race." In Gary Gerstle and John Mollenkopf, eds., *E Pluribus Unum? Contemporary and Historical Perspectives in Immigrant Political Incorporation.* New York: Russell Sage Foundation, pp. 143–72.

Lind, Michael (1995). *The Next American Nation: The New Nationalism and the Fourth American Revolution.* New York: Free Press.

Lopez, David and Richard Stanton-Salazar (2001). "Mexican Americans: A Second-Generation at Risk." In R. Rumbaut and A. Portes, eds., *Ethnicities: Children of Immigrants in America.* Berkeley: University of California Press, pp. 57–90.

Mann, Arthur (1979). *The One and the Many: Reflections on the American Identity.* Chicago: University of Chicago Press.

Marty, Martin E. (1997). *The One and the Many: America's Struggle for the Common Good.* Cambridge, MA: Harvard University Press.

Miller, David (1995). *On Nationality.* Oxford: Clarendon Press.

—— (2004). "Immigrants, Nations, and Citizenship." Unpublished paper presented to CRASSH conference on "Migrants, Nations, and Citizenship." New Hall, Cambridge, July 5–6, 2004.

Miller, John J. (1998). *The Unmaking of Americans: How Multiculturalism Has Undermined America's Assimilation Ethic.* New York: Free Press.

Moruzzi, Norma Claire (1994). "A Problem with Headscarves: Contemporary Complexities of Political and Social Identity." *Political Theory* 22(4): 653–72.

Myrdal, Gunnar, with the Assistance of Richard Sterner and Arnold Rose (1944). *An American Dilemma: The Negro Problem and Modern Democracy.* New York: Harper and Brothers.

Nee, Victor and Richard Alba (2004). "Toward a New Definition." In Tamar Jacoby, ed., *Reinventing the Melting Pot: The New Immigrants and What it Means to be American.* New York: Basic Books, pp. 87–95.

NPR/Kaiser/Kennedy School Poll (2004). *Immigration: Summary of Findings.* http://www.npr.org/news/specials/polls/2004/immigration/summary.pdf

Olneck, Michael R. (1989). "Americanization and the Education of Immigrants, 1900–1925: An Analysis of Symbolic Action." *American Journal of Education* 97: 398–423.

—— (1990). "The Recurring Dream: Symbolism and Ideology in Intercultural and Multicultural Education." *American Journal of Education* 98: 147–74.

—— (2001). "Re-naming, Re-imagining America: Multicultural Curriculum as Classification Struggle." *Pedagogy, Culture, and Society* 9: 333–55.

Olsen, Laurie (1997). *Made in America: Immigrant Students in Our Public Schools.* New York: The New Press.

Ono, Kent A. and John M. Sloop (2002). *Shifting Borders: Rhetoric, Immigration, and California's Proposition 187.* Philadelphia: Temple University Press.

Parks, E. Taylor and Lois F. Parks (1965). *Memorable Quotations of Franklin D. Roosevelt.* New York: Thomas Y. Crowell.

Pew Hispanic Center/Henry J. Kaiser Family Foundation (2004a). "Survey Brief: Assimilation and Language." Report #7052. Washington, DC: Pew Hispanic Center. Available at: http://www.pewhispanic.org/site/docs/pdf/ASSIMILATION%20AND%20LANGUAGE-031904.pdf

Pew Hispanic Center/Henry J. Kaiser Family Foundation (2004b). "Survey Brief: Generational Differences." Report #7054. Washington, DC: Pew Hispanic Center. Available at:

http://www.pewhispanic.org/site/docs/pdf/GENERATIONAL%20DIFFERENCES-031904.pdf

Portes, Alejandro (2004). "For the Second Generation, One Step at a Time." In Tamar Jacoby, ed., *Reinventing the Melting Pot: The New Immigrants and What it Means to be American.* New York: Basic Books, pp. 155–66.

Portes, Alejandro and Lingxin Hao (1998). "*E Pluribus Unum*: Bilingualism and Loss of Language in the Second Generation." *Sociology of Education* 71: 269–94.

Portes, Alejandro and Ruben Rumbaut (1996). *Immigrant America: A Portrait,* 2nd ed. Berkeley: University of California Press.

Portes, Alejandro and Ruben Rumbaut (2001). *Legacies: The Story of the Immigrant Second Generation.* Berkeley: University of California Press.

Portes, Alejandro and Richard Schauffler (1996). "Language and the Second Generation: Bilingualism Yesterday and Today." In A. Portes, ed., *The New Second Generation.* New York: Russell Sage Foundation, pp. 8–29.

Rodriguez, Gregory (2004). "Mexican-Americans and the Mestizo Melting Pot." In Tamar Jacoby, ed., *Reinventing the Melting Pot: The New Immigrants and What it Means to be American.* New York: Basic Books, pp. 125–38.

Rumbaut, Ruben (1997). "Assimilation and Its Discontents: Between Rhetoric and Reality." *International Migration Review* 31 (Winter): 923–60.

Salins, Peter D. (1997). *Assimilation American Style.* New York: Basic Books.

—— (2004). "The Assimilation Contract: Endangered But Still Holding." In Tamar Jacoby, ed., *Reinventing the Melting Pot: The New Immigrants and What it Means to be American.* New York: Basic Books, pp. 99–109.

San Miguel, Guadalupe, Jr. (2004). *Contested Policy: The Rise and Fall of Federal Bilingual Education in the United States, 1960–2001.* Denton: University of North Texas Press.

Sanchez, George J. (1997). "Face the Nation: Race, Immigration, and the Rise of Nativism in Late Twentieth Century America." *International Migration Review* 31(4): 1009–30.

Santa Ana, Otto (2002). *Brown Tide Rising: Metaphors of Latinos in Contemporary American Public Discourse.* Austin: University of Texas Press.

Schmidt, Peter (2003). "Affirmative Action Fight is Renewed in the States." *Chronicle of Higher Education* 49(45): A19.

Schmidt, Ronald, Sr. (2000). *Language Policy and Identity Politics.* Philadelphia: Temple University Press.

Skerry, Peter (2004). " 'This Was Our Riot, Too': The Political Assimilation of Today's Immigrants." In Tamar Jacoby, ed., *Reinventing the Melting Pot: The New Immigrants and What it Means to be American.* New York: Basic Books, pp. 221–32.

Smith, Rogers M. (1987). "The 'American Creed' and American Identity: The Limits of Liberal Citizenship in the United States." *Western Political Quarterly* 47: 225–51.

Stepick, Alex, Carol Dutton Stepick, Emmanuel Eugene, Deborah Teed, and Yves Labissiere (2001). "Shifting Identities and Intergenerational Conflict: Growing up Haitian in Miami." In Ruben Rumbaut and Alejandro Portes, eds., *Ethnicities: Children of Immigrants in America,* Berkeley: University of California Press, pp. 229–66.

Takaki, Ronald (1993). *A Different Mirror: A History of Multicultural America.* Boston: Little, Brown.

Thernstrom, Stephan (2004). "Rediscovering the Melting Pot – Still Going Strong." In Tamar Jacoby, ed., *Reinventing the Melting Pot: The New Immigrants and What it Means to be American.* New York: Basic Books, pp. 47–59.

Triandafyllidou, Anna (2001). *Immigrants and National Identity in Europe.* London: Routledge.

US Department of Education, National Center for Education Statistics (2001). *Educational Achievement and Black–White Inequality,* NCES 2001-061, by Jonathan Jacobson, Cara

Olsen, Jennifer King Rice, and Stephen Sweetland. Project Officer: John Ralph. Washington, DC.

Valenzuela, Angela (1999). *Subtractive Schooling: U.S.–Mexican Youth and the Politics of Caring.* Albany: State University of New York Press.

Vila, Pablo (2000). *Crossing Borders, Reinforcing Borders: Social Categories, Metaphors, and Narrative Identities on the U.S.–Mexico Frontier.* Austin: University of Texas Press.

Waldinger, Roger (2004). "The 21st Century: An Entirely New Story." In Tamar Jacoby, ed., *Reinventing the Melting Pot: The New Immigrants and What it Means to be American.* New York: Basic Books, pp. 75–85.

Walzer, Michael (1980). "Pluralism: A Political Perspective." In S. Thernstrom, ed., *Harvard Encyclopedia of American Ethnic Groups.* Cambridge, MA: Belknap Press, pp. 781–7.

—— (1996). *What It Means to be an American.* New York: Marsilio.

Washington Post/Henry J. Kaiser Family Foundation/Harvard University National Survey on Latinos in America (1999). Available at: http://www.kff.org/kaiserpolls/loader.cfm?url=/commonspot/security/getfile.cfm&PageID=13509

Wiebe, Robert H. (1975). *The Segmented Society: An Introduction to the Meaning of America.* London: Oxford University Press.

—— (2002). *Who We Are: A History of Popular Nationalism.* Princeton, NJ: Princeton University Press.

Wills, John S., Angela Lintz, and Hugh Mehan (2004). "Ethnographic Studies of Multicultural Education in U.S. Classrooms and Schools." In J. Banks and C. Banks, eds., *Handbook of Research on Multicultural Education.* San Francisco: Jossey-Bass, pp. 163–83.

Wodak, Ruth, Rudolf De Cillia, Martin Reisigl, and Karen Liebhart (1999). *The Discursive Construction of National Identity.* Edinburgh: University of Edinburgh Press.

Wuthnow, Robert, ed. (1992). *Vocabularies of Public Life: Empirical Essays in Symbolic Structure.* London: Routledge.

Zolberg, Aristide R. and Long Litt Woon (1999). "Why Islam is Like Spanish: Cultural Incorporation in Europe and the United States." *Politics and Society* 27(1): 5–38.

CHAPTER TEN

Internationalization and Transnationalization

DAVID GERBER

The Transnational Moment

In the late twentieth century analysts of contemporary developments awoke to the consciousness of an increasingly transformed world, in which old structures were losing their conventional meanings and were being forced to assume new identities and purposes. Interrupted for most of the twentieth century by two world wars, the devastating world economic depression of the 1930s, decolonization, and the Cold War, the world market had begun at last to reintegrate itself throughout the globe, and thus to accelerate a process begun with the European voyages of exploration in the fifteenth century. The consequences were most obvious in daily life in the rise and proliferation of corporate giants doing business everywhere and seemingly anchored nowhere in particular, global marketing and advertising, systems that promised to bond the world into one integrated web of instantaneous, electronic communications, an international consumer culture, and environmental problems of planetary proportions. These new patterns asserted themselves as both *international* and *global* realities. They were international in that they involved new types of relationships between individual nation-states, and global in that they took root everywhere, independent of borders and boundaries (Sassen 1998; Tomlinson 1999). To the extent that they seemed deterritorialized – not bound by the constraints of the traditional boundaries and borders of nation-states and existing in new types of spaces dedicated to the production of power, goods, and meanings – they also asserted themselves as *transnational* realities. These new transnational patterns especially caught the eye of analysts, because they threatened in subtle ways to disrupt traditional state sovereignties, and because they were being produced not only from the top-down, as was the case with the globalizing capitalist economy, but from the bottom-up, through the activities of ordinary people in daily life (Wakeman 1988).

Nowhere in the transnational moment of the late twentieth century was this assertion of new patterns through the agency of ordinary individuals, families, and small groups more apparent than in the rapid expansion of the scope and scale of international migration. By the 1980s, citizens of every corner of the world were on the move, as global economic development simultaneously destabilized economies in the developing countries and created a global labor market, especially for low-skill workers, in the developed world. The political conflicts that attended decolonization, which were exacerbated by Cold War geopolitical rivalries and interventions, further destabilized life in many areas of the developing world. Changes in American immigration law in 1965 facilitated the entrance of peoples from outside the regions of Europe that had traditionally formed the core areas for immigration to the United States. But legal immigration was only part of the picture, as illegal entrances, especially across the southwestern border, reached massive proportions.

By the 1990s, American analysts of this new immigration from Asia, Latin America, and the Caribbean basin professed to find patterns that were fundamentally different from those that characterized the historical immigrations of the nineteenth and early twentieth centuries (Basch, Glick Schiller, and Szanton Blanc 1994; Glick Schiller, Basch, and Blanc-Szanton 1992; Smith and Guarnizo 1999; Portes 1997; Portes, Guarnizo, and Landholt 1999). Instantaneous electronic communications and jet air travel and job markets in the developed world that no longer provided stable and long-term employment were said to be creating a population of *transmigrants*. Transmigrants are defined as those individuals "who migrate and yet maintain or establish familial, economic, religious, political, or social relations in the state from which they moved, even as they also forge such relationships in the new state or states in which they settle" (Glick Schiller and Fouron 1999, p. 344). The transmigrant creates a way of life, in other words, that leads to simultaneous incorporation in two, and sometimes even more, societies at once. Dual incorporation – incorporation in a receiving society and reincorporation in the homeland – is the fundamental tenet of transnational migration theory. Transmigrants are not thought of as belonging to any one society, but rather are said to inhabit unique deterritorialized spaces, which are social rather than physical, and created by their own agency in maintaining ties that cross and defy borders. Transnational migration fulfills the new understanding of *diaspora*. The concept no longer describes forced exile, in the classic definition that arose out of the expulsion of the Jews from ancient Palestine, but rather the experience by a people of widespread dispersion across international space in which the dispersed group, rather than the nation-state of residence, becomes the primary focus of activity and meaning (Cohen 1997; Laguerre 1998; Lie 1995; Tölöyan 1998).

Lines of Direction in Transnational Analysis of International Migration

Looking more closely at the conceptual structure of transnational theory, Vertovec has identified six lines of current analysis (Vertovec 1999; see also Kivisto 2001).

1 The social morphology of transnationalization[1]

Transnational migration creates social formations that span borders, and involves relations bringing together homelands, receiving societies, and, as peoples spread themselves out among receiving societies, ethnic groups in the diaspora. In consequence, dense webs of *transnational social fields* are created that bring together the migrant, those he or she has left behind, and possibly other migrants, who may be friends or kin, in yet other receiving societies (Basch, Glick Schiller, and Szanton

Blanc 1994). Thus, to take a contemporary example, a transnational social field ultimately brings together not only Gujarati from western India living in Houston with their family and friends in India, but both of these parties with the Gujarati living in The Hague, London, and Boston (Levitt 2001). An especially powerful analytical concept, "transnational social field" describes not only the usual chains and networks by which we have metaphorized processes of immigration, but webs of families and friends and, linked to them, all of the public and private organizations, agencies, businesses, that provide arenas for facilitating transnational activities. The latter might include: hometown associations and homeland governments that encourage civic engagement, dual citizenship, and investment by migrants; travel and shipping agencies facilitating passage of people and goods between the migrant's various sites of engagement; and banks that facilitate the transfer of monies.

2 Transnationalization and the transmission of capital

International migration is a strategy on the part of individuals, families, and groups for gathering together the material resources to survive and to prosper in periods of economic change that are experienced as destabilizing and a source of insecurity. Therefore, international migration involves the frequent exchange of money, whether in the form of remittances sent by migrants to homelands or subsidies sent to migrants from homelands. Transnational social fields are sites for the transmission of this personal capital, just as global financial institutions are sites for securing the capital needs of global corporations. Social and cultural capital – feelings of solidarity, obligation, and mutuality and habits of mutual assistance – are the values that make this material cooperation possible (Faist 2000a, 2000b).

3 Transnational civil and political engagement

Dual incorporation becomes especially apparent when transmigrants participate simultaneously in the public life of the homeland and that of the receiving society. Contemporary states are increasingly making dual citizenship possible, and allow for, and actively solicit, electoral participation by their nationals who permanently reside outside the country (Baubock 1994; Foner 1997, 2000; Laguerre 1998; Porter 2002; Sontag 1997). In the United States, legal aliens have been allowed to vote in school board elections in a number of localities (Jones-Correa 1998). Subpolitical engagements in neighborhood and community or regional organizations that span the homeland and the receiving society have also emerged, and are independent of laws governing political rights or naturalization status. Though electoral participation and, hence, political power are not at stake, these civic engagements make it possible to play the role of citizen in two places at once.

4 Transnational consciousness and self-identification

Immigrants aspiring to stay permanently in the receiving society are assumed to be engaged in a process of assimilation, however it may be defined precisely. Transmigrants, on the other hand, are said to resist the cultural and psychological implications of geographical fixity and of assimilation. Transnational analysts seek evidence of diasporic consciousness that understands itself in terms of peoplehood (i.e. a common ethnic identity across borders) more than a bounded national identity within nation-state boundaries.

5 Transnational modes of cultural representation

Transmigrants are said to develop modes of representation of experience, history, and identity, which become embedded in the character of their voluntary institutions and societies and in such elements of the expressive styles of transmigrant young people as music and dress. These express the diasporic and hybrid aspects of the lives of individuals and groups that are often spent in cycles of residence in greatly contrasting circumstances, encompassing, for example, agricultural villages in Oaxaca in southwestern Mexico and megalopolitan Los Angeles (Appadurai 1991, 1996; Garcia Canclini 1990).

6 The deterritorialization of meaning

Lack of geographical fixity in transmigrant experience is said to influence a mentality that invents a transnational landscape, characterized less by physical space and situated communities than by separation of territory and loyalty, and an emergence of virtual communities existing in transnational social fields and in cultural representation (Appadurai 1991, 1996).

Implications of Transnational Theory

Stated even this concisely, it is evident that transnational theory lays out a far different conceptual map than immigration studies in the past. Two implications especially need to be spelled out. First, transnational theory challenges the unity of immigration history by its contention of a fundamental break in the nature of international migration that separates, in the American case, the historical migrations of the nineteenth and early twentieth centuries and the contemporary migrations of the late twentieth and twenty-first centuries (Foner 1997, 2000). Second, and related, transnational theory is greatly at odds with reigning conceptual models. Transnational theorists speak directly and critically about the contemporary relevance of assimilation theories in all of their variety, including cultural pluralism, because, they argue, bounded categories that tie the migrant's destiny to the confines of one society cannot adequately describe the lives transmigrants are now making for themselves. In so doing, they have assisted greatly in stimulating reinterest in and formulation of significant restatements of assimilation theory (Alba and Nee 1997; Barkan 1995; Morawska 1994; Portes and Rumbaut 1990).

To interrogate the second of these implications is to strike at the heart of the intricacies of the hypothesis of dual incorporation. It is ultimately to ask whether incorporation into the receiving society, often conceived in the American historical literature in group terms as *ethnicization*, is actually furthered by the formation and maintenance of transnational social fields and homeland involvements. These fields may enhance identity and provide unity for a group, and lead to numerous mobilizations in the receiving society on behalf of the homeland that may take the form in

democratic states, for example, of lobbying and electoral participation, which ultimately have the impact of drawing the group into the major processes of the new
society. We will conjure with this paradox throughout this chapter.

Now, however, we must address the question of the unity of American immigration
history in light of transnationalism analysis. We find that while transnational theorists
may be incorrect about the unprecedented nature of contemporary patterns, the
discussion productively opens up possibilities for revising our understanding of the
evolution of immigration historiography and for understanding old knowledge within
new frames of reference.

The Novelty of Contemporary Patterns
of International Migration

Historians tend to find transnational theory ahistorical and transnational work
shallow in its depictions of historical international migration. While transnational
analysis has become more nuanced in its engagement with history, early statements
may justifiably be criticized for exaggerating the differences between present and
past (cf. Glick Schiller, Basch, and Szanton Blanc 1992; Portes 1997; Glick Schiller
1999; Guarnizo 1998; R. Smith 1997). The early statements have become canonical,
however, and are the ones that more or less influence the conversation between
historians and social scientists who have created transnational theory, so to understand them is to understand the evolution of a critical discussion (Kivisto 2001).
A more important reason for reviewing them, however, is that, exaggerated or not,
the claims for novelty may help to sharpen our understanding of the past. There are
indeed, as we shall see at considerable length, ample precedents for most of today's
patterns in historical migrations. If the transnationalists have neglected to understand
these, historians have been deficient in understanding their relevance to their own
projects. Indeed, the historical literature presents us with a paradoxical situation: it is
rich in underconceptualized, unappreciated detail that documents the existence of
nineteenth- and early twentieth-century transnationalism, and suggests productive
lines for future analysis. This detail may be reinterpreted using the categories and
general orientations of transnational theory. Recent historical literature does this
explicitly, forcing previously analyzed experiences in new directions (e.g. Baily 1998;
Chen 2000; Gabaccia 2000; Hsu 2000; McKeown 2001).

What are the claims for the novelty of present patterns, and, explicitly or implicitly,
the irrelevance of past patterns, that emerge from statements of transnational theory?

1 Transnationalism is a new phenomenon, and cannot be adequately captured by
   a preexisting concept. In particular, the experience of transmigrants cannot be
   explained by the varieties of assimilation theory, which is limited for the purpose
   of analyzing contemporary patterns because of its emphasis on categories bound
   by the geographical, political, social, and economic borders of the nation-state
   (Portes, Guarnizo, and Landholt 1999).
2 In the past, prior to the era of instantaneous electronic communication and jet
   transportation, it was not possible to carry on significant transnational activity,
   such as creating and maintaining transnational social fields (Portes, Guarnizo,
   and Landholt 1999).

3   In the past, there were homeland visits, re-emigration, political diasporas in the
     form of exile and refugee populations, and trade diasporas in foreign enclaves.
     But the difference is found to be that past examples of transnationalization
     lacked the "regularity, routine involvement, and critical mass" of contemporary
     patterns. Few could live simultaneously in two countries at once in terms of
     "routine daily activities" (Portes, Guarnizo, and Landholt 1999).

4   Similarly, though migratory populations have always been characterized by net-
     works for mutual support and the exchange of information and resources, today,
     as a consequence of contemporary transportation and communication tech-
     nologies, the spread, intensity, and simultaneity of network activities create a
     qualitatively different phenomenon (Vertovec 1999).

5   In the historical past, transnationalization did not constitute the dominant pattern
     in immigrant life, while in some contemporary immigrant contexts the social
     structures and ordinary activities of daily life are now said to be transnational. In
     the past, these patterns were ethnic and oriented toward assimilation in the
     receiving society (Vertovec 1999).

6   Immigrant involvements in civic and political life of homelands existed in the past,
     but the opportunity for dual incorporation was limited by the lack of government
     involvement in immigrant homelands in encouraging such engagement. Recog-
     nizing immigrants as assets, especially in economic development, contemporary
     governments directly encourage their diasporas to take an active interest in
     homeland public life (Lessinger 1992; Vertovec 1999).

Historians' understandings of transnationalization

As we have observed, American historians have been quick to resist the validity of
these claims, and rightly point out that much that is said to be unique in present
patterns has ample precedent in the historical past. Yet, for at least two reasons,
historians' criticisms of the claims of transnational theory about history have not
always been on target. First, historians have often been confused about what
transnationalization is represented as being. A common confusion is that transnational
theory is fundamentally either an origins or a contact model, such that any link to
the migrant's homeland is evidence of transnational activity. In an otherwise analy-
tically astute essay, Gjerde, for example, finds a branch of American immigration
historiography associated with those, such as Marcus Lee Hansen, whom he calls
"ethnic Turnerians," to be a precursor of contemporary transnational theory (Gjerde
1999). The claim is made on the basis of the fact that Hansen, who had been a
student of Frederick Jackson Turner and had absorbed Turner's interest in ordinary
folk and rural life, was the first historian to pay serious attention to the Old World
origins of nineteenth-century European immigration to the United States (Hansen
1940). For Hansen, immigrant life did not begin for the Norwegians in Iowa, but in
Varmland, and for the Germans, not in Wisconsin but in Württemberg, with the
economic and social circumstances, including the spread of information about the
United States, that inspired their immigration and assisted in framing their aspirations.
In light of what we have noted that transnational theory contends, Hansen cannot
be said to be pointed in a direction that suggests transnationalization. Indeed, far
from imagining dual incorporation or alternatives to assimilation theory, Hansen

believed that by experience, agency, and aspirations his nineteenth-century European peasant immigrants were Americans before they arrived – sturdy, independent, and democratic, in contrast to those they left behind – and their destiny was happily to become more American.

Similar problems arise from thinking of re-emigration as transnationalization. In itself, the return to live in the homeland is not necessarily transnationalization, but its opposite, for it may represent a turning away from the possibility of dual incorporation. Transnationalization cannot be understood simply in terms of movement.

Faist, one of the foundational transnational theorists, speaks precisely to this point in distinguishing between three generations of theory about the processes of immigration (Faist 2000a). First, there were the one-dimensional push-pull models associated in history with the work of those such as Hansen and Handlin, who analyzed political, economic, and social forces existing simultaneously in time that accounted for emigration from Europe and the attraction of the United States (Hansen 1940; Handlin 1951). A second generation went considerably beyond this model in analyzing structured dependencies and abiding linkages between cores and peripheries and undeveloped and developing regions and states. Associated in historiography with the influential conceptual essay by Thistlethwaite (1964) and with quantitative analysis of massive data sets from Thomas (1973), Baines (1985), and Erickson (1994) to Hatton and Williamson (1998), such work has discovered complex patterns of migratory movement within and among societies, of which permanent resettlement in a receiving society is merely one among many patterns. Thistlethwaite's essay was a revelation to many immigration historians, because it convincingly conceptualized the seasonal labor migrations and re-emigrations in the late nineteenth and early twentieth centuries of, for example, British industrial workers and artisans to Australia and New England, Polish peasants to the Ruhr Valley and to Chicago, and southern Italian peasants to Argentina and New York City, as evidence of the internationalization of labor markets in an emerging Atlantic economy, the units of which were increasingly integrated and governed by the rhythms of the same economic cycles.

But the internationalization of immigration history is not the same thing as its transnationalization. Thistlethwaite and others have not addressed the issues of the transnational theorists, whom Faist identifies as the third generation of theorists of international migration. The third generation analyzes the transnational practices of migrants and those left behind in homelands that connect their two worlds and create a third, transnational space out of that connection. They address the ideas and symbols and the social and symbolic ties that give meaning to these transnational spaces. Moreover, while the internationalists emphasize macro-analysis of states and economic systems, the transnationalists analyze immigration at the meso-level, that is, individuals in their relation to families, friends, and neighbors (Faist 2000a).[2] It is a short step conceptually from international to transnational analysis. By taking it, we move from noting the rhythms of migratory movement within the larger context of economic forces to analyzing the transnational social fields, in the form of individual networks that do the planning and make the resources available and the institutions, businesses, and agencies facilitating movement. It is justifiable not to take this step, in which case one writes about international migration from within another framework. Certainly, without the work of the internationalists, the conceptual breakthroughs of transnationalists would not have been possible. Transnational analysis is based on three-dimensional models conceived by internationalists for understanding the relationships between capitalist modernization and international labor markets.

Failure to identify transnationalization may take another form, too, that leads to the confusion of historians, for a second problem in the historian's confrontation with transnational theory has been the lack of a conceptual language for identifying transnationalization where it actually appears in the literature of present and past immigration history. Ultimately this is a reflection of the direction – assimilation theory – that American immigration studies in history and in urban sociology took in the early twentieth century. Assimilation is certainly a plausible paradigm for seeking to understand immigrants, but in the American case the power of assimilation theories has been overdetermined by national anxieties about the spectacular diversity of the American population. Reflecting American preoccupations with national unity, social order, and cultural coherence during the massive immigrations of the early twentieth century, Americans began almost from the start of systematic, academic immigration research to be concerned with the prospects for the assimilation of the immigrant (Park 1930, 1950; Park and Burgess 1921; Wirth 1928). A countercurrent soon developed in this discourse that put forward a culturally pluralistic formulation of immigrant life in the United States, which did not necessarily ultimately contradict assimilation, but offered a more nuanced understanding of the processes of immigrant life that emphasized the maintenance of memories, identities, and social solidarity based on common homeland origins (Kallen 1924). The maintenance of group life, in fact, could be interpreted as offering the possibility that assimilation might ultimately occur through the mixing and melting of groups (Gordon 1964; Herbert 1960; Kennedy, 1944, 1952).

The preoccupation with assimilation processes and with issues of homogeneity and diversity had various effects on immigration studies that served, among other things, to limit the ability to see transnationalization where it occurred in history or society, or, if it was recognized and acknowledged, to see it as a problem to be exposed rather than an opportunity for analysis. The latter is apparent, for example, in the closely argued work of the political scientist Louis Gerson. Reflecting concerns about the influence of special interest groups on the ability of the United States to frame realistic and effective foreign policies during the Cold War, Gerson's two historical studies of the influence of American ethnic groups in American politics identify homeland loyalties of "hyphenated" (i.e. ethnic) Americans as impairing the process of policy making (Gerson 1953, 1964). Transnationalists interpret ethnic groups identifying with and participating in homeland political and civic movements and lobbying and voting on their behalf in the United States, which Gerson documents amply for the nineteenth and first half of the twentieth century, as evidence of dual incorporation. Gerson's goal, however, is to reveal these to be a *problem* deeply ingrained in American partisan politics, and hence a danger in the world of bitter nuclear rivalries in which he wrote during the most dangerous years of the Cold War. The point may be correct, and the desire to make it is certainly a legitimate goal for a scholar, but pursuing it cuts off analysis about the processes of immigrant and ethnic life.

More pervasive in the literature than the desire to expose the dangers of transnational practices has been the desire to see them exclusively in the light of *American* incorporation. Though he lacked the vocabulary of transnationalization, Gerson gave evidence that he understood dual incorporation. Because he conceived of it as a problem to be exposed, he went no further than conceptualizing it as evidence of divided loyalty that was dysfunctional for the effective functioning of the American political system. This, however, has not been the dominant approach to what, in effect, has been arguing away evidence of transnationalization. Most historians, who use analytical frameworks descended from the varieties of assimilation theory, have conceptualized dual incorporations exclusively from the perspective of the immigrant's and ethnic's life in the United States. While this appears to be a contradiction in terms, it has been deftly argued, and has led to a better understanding of ethnic group processes.

How this has emerged in the historical literature requires some explanation. At the heart of the matter is the problem of *ethnicization*, a concept that describes a process by which immigrant group formation and ethnic incorporation occur simultaneously. It is the process by which unorganized immigrant peoples, to one extent or another lacking in self-consciousness as a group, attain identity, become organized, and are then incorporated into American society as groups (Gerber 1989; Greene 1975; Conzen, Gerber, Morawska, Pozzetta, and Vecoli 1992). It is the process by which, for example, in the late nineteenth and early twentieth centuries Sicilian immigrants, with their background of undeveloped national consciousness and intense regionalism and localism in Europe, came to be *Italian* Americans, or Polish-speaking immigrants from Galicia, who had no state of their own and whose homeland was divided between the German, Russian, and Austro-Hungarian empires, came to be *Polish* Americans (Bukowczyk 1987; Greene 1975; Lopata 1994). The model understands group organization and group incorporation to possess a dialectical relationship, such that the group formation and identity and the capacities to think and act as a group, possessing an understanding of group interests and goals, ultimately become the necessary foundation for entering the processes of American society. Group formation and identity may be established in internal processes, such as Greene suggested in a study of the role of disputes over church governance among Slavic immigrants in leading to an understanding of the need for ethnic solidarity (Greene 1975). Group identity might be based on psychological processes resulting from ascription, as Sarna has suggested in an analysis of how being regarded by others as one people, as a consequence of common language or general geographical origins or stereotypes, brought Sicilians and Calabrians or Galician and Prussian Poles into a consciousness of what had not been assumed in Europe – their unity of history and of identity (Sarna 1978).

Ultimately, however, the literature has assumed that this process attains its fullest realization when it is joined to the social, public processes of American society. It is as a group, for example, that ethnics come to be integrated into American politics. Since the enfranchisement of the white male citizenry in the early nineteenth century, electoral campaigns have been organized for the sake of efficient mobilization on the basis of approaching individual voters in a mass electorate, not as individuals, but as members of ethnic groups. Political resources, such as public employment, nominations for office, public services, and block grants, have often been distributed to ethnic groups to court their vote or to reward their partisan loyalties (Bridges 1984; Katznelson 1981). These mobilizations and the distribution of rewards that they entail, in turn, reinforce ethnic group solidarity and identity, such that the ethnicization model comes to understand ethnic organization and incorporation as constitutive of each other: organization as a group enables the ethnic group to be incorporated, and through incorporation the ethnic group develops its institutions, identity, and interests.

Historians employing the ethnicization model have given ample evidence of understanding that a variety of engagements, especially political and civic, with the homeland have assisted greatly in furthering the process of ethnicization. Studies of ethnic leadership, for example, demonstrate how deeply ethnic intellectuals and activists among such European immigrant peoples as Irish, Poles, or Jews were involved in European affairs on behalf of their beleaguered peoples (Higham 1978; Greene 1987; Jacobson 1995). But the analysis has not taken the form of understanding how American Poles' involvements on behalf of Polish national independence before the rebirth of the Polish state in 1918 reincorporated them in *Polish* affairs, for example, as partisans of two outstanding leaders of the struggle for Polish national self-determination of the era, the socialist Josef Pilsudski or the nationalist Roman Dmowski, and led them to become assets in the power struggles of these men in ways that ultimately influenced the outcome of European events. Instead the analysis has been of the ways in which such engagements influenced ethnicization by effecting the formation, growth, and ideological development of ethnic organizations and leadership within the United States. Lobbying and voting on behalf of homeland causes integrates Poles into American politics, and hence makes them act more American, even as they become more ethnic. So, too, does the ideological development noted in such activities function to make ethnics Americans. As O'Grady argued in his aptly named *How The Irish Became American*, the advocacy for Ireland in its struggle against Britain for national self-determination, democratic self-government, and constitutional liberty, brought the Irish immigrant into closer ideological alignment with Americans, precisely because these political values were widely identified as *American* values (O'Grady 1973).

To one extent or another, these are the arguments that implicitly underlie the analysis in the two most important volumes on ethnic leadership published in the recent past. In Greene's monograph and Higham's collection, in the case of one group after another, homeland engagements, when they arise, are seen in terms of their multiple *American* contexts and consequences (Higham 1978; Greene 1987).

If we hold most of this literature up to the light of a transnational analysis, as we shall do in the next section of this chapter, we might get a more complicated and certainly richer picture that projects dual rather than single incorporation. In doing so, we come to understand the extent to which the claims of transnational theory to the novelty of present transnationalization are incorrect. Though there are still many questions to be addressed, there is much evidence of transnationalization in the historical past, even within the confines of more rudimentary travel and communication technologies.

A number of qualifications are first needed. All groups have not equally experienced dual incorporation. As Foner notes in her careful comparison of Russian Jews and Italians in nineteenth- and early twentieth-century New York City, the Italians were more involved in transnational activities, especially of the private and familial type that involved the exchange of resources, than were the Russian Jews, to a great extent because the Jews had much less desire to return permanently to or be connected to their homeland, where they had experienced a long history of anti-Semitic oppression (Foner 2000). Nor has each set of incorporations been equal in the power of its consequences. It is certainly important in its effects upon the history of various European societies that from their residence in the United States immigrants sent hundreds of millions of dollars in remissions home to their families, or that immigrants played vital roles in national liberation struggles fought in Europe. It is less clear, however, how the consequence of these engagements can explain the lives of the immigrants. Whatever the largely unacknowledged strength of these homeland engagements, in the nineteenth and early twentieth centuries approximately 45 to 55 million largely European immigrants did ultimately choose to make lives for themselves permanently in the United States, and thus became deeply involved in the processes of American society. Over time their children and grandchildren became even less foreign and even more deeply involved in the same processes. It is fruitless to understate the significance of permanent settlement (Foner 2000). An artifact of their permanence is the ethnic groups they formed, which came not only to organize immigrants and their descendants, but to assist in defining the character of American society itself.

We may trace one effect of the power of this ongoing process of ethnicization in the waxing and waning of homeland engagements and of the transnational social fields that sustain them, and alongside these developments, the transformation of the meanings of such engagements. Polish immigrants were deeply engaged in the Polish struggle for self-determination before, during, and just after World War I, but curiously drew back from such engagements in the 1920s, after an independent Poland actually emerged (Pienkos 1984, 1987, 1991). The reasons were complex, but ultimately they reflect less on Poland than on their American home. They experienced a degree of disillusionment when it became clear that the new Polish nation-state was significantly economically and socially underdeveloped and less modern, especially relative to their new American homes. But they also needed to address issues thrust on them in the postwar period by American developments, principally the passage of federal immigration restriction legislation and the rise of anti-immigrant and anti-Roman Catholic nativist movements, especially the Ku Klux Klan, that threatened their security as individuals and as a group. In this mood, the national chairman of the Polish National Congress denounced the effort of the new Polish state to undertake, through its embassies and consulates, the social and political organization of the immigrants. Carefully negotiating the twin poles of Polish American concern, he made it clear nonetheless where their future ultimately lay: "Polonia in America is neither a Polish colony nor a national minority but a component of the great American nation, proud of its Polish origins and careful to implant in the hearts of the younger generation a love for all that is Polish" (Pienkos 1991, p. 73). The repartition of Poland in 1939, World War II, and the Cold War revived engagement with Poland by the aging immigrant generation and now their American-born children and grandchildren, and revitalized the transnational social fields that sustained it. By the late 1930s, however, they and their communities and organizations had taken a decisive turn toward the embrace of American life. However much they cared about Poland, for many Polish Americans, it had become a symbol and memory not a primary loyalty, alternative residence, or place to realize a political mission.

The acknowledgment of dual incorporation and its description, therefore, do not seem sufficient in themselves for analytical purposes, because they cannot help us to understand the finality of such immigrations. We must understand that each of these dual incorporations might have different types of consequences, and that these consequences might exert different degrees of power in different arenas, and hence affect the actors in vastly different ways. We need also to grant the possibility that it was the cunning of the dialectical processes of this history of incorporations that ultimately led, as in O'Grady's formulation, one set of engagements that involved transnationalization to be the servant of the other that involved ethnicization.

We now turn to a more extensive analysis of transnationalization in the historical past, and, in particular, of the dual incorporations manifested among nineteenth- and early twentieth-century immigrants.

New Directions, Old Knowledge

There are at least two difficulties in the way of interrogating historical literature to find evidence of transnationalization in the historical past. First, until recently there have been no studies of historical transnationalization that analyze and describe the phenomenon in the conceptual language of contemporary theory. We must, there- fore, lay out a very different grid for understanding the experiences of the past than that on which they were originally depicted, and interpret evidence carefully gathered by others in ways they did not intend for it to be understood. Second, if, as Foner notes, we lack a sufficient number of close empirical studies of the strength, incidence, and durability of contemporary transnationalization to make confident generalizations about the present (Foner 1997, 2000), the same is even truer of the past.

Even with such limitations, however, there are two areas of immigrant experience emerging from the historical literature that give clear evidence for the presence of dual incorporation on a routine basis and a significant scale: international population movements, and political and civic participation.

Exchanges of Resources, Transnational Social Fields, and Dual Incorporations

The interpretive move toward internationalizing the analysis of international popula- tion movements prepared us to understand, as push-pull models could not, that migration for the purpose of permanent resettlement in a receiving society was only one type of international migratory experience, and that the experience of inter- national migration, encompassing leave-takings of all sorts (emigration, immigration, re-emigration, seasonal migration, etc.), was characterized by strategic planning that encompassed simultaneously homelands and receiving societies. Two metaphors were developed for describing these movements and the planning by which they were realized. Migration sequences were said to resemble a *chain*: links were established by pioneer migrants to those whom they left behind, who were inspired to migrate themselves and given practical assistance to accomplish that end. These migrants, in turn, did the same for those coming after them, adding more links to the chain (MacDonald and MacDonald 1964). Historians interested in the communications among participants in planning migration and exchanging resources object to the limited utility of *chain*, with its implication of linear progression and typically of individual rather than group cooperation, for describing the dense, complex webs of relationships among participants in sending and receiving societies. They offer instead the concept of *network* (Baily 1998; Moya 1998; Tilly 1990). *Network* does enable the analyst to go beyond micro-analysis of individuals and to conceptualize the meso-level of activity encompassing family, kinship, and village. But it does not suggest ways to understand the relevance of institutions and systems to the work of the network. *Transnational social field* enables the next step, which links the meso-level of activity to the macro-level, which involves governments, businesses, and public agencies in the activities of the network.

This becomes evident in looking at the exchange of resources within networks, and specifically in seeking to understand how the transfer of monies enabled both the practice of remittances within networks and the process of re-emigration, and simultaneously incorporated migrants in two societies.

Many studies have demonstrated that, like contemporary immigrants, those in the past sent significant sums of money to their homelands (Cinel 1991; Chen 2000; Foner 1997, 2000; Hsu 2000; Salutos 1956; Wyman 1993). The gross amounts reached impressive proportions, and indeed became in themselves, as was said of Italy at the turn of the last century, a "major industry" for their homelands (Cinel 1991, p. 141). For example:

- Greeks in the United States were said to have sent $4.6 million to Greece in 1910, and in 1920 alone, after a decade of steadily growing numbers in the US, $110 million (Salutos 1956, p. 119);
- Slovaks, a total of $200 million between 1870 and 1912 (Wyman 1993, p. 61);
- Swedes, a total of $192 million between 1906 and 1930 (Wyman 1993, p. 61);
- Italians, a total of $100 million in the brief period from 1897 to 1902 (Wyman 1993, p. 61).[3]

It is no wonder that a contemporary commentator concluded that "it [is] quite probable that 'Little Italy' in New York City contributes more to the tax roll of Italy than some of the poorer provinces in Sicily and Calabria" (Foner 2000, p. 171). In fact, by 1913, remittances, which then totaled $1 billion lire, were 25 percent of Italy's international balance of payments (Cinel 1991, p. 147).

This money was intended for at least three purposes. First, inspired by family loyalty, there was the desire to assist those left at home. The second, relatedly, involved individual aspirations, whether within or outside the context of the domestic economy of the family. Remittances represented personal savings for the future. Increasingly in the late nineteenth and early twentieth centuries, the international migrant population was composed of many single males from rapidly modernizing rural areas, who emigrated without expectation of permanently resettling abroad, and who wished to acquire resources to return to their homelands with the means to withstand the pressures of changing rural economies (Moch 1992). The remittance thus might represent a personal investment, usually for the purpose of purchasing land or a house. Such income rarely enabled dramatic upward mobility, let alone insured protection from losing one's independence and becoming a rural or urban wage-earner. Third, remittances were a basis for individual investment in homeland community improvement projects to develop the local infrastructure, encompassing projects from railroad lines to improving the marketing of crops and new community centers to new bells for the village church (Hsu 2000; Wyman 1993).

While the volume of these remittances is well known, less well appreciated are the systems developed to convey them from the diaspora to the homeland. These systems linked individuals, families, villages, and international institutions into a unified field of transnational activity. Remittances were conveyed in two ways, the mastery of either of which required the international migrant to learn to use the emerging international systems for the exchange of information and money. The first involved postal arrangements. Migrants could send cash, or postal money orders convertible to homeland currency, directly through the international mail. The number of postal money orders sent from the United States to Greece, for example, rose from 409 in 1902 to 10,000 in 1905, during which time their value rose from \$13,295 to \$346,993. In 1909, the value of these money orders sent to Greece increased to \$2,219,297. Whether sent in cash or as a money order, most came to see the value of paying for registered mail, which allowed for tracking the individual envelope on its route across the ocean. In 1901, just over 52,000 pieces of registered mail came to the Athens Post Office from the United States; by 1905, that number had grown to 162,895 (Salutos 1956, p. 118). Hungarian postal authorities estimated that Slovak migrants sent \$42 million from the United States through the mail during 1900–12 (Wyman 1993, p. 61). Doubtless, the heaviest mail traffic in remittances came through the major American industrial cities. The New York Post Office sent \$12.3 million in individual money orders to countries outside the United States between 1900 and 1906, with half going to Hungary, Italy, and Slavic lands, and thus representing the heavy prominence of Italians and East European Jews in the New York City population (Foner 2000, p. 171).

The other method for conveying money involved savings banks. The virtue of immigrant savings banks was that they were managed by countrymen who spoke the migrant's language, and could convey money to the homeland on the migrant's behalf. In 1897, there were 2,625 immigrant savings banks in 146 American cities. Italians were especially heavily engaged in these small banks: 684 (25 percent) of them were owned by Italians, 150 of them in New York City alone (Cinel 1991, p. 31). They did an impressive volume of business. In 1908, for example, a Serbian banker serving countrymen residing in Pittsburgh's industrial South Side estimated that \$20,000 to \$25,000 daily was sent from his bank to Serbia (Wyman 1993, p. 61). But these small banks often perpetrated a variety of frauds that kept this money from reaching its intended recipients. Though slow to realize the importance of remittances to the national economy, the Italian government moved in 1901 to offer migrants an alternative to the neighborhood *banchisti*. The Bank of Naples was authorized to serve as a third party in the transmission of remittances (Cinel 1991). But it never got control of more than 25 percent of monies sent from abroad. Migrants apparently trusted those from the same village or region who lived amongst them in the United States more than they did bankers and government officials in distant cities in their homelands, from which historically little good came to the peasantry.

This choice is a reminder that, though they may have come to different conclusions on what process could best convey their money homeward, the migrants' own agency is at the heart of the formation and maintenance of such transnational social fields. To be sure, in these circumstances the migrants' agency was tightly constrained by institutions and their representatives, and ultimately by the impersonal, modern bureaucratic systems on which they depended. They could learn how to use the international mail, keep a bank account, and buy a postal money order or secure a bank's cooperation in transferring their funds to the homeland; and they could double-check to make sure that their monies were indeed ultimately in the hands of those who were intended to receive them. But in the final analysis these activities involved the exercise of trust which marks much of the public functioning of people who inhabit modernity and cannot depend on face-to-face relations to achieve their ends (Giddens 1990). Here we need to note a necessary qualification to the migrant's otherwise conservative aspirations, for the migrants used modern means to achieve the traditional end of ensuring security, defined along traditional lines, in their homelands. But amidst the impersonal circumstances of these international systems, migrants sought to gain as much control as possible over the processes that assisted them in fulfilling their aspirations. In doing so, they experienced a type of dual incorporation, participating in and using institutions, agencies, and businesses on both sides of the ocean to create a field of activity that enabled the transfer of resources.

Another type of dual incorporation was experienced by a growing segment of the twentieth-century re-emigrant population – retirees with pensions – in maintaining the transnational social fields on which they depended for their security after returning to their homelands. In the twentieth century, federal government pensions for railroad workers, war veterans, and retired employees or their survivors became available, under the social security program, to those, citizens and non-citizens alike, who had worked in the United States and put money into federal pensions funds through payroll deductions, or who had served in the American military in wartime. All of these programs had portability features allowing recipients to receive benefits abroad. Recipients had to see to the paperwork of getting their benefits and having them sent to their homeland residence. The number of those living outside the United States and receiving social security benefits, whether as pensions or survivors' benefits, grew rapidly after 1940, when payments under the federal retirement scheme became available. Workers' pensions required 10 years of work, so the early 1950s saw a rapid rise in recipients, as the inaugural cohort attained age 65. By 1953, 30,145 former residents of the United States, of whom the large majority were re-emigrants living abroad, were receiving a total of $15,800,000 in benefits under the social security program (83rd US Congress 1953, p. 81). The number rose steadily thereafter. The social security administration sent out millions of dollars monthly in pension checks to destinations throughout the world, including some of them, most prominently Poland, behind the Cold War Iron Curtain. The steady increase is attested to in the case of Ireland, for example, in which the number of social security recipients increased from 1,463 in 1955 to 6,528 in 1994; most of them were re-emigrants who had become United States citizens (75 percent) and had returned to Ireland to spend the rest of their lives (Almeida 2001, p. 51).

Between social security, federal railroad workers' pensions, and benefits available to veterans of World War I, 2,739 Greeks were obtaining $1.66 million from the American welfare state in 1952 (Salutos 1956, pp. 85–6). As the sum of $607 in per capita payments from all of these sources makes clear, the monies involved hardly established these Greeks in luxury. Retirement under such circumstances required significant amounts of personal savings, even with the relatively cheaper cost of living abroad. Moreover, re-emigrants often had developed a standard of domestic comfort and hunger for consumer goods in America that made life more expensive than it was for those who had never lived outside the homeland (Cinel 1991; Salutos 1956; Virtanen 1979; Wyman 1993). Some continued to work after re-emigrating. Working or retired, they became reincorporated in their homelands, while remaining integrated into the American welfare state, on which they depended for a variable percentage of their income.

What stands out about such evidence of dual incorporation is how little it has been addressed in the existing historical literature. Studies certainly exist of temporary international migration and re-emigration, and note has been taken extensively of remittances and, to a much lesser extent, that federal pensions possess an international reach. But studies that bring these subjects together into one unified field of analysis, in which the transnational linkages are not assumed but become the problem to be analyzed, have not been undertaken.

Political and Civic Engagements, Transnational Social Fields, and Dual Incorporations

This neglect becomes clear, too, when we revisit the problem of the political and civil engagements of international migrants of the late nineteenth and early twentieth centuries in their homelands. The evidence from historical literature is enormous. It largely follows three lines of analysis.

1 Involvement of international migrants in movements to liberate their homelands

There has been extensive documentation of the involvement of international voluntary migrants and small populations of involuntary political refugees and exiles in movements to liberate their homelands from colonial occupation and political oppression. These movements engaged in propaganda, fundraising, terrorism, and participation in civil wars, wars of liberation, and international conflicts, such as World War I, that were thought to pave the way for homeland liberation. In the nineteenth and early twentieth centuries, most of the significant European imperial powers – Great Britain, Imperial Germany, Austria-Hungary, Czarist Russia, and Spain – and the non-European presence in Europe, the Ottoman Turks, were challenged by anti-colonial political movements, which were often divided by puzzling arrays of organizations and ideologies, formed in the United States. The activities of the Irish against Great Britain (Brown 1966; O'Grady 1973) and the Poles against Germany, Russia, and Austria-Hungary (Pienkos 1984, 1987, 1991) are especially well known, but also documented are the activities of Croats and other South Slavs against Austria-Hungary (Pripic 1971; Wyman 1993), Slovaks against Hungary (Higham 1978; Wyman 1993), Serbs, Bulgarians, Greeks, and Montenegrines against the Ottomans (Salutos 1956; Wyman 1993), and, in a complex variation on national liberation, Jews against both anti-Semitic oppression throughout Europe and on behalf of

Zionist efforts to restore Israel as a Jewish homeland (Urofsky 1975, 1978). These European peoples hardly exhaust the historical record, as research suggests on the efforts from the United States of Chinese against Imperial Japan (Chen 2000; Yung 1999), Punjabis against Great Britain (Jurgensmeyer 1982; Puri 1983), and Cubans against Spain (Thomas 1971; Proctor 1950). The literature further documents the return of some migrants to the restored homeland under a variety of circumstances, such as Poles following Polish independence in 1918, or the American Zionists, who went to the new state of Israel during its War of Independence and following the proclamation of statehood in 1948 (Pienkos 1991; Urofsky 1978). Investments in the restored homeland are also noted, and not all of them, by any means, involved wealthy ethnics with large amounts of capital. The Polish Mechanics Association of Toledo, Ohio began to collect small sums from immigrant workers and owners of small businesses in 1919, and by 1921, when it transferred its work to Poland, had over 18,000 members and $3 million in investment capital, about $164 per member. It eventually began a bank in Warsaw, opened a factory and two brick works, and had its own publication. Some 200 other cooperative enterprises and private corporations were launched by Polish re-emigrants, many of which failed amidst the economic difficulties of the early years of Polish independence (Wyman 1993). Not all returns were motivated by nationalism. The Communist Finns who returned to Soviet Karelia following the Bolshevik Revolution of 1918 were not returning to help build up newly independent Finland, for which the nationalist Finns in the United States had been working, but rather to create socialism in the Finnish province of the new Soviet Union just to the east of the new Finnish state (Hoglund 1960; Wyman 1993). Finally, it needs to be noted that history did not stop for any of these peoples with the achievement of self-determination, which in some cases was usurped almost as quickly as it was attained. The Spanish-American War did not free Cuba from American interference and the rule of a succession of corrupt puppet regimes, which then were replaced in 1959 by Soviet hegemony and the Castro dictatorship. The involvement of Cubans in the United States in the struggles for Cuban self-determination continued from a variety of ideological perspectives, both anti-American and anti-Soviet, throughout the twentieth century (Fagan, Brody, and O'Leary 1968; Portes and Stepick 1993). Similarly, the same organizations, such as the Polish Falcons and the Polish National Alliance, that had worked for Polish independence before and during World War I found themselves two decades later, after World War II, and for the next 30 years, actively contesting Soviet hegemony (Pienkos 1984, 1987, 1991).

2 Efforts of homeland governments in relation to international migrants

Homeland governments have taken a wide variety of interests in their diaspora communities, and sought to reincorporate migrant populations. They have seen them as an economic asset capable of sending home millions of dollars in remittances and, as such, worthy of protection. With this investment in migratory labor in mind, the Italian government moved, unevenly and often ineffectively, to conserve the migrants' labor through regulating migrant-carrying steamship lines, providing migrants with information about labor markets in the United States, directly subsidizing private organizations in the United States engaged in social service work with migrants, and protecting their remittances through authorizing the Bank of Naples to handle the transfer of the migrants' funds (Cinel 1991). The Mexican government and its consular officials in California worked with American local, state, and federal officials in regulating the flow of Mexican agricultural labor into and out of the United States throughout the first half of the twentieth century (Garcia 2001).

Migrants were also recognized as bearing less material potentialities for their homelands. In its bid to become recognized as a great power, the Japanese government in the early twentieth century saw international migrants from Japan as a reflection of national prestige. It worked to screen migrants, so that only hardworking and law-abiding people were given passports; it wanted no criminals and prostitutes representing Japan abroad. It kept watch on the migrants themselves once in the United States through its control of the local branches of the Japanese Association of America, an agent of the Japanese consular service, which registered men for potential military service in Japan, controlled the access of the migrants to official papers, such as birth and marriage certificates that were essential to reuniting families in the United States, and screened the granting of official permissions to return to Japan to visit or to establish families. Finally, Japan took an interest in the civil and economic status of migrants in the United States, less out of humanitarian feeling than a belief that if they were oppressed and exploited, it was a blow to Japan's national standing (Daniels 1978). The lesson of the weakness of the Chinese state, which could do little to protect its citizens abroad from racial violence and economic exploitation (Chen 2000; McKeown 2001; Yung 1999), played heavily into the understanding of its responsibilities by the Japanese state, which moved through the Japanese Association of America to finance the legal defense of the rights of migrants in the cases challenging California laws restricting the right of aliens to own land. The Japanese government protested to President Theodore Roosevelt against the San Francisco Board of Education's imposition of racial segregation on Japanese children, and succeeded in obtaining reversal of the policy (Daniels 1978).

International migrants have also been conceived of as political assets by governments in their homelands. Homeland political parties seeking to form electoral coalitions and to raise funds to finance their campaigns have, like the Jamaican People's National Party, formed American auxiliary organizations, such as, in 1936, the Jamaica Protective League (Kasnitz 1992). Governments have sought to organize migrant populations to have them function as electoral assets in representing their interests in American politics, propagandists, spies, opponents of anti-government exiles and refugees, and even street fighters. The examples of the activities of Nazi Germany and Fascist Italy in the United States in the years before American entry into World War II are particularly well known. Both governments created an elaborate political infrastructure to function in a variety of both public and legal and clandestine and illegal ways to serve homeland interests (Diamond 1974; Diggins 1972; Salvemini 1977). While Italian and German government propaganda efforts in the ethnic press and on foreign language radio doubtless reached significant numbers of the migrant population, the base of activists upon which the larger "fifth column" efforts depended was quite narrow. Salvemini, an eminent historian and anti-Fascist exile, estimated that of 6 million Italian Americans perhaps only 300,000 were ideological Fascists and only 10,000 members of Mussolini's Black Shirt Legions (Salvemini 1977, p. xxxviii). For its part, the Nazi government grew so disenchanted with the

German-American Bund, because of its crude methods, political stupidity, and distance from the mainstream of German America and the United States in general, that it increasingly used the German consular service working in tandem with organs of the German government as the tourist office, the railroad information office, and the Foreign Institute, to serve its purposes. Equally imposing was the opposition to both regimes that took root among not only exiles and refugees, but also liberal, left, and trade union elements in the Italian and German ethnic communities. The Americanization of these ethnic groups, which proceeded apace after 1920 because restrictive quotas and the 1930s depression greatly reduced immigration, did not present either government with fertile grounds for controlling the principal institutions of ethnic communities and suppressing dissent. But German and Italian state activities in ethnic communities revitalized engagement with homelands, even if not to the ends both dictatorships sought.

A generation and more before, the Hungarian government, which feared the organization in the United States of Slovakian national liberation politics among recent migrants, had gone considerably further in subverting ethnic institutions. The Hungarians instituted "American Action," a program combining bribes, bonuses, threats, mail seizures, and espionage across a broad front of Slovakian ethnic institutions, from the Catholic Church to the ethnic press, that was intended to identify and to neutralize the nationalists (Puskas 1983; Wyman 1993). When these efforts failed to check the spread of nationalist activities, the Hungarian government instituted selective procedures for approval of return migration, in effect barring the nationalists from returning to their homeland. But this comprehensive program of subversion and buying influence did not succeed in uprooting Slovak nationalism, which flowered during and after World War I, as the Austro-Hungarian Empire collapsed, and found new sources of grievance in the conflict that arose in the 1920s between Czechs and Slovaks in the new state of Czechoslovakia (Stolarik 1980).

3 American politics and the organization of "nationalities"

While in a variety of ways international migrants were being reincorporated into homeland affairs through nationalist and other political movements and the activities of homeland governments, American political parties were busy seeking to incorporate them into American politics. From the dawn of mass democracy in the 1820s and 1830s, it was evident to party leaders that voters could not be approached efficiently as individuals. Appeals to the wage-earning and family farming majority based on the inequalities of power and wealth among social classes might be destabilizing for American capitalism (Katznelson 1981). On the other hand, party leaders quickly discovered that electoral coalitions could be formed through appeals to ethnic groups, and beginning in the port cities of the eastern seaboard, with their large immigrant populations, they rapidly grew adept in the tactics of forming ethnic coalitions (Bridges 1984). Such appeals were based on nostalgia and flattery, but also on material interests, such as the distribution of political resources (nominations to office, public employment, and social services), and on domestic and often homeland social, political, and diplomatic issues. First employed on a wide scale with Irish and German immigrants in the decades before the Civil War, such appeals quickly became a staple of electoral politics at every level of the federal system. They grew so integral to the normal functioning of politics that they were permanently fixed within the highest levels of the party bureaucracies in the 1880s, when both the Republicans and the Democrats established a "nationalities division" to formulate and coordinate appeals to ethnic communities (Gerson 1964). Perhaps no force in American life has been more responsible for the dual, and thought to be conflicting, loyalties ethnic groups are criticized for maintaining, than American politics itself, which incorporated ethnics into American life by reminding them of their foreign origin and evoking their concern for their homeland.

These appeals to ethnics generated opposite ideological appeals as well: the effort to unify native-born elements around opposition to ethnic interests and the protection of what was assumed to be the original Anglo-American ideological, cultural, and biological constitution of society. Thus, not only have homeland interests been at the heart of electoral politics, but so, too, have issues, such as the social control of alcohol, the public observance of the Christian Sabbath, and the place of the English language in public affairs and the public school curriculum, which have frequently separated native and foreigner, and which have been directly concerned with organizing the public life of a multicultural democracy that is populated by people of different cultures. We might think of the latter issues, which have been staples of American domestic politics and electoral campaigns for almost two centuries, as *ethnic* insofar as they deal exclusively with the immigrant's interaction with other groups within American society. In contrast, homeland-oriented election issues, which have manifested themselves with less regularity, might be thought of as *transnational* to the extent they have concerned the effort to influence American diplomacy on external issues. Historically, a transnationalized agenda has been prominent at times of international crisis. Thus, the presidential elections of 1916 and 1920 witnessed strong appeals to immigrant populations based on, in 1916, the politics of neutrality and planning for the post-World War I era, and in 1920, the politics of the peacemaking that grew out of the Wilson administration's support for self-determination of the peoples of the ruined German, Russian, Austro-Hungarian, and Ottoman empires. The election of 1940 was a reprise of 1916 to the extent that appeals were formed on the basis of ethnic interests in the war in Europe. As the Cold War emerged, ethnic issues re-entered national politics in the presidential elections of 1948 and 1952, when both parties competed with one another to secure the support of those ethnic populations whose eastern and central European homelands had been overrun by the Soviet Union as it advanced on Nazi Germany, by promising to oppose Soviet power. These anti-communist appeals based on emotions about the homeland had enormous power to the extent that they produced a "blowback" effect. Republican rhetoric about "rolling back Communism" not only encouraged the Hungarians to revolt against their Stalinist regime in 1956, only to find the Eisenhower administration unwilling to risk nuclear war to assist them, but they created expectations in the domestic, especially the ethnic, electorate that ultimately caused politicians to shudder at the forces they had unleashed. Republican foreign policy makers came to fear the electoral consequences of seizing opportunities to create small dents in the Iron Curtain by taking advantage of openings to the west offered by Soviet satellite regimes. Thus, when the communist Gomulka government in Poland tentatively approached the United States in an effort to withstand Soviet military pressure, one fear among the Republicans was losing the

Polish American vote, if the administration dealt with Gomulka. Ultimately, however, Polish American leadership and organizations proved willing to support extending aid to Gomulka, as part of a larger humanitarian posture of assisting the impoverished people of postwar Poland (Gerson 1964).

In the historical literature on what we now think of as transnationalized politics, it is often assumed that the source of the success of partisan appeals to immigrant populations has ultimately been a minority group psychology, which requires flattery and nostalgia in proportion to feelings of weakness, alienation, and inferiority prompted by the low socio-economic status and social prestige that attend resettlement at the bottom of a new society (e.g. Diggins 1972; Gerson 1964; O'Grady 1973). But, as the organization of electoral politics around homeland issues suggests, the matter is far more complicated. Party machinery and political campaigns worked constantly to formalize, perfect, and disseminate such appeals, and hence, in effect, to stimulate engagement by ethnic voters and their organizations in homeland affairs. If such a psychology actually existed (for it is asserted rather than proven), American politics gave it a language to express itself, issues to vent its frustrations and aspirations, and election campaigns to serve as a course of action. In this sense, while American politics incorporated ethnic voters, as it did so, it inspired their reincorporation in their homelands, and stimulated the development and strengthening of transnational social fields providing linkages for such reincorporation.

The Transnational Present as History

In analyses of such present international migrant populations as Dominicans, Guatemalans, Haitians, Mexicans, South Asians, Salvadoreans, and West Indians, a broad range of transnationalized activities, facilitated by instantaneous electronic communications, jet air travel, and the cooperation of homeland governments, has been demonstrated. These activities span the familiar spectrum of public and private endeavors from remittances to political and civic engagements. Are the predictions of the permanency of these patterns as exaggerated as were the original claims about their historical novelty? Are the bounded categories of assimilation theory anachronistic for understanding the trajectory of the lives of contemporary international migrants? Is the dialectic between transnationalization and ethnic incorporation, in which engagement with the homeland simultaneously serves both homeland reincorporation and American incorporation, no longer relevant for understanding the path to assimilation?

Certainly the shortcomings of the classic formulations of assimilation are evident, when we observe manifestations of transnationalization among many contemporary migrants. These statements did not place homeland-oriented consciousness and actions at the center of the migrant's concerns, let alone explore the relevance of transnational social fields and dual incorporations. But just as some assimilation theories, by themselves, have proven inadequate to account for the complex patterns generated by past international migrations, the power of transnational theory to explain present international migrations has limitations. Bounded categories and host society realities continue to have profound meanings for the lives of international migrants. To the extent that for millions of people *migration* continues to take on the dimensions of *immigration*, of permanence and finality, the prospect is raised that assimilation, by whatever circuitous path, will re-enter the debate, even now that such inadequacies as neglect of past transnationalization by assimilation theory are understood.

What are these elements of the contemporary international migrant's experience that appear to limit transnationalization? First, we must take note of the economic realities of the lives of the majority of migrants. Jet travel and electronic communications may now be pervasive, but they are also expensive, and often most available to an affluent minority. The poor and marginal, in contrast, continue to remain rooted of necessity where they work, and to communicate by letter through the mail and by personal couriers, such as friends who are returning to their homelands, as well as occasionally by telephone, as international calling rates fall.[4] That contemporary international migrants, like their predecessors of previous migrations, have to make lives for themselves in the receiving society, until they are faced with or are able to create other options, such as re-emigration, suggests the emotion-laden difficulties and complex choices they confront, as they contemplate long-term separation (Foner 2000; Torres-Saillant 1999; Waters 1999).

In the transnational literature, these difficulties are sometimes lost in celebratory discussions of the migrant as a strategizing cosmopolitan, who is waging a campaign against hegemonic political and economic forces in the developed world that seek control over the vast and exploitable, non-white labor pool in the developing countries of Asia, Africa, the Middle East, and the Americas. Transnational activity is seen as a means to resist this hegemony, and assert the migrant's control over his or her labor by seeking, in the rejection of rootedness, to blunt the force of exploitation, oppression, and racism (Basch, Glick Schiller, and Szanton Blanc 1994; Glick Schiller, Basch, and Blanc-Szanton 1995). If we employ conventional understandings that insist that political acts are ones that are consciously directed at achieving formal, institutional, public power, however, there was much more resistance accompanying the historical international migrations, because the late nineteenth and early twentieth centuries were a high point in the activity of the socialist and communist Left throughout the world in organizing wage labor, across national and racial lines (Kivisto 2001). Contemporary organized labor in the developed, receiving societies has been slow to awaken to the need to incorporate contemporary international migrants into the labor movement; and the historic Left is moribund. Thus, a vital element in the improvement of life for international migrants and resident ethnic communities in the past is less active than previously. Partly because of this lack of political institutions and social movements posing alternatives, contemporary international migrants are seldom engaged in active political resistance, let alone large-scale challenges to international capitalism. Instead the wage-earning majority of labor migrants seek a small niche for themselves based on narrow opportunities within international capitalist labor markets and small business sectors. Various strategies of transnationalization, such as sending money to the homeland to be saved for the purchase of a house, may offer the long-term prospect of eventual re-emigration, as it did for previous waves of migrants, but the duration of residence needed to bring this about remains now, as in the past, indeterminate for most individuals, opening them to the forces that worked toward assimilation in the past.

One cannot overestimate the difficulties they face along whichever road they embark on. The newest immigrants are overwhelmingly people of color, and race continues to play a significant role in the structuring of opportunity in American life. To be sure, race plays this role unevenly to the extent that a new racial hierarchy seems in the midst of formation which finds affluent, educated Asian and lighter-skinned Latino professionals and business owners enjoying the economic, social, and cultural privileges of whites of equivalent class position. But for millions of darker-skinned Latino and Afro-Caribbean immigrants, their future in this emerging hierarchy is a source of deep concern (Alba and Nee 1997; Portes and Rumbaut 2001; Vickerman 1999). The old high-paying and secure industrial jobs of the mid-twentieth century that sustained the European immigrants of the past are no longer widely available. The welfare state that once benefited the immigrants and their children, through such large-scale mid-twentieth-century programs as those created by the GI Bill of Rights for veterans of World War II and through virtually free public higher education, has deteriorated amidst neo-liberal policies that starve the public sector in order to stimulate private investment. Moreover, the group solidarity that once assisted immigrants through the sharing of resources for mutual benefit and community-building may be sapped by transnationalization itself, if those migrants with the material and social resources to assist ethnic community formation are focused on maintaining a transnational lifestyle that seeks to span two societies at once (Foner 2000; Torres-Saillant 1999).

Even if the more affluent minority of contemporary international migrants thus seems to have the potential to resist assimilation, it remains an open question whether that resistance can be sustained into the second generation. The question is just as valid for the poorer migrants who might adopt the goal of keeping alive in their families a vision of return to the homeland, and seek to safeguard their children from assimilative forces. The precedents found in immigration history suggest that the second generation may choose another path. Salutos found retired re-emigrants in Greece whose children had refused to return to the old country, leaving the parents eventually to return by themselves and depend on their ability to travel to America to see their children and grandchildren (Salutos 1956). Cinel noted the same conflict in interviews in southern Italy with elderly re-emigrants whose children had also refused to return (Cinel 1991). The trajectory of these second-generation lives had been set in the United States, and there was no desire to deviate from it. Ultimately, when faced with the choice, the children of these contemporary migrants may also opt to make lives for themselves in the United States, where their opportunities and personal freedoms are greater than in villages in Mexico or Pakistan, and to reject binational activities and consciousness for more conventional, bounded conceptions of identity based on the continuity of their American experience. Peer-group pressures within school and youth cultures popularized by electronic media may propel them in that direction.

Intimations that this is happening are confirmed by the most comprehensive analytical study of today's immigrant second generation (Portes and Rumbaut 2001). The authors analyze the experience of youth in the traditional categories – family, parental expectations and pressures, peer group, community, public schools, peer groups, language shift, etc. – of the sociology of immigration, as these have descended out of assimilation theories, and spend little time tracing transnational activity or consciousness, largely because it is so rare. They note that some Vietnamese and Dominican parents send children to their homelands in the summer to stay with relatives to impede their Americanization, but this strategy is recognized as exceptional, if only because of its expense. But the authors go beyond identifying transnationalization as rare, to maintain it has negative effects. They find it manifest in homeland political and civic engagements, which they dismiss as "ethnic mobilizations under foreign flags" (p. 279), "that are essentially defensive reactions to American nativist prejudices and bigoted, public campaigns for rapid assimilation." These might yield some positive short-run gains, but are said to have negative long-term effects for individuals, and especially for youth. In an embrace of what Gans terms "straight-line" assimilation theory (Gans 1992),[5] Portes and Rumbaut maintain that ultimately today's transnationalization creates an adversarial, defensive stance toward the mainstream social institutions, especially the public schools, that are key to the second generation's American future. They reject, therefore, the more complex formulation that sees homeland reincorporation ultimately serving the needs of American incorporation, which informs the historical literature. In the end, along with other commentators who believe that the second generation's destiny lies in the United States, they leave room for the more traditional homeland ties – memory, family history, and occasional contact with and visits to the old country (Reimers 1999).

These understandings of the continuing relevance of assimilation theory do not begin to address the larger economic, political, and social contexts that provide the outer boundaries within which the migration decisions of individuals are possible. Crises in the international economy that depress labor markets as well as the rise in receiving societies of anti-immigration nativist movements that seek to bar the gates to international migrants might well combine to foreclose access to work, residence, and security in the United States and other developed societies. While not all of them are influenced by nativist prejudices, a number of well-financed advocacy organizations have arisen in recent years to put the demographic, environmental, economic, and cultural cases for immigration restriction (Reimers 1998). Patrick Buchanan sought to forge a political career, though by no means very successfully, throughout the 1990s trying to create a national nativist movement similar to the ones created in Europe by such right-wing populist politicians as Jörge Haider, Jean-Marie Le Pen, and Pym Fortun. Such a politics exploits fears about cultural dissolution, low birth rates among native-stock citizens relative to recent immigrants, a relative decline of native political power, and, in a reprise of a long-time source of anxiety, conflicting, dual loyalties. No matter how fragmentary, anecdotal, unthreatening, or misinterpreted the evidence of contemporary transnationalization, it has served to fuel nativism (Bouvier 1991; Brimelow 1995; Chavez 2001; Suro 1996). Today, it is further fueled by fears of domestic subversion and terrorism associated with unassimilated, transnationalized international migrants.

To appreciate the possibility of the triumph of a restrictionist political agenda, it is necessary to understand that, contrary to the claims of many interpreters of contemporary globalization and some transnational theorists, the nation-state, with all of its formidable powers, is hardly in its death throes. National sovereignty and physical boundaries continue to matter – much more so, in fact, when it comes to people, especially as bearers of different habits, languages, and cultures, than to capital, which migrates much more freely (Lee 1999; Soysal 2000). American immigration law is very much relevant to the lives of contemporary international migrants. For all of the contemporary opportunities for transnationalization, as Reimers notes, most contemporary international migrants who enter the country legally come under the law's family preference categories, and thus represent an effort to reconstitute in one place families that have been separated. Other rights and benefits under law accrue to those who permanently cast their lot with American society and become naturalized citizens (Reimers 1999). Law and the power of the state to enforce it by creating positive and negative incentives in the path of international migrants thus assist significantly in creating the boundaries around which immigration decisions are conceived by individuals.

Any successful effort at barring the gates to international migration would place today's recent arrivers in the same position as their predecessors from Europe after the passage of the 1924 Johnson–Reid Act. This law established strict quotas on migrants from southern and eastern Europe, and reaffirmed the total ban on immigrants ineligible for citizenship, which reaffirmed the exclusion of Chinese, and barred Asians, such as the Japanese, who had been declared ineligible for naturalization by court decisions because of race (Bernard 1980). Without the reinforcement of cultural and identificational difference prompted by new immigration, such restrictions speeded the assimilation of southern and central European and Asian immigrants and their children. How such forces will play themselves out in the future, we cannot know. But in contrast to the predictions of a transnationalized population of international migrants who are successful over the long term in living neither here nor there, it is equally plausible to consider that the future may not differ much from the past, with its record of assimilation.

NOTES

1 I do not employ the common usage, "transnationalism," which suggests an ideology or belief system, rather than a process or a behavior, either of which seem more adequately described by the term "transnationalization."

2 Micro-analysis of immigration is associated with rational choice theory, which studies immigration decisions, as they are rarely made, strictly from the perspective of the individual (Faist 2000a).

3 Of the 350 million lire in remittances handled by the Bank of Naples in 1904, 43 percent (150 million) of the money came from the United States, with Italians in Germany contributing the next largest sum, which amounted to 14 percent (49 million) (Cinel 1991, p. 145).

4 Levitt (2001, p. 23) notes that phone rates to the Dominican Republic from the United States for the Boston area Dominicans she has studied have fallen from $10.59 for three minutes in 1965 to $2 in 2000, which comes to approximately $28 a month for a once a week ten-minute or $56 a month for a once a week twenty-minute conversation. Whether these sums are really negligible, however, can only be understood in the context of the study of household budgets.

5 Gans had in mind the difference between formulations of assimilation that saw the process as unidirectional and sequential ("straight-line") and uneven and occasionally contradictory ("bumpy-line"). His embrace of the latter, a rejection of mechanistic understandings of assimilation, is especially intended to accommodate the findings of studies that reveal the malleability of the ethnic *group* and the waxing and waning of its relevance in inspiring activity on the part of individuals (Gans 1992).

REFERENCES

83rd United States Congress (1953). *Analysis of the Social Security System, Part 2.* Washington, DC: Government Printing Office, Table 1, p. 81.

Alba, Richard D. and Victor Nee (1997). "Rethinking Assimilation Theory for a New Era of Immigration." *International Migration Review* 31: 826–74.

Almeida, Linda Dowling (2001). *Irish Immigrants in New York City, 1945–1995.* Bloomington: Indiana University Press.

Appadurai, Arjum (1991). "Global Ethnoscapes: Notes and Quotes for a Transnational Anthropology." In R.G. Fox, ed., *Recapturing Anthropology: Working in the Present.* Santa Fe, NM: School of American Research Press, pp. 191–210.

—— (1996). *Modernity at Large: Cultural Dimensions of Globalization.* Minneapolis: University of Minnesota Press.

Baily, Samuel L. (1998). *Immigrants in the Land of Promise: Italians in Buenos Aires and New York City, 1870–1914.* Ithaca, NY: Cornell University Press.

Baines, Dudley (1985). *Migration in a Mature Economy.* New York: Cambridge University Press.

Barkan, Elliott (1995). "Race, Religion and Nationality in American Society: A Model of Ethnicity – from Contact to Assimilation." *Journal of American Ethnic History* 14: 38–75.

Basch, Linda, Nina Glick Schiller, and Cristina Szanton Blanc (1994). *Nations Unbound: Transnational Projects, Postcolonial Predicaments and Deterritorialized Nation-States.* Amsterdam: Gordon & Breach.

Baubock, Rainer (1994). *Transnational Citizenship: Membership and Rights in International Migration.* Brookfield, VT: E. Elgar.

Bernard, William S. (1980). "Immigration: History of U.S. Policy." In Stephen Thernstrom, ed., *Harvard Encyclopedia of American Ethnic Groups.* Cambridge, MA: Harvard University Press.

Bouvier, Leon (1991). *Peaceful Invasions: Immigration and Changing America.* Lanham, MD: University Press of America.

Bridges, Amy (1984). *A City in the Republic: Antebellum New York and the Origins of Machine Politics.* Ithaca, NY: Cornell University Press.

Brimelow, Peter (1995). *Alien Nation: Common Sense about America's Immigration Disaster.* New York: Random House.

Brown, Thomas N. (1966). *Irish American Nationalism, 1870–1890.* Philadelphia: Lippincott.

Bukowczyk, John J. (1987). *And My Children Did Not Know Me: A History of Polish Americans.* Bloomington: Indiana University Press.

Chavez, Leo R. (2001). *Covering Immigration: Popular Images and the Politics of the Nation.* Berkeley: University of California Press.

Chen, Yong (2000). *Chinese San Francisco, 1850–1943: A Trans-Pacific Community.* Stanford, CA: Stanford University Press.

Cinel, Dino (1991). *The National Integration of Italian Return Migration, 1879–1929.* New York: Cambridge University Press.

Cohen, Robin (1997). *Global Diasporas: An Introduction.* Seattle: University of Washington Press.

Conzen, Kathleen Neils, David Gerber, Ewa Morawska, George Pozzetta, and Rudolph Vecoli (1992). "The Invention of Ethnicity: A Perspective from the United States." *Journal of American Ethnic History* 12: 3–41.

Daniels, Roger (1978). "The Japanese." In John Higham, ed., *Ethnic Leadership in America.* Baltimore, MD: Johns Hopkins University Press, pp. 36–63.

Diamond, Sander A. (1974). *The Nazi Movement in the United States, 1924–1941.* Ithaca, NY: Cornell University Press.

Diggins, John P. (1972). *Mussolini and Fascism: The View from America.* Princeton, NJ: Princeton University Press.

Erickson, Charlotte (1994). *Leaving England: Essays on British Emigration in the Nineteenth Century.* Ithaca, NY: Cornell University Press.

Fagan, Richard F., Richard A. Brody, and Thomas J. O'Leary (1968). *Cubans in Exile: Disaffection and the Revolution.* Stanford, CA: Stanford University Press.

Faist, Thomas (2000a). *The Volume and Dynamics of International Migration and Transnational Social Spaces.* Oxford: Clarendon Press.

—— (2000b). "Transnationalization in International Migration: Implications for the Study of Citizenship and Culture." *Ethnic and Racial Studies* 23: 189–222.

Foner, Nancy (1997). "What is New about Transnationalism?: New York Immigrants Today and at the Turn of the Century." *Diaspora* 6: 355–76.

—— (2000). *From Ellis Island to JFK: New York's Two Great Waves of Immigration.* New Haven and New York: Yale University Press and Russell Sage Foundation.

Gabaccia, Donna R. (2000). *Italy's Many Diasporas.* London: UCL Press.

Gans, Herbert (1992). "Comment: Ethnic Invention and Acculturation: A Bumpy-Line Approach." *Journal of American Ethnic History* 11: 42–52.

Garcia Canclini, Nestor (1990). *Culturas Hibridas: Estrategias para Entras y Salir de la Modernidad.* Mexico City: Grijalbo.

Garcia, Matt (2001). *A World of Its Own: Race, Labor, and Citrus in the Making of Greater Los Angeles, 1900–1970.* Chapel Hill: University of North Carolina Press.

Gerber, David A. (1989). *The Making of an American Pluralism: Buffalo, New York, 1825–1860.* Urbana: University of Illinois Press.

Gerson, Louis L. (1953). *Woodrow Wilson and the Rebirth of Poland, 1914–1920: A Study in the Influence on American Policy of Minority Groups of Foreign Origin.* New Haven, CT: Yale University Press.

—— (1964). *The Hyphenate in Recent American Politics and Diplomacy.* Lawrence: University of Kansas Press.

Giddens, Anthony (1990). *The Consequences of Modernity.* Stanford, CA: Stanford University Press.

Gjerde, Jon (1999). "New Growth on Old Vines – the State of the Field: The Social History of Immigration and Ethnicity in the United States." *Journal of American Ethnic History* 18: 40–65.

Glick Schiller, Nina (1999). "Who Are These Guys? A Transnational Reading of the U.S. Immigrant Experience." In Lilliana Goldin, ed., *Identities on the Move.* Austin: University of Texas Press.

Glick Schiller, Nina and Georges E. Fouron (1999). "Terrains of Blood and Nation: Haitian Transnational Social Fields." *Ethnic and Racial Studies* 22: 340–66.

Glick Schiller, Nina, Linda Basch, and Christina Blanc-Szanton, eds. (1992). *Towards a Transnational Perspective on Migration: Race, Class, Ethnicity, and Nationalism Reconsidered,* Vol. 645, *Annals of the New York Academy of Sciences.* New York: New York Academy of Sciences.

—— (1995). "From Immigrant to Transmigrant: Theorizing Transnational Migration." *Anthropological Quarterly* 68: 48–63.

Gordon, Milton (1964). *Assimilation in American Life: The Role of Race, Religion, and National Origins.* New York: Oxford University Press.

Greene, Victor R. (1975). *For God and Country: The Rise of Polish and Lithuanian Ethnic Consciousness in America, 1860–1910.* Madison: State Historical Society of Wisconsin.

—— (1987). *American Immigrant Leaders, 1800–1910: Marginality and Identity.* Baltimore, MD: Johns Hopkins University Press.

Guarnizo, Luis Edward (1998). "The Rise of Transnational Social Formations: Mexican and Dominican State Responses to Transnational Migration." *Political Power and Social Theory* 12: 45–94.

Handlin, Oscar (1951). *The Uprooted: The Epic Story of the Great Migrations that Made the American People*. Boston: Little, Brown.

Hansen, Marcus Lee (1940). *The Atlantic Migration, 1607–1860: A History of the Continuing Settlement of the United States*. Cambridge, MA: Harvard University Press.

Hatton, Timothy J. and Jeffrey G. Williamson (1998). *The Age of Mass Migration: Causes and Economic Impact*. New York: Oxford University Press.

Herbert, Will (1960). *Protestant–Catholic–Jew*. New York: Anchor.

Higham, John, ed. (1978). *Ethnic Leadership in America*. Baltimore, MD: Johns Hopkins University Press.

Hoglund, A. William (1960). *Finnish Immigrants in America – 1880–1920*. Madison: University of Wisconsin Press.

Hsu, Madeline Yuan-Yin (2000). *Dreaming of Gold, Dreaming of Home: Transnationalism and Migration between the United States and South China, 1882–1943*. Stanford, CA: Stanford University Press.

Jacobson, Matthew Frye (1995). *Special Sorrows: The Diasporic Imagination of Irish, Polish and Jewish Immigrants in the United States*. Cambridge. MA: Harvard University Press.

Jones-Correa, Michael (1998). *Between Two Nations: The Political Predicament of Latinos in New York City*. Ithaca, NY: Cornell University Press.

Juergensmeyer, Mark (1982). "The Gadar Syndrome: Ethnic Anger and Nationalist Pride." *Population Review* 25: 48–58.

Kallen, Horace M. (1924). *Culture and Democracy in the United States*. New York: Boni & Liveright.

Kasnitz, Philip (1992). *Caribbean New York*. Ithaca, NY: Cornell University Press.

Katznelson, Ira (1981). *City Trenches: Urban Politics and the Patterning of Class in the United States*. Chicago: University of Chicago Press.

Kennedy, Ruby Jo Reeves (1944). "Single or Triple Melting Pot? Intermarriage Trends in New Haven, 1870–1940." *American Journal of Sociology* 49: 331–9.

—— (1952). "Single or Triple Melting Pot? Intermarriage Trends in New Haven, 1870–1950." *American Journal of Sociology* 58: 56–9.

Kivisto, Peter (2001). "Theorizing Transnational Immigration: A Critical Review of Current Efforts." *Ethnic and Racial Studies* 24: 548–77.

Laguerre, Michel (1998). *Diasporic Citizenship: Haitian Americans in Transnational America*. New York: St. Martin's Press.

Lee, Erika (1999). "Immigrants and Immigration Law: A State of the Field Assessment." *Journal of American Ethnic History* 18: 85–114 and 157–66.

Lessinger, Johanna (1992). "Investing or Going Home: A Transnational Strategy among Indian Immigrants in the United States." In Nina Glick Schiller, Linda Basch, and Christina Blanc-Szanton, eds., *Towards a Transnational Perspective on Migration: Race, Class, Ethnicity, and Nationalism Reconsidered*. Vol. 645, *Annals of the New York Academy of Sciences*. New York: New York Academy of Sciences, pp. 53–80.

Levitt, Peggy (2001). *The Transnational Villagers*. Berkeley: University of California Press.

Lie, John (1995). "From International Migration to Transnational Diaspora." *Contemporary Sociology* 24: 303–6.

Lopata, Helena Znaniecka (1994). *Polish Americans*, 2nd ed. New Brunswick and London: Transaction Publishers.

Luconi, Stefano (2001). *From Paesani to White Ethnics: The Italian Experience in Philadelphia*. Albany: State University of New York Press.

MacDonald, John S. and Leatrice D. MacDonald (1964). "Chain Migration, Ethnic Neighborhood Formation, and Social Network." *Milbauk Memorial Fund Quarterly* 42: 82–97.

McKeown, Adam (2001). *Chinese Migrant Networks and Cultural Change: Peru, Chicago, and Hawaii, 1900–1936.* Chicago: University of Chicago Press.

Moch, Leslie Page (1992). *Moving Europeans: Migration in Western Europe since 1650.* Bloomington: Indiana University Press.

Morawska, Ewa (1994). "In Defense of the Assimilation Model." *Journal of American Ethnic History* 13: 76–87.

Moya, José C. (1998). *Cousins and Strangers: Spanish Immigrants in Buenos Aires, 1850–1930.* Berkeley: University of California Press.

O'Grady, Joseph (1973). *How the Irish Became American.* New York: Twayne.

Park, Robert (1930). "Assimilation, Social." In Edwin Seligman and Alvin Johnson, eds., *Encyclopedia of the Social Sciences.* New York: Macmillan, pp. 281–3.

—— (1950). *Race and Culture.* Glencoe, IL: Free Press.

Park, Robert and Ernest W. Burgess (1921). *Introduction to the Science of Sociology.* Chicago: University of Chicago Press.

Pienkos, Donald E. (1984). *Centennial History of the Polish National Alliance of the United States of North America.* Boulder, CO: Eastern European Monographs.

—— (1987). *One Hundred Years Young: A History of the Polish Falcons of America, 1887–1987.* Boulder, CO: Eastern European Monographs.

—— (1991). *For Your Freedom through Ours: Polish American Efforts on Poland's Behalf, 1863–1991.* Boulder, CO: Eastern European Monographs.

Porter, Eduardo (2002). "Mexico Woos its Citizens Living in the U.S." *Wall Street Journal,* October 24.

Portes, Alejandro (1997). "Immigration Theory for a New Century: Some Problems and Opportunities." *International Migration Review* 31: 799–825.

Portes, Alejandro and Ruben G. Rumbaut (1990). *Immigrant America: A Portrait.* Berkeley: University of California Press.

—— (2001). *Legacies: The Story of the Immigrant Second Generation.* Berkeley and New York: University of Chicago Press and Russell Sage Foundation.

Portes, Alejandro and Alex Stepick (1993). *City on the Edge: The Transformation of Miami.* Berkeley: University of California Press.

Portes, Alejandro, Luis Eduardo Guarnizo, and Patricia Landolt (1999). "The Study of Transnationalism: Pitfalls and Promise of an Emergent Research Field." *Ethnic and Racial Studies* 22: 217–33.

Pripic, George J. (1971). *The Croatian Immigrants in America.* Philadelphia: Philosophical Library.

Proctor, Samuel (1950). *Napoleon Bonaparte Broward, Florida's Fighting Democrat.* Gainesville: University of Florida Press.

Puri, Harish K. (1983). *Ghadar Movement.* Amritsar: Guru Nanak Dev University Press.

Puskas, Julianna (1983). *From Hungary to the United States, 1880–1914.* Budapest: Akademiai Kiado.

Reimers, David (1998). *Unwelcome Strangers: American Identity and the Turn against Immigration.* New York: Columbia University Press.

—— (1999). "The: New Immigrants Neither Here Nor There?" *Culturefront* 8: 4–8, 13–14.

Salutos, Theodore (1956). *They Remember America: The Story of Repatriated Greek-Americans.* Berkeley: University of California Press.

Salvemini, Gaetano (1977). *Italian Fascist Activities in the United States,* ed. Philip V. Cannistraro. New York: Center for Migration Studies.

Sarna, Jonathan (1978). "From Immigrants to Ethnics: Toward a New Theory of Ethnicization." *Ethnicity* 5: 73–8.

Sassen, Saskia (1998). *Globalization and Its Discontents: Essays on the New Mobility of People and Money*. New York: New Press.

Smith, Michael Peter and Luis Eduardo Guarnizo (1999). *Transnationalism From Below*, Vol. 6, *Comparative Urban and Community Research*. New Brunswick, NJ: Transaction (second printing).

Smith, Robert (1997). "Transnational Migration, Assimilation, and Political Community." In Margaret Crahan and Alberto Vourvoulias Bush, eds., *The City and the World: New York's Global Future*. New York: Council on Foreign Relations.

Sontag, Deborah (1997). "Advocates for Immigrants Exploring Voting Rights for Noncitizens." *New York Times*, July 31.

Soysal, Yasemin Nuhoglu (2000). "Citizenship and Identity: Living in Diasporas in Post-War Europe?" *Ethnic and Racial Studies* 23: 1–15.

Stolarik, Mark M. (1980). "The Slovaks." In Stephen Thernstrom, ed., *Harvard Encyclopedia of American Ethnic Groups*. Cambridge, MA: Harvard University Press, pp. 926–34.

Suro, Robert (1996). *Watching America's Doors: The Immigration Backlash and the New Policy Debate*. New York: The Twentieth Century Fund.

Thistlethwaite, Frank (1964). "Migration from Europe Overseas in the Nineteenth and Twentieth Centuries." In Herbert Muller, ed., *Population Movements in Modern European History*. New York: Macmillan, pp. 73–92.

Thomas, Brinley (1973). *Migration and Economic Growth: A Study of Great Britain and the Atlantic Economy*. Cambridge: Cambridge University Press.

Thomas, Hugh (1971). *Cuba: The Pursuit of Freedom*. New York: Harper & Row.

Tilly, Charles (1990). "Transplanted Networks." In Virginia Yans-McLaughlin, ed., *Immigration Reconsidered: History, Sociology, and Politics*. New York: Oxford University Press, pp. 79–95.

Tölöyan, Khachig (1998). "(Re)Thinking Diasporas: Stateless Power at the Transnational Moment." *Diaspora* 5: 3–37.

Tomlinson, John (1999). *Globalization and Culture*. Chicago: University of Chicago Press.

Torres-Saillant, Silvio (1999). "Nothing to Celebrate." *Culturefront* 8: 41–4.

Urofsky, Melvin (1975). *American Zionism from Herzl to the Holocaust*. Garden City, NY: Doubleday.

—— (1978). *WE ARE ONE! American Jewry and Israel*. Garden City, NY: Doubleday.

Vertovec, Steven (1999). "Conceiving and Researching Transnationalism." *Ethnic and Racial Studies* 22: 447–56.

Vickerman, Milton (1999). *Crosscurrents: West Indian Immigrants and Race*. New York: Oxford University Press.

Virtanen, Keijo (1979). *Settlement or Return: Finnish Emigrants (1860–1930) in the International Overseas Migration Movement*. Vol. 5, *Migration Studies*. Turku: The Migration Institute.

Wakeman, Frederic E., Jr. (1988). "Transnationalism and Comparative Research." *Items* 35: 85–9.

Waters, Mary (1999). *Black Identities: West Indian Immigrants' Dreams and American Realities*. Cambridge, MA: Harvard University Press.

Wirth, Louis (1928). *The Ghetto*. Chicago: University of Chicago Press.

Wyman, Mark (1993). *Round-Trip to America: The Immigrants Return to Europe, 1880–1930*. Ithaca, NY: Cornell University Press.

Yung, Judy (1999). *Unbound Feet: A Social History of Chinese Women in San Francisco*. Berkeley: University of California Press.

CHAPTER ELEVEN

Immigration and Race Relations

JEFFREY MELNICK

It seems straightforward enough: "Immigration and Race Relations." There is a neat tale promised by such a title, a promise of a linear history that tells how various people have come to the United States, how they have interacted with African Americans (and, perhaps, Native Americans), how they have helped shape the customs and state policies that constitute "race" in the United States and how they have in turn been changed by the racial system they found here. It is a simple enough narrative, on the face of it, and one that has been sustained by nearly a century's worth of academic and creative work in the field. This story has acquired a form with defining images: left Europe to escape religious or ethnic persecution; came to America with nothing, searching for economic opportunity; saw the Statue of Liberty as they leaned over the railing of their ship; settled usually on the east coast (or maybe Chicago); worked hard and made a better life for their children; ended up in the suburbs; usually as white people.

The subjects of this familiar immigration story – and very often the creators of it – were Euro-Americans who embraced, promoted, and elaborated upon a founding myth of America. This mythic narrative, still taught to many American schoolchildren in the form of the story of the first Thanksgiving and in the Pocahontas story, places "love" at the center: white newcomers, at first wary of and hostile toward the "darker" people they meet on the American content, come to appreciate the gifts offered by them and find their way into alliances of one sort or another. Werner Sollors has explained in detail how tales of Indian–white romantic love have acted as one major form for articulating the idea that "consent" (the willingness to invent and act out a new social identity) has often trumped "descent" (actual position by birth) in the American imagination – even in the face of all kinds of evidence that things have not actually worked this way (Sollors 1986, pp. 111, 128). While rarely articulating their concerns in the language of voluntary affiliation, even apologists for slavery in the nineteenth century drew on the language of love – in this case, usually the language of parental care: in 1861, for instance, one southern minister suggested that his slaves stood to him "in the relation of a child . . . I am to him a guardian and a father" (Osofsky 1967, p. 93).

It is no surprise that over time Americans have constructed a durable narrative of migration(s) and peaceful intergroup contact. Reconciling a foundational Declaration of Independence that demands equality and liberty with a historical reality that includes genocide, mass enslavement, annexation, and other forms of colonial and neocolonial violence, has led to the development of a sort of culture-wide reaction formation. Where in reality there has been intense racial hatred, the mythology gives us stories of black–white love of one form or another – from *Uncle Tom's Cabin* through whatever *Lethal Weapon* movie we are currently up to. In the face of closely guarded borders, the mythology substitutes "Give me your tired, your poor, Your huddled masses." Above all, the combined narratives of immigration and race relations that have dominated the telling of American history give us a picture of a world in which certain types of migrants (i.e. African Americans) loom as a problem, and others stand as the model of success – the solution! – to the problem of race in America (Prashad 2000, p. viii).

I want to propose that the very title I have chosen, commonplace as it is, holds in it centuries of pernicious – even violent – cultural work. I have chosen the title for its very familiarity; on the face of it "Immigration and Race Relations" portends nothing more controversial than a survey of the various ways that the United States has come to be populated and how its many constituent groups have interacted with each other. In the American historical lexicon, "immigration" has frequently been deployed as an ennobled keyword: its crosslinks, in virtual terms, include "Promised Land," "American Dream," and "liberty." Its most important court attendant is the hazy but crucial concept, "ethnicity," with "culture" also performing an important function. This is not to ignore the fact that American peoplehood has often been conceptualized precisely in terms of keeping out "undesirable" others, whether they be Chinese migrants in the 1880s or Mexican migrants in the 1980s. But even so, race and race relations have come to seem as the evil (darker?) twin of the more hopeful figure of immigration.

This cultural movement in favor of immigration privileges traceable roots, Atlantic passage (of the relatively voluntary kind), and uplift. While the roots of the immigration paradigm stretch back quite directly to the initial exploration of the "New World" by Europeans, its modern formulation derives from migration patterns established, roughly, between the 1830s and 1950s. This period brought all manner of "worthy" immigrants from Europe: Irish famine victims, Jews escaping pogroms, Italians leaving behind political and economic insecurity, Armenians fleeing the genocide. These were the immigrants who would become "white ethnics" by the middle of the twentieth century – hyphenated denizens of what would later be reconfigured as "multicultural" America.

It is "multiculturalism" which has, of course, come to serve as the umbrella under which "immigration" and "race relations" – and all their minions – are now operating in the United States. The history of "multiculturalism" as a social movement, pedagogical approach, and so on, is beyond the purview of this chapter, but it is worth noting that this innovation, for good and ill, does represent one kind of effort to bridge the gap between immigration and race relations. In other words, at its best, multiculturalism includes the requirement that each group identity can be understood only when placed in the dynamic context of all group identities. At its worst, of course, multiculturalism can, and has, devolved into a kind of mindless celebration of all "difference."

In the 1990s "diversity" was transformed from a national motto ("E Pluribus Unum") describing the multiple roots of the American union into an easy-toswallow prescription – something Americans could be "trained" in to make a better workplace, or something they could sing about at grade school musical events, or celebrate during various federally (or at least culturally) sanctioned holidays. The untenable nature of "multiculturalism" as a way to map the social realities of life in the United States (both current and historical) comes most clear, perhaps, with the holidays, especially those – for example, Thanksgiving – that involve more than one major constituency. While the complexities surrounding Thanksgiving are fairly well known, perhaps less publicized have been intergroup contretemps having to do with Columbus Day, a national holiday in the United States.

Columbus Day became a federal holiday in 1971, but its history stretches back at least as far as 1792, when the 300th anniversary of Christopher Columbus's journey to the Bahamas was commemorated in New York. In the 1860s, Italians in New York and San Francisco organized celebrations in his honor. President Franklin Roosevelt proclaimed October 12 as Columbus Day in 1937; 34 years later it was entered onto the United States calendar as an official national holiday (www.thebearbyte.com/Columbus). By the time it became a *national* holiday it was also clear that Columbus Day was an *ethnic* holiday as well: in short, it is a day to celebrate Italian immigration to the United States. Columbus, of course, never made it exactly to the land mass that we now call the United States. But he has been adopted (or invented, really) as a kind of patron saint of Italian immigration to the United States, and there is no doubt that the early autumn holiday in his honor is securely ensconced.

As with the more or less unconscious yearly revival of the Thanksgiving myth as an immigration "Happy Meal" (football included!), Columbus Day, for the most part, slipped into the American imaginary without much fanfare. But of course there is at least one major group of people who refute not only the logic of the holiday (what does Christopher Columbus have to do with the United States anyway?) but also the moral rightness of it. For the last few decades a number of American Indians in advocacy groups and on their own have loudly protested the slippage from particularist pride to the generalized enshrinement that constitutes Columbus Day. In recent years numerous cities have seen their Columbus Day parades met by major protests: in Denver, in 2000, for instance, nearly 150 American Indians were arrested during a street action (http://www.thebearbyte.com/Columbus). American Indian journalists have come to more or less automatically suggest that Columbus Day is a way of "Celebrating a Holocaust" (see, for instance, Brenda Norrell, in *Indian Country Today*, October 11, 2004).

The slippage from the ethnic/particular to the national/general in the case of Columbus Day (that is, how an Italian American pride day got turned into a federal holiday) stands as an emblem of what is usually wrong with the "immigration and race relations" formulation: more often than not it configures "immigration" as good and relatively unproblematic, a story of uplift and progress – immigration as *the* national saga. Oscar Handlin codified this approach in the opening of his 1951 book *The Uprooted*: "Once I thought to write a history of the immigrants in America. Then I discovered that the immigrants were American history" (Handlin 1951, p. 3). This bright and sunny version of the peopling of America is disturbed only when the dark shadow of "race relations" appears. Most commonly this happens when people left out of the standard immigration saga (e.g. Native Americans and

African Americans) demand either to have standing in the narrative (i.e. "we are all immigrants, at least originally") or, more radically, to rewrite the narrative altogether.

What has been lost in all of the triumphalist narratives of American identity is any sense of how "race" and "immigration" have mutually constituted each other, in the bloodsoaked contexts of colonization, slavery, and xenophobia. The burden of this chapter then is to separate out each term in the title "Immigration and Race Relations" in order to perform a brief archaeology of each one. Doing so will allow us to explore the obfuscating work performed by each element in the equation and will open up at least some provisional routes leading to a more useful formulation.

"Immigration"

It took a little time – five centuries, give or take – for a loose coalition of artists, activists, and scholars to begin effectively to rewrite the age-old narrative of immigration as an area of activity that had been characterized above all by individual motivation, directionality, and a quasi- (and often fully) religious sense of purpose. The story of America's founding by "pilgrims" is the ur-narrative that has generated, at least in part, most successive immigration narratives. As Valerie Babb has shown, a large body of early American writings worked to mythologize "English experiences, turning migrants into pilgrims sharing a special bond with God as they settle a new land" (Babb 1998, p. 59). Many modern scholars (see Sollors 1986, pp. 54–6, for instance) have noticed how invested the earliest English migrants to the "New World" were in the notion that their move to a new land was at once divinely sanctioned *and* marked by their own individual (and group) bravery.

What these early migrants and their literal and symbolic descendants chose to forget (or never knew) is that their pilgrimage to the "Promised Land" (as they often called it, as Russian Jewish immigrant Mary Antin called her 1912 autobiography, and so on) was enmeshed in an ever-growing worldwide economic system, racial and religious conceptualizations, and contests over political power. To put it more baldly, as globalization theorist Saskia Sassen has, most narratives of immigration to the United States have acted as if such migrations "just happen" (Sassen 1998, p. 56). It is stunning, really, to observe the way that Americans have come to understand the peopling of their land as a kind of haphazard series of decisions made by a few hearty pioneers who finally had just had enough of the old world and decided to pick up sticks and make a better life for themselves. And so on.

But as Sassen and other theorists of what we have learned to call "globalization" have taught us, these world-changing migrations do not, "just happen." They are, Sassen writes, "produced" and "patterned" (p. 56). Again, Sassen writes:

> What we still narrate in the language of immigration and ethnicity . . . is actually a series of processes having to do with the globalization of economic activity, of cultural activity, of identity formation. Too often immigration and ethnicity are constituted as otherness. Understanding them as a set of processes whereby global elements are localized, international labor markets are constituted, and cultures from all over the world are de- and reterritorialized, puts them right there at the center along with the internationalization of capital as a fundamental aspect of globalization. (p. xxxi)

It is, of course, anachronistic to speak of the earliest migrants to the Americas in the context of "globalization" as we use that term today. But Sassen and her colleagues who have developed globalization as a field of study have correctly pointed to some core problems with the immigration paradigm that has ruled American consciousness for so long.

Above all, the challenge made by globablization theory has to do with the old sense of immigration as a more or less individual life choice, as opposed to the result of an interwoven set of processes – most of which originate from outside the self. To narrate English settlement of the "New World" outside of a linked exploration of the slave trade, or of the simultaneous development of instrumental notions of the hierarchy of the "races," is to detach that movement from the very context that gives it any meaningful specificity.

But of course the languages of immigration and ethnicity have been instrumental themselves. The old-fashioned, linear notion of immigration as something that the individual simply *does* removes the entire complex of issues from the realm of political and economic interests. This is not simply the stuff of academic debate and arguing over shades of meaning. "There is a strong tendency in immigration policy in developed countries," according to Sassen,

> to reduce the process to the actions of individuals. The individual is the site for accountability and enforcement. Yet it can be argued that international migrations are embedded in larger geopolitical and transnational economic dynamics. . . . Economic internationalization and the geopolitics resulting from older colonial patterns suggest that responsibility for immigration may not be exclusively the immigrant's. (p. 8)

Even the most cursory look at United States "immigration" history in the modern age shows how the machinery of state and industrial power helped shape what Sassen calls the "patterning" of migrations. This "patterning" is perhaps nowhere more striking than in the way that Puerto Ricans and Mexicans have been alternately incorporated into and rejected by the dominant culture of the United States. A brief sketch of how Mexicans and Puerto Ricans have become American reveals, in one suggestive way, how insufficient and obfuscatory the "immigration" concept is when concretely applied to the peopling of the United States. At the same time, a thumbnail history of both groups in relation to official state policy (and less official but equally powerful cultural behaviors and representations) makes it clear that inventing a Eurocentric immigration narrative has been crucially important to Americans' sense of their nation as a sanctuary for the (worthy) downtrodden people of the world. The "immigration" narrative that is so crucial to American grade school pedagogy and July 4th celebrations – to all the constituents of the most optimistic variant of American nationalism as a pluralistic venture – shows itself in the light of America's Latino people to be little more than a way to avoid talking about war and labor needs as the major factors in the peopling of the United States.

Mexicans, of course, did not originally come to the United States: the United States came to them in the mid-nineteenth century, as one outcome of the Mexican–American War:

> Under the terms of the Treaty of Guadalupe Hidalgo . . . Mexico ceded to the United
> States a vast territory, including California, Arizona, New Mexico, and other large

fragments, and also approved the prior annexation of Texas. The lands which Mexico ceded to the United States were greater in extent than Germany and France combined and represented one-half of the territory which Mexico possessed in 1821. All citizens of Mexico residing within the ceded domain were to become citizens of the United States if they failed to leave the territory within one year after ratification of the treaty. Only a few thousand Mexican nationals . . . took advantage of this provision. (McWilliams 1969, p. 51)

The first mass movement of Mexicans to the United States, then, was entirely the result of political and military arrangements. Individual will and personal desire had little or nothing to do with how these thousands of Mexicans became Mexican Americans – later to be known as Chicanos. The lands annexed by the United States in 1848 would become important again in the late 1960s when young Chicano writers and activists began speaking of Aztlán – the mythologized version of the homelands that had been lost over a hundred years earlier.

It was war that first brought masses of Mexicans into the body of the American nation and it was war again – this time World War II – that multiplied the number of Mexicans who would become (at least temporarily) Americans. Thousands of Mexican immigrants arrived in the United States in the early 1940s under the auspices of the United States government, which was responding to pressure from farm interests in the western region to import temporary workers in order to solve the immediate shortage of farm labor. (Some of the same farm interests, such as those represented by the Grower-Shipper Vegetable Association, were among the first and most vocal to call for the internment of Japanese and Japanese Americans living in the west coast states – many of whom were their competitors in farming.) To deal with the labor shortage, the federal government drafted in 1942 the Bracero Program, an emergency farm labor plan.

During its inception, the Bracero Program was overseen by the Farm Security Administration (FSA). Many growers, though, considered the FSA, which had been created as part of Roosevelt's New Deal, to be too pro-union and too politically progressive for their liking. Instead, they persuaded the government to transfer control of the plan to the War Food Administration, which was known as a far more conservative organization – and on whose policies agribusiness had much more influence. The Bracero Program was extremely and promptly successful at meeting its goal of supplying cheap labor for agribusiness: between 1942 and 1947, 219,000 Mexican agricultural workers entered the United States from Mexico (Lorey 1999, p. 90). Following on the heels of this success, the United States and Mexico signed another agreement in 1943 for a similar plan to provide the United States with railroad workers. This new plan allowed the United States to import 20,000 additional Mexican workers in 1943, 50,000 in 1944, and 75,000 in 1945.

The Bracero Program and its successors marked the beginning of a massive movement of Mexicans to border states in both Mexico and the United States, one that continues into the twenty-first century. In addition to the major population shifts that the programs brought about, the social and cultural consequences of the programs were profound. In other words, not only did these labor programs bring hundreds of thousands of Mexican persons to the United States, but they established powerful narratives concerning the status and entitlement of these individuals once they entered

United States society. The Bracero Program fostered the notion that Mexican workers were entirely dispensable, and that once they were no longer needed, they could simply be returned to Mexico. The government's notorious Operation Wetback is a prime example: under its auspices, 2 million Mexicans – and Mexican Americans who were actually US citizens or legally resident aliens – were deported back across the border between 1953 and 1955. (More than 300,000 Mexicans and Mexican Americans – some historians set the number at twice that – were likewise deported from the United States during the 1930s.) Furthermore, the apparently inexhaustible supply of Mexican laborers allowed large agribusinesses to keep wages low for non-Mexican and Mexican workers alike. Because of the vulnerability of Mexican workers, it was common for growers to refuse to pay their wages, to demand excessive hours in the field, to ignore hazardous working conditions (especially pertaining to poisoning from pesticides and herbicides), and to violate provisions for housing and transportation. In short, the braceros and their children lived in poverty, with few opportunities to seek relief.

The Mexican experience with (and in) the United States demonstrates in a stark way that the "immigration" paradigm is not applied to migrant groups to the United States (or its precursor colonies) in an uncomplicated way. Of course the early peopling of the North American continent with Africans kidnapped into slavery made that clear from the earliest days of settlement. But it is useful to tally up some of the major exceptions to the standard immigration narrative as a way of closing in on its ultimate meaning as a false promise and a dodge, a fairy-tale Americans have told themselves since early colonial days as a way to avoid the difficult realities of war and unfree labor.

Just as much of Mexico became part of the United States through the Mexican–American War, so did Puerto Rico become a colony of the United States as one result of the Spanish–American War. The Foraker Act of 1900 denied, "for the first time in U.S. history, both territorial status and constitutional protection and citizenship to a newly acquired territory" (Oboler 1995, p. 37); citizenship would not come until the 1917 passage of the Jones Act. The political issues marked off by these two dates can only hint at the complex ways in which the United States took control over Puerto Rico in these years. As Virginia Sánchez Korrol has explained, the "penetration of United States capital into the Puerto Rican economy since 1898 virtually destroyed the traditional pattern of land ownership and consolidated the dominance of large continental corporations" (Sánchez Korrol 1983, p. 25). Capital was just one part of the bigger picture, though: American "commodities, laws, and customs" were all foisted on Puerto Ricans busily being incorporated into the American empire (Duany 2002, p. 1). American domination was expressed in virtually every area of Puerto Rican life; officers of the United States government "pressured Puerto Rican municipal and school bands to change their calendars and their repertoires to conform with American holidays and patriotic songs," for instance (Glasser 1995, p. 37).

There were a number of major causes of increased Puerto Rican migration to the mainland. Curtailment of European immigration just after World War I (particularly through the National Origins Act of 1924) created more job opportunities for Puerto Ricans in New York and elsewhere in the continental United States; by 1930 at least 52,000 island Puerto Ricans had settled on the mainland (Sánchez Korrol

1983, p. 31; Cofer 1993, p. 213). A devastating hurricane in 1928, combined with the increasing control exerted by United States corporations over Puerto Rican agriculture, encouraged more and more Puerto Ricans to leave the island for New York (Glasser 1995, p. 50).

Operation Bootstrap (officially called the Industrial Incentives Act of 1947) converted what had been a steady migration of Puerto Ricans to New York into what Victor Hernández Cruz has called "one of the great exoduses of recent times" (1991, p. 92). Between 1940 and 1950 migration from Puerto Rico to New York increased by over 200 percent (Padilla 1964, p. 21). While New York had some 45,000 Puerto Rican inhabitants in 1930, by 1950 it would have around 250,000; this number would more than double again (577,000) by 1956 (Handlin 1962, p. 143; Schneider 1999, p. 32). Operation Bootstrap represented a major economic and cultural assault on Puerto Rico; it also, on some level, reinvented New York as a cultural colony of Puerto Rico. Operation Bootstrap "combined a massive industrialization program on the island based on long-term tax breaks for U.S. corporation and the export of thousands of displaced workers to the United States" (Oboler 1995, p. 39). The Puerto Ricans whose migration was predestined by this act of social engineering (the "cheap labor pool") were also prepared to serve the needs of US corporate interests through a variety of educational protocols.

The incorporation of Puerto Rico, along with the Philippines, marked an important moment in the development of American empire at the end of the nineteenth century. This military expansion abroad and economic expansion at home made it clear (as it should have been from the very founding of the nation) that, as Matthew Jacobson has nicely summarized, the putative "greatness" of the United States depended on "the dollars, the labor, and not least, the very *image* of the many peoples with whom Americans increasingly came in contact and whom they blithely identified as inferiors" (Jacobson 2000, p. 5). Those people were not just Puerto Ricans and Mexicans, but a variety of Asians as well: Lisa Lowe has noted that immigration has been a "crucial *locus* through which U.S. interests have recruited and regulated both labor and capital from Asia" (1996, p. 7).

But insofar as "immigration" has stood as a keyword for movement to the United States, it begins to come clear that it has been reserved (in opposition to "race relations") as a benefit of citizenship for a relatively small and elect group of Americans who labor properly as white people. Chinese workers on the railroad represent a "yellow peril" and Mexican immigrants to the Untied States are viewed, as Leo Chavez argues, as an "invasion" (2001, p. 231). Again and again it seems that immigration to the United States as a positive, constructive activity is reserved for certain white Europeans. According to Doreen Alvarez Saar, this sentiment was expressed as early as 1782, with the publication of J. Hector St. John de Crèvecoeur's *Letters from an American Farmer*. As Saar reads it, Crèvecoeur could only imagine that the personal metamorphosis we have come to call "Americanization" depended "upon a notion of individual responsibility called industry" that only certain immigrants possessed. But even more crucially, as Saar explains, "certain groups are excluded from even being considered for Americanization. Because of the Anglocentricity of the principles, both Native Americans and Africans brought to America as slaves remain outside the assimilation process" (1993, p. 252).

From the very earliest consideration of how Americans are "made," the immigration concept has been saturated with racialized notions of proper free labor. It has become something of a commonplace for scholars of American history to point out that the very concept of honorable labor in the United States has always been defined in large part by its (at least) implicit comparison to all the unfree labor – in the form of indentured servitude and slavery especially – surrounding it. This cultural process has donated much energy to the project of defining immigrants by who they are not. As Frank Shuffleton usefully summarizes,

> [for] European immigrants on their way to being ethnically transformed as Americans, the seemingly most obvious cultural others in early America, both in terms of difference and numbers, were the Native Americans and the African slaves, and it is impossible to understand later phenomena of American ethnicity without considering always the power of ethnic representations of and by these groups of people. (1993, p. 9)

The "immigration" in the title of this chapter, then, comes to fullest light as best a hedge, and at worst, a motivated misnomer. The burden of "immigration" as a concept – especially in the phrase "immigration and race relations" – seems simple: to mark off those "foreigners" who move to the United States and there come into interesting and productive contact with "others" who are neither immigrants nor white. But by defining who counts as an "immigrant," this paradigm is already making a strong cultural argument about respect and belonging in the United States. Without the African Americans forced to migrate in chains, without the Native Americans and Puerto Ricans (often forced, as Rachel Buff has noted, "by public policy or economic circumstances to move without crossing national borders" (2001, p. 176)), without the Mexicans annexed into the United States, "immigration" begins to look more and more like an exclusive club in this country, and not "American history" itself, as Oscar Handlin and so many others would have us believe.

"And"

The problem with "and," as should be clear by now, is that it promises too much and delivers too little (or, looking at it a different way, it delivers more than it means to!).

What the formulation promises – as social science paradigm, public policy occasion, and so on – is a straight line. "And" suggests chronological clarity and conceptual neatness: it is the heart of an analogy and an allegory that continue to shape Americans' ability to understand themselves. The problem with "and" is that it pretends that what really matters is the firm boundary separating "immigration" from "race relations" when in reality the action is inside of each term and in the dynamic interplay between them.

Immigration *is* race relations, as scholars of American history have been more and more able to discover, in the last decade or so. The "hyphen" that has been so crucially defining for so many migrants to the United States has itself been an "and" that has been functional in defining the racial identity of many new Americans. While immigration restrictionists have at various times of crisis attempted to define the hyphen as a minus sign, it has been far more common for Americans to construe the hyphen as a symbol of potent synergism – at least in the case of European immigrants to the United States.

That it has been so possible, so necessary really, to imagine European immigrants riding the hyphen to a successful both/and identity has, for some time, been a way to make oblique (at least) commentary on what separates white immigrants from the darker others they are so often pit against. Another way of saying this is to note that a kind of "and" work has already been done under the rubric of the keyword "immigration" – before we even get to the "and" that connects up immigrants to the world of "race" and race relations. Labor historian David Roediger has elaborated on this idea in a number of places, but especially in an essay in which he builds on work done by Richard Williams to argue that "ethnicity" (the category Americans use for fully domesticated immigrants and their children) is "made possible by race": "ethnicity is a social status assigned to those immigrants, who, though slotted into low-wage jobs, were *not* reduced to the slavery or systematic civil discrimination that 'racial' minorities suffered" (Roediger 1994, p. 182).

Here the analogical function of the "and" is revealed. Roediger and others have done important work to uncover the terms of the analogy in the labor context. In the early to mid-nineteenth century, for instance, a whole vocabulary developed (including phrases "work like a nigger" and "white slavery") to compare the work done by immigrants to that done by enslaved Africans in America (Roediger 1991, p. 68). This language was used, as Roediger makes clear, not as "an act of solidarity with the slave but rather a call to arms to end the inappropriate oppression of whites" (ibid.).

The premise that "immigrants" (and then "ethnics" or white ethnics) could gain – materially or at least symbolically – from the comparison has been at the heart of management strategies to keep immigrants and African Americans from making threatening alliances. As Matthew Jacobson discusses in the context of the late nineteenth- and early twentieth-century social engineering, immigrants served not only "to fill the positions and staff the factories as the nation's economy expanded, but monitoring and tapping the immigrant streams became an important element of workforce management, as employers sought just the right kind of workers and the right combinations of workers to maximize productivity and to minimize labor's stridence and solidarity." Even more important, as Jacobson notes, the deployment of the "and" in "immigration and race relations" as a "versus" meant "using ethnic or racial difference itself in engineering a workforce that was usefully divided against itself" (2000, p. 69).

Always implicit (when not expressed outright) in this Manichean structuring of American social life was a set of linked analogies: immigrant is to racial minority as freedom is to slavery, and so on. The "and" is the engine of a pernicious analogy, one that has been adopted by literary artists, government officials, and social scientists alike. Stephen Steinberg argues that the American tradition of sociology relies heavily, at least in certain of its branches, on this "and," which puts "ethnic heroes" against "racial villains" (1989, p. 263). The analogical "and" of "immigration and race relations" promotes a zero-sum game, in which, recent history tells us, worthy immigrants (i.e. model minorities) will be used as a weapon to be deployed against unworthy racial minorities. This is complicated, of course, by the increasing number of black immigrants coming from Africa, Latin America, and the Caribbean to the

United States in the wake of changing immigration laws (especially in 1965). And it is complicated too by the reality that in certain times and places, native-born people of color have been promoted as the antidote to the dangerous incursion of "foreigners." But above all, the "and" that connects immigration to race relations insists upon a stable and neatly unfolding narrative of demographic change that acts as a smokescreen hiding the state policies and corporate strategies that have had the greatest influence on changing demographic patterns.

The "and" also anchors a powerful allegory about American life, an allegory about the "ordinary" goodness of immigrants. Judith Smith has recently demonstrated in convincing detail how a cohort of American writers and filmmakers in the post-World War II era converted the immigrant family story into *the* story of proper American cosmopolitanism, and in doing so wrote African American families out of the normative category of the "healthy." Writers as diverse as Betty Smith and Arthur Miller began to insist that groups of immigrants formerly seen as "racialized outsiders" (Smith 2004, p. 4) must now be understood as avatars of a new pluralistic reality. But this cultural work was rooted, of course, in a set of ideas about "race" that were in flux: one of the problems with the title "immigration and race relations," we come to see, is that American definitions of "race" change constantly and involve a steady process of migration. Naming who "counts" as white, black, brown, or other, is an activity and not a fact. "Immigration and Race Relations" cannot serve well, then, because the "race" in the title begs more questions than it answers.

"Race"

The problem with the "race" in "Immigration and Race Relations" is that it puts race "on the other side of the tracks" from immigration, as legal scholar Patricia Williams has written (1997, p. 7). But "race" and racial formation are everywhere, as an influential set of scholars in sociology, postcolonial studies, American labor history, and literary criticism (to name just a few areas) have demonstrated conclusively. Race, as Thomas Guglielmo has recently made clear, is not "simply an idea, an attitude, a consciousness, an identity, or an ideology. . . . It is also rooted in various political, economic, social, and cultural institutions and thus very much about power and resources" (2003, p. 7). Racial thinking has been at the heart of virtually all American immigration laws, for instance, at least up until the second half of the twentieth century. And the practice of racial naming (and unnaming) has acted as a gatekeeping force in American life, determining who can live in this country, where they can live, what work opportunities will be open to them, and what their legal rights and status will be.

But as Patricia Williams has so eloquently explained, the joined social processes that contribute to the racial naming of certain individuals and groups of people have also been involved in "exnomination" – that is the unnaming of whiteness as itself a racial identity. Further, to achieve the powerful status of "white" in modern American history has also meant, as Williams notes, to gain access to the dominant form of nationalism the country offers to and demands from its citizens (1997, pp. 7, 56).

For the most part, European immigrants to the United States have covered the legal and cultural ground necessary to achieve whiteness. Many came in with whiteness as a given aspect of their identities and social standing; Thomas Guglielmo's recent work on Italian immigrants in Chicago suggests that even when Italians were understood by other Americans as belonging to a distinct "Latin" race, their position as white people was rarely challenged (2003, p. 10). This has been less true for other groups of European immigrants to the United States, most notably Irish and East European Jews. Irish immigrants, as David Roediger and other historians have discovered, experienced a long and painful process of racialization (and then ethnicization) as they struggled to be accepted as at least provisionally white – and definitely not black. But this was a long process and one with indeterminate starting and ending points. To speak of "Immigration and Race Relations" makes it impossible to focus on race formation and revision as themselves historically dynamic areas of concern, scrutiny, and challenge.

Coming to the United States in large numbers decades after the Irish began their "race" journey, East European Jews faced similarly complex issues having to do with their fluid racial identity. Noticeably distinct from their German Jewish immigrant predecessors in terms of language acquisition, settlement patterns, and a variety of physical markers, the East European Jews presented a difficult conundrum for American social scientists, politicians, and concerned citizens. While they obviously did not belong to the Anglo-Saxon or Nordic races (as the racial anthropologists of the early twentieth century would have put it) they also were clearly distinct from African Americans. A number of Jewish Americans were able to manipulate to their advantage what Robert Orsi, in a different context, has called the "Inbetween" status of certain immigrant groups. Many Jewish songwriters and musical performers, in fact, traded on just this status, using their perceived placement as somewhere in between white and black people as a way to promote their own productions as somehow "natural" expressions of blackness while maintaining their own plausible claim on a white social status for themselves (Melnick 1999).

But taking advantage of the instability of "race" in American life was not without dangers, and these dangers ranged from social opprobrium to outright violence. For instance, in 1913, a Jewish factory manager in Atlanta named Leo Frank was accused and convicted of murdering (and perhaps sexually abusing) a young white woman, Mary Phagan, who worked at the National Pencil Company. When the crime was first discovered, Frank adopted a number of postures that made it clear that he assumed that the crime would be pinned on Jim Conley, the African American janitor in the factory. Many of Frank's statements and actions in the immediate aftermath made it clear that he thought he would be taken as a white man no different from any other southern white man and would be extended the courtesies and social practices therein. But in the court case Frank's Jewishness was racialized in a way that made him seem a more likely villain in the crime: he was convicted in 1913 and sentenced to death. After a number of appeals that brought his case all the way to the United States Supreme Court, Frank finally had his sentence commuted in the summer of 1915 by the governor of Georgia. Soon after, Frank was kidnapped from the prison farm where he was being held and taken to the town of Marietta, Mary Phagan's hometown, where he was lynched (Melnick 2000). The negotiations – explicit or not – that must have taken place among police officers, lawyers, politicians, and lynchers (with some holding membership in more than one category) as they decided who to punish for Mary Phagan's death reveal to us that race has been a slippery, shape-shifting force in American life.

But "race," as Thomas Guglielmo reminds us, is not some social abstraction (or "construction") as so many of us have gotten in the bad habit of acting. It has been important for many scholars of American history to examine how ideas about, and consciousness of, race have changed over time, and how these arguments (whether about original creation of the human peoples, or about the group characteristics of the various populations on the American landscape) have relied on wildly different assumptions about how race gets constructed. But this archaeological work, for all its usefulness, too often leads down an intellectual path where it seems as if any particular definition of race doesn't matter. This is what Patricia Williams realized when a number of her son's nursery school teachers worried that her son was literally color-blind: Williams's child seemed unable to name different colors when prompted to do so by his teachers. But, as Williams discovered after some investigation, her son could see colors perfectly well; having been taught, however, that it doesn't matter "whether you're black or white or red or green or blue" (1997, p. 3) by his well-meaning, progressive teachers, her young son decided to apply that lesson to all matters colorful. Williams rightly notes that such corrective pedagogy is rooted in the reality that race continues to be functional in the United States, and continues to inflict daily hurts on its most vulnerable citizens.

So, while we can never conclusively say in any particular moment "This is what race means now," it is also important, following Barbara Jeanne Fields's paradigm-shifting work, not to treat race as some transhistorical or metaphysical force in American life (Fields 1982, p. 144). The meaning of race constantly changes, and is always under construction; the reality of racism, however, is always with us (Omi and Winant 1986). The context of immigration makes the stakes of constantly noticing (and agitating around) how race gets defined especially high. Gary Gerstle, among others, has explained how pseudoscientific definitions of race in the first few decades of the twentieth century were crucially important not only in helping to develop a functional sense of "racial nationalism" in American life, but also in working quite materially to support claims made by advocates of immigration restriction (Gerstle 2001, p. 104). In our time, anti-immigrant biases, in legislation (as with the notorious passage of Proposition 187 in California in 1994) and in public rhetoric (as with Peter Brimelow's hatemongering 1996 book *Alien Nation*), continue to rely on "common sense" understandings of how immigration and race are mutually constitutive (Chavez 2001, p. 147). These common sense understandings of race and immigration pivot on overly simplified (and highly motivated) ideas about what sorts of "relations" should exist among various populations and individuals in the nation and beyond.

"Relations"

What could be less precise – or more important – than "relations"? In the many possible contexts suggested by "Immigration and Race Relations" this keyword has meant everything from the most private of romantic and sexual contact, to the largest-scale questions of international political and economic development. "Relations" is the crux of the matter at hand, the site where every "we" meets its significant "other." Not surprisingly, every major shareholder in the development of American identity – from the worlds of government, religion, education, entertainment, and so on – has vigorously entered into discussions about the proper ways to engineer contact between "us" and "them" (or "them[1]" and "them[2]" and so on). Not surprisingly, there is not one neat tale to tell of how "relations" have been managed in the United States context. Insofar as we can map "relations" in any useful, historically-grounded way, it is best to understand the major action developing along the lines of the axis of "natural/unnatural" contact, rather than along any more traditional trajectories (i.e. by ethnic/racial group).

For a long time, for instance, many have assumed that some "natural" relationship exists linking Jews and African Americans. Evidence is found erratically but regularly in shared histories of oppression, joint efforts working for civil rights, and so on. But, for at least the last few decades of the twentieth century, it has puzzled many observers that African Americans and Jews do not always get along so well when they actually come into contact with each other. This became especially clear in the context of a divisive teachers' strike in Brooklyn in the late 1960s, when the interests of Jewish teachers came into direct conflict with those of African American parents. "Relations," we learned from this moment, had been a misnomer all along. There *were* historical links joining African Americans and Jews, but the relationship they were brought into was better understood as "relatedness" rather than some naturally positive "relations."

Perhaps this could be illustrated more clearly with a contemporary musical example. Sometime in the mid-1990s, jazz musician Steve Bernstein was asked by John Zorn to make a record for Zorn's Radical Jewish Culture series. Bernstein is a downtown New York avant-garde jazz trumpeter and bandleader – a member of John Lurie's Lounge Lizards and leader of his own Sex Mob, a group that specializes in free jazz versions of James Bond theme songs and covers of Abba and Prince. Bernstein recounts initially being puzzled by Zorn's invitation. He writes in the liner notes to *Diaspora Soul*, the record he finally made for Zorn: "I was left with an enigmatic question. How does a Jewish musician who has spent his life studying 'other' musical cultures make a 'Jewish' record, when, by nature, all of one's music is already 'Jewish'?" Bernstein, by his own account, struggled for three years with this question, and then finally has what he calls his "Gulf Coast epiphany": "I had been doing a lot of reading and listening for the past few months to the music of New Orleans, and had been developing a theory about the evolution of New Orleans marching band music not into what we call jazz, but into rhythm and blues." Those of us familiar with the discourses of black–Jewish likeness see now where this is going and we are cringing: somehow Bernstein will punctuate this musicological genealogy with some definitive proof that the diasporic souls of black folk and Jewish folk are linked and that these links take musical forms which, if not identical, exist at least in some kind of natural harmony. This is a line of thought that has been promoted for almost a century now

But Bernstein has some tricks up his sleeve. His musings on the Gulf Coast lead him to "thinking not just about a New Orleans sound, but rather the Gulf Coast sound, encompassing Texas and Cuba – and the last part of the Gulf Coast was Miami. And who retired to Miami?" Now it's clear that Bernstein has been setting us up all along, playing on our expectation that black/Jewish sympathy is a given, natural, and essential fact of American musical life. Bernstein's left turn has taken us not to the usual imaginary place where Jews make beautiful music out of raw black materials: "And who retired to Miami? The most popular Cuban export of the '50s was the cha-cha.

In New Orleans there is a rhythm called the half a cha. And who loves a cha-cha more than the Jews? And the final piece of the grail – the hora bass pattern . . . is the first half of clave, the heart of Afro-Cuban music." Bernstein's liner notes to *Diaspora Soul* lay waste to a long tradition of drawing false parallels between Jewish American and African American life. Bernstein's hilariously false logic – bordering almost on cabalistic numerology (half a cha = half a clave = I just had to make this record!) – is a sharp reminder that the "relations" in "Immigration and Race Relations" can only have meaning as a culturally-situated and historically-precise proposition.

Adolph Reed long ago made the point that there "is no simple 'historical and political relation between blacks and Jews'" but instead a rather large set of intersecting activities, rhetorical tendencies, and so on. Reed goes even further, noting that insofar as what we call "black–Jewish relations" is about rhetoric, it has been a "dialogue" that found Jews – as major players in black civil rights organizations – able to "steer" from both sides (Reed 1986, pp. 88–9). If "relations" is going to have any meaning, then, in the context of immigration and race, it will have to be as a process, a web of power relations, and not as a thing in itself.

Investigations of these power relations will have to take place on the most local level of interpersonal contact as well as on the global level: of course these two planes of human activity cannot be separated out from each other. For instance, one of the most fascinating indices of changing American ideas about immigrants is found in state policies regarding marriage. In 1907, for instance, the United States Congress passed a law that established that any American woman who married a foreigner would take the nationality of her husband. While on the face of it this seems like an attempt mainly to discipline American women *vis-à-vis* their freedom to make romantic choices, the law had a more direct target, as Lawrence Fuchs reminds us: since Asian immigrants were the only "foreigners" at the time who were not allowed to become "Americans" this law was, in addition to its function as gender policing, also a form of immigration control (Fuchs 1990, p. 115).

The "relations" in "Immigration and Race Relations" works in strange and unpredictable ways. Japanese American writer David Mura has written in painful detail about his status as a second-generation Asian American and how the constellation of images surrounding Asian American men (especially in *relation* to African American men) has perverted his sense of himself as a sexual being. Mura describes his one-time obsession with American pornography, rooted mostly in his desire to come to grips with his own feelings of erasure that develop when confronted with the "stereotype of the asexual Asian man" (Mura 1996, p. 189). Mura realizes that in the dyadic American imaginative system of black/white relations, Asian (or Asian American) men have no place. He develops a "secret fear" that his wife will betray him with a white man and "a secret desire" that this imaginary man "will not be white, but black" (p. 186). Mura's honest and terrifying testimony about his internal landscape of immigration and race relations serves as a reminder that individual consciousness is shaped by a host of conflicting external forces, most of which are largely outside of each person's control. His words also serve to instruct that the most important function of "relations" is not as a collection of real world facts, but rather as a sort of internalized instruction manual for proper racial behavior. Mura learns early that black sexuality is somehow "natural," white sexuality is "repressed," and his own sexuality is nonexistent. This colonization of Mura's internal life bears easy-to-see traces of the history of American enslavement (with its reality of unrestricted access to African American bodies for white slave-owners and the attendant ideology/rationalization that African Americans were oversexed) and American military imperialism (with its attendant ideology/rationalization that Asian women are available and oversexed, largely *because* Asian men are perceived as asexual).

The history of "relations" in the context of immigration and race depends on deep structures of belief about what anthropologist Mary Douglas long ago described as the mutually constitutive social poles of purity and danger. On the American scene one only has to look at the baroque vocabulary of slur words that have been invented to discipline those racial misfits who refuse to fit (or cannot fit) into the more approved social categories of identity. "Pocho" for Mexicans who become "too" American, "Banana" for the Asian American who becomes too white, "Oreo" for the not-black-enough African American. All these terms act as reminders of how harshly conceived the idea of "relations" has been in United States history, and how contingent. All manner of sexual border-crossings have been unofficially ignored, if not officially approved, through the course of American history. But those relations can just as soon lead to punitive measures (judicial, mob, other) as they can to smirking acceptance. It just depends when they happen, and where.

In recent days there has been a fairly concerted, if disorganized, effort by activists and scholars to reclaim "relations" as a positive reality. Nowhere has this been more apparent than in the development of a field of study and political activism surrounding the US–Mexico border. Inspired by the crucial imaginative work done by Gloria Anzaldúa (especially in her 1987 book *Borderlands/La Frontera*), many Americans have attempted to put hybridity, mestizo/a consciousness, and multilinguality back at the center of American history. This has been important work and has helped put "relations" back into play as an open question in the history of the peopling of the Americas. But this work has also been guilty, as Marcial González has recently pointed out, of "romanticizing the border" as a place of almost mystical intergroup contact and creativity, rather than as "an instrument of political manipulation to control the supply of labor for certain industries in the United States" (González 2003, pp. 284, 281). Freezing the border as a place of fruitful multiplicity has obvious political work to do, but it has the danger of locking these particular (and time-bound and culturally-specific) relations into a new melting-pot narrative of happy intergroup contact. What we need instead are new words and approaches that help us get out of the "Immigration and Race Relations" trap altogether.

New Words

Fortunately, new strategies are in place already that will help us out of the "Immigration and Race Relations" trap. Most promising are those that track movement of the world's people as both a cause and a result of major social changes. Movement, as seen under these new lenses, is constant and multidirectional. It is, to use Saskia Sassen's word, "patterned." Sassen explains that,

> the emergence of a global economy . . . contributed both to the creation abroad of pools of potential emigrants and to the formation of linkages between industrialized and developing countries that subsequently were to serve as bridges for international

migration. Paradoxically, the very measures commonly thought to deter immigration –
foreign investment and the promotion of export-oriented growth in developing countries
– seem to have had precisely the opposite effect. (1998, p. 34)

Sassen's work is joined by that of Arjun Appadurai, who has fruitfully called
attention to the ways that global movement of people, commodities, capital, and
knowledge is now controlled through a series of "scapes" – ethnoscapes, mediascapes,
financescapes, technoscapes, and ideoscapes – in opposition to previous organization
schemes that were basically defined by national borders (Appadurai 1996, p. 33).

The work of Sassen, Appadurai, and other theorists of globalization (along with
other scholars whose keywords are "diaspora," "postcolonial," and so on) corrects
the no longer useful picture of "Immigration and Race Relations" by insisting on
interpenetration and flux as first principles. Lisa Lowe, for instance, has explained
how post-1965 Asian immigrants were often seen by native-born Americans as
having come from "stable, continuous, 'traditional' cultures" but that in reality they
had mostly come "from societies already disrupted by colonialism and distorted by
the upheavals of neocolonial capitalism and war" (Lowe 1996, p. 16). Dub poet and
reggae performer Linton Kwesi Johnson said the same thing more sharply in an
interview when asked whether signing with Island Records gave him an international
base: "Island did *not* give me an international base from which to operate. [The]
fact that I'm a black person from the Caribbean who lives in Britain means that
I *have* an international base. Y'know?" (quoted in Davis and Simon 1982, p. 163).

Paul Gilroy's work on black diasporas of the Atlantic world has opened up a deep
historical context for approaching these matters. What Gilroy has done is provide an
analytical framework for plotting more than 500 years of migrations of black people
traveling in many directions through the Atlantic and coming into contact with a
variety of other populations, and in the process forging new identities, cultural
forms, and so on. Gilroy's work (which also happens to plot black–Jewish relations
as a major expression of the interplay of global migrations and local innovations) is
joined by a number of important creative works (including Michelle Cliff's *Free
Enterprise* and Caryl Phillips's *The Nature of Blood*) that insist upon the primacy of
hybridity and the multidirectionality of all the most significant migrations.

The anthropologist Ulf Hannerz has been arguing for this theoretical shift for
quite a while. In 2000 he summarized the new approaches:

> here we are now with hybridity, collage, mélange, hotchpotch, montage, synergy,
> bricolage, creolization, mestizaje, mongrelization, syncretism, transculturation, third
> cultures and what have you; some terms used perhaps only in passing as summary
> metaphors, others with claims to more analytical status, and others again with more
> regional or thematic strongholds. (quoted in Sheller 2003, p. 192)

This slightly flippant cataloging does not hide the important point that Hannerz
wants to make about how older ideas about migration that rely on simply-drawn
and distinct trajectories of individual (or small group) movement need to be replaced by more nuanced renderings. Replacing "Immigration and Race Relations"
with new keywords like globalization, creolization, diaspora, and so on is not only
historically necessary, but also opens up the possibility, as outlined by David Hollinger

and others, that "voluntary" identities will now become real options alongside (and maybe someday instead of) the usual compulsory ones.

REFERENCES

Anzaldúa, Gloria (1987). *Borderlands/La Frontera: The New Mestiza*. San Francisco: Spinster's/ Aunt Lute.
Appadurai, Arjun (1996). *Modernity at Large: Cultural Dimensions of Globalization*. Minneapolis: University of Minnesota Press.
Babb, Valerie (1998). *Whiteness Visible: The Meaning of Whiteness in American Literature and Culture*. New York: New York University Press.
Bernstein, Steven (1999). Liner notes, *Diaspora Soul*. New York: Tzadik.
Buff, Rachel (2001). *Immigration and the Political Economy of Home: West Indian Brooklyn and American Indian Minneapolis*. Berkeley: University of California Press.
Chavez, Leo (2001). *Covering Immigration: Popular Images and the Politics of the Nation*. Berkeley: University of California Press.
Cofer, Judith Ortiz (1993). *Telling the Lives of Barrio Women*. New York: W.W. Norton.
Cruz, Victor Hernández (1991). *Red Beans*. Minneapolis: Coffee House.
Davis, Stephen and Peter Simon (1982). *Reggae International*. New York: R & B.
Douglas, Mary (1966). *Purity and Danger: An Analysis of Concepts of Pollution and Taboo*. New York: Praeger.
Duany, Jorge (2002). *The Puerto Rican Nation on the Move: Identities on the Island and in the United States*. Chapel Hill: University of North Carolina Press.
Fields, Barbara J. (1982). "Ideology and Race in American History." In J. Morgan Kousser and James McPherson, eds., *Region, Race, and Reconstruction: Essays in Honor of C. Vann Woodward*. New York: Oxford University Press, pp. 143–77.
Fuchs, Lawrence (1995). *The American Kaleidoscope: Race, Ethnicity, and the Civic Culture* [1990]. Hanover, NH: University Press of New England.
Gerstle, Gary (2001). *American Crucible: Race and Nation in the Twentieth Century*. Princeton, NJ: Princeton University Press.
Gilroy, Paul (1993). *The Black Atlantic: Modernity and Double Consciousness*. Cambridge, MA: Harvard University Press.
Glasser, Ruth (1995). *"My Music is My Flag": Puerto Rican Musicians and Their New York Communities, 1917–1940*. Berkeley: University of California Press.
González, Marcial (2003). "A Marxist Critique of Borderlands Postmodernism: Adorno's *Negative Dialectics* and Chicano Cultural Criticism." In Bill Mullen and James Smethurst, eds., *Left of the Color Line: Race, Radicalism, and Twentieth-Century Literature of the United States*. Chapel Hill: University of North Carolina Press, pp. 279–97.
Guglielmo, Thomas (2003). *White on Arrival: Italians, Race, Color, and Power in Chicago, 1890–1945*. New York: Oxford University Press.
Handlin, Oscar (1962). *The Newcomers: Negroes and Puerto Ricans in a Changing Metropolis*. Garden City, NY: Doubleday.
—— (1971). *The Uprooted* [1951]. New York: Little, Brown.
Hollinger, David (1995). *Postethnic America: Beyond Multiculturalism*. New York: Basic Books.
Jacobson, Matthew Frye (2000). *Barbarian Virtues: The United States Encounters Foreign Peoples at Home and Abroad, 1876–1917*. New York: Hill and Wang.
Lorey, David. E. (1999). *The U.S.–Mexican Border in the Twentieth Century*. Wilmington, DE: Scholarly Resources, Inc.
Lowe, Lisa (1996). *Immigrant Acts: On Asian American Cultural Politics*. Durham, NC: Duke University Press.

McWilliams, Carey (1969). *North From Mexico: The Spanish Speaking People of the United States* [1949]. New York: Praeger.

Melnick, Jeffrey (1999). *A Right to Sing the Blues: African Americans, Jews, and American Popular Music*. Cambridge, MA: Harvard University Press.

—— (2000). *Black-Jewish Relations on Trial: Leo Frank and Jim Conley in the New South*. Jackson, Miss.: University Press of Mississippi.

Mura, David (1996). *Where the Body Meets Memory: An Odyssey of Race, Sexuality and Identity*. New York: Anchor.

Norell, Brenda (2004). "Columbus Day: Celebrating a Holocaust." *Indian Country Today*, October 11. Found at http://ccmep.org/2004_articles/local/101104_columbus_day.htm.

Oboler, Suzanne (1995). *Ethnic Labels, Latino Lives: Identity and the Politics of (Re)Presentation in the United States*. Minneapolis: University of Minnesota Press.

Omi, Michael and Howard Winant (1986). *Racial Formation in the United States: From the 1960s to the 1990s*. New York: Routledge & Kegan Paul.

Orsi, Robert (1992). "The Religious Boundaries of an Inbetween People: Street *Feste* and the Problem of the Dark-Skinned Other in Italian Harlem, 1920–1990." *American Quarterly* 44: 313–47.

Osofsky, Gilbert (1967). *The Burden of Race: A Documentary History of Negro–White Relations in America*. New York: Harper & Row.

Padilla, Elena (1964). *Up from Puerto Rico* [1958]. New York: Columbia University Press.

Prashad, Vijay (2000). *The Karma of Brown Folk*. Minneapolis: University of Minnesota Press.

Reed, Adolph (1986). *The Jesse Jackson Phenomenon: The Crisis of Purpose in Afro-American Politics*. New Haven, CT: Yale University Press.

Roediger, David (1991). *The Wages of Whiteness: Race and the Making of the American Working Class*. New York: Verso.

—— (1994). *Towards the Abolition of Whiteness*. New York: Verso.

Saar, Doreen Alvarez (1993). "The Heritage of American Ethnicity in Crèvecoeur's *Letters from an American Farmer*." In Frank Shuffleton, ed., *A Mixed Race: Ethnicity in Early America*. New York: Oxford University Press, pp. 241–56.

Sánchez Korrol, Virginia E. (1994). *From Colonia to Community: The History of Puerto Ricans in New York City* [1983]. Berkeley: University of California Press.

Sassen, Saskia (1998). *Globalization and its Discontents: Essays on the New Mobility of People and Money*. New York: New Press.

Schneider, Eric (1999). *Vampires, Dragons, and Egyptian Kings: Youth Gangs in Postwar New York*. Princeton, NJ: Princeton University Press.

Sheller, Mimi (2003). *Consuming the Caribbean: From Arawaks to Zombies*. New York: Routledge.

Shuffleton, Frank, ed. (1993). *A Mixed Race: Ethnicity in Early America*. New York: Oxford University Press.

Smith, Judith (2004). *Vision of Belonging: Family Stories, Popular Culture, and Postwar Democracy, 1940–1960*. New York: Columbia University Press.

Sollors, Werner (1986). *Beyond Ethnicity: Consent and Descent in American Culture*. New York: Oxford University Press.

Steinberg, Stephen (1989). *The Ethnic Myth: Race, Ethnicity, and Class in America* [1981]. Boston: Beacon.

Williams, Patricia (1997). *Seeing a Color-Blind Future: The Paradox of Race*. New York: Noonday.

PART III

POPULATION AND SOCIETY

CHAPTER TWELVE

Demography and American Immigration

MICHAEL S. TEITELBAUM

Human populations are complex, even many-splendored things. As studied by demographers, they embody within them all of the multifaceted human characteristics that are important in both conceptual and practical terms. Such characteristics include, for example, population size, rate of growth or decline, sex composition, family structure, race, ethnicity, language, religion, national origins, education and skill composition, geographical distribution, and so on. It is no exaggeration to say that the categories embodied within demographic data and analysis include many of those with the greatest salience over the sweep of human history. This chapter addresses the extent to which the demography of the United States has been and may be affected by immigration.

The Three Forces of Demographic Change

Notwithstanding the complexities and (often) passions that surround many of the demographic categories, there is at the same time an attractive simplicity embodied within demographic analysis. In particular, there are only three plausible drivers of demographic change: births, deaths, and migration. Put another way, a defined human population can change only by the increment of births ("fertility"), the decrement of deaths ("mortality"), or the migration of its own members or those of other population groups.

For much of the history of the human species, mortality rates were generally high and also erratic, with periodic decimations resulting from drought, war, famine, or disease. Fertility rates were also high, though likely not as high as the theoretical maximum set by biological factors. Suffice it to say that for most of human existence, there was an approximate balance over the long term between high mortality and high fertility, resulting in only the slightest rates of increase in human population numbers. Moreover, because fertility rates were generally high, we can estimate that human populations over this lengthy period were heavily comprised of younger age groups, that is, children and young adults.

Migration certainly was also a significant factor in human history, with lengthy treks suggested by molecular and other studies of early human origins and evolution.

Early humans were most likely nomadic, implying that seasonal migration was central to their societies. Later, with the rise of sedentary agriculture as an evolutionarily superior form of food production, repetitive migrations no doubt became less common. Nonetheless there continued to be large population movements across space, in response to weather, soil degradation, military conquest, and other forces. It is only fair to say that we know rather little still about the magnitudes and directions of migration patterns in the ancient world. More specifically for the purposes of this volume, there is broad consensus among archaeologists that the original human inhabitants of the Americas were themselves migrants from Asia, but the details of such migrations have yet to be resolved.

American Demography

As we move to the modern period and to the early days of European settlement in North America, there are more sources of information and insight. Data on the colonial period are quite limited, but in its new Constitution the fledgling republic of the United States that emerged out of the Revolutionary War required the taking of a decennial census of population. The reason – apportionment of seats in the House of Representatives under the terms of the Great Compromise – was political rather than analytic. Nonetheless every 10 years the census provided an otherwise unavailable demographic portrait of the population resident within the expanding boundaries of the republic.

Some Americans are fond of calling their country "a nation of immigrants," or one "built by immigrants." There is a good deal of mythology in this view: since 1850, the percentage of the US population foreign-born has never exceeded 15 percent; the peak was 14.7 percent in 1910 (US Bureau of the Census 1999). Even today, despite the largest wave of immigration ever experienced by the United States, that percentage is still 12 percent (though increasing rapidly).

This is not to say that immigration to the United States has not been a powerful demographic force. On the contrary. Indeed, a statement far more accurate than the "nation of immigrants" slogan would be that the United States is a nation of the children, grandchildren, and great-grandchildren of immigrants – a large fraction of the US population can identify an immigrant forebear in their family tree.

Moreover, successive waves of foreign immigration, followed by internal migration of these immigrants' progeny, have greatly transformed American demographic composition: its structure in terms of age groups, urban vs. rural residence, distribution of population among states, education and skills, and national/ethnic/religious/racial characteristics. For example, in 1900 the population of the south was nearly one-third African in origin. By 2000, this proportion was down to less than 19 percent, following in-migration by non-Africans both domestic and foreign, and out-migration to the industrial north by the children, grandchildren, and great-grandchildren of African slaves. In the northeast region, the percentage black increased from 1.8 percent in 1900 to 11.4 percent in 2000. In 1900 nearly 60 percent of the populations of both Mississippi and South Carolina were black, whereas in 2000 this percentage had declined to 36 and 30 percent respectively (Hobbs and Stoops 2002, Table 3.1). More recently, in the period 1980 to 2000, immigration from Latin America and higher fertility among Hispanics have shifted the demographic composition of the west region from 14.5 percent Hispanic in 1980 to 24.3 percent in 2000 (the first "Hispanic" question appeared in the 1980 census) (Hobbs and Stoops 2002, Figure 3.11).

Since World War II, the population of the United States has again been transformed. There are four identifiable elements that have been at work in this regard.

The first is the dramatic "baby boom" that followed the war, but unlike in most postwar countries, the US baby boom turned into a sustained rise in fertility to wholly unanticipated levels, over a period of two decades or more. To put some numerical flesh on these prose bones, US fertility as measured by the annual total fertility rate (TFR) increased by 28 percent in just over one decade, from 2.94 in 1946 to a peak of 3.77 in 1957. It then remained at high levels for nearly a decade longer, before it began to decline sharply in the mid-1960s. This decline, known now in journalistic usage as the "baby bust," is the second key element of recent US demographic change. It was a quite rapid decline, yet the TFR did not decline down to the 1946 level of 2.94 until 1965 (Teitelbaum and Winter 1985, Appendix A). Further declines then ensued, with a low of 1.80 in 1983. Then – to the surprise of many – US fertility began to increase, and as of 2001 had risen to over 2.11 (US National Center for Health Statistics 2003, Table 88).

The result of the large and sustained burst of fertility, followed by a decline to levels closer to those of the 1920s – i.e. relatively low by historical standards, but relatively high by comparative international standards – is a sharply distorted age structure for the United States, with very large age cohorts born during the baby boom gradually working their way up the age scale. As of 2005, the 1947–65 baby boomers will be in their thirties, forties, and fifties, with smaller age cohorts both ahead of them and behind them. Hence the first and second of the four elements of recent US demographic change, the baby boom from 1947 to 1965 and the baby bust of 1966 to the present, together have had powerful impacts on the composition of the US population of today.

The third element is the increase (again, unexpected in its scale) in longevity. Life expectancy at birth rose from 68.2 in 1950 to 77.0 in 2000, an increase of 11.3 percent. Over the same period, US life expectancy at age 65 increased by 29.5 percent, from 13.9 to 18.0 (http://www.cdc.gov/nchs/data/hus/tables/tables/2003/03hus027.pdf). Exactly which factors account for this improvement in older life expectancy are in dispute, but many observers believe that it is less due to the expensive and high-tech interventions of the heavily therapeutic US medical system, and more related to preventive health measures such as reduction in smoking and effective pharmaceuticals to control high blood pressure, thereby preventing many cases of cigarette-related cancer and serious cardiovascular accidents such as strokes and heart attacks. Other factors would surely include healthier diet and lifestyle, along with successful curative medicine in some domains.

The fourth element, which used to be of relatively small impact in demographic terms but has become increasingly dominant, is immigration. The United States was, in the nineteenth century, one of the classic examples of a resource-rich but sparsely populated country. With the Louisiana Purchase of 1803, the fledgling republic had with a stroke of the pen (for a purchase price of 60 million francs, or about $15 million) added some 2 million square kilometers (800,000 square miles) of land extending from the Mississippi River to the Rocky Mountains. The Purchase nearly doubled the land area of the United States, and later large acquisitions followed with the cession of what is now the US southwest following the United States-Mexico War of 1846–8.

As the American industrial revolution accelerated during the late nineteenth century, industrial employers aggressively recruited labor from the then desperately poor countries of western Europe – Germany, Sweden, Ireland – and later from the largely agrarian countries of eastern and southern Europe – Italy, Poland, Greece, Russia, etc. Indeed there were essentially no numerical limits on immigration numbers to the United States during the nineteenth century, and the combination of energetic labor recruitment by employers in American industrial cities (New York, Boston, Philadelphia, Baltimore, Bridgeport, Detroit, Chicago, etc.), aggressive marketing of low-cost "steerage" transportation by Atlantic steamship companies, and the Homestead Act's offer to European landless peasants of large tracts of land (which they had to be willing to farm) for a nominal fee in the American midwest, proved to be highly attractive. Meanwhile the swashbuckling entrepreneurs of the great railroad boom of the 1870s and 1880s (during which some 110,000 miles were added to the rail system) found an ample supply of contract laborers in China and Mexico.

Both the foreign-born and native-born populations of the United States grew rapidly through the late nineteenth and early twentieth centuries. The foreign-born population increased by over 350 percent between 1850 and 1900, rising from about 2.2 million to 10.3 million. The trend continued through to 1930, increasing by nearly 40 percent more before reaching a peak of 14.2 million. As to the percentage foreign-born, this measure too increased rapidly, but more slowly than for absolute numbers because the native-born population was also growing over the period. As may be seen in Table 12.1, in 1850 less than 10 percent of the US population was foreign-born. This percentage increased from 1850 through 1910, reaching a peak of 14.7 percent.

As the numbers of immigrants grew, political opposition to this *laissez-faire* immigration policy appeared. The first restrictions imposed were qualitative, with certain categories excluded such as indentured servants, the blind, those ill with contagious diseases, paupers, and convicts. In 1882, under pressure from activist movements especially in California, Chinese laborers were excluded, and later under the Gentlemen's Agreement of 1907 the Japanese government agreed to halt emigration of Japanese male laborers to the United States and the United States agreed to stop segregated schooling of Japanese children living in the United States.

With respect to immigration from Europe, no quantitative limits were imposed until 1921, but would-be immigrants were screened upon arrival. For this purpose, the immigration station at Ellis Island in New York harbor was constructed in 1892, although only very small percentages of those screened there were excluded.

But the numbers entering from eastern and southern Europe continued to swell, and an increasingly strident anti-immigration movement emerged during the first decade of the twentieth century. Rising labor unrest during the period was blamed upon eastern and southern European immigrants, claims rendered more effective given the visibility of foreign-born radicals who played active roles in the socialist, communist, and anarchist movements of the period. After much political rhetoric and conflict, and during the convulsions of World War I, the first requirements for

Table 12.1 Nativity of the population and place of birth of the native population: 1850 to 1990

Year[1]	Total population	Native population Total	Born in the United States	Born abroad Total	In outlying areas 2[2]	Foreign-born population Of American parents
Number						
1990*	248,709,873	228,942,557	225,695,826	3,246,731	1,864,285	19,767,316
1980*	226,545,805	212,465,899	210,322,697	2,143,202	1,055,030	14,079,906
1970*[3]	203,210,158	193,590,856	191,329,489	2,261,367	1,370,101	9,619,302
1960*[1]	179,325,671	169,587,580	168,525,645	1,061,935	401,510	9,738,091
1950*	150,216,110	139,868,715	139,442,390	426,325	96,355	10,347,395
1940	131,669,275	120,074,379	119,795,254	279,125	122,169	11,594,896
1930	122,775,046	108,570,897	108,304,188	266,709	130,677	14,204,149
1920	105,710,620	91,789,928	91,659,045	130,883	92,863	13,920,692
1910	91,972,266	78,456,380	78,381,104	75,276	67,911	13,515,886
1900	75,994,575	65,653,299	65,583,225	70,074	67,151	10,341,276
1890[1]	62,622,250	53,372,703	53,362,371	10,332	10,010	9,249,547
1880	50,155,783	43,475,840	43,475,498	342	291	6,679,943
1870	38,558,371	32,991,142	32,990,922	220	169	5,567,229
1860[4]	31,443,321	27,304,624	27,304,624	—	—	4,138,697
1850[4]	23,191,876	20,947,274	20,947,274	—	—	2,244,602

Table 12.1 (cont'd)

Year[1]	Total population	Native population		Born abroad			Foreign-born population
		Total	Born in the United States	Total	In outlying areas 2[2]	Of American parents	Of American parents
Percentage distribution							
1990*	100.0	92.1	90.7	1.3	0.7	0.6	7.9
1980*	100.0	93.8	92.8	0.9	0.5	0.5	6.2
1970*[3]	100.0	95.3	94.2	1.1	0.7	0.4	4.7
1960*[1]	100.0	94.6	94.0	0.6	0.2	0.4	5.4
1950*	100.0	93.1	92.8	0.3	0.1	0.2	6.9
1940	100.0	91.2	91.0	0.2	0.1	0.1	8.8
1930	100.0	88.4	88.2	0.2	0.1	0.1	11.6
1920	100.0	86.8	86.7	0.1	0.1	–	13.2
1910	100.0	85.3	85.2	0.1	0.1	–	14.7
1900	100.0	86.4	86.3	0.1	0.1	–	13.6
1890[1]	100.0	85.2	85.2	–	–	–	14.8
1880	100.0	86.7	86.7	–	–	–	13.3
1870	100.0	85.6	85.6	–	–	–	14.4
1860[4]	100.0	86.8	86.8	–	–	–	13.2
1850[4]	100.0	90.3	90.3	–	–	–	9.7

* Indicates sample data.

– Represents zero or rounds to zero.

1 Starting in 1960, includes population of Alaska and Hawaii. For 1890, excludes population enumerated in the Indian Territory and on Indian reservations for whom information on most topics, including nativity, was not collected.

2 Puerto Rico is the only outlying area for which the number has ever exceeded 100,000. The numbers for Puerto Rico: 1,190,533 in 1990; 1,002,863 in 1980; 810,087 in 1970; 617,056 in 1960; 226,010 in 1950; 69,967 in 1940; 52,774 in 1930; 11,811 in 1920; 1,513 In 1910; and 678 in 1900.

3 The data shown in Table 12.1 are based on the 15 percent sample. For 1970, data based on the 5 percent sample show total population as 203,193,774, native population as 193,590,856, born in the United States as 191,836,655, born abroad as 1,617,396, in outlying areas as 873,241, of American parents as 744,155, and foreign-born population as 9,739,723.

4 In 1850 and 1860, information on nativity was not collected for slaves. The data in the table assume, as was done in 1870 census reports, that all slaves in 1850 and 1860 were native. Of the total black population of 4,880,009 in 1870, 9,645, or 0.2 percent, were foreign-born (1870 census, Vol. I, Dubester #45, Table XXII, pp. 606–15).

Source: US Bureau of the Census 1999 (see text for sources, definitions, and explanations).

literacy were imposed, and following the end of the war, in 1921 the first numerical limits were imposed, primarily by means of what came to be the national origins quota system which was designed by its authors to sharply constrain the large-scale immigration flows from eastern and southern Europe.

The Great Depression of the 1930s, more severe in the United States than in much of Europe, led to declines in immigration numbers well below the limits of these quotas, and indeed in some years during that decade net immigration to the United States was actually negative. Finally, the outbreak of World War II imposed additional forms of constraint on Atlantic migration movements.

Following the war, the percentage foreign-born had declined to less than 7 percent by 1950, from its peak 1910 figure of 14.7 percent. This measure reached a low of 4.7 percent in 1970. Legislative actions in 1965 that expanded and liberalized legal immigration, followed by accelerating unauthorized immigration flows during the 1970s, 1980s, and 1990s, caused this trend to reverse direction and the percentage has increased rapidly to the present time. Estimates from the 2000 census suggest that the enumerated foreign-born population had reached approximately 31.1 million, an all-time high in absolute terms. This estimate represents 11.1 percent of the total enumerated population in 2000, well over twice that in 1970, though still less than the peak percentage in 1910 (http://www.census.gov/prod/2003pubs/c2kbr-34.pdf).

As immigration volumes have increased over the past few decades, they have also tended to become increasingly concentrated, in two senses. First, although the national origins/languages/religions of legal immigrants have been very diverse in a qualitative sense, with some number of immigrants and refugees entering from perhaps all of the world's nearly 200 nations, in quantitative terms the flows of legal and illegal migrants taken together have been very large from the relatively small region represented by Latin America and the Caribbean. The US Census Bureau estimates that over one-half of the foreign-born population in 2003 came from this region, which accounts for less than 10 percent of the world population (Larsen 2003). Second, the US destinations of both legal and illegal immigrants have been highly concentrated in just a few states, and within these in just a few metropolitan areas. Of 31.1 million foreign-born persons enumerated in the 2000 census, 21.4 million or 69 percent resided in just six states (California, New York, Texas, Florida, Illinois, and New Jersey) (US Congress, Congressional Budget Office 2004, p. 12). Indeed only four metropolitan areas accounted for over 37 percent of this six-state total (Los Angeles County, California; New York City; Cook County, Illinois; and Miami-Dade County, Florida) (US Congress, Congressional Budget Office 2004, p. 12). This pattern of internal concentration may have been somewhat moderated in recent years since there are signs that recent immigrants are migrating increasingly to other areas, or re-migrating from their original destinations to others.

The Near-Universality of Fertility Decline

The United States was one of a few industrialized countries (others included Canada, Australia, and New Zealand) that experienced a large and sustained "baby boom," as discussed above. The boom began a few years after World War II, and continued for nearly two decades thereafter. Fertility rates in most other industrialized countries generally declined over the period, in some cases gradually, in others sharply. (Although one often reads of postwar "baby booms" in Europe, typically these were more "boomlets" than booms – short-term spikes in fertility that continued for only a few years before declining.)

In fact, fertility declines have been widespread. Especially since the 1970s, there have been fertility declines in much of the developing world, with notable exceptions in regions such as sub-Saharan Africa, the Arab Middle East, and Pakistan. In some regions, including much of Europe and East Asia including China, fertility rates have declined to record lows, often below the notional "replacement level" of 2.1 children per woman required for replacement of a low mortality over the long term.

The Demographic Significance of Immigration

The demographic significance of immigration has been amplified by such declines in fertility. Divergent trends of rising immigration and declining fertility have resulted in increasing proportions of net population change attributable to immigration. Indeed, in a few countries, such as Germany – in which fertility rates have been below 1.5 children for an extended period – deaths have come to somewhat exceed births and hence all of net population increase is due to net immigration.

Fertility rates in the United States are at the high end of the range for industrialized countries – i.e. very near to the "replacement" level of 2.1 children per woman – for reasons that we do not fully understand. Still, the convergence in the US case of large and increasing immigration flows with fertility declines to low levels implies that net immigration in recent years has accounted for one-third to one-half of net population growth (this wide range of uncertainty is due mainly to the absence of credible US data on the actual numbers of immigrants, both legal and illegal).

This generally increasing demographic significance of immigration, coupled with the high degree of concentration of US immigration in terms of both origin and destination, has produced some dramatic impacts in terms of demographic composition in some US regions and metropolitan areas.

It seems clear enough that immigration can represent an important driver of demographic change, especially when there are substantial immigration flows into settings of low fertility. To what extent might it be said that demography represents an important "cause" or "driver" of immigration movements? Here the answer is far hazier. Empirically, we know that many of the world's most significant source countries of immigrants are low- or moderate-income countries of the developing world. Obvious examples would include Mexico, Haiti, Morocco, El Salvador, the Philippines, and many others. More generally, according to UN estimates the areas with the largest net outflows (immigrants less emigrants) have been Asia, Africa, Latin America, and the Caribbean. This is true in both absolute terms and in terms of rates per 1,000 population (United Nations, Population Division 2002).

On average, such countries experienced high rates of both fertility and demographic increase during the postwar period. As a result, most have been characterized by relatively youthful age compositions, and it is well established that young adults generally show the highest propensity for migration. To this extent it might be concluded that demography does indeed represent an important driver favoring international migration.

On the other hand, there are many countries with high fertility rates and high proportions of young adults which have not generated large-scale migratory flows. And there are a substantial number of cases of exceptionally high migration propensities that seem to be more related to political forces (including civil strife, systematic abuses of human rights, ethnic cleansing, failed states, and even genocide), and others that seem tied more to active recruitment of migrants by employers in destination countries than to demographic drivers in countries of origin. Meanwhile, there are some very large developing countries such as China and India that have produced large absolute numbers of migrants, but only moderate rates of outflow relative to their enormous population bases.

Demographic Interactions between Low Fertility and Immigration: "Replacement Migration"

Other things being equal, a lower-fertility population will have an "older" age distribution than a higher-fertility population. Hence as fertility rates have declined around the world, to low levels in most industrialized and some rapidly developing countries, and to moderate levels in most other regions, one effect has been a decline in the percentage of children and (after a lengthy lag) an increase in the percentage over age 60 or 65.

Meanwhile, flows of immigrants tend to consist disproportionately of young adults, typically in their twenties and thirties. Some have interpreted these demographic tendencies, often without much in the way of quantification, to imply that if a shift toward an older age composition is deemed undesirable, this can be counteracted by increased admissions of international migrants.

A useful set of quantitative simulations of these phenomena has been conducted by the United Nations Population Division, published in *Replacement Migration: Is it a Solution to Declining and Ageing Populations?* (United Nations, Population Division 2000). The report simulates a series of hypothetical scenarios to the year 2050, exploring what numbers of immigrants would be required over this 50-year period in selected countries in order to meet certain specified outcomes:

- Prevent a decline in the total population size.
- Hold constant the size of the population between ages 15 and 65.
- Hold constant the "old age dependency ratio" (defined as persons 65+ to those 15–64).

Press attention to these simulations is an interesting story in itself (Teitelbaum 2004), with exaggerated headlines such as the *New York Times*'s "Europe Stares at a Future Built by Immigrants: It's the American Way" (Crosette 2000) and *Le Figaro*'s "The Report That Alarmed Europe" (2000). In translating the English title of the UN report into French, the elite Paris newspaper *Le Monde* deleted the question mark from its subtitle, rendering it as a declarative "Replacement Migration: A Solution to Declining and Aging Populations" (2000a), and interpreted the report as indicating that "Europe Would Need 159 Million Immigrants by 2025" (2000b). Presumably based upon such press coverage rather than a reading of the actual analyses, there was harsh criticism from politicians such as Jean-Pierre Chevenement, then the French

Minister of the Interior, and from the European Union's Representative to the United Nations. (Approvals by governments are not required for publication of reports by the UN Secretariat.)

Had these critics based their assessments on the report itself rather than on the garbled press coverage it evoked, they would have understood that its conclusions were very different from what they had supposed. In particular, the report's UN authors concluded rather declaratively that in countries with very low fertility rates, halting demographic aging via immigration would require such "extraordinarily large numbers of immigrants" as to seem "out of reach" in social and political terms.

Consider for example the report's "Scenario V," which is closest to specifying a halt to demographic aging in that it requires that the ratio of working age to "dependent" population (defined respectively as 15–64 and 65+) be held constant over the scenario period 1995–2050. For the United States, this scenario would require admission of some 593 million immigrants, an average of 10.8 million per year. The assumptions of this scenario imply that the US population in 2050 would have increased to 1.1 billion (from about 295 million in 2004). Of these 1.1 billion, 775 million or 73 percent would be accounted for by post-1995 immigrants or their descendants.

The United States, as noted earlier, represents a relatively high-fertility case among industrialized countries. For Germany, a relatively low-fertility case, the comparable number of immigrants implied by this scenario would be 188 million by 2050, who then would account for some 80 percent of the population in Germany. For Italy, the comparable number under this scenario would be 120 million immigrants (79 percent of the 2050 population). For the EU as a whole, the scenario posits a flow of 700 million immigrants (accounting for 75 percent of the 2050 EU population). For Japan, the scenario implies 553 million immigrants over the period, who by 2050 would account for 87 percent of the population in Japan (United Nations, Population Division 2000, Tables IV.4 and IV.7).

Although the calculations produced by the Replacement Migration exercise are hypothetical, they do offer useful quantitative illustrations of how low-fertility rates when combined with substantial immigration can produce dramatic transformations of national populations, and hence why the UN authors pronounced such "extraordinarily large" immigration flows as likely "out of reach". They also illustrate how very large the numbers of immigrants would have to be in order to counter the effects of low fertility rates on demographic aging.

Summary and Conclusions

Human population can change in size or composition only by the increment of births ("fertility"), the decrement of deaths ("mortality"), or migrations. Of these, the most powerful demographic force over the past two centuries has been change in fertility. Fertility rates fluctuated rather substantially during the twentieth century in the United States, declining to low levels during the 1930s, followed by an unusually large and sustained baby boom after World War II, followed by a "baby bust" post-1965 to levels below those of the 1930s.

In its early colonial days, the territory that later became the United States was dramatically transformed in demographic terms by immigration. Though some today are fond of characterizing the United States as still "a nation of immigrants," the quantitative data reveal otherwise: since 1850, the percentage of the US population foreign-born has never exceeded 15 percent, a peak reached in 1910; the percentage at present is about 12 percent, though up sharply from the 1950s and still rising rapidly.

The United States of today may not be "a nation of immigrants," but immigration nonetheless has been a powerful force in US demographic change. Successive waves of foreign immigration, accompanied by subsequent internal migration of both immigrant groups and native-born persons, have greatly transformed American demographic composition: its structure in terms of age groups, urban vs. rural residence, distribution of population among states, education and skills, and national/ethnic/religious/racial characteristics.

Since World War II, the US population has increased substantially in size, and has been transformed substantially in composition. Three factors – the large and sustained postwar baby boom, the subsequent baby bust post-1965, and substantial extension of life expectancy after age 65 – jointly produced a distorted and rapidly changing age composition. Since the 1970s, rapid growth in immigration, coupled with fertility rates that have declined to moderately low levels, has meant that immigration patterns have again become a very prominent factor in US demographic change.

Immigrants to the United States are predominantly young adults. Unfortunately this has led some to make vague but ill-informed arguments that immigration policies can halt or reverse the shift toward the "older" age structures that inevitably result from fertility declines. Empirical calculations based upon alternative scenarios suggest that such effects upon age structures can be achieved only with extraordinarily high numbers of annual immigrants.

REFERENCES

Crosette, Barbara (2000). *New York Times, Week in Review*, January 2, Section 4: 1.

Hobbs, Frank and Nicole Stoops (2002). *U.S. Census Bureau, Census 2000 Special Reports, Series CENSR–4, Demographic Trends in the 20th Century*. Washington, DC: US Government Printing Office, Figure 3.9. http://www.census.gov/prod/2002pubs/censr–4.pdf

http://www.cdc.gov/nchs/data/hus/tables/2003/03hus027.pdf

http://www.census.gov/prod/2003pubs/c2kbr–34.pdf

Larsen, Luke J. (2004). *The Foreign-Born Population of the United States, 2003. Current Population Reports, P20–551*. Washington, DC: US Census Bureau.

Le Figaro (2000). "Le rapport qui alarme l'Europe." 10 January.

Le Monde (2000a). "Migration de remplacement: une solution aux populations en declin et viellissantes." 6 January.

Le Monde (2000b). "L'Europe aurait besoin de 159 millions d'immigrés d'ici à 2025." 6 January.

Teitelbaum, Michael S. (2004). "The Media Marketplace for Garbled Demography." *Population and Development Review* 30(2): 317–327.

Teitelbaum, Michael S. and Jay M. Winter (1985). *The Fear of Population Decline*. New York and London: Academic Press, Appendix A.

United Nations (2000). *Replacement Migration: Is It a Solution to Declining and Ageing Populations?* New York: UN Population Division.

—— (2002). *International Migration* (ST/ESA/SER.A/219). New York: UN Population Division, Department of Social and Economic Affairs.

US Bureau of the Census (1999). "Nativity of the Population and Place of Birth of the Native Population: 1850 to 1990." Internet release of March 9.

US Congress (2004). *A Description of the Immigrant Population*. Washington, DC: Congressional Budget Office, November, p. 12.

US National Center for Health Statistics (2003). *Vital Statistics of the United States* (annual). In *Statistical Abstract of the United States*. Washington, DC: US Census Bureau, Table 88.

CHAPTER THIRTEEN

Gender and Immigration

SUZANNE M. SINKE

All cultures recognize gender, a system of meaning based on sexual differences, but the meanings vary substantially both from one society to another and across time, as do the meanings of sexual differences. Gender intertwines with migration in a variety of ways. On a basic level international migration brings different gender systems in contact. Immigrants face variations to their own systems of belief and behavior as they encounter the role ideologies of others: earlier arrivals, other groups, and the dominant society. Moreover, the dominant group in the United States at various points in time has had to rethink gender ideology in the face of "foreign" challenges which then became internal ones. Second, gender guides migration patterns. Differing sex ratios reflect not only labor market segmentation – different job opportunities for men and women – but also different cultural norms. The demographic imbalances that result often rearrange gender roles, in some cases by stretching family functions across borders, such as having a wage-earner in one country and child care in another. Even persons who wish to maintain gender roles may find this difficult if not impossible as disproportionate numbers of young men or women enter or exit a society, and as mainstream ideals from a homeland clash with cultural currents from the new location, as, for example, on the issue of dating before marriage.

Finally, gender helps create and sustain hierarchies of power. In terms of international migration to the United States, policies of family formation and reunification have been tied not only to shifting patriarchal norms, but also to racial and ethnic standings, reinforced by colonialism in some cases. People from a particular country or immigrants generally can be portrayed in more masculine or feminine ways, their gender relations as more or less "natural" by American standards, which in turn affects reception, treatment, and policy making. Differences undergird and later justify who can immigrate, who earns more, who can be trusted by authorities, who can move up the social ladder, who can live in a certain area, who can marry whom. The images of "alien," "immigrant," and "migrant" – from the cartoons of drunken Irish men with simian faces of the mid-nineteenth century, to the theatrical character of the Chinese prostitute of the late nineteenth century, to the poignant images of European immigrant working women in Progressive-era photography, to the triumphant Cuban refugee families arriving in south Florida, to videos of men crossing the border from Mexico illegally, to mugshots of male Middle Eastern immigrant terrorists in the early twenty-first century – all contribute to a way of thinking about a group of migrants and to impressions of international migration more generally. Not surprisingly, immigrants themselves have created competing images, from exemplary military service of men in ethnic regiments in war to separate beauty pageants for Asian American women (e.g. Chang 1996; Wu 1997).

As a key element of social identity, gender informs individual and familial decision making, as well as national and international policies. For men, restrictions on migration were sometimes tied to expected military service (and thus some young men had to emigrate illegally to avoid conscription, whether in Prussia in the early nineteenth century or in El Salvador in the 1980s). For women, fear of moral degradation in the form of pregnancy or prostitution has often steered both families and the US government to limit the migration of single women arriving on their own. Women have sometimes sought out migration specifically to avoid such proscriptions (e.g. Puskás 2000). Up until the early twentieth century, married women who migrated on their own leaving husbands behind, even if they were in good health might face deportation, a practice that did not apply to married men on their own. Policies requiring "good moral character" of immigrants made the migration of openly gay men and lesbians difficult (Luibhéid 2002). Even apparently neutral legislation often had gendered applications, as in determining what constituted "persecution" to qualify for refugee status, whether one was likely to become a public charge, or if a person held suspect political views.

Developing the Concept of Gender 1960–2000

In 1960 an American scholar who wrote about gender might have defined it as (1) a synonym for sex, a biological category; or in its alternative meaning, (2) an (often arbitrary) linguistic division present in many languages. It was rare for a historian to use the term at all, and gender-related topics were absent from major publications, the curriculum, and scholarly discussion. By 1970 the women's movement and other social changes sparked interest in what sociologists and psychologists then termed sex roles. Among historians, the "history from the bottom up" approach included the genesis of two major subfields – family history and the history of women – both of which would eventually contribute to knowledge of gender as they documented patterns of ideology and behavior from the past. At first, however, they tended to augment the existing historiography (e.g. Kerber 1980). There were studies of exceptional women who fit the definitions of historical leaders, studies of communities which included women at least on a demographic level (i.e. how many were married, at what age), and studies of the "private sphere" – typically activities carried out in households by women and children. Many of the studies focused on British-descended middle-class women of the northeast, ignoring much of the racial and ethnic population of the nation, including most immigrants.

A third trajectory, more specifically tied to the history of sexuality, began to explore the definition of sexual deviance. Gay rights activists persuaded the American Psychiatric Association to stop labeling homosexuality as a disorder in 1974, and their efforts to change other anti-gay measures continued thereafter. Around the same time French philosopher Michel Foucault published his path-breaking *History of Sexuality*, Volume 1, which became the basis for a great deal of scholarship on gender. Interest in gender-related topics led to the launch of several journals in the 1970s, among them *Feminist Studies, Sex Roles, Signs,* and the *Journal of Homosexuality*. Women's studies programs began to form at various universities as instructors noted both the lack of support within traditional disciplines and the benefits of interdisciplinary collaboration. Historians, meanwhile, were beginning to take increased interest in both women and immigrants, but the two categories remained largely separate. Scholars of immigration generally wrote about men as the norm, and those who included women tended to do so under the rubric of family.

By the 1980s the burgeoning field of women's history had reworked the first definition so that gender typically appeared as the social role associated with being biologically male or female. In practice, if a title included "gender" it was often primarily about women. A decade later attention to masculinity and to sexuality as well as attention to divisions in the category "woman" led to another revision. In this turn-of-the-twenty-first-century rendition, gender still referred to meanings associated with sexual differences, but scholars further argued that sexual differences were also culturally constructed, and hence some used the term sex-gender to show the interplay of biological and social processes. "Man" and "woman" no longer had consistent meanings in this post-structural world. People who according to western cultural norms at particular points in time were deviant or abnormal (e.g. homosexual or hemaphrodite) sometimes appeared as different gender categories in other cultural contexts. Scholars noted how racial ideology complicated categories even more, sometimes creating a "third gender," as with early twentieth-century "feminized" Filipino migrant men (Lee 1999). In other words, gender became an (often arbitrary) social division. In all versions gender was a key element of personal and social identity, and in the recent renditions one often associated with hierarchies of power. For most US undergraduates and the public at large, however, gender remains what men and women "naturally" should be or do, a biological given, perhaps ordained by God.

Meanwhile studies of women also shifted to more diverse racial and ethnic backgrounds. Scholars of African American life argued convincingly that race made at least as much if not more difference than gender in determining life patterns. Others, particularly students of Asian and Latino/a migration, echoed the sentiment, adding other caveats about class and legal (immigration) status (Ngai 2004). Both women's studies and ethnic studies typically charted women's experiences from a divide based on race, though by the 1990s studies of what constituted whiteness suggested the divide was perhaps better described as a shifting continuum (López 1996). Further, as more studies of European immigrant women appeared, the chorus of dissent from one standard model of American women's history rose (Gabaccia and Iacovetta 2002; Sinke 2002).

Greater attention to men as men reinforced these challenges to a unified category. E. Anthony Rotundo demonstrated how the dominant masculinity of any era intertwined with key political and economic institutions – with power relations, from the communal masculinity of Puritan New England to self-made manhood in the nineteenth century, to passionate manhood in the twentieth century. He and other scholars helped broaden scholarship in many fields, from diplomacy to economics, to see the relationship of private life, and of gender relations in it, to public activities.

So, for example, scholars examining foreign relations in the early Cold War wrote about "war brides," and those studying early twentieth-century colonialism looked at Theodore Roosevelt's private life (Yuh 2002; Bederman 1995). In many of these engendered stories, migrants from other countries and ethnic minorities within the United States complicated dominant visions – if they appeared at all. In the chapter that follows I examine a few case studies of gender as it relates to immigration, not as a comprehensive chronicle, but as an introduction to how scholars think about gender in this field and how gender scholarship enhances and reconfigures studies of migration.

Early National Period

The American Revolution, like most wars, revised gender roles, at least temporarily, calling on men to take up arms and abandon various family activities, and on women to join the military entourage as service workers, and on housewives to use their consumption decisions to support the cause as well as to substitute for their absent husbands in some family economic endeavors. After the war many Anglo women who had supported the British cause faced emigration, either north to Canada or back to England. For the rest of the European-descended population, one of the tasks was defining womanhood and manhood in a nation no longer tied to a system of nobility and where individual (manhood) rights prevailed. For many (especially white) men of limited or no means this meant an increase in rights. For women, it was as likely to limit their access to family resources (Rosen 2003).

American Indian women faced further challenges as the new nation backed geographic expansion into new territories. One of the justifications used to conquer new lands was the lack of civilization of the native populations, and gender roles were a key part of that ideal. To counter this, some groups, particularly in the southeast, adopted elements from the white population, including many which favored male rule. As Theda Perdue has shown for the Cherokee, a group with matrilineal kinship in which clan mothers played a major role in determining land use, this meant a formal loss of power, though women's claims to be able to represent their clans continued within the group. At the same time, at least some Anglo women may have taken note of alternative gender systems. Sally Roesch Wagner argued that it was not just a coincidence that many of the early European-descended women's rights activists lived in proximity to and with some knowledge of Haudenosaunee women, who were fighting to retain their rights to suffrage and to other forms of power within their communities.

In a system Linda Kerber described as "revolutionary motherhood," dominant culture began to define women as crucial to citizenship through training sons to be good citizens and daughters to be good mothers. In sharp contrast to the earlier colonial pattern whereby fathers were primarily responsible for children's socialization, even if mothers handled many of the everyday tasks, this new version of motherhood tied into romantic rhetoric that saw women as more nurturing and "naturally" suited to care for children. It was an ideal less suited to working-class life and family-based farming, both of which were common among immigrants.

The gender shift already begun by the time of the American Revolution continued to reconfigure gender roles in the early national period around a presumed division of private and public space. With industrialization and increased urban life, the separation became enshrined in a cult of domesticity which saw women as keepers of the home, while men went outside this haven to earn the family wages. This middle-class ideal rested on the shoulders of immigrants and slaves. Increasingly immigrant domestic servants rather than daughters did the dirty "female" work for wages, creating a visual class divide that accentuated racial and ethnic difference (O'Leary 1996).

One of the major streams of migration into the United States officially ended in 1808 when the importation of slaves became illegal. For these forced migrants, notions of gender and of gender roles came with strict parameters. The inability to marry legally, the absence of freedom of movement in the context of unequal sex ratios, and the imposition of work regimens which separated men and women according to particular tasks, for example, made it difficult to maintain ideas or practice of gender as many knew them prior to capture. At the same time, the white population used the idea of less restrained sexuality among the black population to justify sexual abuse of slave women. This was one of the few areas of US law where matrilineal kinship prevailed, for the child of a female slave became a slave unless the owner chose to free the individual. Anti-miscegenation statutes and social control insured that partnerships of black men and white women, however, were much less common, and in fact were typically viewed as rape (Hodes 1997). This was one of many inequalities which undermined the manhood of male slaves. The enforcement of sexual relations in one gender pattern only – high-status men with low-status women under patriarchy in this case – typifies how gender reinforces and embodies unequal power arrangements.

Mid-Nineteenth Century

Major immigration of German-speaking and Irish Catholic groups in the mid-nineteenth century faced challenges on various grounds. One of them was from women's reform movements. Middle-class American women, many of Anglo back-ground, resented the drinking habits of newcomers, and they sometimes stereotyped immigrant familial relations as abusive. The degree to which women should have custody of children, control of their own earnings, independent ownership of property, and the right to bodily integrity, was in flux. In trying to gain political and social power for themselves, Anglo women reformers sought to control working-class men and women, many of whom were immigrants, and to stereotype their familial relations as less civilized. Yet men remained the representatives of their households in many ways, including the automatic naturalization of wives if their husbands became US citizens.

What constituted a family? This became a major issue when followers of the Church of Jesus Christ of Latter Day Saints, many of whom were immigrants from Britain and Scandinavia, began to advocate polygyny (e.g. Bartholomew 1995). In reality polygyny was probably a more widespread ideal worldwide than monogamy, but it went strongly against the norm for US policy makers in the mid-nineteenth century, who outlawed it. The unusually large numbers of women moving to Mormon-dominated areas contrasted with typically highly male-skewed western migrations. Further, Mormon women's support of suffrage and public advocacy of their religion and its marital practices provided a strong contrast to other suffrage supporters of the day.

When the Dillingham Commission reported on the past from the perspective of the early twentieth century, the stereotypical immigrant of this "old immigration" period was male, but came as a settler, meaning with family either in tow or following him. There were, in fact, quite a number of such migrants, especially among Norwegians, Dutch, and other northwestern Europeans. Migration for those groups sometimes upheld and reinforced gender relations. In some cases a young adult son or father would pioneer the family chain, only to be joined later by others. Rarely, in this period, would a daughter be the initial migrant, and even less often a wife. Women could engage in subsistence agriculture, work in cottage industries, and take part in kin networks in the homeland. But authorities considered a woman alone suspect, and her earnings rarely could match those of a man or even a boy. For most immigrant groups, the idea of an independent woman was not acceptable. For that reason it is useful to consider the Irish migration.

One of the most striking examples of the need to keep gender in mind in the historiography was the example of Irish immigrant women. As Hasia Diner reported in 1983, the image of Irish immigration up to that time was one of men involved in harsh manual labor. The majority of Irish immigrants in the late nineteenth century, however, were women, and their experiences were often more positive than those of Irish immigrant men. As domestic servants, the most common occupation for this group, Irish immigrant women typically had better opportunities than in their home-lands, and they recognized it. Irish women, to a greater degree than many women in this period, migrated to engage in waged labor. "Bridget," the Stereotypical Irish domestic who did the dirty work, helped make possible the ideal woman of the Victorian middle class.

Irish migrant women also illustrated some of the factors that would lead to higher rates of female out-migration from a homeland. As in most areas, Irish rural economic activities were divided according to sex and age. Changes in inheritance patterns to male primogeniture reduced chances of either inheritance or marriage for both men and women and created an expectation that both would go elsewhere to work. Moreover, industrial production replaced cottage industry, leaving fewer opportun-ities for women as "spinsters" (literally those who spun thread). Late marriage and high rates of persons never marrying after the famine years of the late 1840s made it easier to envision a woman on her own, as did strict segregation according to gender in society generally.

Once women's international emigration networks were established, not only did the networks foster migration by providing money and information, but they made it easier for other women to envision migration, and for people to accept it. Another element that assisted in this was the presence of Irish and Irish-descended women in Catholic sisterhoods in the United States. As a key line of defense against poverty and other problems, nuns were a key link in the female networks women created and main-tained. Irish men also created networks, ones which were more likely than those of women to lead to mines, to lumber camps, and to construction projects. Though most Irish immigrants at mid-century lived in cities, women were much more likely to be city dwellers than men, a pattern common for most immigrant groups, but exaggerated by the large numbers of single Irish women who sought domestic service jobs.

As the United States took over much of northern Mexico at mid-century, many Mexicans found the border crossing their land. Not only did this result in almost total loss of land within a decade for Spanish Mexicans, but it meant the loss of legal rights for women, such as rights to sue and be sued and to own property within marriage, which were much more limited, if they existed at all, in other parts of the country. As Deena J. González has shown, some women, such as Gertrudis Barceló, tried to make the best of the situation, in her case using her influence in local politics and capitalizing on the newcomers by running a saloon. Such economic activity was often suspect for women, and might add to a negative general image of Mexican women, one reinforced by racial prejudice and Protestant–Catholic antagonism.

Racial ideology combined with gender ideals to spur restrictive legislation. Chinese migrants faced massive discrimination on the west coast, where most settled. Highly uneven sex ratios combined with various measures which kept Chinese men from owning land, testifying in court, or marrying whites, and helped create gendered stereotypes. Migration patterns changed the gender roles of Chinese immigrants. In the Chinatowns that developed the most prevalent public image of women was as prostitutes, who constituted the majority of Chinese women in the United States at mid-century. This association of Chinese women with prostitution, which became a major justification for the Page Law of 1875, outlawing the immigration of prostitutes, would come to affect various other Asian immigrant groups in subsequent years.

The image of Chinese immigrant men, on the other hand, reflected two aspects of the demographics of gender: (1) the growth of a service sector to assist not only the Chinese population, but also others in a region where there were few female workers; and (2) the concentration of questionable activities associated with young men. The first resulted in the feminized image associated with men working in laundries and as domestic servants. It also related to the stereotypical physical image of Chinese migrant men – long queues and baggy clothing – which set them off from dominant "manly" ideals. The second demographic image of Chinese men was one common to migrant communities with a large disproportion of young men. Chinatown, San Francisco, for example, was noted for disease, gambling, prostitution, opium, organized crime, and other vices. The fear of a growing Chinese American presence in the context of increasing concern for race fueled the Chinese Exclusion Acts, beginning in 1882. Some migrants selectively embraced western gender ideals. A few women began challenging their contracts as indentured prostitutes, going for example to the "rescue" home in San Francisco, where they appealed to the middle-class gender norms of missionaries (Pascoe 1990).

Like most immigrants in this era, Chinese men rarely married in the United States. Even less common, few sent for their spouses. They were often engaged in a dual strategy of male migration that complemented women's work in Cantonese households – a pattern that would be repeated in other sending regions later in the century. Women could and did handle agricultural tasks and ongoing childcare and household tasks, but the families sought cash from a male migrant wage-earner. Sucheta Mazumdar argued that some of the Chinese male migrants may have left due to shifting patriarchal norms, particularly the loss of power men experienced associated with religious groups giving women options outside marriage (Mazumdar 2003). This highlights a debate in the historiography of gender and migration generally over to what extent the women "left behind" were dependent on migrants' earnings, and to what extent they sparked and supported migration decisions (e.g. Reeder 2002; Khatar 2001). Among the Chinese migrant population those men who did want to stay in the United States faced difficulty reuniting with spouses, recruiting spouses from their homeland, or marrying local women given anti-miscegenation sentiments and statutes.

Shifts from the Late Nineteenth Century

As steam transportation and railroad building eased travel to and from the United States, more immigrants undertook transnational economic paths, and others joined into the familial and village networks that crossed borders. Most common was the pattern by which young men came to the United States to work temporarily, perhaps for a season, but more likely for a few years. Some eventually stayed, but return migration was widespread, with estimates running up to 90 percent for some groups in the early part of the twentieth century. For single men, the absence of women whom they considered suitable for marriage (or who considered them suitable) sometimes sparked return migration, either to find a bride and bring her over, or to use the money earned in the United States to set up a more prosperous household in the homeland (Sinke 1999). Married men from southern and eastern Europe often left spouses and children behind, going back or sending for them at a later date if desired. The division of wage-earning from family life across an international border was not entirely new, but it expanded in scope in this period. For women return rates were more limited. Fewer women earned enough to return given lower wages, and moreover, many did not want to. Women were more likely to come after family connections were already established in the United States, or to marry within a few years of migrating as young adults, meaning that family motives were as likely to keep them in the new country as to entice them back. Moreover, there were strong cultural incentives to stay for many women. Whether accurately or not, many viewed the United States as a more "liberated" land for women (Harzig 1997).

Migrants filled a particular niche in the US gender transformation of the era. Just as dominant masculinity came to associate masculine physicality largely with leisure and sports rather than with heavy manual labor in the workplace, immigrants engaged in the physical tasks of the industrial world. The maternalist rhetoric of some Progressive-era reformers assumed a breadwinner/homemaker distinction, and tried to impose it. They also targeted immigrants for reform, assuming their gender roles were suspect.

Early social scientists who studied gang activity, such as Frederick Thrasher for Chicago and William Foote Whyte for Italian Americans in Boston, reinforced an image that popular culture magnified over time, one of immigrant men and illegal activity. Likewise, the campaign against piecework at home as child abuse recognized the financial necessity, but nonetheless berated immigrant families for allowing women and children to work for wages under such conditions. Countering such images was a reason to stress men's leadership roles in families and women's ties to children and home rather than immigrant women's activism.

The connotation of "American," a term adapted in various languages to apply to those who had lived in the United States, differed for men and women. For both it included a lack of deference to traditional authority and often monetary riches as well as a more cosmopolitan outlook (Wyman 1993). While these could be ambiguous for men, for women they were typically much more negative. In particular a taint of worldliness often applied to moral character. A woman who either migrated or returned on her own often illustrated a degree of independence people interpreted as lack of deference to patriarchy, which in many settings could challenge existing gender roles.

For East European Jews, the situation was somewhat different owing to much lower rates of return – a consequence of ethno-religious persecution – and more balanced sex ratios. Two very significant shifts in gender roles took place on the group level, if not always for individuals, around the turn of the century. First, the emphasis on religious education for men diminished as idealized masculinity became more associated with money-making endeavors. As a result, women's roles as money-earners even after marriage became less acceptable, and the idea of a woman supporting her husband became a source of ridicule not only for the surrounding society, but also within the ethnic group. Second, young adults used migration to speed a shift towards independence, epitomized by the transition from arranged marriage to love matches. Young adults engaged in leisure activities in urban centers that brought young men and women together, in mass amusements, dance halls, and later social clubs (S. Glenn 1990). The overbearing father who refused to acquiesce to a daughter's interest in a particular young man she met on her own was a staple in the stories of the second generation. Young men sometimes sought "manly" acceptance through sports, particularly baseball, though anti-Semitism also made for difficulties there.

US society generally was in the midst of redefining gender roles concurrently with the major wave of international migration. A significant cohort of college-educated women sought acceptance through public activism. They completed and undergirded the changes under way, primarily on a state by state basis, through the end of the nineteenth century, in providing women with individual property rights, guardianship of children, and – particularly late in the century – more opportunities for divorce in cases of abuse and neglect. As campaigns for suffrage increased, immigrant women sometimes joined, but more often looked with skepticism, for progressive reformers were as likely to degrade immigrant women for various cultural failings as to support their interests. Progressive reformers decried the authority of immigrant men over their households, taking on wife-beating in particular. Immigrant men resented this intrusion on what some considered appropriate patriarchal privilege. Immigrant women were also ambivalent about giving up the support and protection which were tied to ethnic solidarity. The reformers who advocated Americanization along the lines of middle-class society ignored the realities of working-class life, the realities of women's economic contributions, and – often – racial and/or ethnic discrimination (Lissak 1989). Likewise, reformers who sought to cut immigrant birth rates through voluntary motherhood made their arguments on the basis of the racial inferiority of this "new" immigrant stock. Immigrant organizers were more likely to focus on ethnic and/or class solidarity.

To a greater degree than the general population, immigrants gravitated to cities. Urban residence often entailed a degree of anonymity and a lack of collective control on morality that challenged former residents of rural areas. Most cultural traditions in the United States connected family honor to female morality on some level, but the stress placed on female virginity at marriage varied. Yet there was also a sense among many that men should have sexual experience prior to marriage. The need for "bad" women fueled what some perceived as an explosion of prostitution and pornography (Murphy 1997). It also fueled a hysteria over white slavery, defined as the kidnapping or enticement of single white women into prostitution. The fear of moral degradation of women led to much stricter controls on young women immigrants on their own than those applied to young men. Inspectors might ask when a woman last menstruated and if she had slept with anyone. Single men were unlikely to face this level of scrutiny unless they accompanied unrelated women.

Policies which gave preference to women when they arrived as dependants under the protection of men reinforced existing patriarchal norms, but they also came into conflict with racial ideology. This was clearest in the case of Japanese immigrants on the west coast. Japanese immigrant men began arriving in significant numbers in the 1890s. Though the Japanese government was better equipped to take on the United States in terms of discrimination, the attitudes of many US citizens (which excluded most Japanese-born by law) were similar to those that applied to the Chinese. In this setting the government and society weighed the value of upholding patriarchal norms against racial prejudice. After the Japanese government had agreed to stop sending laborers in the Gentlemen's Agreement of 1907–8, US attention focused on the so-called "picture brides." Like many immigrants, Japanese men often arrived as single adults, and over time many of them sought spouses. Like most other groups of the era, they preferred women close to their own background, a trend reinforced by anti-miscegenation laws and social prejudice against Asians, particularly on the west coast. Japanese men, like those of many other groups, wrote back to the homeland for spouses, arranging marriage through accepted channels. Unlike most groups, Japanese men could marry in absentia, a practice that some white activists labeled uncivilized. Many white leaders feared Japanese women settling in the United States and having children who would be US citizens. The rising racism eventually led to elimination of all migration from Japan.

Several other legal changes in the late 1910s and 1920s changed gender relationships for immigrants. World War I offered immigrant men a quick road to naturalization by joining the military, though the courts still denied this to Asians based on race, and denied migration from the Asian barred zone. The Immigration Act of 1917 also reinforced exclusion of homosexuals under the "psychopathic inferiority" clause. The institution of national origin quotas in the early 1920s cut back migration from Europe substantially, and set up a particularly difficult problem of how to deal with immigrant dependents. As in the Chinese and Japanese cases earlier, the laws at first allowed some exceptions for wives and minor children, protecting patriarchal privilege, but as it became clear that this would subvert the exclusion principles, they too became subject to greater scrutiny and exclusion. This tied into a second shift. Once US women had the vote on a national level in 1919, naturalization law also changed to make a woman's citizenship less dependent on her husband (Bredbenner 1998). In part this shift helped underscore restrictive quota laws, because as long as women's citizenship depended on spousal status, naturalized male immigrants could bring over their spouses as US citizens, with the exception of female "aliens ineligible to citizenship" – mainly Asians.

Immigrants, a disproportionate group in the working population, also formed a disproportionate share of labor activists in the early twentieth century. Immigrant women, particularly Jewish immigrant women, became associated with union organizing, though Italian women became key figures when other radical options closed (J. Guglielmo in Gabaccia and Iacovetta 2002). But it was immigrant men who were most often stereotyped as radicals. In the context of the Red Scare following World War I, this association of immigrants with the Left helped fuel anti-immigrant legislation. Within the labor movement, immigrants promoted their own gender ideals, whether as Italian syndicalist men or anarchist mothers, each of which had transnational meaning (Topp 2001; Merithew in Gabaccia 2002). Pursuing the gendered dimensions of transnational ties for this period of mass migration, whether in labor, religion, or foreign policy, has become a major part of scholarship.

Changing the Balance

The 1920s witnessed a major generational divide concerning gender roles. In part this was the result of the country becoming predominantly urban in terms of population for the first time. Mass entertainment was available in urban spaces to a greater degree than in rural ones, and with it came new images of gender and ethnicity. Immigrant parents sought to protect their children from the problems as well as the stigma associated with parts of urban life. The flapper of the 1920s, with her relatively short skirts, alcohol consumption, and dating subculture, was a particularly difficult challenge for some. Italian- and Mexican-born parents, for example, would demand that chaperones accompany their daughters to social settings (e.g. Ruiz 1998). Adjusting gender roles to a dating situation became difficult, and for many it became a point of pride that men could "protect their women" against the sexual norms of the dominant society, and that women adhered to a different vision of femininity (Espiritu 2001). This reinforced the image of women as cultural conservators, and placed much stricter limits on them in the name of ethnic existence than it did for men.

For some immigrant men, proving manhood in a society where racial discrimination limited opportunities and negated patriarchal hierarchy, at least in some settings, meant finding niches for "manly" behavior. Sport, particularly baseball, was one of those avenues. As José Alamillo showed for Mexican Americans in southern California, for example, a combination of aggressive play, abusive language, gambling, game brawls, and post-game drinking parties helped reinforce an ideal of masculinity for a group which faced limited opportunities for recreation elsewhere. This form of hierarchy based on manliness in turn carried over to labor organizing and to the home.

For other immigrant men and their sons, opportunities for respect came through family or village associations, whether Chinese *fongs*, East European Jewish *Landsman-schaftn*, or Mexican American *parentesco*. Religious and fraternal organizations also allowed men leadership roles and opportunities for activities defined as manly. These groups sometimes allowed women in auxiliary roles, and in many cases women expanded those activities early in the twentieth century, but men retained the leadership positions and typically the groups specifically reinforced patriarchal language and worldview.

Other young men, faced with poor opportunities and often racial or ethnic discrimination as well, turned to gangs. While there had been large Irish and German gangs in the nineteenth century in some major cities, social scientists began to study them as distinct subcultures in the early twentieth century: Jewish, Polish, and

Italian American gangs to name a few. What many shared, according to researchers, was the competition for space and resources in poor, often deteriorating communities. Boys and young men stressed toughness and bravado while gaining social networks and respect that they did not get through standard occupational or educational avenues. They could be manly by showing themselves as gang members walking, or later cruising, on the street, a particular way of posing. Girls in the same neighborhoods, however, were rarely gang members in this period.

A shift in the sex ratio balance of formal immigration was under way by 1930. In the context of greater migration back to sending areas, sometimes in the form of repatriation or expulsion during the Great Depression, women came to form the majority of immigrants. In part this was a function of spouses joining husbands, but it also reflected the growth of the service sector in the US economy, a trend that would gain impetus after World War II as the country relied less on heavy industry for economic advancement. The greatest female majority, however, occurred in the aftermath of World War II, as US servicemen brought back spouses they married while stationed in other countries. The War Brides Acts primarily affected women from allied nations, especially Great Britain. They reinforced one of the central themes of gender in immigration policy, that of married women being classified as dependents, whether they worked for wages or not. Further, the marriages were one end of a continuum of relations between US service personnel, almost exclusively male, and foreign women, one in which more casual liaisons were more common.

World War II, as with most wars, offered some immigrant men a chance to prove their patriotism. European immigrant men fought side by side with other white Americans, a key experience in breaking down ethnic distance. Some Japanese American men left internment camps to join up. After the war, former soldiers – male and usually white – benefited from home loans and education, setting the stage for massive social mobility. A family wage prevailed in some industries, though women still tended to work, both as single young adults and, if married, a bit later in life. Women's jobs were highly segregated, particularly compared to wartime openings. In the declining rural communities of the midwest, as Jon Gjerde illustrated, ethnic values transmitted over several generations, particularly the subordination of women's interests to family goals, kept German and other northwestern European-descended families on the land long after Yankees had left and well beyond when family farming seemed economically tenable (Gjerde 1997).

Though the troops came home after World War II, the US presence outside US borders continued in the context of the Cold War. US bases brought a steady stream of young men (and a handful of women as well) into contact with foreign nationals. Military leaders, who had often relied on an appeal to hyper-masculinity, implicitly and later explicitly advocated heterosexual outlets for servicemen, primarily in the form of prostitution, as part of rest and relaxation. In line with the scientific thinking of their day, they assumed men had greater needs for sexual release than did women, and that keeping those needs in check too long would be bad. The image that many servicemen got of the Philippines or Thailand was of a place where many young women were prostitutes. It fueled an already-existing stereotype of exotic women from Asia and the Pacific, and contributed to an onus on women from this region who married US servicemen. For Korea, military wives were the pioneers of a major late twentieth-century migration, sponsoring other family members over time and operating as model housewives in part to counter the camptown stigma (Yuh 2002).

World War II also ushered in another program with important gender implications, the Bracero Program, which continued in spurts until 1964. The use of Mexican labor under contract was not entirely new, but the scale of this program was unusual. Somewhere between 4 and 5 million men – and contracts went to men – came to the United States under this program, working especially in seasonal agriculture and ranching. Men from marginal social positions gained status in the Mexican state just as they embodied the unequal national positions (Cohen 2000). Though the conditions of employment were spelled out, many employers did not abide by them, and though workers officially could bring families under some contracts, many did not. The program created a pool of Mexican men who were not considered immigrants, but whose experience in the United States combined with poor conditions in the homeland to make it likely they would return to work again. It also supported a male tradition in Mexico of traveling off for a job, leaving behind the women. Because the jobs were for men, the networks that formed also linked primarily to male employment. Mexican women had worked in some agricultural employment in the United States, particularly in food canneries, but under the contract system they were most likely to migrate as dependents, even if they hoped to work for wages in the United States as well.

The emphasis on heterosexual couples with men as wage-earners and women as dependants was a hallmark of the postwar era. In the consensus atmosphere of the 1950s the fear of homosexuality made its way into both law and policy regarding immigration. The McCarren–Walter Act of 1952 reiterated that immigration officials should exclude those who had a "psychopathic personality" or "mental defect." As Eithne Luibhéid illustrated, this language was used to exclude some women presumed to be lesbian along the United States–Mexico border, primarily if they acted or looked "masculine." Women who crossed the border regularly for work, such as domestic servants at the Juarez–El Paso post, could and did face regular scrutiny of their femininity as well as general health.

Late Twentieth Century

The Hart–Cellar Act of 1965, which sparked the late twentieth-century wave of migration, made (heterosexual) family reunification its highest priority, which contributed to female majorities among immigrants in a number of ways. Spouses (at least as the United States defined spouses) had first priority. Unmarried minor children and parents followed. Whereas the preference for children a century earlier almost always ran to sons, the economy of the late twentieth century was as likely to attract daughters. Further, immigrant children were more likely to bring over mothers than fathers, both because women tended to marry older men and outlive them, and because elderly men were more likely to be able to afford to remain on their own longer. But family reunification, which was worded as gender neutral, also worked to bring in men. Filipina nurses were often the first in their families to migrate, sending later for husbands and children (Choy 2003). Thus a policy initially built on the idea of dependent wives and children came to be the most common way for individuals to enter the United States as immigrants, regardless of and often in contrast to their employment ambitions. It set up a situation in which at least some would try to create family ties in order to migrate.

While this strengthened women's role as key players in migration streams, it remained clearly tied to heterosexual marriage as understood in the United States. In fact, "sexual deviation" was added to the Immigration and Naturalization Service's (INS) list of characteristics which warranted exclusion in 1965, and court cases reinforced this intent. Despite the fact that homosexuality was no longer listed as a disorder by the American Psychiatric Association after 1974, the INS continued to officially bar people on these grounds until 1990. The ambivalence of US legal policy concerning same-sex relationships was evident in the 1990s as Congress passed the Defense of Marriage Act – stating that a spouse could only be of a different sex. This was followed in 1999 by the US Supreme Court ruling in favor of granting certain rights to same-sex partnerships. But as far as immigration was concerned same-sex relationships did not warrant consideration. Though gay and lesbian couples have been able to marry or register as partners legally in several countries as well as in various locations in the United States, as of 2000 such marriages, like polygynous marriages in other countries, were not considered valid for immigration purposes. Moreover, gay HIV activists found themselves the targets of immigration bans based on medical status (Dueñas 2000). Both the ability of women to sponsor husbands and the inability of gay men and lesbians to sponsor partners served as gauges of US gender ideology in the law, as well as of how the United States measured up in terms of international human rights.

Another shift in migration patterns late in the century was the importance of legality in migration status. Crossing the border illegally entailed different threats compared with doing so legally. Families from Mexico and beyond were often more hesitant to send daughters and wives into situations where physical violence was possible, for the threat of sexual abuse would then be a possibility. Men who left wives behind, as in migrations of the past, might prefer to have them stay in communities where extended kin could watch their behavior, while the men lived without as much supervision in male spaces. Women got around some of these constraints by developing their own networks (Hondagneu-Sotelo 1994).

The new wave of migration coincided, as with the previous wave, with a major women's rights movement. And as in the earlier period, most immigrant women were suspicious of how the movement dealt with the issue of immigration, though they were often in accord with some of its goals, particularly regarding workplace treatment and equal wages for equal work, at least if they knew about them. In another parallel, many reformers of the late twentieth century labeled the family relations of immigrant communities dysfunctional. The image of a Mexican immigrant man as tied to a "machismo" ideal or of a Nuer refugee man as a potential wife-beater assisted some immigrant women at the cost of stereotyping whole groups. The difficulty of moving from a culture with one standard of gender relations to a country with another standard remained. While a late twentieth-century migrant from Finland or Sweden might have found US gender relations rather traditional, those from many countries were more likely to label them too liberal. As the religious Right in the 1980s and beyond bolstered its efforts to undergird patriarchy – to ensure men were heads of households – feminists sought to assure their own rights and sometimes those of immigrants as well. The stereotype of the submissive foreign-born wife serving her US-citizen husband epitomized the battle, as well as a vision of foreign relations generally in which the United States ruled.

As many US middle-class wives took advantage of better job opportunities opened by the women's movement, or simply sought to maintain or improve economic status, they found husbands reluctant to assist with household tasks. Couples turned to immigrant women as the solution. The late twentieth-century image of the successful American woman who combined career and family was often predicated on immigrant and/or ethnic women handling service tasks: childcare, food preparation, housecleaning, elder care, and nursing. In part this was through factory work, in food processing and clothing manufacturing fields, for example, but it also took place in less formal workplaces. Work in private households was one of the most common occupations for immigrant women in the late twentieth century. This was especially true for women from less industrialized countries, who were more often associated with "traditional" motherhood, a stereotype that goes back to early urbanization, when women from the countryside had an edge over city women for domestic service jobs.

Once again the social reproduction of the family took place across a national border, except that in the late twentieth-century context it was more likely a mother who left the children behind with the family. The long hours required to make a living both for domestics and for other workers at the lower end of the economic scale made it difficult for them to supervise their own children. For this reason some migrant parents never sent for their children. Others sent children back to their homelands, not only to fight discrimination and independence built into US culture, but also to avoid the gendered risks of gang activity for boys (and a few girls as well) and sexual experimentation for girls as they reached teenage years. The sense of trying to maintain a different gender system against terrible odds appeared often in sociological studies (Hondagneu-Sotelo 2001).

Some Filipina and Cuban women could make the point that they consciously rejected American sexual freedom and sought spouses who respected them for it. A Lebanese-born man might complain that he was supporting five households of extended kin, many of them immigrants, on his income. A Vietnamese man might seek a spouse from the homeland in hopes that she would accept the obligation to care for his parents in old age. In other words, the ethnic ethic, one that did not correspond to the "independent" familial ideals many associated with the United States because of the mass media, was a rallying point for some. The examples illustrated that there was a range of gender roles that existed, though it was less clear to what extent that range was imported. Immigrant self-selection continued as well. And the image of less traditional US men (compared to those of Russia or Vietnam for example), of women having better opportunities to make a living and get an education than in a homeland, and of freedom from bodily harm based on gender often operated as an attraction for migrants (e.g. Thai 2003). It also began to play a role in refugee policy as the United Nations recognized certain forms of activity targeted at women, such as female genital mutilation/circumcision, as abusive under certain circumstances.

As in the past, migrants often faced a loss of status in migration, and this loss, particularly for men without significant education, might mean a reversal of economic roles. While in some cases this might lead to more egalitarian family roles, it could also lead, as in Cecilia Menjívar's study of undocumented migrants from Central America, to a withdrawal of men from household responsibilities. Further, while women employed as domestics in the United States might see and aspire to a more equal gender division of labor in the household (except for their own paid work), men employed in manual labor might see primarily more "traditional" gender relations. In other words, women's paid employment often provided a basis for power within the family, but did not do so automatically. Men who lost status as breadwinners might seek to regain it through stricter patriarchal control over the household.

Scholars often refer to a bifurcation of the migration streams of the post-1965 era into the highly educated and skilled on the one hand and those with minimal training on the other. Gender has guided each migration stream and complicated the pattern. As Yen Le Espiritu has shown, women have been somewhat more successful than men in transferring skills to the new location, though this differs by group. The literature on ethnic enclaves of the late twentieth century often portrayed certain groups such as Chinese or Cubans as particularly successful. Those who examined the gender dimensions of these self-employed occupations, however, often found that the success was gender-specific, with better positions reserved for men. Likewise, business success often relied upon the exploitation of family members, particularly female family members, for little or no wages. For Cubans, Yolanda Prieto (1987) noted the trend of married women working for wages outside the home in order to maintain at least middle-class status (a general US trend for the late twentieth century), but also a tendency to downplay this activity and to remain in charge of most household work. For many elite groups, a stay-at-home wife remained an ideal on some level, sometimes to the chagrin of women, such as the highly educated Asian Indians, who came with the idea of better career opportunities.

One of the characteristics of some late twentieth-century migrants was a commitment to transnational ties, not unlike those of the past, but reinforced by better transportation and communication linkages between sending and receiving areas. How people used those links remained gendered. As Sarah J. Mahler illustrated for Salvadorean migrants in New York, access to communication technology could still be controlled by one partner, in this case typically a man. Moreover, communications and transportation infrastructure remained unequal, meaning that instantaneous calls and quick trips back and forth were not possible for all.

Conclusion

Throughout US history gender has guided migration streams and perceptions of immigration, and migration has affected gender roles for the US more generally. The scholarship on gender and international migration has moved beyond simply family roles or economic roles, though these remain important themes. In the literature, studies of women, meant to redress the imbalance in earlier literature, have begun to find counterparts in studies of masculinity and of more integrated gender treatments. The future of gender studies remains promising, particularly as scholars of migration explore themes of gender in areas such as religion, foreign policy, and popular culture.

NOTE

The author would like to thank Linda Heidenreich for insightful comments on a draft of this chapter.

REFERENCES

Alamillo, José M. (2003). "Peloteros in Paradise: Mexican American Baseball and Oppositional Politics in Southern California 1930–1950." *Western Historical Quarterly* 34 (Summer): 191–211.

Alvarez, Robert R. (1987). *Familia: Migration and Adaptation in Baja and Alta California, 1800–1975*. Berkeley: University of California Press.

Bartholomew, Rebecca (1995). *Audacious Women: Early British Mormon Immigrants*. Salt Lake City: Signature Books.

Bederman, Gail (1995). *Manliness and Civilization: A Cultural History of Gender and Race in the United States, 1880–1917*. Chicago: University of Chicago Press.

Bredbenner, Candice Lewis (1998). *A Nationality of Her Own: Women, Marriage, and the Law of Citizenship*. Berkeley: University of California Press.

Chang, Thelma (1996). *"I Can Never Forget": Men of the 100th/442nd* [1991]. Tucson: University of Arizona Press.

Charles, Carolle (1995). "Gender and Politics in Contemporary Haiti: The Duvalierist State, Transnationalism, and the Emergence of a New Feminism (1980–1990)." *Feminist Studies* 21 (Spring): 135–64.

Choy, Catherine Ceniza (2003). *Empire of Care: Nursing and Migration in Filipino American History*. Durham, NC: Duke University Press.

Cohen, Deborah (2000). "Masculinité et visibilité sociale: le spectacle de l'Etat dans la construction de la nation mexicaine." *Clio: Histoire, Femmes, et Sociétés* 12: 163–76.

Cott, Nancy F. (2000). *Public Vows: A History of Marriage and the Nation*. Cambridge, MA: Harvard University Press.

D'Emilio, John and Estelle Freedman (1988). *Intimate Matters: A History of Sexuality in America*. New York: Harper & Row.

Diner, Hasia R. (1983). *Erin's Daughters in America: Irish Immigrant Women in the Nineteenth Century*. Baltimore: Johns Hopkins University Press.

Dueñas, Christopher A. (2000). "Coming to America: The Immigration Obstacle Facing Binational Same-Sex Couples." *Southern California Law Review* 73 (May): 811–41.

Enloe, Cynthia (2000). *Bananas, Beaches, and Bases: Making Feminist Sense of International Politics*. Berkeley: University of California Press.

Espiritu, Yen Le (2001). "'We Don't Sleep Around Like White Girls Do': Family, Culture, and Gender in Filipina American Lives." *Signs: Journal of Women in Culture and Society* 26(2): 415–40.

Gabaccia, Donna, ed. (1992). *Seeking Common Ground: Multidisciplinary Studies of Immigrant Women in the United States*. Westport, CT: Greenwood Press.

—— (1998). *From the Other Side: Women, Gender, and Immigrant Life in the U.S. 1820–1990*. Bloomington: Indiana University Press.

Gabaccia, Donna and Franca Iacovetta, eds. (2002). *Women, Gender, and Transnational Lives: Italian Workers of the World*. Toronto: University of Toronto Press.

Gjerde, Jon (1997). *The Minds of the West: Ethnocultural Evolution in the Rural Middle West 1830–1917*. Chapel Hill: University of North Carolina Press.

Glenn, Evelyn Nakano (2002). *Unequal Freedom: How Race and Gender Shaped American Citizenship and Labor.* Cambridge, MA: Harvard University Press.

Glenn, Susan A. (1990). *Daughters of the Shtetl: Life and Labor in the Immigrant Generation.* Ithaca, NY: Cornell University Press.

González, Deena J. (1999). *Refusing the Favor: The Spanish-Mexican Women of Santa Fe, 1820–1880.* New York: Oxford University Press.

Grasmuck, Sherri and Patricia Pessar (1991). *Between Two Islands: Dominican International Migration.* Berkeley: University of California Press.

Harzig, Christiane, ed. (1997). *Peasant Maids – City Women.* Ithaca, NY: Cornell University Press.

Hodes, Martha, ed. (1997). *Sex, Love, Race: Crossing Boundaries in North American History.* New York: New York University Press.

Hondagneu-Sotelo, Pierrette (1994). *Gendered Transitions: Mexican Experiences of Immigration.* Berkeley: University of California Press.

—— (2001). *Doméstica: Immigrant Workers Cleaning and Caring in the Shadows of Affluence.* Berkeley: University of California Press.

—— ed. (2003). *Gender and U.S. Immigration: Contemporary Trends.* Berkeley: University of California Press.

Hune, Shirley and Gail M. Nomura, eds. (2003). *Asian/Pacific Islander American Women: A Historical Anthology.* New York: New York University Press.

Joe, Karen A. and Meda Chesney-Lind (1995). "'Just Every Mother's Angel': An Analysis of Gender and Ethnic Variations in Youth Gang Membership." *Gender and Society* 9(4): 408–31.

Jones-Correa, Michael (1998). "Different Paths: Gender, Immigration, and Political Participation." *International Migration Review* 32 (Summer): 326–49.

Kerber, Linda (1980). *Women of the Republic: Intellect and Ideology in Revolutionary America.* Chapel Hill: University of North Carolina Press.

Khatar, Akram Fouad (2001). *Inventing Home: Emigration, Gender, and the Middle Class in Lebanon, 1870–1920.* Berkeley: University of California Press.

Kimmel, Michael (1996). *Manhood in America: A Cultural History.* New York: Free Press.

Lee, Robert G. (1999). *Orientals: Asian Americans in Popular Culture.* Philadelphia: Temple University Press.

Lieu, Nhi T. (2000). "Remembering 'The Nation' Through Pageantry: Femininity and the Politics of Vietnamese Womanhood in the *Hoa Hau Ao Dai* Contest." *Frontiers* 21(1–2): 127–51.

Lissak, Rivka Shpak (1989). *Pluralism and Progressives: Hull House and the New Immigrants, 1890–1919.* Chicago: University of Chicago Press.

López, Ian F. Haney (1996). *White By Law: The Legal Construction of Race.* New York: New York University Press.

Luibhéid, Eithne (2002). *Entry Denied: Controlling Sexuality at the Border.* Minneapolis: University of Minnesota Press.

Mahler, Sarah J. (2001). "Transnational Relationships: The Struggle to Communicate Across Borders." *Identities* 7(4): 583–619.

Mazumdar, Sucheta (2003). "What Happened to the Women? Chinese and Indian Male Migration to the United States in Global Perspective." In Shirley Hune and Gail M. Nomura, eds., *Asian/Pacific Islander American Women: A Historical Anthology.* New York: New York University Press, pp. 58–74.

Menjívar, Cecilia (2000). *Fragmented Ties: Salvadoran Immigrant Networks in America.* Berkeley: University of California Press.

Meyerowitz, Joanne, ed. (1994). *Not June Cleaver: Women and Gender in Postwar America.* Philadelphia: Temple University Press.

Mullan, Michael L. (1999). "Ethnicity and Sport: The Wapato Nippons and Pre-World War II Japanese American Baseball." *Journal of Sport History* 26(1): 82–114.

Murphy, Mary (1997). *Mining Cultures: Men, Women, and Leisure in Butte, 1914–1941.* Urbana: University of Illinois Press.

Ngai, Mae M. (2004). *Impossible Subjects: Illegal Aliens and the Making of Modern America.* Princeton, NJ: Princeton University Press.

O'Leary, Elizabeth L. (1996). *At Beck and Call: The Representation of Domestic Servants in Nineteenth-Century American Painting.* Washington, DC: Smithsonian Institution Press.

Parreñas, Rhacel Salazar (2001). *Servants of Globalization: Women, Migration, and Domestic Work.* Stanford, CA: Stanford University Press.

Pascoe, Peggy (1990). *Relations of Rescue: The Search for Female Moral Authority in the American West, 1874–1939.* New York: Oxford University Press.

Pedraza, Silvia (1991). "Women and Migration: The Social Consequences of Gender." *Annual Review of Sociology*: 303–25.

Peiss, Kathy and Christina Simmons, eds., with Robert A. Padgug (1989). *Passion and Power: Sexuality in History.* Philadelphia: Temple University Press.

Perdue, Theda (1998). *Cherokee Women: Gender and Culture Change, 1700–1835.* Lincoln: University of Nebraska Press.

Pickle, Linda Schelbitzki (1996). *Contented Among Strangers: Rural German-Speaking Women and Their Families in the Nineteenth-Century Midwest.* Urbana: University of Illinois Press.

Prieto, Yolanda (1987). "Cuban Women in the U.S. Labor Force: Perspectives on the Nature of Change." *Cuban Studies* 17: 73–91.

Puskás, Julianna (2000). *Ties that Bind, Ties that Divide: One Hundred Years of Hungarian Experience in the United States.* New York: Holmes & Meier.

Reeder, Linda (2002). *Widows in White: Migration and the Transformation of Rural Women, Sicily, 1880–1928.* Toronto: University of Toronto Press.

Rosen, Deborah A. (2003). "Women and Property Across Colonial America: A Comparison of Legal Systems in New Mexico and New York." *William and Mary Quarterly* 60(2): 355–81.

Rotundo, E. Anthony (1993). *American Manhood: Transformations in Masculinity from the Revolution to the Modern Era.* New York: Basic Books.

Ruiz, Vicki L. (1998). *From Out of the Shadows: Mexican Women in Twentieth-Century America.* New York: Oxford University Press.

Scott, Joan W. (1986). "Gender: A Useful Category of Historical Analysis." *American Historical Review* 91: 1053–75.

Sharpe, Pamela, ed. (2001). *Women, Gender and Labour Migration: Historical and Global Perspectives.* London: Routledge.

Simon, Rita J. and Caroline Brettell, eds. (1986). *International Migration: The Female Experience.* Totowa, NJ: Rowan & Allenheld.

Sinke, Suzanne M. (1999). "Migration for Labor, Migration for Love: Marriage and Family Formation across Borders." *OAH Magazine* (Fall): 17–21.

—— (2002). *Dutch Immigrant Women in the United States, 1880–1920.* Urbana: University of Illinois Press.

Tchen, John Kuo Wei (1999). *New York Before Chinatown: Orientalism and the Shaping of American Culture, 1776–1882.* Baltimore: Johns Hopkins University Press.

Thai, Hung Cam (2003). "Clashing Dreams: Highly Educated Overseas Brides and Low-Wage U.S. Husbands." In Barbara Ehrenreich and Arlie Russell Hochschild, eds., *Global Woman: Nannies, Maids, and Sex Workers in the New Economy.* New York: Metropolitan Books.

Topp, Michael Miller (2001). *Those Without A Country: The Political Culture of Italian American Syndicalists.* Minneapolis: University of Minnesota Press.

Wagner, Sally Roesch (1996). *The Untold Story of the Iroquois Influence on Early Feminists.* Aberdeen, SD: Sky Carrier Press.

Wu, Judy Tzu-Chun (1997). "'Loveliest Daughter of Our Ancient Cathay!' Representations of Ethnic and Gender Identity in the Miss Chinatown U.S.A. Beauty Pageant." *Journal of Social History* 31(1): 5–31.

Wyman, Mark (1993). *Round-Trip to America: The Immigrants Return to Europe, 1880–1930.* Ithaca, NY: Cornell University Press.

Yuh, Ji-Yeon (2002). *Beyond the Shadow of Camptown: Korean Military Brides in America.* New York: New York University Press.

Yung, Judy (1995). *Unbound Feet: A Social History of Chinese Women in San Francisco.* Berkeley: University of California Press.

Zavella, Patricia (2003). "Talkin' Sex: Chicanas and Mexicanas Theorize about Silences and Sexual Pleasures." In Gabriela F. Arredondo, Aída Hurtado, Norma Klahn, Olga Nájera-Ramírez, and Patricia Zavella, eds., *Chicana Feminisms: A Critical Reader.* Durham, NC: Duke University Press, pp. 228–53.

CHAPTER FOURTEEN

Immigrant Residential and Mobility Patterns

BARRY R. CHISWICK AND PAUL W. MILLER

A common characteristic of immigrants in various destinations and in various time periods is that they tend to be geographically concentrated.[1] Immigrants from a particular origin tend to live in areas where others from the same origin live, rather than distributing themselves across the regions of the destination in the same proportion as the native-born population. The result of this tendency to settle among others from their country of origin is the formation of immigrant and ethnic concentrations or enclaves.

There are consequences of these geographic concentrations (see, for example, Case and Katz 1991; Chiswick and Miller 1995, 2005; Goddard, Sparkes, and Haydon 1985; Le 1999; Veltman 1983). The geographic concentration appears to have adverse effects on immigrants acquiring destination language skills, but they may have favorable effects on immigrant groups maintaining and passing their mother tongue and ethnic culture on to their children. Enclaves may facilitate immigrant entrepreneurship, although they appear to depress the nominal earnings of immigrants. Enclaves have an effect on the supply and demand for "ethnic goods," as well as on the demand for publicly provided goods and services.[2] Moreover, enclaves may affect the political strength of immigrant groups at local and national levels. Finally, these enclaves affect the demand for housing among immigrants and are sometimes associated with slum or ghetto neighborhoods.

It is well known that immigrants adjust to the circumstances of the US economy the longer they have lived in the United States. This immigrant adjustment has generally been measured using information on earnings, occupational status, or employment, and the changes in these measures with duration of residence have been intensively researched, with the major issues being outlined in Chiswick (1978, 1980, 1982). Comparatively less is known, however, of the other adjustments that immigrants might make, such as in the location of their residence. Yet these types of adjustment may be as important as the earnings and occupation measures generally studied. Massey argues,

> An important aspect of assimilation is the degree to which immigrant groups are spatially isolated from the mainstream of US society. Residential segregation is not only

important as an indicator of assimilation in its own right, but also has implications for other dimensions of sociocultural integration that are highly related to propinquity – e.g., intermarriage. (1981, p. 67)

Changing patterns of immigrant social geography have received treatment by historians such as Ward (1971), Thernstrom (1973), and Zunz (1982). This chapter presents information on immigrant concentrations in the United States in the year 2000, with some comparisons to a decade earlier.[3] The study has two main sections, the first dealing with residential location and the second with internal mobility. It ends with a summary and discussion.

Immigrants' Residential Location

Distribution Across States

Perhaps the easiest way of illustrating the geographic concentration in the United States is to consider the distribution across the states. One of the factors that research has shown as being important in influencing the settlement pattern of immigrants is the language spoken at home. The Spanish language is so dominant among the languages other than English spoken at home in the United States that it is analyzed separately from all other languages (see, for example, Chiswick and Miller 1996, Table 2). Data are available in the 2000 census on the language spoken at home for all persons aged 5 and over.

In 2000, about 83 percent of the foreign-born population in the United States spoke a language other than or in addition to English at home. Of those who did so, just over one-half spoke Spanish, and are primarily immigrants from Mexico, Central and South America, and the Caribbean. The next most frequently spoken language was Chinese, but it is spoken by only about 5 percent of the non-English-speaking immigrants. The Chinese speakers had a variety of origins, although they primarily came from China (62 percent), Taiwan (12 percent), Hong Kong (9 percent), and Vietnam (7 percent). In contrast, only about 9 percent of those aged 5 and over who were born in the United States spoke another language at home, and these are predominantly second-generation Americans, that is, the US-born children of immigrants.

Table 14.1 reports the distribution of the native-born and the foreign-born across the states. The distribution of the native-born across states serves as the benchmark against which concentrations of the foreign-born may be assessed. For the foreign-born there are three subgroups: those who speak only English at home, those who speak Spanish at home, and those who speak a language other than English or Spanish at home.

It is seen that, according to the 2000 census, 9.8 percent of the native-born live in California, 5.9 percent in New York, 7.1 percent in Texas, 4.4 percent in Illinois, and close to 5 percent in each of Florida and Pennsylvania. A total of 37 percent of the native-born live in these six states. In comparison, more than one-quarter of the foreign-born live in California (28.5 percent), 12.3 percent live in New York, 9.3 percent in Texas, and 8.6 percent in Florida. A further 5 percent of the foreign-born live in Illinois and 4.8 percent in New Jersey. Thus, the six states with the largest

Table 14.1 State of residence of persons aged 5 and over by nativity and language spoken at home, 2000 US Census (percent distribution)

State	Native-born[a] Total	Foreign-born Only English	Spanish	Other	Total
Alabama	1.77	0.43	0.24	0.27	0.28
Alaska	0.23	0.14	0.04	0.17	0.11
Arizona	1.78	1.91	3.21	0.90	2.08
Arkansas	1.06	0.27	0.29	0.16	0.23
California	9.79	18.17	33.79	27.05	28.48
Colorado	1.56	1.36	1.49	0.86	1.22
Connecticut	1.18	2.03	0.54	1.60	1.21
Delaware	0.30	0.17	0.09	0.16	0.13
Dist. Columbia	0.20	0.32	0.20	0.22	0.23
Florida	5.27	10.31	10.80	5.36	8.56
Georgia	3.04	2.06	1.84	1.75	1.84
Hawaii	0.39	0.58	0.03	1.47	0.69
Idaho	0.49	0.22	0.27	0.13	0.21
Illinois	4.35	3.47	4.91	5.62	4.95
Indiana	2.37	0.74	0.54	0.68	0.63
Iowa	1.15	0.30	0.18	0.36	0.27
Kansas	1.03	0.46	0.50	0.38	0.45
Kentucky	1.61	0.36	0.15	0.33	0.26
Louisiana	1.76	0.41	0.28	0.43	0.36
Maine	0.50	0.33	0.01	0.17	0.13
Maryland	1.92	2.31	0.91	2.35	1.71
Massachusetts	2.22	3.19	0.91	3.93	2.49
Michigan	3.81	2.55	0.59	2.53	1.69
Minnesota	1.89	1.09	0.44	1.16	0.84
Mississippi	1.13	0.25	0.09	0.12	0.13
Missouri	2.21	0.69	0.26	0.62	0.48
Montana	0.36	0.16	0.01	0.04	0.05
Nebraska	0.66	0.24	0.26	0.22	0.24
Nevada	0.67	0.93	1.28	0.69	0.99
New Hampshire	0.48	0.32	0.06	0.22	0.17
New Jersey	2.72	4.72	3.54	6.16	4.78
New Mexico	0.67	0.40	0.77	0.18	0.47
New York	5.90	18.25	8.22	14.32	12.33
North Carolina	3.08	1.45	1.61	1.14	1.40
North Dakota	0.26	0.06	0.00	0.06	0.03
Ohio	4.46	1.64	0.28	1.74	1.09
Oklahoma	1.34	0.46	0.47	0.37	0.43
Oregon	1.26	1.15	0.90	0.94	0.96
Pennsylvania	4.78	2.51	0.44	2.49	1.60
Rhode Island	0.37	0.37	0.30	0.54	0.41
South Carolina	1.58	0.49	0.34	0.36	0.37
South Dakota	0.30	0.08	0.01	0.07	0.05
Tennessee	2.24	0.62	0.48	0.57	0.54

Table 14.1   (cont'd)

	Native-born[a]	Foreign-born			
State	Total	Only English	Spanish	Other	Total
Texas	7.08	5.77	14.89	4.67	9.30
Utah	0.81	0.52	0.59	0.42	0.51
Vermont	0.24	0.21	0.01	0.11	0.08
Virginia	2.60	2.02	1.27	2.50	1.88
Washington	2.11	2.60	1.20	2.57	1.98
West Virginia	0.73	0.09	0.02	0.09	0.06
Wisconsin	2.10	0.77	0.46	0.70	0.61
Wyoming	0.20	0.06	0.03	0.02	0.03
Total	100.00	100.00	100.00	100.00	100.00
% of foreign-born	–	16.88	43.46	39.66	100.00

(a) Among the native-born, 91.4 percent speak only English, 5.8 percent speak Spanish, and 2.8 percent speak other languages.

Source: 2000 US Census Public Use Microdata 1% Sample.

number of the foreign-born accounted for over two-thirds (69 percent) of all foreign-born residents in the United States in 2000, while only 35 percent of the native-born lived in these states. Hence, immigrants are geographically concentrated by state. Moreover, they are concentrated in or near the major international airports for entry into the United States (New York, Los Angeles, San Francisco, Chicago, and Miami).

The Big Six immigrant states – California, Texas, New York, Florida, Illinois, and New Jersey – have high concentrations of immigrant foreign language speakers.[4] The data in Table 14.1, columns 2 to 5 show that the geographic concentration of the foreign-born who speak only English at home is less intense than for foreign language speakers. For example, 61 percent of immigrants who speak only English live in the Big Six immigrant states, compared to around 69 percent for all the foreign-born: 76 percent for those who speak Spanish and 63 percent for those who speak a language other than English or Spanish at home.

Yet these data also show that these six states differ in importance as destinations for the foreign-born according to their language usage. For example, whereas 49 percent of immigrant Spanish speakers live in California and Texas, only 24 percent of the monolingual English-speaking immigrants and 17 percent of the native-born live in these two states. Whereas 8 percent of foreign-born Spanish speakers live in New York, and a further 4 percent in New Jersey, 18 percent of the foreign-born who speak only English live in New York and a further 5 percent live in New Jersey. For the foreign-born who speak a language other than English or Spanish at home, 14 percent live in New York and 6 percent in New Jersey. Similarly, Florida has high proportions of immigrants who speak either only English (10 percent) or Spanish (11 percent), but a relatively low proportion of the foreign-born who speak another language at home. These data suggest that knowledge of the language mix of residents

Table 14.2 Six main immigrant-receiving states for immigrants aged 5 and over, by nativity and language spoken at home, 2000 and 1990 US Censuses (percent distribution)

State		Native-born Total	Foreign-born Only English	Spanish	Other	Total
California	2000	9.8	18.2	33.8	27.1	28.5
	1990	10.2	19.2	43.5	29.8	32.8
Florida	2000	5.3	10.3	10.8	5.4	8.6
	1990	5.0	10.1	11.9	4.5	8.5
Illinois	2000	4.4	3.5	4.9	5.6	5.0
	1990	4.6	3.4	4.6	5.7	4.8
New Jersey	2000	2.7	4.7	3.5	6.2	4.8
	1990	2.9	5.3	3.7	6.0	5.0
New York	2000	5.9	18.3	8.2	14.3	12.3
	1990	6.5	19.7	9.7	16.3	14.5
Texas	2000	7.1	5.8	14.9	4.7	9.3
	1990	6.8	4.4	13.9	3.7	7.7
Other states	2000	64.8	39.2	23.9	36.7	31.5
	1990	64.0	37.9	12.7	34.0	26.7
Total		100.00	100.00	100.00	100.00	100.00

Source: 1990 and 2000 US Census Public Use Microdata 1% Sample.

in a location may be helpful in understanding the location decisions of immigrants.

There have been few changes in the location choices of immigrants over the past decade. Table 14.2 reports the data for 2000 for each of six main immigrant-receiving states and all other states combined, in bold type, followed by comparable data for 1990 in normal type. These data show a small drift away from California, New York, and New Jersey for both the native-born and foreign-born, and a small drift towards Texas and Florida. The Big Six immigrant-receiving states, however, were home to relatively fewer immigrants (69 percent in 2000 compared to 73 percent in 1990), even though their share of the native-born population did not change appreciably over the decade of the 1990s.

Residential Patterns Among the Foreign Born by Immigration Cohort

Table 14.3 presents data on the degree of concentration of the foreign-born by immigrant cohort. Only the six states with the largest number of the foreign-born are separately identified in this table. Five categories for period of arrival are specified for the foreign-born. It is seen that almost one-quarter of the foreign-born living in the United States in 2000 arrived in the period 1995–2000. The proportions in three other five-year periods, 1990–4, 1985–9, and 1980–4, are 18 percent, 15 percent, and 12 percent, respectively. The remaining immigrants (31 percent) arrived before 1980. While there is some variation in the proportion of the foreign-born living in the six states for each of the arrival cohorts in Table 14.3, the proportion is relatively

Table 14.3 State of residence of persons aged 5 and over by nativity and period of immigration, 2000 US Census (percent distribution)

State	Native-born Total	Foreign-born: arrival year					
		1995–2000	1990–4	1985–9	1980–4	Before 1980	Total
California	9.79	22.14	28.16	34.10	33.69	28.63	28.48
Florida	5.27	7.99	7.47	7.32	8.93	10.09	8.56
Illinois	4.35	5.34	5.30	4.57	3.76	5.11	4.95
New Jersey	2.72	4.64	4.87	4.97	4.46	4.87	4.78
New York	5.90	10.46	13.72	12.80	11.95	12.87	12.33
Texas	7.08	10.43	9.70	8.58	10.37	8.13	9.30
Other states	64.90	39.00	30.78	27.66	26.84	30.31	31.60
Total	100.00	100.00	100.00	100.00	100.00	100.00	100.00
% of foreign-born	–	23.48	18.07	15.15	12.39	30.90	100.00

Source: 2000 US Census Public Use Microdata 1% Sample.

high for each group, ranging from 73 percent for the 1980–4 cohort to 61 percent for the 1995–2000 cohort, considerably in excess of the 35 percent of the native-born living in these states.

Examination of the proportion of the foreign-born in each of the six major immigrant-receiving states for each of the arrival cohorts shows two main patterns. The first is that immigrants in the post-1990 cohorts appear to be less concentrated in the major immigrant-receiving states than was the case for the earlier arrival cohorts. In large part this arises from the relatively smaller number living in California among the more recent arrival cohorts, although the trend towards smaller percentages of immigrants locating in Florida and New York also contributes to this finding. The second pattern is that there has been a rise in the proportion of immigrants locating in Illinois since 1980, and a rise in the proportion locating in Texas since 1985.

These patterns could be due to a number of factors. First, economic conditions in the states may have varied over time, so that California was a relatively less prosperous state, and hence a less attractive destination for the foreign-born in the late 1990s than before 1995. Indeed, for much of the 1980s the unemployment rate in California was at or below the national unemployment rate, whereas for most of the 1990s the unemployment rate in California was above the national unemployment rate. In the mid-1990s, for example, the unemployment rate in California (of 8 to 9 percent) was two percentage points higher than the national unemployment rate (6 to 7 percent). Second, the patterns may be a consequence of variations across states and across time in the relative availability of public infrastructure and in the affordability of housing. Third, the data may be a reflection of internal migration. That is, immigrants may move from their state of initial settlement. Patterns of internal migration are explored below. Fourth, and perhaps most importantly, the countries of origin of the immigrants to the United States have changed in recent years, and with that there has been a change in the area of initial settlement.

Table 14.4 Distribution of foreign-born persons by period of immigration and major birthplace region, 2000 US Census (percent distribution)

Country or region	Arrival cohort					
	1995–2000	1990–4	1985–9	1980–4	Before 1980	Total foreign-born
UK & Ireland	1.64	1.52	1.67	1.88	5.10	2.72
Canada	2.13	1.76	1.22	1.28	5.06	2.72
Mexico	34.48	32.59	33.90	26.58	22.63	29.41
Other Europe[a]	11.16	10.79	7.08	6.32	22.88	13.50
Asia	25.13	27.82	27.85	33.85	22.08	26.17
S & C America	13.36	13.13	16.20	15.31	8.75	12.57
Caribbean	6.77	9.09	9.06	11.40	11.28	9.50
Other	5.34	3.30	3.02	3.38	2.22	3.41
Total	100.00	100.00	100.00	100.00	100.00	100.00
% of foreign-born	23.48	18.07	15.15	12.39	30.90	100.00

(a) Other Europe excludes UK and Ireland.

Source: 2000 US Census Public Use Microdata 1% Sample.

The Birthplace Mix of Immigrants

Data on the birthplace mix of the immigrants are presented in Table 14.4. Immigrants in the "Before 1980" cohort are mostly from Other Europe (23 percent), Asia (22 percent), Mexico (23 percent), and the Caribbean (11 percent).[5] The 1980s and 1990s and into the 2000s have seen a strong growth in the importance of Asia, Mexico, and South and Central America as immigrant source regions, and a decrease in the relative importance of immigrants from the UK and Ireland, Canada, Other Europe, and the Caribbean. Among the immigrants who arrived over the period 1995–2000, 25 percent were from Asia (compared to 22 percent in the Before 1980 cohort), 34 percent from Mexico (23 percent in the Before 1980 cohort), and 13 percent from South and Central America (9 percent in the Before 1980 cohort). Only 11 percent of the 1995–2000 cohort were from Other Europe (compared to 23 percent for the Before 1980 cohort), 2 percent from the UK and Ireland (5 percent in the Before 1980 cohort), 2 percent from Canada (5 percent in the Before 1980 cohort), and 7 percent from the Caribbean (11 percent in the Before 1980 cohort). There have not been any major changes in the relative importance of the major immigrant source regions over the past 15 years.

Residential Location and Birthplace

Given the size of these shifts in the countries of origin of the immigrants, it is possible that the birthplace mix could impact on the data presented in Table 14.3. Table 14.5 reports the distribution of the state of residence of the foreign-born by the immigrants' birthplace. It is apparent that the geographic concentration by state varies by birthplace group. At the most aggregate level, the concentration among immigrants from the British Isles and Canada is quite low, with 45 percent of

Table 14.5 State of residence of immigrants by birthplace, 2000 US Census (percent distribution)

State	Birthplace							
	UK & Ireland	Canada	Mexico	Other Europe[a]	Asia	S & C America	Caribbean	Other
California	18.18	16.09	42.52	14.30	35.27	23.99	2.53	18.34
Florida	9.97	12.06	2.07	6.36	2.90	16.60	37.18	3.31
Illinois	3.81	2.42	6.65	8.82	4.44	2.13	1.01	3.07
New Jersey	5.25	2.14	0.70	7.74	5.15	7.96	8.19	5.92
New York	12.91	6.96	1.86	18.55	11.10	17.54	34.34	10.87
Texas	4.54	4.75	20.50	2.86	5.64	6.31	1.38	6.71
Other states	45.34	55.57	25.70	41.37	35.49	25.46	15.38	51.78
Total	100.00	100.00	100.00	100.00	100.00	100.00	100.00	100.00
% of foreign-born	2.72	2.72	29.41	13.50	26.17	12.57	9.50	3.41

(a) Other Europe excludes UK and Ireland.

Source: 1990 US Census Public Use Microdata 1% Sample.

immigrants from the UK and Ireland living outside the Big 6 states, and 56 percent of immigrants from Canada living in states other than these six. In comparison, only 26 percent of immigrants from Mexico, 15 percent of those from the Caribbean, and 25 percent of those from South and Central America live in states other than the Big 6 immigrant destinations.

Among Mexican immigrants in 2000, 43 percent live in California. 21 percent live in Texas, followed by Illinois with 7 percent. This clustering involves factors other than just proximity to the border with Mexico, as in the case of Illinois, although obviously this proximity is very important. The other two states that border Mexico (Arizona and New Mexico) are, respectively, home to only 4.7 percent and 1.1 percent of immigrants from Mexico (1.8 percent of the native-born live in Arizona and 0.7 percent in New Mexico). In total, 69 percent of immigrants from Mexico are found in the four states that border Mexico. This compares with just 19 percent of the native-born population.

Among immigrants from the Caribbean, 37 percent live in Florida, while 43 percent live in the other eastern seaboard states in Table 14.5, New York and New Jersey. Only 3 percent live in California. Immigrants from South and Central America are concentrated in California (24 percent), New York (18 percent), and Florida (17 percent). It is interesting to note that the Asian immigrants, who have been numerous in recent immigration flows, are also heavily concentrated in California (35 percent).

Internal US Mobility

Knowledge of the pattern of internal US mobility of immigrants (and also of the native-born) is important for a number of reasons. If immigrants relocate from the initial place of settlement, there will be implications for planning for public infrastructure and other amenities. This internal mobility will also have implications for the demand for housing, and the demand for goods more generally, as it will for the labor market, perhaps most obviously in terms of labor supply, but also in terms of the demand for labor, given that this is a derived demand. There may also be implications for the wages and unemployment outcomes for immigrants (as well as for natives) who move, as well as for members of local labor markets who do not move.

Tendencies towards relocation will also be relevant for understanding the importance of concentrations of immigrants, the so-called ethnic or language enclaves referred to above. If immigrants tend to disperse with duration of residence in the United States, then any geographic concentrations observed among new immigrants will be less of an issue. Moreover, if any tendency for immigrants to become less geographically concentrated with duration of residence in the United States varies by immigrant group, then this has implications for immigration policy and also for settlement policy. For example, the immigrants who are better educated or more proficient in English may be more mobile than less educated immigrants or those without English proficiency. Immigrants who have a greater attachment to the labor market may similarly be more mobile than immigrants with a lesser attachment. If so, the acquisition of post-migration education and English language skills, and the ensuing labor market success, can lead to greater mobility among immigrants and less geographic concentration.

Immigrant Mobility: A Cross-Sectional Analysis

Mobility and immigrant adjustment may be assessed in a number of ways. The method employed in much of the research to date on immigrant adjustment has involved comparison of immigrants who have lived in the United States for varying periods of time. For example, the outcomes (income, unemployment, location) at a specific point in time (e.g. 2000) for recent arrivals who entered the United States between 1995 and 2000 can be compared with the same outcomes at the same point in time (i.e. 2000) for immigrants who entered the United States earlier, for example between 1990 and 1994. The differences in outcomes for these two arrival cohorts can be attributed to having lived in the United States for, on average, around five additional years.

Data on the location of immigrants according to arrival cohort were presented in Table 14.3. Immigrant mobility and hence adjustment is inferred from these data by comparing the distributions of immigrants reading from left to right in the table. Thus, interpreting the table this way, it is observed that between 22 and 34 percent of immigrants reside in California for the first 15–20 years of residence in the United States.[6]

There are U-shaped patterns with duration of residence in the percentage of immigrants who live in Florida and Illinois, but there is no obvious pattern observed for Texas, New Jersey, and New York. However, the cross-sectional patterns of internal mobility of immigrants in Table 14.3 are quite irregular. Bartel and Koch also conducted an analysis along these lines and concluded, "the evidence . . . gives only limited support for the hypothesis that, as time elapses in the United States, the immigrants will become more dispersed throughout the country" (1991, p. 124; see also Bartel 1989).

The absence of systematic patterns of immigrant mobility in Table 14.3 may be due to deficiencies in the cross-sectional data for the study of mobility patterns. This issue is addressed in the following section.

Immigrant Mobility: A Longitudinal Analysis

Inferring immigrant adjustment from cross-sectional data may result in misleading conclusions because the composition of the immigrant groups in each of the arrival cohorts may differ. These differences can be due to obvious factors, such as the changes in the birthplace mix of recent immigrants addressed above. They could also be due to less obvious, but equally important, factors, such as selective emigration, and the difficulty of disentangling the changes associated with different economic and social conditions at the time of entry into the United States from the longitudinal changes that the analysis is attempting to quantify.

Given these problems with the study of cross-sectional data, analyses of immigrant adjustment using longitudinal data may have much to offer. Chiswick (1977) attempted to overcome the biases inherent in the use of cross-sectional data in a study of the occupational attainment of immigrants by using the retrospective information on occupation collected in the 1970 census.[7] A similar approach can be used in the study of immigrant mobility in the United States. The 2000 census collected information on the place of residence of each individual five years before the census.

Table 14.6 presents information on the state of residence in 1995 and in 2000 of the native-born and foreign-born aged 5 years and over in 2000. Note that this is the actual state of residence in 2000 for each individual and the retrospective account of the state of residence in 1995. While the data may be subject to recall error, it would be expected that for such an obvious issue as state of residence, the extent of recall error would be slight.

Table 14.6 State of residence in 1995 and 2000 of persons aged 5 and over by nativity, 2000 US Census (percent distribution)

	Native-born		*Foreign-born*[a]	
State	*Location in 1995*	*Location in 2000*	*Location in 1995*	*Location in 2000*
California	10.01	9.79	31.40	30.42
Florida	5.01	5.27	8.40	8.73
Illinois	4.47	4.35	4.88	4.83
New Jersey	2.81	2.72	4.82	4.82
New York	6.17	5.90	13.74	12.91
Texas	7.00	7.08	8.86	8.95
Other states	64.52	64.90	27.90	29.33
Total	100.00	100.00	100.00	100.00

(a) The foreign-born are restricted to those who arrived before 1995.

Source: 2000 US Census Public Use Microdata 1% Sample.

It is quite clear that the distributions across these states for the native-born and the foreign-born are quite stable over the five-year period. The only point of note for the native-born is a slight drift to Florida and away from California, New York, and Illinois. The data for the foreign-born are also characterized by a high degree of stability, although there is some evidence of a shift out of California and New York, and to a lesser extent Illinois, and a shift into Florida and Texas. Moreover, the patterns evident from comparison of the actual states of residence in 2000 with the retrospective account of the state of residence in 1995 are broadly in line with the patterns that emerge from study of the actual states of residence in 2000 and 1990 (see Table 14.2). In other words, the use of the retrospective account does not appear to result in any obvious problems at this aggregate level.

Table 14.7 lists data on the state of residence in 2000 and 1995 for three arrival cohorts among the foreign-born: those who arrived during 1990–4, 1985–9, and 1980–4. There are two main features of these data. First, at this more refined level, there is less evidence of a shift of immigrants towards Texas, though the evidence for the shift towards Florida and away from New York and California is as strong as in Table 14.6. Second, there are no major changes across arrival cohorts in mobility patterns. There are, however, quite distinct changes across cohorts in location patterns. The data in Table 14.3, show, for example, that a major difference in the proportions of immigrants residing in California among the more recent arrival cohorts and the earlier arrival cohorts is driven by the initial location decisions of immigrants rather than by internal mobility after they have arrived in the United States.

The data presented in Tables 14.6 and 14.7 are the net outcomes of gross flows into and out of the states. Gross flows into and out of the states provide richer detail. For example, it may be that a particular area has a stable share of the immigrants in an arrival cohort, but over time this is progressively being made up of

Table 14.7 State of residence of foreign-born persons aged 5 and over, by duration of residence in the United States, 2000 US Census (percent distribution)

| State | Arrival cohort | | | | | |
| | 1990–4 | | 1985–9 | | 1980–4 | |
	Location in 1995	Location in 2000	Location in 1995	Location in 2000	Location in 1995	Location in 2000
California	29.54	28.16	35.64	34.10	34.83	33.69
Florida	7.31	7.47	7.07	7.32	8.69	8.93
Illinois	5.27	5.30	4.59	4.57	3.83	3.76
New Jersey	4.74	4.87	4.93	4.97	4.40	4.46
New York	14.73	13.72	13.78	12.80	12.87	11.95
Texas	9.69	9.70	8.43	8.58	10.28	10.37
Other states	28.72	30.78	25.55	27.66	25.11	26.84
Total	100.00	100.00	100.00	100.00	100.00	100.00

Source: 2000 US Census Public Use Microdata 1% Sample.

a different group of immigrants. The demands that this new group have on public and community services, and the types of housing they use now and are likely to seek in the future, may differ from those of the original immigrants. These issues are best addressed through a gross flows analysis.

Immigrant Mobility: Gross Flows

The gross flows analysis presented here is based on cross-tabulating the current state of residence and the state of residence five years ago. This provides information on (1) the way that residents of a particular area five years ago disperse; (2) the areas (five years ago) from which the current members of a particular region originated; (3) differences across immigrants of different backgrounds (e.g. language) in the tendencies towards concentration.

Table 14.8 presents information on the proportions of the various groups who moved over the five-year period 1995 to 2000. Three categories are identified: those who did not move house; those who moved house within the same state, and those who moved inter-state.[8] In order to abstract from the issues associated with teenagers and school children leaving home for the first time, the analyses in this section are restricted to those aged 25 and over.

Among the native-born aged 25 and over, around 60 percent did not change their residence over the five-year period 1995–2000. Around 32 percent moved house within their existing state, and 8 percent moved inter-state. The mobility patterns for the total foreign-born are similar to those for the native-born, with around 55 percent not moving, 37 percent moving intra-state, and 8 percent moving inter-state. It is important to recognize the magnitudes of the movements of people that these figures represent. Thus, these data indicate that some 57 million people in the 25-and-over age group moved intra-state within the five-year period studied. Of these, 50 million were native-born and 7 million were foreign-born. These data also indicate that around 14 million people aged 25 and over moved inter-state within

Table 14.8 Mobility rates 1995–2000 by nativity and duration of residence, persons aged 25 and over, 2000 US Census (percent distribution)

		Foreign-born: arrival year				
Mobility status	*Native-born*	*1990–4*	*1985–9*	*1980–4*	*Before 1980*	*Total*[a]
Did not move house	59.37	36.03	44.77	53.13	67.79	55.30
Moved house but not state	32.39	52.14	46.25	39.06	26.27	36.81
Moved state	8.24	11.83	8.99	7.81	5.94	7.89
Total	100.00	100.00	100.00	100.00	100.00	100.00

(a) Total is for immigrant arrivals before 1995.

Source: 2000 US Census Public Use Microdata 1% Sample.

the five-year period (12.7 million native-born and 1.6 million foreign-born). In other words, there are about 11 million people aged 25 and over moving home intra-state each year, and close to 3 million people moving inter-state. The internal mobility within the United States is of a massive scale.

Analysis of the degree of mobility by arrival cohorts reveals an interesting pattern. The proportion of an arrival cohort that moved over the five-year period before the 2000 census decreases the longer the cohort has lived in the United States. Movers are 64 percent among immigrants who arrived in 1990–4, and 32 percent among immigrants who arrived before 1980.[9] The intra-state and inter-state mobility rates for the more recent group of arrivals (1990–4) are therefore about double the rates among the more established cohort that arrived before 1980. The mobility rates of the foreign-born who arrived around 1980 to 1984 and earlier closely resemble those of the native-born. In the language of the immigration assimilation literature, this implies immigrant "catch-up" after around 15 years, which is about the same as in studies of earnings.

Table 14.9 presents information on the state of residence in 2000 of the native-born who lived in the six major immigrant states and in all other states in 1995. Reading down the columns in Table 14.9 indicates where individuals living in each of the states in 1995 were living in 2000.[10] Consider the column for the residents of California in 1995: 92 percent of those who lived in California in 1995 also lived in California in 2000. The approximately 8 percent of 1995 residents of California (about 1.1 million people in the 25-years-and-over age group) who left the state dispersed over a wide range of states, although there are minor concentrations in Florida and Texas. The relatively high rate of movement out of New York and New

Table 14.9 State of residence in 2000 by state of residence in 1995, native-born persons aged 25 and over, 2000 US Census (percent distribution)[a]

State of residence in 2000	State of residence in 1995						
	California	Florida	Illinois	New Jersey	New York	Texas	Other states
California	92.21	0.53	0.61	0.38	0.58	0.58	0.61
Florida	0.36	90.82	0.82	1.50	1.78	0.39	0.77
Illinois	0.21	0.28	91.82	0.15	0.14	0.18	0.29
New Jersey	0.11	0.22	0.08	91.44	1.03	0.06	0.13
New York	0.25	0.48	0.15	1.00	91.28	0.12	0.25
Texas	0.61	0.44	0.41	0.22	0.20	93.74	0.56
Other states	6.26	7.22	6.10	5.31	4.99	4.92	97.39[b]
Total	100.00	100.00	100.00	100.00	100.00	100.00	100.00
% of foreign-born	9.22	5.20	4.43	2.83	6.03	6.67	65.61

(a) The foreign-born population is restricted to those who entered the United States before 1995.
(b) Of this group, 60 percent did not move house, 32 percent moved house but not state, and 8 percent moved state.

Source: 2000 US Census Public Use Microdata 1% Sample.

Jersey to Florida may simply be a post-retirement phenomenon. However, the major features of the gross flows between states for the native-born are the small variations in the percentage that remain within the state over the period 1995–2000, and the wide spread across states of those who move inter-state.

Table 14.10 presents data on the state of residence in 2000 of the foreign-born who lived in the United States in 1995. The proportion of immigrants who lived in either California or Florida in 1995 who did not move inter-state is greater than the corresponding figures for the native-born (see Table 14.9). This lower degree of inter-state mobility among the foreign-born does not, with the possible exception of Illinois, extend to the other states listed in the table. That is, not only do California and Florida have drawing power in terms of the location of new immigrants (see second section of chapter), but they also retain relatively more of their immigrants than other states. Moreover, California and Florida are more likely to be destinations for immigrants who move from other states than they are to be destinations for the native-born who move from other states.

The gross flow data for the foreign-born as in Table 14.10 can be analyzed separately by duration of residence in the United States. The analysis was done for those who arrived in the United States during the 1990–4 period, and those who arrived a decade earlier, 1980–4. These data show that among each arrival cohort, residents of California, Florida, and Texas are less likely than the residents of other states to move inter-state. They also show that the flows into California are slightly more pronounced among the groups of more recent arrivals (1990–4) than among the immigrants who have resided longer in the United States (1980–4).

Table 14.10 State of residence in 2000 by state of residence in 1995, foreign-born persons aged 25 and over, 2000 US Census (percent distribution)[a]

State of residence in 2000	State of residence in 1995						
	California	Florida	Illinois	New Jersey	New York	Texas	Other states
California	94.99	0.71	1.20	0.89	0.66	0.84	1.96
Florida	0.28	94.26	0.74	2.03	1.77	0.42	1.12
Illinois	0.20	0.17	93.26	0.20	0.15	0.27	0.49
New Jersey	0.12	0.37	0.08	91.61	1.74	0.13	0.45
New York	0.17	0.43	0.25	1.34	91.68	0.25	0.60
Texas	0.46	0.64	0.62	0.35	0.28	94.09	1.07
Other states	3.79	3.42	3.86	3.59	3.72	4.00	94.31[b]
Total	100.00	100.00	100.00	100.00	100.00	100.00	100.00
% of foreign-born	30.98	8.70	4.90	4.91	13.95	8.65	27.92

(a) The foreign-born population is restricted to those who entered the United States before 1995.
(b) Of this group, 54 percent did not move house, 34 percent moved house but not state, and 12 percent moved state.

Source: 2000 US Census Public Use Microdata 1% Sample.

Table 14.11 Lived in the same state in 1995 and 2000, adult native-born and adult foreign-born persons who arrived in the United States in 1990 to 1994, 2000 US Census (percent distribution)

| State | Native-born | Foreign-born | | |
		Speak only English	Speak Spanish	Speak another language
California	94.1	89.6	91.9	94.1
Florida	86.3	88.8	93.2	91.3
Illinois	94.3	91.3	93.1	89.0
New Jersey	93.5	79.3	89.2	89.3
New York	95.6	89.7	91	87.9
Texas	92.9	85.7	93.8	87.7
Other states	97.0	89.5	94.5	90.1

Source: 2000 US Census Public Use Microdata 1% Sample.

Table 14.11 reports for the adult native-born and for the adult foreign-born (by language group) who arrived in the United States between 1990 and 1994 the extent to which they lived in the same state in 1995 and 2000. The native-born showed the least mobility. Among the foreign-born those who spoke only English at home were least likely to be living in the same state, while those who reported that they spoke Spanish at home were most likely to do so. Apparently, the absence of proficiency in English inhibits inter-state mobility.

Summary and Discussion

This chapter uses data from the 2000 Census of Population of the United States to explore the residential patterns in 2000 and the internal mobility from 1995 to 2000 of the foreign-born or immigrant population.

The foreign-born are far more geographically concentrated than are the native-born. The "Big Six" immigrant-receiving states – California, Texas, Florida, New York, New Jersey, and Illinois – accounted for 69 percent of the foreign-born population (with 29 percent of the foreign-born living in California) in 2000, but only 35 percent of the native-born. Among the foreign-born who speak only English at home, 61 percent live in the Big Six, in contrast to 76 percent for those who speak Spanish at home, and 63 percent for immigrants who speak other languages. Thus, Spanish speakers are even more highly concentrated than immigrants with other linguistic practices at home.

The concentration in these six states was somewhat less intense in 2000 than it was in 1990 (73 percent in 1990 in contrast to 69 percent in 2000), with the concentration decreasing slightly in California, New York, and New Jersey, but increasing slightly in Texas and Florida. This appears to be due to a smaller degree of geographic concentration among the post-1990 cohorts of immigrants.

The geographic concentration of immigrants in 2000 varied by country of birth. Those from the British Isles and Canada were the least concentrated in these six states, while Mexican, Caribbean, and other Latin American immigrants were the most intensely concentrated in these states. Among the foreign-born from Canada, only 44 percent lived in the Big Six immigrant-receiving states. Among Mexican immigrants in 2000, 43 percent lived in California, 21 percent in Texas, and 7 percent in Illinois, with only 5 percent in total in Florida, New York, and New Jersey, for a total of 74 percent.

Analyzing data on state of residence in 1995 and 2000 for the same individuals provides insights on internal mobility over this five-year period. Overall, mobility propensities did not differ by nativity. Among the adult foreign-born, 35 percent moved within their state and 8 percent moved inter-state, in contrast to 32 percent and 8 percent, respectively, for the native-born. However, propensities for internal mobility among the foreign-born decrease with duration of residence in the United States and reach the native-born level after about 15 years. Immigrants in California and Florida were less likely to move out of these states than were the native-born. These states were also more likely to be destinations for immigrants living in other states in 1995 than was the case for the native-born. The foreign-born who speak only English at home were most likely to move inter-state between 1995 and 2000, while those who speak Spanish at home were the least likely to move.

Thus, the foreign-born in the United States in 2000 were highly geographically concentrated, although somewhat less so than in 1990. There was a high degree of internal mobility among the foreign-born, with this mobility decreasing with duration of residence in the United States and being highest for those who speak English at home. California and Florida were particularly successful in retaining their foreign-born populations and attracting the foreign-born from elsewhere in the United States.

The work reported in this chapter draws attention to several key issues requiring further research. First, there is a need for further summary information, using detailed geographic data, on the way that geographic concentration varies across groups of immigrants defined with respect to country of origin, level of education, duration of residence, ethnicity, and gender. Such summary information can be obtained using the indices developed by economists, sociologists, and geographers to measure such diverse issues as occupational segregation and industrial concentration. This work has the potential to show the nature of the links that bind immigrants together and lead to the formation of concentrations of individuals from the same birthplace, ethnic group, or language group in distinct locations.

Second, much of the detailed behavioral modeling of immigrant residential location and mobility (e.g. Bartel 1989) has been based on 1980 census data. This work yielded many key findings, including the finding that the percentage of the particular ethnic population that resides in a given location was the most important determinant of the location choice of immigrants. There is a clear need to update this work, and to explore additional behavioral determinants of location choice: for example, the language used at home by the immigrants. Moreover, Bartel (1989) did not address why some areas have virtually no members of particular ethnic groups that are well represented elsewhere. This is clearly important in terms of establishing the likely demands on local services as a result of immigrant location decisions.

Third, additional research is needed into the factors that give rise to the considerable inter-state and intra-state mobility documented above. In conducting this type of work there needs to be a greater emphasis on family characteristics than there has been in the research to date. In other words, rather than having the individual as the unit of analysis, the unit of analysis could be the family unit. Are large families more likely to move than small families? Are families with young children more likely to move than childless families, or families with only older children? Does it matter for internal mobility if there is more than one labor-force participant in the family? Do these characteristics of mobility patterns across family units vary according to country of birth, duration of residence in the United States, citizenship, ethnicity, and language background?

This research should also analyze whether the ethnic characteristics of the region are important to understanding internal mobility. This theme has been a major focus in recent research on immigrant assimilation (see, for example, Chiswick and Miller 2005; Lazear 1999). Hence, the research on internal mobility could study the movements of people into and out of communities according to the match between the characteristics of the individual and the characteristics of the community. For example, do Hispanics move to areas of Hispanic concentration? Do individuals who are not Hispanic tend to move out of areas of growing Hispanic concentration?

Immigrant residential location and mobility patterns are important behavioral phenomena that are helping shape the character of America's cities. Pursuing these research themes will help us to understand the composition of the cities in which we live.

NOTES

We thank Derby Voon for research assistance. Barry Chiswick acknowledges research support from the Institute of Government and Public Affairs, University of Illinois. Paul Miller acknowledges financial assistance from the Australian Research Council.

1   For economic analyses of the location choice of immigrants see Bartel 1989; Chiswick, Lee, and Miller 2001; Funkhouser 2000; Zavodny 1999.

2   "Ethnic goods" are market and non-market goods and services consumed by members of an immigrant or ethnic group that are not consumed, or not consumed in the same manner or to the same extent, by members of other groups. These include ethnic churches and marriage markets, as well as food, clothing, and festivals specific to immigrant or ethnic groups. For an application of this concept, see Chiswick and Miller 2005.

3   For the purpose of this study the native-born are those born in one of the 50 states or the District of Columbia. The foreign-born are those born in a foreign country and whose parents were not Americans (US citizens) at the time of their birth. Persons born in a territory or "outlying area" of the United States (e.g. Puerto Rico or the US Virgin Islands), those born abroad of American parents, and those born at sea are considered neither native nor foreign-born and are excluded from this analysis.

4   These states also account for 70 percent of native-born Spanish speakers. Both New York and California have relatively high proportions of the native-born who speak languages other than English or Spanish at home.

5   The main turning point in the countries of origin of immigrants is the Immigration and Nationality Act of 1965, which abolished discriminatory "national origins" restrictions on migration, particularly from Asia (see Chiswick and Sullivan 1995).

6   This corresponds to the time period at which immigrants typically catch up with the native-born in terms of their earnings in cross-sectional studies. See, for example, Chiswick's (1978) study of this earnings "cross-over" concept.

7 This was the one and only census to ask occupation, in addition to the standard question on current occupation.

8 The census provides information on the state of residence in 2000 for all people, identifies people who lived in the same house in 1995 and 2000 (non-movers), the state of residence in 1995 for those who did not live in the same house in 1995 and 2000 (movers). Intra-state and inter-state mobility are determined through comparison of the state of residence of movers in 1995 and 2000.

9 It is instructive to consider the numbers of people involved in these moves. Data in Table 14.9 data indicate that of the 3.6 million recent (1990–4) arrivals aged 25 and over, 1.9 million moved intra-state and 0.4 million moved inter-state over the period 1995–2000.

10 The greater percentage of non-movers in the final column for the "Other" group of states should be recognized as a result of the level of aggregation in these data. As outlined in the notes to the tables, inter-state mobility for this "Other" group is comparable to that for the states separately identified in the table for the native-born, and slightly greater than that for the states separately identified for the foreign-born.

REFERENCES

Bartel, Ann P. (1989). "Where Do the New U.S. Immigrants Live?" *Journal of Labor Economics* 7(4): 371–91.

Bartel, Ann P. and M.J. Koch (1991). "Internal Migration of U.S. Immigrants." In John. M. Abowd and Richard B. Freeman, eds., *Immigration, Trade and the Labor Market*. Chicago: University of Chicago Press, pp.121–34.

Case, A.C. and L.F. Katz (1991). "The Company You Keep: The Effects of Family and Neighborhood on Disadvantaged Youths." Harvard Institute of Economic Research, Discussion Paper No. 1555.

Chiswick, Barry R. (1977). "A Longitudinal Analysis of the Occupational Mobility of Immigrants." In Barbara D. Dennis, ed., *Proceedings of the 30th Annual Winter Meetings*. Madison: Industrial Relations Research Association, pp. 20–7.

—— (1978). "The Effect of Americanization on the Earnings of Foreign-Born Men." *Journal of Political Economy* 86(5): 897–922.

—— (1980). *An Analysis of the Economic Progress and Impact of Immigrants*. Department of Labor Monograph, NTIS No. PB80–200454. Washington, DC: National Technical Information Service.

—— (1982). *The Employment of Immigration in the United States*. Washington, DC: American Enterprise Institute, pp. 289–313.

Chiswick, Barry R. and Paul W. Miller (1995). "The Endogeneity Between Language and Earnings: An International Analysis." *Journal of Labor Economics* 13(2): 246–88.

—— (1996). "The Languages of the United States: Who Speaks What and What it Means." *READ Perspectives* 3(2): 5–41.

—— (2003). "Issue Paper on the Impact of Immigration for Housing." In Jennifer Johnson and Jessica Cigna, eds., *Issue Papers on Demographic Trends Important for Housing*. Office of Policy Research and Development, US Department of Housing and Urban Development (February), pp. 1–78. (http://www.huduser.org/publications/econdev/demographic_trends.html)

—— (2005). "Do Enclaves Matter in Immigrant Adjustment?" *City and Community* 4(1): 5–36.

Chiswick, Barry R. and Teresa Sullivan (1995). "The New Immigrants." In Reynolds Farley, ed., *State of the Union 2, Social Trends*. New York: Russell Sage Foundation, pp. 211–70.

Chiswick, Barry R., Yew Liang Lee, and Paul W. Miller (2001). "The Determinants of the Geographical Concentration Among Immigrants in Australia." *Australasian Journal of Regional Studies* 7(2): 125–50.

Funkhouser, Edward (2000). "Changes in the Geographic Concentration and Location of Residence of Immigrants." *International Migration Review* 34(2): 480–510.

Goddard, R.F., L.H. Sparkes, and J.A. Haydon (1985). "Demographic Consequences of Immigration." In Neville R. Norman and Kathryn F. Meikle, eds., *The Economic Effects of Immigration on Australia*. Melbourne: Committee for Economic Development of Australia, pp. 47–161.

Lazear, Edward P. (1999). "Culture and Language." *Journal of Political Economy* 107(6, part 2): S95–S126.

Le, Ahn T. (1999). "Empirical Studies of Self Employment." *Journal of Economic Surveys* 13(4): 381–416.

Massey, Douglas (1981). "Dimensions of the New Immigration to the United States and the Prospects for Assimilation." *Annual Review of Sociology* 7: 57–85.

Thernstrom, Stephan (1973). *The Other Bostonians: Poverty and Progress in the American Metropolis, 1880–1970*. Cambridge, MA: Harvard University Press.

Veltman, C. (1983). *Language Shift in the United States*. Berlin: Moulton.

Ward, David (1971). *Cities and Immigrants: A Geography of Change in Nineteenth Century America*. New York: Oxford University Press.

Zavodny, Madeline (1999). "Determinants of Recent Immigrants' Locational Choices." *International Migration Review* 33(4): 1014–30.

Zunz, Olivier (1982). *The Changing Face of Inequality: Industrial Development and Immigrants in Detroit, 1880–1920*. Chicago: University of Chicago Press.

CHAPTER FIFTEEN

Characteristics of Immigrants to the United States: 1820–2003

GUILLERMINA JASSO AND MARK R. ROSENZWEIG

As the great American experiment unfolds, curiosity grows about the persons who in successive centuries have built the country. Most came from someplace else – some eager, some in chains, some in between. They thought they were building new lives, chosen or not. But they were building the first new nation. By a strange alchemy that Adam Smith had explored and that turned classical ideas upside down, building a country was what they did, when they built their lives.

There is much we would like to know about them, much we wish we could ask them. Most did not realize how momentous would be the product of their daily lives.

In this chapter we consider a part of the story, the part involving immigrants to the United States. The two other great parts, involving Native Americans and the great slave migration, must unfortunately remain outside our purview.

Who came? And why? What did they bring with them, besides that ineffable and peculiar migrant energy? What happened when they were thrown with many others like themselves? What laws and norms were they abandoning? And which were they embracing, or inventing? Who stayed? And who left? What were the trajectories of religion and language, not to mention schooling and earnings?

This territory, of course, has received rich and abundant treatment. Our approach in this chapter is to highlight some of the personal characteristics and some aspects of the legal environment which from the vantage point of the models and frameworks developed in social science appear important. Accordingly, we specify four immigration eras, starting with the Pre-Restriction Era which ended in 1875, and culminating in the Era of Both Qualitative and Quantitative Restrictions on Both Hemispheres which has characterized US immigration since 1965. And we contrast a variety of characteristics, such as origin country, mother tongue, and literacy and schooling, across the period. Immigration statistics date to 1820, and thus our examination begins in 1820. For the contemporary period, we draw on the new data collected by the New Immigrant Survey (NIS), which provides extensive information on characteristics of immigrants.

As will be discussed, many of the important immigration questions cannot be answered without microdata based on probability samples of cohorts of new immigrants. Like other scholars who have examined historical data (for example, Carter and Sutch 1998), we are struck by the possibilities for rich new research, inclusive of constructing data sets based on probability samples drawn from historical cohorts, to simulate the NIS data.

The chapter is organized as follows: section 1 summarizes the major questions, models, and frameworks in the social scientific study of migration. In section 2 we review the major legislation shaping immigration to the United States, focusing on four major immigration eras. Section 3 turns to the data sources available for empirical research on US immigration, distinguishing between data sources with three differing levels of specificity and including a brief description of the New Immigrant Survey which will provide longitudinal data on probability samples of new legal immigrants from selected cohorts (starting with the cohort of 2003). Section 4 describes and discusses 16 characteristics of US immigrants, ranging from origin country, sex ratio, and race to language, religion, and financial resources. A short note concludes the chapter, the theme of which concerns the possibility of constructing new longitudinal microdata sets based on probability samples drawn from historical cohorts of new immigrants.

1 Questions, Models, and Frameworks

In the study of migration there are four central questions. These are:

1 What are the migrant's characteristics and behavior at entry?
2 How do the migrant's characteristics and behavior change with time in the destination country?
3 What are the characteristics and behavior of the children of immigrants?
4 What are the impacts on the origin and destination countries?

For example, questions about the characteristics of immigrants at entry and the forces of selectivity, such as whether immigrants are selected from among higher-skilled or lower-skilled or whether there is change in immigrant quality across cohorts (Barrett 1996; Borjas 1985; Carter and Sutch 1998; Cobb-Clark 1993; Jasso, Rosenzweig, and Smith 2000; Loaeza Tovar, Planck, Gómez Arnau, Martin, Lowell, and Meyers 1997; Smith and Edmonston 1997) exemplify the first central question. Similarly, questions about what happens to immigrants post-immigration – discussed variously as assimilation, acculturation, adaptation, integration, incorporation, convergence, etc., and encompassing broad domains from employment and earnings to health and fertility to language, religion, and identity – exemplify the second central question (Loaeza Tovar, Planck, Gómez Arnau, Martin, Lowell, and Meyers 1997; Smith and Edmonston 1997). All questions concerning immigrant children and the children of immigrants, including questions about their initial characteristics as well as their progress over time, obviously fall under the third central question (Committee on the Health and Safety Implications of Child Labor 1998; Hernandez and Charney 1998; Portes and Rumbaut 2001). And, finally, questions about the impacts of immigration seek to assess impacts of various kinds on both individuals and societies in both origin and destination countries; examples include questions about remittances, the "brain drain," prices of consumer goods, and artistic excellence (Loaeza Tovar, Planck, Gómez Arnau, Martin, Lowell, and Meyers 1997; Smith and Edmonston 1997).

Of course, the four central questions are interrelated, and many studies address more than one of them; for example, studies comparing the skills of immigrants by their class of admission (the provision of US immigration law which made them eligible for an immigrant visa) may both compare skills at entry and also compare skill trajectories over time (Duleep and Regets 1996; Jasso and Rosenzweig 1995; Jasso, Rosenzweig, and Smith 2000).[1]

As even the foregoing abbreviated look at the four central questions suggests, there are three fundamental actors in the study of migration: the migrant, who is usually thought of as the chief protagonist; others at the place of origin; and others at the place of destination. All three kinds of actors make pertinent decisions, play parts in migration processes, and experience migration impacts. Moreover, migration involves special relations between different kinds of actors. For example, consider the relation between migrant and others at origin – others may force or, alternatively, make possible the migration; and the migrant may, in turn, provide financial assistance and information, leading to diffusion of ideas and practices from the migrant's destination. Similarly, consider the relation between migrant and others at destination – migration may originate with, or be made possible by, actions of others at destination, who act as sponsors of desired workers or spouses; and more distant others at destination may experience a variety of gains and losses as workers, consumers, owners of capital, taxpayers, artists, and biological beings with healthiness to develop and protect.

Migration analysis encompasses the totality of immigrant and societal characteristics, and thus the quantities of interest span broad topical domains, including not only migration-centered phenomena – such as emigration and naturalization – but also phenomena from the larger sociobehavioral world – such as language acquisition, identity formation, skill prices and skill transferability, religion, and so on. As well, the quantities of interest span varying levels of generality, from the characteristics of individual immigrants to the social, economic, and political characteristics of both origin and destination countries, including, importantly, their laws on exit and entry.

Reasoning about the central questions leads quickly to specification of relations between basic quantities and thus to basic overarching models that embed several relations.

For example, the first central question focuses on the selection of immigrants and their characteristics at entry – how a given individual becomes a migrant, moving from origin to destination. Understanding the selection of immigrants requires understanding the decision to migrate, in the context of social, economic, and political conditions in both origin and destination countries, including laws governing exit and entry. Models that have been advanced suggest that the underlying behavioral principle may be, as the Romans put it, "ubi bene, ibi patria" – where one is well-off, there is one's country. The prospective migrant compares his or her expected well-being in the two locales. Both the decision to migrate and the strategy for achieving migration are shaped by both the migrant's own characteristics and conditions in the origin and destination areas, together with the migrant's information about them. The basic models quickly become complicated when the migrant is modeled with a family; for example, not all family members may gain from migration, and, alternatively, an adult migrant's decision may be based on the expected well-being of his or her children.

Similarly, reasoning about the second central question not only suggests the continuing operation of both the migrant's characteristics and conditions in the origin and destination countries, but also introduces a dynamic element. An important new conceptual tool is the trajectory, for example, the skill trajectory, earnings trajectory, health trajectory, language trajectory, religion trajectory, and so on.[2]

2 Legislation Pertaining to Immigration and Naturalizaiton

From the start of the Republic, the federal government assumed the right to regulate citizenship and naturalization. It was not clear, however, whether responsibility for regulating immigration belonged to the states or to the federal government. That is, it was not clear whether immigration was included under "foreign commerce," which Article I, Section 8 of the Constitution gave Congress the power to regulate. Thus, although Congress passed legislation covering vessel reporting requirements and passenger safeguards (the Steerage Act of 1819 and the Passenger Acts of 1847 and 1855), the issue was not resolved until 1875 when the Supreme Court (*Henderson v. City of New York*) ruled that regulation of immigration is a federal power under the foreign commerce clause and declared state restrictions on immigration unconstitutional.

Legislation on Citizenship and Naturalization

The first immigration era – before 1875 – may be called the Pre-Restriction Era because immigration was largely unrestricted (Table 15.1). Naturalization, however, was not unrestricted. The Naturalization Act of 1790 limited naturalization to "free

Table 15.1 Major US legislation pertaining to criteria for immigration and naturalization: 1789–2005

Legislation	Date	Major provision(s)
A. Pre-Restriction Era (1789–1874)		
Naturalization Act	1790	Limits naturalization to "free white persons"; requires two-year residence in US
Santo Domingo Refugee Act	1794	Provides relief for Santo Domingo refugees
Naturalization Act	1795	Requires five-year residence in US for naturalization
Alien and Sedition Acts	1798	Empowers President to deport aliens considered dangerous to US
Naturalization Act	1798	Requires 14-year residence in US for naturalization
Act of April 14, 1802	1802	Restores naturalization provisions of 1795 Act
Steerage Act of March 2, 1819	1819	Establishes vessel reporting requirements and passenger safeguards
Passenger Act of February 22, 1847	1847	Revises passenger safeguards
Act of February 10, 1855	1855	Grants citizenship to alien women who marry a US citizen or whose husbands naturalize, regardless of place of residence

Table 15.1   (*cont'd*)

Legislation	Date	Major provision(s)
Passenger Act of March 3, 1855	1855	Repeals earlier Passenger Acts, codifying reporting requirements and passenger safeguards
Act of April 9, 1866	1866	Extends citizenship to US-born children of aliens ineligible to naturalize
Nationality Act	1870	Extends naturalization to "aliens of African nativity and to persons of African descent"

B. Era of Qualitative Restrictions (1875–1920)

Immigration Act	1875	Bars prostitutes and convicts
Chinese Exclusion Act	1882	Bars Chinese laborers; prohibits naturalization of Chinese persons
Immigration Act	1882	Increases list of inadmissibles and imposes head tax
Alien Contract Labor Law	1885	Bars importation of contract labor
First Deportation Law	1888	Authorizes deportation of contract laborers
Immigration Act	1891	Increases list of inadmissibles; authorizes deportation of illegal aliens
Immigration Act	1903	Increases list of inadmissibles
Basic Naturalization Act	1906	Requires knowledge of English for naturalization
Immigration Act	1907	Increases list of inadmissibles (including unaccompanied children under 16)
[Gentlemen's Agreement]	1907	Restricts Japanese immigration
Immigration Act	1917	Increases and codifies list of inadmissibles; requires literacy for those over 16; bars Asia–Pacific Triangle aliens

C. Era of Qualitative Restrictions Plus Quantitative Restrictions on Eastern Hemisphere (1921–64)

First Quota Law	1921	Limits immigration to 3% of national origin of 1910 foreign-born: 357,000
Married Women's Act	1922	Gives women their own nationality, independent of their husband's
National Origins Act	1924	Limits immigration to 2% of national origin of 1890 foreign-born: 164,000. In 1929, shifts quota formula to reflect national origin of white US population in 1920: 154,000. Bars from immigration aliens ineligible for citizenship. Defines "immigrant" and establishes new class of "nonimmigrant"
Philippine Independence Act	1934	Limits Filipino immigration to 50
Nationality Act	1940	Extends naturalization of military personnel regardless of race
Act of October 14, 1940	1940	Permits indigenous races of WH to naturalize

Table 15.1   (cont'd)

Legislation	Date	Major provision(s)
Act of December 17, 1943	1943	Extends naturalization to Chinese persons and persons of Chinese descent
War Brides Act	1946	Facilitates immigration of spouses and children of military personnel
Act of July 2, 1948	1948	Extends naturalization to Filipino persons or persons of Filipino descent and to persons of races indigenous to India
Internal Security Act	1950	Increases grounds for exclusion
Immigration & Nationality Act	1952	Establishes preference category system; retains national origins quotas; total about 154,000 plus 2,000 from Asia–Pacific Triangle; eliminates all racial and gender bars to naturalization

D. Era of Both Qualitative and Quantitative Restrictions on Both Hemispheres (1965–)

Immigration Act	1965	Abolishes national origins quotas; for EH, establishes uniform per country limit of 20,000 and preference-category system with overall ceiling of 170,000; for WH, effective 1968, places overall ceiling of 120,000
Immigration & Nationality Act	1976	Extends per country limit and preference-category system to WH
Act of October 12, 1976	1976	Places restrictions on foreign medical graduates coming to the United States for practice or training in the medical profession
Worldwide Ceiling Law	1978	Brings both hemispheres under single worldwide ceiling of 290,000
Refugee Act of 1980	1980	Reduces worldwide ceiling to 270,000
Immigration Reform and Control Act	1986	Grants conditional legalization to certain aliens resident in the US; imposes employer sanctions
Immigration Marriage Fraud Amendments	1986	Aliens deriving immigrant status based on a marriage of less than two years are conditional immigrants; conditionality may be removed upon application within 90 days of two-year anniversary of admission to conditional status
Immigration Act	1990	Restructures numerical ceilings and preference category system; establishes lottery-based Diversity Visa Program; revises and recodifies the 32 grounds for exclusion into nine categories
Illegal Immigration Reform and Responsibility Act	1996	Tightens requirements for affidavit of support for sponsored immigrants and makes contract legally binding; recodifies grounds for exclusion into grounds for inadmissibility

Note: For further information on immigration and naturalization legislation, see the USCIS website (www.uscis.gov).

white persons," a class excluding nonwhites, indentured servants, and married women. Thus, there were two kinds of immigrants in the United States – those eligible to naturalize and those not. Accordingly, there would be three kinds of legislative activity, pertaining, respectively, to: (1) definition of the class of aliens ineligible to naturalize; (2) the citizenship status of children of aliens ineligible to naturalize; and (3) the immigration prospects of aliens ineligible to naturalize.

In establishing the class of aliens ineligible to naturalize, Congress noticed three personal characteristics – race, sex, and marital status.

Race and naturalization

With respect to race, the Civil War and the Fourteenth Amendment paved the way for the 1870 Nationality Act, which extended naturalization to "aliens of African nativity and to persons of African descent." And in 1940, naturalization was extended to persons of indigenous Western Hemisphere races. Meanwhile, the Chinese Exclusion Act of 1882 explicitly barred the naturalization of Chinese persons.

During the long period of racial bars to naturalization, a major concern had been how to define "white" – a concern which prompted such colorful highlights as a 1909 query whether "Jesus of Nazareth himself" would be denied naturalization, and an INS circular in 1937 stipulating that Mexicans were considered white for purposes of immigration and naturalization (Smith 2002).

But the days of racial bars to naturalization were numbered. Since World War I, there had been a tradition of naturalizing military personnel regardless of their race. Legislation in 1940 codified the practice. It was quickly followed by repeal of the bars to Chinese naturalization (1943), extension of naturalization privileges to persons of Filipino birth or descent and persons of races indigenous to India (1948), and, finally, in 1952, repeal of all racial bars to naturalization.

As for the US-born children of aliens ineligible to naturalize, legislation in 1866 extended citizenship to them, regardless of race. The *jus soli* of US nationality law trumped race.

Finally, the two legislative strands covering immigration and naturalization had converged in 1924, when the National Origins Act stipulated that aliens ineligible to naturalize would not be permitted to become immigrants. Termination of racial bars to naturalization in 1952 terminated racial bars to immigration.

Gender, marital status, and naturalization

All males were subject to the laws governing citizenship and naturalization. Women, however, were a class apart, with special rules depending on their marital status – rules, moreover, which appear to have varied considerably and been interpreted (and implemented) diversely (Smith 1998). The Nationality Act of 1790 had restricted naturalization to "free white persons," and soon married women had come to be considered unfree and thus either barred from naturalization or granted citizenship as the spouse of a naturalizing husband. Indeed, legislation enacted in 1855 granted citizenship to alien women who married a US citizen or whose alien husband naturalized, regardless of the wife's place of residence. Thus, a foreign-born wife might enter the United States for the first time as a citizen.

Women's suffrage and passage of the 19th Amendment to the Constitution led to unforeseen consequences which doomed the intertwining of women's and men's nationality. Specifically, now that the wife of a naturalizing alien could vote, the wife's characteristics (such as her knowledge of English) were noticed when her husband applied to naturalize, sometimes destroying his chances. The Married Women's Act of 1922 put an end to the link between gender, marriage, and nationality (except for minor procedural issues), and henceforth alien women applied to naturalize and naturalized on their own.[3]

Legislation on Immigration

For almost a century, immigration to the young country had been unrestricted. The year 1875 marked the start of the second immigration era, which may be called the Era of Qualitative Restrictions (Table 15.1, part B), the period when there were no numerical limitations on immigration, only a growing set of exclusion criteria based on personal characteristics or behavior. Prostitutes and convicts were the first to be barred as undesirable immigrants (1875). Next, the Chinese Exclusion Act of May 6, 1882 suspended the immigration of Chinese laborers. Within three months, the Immigration Act of August 3, 1882 established the first financial test, declaring inadmissible anyone likely to become a public charge and imposing a head tax of 50 cents per passenger. The list of inadmissibles would continue to grow – persons with certain contagious diseases, further classes of convicts, polygamists (1891); anarchists and persons advocating overthrow of the government of the United Sates (1903); persons with mental or physical handicaps and unaccompanied children under 16 (1970); and on and on. The high-water mark of the Era of Qualitative Restriction came in 1917 with passage of legislation which imposed a literacy test on adult immigrants (albeit with waivers for the illiterate wives of literate immigrants), and barred persons from the Asia–Pacific Triangle zone.[4]

Though the list of inadmissibles would continue to grow – and to shrink from time to time, as with repeal of homosexuality as a ground for exclusion (1990) – so that today there are nine broad categories of grounds for inadmissiblity, after 1917 the qualitative restrictions would be joined by quantitative restrictions, at least on natives of one hemisphere.

The link between immigration and naturalization remains, codified in the grounds for inadmissibility: "Any immigrant who is permanently ineligible to citizenship is inadmissible" (Section 212(a)8(A) of the Immigration and Nationality Act).

Purely qualitative restrictions based on personal characteristics and behavior proved insufficient to quell the discontent with an open immigration policy. The third immigration era, the Era of Qualitative Restrictions Plus Quantitative Restrictions on the Eastern Hemisphere (Table 15.1, part C), was inaugurated with passage of the Quota Law of May 19, 1921, also known as the First Quota Law and the Emergency Quota Act. The 1921 act limited the number of immigrants of any Eastern Hemisphere nationality to 3 percent of the foreign-born of that nationality residing in the United States in 1910, for a total of 357,000; the law exempt persons who had resided in a Western Hemisphere country continuously for at least one year. Within a year, the act of May 11, 1922 extended the 1921 law for two years and increased to five years the period of Western Hemisphere residence necessary for a waiver. The 1922 act was followed by the Immigration Act of May 26, 1924, also known as the National Origins Act, which provided for a transition quota system to be followed by a permanent system with a quota of 154,000 reflecting the national origins of the white US population in 1920. Provision was made for the unlimited immigration of wives and minor children of US citizens and for preferences within the quotas for close relatives and highly skilled individuals. As well, immigration from the Western Hemisphere remained numerically unlimited.

World War II brought with it repeal of the anti-Chinese immigration provisions, for China was a wartime ally and, after the war, a series of laws to permit immigration of refugees and of spouses and children of military personnel, as well as new security legislation. These and all existing laws were consolidated into a comprehensive new Immigration and Nationality Act, which was passed on June 27, 1952, over the veto of President Harry S. Truman. The new act retained the national origins quotas but established a new preference category system; it also eliminated all gender bias in immigration.

The Immigration and Nationality Act of 1952 was the culmination of the third immigration era. But it aroused profound discontent. President Truman quickly appointed a Commission on Immigration and Naturalization. Its report, titled *Whom We Shall Welcome*, after a memorable phrase of George Washington, was issued in January 1953. It featured a stirring Introduction which argued that the act of 1952 "fails to embody principles worthy of this country" (p. xi) and concluded "that our present immigration law should be completely rewritten" (p. xv).

The rewriting would come, but not for 13 years and not without a large price: placing numerical limitations on immigration from the Western Hemisphere. The Immigration Act of 1965 ushered in the fourth immigration era – the Era of Both Qualitative and Quantitative Restrictions on Both Hemispheres (Table 15.1, part D).

The 1965 Act established a two-tiered immigration system, in broad brush a numerically unlimited tier for the immediate relatives of US citizens, and a numerically limited tier of visas for other relatives and employment-based immigrants allocated via preference categories. The preference category system was initially applied only to the Eastern Hemisphere but was extended to the Western Hemisphere in 1976. Meanwhile, the 1965 Act had assigned separate ceilings for the numerically limited visas in the two hemispheres (170,000 for the Eastern Hemisphere, 120,000 for the Western Hemisphere), but the Worldwide Ceiling Law of 1978 brought both hemispheres under a single worldwide ceiling of 290,000, a ceiling subsequently reduced to 270,000 when the Refugee Act of 1980 set up separate mechanisms for the admission of refugees.

The preference category system for allocating numerically limited visas was restructured by the Immigration Act of 1990, effective in fiscal year (FY) 1992. The new system provides separate ceilings and preference categories for family-based and employment-based visas. The number of visas available annually in the family preference categories is at least 226,000, but may be larger (though never larger than 480,000) depending on the previous year's volume of numerically-unrestricted immigration); in the employment-based categories, the annual number of visas available is at least 140,000, but may be larger if there are unused family preference visas).[5]

Additionally, US immigration law provides for immigration on humanitarian and diversity grounds. On humanitarian grounds, persons admitted to the United States with refugee visas or given asylee status (both refugee and asylee visas are temporary "nonimmigrant" visas) may adjust to legal permanent residence after residing in the United States for one year. There is no ceiling on refugee adjustments to permanent residence, and the number has ranged in recent years from a low of 39,495 in FY 1999 to 118,528 in FY 1996; in contrast, asylee adjustments are constrained to 10,000 per year. On diversity grounds, the United States grants 50,000 visas annually to nationals of countries from which the number of numerically-limited immigrants is less than 50,000 in the preceding five years. Eligibility requirements include a high school degree or equivalent, or two years' work experience (within the preceding five years) in an occupation requiring two years of training or experience; selection is by lottery.[6]

Table 15.2 summarizes visa allocation law in the third and fourth immigration eras, providing information on numerically limited and unlimited categories, preference categories for family- and employment-based visas, and numerical ceilings.

3 Data for Studying Migration

Studying migration empirically presents formidable data challenges. To appreciate these, consider the following aspects of migration: (1) There may be important differences across entering cohorts of new legal immigrants – reflecting both changes in the United States and its immigration laws and also changes in countries around the world (including natural disasters and political upheavals). (2) Assimilation occurs over time. (3) Immigrants leave, and entering cohorts are thinned over time by nonrandom emigration. (4) Both migration and assimilation behaviors are shaped by individual and family characteristics and responsive to conditions in both countries, including the legal environment faced by the migrant. Together, these features dictate the data requirements.

In brief, the data should consist of probability samples drawn periodically from entering cohorts of immigrants of identifiable legal status – of identifiable legal status so that the context and the environment they face may be correctly characterized; of entering cohorts so that they can be examined before the nonrandom emigration begins; and of multiple cohorts because conditions change in both origin and destination countries. The design should be longitudinal (not only to study assimilation but also to distinguish between effects associated with year of immigration and effects associated with length of time in the United States). Information should be obtained both from the sampled individual and from or about all other persons in the household and the (extended) family, including persons living abroad and new members added over time. Finally, the information collected should cover pre-migration experience and include complete retrospective and prospective histories of schooling, work, migration (including legal status), sponsorship, and health, and of linguistic, marital, and reproductive behaviors.

In principle, the earlier in the migration process the migrants enter the study the better. For example, one can envision a sampling design in which a random sample is drawn from among all first-time entrants to the United States. Such a set would include not only legal immigrants but also a variety of temporary nonimmigrants (students, diplomats, temporary workers, etc.). Following them over time, one would observe the process by which some among them decide to seek permanent residence in the United States, as well as the process by which some among them become illegal (by overstaying a temporary visa or by violating the terms of their visa, say, by

Table 15.2 Summary of US law governing immigrant visa allocation since 1924, by nativity and kinship ties to US citizens and residents

Visas Hemisphere	1924–1952 EH	1924–1952 WH	1952–1965/68 EH	1952–1965/68 WH	1965/68–1977 EH	1965/68–1977 WH	1977–1992 Worldwide	1992– Worldwide
Kin of US Citizen								
Husband	U|1P	U, NS	U	U, NS	U	U	U	U
Wife	U	U, NS	U	U, NS	U	U	U	U
Parent	1P	U, NS	2P	U, NS	U	U	U	U
Minor child	U	U	U	U	U	U	U	U
Adult unmarried child	NP	U, NS	4P/2P	U, NS	1P	L, NS	1P	F-1P
Adult married child	NP	U, NS	4P	U, NS	4P	L, NS	4P	F-3P
Sibling	NP	U, NS	4P	U, NS	5P	L, NS	5P	F-4P
Kin of US permanent resident alien								
Husband	NP	U, NS	3P	U, NS	2P	L, NS	2P	F-2P
Wife	2P	U, NS	3P	U, NS	2P	L, NS	2P	F-2P
Minor child	2P	U	3P	U	2P	L	2P	F-2P
Adult unmarried child	NP	U, NS	NP/3P	U, NS	2P	L, NS	2P	F-2P
Adult married child	NP	U, NS	NP	U, NS	NP	L, NS	NP, NS	
Other kin and non-kin								
Employment-based	1P	U, NS	1P	U, NS	3P/6P	L, NS	3P/6P	E-1,2,3,4,5P NS in E-4,5 & some E-1,2
All others	NP	U, NS	NP	U, NS	NP	L, NS	NP, NS	
Ceiling on numerically limited visas (in thousands)	165/154		156		170	120	290 worldwide 270 after 1981	366

Notes:

1 The symbol **U** denotes an unlimited supply of visas. All other visas are numerically limited, and denoted either by the corresponding preference category (such as **1P**), or by the residual nonpreference **NP**. The symbol **NS** denotes the case where no visa sponsorship is required; such persons may apply for an immigrant visa without the action of a US citizen or permanent resident.

2 A slash between two visa categories indicates a change in the law during the period. A slash between two dates indicates different end-dates for some of the provisions in the table. The symbol **l** indicates the possible relevance of both visa categories.

accepting unauthorized employment). Unfortunately, the requisite sampling frame for such a study does not yet exist.[7]

The United States does maintain excellent records on all persons newly admitted to legal permanent residence. Moreover, in its annual reports – the *Annual Report of the Commissioner General of Immigration* (published 1898–1932), the *Annual Report of the Immigration and Naturalization Service* (published in the years 1943–78), the *Statistical Yearbook of the Immigration and Naturalization Service* (published in the years 1979–2001), and the *Yearbook of Immigration Statistics* (published since 2002) – the US Immigration and Naturalization Service, and its successor, the Office of Immigration Statistics (OIS) within the Department of Homeland Security, has published tabulations describing basic characteristics of each annual cohort of immigrants; the volumes for recent years are posted on the OIS website.

We may distinguish between three levels of specificity in the data for studying legal immigrants.

Data with Level 1 specificity

At Level 1, data consist of published tabulations based on new immigrant cohorts. For example, the INS *Statistical Yearbooks* and OIS *Yearbooks of Immigration Statistics* make it possible to track the total volume of immigration from year to year, as well as the volume by origin country and by class of admission. To illustrate, information posted on the OIS website indicates that the total number of persons admitted to legal permanent residence in FY 2003 was 705,827; that of these, 51 percent were new arrivals and 49 percent were adjusting from a nonimmigrant visa; that 55 percent were female; and that the most popular state of intended residence was California, attracting almost 25 percent, followed by New York, attracting 12.7 percent. Similarly, the information from the turn of the twentieth century compiled by the US Immigration Commission of 1911 (known as the Dillingham Commission), examined below, is based on published tabulations.

Data with Level 2 specificity

Suppose, however, that interest centers on more detailed information, such as the sex ratio among immigrants admitted as spouses of US citizens. After 1979, the official yearbooks ceased reporting husbands and wives separately. Accordingly, it is now necessary to go beyond published tabulations and obtain the complete microdata sets from the annual immigrant cohorts. These, which exemplify what we may call Level 2 specificity, are available for sale by the National Technical Information Service, suitably devoid of personal identifiers. With the public-use microdata, many new kinds of analyses become possible, for example, analysis of the sex ratio of immigrants by country, class of admission, and age group, and of intended residence by origin country and class of admission.

Data with Level 3 specificity

The public-use immigrant cohort data sets, however welcome they are for providing information on a complete set of each year's new legal immigrants, leave much to be desired. They have no information on schooling or on earnings; the information is organized by individuals, and thus it is not possible to reconstitute family groupings; and so on. The solution is obvious: use INS/USCIS administrative records as a sampling frame, draw a random sample, and carry out interviews, not only soon after admission to legal permanent residence but also, in a panel design, periodically for many years. We may think of such data as exhibiting Level 3 specificity – like Level 1 data, Level 3 data cover legal immigrants newly admitted to permanent residence; like Level 2 data, Level 3 data are microdata with observations on individuals; and, now, at Level 3, the records-based data are augmented by information collected in personal interviews.

Many panels and workshops assembled in both the public and private sectors – for example, panels of the National Academy of Sciences, the National Institutes of Health, the Rockefeller Foundation – contributed to the evolving vision of the required data. With contributions from many scholars, a new plan was formulated for collecting immigrant data that would enable research that substantially advances understanding of the social and economic characteristics of immigrants and the effects of immigration in the United States. This new plan – the New Immigrant Survey (NIS) – has a prospective-retrospective design in which large probability samples are drawn from new cohorts of legal permanent resident aliens, using government administrative records. Sampled immigrants are interviewed immediately after admission to permanent resident status and re-interviewed periodically thereafter; information is collected on the sampled immigrants' spouses and family and household members, including their children, both the immigrant children they brought with them and the US citizen children born to them in the United States.[8]

Because such a design had never been tried before, a pilot – the NIS-P – was carried out, with support from National Institutes of Health, the National Science Foundation, and the Immigration and Naturalization Service. The pilot survey confirmed the soundness of the design, highlighted the importance of contacting sampled immigrants immediately after admission to permanent residence, and provided new information on immigrants never before available (for example, on the schooling of new legal immigrants, on assortative mating in schooling, on religion).[9]

The first full cohort of the NIS was fielded in 2003. The baseline round was in the field from May of 2003 to June of 2004. Plans are under way for a summer 2005 release of public-use data from the baseline round and for an autumn 2005 start for the second-round fieldwork.[10]

An important feature of NIS data will be the longitudinal nature of the surveys. As information accumulates over time, it will be possible to address questions on incorporation and on impacts, for both the immigrant generation and the descendants of immigrants, with unprecedented rigor and sharpness. Until the NIS surveys accumulate several rounds, only two sources permit a glimpse of incorporation processes. These are the Matched Immigrant-Naturalization Cohorts prepared by INS (used, for example, in Jasso and Rosenzweig 1995 and Jasso 2004) and data from the US decennial censuses, which cover the survivors of immigrant cohorts after they have been thinned and altered by emigration and emigration selectivity, and which do not distinguish among legal immigrants (and those who have naturalized) and other foreign-born such as temporary nonimmigrants and illegal migrants.

As already noted, our review of the characteristics of immigrants renders vivid the possibility of preparing new data, to parallel the NIS data, based on historical cohorts. Probability samples could be drawn from ship manifests, linked to census data (and possibly to other official data sources), and possibly combined with data obtained from their descendants. Such data would constitute a remarkably rich source for new research.

4 Characteristics of US Immigrants in the Years 1820 to 2003

In this section we turn to the composition of US immigrants in the period of almost 200 years since information on immigrants was first recorded. The volume and composition of immigrant flows both reflect and engender immigration law regimes. And they shed light on the remarkable story of the great American experiment, as people came from all over the world to build new lives and in the process built a new country.

Volume of US Immigration and Emigration

The general outlines of the volume of US immigration are well known. Graphs are ubiquitous, published, for example, every year in the official reports (the *Yearbook of Immigration Statistics* and its predecessors). Figures 15.1a and 15.1b present these graphs, distinguishing between volume with and without inclusion of the persons admitted to lawful permanent residence via amnesty provisions of the Immigration Reform and Control Act of 1986. The graphs feature vertical lines to separate the four immigration eras.

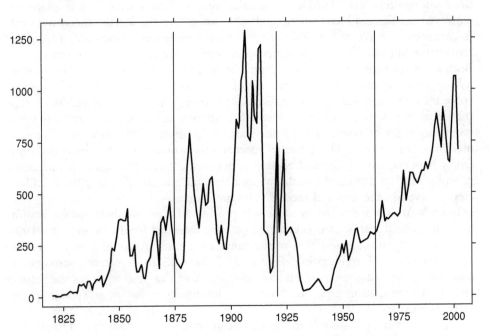

Figure 15.1a Immigration to the United States, excluding IRCA immigrants

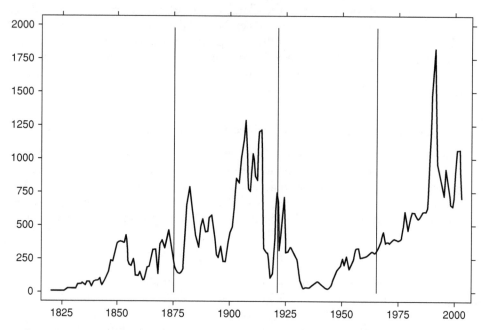

Figure 15.1b Immigration to the United States, including IRCA immigrants

As expected and already known, there is a disjuncture shortly after the start of the third immigration era (1921), as quantitative restrictions were put in place for natives of the Eastern Hemisphere (and subsequently, in the fourth immigration era, for natives of the Western Hemisphere). But another feature stands out. This is the remarkable similarity in both placement and slope of the two segments of the graph. Both segments begin with very low immigration and quickly accelerate. This similarity suggests that once an immigrant flow gets started, sociobehavioral mechanisms come into play and generate a predictable increase. The further suggestion is that the initial regime is unimportant – whether unrestricted as at the start of the first immigration era or restricted as at the start of the third immigration era. The new mechanisms take over. These further mechanisms probably involve networks, both family networks and social and economic networks. Thus, the family reunification provisions of the third and fourth immigration eras may mimic the natural tendencies observed in the first and second immigration eras.

But migration was not purely a one-way process. There was substantial emigration from the United States. Data on emigration were recorded for the period from 1908 to 1958. Estimates suggest that in the nineteenth century, emigration hovered at about one-third of immigration. Figures 15.2a and 15.2b depict net immigration and both gross and net immigration combined. A vertical line separates the second and third immigration eras. As shown, net immigration was negative during the Depression years of 1932–5.

The chief striking feature is the reduction in emigration, relative to immigration, after World War II. A possible interpretation is that after the start of numerical

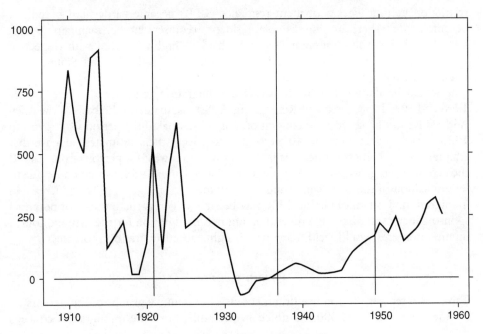

Figure 15.2a Net immigration to the United States: 1908–58

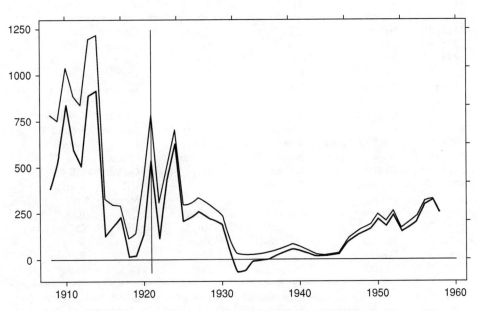

Figure 15.2b Gross and net immigration to the United States: 1908–58

restriction getting legal permanent residence (LPR) became harder and keeping it became harder (there are, for example, residence requirements for maintaining LPR status), and thus the immigrant flow is both more highly selected with respect to expected attachment to the United States and, once in the United States, more reluctant to relinquish LPR status.

It would be illuminating to construct an emigration series for the years before 1908 and after 1958. Jasso and Rosenzweig (1990) estimate, on the basis of the Alien Address Report program, that emigration was substantial in the period from 1961 to 1980 – possibly as high as 40 percent. Moreover, their estimates suggest that emigration was highest for persons from Europe and lowest for persons from Asia. If the gap between gross and net immigration widened after 1958, this could be due to intensification of the same family and network mechanisms generating an increase in immigration. That is, obtaining LPR may become easier as the number of potential sponsors increases. Mapping emigration and net immigration for the first and fourth immigration eras would yield many new insights about migration processes.

Origin Country

Table 15.3 reports the top five origin countries or country groups of immigrants by decade from 1821 to 2000. As noted in the table, both the immigration concept

Table 15.3 Top five immigrant origin countries or country groups, by decade: 1821–2000

Period	1	2	3	4	5
1821–30	Ireland	UK	France	Germany	Mexico
1831–40	Ireland	Germany	UK	France	Canada
1841–50	Ireland	Germany	UK	France	Canada
1851–60	Germany	Ireland	UK	France	Canada
1861–70	Germany	UK	Ireland	Canada	Norway/Sweden
1871–80	Germany	UK	Ireland	Canada	China
1881–90	Germany	UK	Ireland	Canada	Sweden
1891–1900	Italy	Austria/Hungary	Russia	Germany	Ireland
1901–10	Austria/Hungary	Italy	Russia	UK	Germany
1911–20	Italy	Russia/USSR	Austria/Hun	Canada	UK
1921–30	Canada	Mexico	Italy	Germany	UK
1931–40	Germany	Canada	Italy	UK	Mexico
1941–50	Germany	Canada	UK	Mexico	Italy
1951–60	Germany	Canada	Mexico	UK	Italy
1961–70	Mexico	Canada	Italy	UK	Cuba
1971–80	Mexico	Philippines	Korea	Cuba	Vietnam
1981–90	Mexico	Philippines	China	Korea	Vietnam
1991–2000	Mexico	Philippines	FSU	China	India

Notes: Rankings based on seaport arrivals in 1820–67, immigrant arrivals in 1868–91 and 1895–7, and immigrants admitted to lawful permanent residence in 1892–4 and since 1898. Land arrivals not completely enumerated until 1908. Origin country refers to country from whence alien came (prior to 1906), country of last permanent residence (1906–79 and 1984–99), and country of birth (1980–3). Separate figures for Norway and Sweden not available before 1871. Austria-Hungary figures combined for all periods. Canada includes Newfoundland and prior to 1898 includes as well other British possessions in North America.

Source: USCIS *Statistical Yearbook*, 2003, Table 2.

and the country concept changed over the years, and, moreover, land arrivals were not completely enumerated prior to 1908. Nonetheless, the rankings show the shifting composition of US immigrants. First, Canada and Mexico have been import-ant sources of immigration throughout; even when land arrivals were incompletely enumerated, the two neighboring countries appear among the top five (Mexico is fifth in the first period, 1821–30, and Canada appears in either fourth or fifth place in every decade from 1831 to 1890). Second, the lands encompassed by the Russian Empire, the Soviet Union, and the former Soviet Union were important sources of immigration for the last three decades of the second immigration era (1891–1920), and became important again in the 1991–2000 decade. Third, dominance shifts from Ireland and the United Kingdom in 1821–30 to Ireland and Germany in 1831–50, after which Germany dominates for four decades (with, however, UK and Ireland close behind); dominance then shifts to Italy, Austria-Hungary, and, as noted, Russia for the three decades before the end of unrestricted immigration (1891–1920); the 40 years including and surrounding World War II are dominated by the two neighboring countries and by Germany, Italy, and the UK, countries from which new immigrants came as refugees or spouses; thereafter, the Cuban and Vietnam exoduses achieve prominence and a new center of gravity arises in Asia, as the Philippines, Korea, China, and India become major sources of immigrants, together with countries of the former Soviet Union.

In very broad strokes, it could be said that the American continent remains a rich source of immigration to the United States and that the sources of immigration from beyond the Americas have been shifting eastward during the past 200 years.

Sex Ratio

Data compiled by the US Immigration Commission (1911) for the period 1820–67 and incorporated into the series based on official immigration statistics in *Historical Statistics of the United States* (1975), combined with figures from the *Annual Reports* and *Statistical Yearbooks* for the years since 1970, indicate that the percentage male was greater than 50 percent in every year before 1930 (except trivially in 1922) and generally less than 50 percent thereafter (except during the years of IRCA legalizations and trivially in 1984 and 1985). Figure 15.3 depicts the percent male, with vertical lines, as before, representing the boundaries of the four immigration eras.

The plot in Figure 15.3 masks substantial variation in the proportion male across origin countries. The Dillingham Commission (1911, Vol. 3, pp. 47–8) noted that in the 12 years between 1899 and 1910 "races with particularly high proportions of males" included the East Indian (98 percent), Turkish (96.3 percent), and Chinese (96 percent), and those with particularly low proportions of males included the Irish (47.9 percent) and the Hebrew (56.6 percent).

From our vantage point, Figure 15.3 seems to tell two stories. The first is that when immigration is numerically unrestricted, as it was before the start of the third immigration era in 1921, the inflow will include a large number of what we may call temporary sojourners – including young people (mostly males in the time before gender equality) who are in it to seek their fortune or for the adventure. The second is that the specific form of visa allocation the United States has chosen for the numerically restricted third and fourth immigration eras favors family reunification

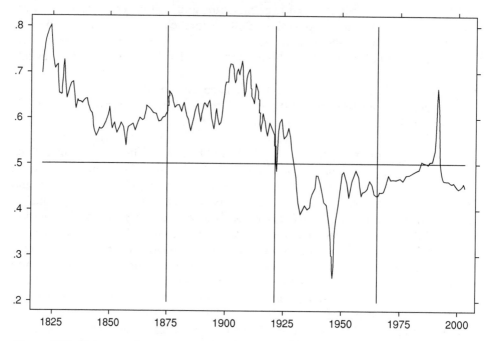

Figure 15.3 Percent male among new immigrants to the United States

and implies the immigration of brides and widowed mothers. Jasso and Rosenzweig (1990, pp. 159–62) report that in every year between 1950 and 1979 the number of new immigrants admitted as wives of US citizens exceeded that of husbands of US citizens – although the predominance of wives was chiefly characteristic of Eastern Hemisphere spouse immigration. The predominance of wives continues to characterize spouse-of-US-citizen immigration in recent immigrant cohorts, including the NIS cohorts of 1996 and 2003.

If the pre-1921 percentage male reflects temporary sojourns, then emigration should also be predominantly male. The Dillingham Commission explored this question for the three years of data it had available to it, beginning in 1908 when emigration statistics were first recorded and ending in 1910. The report (Vol. 3, pp. 374–84) concludes that emigration is overwhelmingly male – 82 percent for the three years.

Consistent with this picture of male sojourning, early data from the NIS-2003 baseline round indicate that the expectation to remain in the United States is lowest among immigrants admitted with employment-based visas (65 percent) and that, within this set, a smaller proportion of men than of women intend to stay (64 percent versus 67 percent).

Race

Preoccupation with race is a classic theme in American immigration history, as evident in the discussion of immigration and naturalization legislation above. The

Bureau of Immigration began collecting data on "race or people" in 1899. According to the Dillingham Commission Report, "This departure was necessitated by the fact that among immigrants from southern and eastern European countries, as well as from Canada and other sources of immigration, the country of birth does not afford a satisfactory clue to the actual racial or ethnical status of such immigrants" (Vol. 3, p. 44). This theme is repeated a few pages later when the report notes that "the country of last permanent residence gives but little clue to the race of immigrants as far as a number of countries is concerned" (Vol. 3, p. 52).

Not surprisingly, the new data were quickly used, and the Dillingham Report observes that "recent statistics and discussions have more and more centered around the racial basis" (Vol. 3, p. 45). Further, the Dillingham Commission prepared a *Dictionary of Races or Peoples* (Volume 5), including designations such as "English," "Scandinavian," "African (black)," "French," "Mexican," "Hebrew," "Italian, North," and "Italian, South."

The report itself noted that in the 12-year period since race data began to be collected (1899–1910), South Italians comprised one-fifth of all immigration and if combined with North Italians the figure reached one-fourth (Vol. 3, p. 45), and provided extensive tabulations including race.

But race and its meaning were to change dramatically in the United States and by the time of the US Select Commission on Immigration and Refugee Policy (1979–81), there was much concern that the family reunification thrust of the visa allocation system operated to exclude blacks and others underrepresented in recent immigration. The Commission considered a lottery option as a way to attract a more diverse set of immigrants (Jasso 1988), and the 1990 Act established a Diversity Visa Program. Under current rules, natives of countries underrepresented in recent immigration (defined as having fewer than 50,000 immigrants during the previous five years) are eligible to apply, and 50,000 visas are awarded each year to the qualified winners of a lottery and their spouses and minor children.

Information on race is no longer published in the *Statistical Yearbooks*, and thus the first indication concerning the outcome of the Diversity Visa Program is provided by data from the baseline round of NIS-2003. The data reveal that the percent black is 33 percent among diversity principals, larger by far than among the other major immigrant subsets (10 percent among spouses of US citizens, 3 percent among employment-based principals, and 13 percent among the remainder). Thus, the Diversity Visa Program is successfully increasing black immigration to the United States.

Mother Tongue and Current Language

Another way to describe immigrants is by their original native language – their mother tongue. Table 15.4 reports in part A the top 10 mother-tongue languages of the white foreign-born populations enumerated in the US censuses of 1910 to 1940 and 1960 and 1970, and in part B of the total foreign-born populations enumerated in the US censuses of 1960 and 1970. These populations reflect earlier immigration flows, possibly thinned by death and emigration. As expected from the figures on origin country composition, the dominant languages across all the census years are English-Celtic, German, and Spanish, followed by Italian, Yiddish, Polish,

Table 15.4 Top 10 mother-tongue languages, foreign-born in the US Censuses and NIS-Pilot FY 1996 immigrants

A. White foreign-born population in the US decennial censuses

1910	*1920*	*1930*	*1940*	*1960*	*1970*
Eng/Celtic	Eng/Celtic	German	Eng/Celt	Eng/Celt	Spanish
German	German	Eng/Celt	German	German	Eng/Celt
Italian	Italian	Italian	Italian	Italian	German
Yiddish	Yiddish	Yiddish	Yiddish	Spanish	Italian
Polish	Polish	Polish	Polish	Polish	Yiddish
Swedish	Swedish	Spanish	Spanish	Yiddish	Polish
French	Spanish	Swedish	Swedish	French	French
Norwegian	French	French	French	Russian	Greek
Spanish	Russian	Norwegian	Russian	Swedish	Hungarian
Hungarian	Norwegian	Russian	Hungarian	Hungarian	Russian

B. All foreign-born population in the US decennial censuses and NIS-Pilot immigrants

Census 1960	*Census 1970*	*NIS-P FY 1996*
English/Celtic	English/Celtic	Spanish
German	Spanish	English
Italian	German	Russian
Spanish	Italian	Chinese
Polish	Yiddish	Vietnamese
Yiddish	Polish	Tagalog
French	French	Polish
Russian	Greek	Arabic
Swedish	Chinese	French
Hungarian	Hungarian	Urdu

Swedish, and French. Spanish displays an interesting ascent among the white foreign-born population, from ninth in 1910 to seventh in 1920, to sixth in 1930 and 1940, to fourth in 1960 and first in 1970; however, among all foreign-born, Spanish reaches only second place in 1970.

The third column of part B reports the mother tongue of the NIS-Pilot immigrants in the FY 1996 cohort. As shown, the ordering of mother tongue begins with Spanish and continues with English, Russian, Chinese, Vietnamese, Tagalog, and Polish.

Mother tongue, of course, describes only the earliest language. New languages are acquired, and immigrants may become dominant in the new language, processes which will be intensively studied in the New Immigrant Survey. Data from the NIS-Pilot provide two important pieces of information, concerning, respectively, the immigrant's preferred language in which to be interviewed and the immigrant's use of English.

Over 40 percent of the NIS-Pilot immigrants preferred to be interviewed in English at the baseline round, although less than 20 percent came from a country one of whose official or dominant languages is English. Another 31 percent preferred Spanish, and 8 percent preferred Russian. Other languages preferred by NIS-Pilot immigrants were, in order of frequency (adjusted for over/undersampling), Chinese, Vietnamese, Polish, French, Tagalog, Korean, Thai, Arabic, Gujarati, Romanian, Albanian, Bengali, Farsi, Ibo, Italian, and Portuguese. In 58 of the 111 countries represented in the NIS-P, all the immigrants preferred English, and in 22 countries all the immigrants preferred a non-English language.

There is substantial use of English among the NIS-P immigrants. Over three-fourths – 78 percent – report that they use English either at home or outside the home. Moreover, almost half – 48 percent – use English both in the home and outside the home, and the proportion who speak only English either at home or outside the home is 34 percent.

Of course, it will be interesting to see how language patterns change with time in the United States.

What Immigrants Were Fleeing

There are many images of immigration. The most important one, of course, is of persons seeking a better life for themselves and their children. But sometimes they are merely seeking life. Famine, war, or persecution may pose mortal threats. Additionally, immigrants may be seeking escape from a life of discrimination based on sex or race or religion. Certainly there is abundant historical evidence of all these processes, from earliest colonial times to the Irish famine to the Russian pogroms.

NIS-2003 asked immigrants in its baseline round the question, "Did you or your immediate family ever suffer any harm outside of the United States because of your political or religious beliefs, or your race, ethnicity or gender?" Eight percent of male immigrants and 5.5 percent of female immigrants responded in the affirmative, for a total of 6.7 percent of the sample. Among these, 25 percent had been imprisoned, 35 percent had received physical punishment by public officials and 32 percent by others, 41 percent had lost a job, 41 percent had property damage and 27 percent had property confiscated, and 70 percent had received verbal or written threats.

Had New Immigrants Been Here Before?

The Dillingham Commission Report observes that "there is a somewhat prevalent belief that the present tide of immigration to the United States is largely composed of persons who have been in the United States before" (Vol. 3, p. 358). However, in the 12-year period examined by the Commission, only 12.4 percent had been in the United States before.

Perhaps public opinion was prescient. For in the current time of full restrictions, qualitative and quantitative, on immigration there has been a substantial amount of adjustment of status from nonimmigrant temporary visas to permanent residence, not only among refugees and asylees (as well as IRCA legalization immigrants) but also among the regular immigration classes, especially after the 1977 legislation which extended adjustment of status privileges to natives of the Western Hemisphere. For example, the number of adjustees exceeded that of new arrivals in every year since 1996 except 1988, 1999, and 2003, years in which administrative and processing conditions produced large backlogs in immigrant visa processing in US immigration offices.

Moreover, new-arrival immigrants may already be living in the United States, in an undocumented status, and return to their origin country for visa processing. As well, many new immigrants may have visited the United States before or even lived in the United States as a temporary nonimmigrant. For example, among the FY 1996 immigrants surveyed in the NIS-Pilot, 55 percent were adjusting status and an additional 14 percent had been in the United States before, for a total of 69 percent with US experience.

Previous Illegal Experience

Before restriction, there was no illegal immigration. Once restrictions were established, illegal immigration began. During the second immigration era, the Era of Qualitative Restriction, illegal immigrants would have consisted largely of inadmissibles. With the advent of numerical restriction, illegal immigration in the third and fourth immigration eras would grow. The question arises whether legals and illegals are drawn from distinct populations or whether instead the two are intertwined. Data from the 1996 cohort of the New Immigrant Survey indicate that one-third of new legal permanent residents have previous illegal experience. Illegal experience may be of several kinds – entry without inspection, visa overstaying, or unauthorized employment. Some observers believe that the rate of previous illegal experience is much higher, judging from the pervasiveness of processing delays and the consequent lapses into illegality.

Family Reunification and Independent Immigration

The heavy emphasis on family reunification in US immigrant visa allocation during the numerically restricted years of the third and fourth immigration eras has prompted many observers to propose a category for "independent" immigrants; the US Select Commission on Immigration and Refugee Policy recommended such a category in 1981. And, indeed, the Diversity Visa Program established by the 1990 Act promotes independent immigration by awarding visas randomly to natives of countries that have been underrepresented in recent migration streams.

There is a real question, however, of what would be the "natural" immigrant mix absent of any restrictions. The Dillingham Commission Report enables a look at this question. The report examined data for the years 1908 to 1910 and found that 79 percent of the new immigrants were going to join relatives and 14.9 percent were going to join friends, with only 6.1 percent not joining either relatives or friends (Vol. 3, p. 362).

Interestingly, the proportion of diversity immigrants in recent years has hovered around 6 percent – reaching 7.4 percent in 1999 and falling to 3.9 percent in 2001, fluctuations which may be attributed to unevenness of US and consular processing times of non-diversity visas (DHS 2003 *Yearbook of Immigration Statistics*, Table 4).[11]

Thus, the sociobehavioral mechanisms associated with family and networks may generate the same mix of immigrants with or without restrictions, as suggested earlier by the similar slope of the immigration increase for the two segments starting, respectively, in the first and third immigration eras.

Literacy and Schooling

The United States achieved an unprecedented level of mass schooling in its first century, as described and analyzed by Goldin and Katz (2003). It is therefore not surprising that illiteracy among immigrants would be viewed with great concern (Goldin 1994). The Dillingham Commission Report notes that a quarter of all new immigrants admitted in the 1899–1910 period were illiterate. This contrasted sharply with literacy rates among the native-born, which, according to *Historical Statistics* (Series 664–8), were 6.2 percent and 4.6 percent among native whites in 1890 and 1900, respectively.

Of course, there was great variation by "race" in illiteracy. Portuguese immigrants in the 1899–1910 period had the highest illiteracy rate – 68.2 percent – followed by Turkish (59.5 percent), Mexican (57.2 percent), and South Italian (53.9 percent) immigrants. At the other end of the spectrum, the lowest illiteracy rates were among Scandinavian (0.4 percent), Scottish (0.7 percent), and English (1 percent) immigrants.

Against this backdrop, the Immigration Act of 1917 which required literacy among immigrants over 16 years of age seems an early courier to be shortly followed by the quota acts.

Schooling among new legal immigrants in the contemporary period is decidedly bimodal. Data from the NIS 1996 and 2003 cohorts indicate that although average schooling is similar to that among native-born, the proportions with very high and very low schooling are about three times as large as among the native-born (Jasso, Massey, Rosenzweig, and Smith 2000b). There are few explicit schooling requirements in current immigration law (exceptions are in the Diversity Visa Program, which requires a high school education, or its equivalent, and in the "advanced degree" subset of the employment second preference category and the baccalaureate subset of the employment third preference category). And the combination of spouse visas – US citizens may marry whomever they want, but they seem to want to marry similarly educated individuals (Jasso, Massey, Rosenzweig, and Smith 2000a) – refugee provisions, and employment opportunities for highly educated persons would seem to promote a bimodal distribution.

Of course, many immigrants acquire additional schooling after immigration. Thus, the longitudinal data from the NIS will provide new information on final schooling attainment.

How Immigrants Achieved Immigration

In the years before restriction, the main challenge was to accumulate the resources for making the trip to the United States. After restrictions were imposed, the challenge expanded to qualifying in one of the visa categories, which in turn means finding a sponsor – a relative or employer who will petition for the prospective immigrant.

The Dillingham Commission Report looked at information on who paid for the passage among immigrants in the three years from 1908 to 1910. In this period, 69 percent of the new immigrants reported paying for the passage themselves, with another 29.9 percent reporting that a relative paid for the passage, with only 1 percent reporting that someone else besides a relative paid for the passage (Vol. 3, p. 359).

Today, the overwhelming majority of new immigrants must be sponsored by a relative or employer. However, the precise nature of the financial arrangements is not known. The New Immigrant Survey is fielding a large battery of questions that will shed light on these possibly elaborate two-way transfer systems. Preliminary information from the NIS-Pilot indicates that in approximately the first 22 to 23 months after admission to lawful permanent residence, 9.4 percent of the sample provided financial help to relatives or friends in the United States, and 3.7 percent received loans from relatives or friends in the United States.

Financial Resources

The Immigration Act of 1882 declared inadmissible anyone likely to become a public charge. Because current financial resources have a bearing on the possibility of becoming a public charge, the Act of March 3, 1893 added to the reporting requirements for vessels that they state whether the prospective immigrant possessed $30 and, if not, the amount possessed. In 1903 this amount was increased to $50. Of course, a prospective immigrant might not reveal the actual amount of money in his or her possession, and thus the figures are said to pertain to "showing money."

The Dillingham Commission Report provides tabulations of the amount of money shown, by race, for each of the years between 1899 and 1910. The figures indicate that 74.5 percent of the immigrants admitted showed money, and that among those showing money, the average was $28.95 (Vol. 3, p. 350). The amount of money shown varied widely across "race" (Vol. 3, pp. 357–8). Groups showing the highest average amounts were the East Indian ($939.48 in the 1899–1903 period), Spanish-American ($160.57 in the 1899–1903 period and $134.82 in the 1904–10 period), and Pacific Islanders ($142.93 in the 1899–1903 period). The lowest average amounts shown were recorded for black Africans ($8.48), Lithuanians ($11.20), and Rumanians ($11.42), all in the 1899–1903 period.

Today there are two sets of financial controls. First, the immigrant must provide evidence that he or she will not become a public charge. This is accomplished by submitting either a letter with an offer of employment stating the rate of pay, or evidence of bank balance, stock portfolio, ownership of real estate, or cash surrender value of insurance policies. The second is the contractually binding affidavit of support that must be provided for all family-based immigrants as well as for employment-based immigrants who will be working for relatives or for companies where relatives own 5 percent or more.

Additionally, the practice of having the immigrant pay a head tax – first established in 1882 – today takes the form of application fees. Fees vary. For example, in the case of a family-based immigrant adjusting status in the United States, the sponsor's petition has a fee of $185; subsequently, the prospective immigrant's application to adjust status has a fee of $220 ($160 if the prospective immigrant is under 14), plus a fingerprinting fee of $25.

Immigration to the United States appears to be worth the expense, on average. The Dillingham Commission Report notes that the total amount of money shown in the 12-year period from 1899 to 1910 was $206,145,738, while the amount of money sent from the United States in one year alone – 1907 – was estimated at $275 million, suggesting augmented earnings (as well as the possibility of concealing money at immigration). Data from the NIS-Pilot indicate that among those immigrants who had worked abroad before immigrating and were working at the time of the first interview after their admission to lawful permanent residence, over 70 percent had experienced a gain in earnings. The gains at this early time in the immigrant career were not trivial – in PPP-adjusted figures, $10,306 for men (a 68 percent increase) and $6,146 for women (a 62 percent increase).

Home Ownership

An important indicator of financial well-being as well as of attachment to the United States is home ownership. High rates of home ownership have characterized immigrants in the United States (Carter and Sutch 1998; Haines and Goodman 1995). Data from the NIS 1996 and 2003 cohorts are consistent with historical experience. For example, NIS-2003 data indicate that, already in the first or second year after admission to LPR, over a quarter of new immigrants own their homes. Of course, the rate is much higher among immigrants who are adjusting status after already being in the United States as a nonimmigrant than among new arrivals – 36.7 percent versus 10.2 percent.

Moreover, there is interesting variation by visa class. For example, 41 percent of spouse immigrants and 38 percent of employment principals in NIS-2003 are homeowners, but only 5 percent of diversity principals and 21 percent of the remainder.

Remittances

An important question in the study of immigrant behavior involves remittances. What fraction of immigrants send money back home? What is the remittances trajectory? What are the amounts? And what is the magnitude of net remittances – after accounting for help received from persons in the origin country? Data from the NIS-Pilot indicate that 26 percent of the new immigrants sent remittances abroad in the first year after admission to LPR. The amount of remittances sent abroad is a little over $350 million. Respondents also reported receiving loans and other financial help from abroad. Excluding loans, on the assumption that they have to be repaid, the estimate of financial help received from abroad is almost $100 million. Thus, the estimated net outflow in the first year of LPR for the FY 1996 cohort is approximately $250 million. Of course, these estimates are for the first year; an important question that the NIS will address, as survey rounds accumulate over time, pertains to the transfer trajectory – do net outflow and its components increase or decrease or remain the same over time? Moreover, different cohorts may have distinctive transfer patterns; by round 2 of NIS-2003, it will be possible to obtain estimates for the 2003 cohort comparable to the estimates for the FY 1996 immigrants, thus beginning to shed light on cohort effects on transfers.

Married Couples at Admission to Lawful Permanent Residence

There seem to have been two major marital patterns among new immigrants in the time of numerically unrestricted immigration. In one pattern, a married couple immigrated together; in the second, the husband tried the United States and, if the environment proved suitable, the wife (and children) joined him. In the time since restriction, there has been a third pattern, which may be numerically quite large; this involves achieving immigration through a new marriage to a US citizen.

The first two patterns continue. The first is visible in all the visas awarded to the spouses and minor children of visa principals (for example, visas awarded to spouses and minor children of employment principals, diversity principals, and such family principals as siblings of US citizens). The second is less clearly visible; it pertains to visas awarded to spouses of permanent residents (family second preference) and naturalized citizens, where the marriage pre-existed the sponsoring spouse's immigration to the United States. Although there is a clue in published tabulations which distinguish between conditional and unconditional visas – conditional visas are awarded to spouses in marriages of less than two years' duration – only direct questioning can provide unambiguous information. The quintessential third pattern involves a native-born US citizen who marries and sponsors the immigration of a foreign-born spouse. Of course, after admission to LPR, there are new types of marriages, some between natives and foreign-born and others between two foreign-born persons.

The existence of these very different kinds of married couples has large implications for the family environments in which children are raised and for the quality of relations between natives and newcomers. If large numbers of immigrants are married to native-born US citizens, the possibility of bitter nativist–immigrant conflicts diminishes.

This is an area in which further research would be most fruitful, including research using historical census data. For many years, there has been a single piece of information pertaining to the nativity of US citizens who sponsor spouses. This is based on a special study carried out by the General Accounting Office (GAO) based on immigrant records for FY 1985 (US GAO 1988). The GAO team obtained information on the nativity of the US citizen sponsors of immediate relatives, and this information led to the estimate that 80 percent of the sponsors are native-born US citizens (Jasso and Rosenzweig 1990, p. 224).

Data from the NIS-Pilot indicate that among the FY 1996 immigrants, the proportion native-born among the sponsors of newly-married immigrants was 59 percent, while among the sponsors of immigrants married more than two years it was 46 percent. The differential is exactly in the correct direction. Because new marriages are more numerous, the overall proportion native-born among the spouse sponsors is 55 percent. Data from the 2003 cohort of the NIS will prove illuminating, as it is not clear whether the 1996 cohort reflects possibly differing mechanisms among new immigrants married to naturalized IRCA amnestied immigrants.

Religion

Religion has played a large part in the immigration history of the United States. Some immigrants came in order to practice their religion freely, others to escape from all religion. Meanwhile, public sentiment sometimes has been highly negative about certain religions; two prime examples are Catholicism and Judaism. Because government surveys may not ask questions on religion, there is no historical series such as the census would provide. The General Social Surveys (GSS) have asked probability samples of the population questions about religion since 1972, and the

NIS asks immigrants questions about religion. Data from these two sources yield interesting results.

Approximately two-thirds of the NIS-Pilot immigrants are Christian, substantially below the 82 percent of the native-born surveyed in the General Social Survey of 1996. However, the proportion Catholic is 42 percent, almost twice as large as among the native-born (22 percent). The proportion reporting themselves outside the Judaeo-Christian fold is over four times larger among recent immigrants than among the native-born (17 versus 4 percent); 8 percent of the new immigrants are Muslim. And as would be expected in a country whose principles include not only the freedom to practice any religion but also the freedom to practice no religion, 15 percent of the new immigrants report no religion, a larger fraction than among the native-born (12 percent). Of course, religious preference may change with time in the United States.

5 Concluding Note

In this chapter we highlighted 16 characteristics of new immigrants to the United States, based on historical and contemporary data, in a framework attentive to the four major immigration eras generated by immigration law. We found some remarkable similarities – for example, in the slope of the immigration increase in the 1820–1920 period and in the restriction third and fourth immigration eras, and in the proportions of immigrants coming to join relatives and friends. We examined financial resources, remittances, language, religion, and a host of other characteristics.

Particularly striking was the growing sense that the longitudinal microdata design of the New Immigrant Survey, which provided much of the information we used to describe current immigrants, could usefully be simulated on historical cohorts of immigrants. The outlines of the design would be simple, although quite challenging to implement. First, probability samples would be drawn from among cohorts of new legal immigrants, using ship manifests and immigration records. Second, these samples would be linked with other sources of data, principally the decennial censuses, but including as well vital registry records, parish records, and other sources. Third, descendants of sampled immigrants would be interviewed concerning additional characteristics, such as health behaviors and religion.

The story of US immigrants is a marvel of industry and courage. Understanding that story more deeply demands the same.

NOTES

1   To illustrate: a recent study addressed the question whether immigrants screened for skills do better than immigrants admitted as the spouses of US citizens, and concluded that while there is a substantial skill differential at entry, the skill differential narrows over time, with employment immigrants experiencing occupational downgrading and marital immigrants experiencing occupational upgrading – possibly the result of the screening process itself: while employers may screen for the short term, Americans marrying a foreigner may screen for the long term (Jasso and Rosenzweig 1995).

2   Our notion of "trajectory" encompasses both sequences of states and continuous increases or decreases in quantitative characteristics. For example, the religion trajectory may be a sequence of realizations of the categorical variable "religious preference," while

the health trajectory may be a curve describing increases and decreases in the quantitative variable "healthiness."

3 See Smith (1998) for elaboration of the link between gender, marriage, and naturalization.

4 For insightful analysis and discussion of immigration restriction in the final 30 years of the Era of Qualitative Restriction and, in particular, the financial test and the literacy test, see Goldin (1994).

5 For succinct description of current US visa allocation law, see the websites of the State Department and of the US Citizenship and Immigration Services (USCIS), one of the successor agencies to the US Immigration and Naturalization Service (INS). For elaboration from a social science perspective and a close look at changes in the law across the period from 1972 to 1995, see Jasso, Rosenzweig, and Smith (2000).

6 The number of persons admitted as refugees is set annually by the President in consultation with Congress; the ceiling has fluctuated in the range of 75,000 to 100,000. The diversity lottery program was begun in FY 1987 on a trial basis and made a part of US immigration law under provisions of the Immigration Act of 1990. For further information on refugees, asylees, and diversity immigrants, see the USCIS and State Department websites.

7 However, complete enumeration of new holders of visas in certain nonimmigrant classes, such as students and temporary workers, may soon become possible, paving the way for feasible sampling designs.

8 For further description of the New Immigrant Survey, see Jasso, Massey, Rosenzweig, and Smith (in press) and the NIS website (http://nis.princeton.edu).

9 Comprehensive exposition of the design of the NIS-Pilot, together with information obtained in the Pilot, may be found in the initial papers from the project (Jasso, Massey, Rosenzweig, and Smith 2000a, 2000b, 2003) and on the NIS website. Public-use microdata and documentation for the NIS-Pilot are available on the NIS website.

10 For description of the design of NIS-2003, see Jasso, Massey, Rosenzweig, and Smith (in press).

11 These proportions are based on the ratio of diversity immigrants to the total number of non-legalization immigrants.

REFERENCES

Barrett, Alan (1996). "Did the Decline Continue? Comparing the Labor-Market Quality of United States Immigrants from the Late 1970s and Late 1980s." *Journal of Population Economics* 9: 57–63.

Borjas, George J. (1985). "Assimilation, Changes in Cohort Quality, and the Earnings of Immigrants." *Journal of Labor Economics* 3: 463–89.

Carter, Susan B. and Richard Sutch (1998). "Historical Background to Current Immigration Issues." In James P. Smith and Barry Edmonston, eds., *The Immigration Debate: Studies on the Economic, Demographic, and Fiscal Effects of Immigration*. Washington, DC: National Academies Press, pp. 289–366.

Cobb-Clark, Deborah A. (1993). "Immigrant Selectivity and Wages: The Evidence for Women." *American Economic Review* 83: 986–93.

Committee on the Health and Safety Implications of Child Labor, Board on Children, Youth, and Families, National Research Council/Institute of Medicine (1998). *Protecting Youth at Work: Health, Safety, and Development of Working Children and Adolescents in the United States*. Washington, DC: National Academies Press.

Duleep, Harriet Orcutt and Mark C. Regets (1996). "Admission Criteria and Immigrant Earnings Profiles." *International Migration Review* 30: 571–90.

Gibson, Campbell J. and Emily Lennon (1999). "Historical Census Statistics on the Foreign-born Population of the United States: 1850–1990." US Bureau of the Census. Population Division Working Paper No. 29.

Goldin, Claudia (1994). "The Political Economy of Immigration Restriction in the United States, 1890 to 1921." In Claudia Goldin and Gary D. Libecap, eds., *The Regulated Economy: A Historical Approach to Political Economy*. Chicago: University of Chicago Press, pp. 223–57.

Goldin, Claudia and Lawrence F. Katz (2003). "The 'Virtues' of the Past: Education in the First Hundred Years of the New Republic." NBER Working Paper 9958.

Haines, Michael R. and Allen C. Goodman (1995). "A Home of One's Own: Aging and Home Ownership in the United States in the Late Nineteenth and Early Twentieth Centuries." In David I. Kertzer and Peter Laslett, eds., *Aging in the Past: Demography, Society, and Old Age*. Berkeley: University of California Press, pp. 203–28.

Hernandez, Donald J. and Evan Charney, eds. (1998). *From Generation to Generation: The Health and Well-Being of Children in Immigrant Families. Report of the National Research Council and the Institute of Medicine*. Washington, DC: National Academies Press.

Jasso, Guillermina (1988). "Whom Shall We Welcome? Elite Judgments of the Criteria for the Selection of Immigrants." *American Sociological Review* 53: 919–32.

—— (2003). "Migration, Human Development, and the Lifecourse." In Jeylan T. Mortimer and Michael Shanahan, eds., *Handbook of the Lifecourse*. New York: Kluwer, pp. 331–64.

—— (2004). "Have the Occupational Skills of New Legal Immigrants to the United States Changed Over Time? Evidence from the Immigrant Cohorts of 1977, 1982, and 1994." In Douglas S. Massey and J. Edward Taylor, eds., *International Migration: Prospects and Policies in a Global Market*. Oxford: Oxford University Press, pp. 261–85.

Jasso, Guillermina and Mark R. Rosenzweig (1990). *The New Chosen People: Immigrants in the United States*. The Population of the United States in the 1980s: A Census Monograph Series. New York: Russell Sage.

—— (1995). "Do Immigrants Screened for Skills Do Better Than Family-Reunification Immigrants?" *International Migration Review* 29: 85–111. Reprinted in Klaus F. Zimmerman, ed., *The Economics of Migration*. Cheltenham, UK: Elgar Press, in press.

Jasso, Guillermina, Douglas S. Massey, Mark R. Rosenzweig, and James P. Smith (2000a). "Assortative Mating among Married New Legal Immigrants to the United States: Evidence from the New Immigrant Survey Pilot." *International Migration Review* 34: 443–59.

—— (2000b). "The New Immigrant Survey Pilot (NIS-P): Overview and New Findings about U.S. Legal Immigrants at Admission." *Demography* 37: 127–38.

—— (2003). "Exploring the Religious Preference of Recent Immigrants to the United States: Evidence from the New Immigrant Survey Pilot." In Yvonne Yazbeck Haddad, Jane I. Smith, and John L. Esposito, eds., *Religion and Immigration: Christian, Jewish, and Muslim Experiences in the United States*. Walnut Creek, CA: AltaMira Press, pp. 217–53.

(In press). "The U.S. New Immigrant Survey: Overview and Preliminary Results Based on the New-Immigrant Cohorts of 1996 and 2003." In UK Home Office, *Longitudinal Surveys and Cross-Cultural Design*.

Jasso, Guillermina, Mark R. Rosenzweig, and James P. Smith (2000). "The Changing Skill of New Immigrants to the United States: Recent Trends and Their Determinants." In George J. Borjas, ed., *Issues in the Economics of Immigration*. Chicago: University of Chicago Press, pp. 185–225.

Lapham, Susan, Patricia Montgomery, and Debra Niner (1993). "We the American . . . Foreign Born." (WE-7). US Bureau of the Census.

Loaeza Tovar, Enrique M., Carlos Planck, Remedios Gómez Arnau, Susan Martin, B. Lindsay Lowell, and Deborah W. Meyers, eds., with contributions by F.D. Bean, R. Corona, R.

Tuirán, K. Woodrow-Lafield, J. Bustamante, G. Jasso, J.E. Taylor, P. Trigueros, A. Escobar Latapí, P. Martin, K. Donato, G. Lopez Castro, M. Tienda, G. Verduzco, M. Greenwood, K. Unger, F. Alba, S. Weintraub, R. Fernández de Castro, M. García y Griego (1997). *Report of the Binational Study of Migration between Mexico and the United States.* Washington, DC, and, in Spanish, Mexico, DF.

Malone, Nolan, Kaari F. Baluja, Joseph M. Costanzo, and Cynthia J. Davis (2003). "The Foreign-Born Population: 2000." US Bureau of the Census.

Portes, Alejandro and Rubén G. Rumbaut (2001). *Legacies: The Story of the Immigrant Second Generation.* Berkeley: University of California Press.

President's Commission on Immigration and Naturalization (1953). *Whom We Shall Welcome? Report of the President's Commission on Immigration and Naturalization.* Washington, DC: US Government Printing Office.

Smith, James P. and Barry Edmonston, eds. (1997). *The New Americans: Economic, Demographic, and Fiscal Effects of Immigration. Report of the National Research Council.* Washington, DC: National Academies Press.

Smith, Marian (1998). "'Any Woman Who Is Now or May Hereafter Be Married . . .': Women and Naturalization, ca. 1802–1940." *U.S. National Archives and Records Administration* 30(2) (available at www.archives.gov).

—— (2002). "Race, Nationality, and Reality: INS Administration of Racial Provisions in US Immigration and Nationality Law Since 1898." *U.S. National Archives and Records Administration* 34(2) (available at www.archives.gov).

U.S. Commissioner General of Immigration (1898–1932). *Annual Reports.* Washington, DC: US Government Printing Office.

US Department of Homeland Security (2002). *Yearbook of Immigration Statistics.* Washington, DC: US Government Printing Office.

US Department of State (various issues). Visa Bulletin. Issued monthly.

US General Accounting Office (1988). *Immigration: The Future Flow of Legal Immigration to the United States.* Washington, DC: US Government Printing Office.

US Immigration Commission (1911). *Reports of the Immigration Commission* (also known as the Dillingham Commission Report), 42 volumes. Washington, DC: US Government Printing Office.

US Immigration and Naturalization Service (1943–78). *Annual Report of the Immigration and Naturalization Service.* Washington, DC: US Government Printing Office.

—— (1979–2001). *Statistical Yearbook of the Immigration and Naturalization Service.* Washington, DC: US Government Printing Office.

CHAPTER SIXTEEN

Marriage Patterns in Historical Perspective: Gender and Ethnicity

ROBERT MCCAA, ALBERT ESTEVE,
AND CLARA CORTINA

Nice Greek girls do three things. Marry Greek boys. Make Greek babies. Feed everybody
until the day we die.
    Toula Portokalos (Nia Vardalos), *My Big Fat Greek Wedding* (IPC Films, 2002)

Gender is fundamental to understanding ethnic marriage patterns, particularly in the case of the United States of America, where immigrant streams have long been sex-selective. While for much of a century (1880–1970) male immigrants typically outnumbered females 110:100, for Greeks and Italians the adult sex ratio averaged 150:100, and Norwegians, Mexicans, Austrians, and others were not far behind at 125:100. In caste societies, polyandry, celibacy, or same-sex unions might be the means for attaining equilibrium in socially constructed marriage markets. In the United States, out-marriage is the escape valve, as far back in the past as census microdata permit us to peer. Nevertheless, breaking the gender squeeze is a two-step or, better, two-generation process with immigrants favoring spouses of their own ethnicity even though born in the United States, shoving, as far as possible, the imbalance onto the second generation.

Toula was expected to marry a Greek to maintain her ethnic ties and traditions. She was constrained by a demographic imperative, the gender squeeze: a surplus of eligible Greek men. Her brothers were free to choose whomever they pleased. The second-generation gender in over-supply, typically males, except for the Irish and a few less well known groups, are faced with three choices: marrying out, marrying late, or not marrying at all. Not surprisingly, as our analysis will show, the favorite choice is to marry out, even for Norwegian farmers in close proximity to Lake Wobegon (data not available for the village; unsubstantiated reports in the liberal media lament the large number of confirmed bachelors). This pattern, detailed by a study of century-long marriage patterns in New York City (McCaa 1993), clearly has national dimensions.

Will the gender squeeze, the demographic dynamo of the past, promote high rates of intermarriage for the newest immigrants from Latin America, Asia, and, most recently, Africa? Are the segmented assimilationists correct that the old rules governing the marriage market no longer apply because the latest streams of

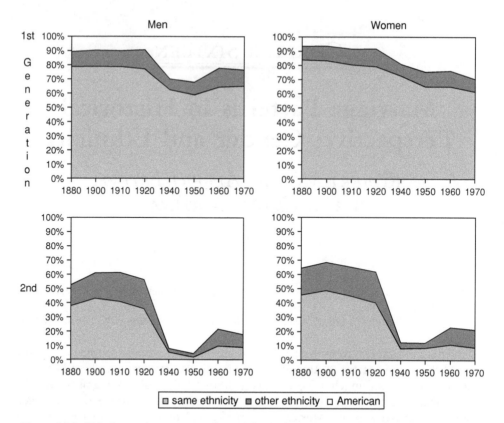

Figure 16.1 Ethnic marriage patterns by gender and generation: Restrictive legislation of the 1920s followed by the Great Depression sharply curtailed immigration and promoted out-marriage.

Note: Sums for 50 countries of origin, Albania to Yugoslavia, excluding native-born of native-stock married to native-born of native-stock.

Source: IPUMS-USA (Ruggles and Sobek 2004), 1% sample extract.

immigrants confront racial in addition to ethnic barriers? We conclude by analyzing census microdata of the last three decades to try to peer into the future. Our analysis suggests that the trends are not entirely different from those of what in 1910 were called the "new" immigrants – Italians, Greeks, and other eastern Europeans – but today refer to ethnicities of Latin American and Asian origins.

Figure 16.1 sums up the ethnic marriage patterns of 50 groups by gender and generation over the space of a century, 1880–1970. Does this figure bring to mind Lieberson's "bumpy line" theory of ethnic marriage assimilation in which the second generation leads the way? Four points stand out, when all groups are thrown into the same plot. First, immigrants always had the highest rates of in-marriage, in part because marriages consummated before immigration are counted here. In 1880, 80 percent of immigrants were in endogamous unions, down to 60 percent a century later. Second, children of immigrants, the "second generation," were always substantially less likely than their parents to take a spouse of their own ethnicity. In 1880, 40 percent were endogamously married versus fewer than 10 percent six decades later. Third, interruption of immigration streams had profound effects on ethnic in-marriage. By 1920, endogamy rates for children of immigrants had declined, but only fractionally. The disruption of immigration flows by World War I caused only a slight drop. Until the 1930 microdata are made available, it is not possible to assay the effects of the restrictive immigration measures of the 1920s. We suspect that these were minor. In any case, by 1940 the rate had plummeted to less than 10 percent, according to the census microdata. Finally, the Great Depression was a watershed. As early as 1950 endogamous unions rose slightly, but they barely attained 10 percent of the total for children of immigrants. At such low levels, strong groupings based on ethnicity are difficult to maintain.

While Figure 16.1 is useful to summarize broad trends, our goal is to illuminate the social geometry of marriage, particularly between the newest and older patterns of ethnic intermarriage. US population censuses, specifically samples disseminated by the IPUMS-USA project, are recognized for their comparability in space and time (Ruggles and Sobek 2004). The IPUMS (Integrated Public Use Microdata Sample) contains responses of individual persons to the decennial US census schedules. Spouses, often listed successively on the forms and in the datafiles, are identified by marital status and relationship to householder. Microdata supplied by IPUMS-USA identify spouses ("SPLOC"), which means that researchers may analyze, as we have in Figure 16.1, husbands and wives according to their combined demographic and social characteristics, including national origins.

Compared with other quantitative sources in the social sciences, census microdata offer unrivaled temporal and sample density. Nevertheless, as for any source with long-term coverage, new variables appear and the meaning, significance, and comparability of old ones change. Country of birth, used here to identify immigrants, is common to all US censuses from 1850 through 2000. To distinguish individuals whose parents immigrated, we rely on country of birth of mother and father, first recorded in 1880 and maintained through the census of 1970. Beginning in 1980, instead of parents' country of birth, the Census Bureau introduced an open-ended ancestry question, which permitted individuals to indicate ethnic identities irrespective of generational depth. Then too, beginning in 1980, the opening up of the "race" question elicited a wide range of responses, including "Japanese," "Philippine," "Korean," etc. Parents' country of birth and ancestry (which we supplement with "race" and "Hispanic origin") are not comparable, so we split our analysis at 1980.

For the first period, 1880–1970, first- and second-generation immigrants are distinguished by means of country of birth for the individual and his or her parents' country of birth (as in Figure 16.1). "Natives" are classified as those born in the United States whose parents were also born in the United States. For individuals with only one parent born abroad, this is assigned as the parents' country of origin. Where both parents were born abroad, the mother's country of birth is favored, even where the country of birth of the father is the same as that of the spouse or the spouse's parents.

For the second period, 1980–2000, country of birth is used to determine first-generation immigrants. Since no question was asked regarding parents' country of birth, we rely on "ancestry," "race," and "Hispanic origin" to classify individual's ethnic origin for second and older generations, including native non-Hispanic whites as well as other non-natives.

Census microdata indicate prevalence, not incidence. They offer no information on the celebration of marriages at specific moments in time, but rather indicate the marital status of individuals at census date. Unions broken by separation, divorce, or widowhood go unnoted. Thus, if ethnically endogamous marriages are less likely to dissolve at younger ages, then any source based on prevalence will overestimate the incidence of such unions (Jacobs and Labov 2002).

In the following analysis, to limit bias we adopt a practice common to research on this topic and focus only on unions of young men, aged 25–34 years (Qian 1997, Qian and Lichter, 2001). For historical research involving decennial censuses, restricting attention to a 10-year age group has the added advantage of avoiding overlapping cohorts in successive censuses. The disadvantage is that we may underestimate ethnically mixed marriages because, as Toula's prolonged courtship shows us, exogamous marriages tend to occur at somewhat older ages (Porterfield 1982). The fact that marital status at the moment of immigration is unknown may also be seen as a limitation of our sources. Unions occurring before immigration are indistinguishable from those formed afterwards because only two censuses (1900 and 1910) inquire about age at marriage. To minimize this effect, we have excluded immigrants whose declared year of immigration (available in all censuses from 1900 to the present) points to an age at immigration of 20 years or more.[1]

Small groups tend to marry out more, simply because they are small – not because of the intrinsic preferences for or against any specific ethnicity (Blau 1977). Log-linear models readily account for group size to reveal broad patterns of in-marriage and intermarriage (see Appendix). Our periodization for the log-linear analysis for the first period (1880–1920) and the second period (1980–2000) responds both to historical developments, as we have seen above, and to the availability of information. Since country of emigration for the first period differs greatly from the second, we have selected different groups for each. For the first period, we focus on immigrants from England, France, Germany, Ireland, Italy, and Sweden, while for the second, we have selected China, Cuba, Japan, Korea, Mexico, and the Philippines. For each period these are the most commonly cited in the literature on ethnic intermarriage (Pagnini and Morgan 1991).

In contrast to Figure 16.1 with its sums for 50 ethnicities, the Appendix describes a set of models in which each ethnic group is analyzed individually. Surprisingly endogamy of the foreign-born is typically higher in the first period than in the second. This suggests that while marriage markets are now transnational, they function to a measurable degree to promote intermarriage rather than in-marriage, as was the almost unbroken rule at the beginning of the twentieth century. For example, consider the Japanese-born. Their exceedingly low endogamy ratio is no longer due to the "war-bride" phenomenon, but rather to a relatively higher proportion of transnational courtships leading to marriage with individuals who do not claim Japanese ancestry on the census form. In the first period, for foreign-born ethnics three degrees of endogamy are discernible: high (log odds below 5, characteristic of the English and "German" from 1910), higher (~5 for the French and Irish), and highest (greater than 6 for the Swedish and Italian). In the second period, aside from the Japanese, most log odds are in the range of 5–6, that is, substantially less than peaks typical of period one.

Second-generation endogamy in period one displays the pattern associated with the assimilationist model. Log odds are typically half those of the first generation of the same ethnic background. Clearly lagging behind in the generational two-step were the Italians (and to a certain extent Germans), but we know from census microdata for 1940 and beyond that Italian (and German) endogamy quickly approached the American assimilationist norm depicted in Figure 16.1. In period two, the ancestry question on the census form means that ethnic endogamy can now be measured regardless of generation. Moreover for individuals of multi-ethnic backgrounds, similar identities may be elected, heightening endogamy. It is unfortunate that we did not model this for the same groups as in period one in order to calibrate this effect. Not surprisingly, endogamy patterns within ancestral groups are much higher than for ethnic endogamy limited to the second generation as in period one. Under the circumstances the odds of endogamy for those of Mexican ancestry are surprisingly low given the flood of Mexican immigrants in recent decades.

By 2002, when *My Big Fat Greek Wedding* opened in theaters, the struggle to marry outside one's ethnic group had become a quaint stereotype. As one reviewer noted, Toula's family could have been Italian, Hungarian, Polish, or even Jewish. No reviewer referred to English, French, or Scottish, among the old immigrants, nor any of the newest immigrants – Mexican, Filipino, or Somali. The difference between the patterns of traditional ethnic assimilation and segmented assimilation experienced by the newest immigrants should be reflected in distinct ethnic marriage patterns. As we have seen, in the first case we found classic assimilation for all the groups, a more or less continuous, progressive increase in marriages with the native-born of native parents. In contrast, in the second case, we found somewhat greater variety of patterns and stronger endogamy, particularly in the second generation. What we were unable to determine was whether this increase was due to the fact that the census now addresses issues of ancestry, Hispanic origin, and race, rather than parental country of birth. Then too, what might have happened to the classic pattern of assimilation through marriage if in the 1920s and 1930s European immigrants had continued to stream into the United States as at the beginning of the twentieth century? For the newest groups the process of assimilation is still unfolding. If the patterns of the past are a guide, political or economic disruptions of immigration flows will substantially impact patterns of marital assimilation. Where no disruptions occur, marital endogamy is likely to persist for decades, if not generations.

Appendix: Methodology for Marriage Models

If all groups had exactly the same number of spouses, there would be no need for log-linear analysis. Since all groups are different, log-linear models are used to remove the effects of unequal group sizes. Throughout we use 1 percent samples of the harmonized census microdata. Table 16.1 lays out the topology of our analysis. For each ethnic group, marital unions are distributed according to the ethnic origins of the husband and wife divided into four categories. For the first period, 1880–1920, these are: (A) native, (B) other non-native, (C) first-generation immigrant, and (D) second-generation immigrant, that is native-born of one or more parents born abroad. For the second period, 1980–2000, to take into account the ancestry information collected by the census, the categories become (A) native non-Hispanic white, (B) other non-native, (C) first-generation immigrant, and (D) second or

ROBERT McCAA, ALBERT ESTEVE, AND CLARA CORTINA

Table 16.1 Model topologies for husband and wife's ethnicity marriage patterns, 1880–1920 and 1980–2000

	1880–1920	1980–2000
A	Native	Native non-Hispanic white
B	Other non-native	Other non-native
C	First generation same ethnicity	First generation same ethnicity
D	Second generation same ethnicity	Second + generation same ancestry

Husband	Wife							
	A	*B*	*C*	*D*	*A*	*B*	*C*	*D*
	M_0 *Independence*				M_1 *Uniform homogamy*			
A	0	0	0	0	1	0	0	0
B	0	0	0	0	0	1	0	0
C	0	0	0	0	0	0	1	0
D	0	0	0	0	0	0	0	1
	M_2 *Discrete homogamy*				M_3 *Discrete homogamy + 2nd generation & 1st*			
A	1	0	0	0	1	0	0	0
B	0	2	0	0	0	2	0	0
C	0	0	3	0	0	0	3	4
D	0	0	0	4	0	0	4	4
	M_4 *Discrete homogamy + symmetry 2nd & 1st*				M_5 *Discrete homogamy + gender asymmetry 2nd & 1st*			
A	1	0	0	0	1	0	0	0
B	0	2	0	0	0	2	0	0
C	0	0	3	5	0	0	3	6
D	0	0	5	4	0	0	5	4

more generations. For both periods, the "other non-native" category is relative to the ethnicity of the reference person. Finally, to take into account census year, we use a series of tables that consist of four rows (husband's ethnicity) by four columns (wife's ethnicity) by four censuses (three for the second period) by six ethnicities (a different set for each period).

A series of six models is tested for each ethnicity and census. The simplest model is M_0, complete independence. It tests the false proposition that there is no relation between the ethnicity of the husband and that of the wife, that ethnicity is not a relevant consideration for nuptial pairings. Its frequencies may be derived as follows.

$$\log f_{ijc} = \mu_0 + \mu_i + \mu_j + \mu_c + \mu_{ic} + \mu_{jc} \tag{1}$$

Where $\log f_{ijc}$ is the natural logarithm of the expected from row i, column j, and the covariable c (census); μ_0 is a constant; μ_i the parameter of row i; μ_j the parameter of column j; and μ_c the parameter of the covariable c.

At the other extreme is the saturated model (not depicted), which assumes a unique interaction for each of the possible combinations of pairings, and therefore we must estimate a parameter for each one. The mathematical expression of this model is:

$$\log f_{ijc} = \mu_0 + \mu_i + \mu_j + \mu_c + \mu_{ic} + \mu_{jc} + \mu_{ij} + \mu_{ijc} \qquad [2]$$

where μ_{ijc} is the parameter representing the interaction between row i, column j, and the covariable c. The saturated model has the unique property of reproducing the data exactly, but it is of no analytical interest because it requires as many parameters as there are interactions to explain. The saturated model offers no parsimony whatsoever. Between the saturated and independence models, numerous combinations exist. Because each yields some degree of parsimony they are of substantive interest. They allow us to test the validity of specific hypotheses with regard to the patterns of ethnic interaction in the formation of marital unions. Throughout, we test the importance of time, in three ways: none, uniform, and significant variation found in each census.

Table 16.1 illustrates the topological structure of the basic parameters of each of the principal hypotheses that we propose to test. All substantive models include homogamy parameters. This is depicted along the diagonal where like-ethnics are shown as married to like-ethnics. These are the endogamous unions and they can be interpreted in terms of marital assimilation or the lack thereof. Model M_1 tests a second false proposition, that homogamy is the same for all combinations, parameter 1: [A,A] = [B,B] = [C,C] = [D,D]. The uniform homogamy model assumes quasi-independence in the off-diagonal cells. Although false, this model provides a better benchmark than M_0 for selecting more parsimonious models. It relaxes the condition of independence by assuming that the cells on the diagonal contain the majority of cases, but restricts this association to be equal for each endogamic combination. This model is a first test of the conventional assimilationist theory of ethnic marriage. Where it fits the data for any ethnic group, neither generation nor gender are important mechanisms for assimilation. Where it does not, our attention must focus on in-marriage parameters and the differences between first- and second-generation pairings and their variations in time.

Model M_2 relaxes even further the condition of homogamy by allowing each cell on the diagonal to take on a unique value, indicating a unique degree of endogamy for each combination. This formulation yields four parameters: [A,A] ≠ [B,B] ≠ [C,C] ≠ [D,D]. M_3 expands on the previous model considering parameter 4, cells [D,C] and [C,D], as also surpassing the condition of independence. Between the first and second generation of a common ethnicity or ancestry, our model 3 proposes a special attraction, indeed a uniform attraction identical to endogamy between second-generation unions of the same enthnicity.

Model M_4 bestows a single, unique parameter on generational exogamy, distinct from ethnic endogamy, that is [D,C] = [C,D] ≠ [D,D]. Finally, M_5 tests the hypothesis of gender assymetry in generationally exogamous unions, [D,C] ≠ [D,C]. If gender squeeze plays a role in promoting exogamy, model 5 should fit the data better than model 4. A more complete testing of this hypothesis might include the parameter [D,A] ≠ [A,D] to measure the interaction between the native-born and second-generation ethnicities. We did not perform this test.

To this typology we add the layers of time, one for each census (C), specific for both husbands (CH) and wives (CW). Tables 16.2 and 16.3 show the results for six ethnicities for the periods 1880–1920 and 1980–2000.

Table 16.2 Modelling fittings for six ethnicities over four censuses: 1880, 1900, 1910, 1920

Best models: M_3 (discrete homogamy with 2nd & 1st generation crossings) for English, Swedish, and French – uniform for all censuses; and M_5 (M_3 with the addition of gender asymmetry) – uniform for Irish and Italians, discrete for each census for Germans

	df	Ireland		England		Sweden		Germany		Italy		France	
		G^2	BIC	G^2	BIC	G^2	BIC	G^2	BIC	G^2	BIC	G^2	BIC
Independence/marginals													
1 CH, CW	36	893140.6	541620.1	567940.5	488120.6	972100.4	483880.2	821060.3	579380.1	134223.0	557160.8	573190.8	446750.1
Time constant association													
2 CH, CW, M_1	35	3345.9	2699.1	1079.2	672.9	4568.3	2358.3	4018.1	3519.2	298490.7	7162.4	1291.7	320.6
3 CH, CW, M_2	32	2828.0	1388.3	695.3	308.6	3435.5	669.3	3404.5	2390.3	150820.9	2407.6	647.7	102.8
4 CH, CW, M_3	32	532.8	163.8	543.7	194.1	412.2	53.1	785.7	462.06	444.9	97.0	386.6	32.3
5 CH, CW, M_4	31	501.2	142.5	542.4	204.0	399.3	45.2	692.8	338.9	428.5	87.8	382.4	40.2
6 CH, CW, M_5	30	458.6	117.4	541.5	214.8	387.3	47.0	672.7	329.7	409.6	87.0	377.3	45.7
Time variant association													
Uniform variation over C													
7 CH, CW, M_{3b}	29	294.4	−61.3	150.2	**−191.7**	111.2	**−224.7**	571.5	252.6	103.8	−259.2	103.7	**−236.7**
8 CH, CW, M_{4b}	28	272.3	−78.2	150.1	−180.4	104.1	−222.8	507.1	174.0	107.7	−265.1	99.8	−227.7
9 CH, CW, M_{5b}	27	228.0	**−99.8**	149.4	−169.2	92.2	−221.9	489.9	168.7	60.9	**−270.4**	95.7	−219.6
Unrestricted variation													
10 CH, CW, M_{5c}	12	64.2	−76.9	113.4	−27.9	31.19	−107.1	164.1	**19.1**	16.4	−119.6	23.0	−115.9

C: Census year; H: Husband's ethnicity; W: Wife's ethnicity; M^1–M^5: model specifications for Husband and Wife's ethnicity association; b: uniform variation over C; c: unrestricted variation over C

df: degrees of freedom

G^2: measure of goodness of fit

BIC: Bayesian Inference Coefficient takes into account the trade-off between degrees of freedom, goodness of fit, and sample size; lowest value signals best fit (in **bold**)

Table 16.3 "Newest" ethnicities' marriage patterns 1980, 1990, 2000: three models
M_3 (discrete homogamy with 2nd & 1st generation crossings) uniform for all censuses for Koreans and Cubans; M_4 (M_3 plus gender symmetry) uniform for all censuses for Chinese, Japanese, and Filipinos; and M_5 (M_3 with the addition of gender asymmetry), discrete for each census for Mexicans (poor fit in any case)

		China		Japan		Korea		Philippines		Mexico		Cuba	
	df	G^2	BIC	G^2	BIC	G^2	BIC	G^2	BIC	G^2	BIC	G^2	BIC
Independence/marginals													
1 CH, CW	27	310904.1	153308.8	224864.4	151632.3	236213.4	151490.0	237561.7	15357.2	400987.0	202024.4	269700.5	152541.1
Time constant association													
2 CH, CW, M_1	26	5336.1	2202.2	1692.2	683.7	2178.8	967.7	3072.3	1364.3	139640.5	12751.3	4534.3	1804.6
3 CH, CW, M_2	23	5339.4	602.2	782.0	198.7	843.8	132.6	3432.1	645.2	156550.1	9506.2	4413.3	647.1
4 CH, CW, M_3	23	353.6	67.3	716.3	412.5	369.4	75.7	345.6	58.5	1498.9	1138.8	313.9	29.6
5 CH, CW, M_4	22	339.3	64.0	403.6	127.0	361.5	84.7	325.7	50.8	1365.6	1060.2	313.8	42.1
6 CH, CW, M_5	21	335.8	75.2	402.4	139.5	361.3	97.4	313.2	51.0	1363.1	1071.9	311.8	52.8
Time variant association													
Uniform variation over C													
7 CH, CW, M_{3b}	21	79.1	**-189.5**	413.3	129.8	123.6	**-171.9**	92.2	-172.9	848.1	544.0	66.4	**-198.4**
8 CH, CW, M_{4b}	20	66.8	**-189.6**	111.1	**-143.4**	114.2	-163.0	74.4	**-180.3**	770.1	509.1	65.8	-186.6
9 CH, CW, M_{5b}	19	62.7	-178.8	109.8	-131.0	114.2	-150.4	60.8	**-181.4**	767.4	520.9	63.4	-176.0
Unrestricted variation													
10 CH, CW, M_{5c}	9	36.6	-77.2	69.3	-45.2	19.5	-96.8	42.3	-73.2	**564.7**	**437.4**	33.3	-80.4

C: Census year; H: Husband's ethnicity; W: Wife's ethnicity; M^1–M^5: model specifications for Husband and Wife's ethnicity association; b: uniform variation over C; c: unrestricted variation over C
df: degrees of freedom
G^2: measure of goodness of fit
BIC: Bayesian Inference Coefficient takes into account the trade-off between degrees of freedom, goodness of fit, and sample size; lowest value signals best fit (in **bold**)

Endogamous marriage patterns in both time periods are remarkably uniform. A small class of models fits the data adequately, even though the degree of endogamy varies considerably as we shall show below. The endogamy rule is the single most important constraint on nuptial pairings, accounting for 90 percent of the fit, as we see by comparing models 1 and 2 (Tables 16.2 and 16.3, BIC or G^2). In both periods history matters. None of the time-constant models fit adequately (models 2–6). On the other hand, while history matters, our models suggest that it does so in a generally uniform way, rather than as a discrete process oscillating from decade to decade. In both periods, the unrestricted time variation model fits best for only one of six ethnicities – Germans in the first and Mexicans in the second (model 10, Tables 16.2 and 16.3). An *ad hoc* explanation in the first instance is that what constituted Germans in the census changed markedly from 1900 to 1920 because of first the incorporation, then devolution, of Poland. In the case of Mexicans born in Mexico and resident in the United States, their numbers approached one million in 1980. Then the Mexican-born population doubled from 1980 to 1990, and doubled again from 1990 to 2000. This explosive growth meant that the Mexican-born population was rejuvenated each decade as were the odds of inter-marriage. To successfully model Mexican marriage patterns, additional parameters are required.

Table 16.4 reports the degree of endogamy by generation for all 12 ethnicities. To control for the disturbing effects of model type, we use model 10 in computing log odds of nuptial pairings, even though this model is not the most parsimonious fit.

Table 16.4 Endogamy estimates for old and newest ethnic groups by generation
Log odds for in-marriage from model M_{5c}: discrete homogamy plus gender asymmetry with unrestricted variation from census to census

	First generation (parameter 3)				Second generation (parameter 4)			
	1880	1900	1910	1920	1880	1900	1910	1920
Ireland	5.0	5.3	5.6	5.3	2.2	2.2	1.8	1.7
England	3.1	2.3	2.5	3.0	0.6	0.8	0.7	0.9
Sweden	7.3	6.3	6.0	5.8	6.4	5.0	3.1	2.8
Germany	4.9	4.7	3.6	3.9	2.2	1.9	1.5	1.2
Italy	8.8	10.4	10.1	8.6	–	–	–	5.7
France	4.8	5.6	6.4	4.6	2.3	1.8	–	1.5
	First generation				Second generation or more			
	–	1980	1990	2000	–	1980	1990	2000
China	–	6.4	6.5	6.4	–	5.7	4.6	5.0
Japan	–	1.2	1.8	3.0	–	5.8	4.5	5.4
Korea	–	4.0	6.0	6.2	–	–	–	5.9
Philippines	–	5.1	4.5	4.8	–	4.5	4.2	4.4
Mexico	–	5.7	5.6	5.2	–	3.9	3.3	2.9
Cuba	–	5.5	5.5	5.8	–	3.9	4.1	4.3

NOTE

1   The 1980 and 1990 censuses report year of immigration in groups rather than single
years. We have taken the last year of the group as the year of immigration.

REFERENCES

Akers, D.S. (1967). "On Measuring the Marriage Squeeze." *Demography* 4(2): 907–24.

Alba, R.D. and R.M. Golden (1986). "Patterns of Ethnic Marriage in the United States."
Social Forces 65(1): 202–23.

Alba, R.D. and V. Nee (1997). "Rethinking Assimilation Theory for a New Era of Immigration." *International Migration Review* 31(4): 826–74.

Blau, P.M. (1977). *Inequality and Heterogeneity.* New York: Free Press.

Blau, P.M., T.C. Blum, and J.E. Schwartz (1982). "Heterogeneity and Intermarriage." *American Sociological Review* 47(1): 45–62.

Botev, N. (1994). "Where East Meets West: Ethnic Intermarriage in the Former Yugoslavia."
American Sociological Review 59: 461–80.

Goldman, N., C.F. Westoff, and C. Hammerslough (1984). "Demography of the Marriage
Market in the United States." *Population Index* 50(1): 5–25.

Gordon, M. (1964). *Assimilation in American Life.* New York: Oxford University Press.

Gray, A. (1987). "Intermarriage: Opportunity and Preference." *Population Studies* 41(3):
365–79.

Hout, M. and J.R. Goldstein (1994). "How 4.5 Million Irish Immigrants Became 40 Million
Irish Americans: Demographic and Subjective Aspects of the Ethnic Composition of White
Americans." *American Sociological Review* 59(1): 64–82.

Jacobs, J.A. and T.G. Labov (2002). "Gender Differentials in Intermarriage Among Sixteen
Race and Ethnic Groups." *Sociological Forum* 17(4): 621–46.

Jones, F.L. and R. Luijks (1996). "Post-War Patterns of Intermarriage in Australia: The
Mediterranean Experience." *European Sociological Review* 12: 67–86.

Kalmijn, M. (1998). "Intermarriage and Homogamy: Causes, Patterns and Trends." *Annual
Review of Sociology* 24: 395–421.

McCaa, R. (1993). "Ethnic Intermarriage and Gender in New York City." *Journal of Interdisciplinary History* 24(2): 207–31.

Massey, D. (1985). "Ethnic Residential Segregation: A Theoretical Synthesis and Empirical
Review." *Sociology and Social Research* 69: 315–50.

Morgan, B. (1991). "A Contribution to the Debate on Homogamy, Propinquity, and Segregation." *Journal of Marriage and the Family* 4: 909–21.

Page, H.J. (1995). "Nuptiality Behaviour of Immigrant Populations." In A.S. Voets,
J. Schoorl, and B. de Bruin, eds., *Demographic Consequences of International Migration.*
The Hague: Nidi, pp. 163–75

Pagnini, D.L. and S.P. Morgan (1990). "Intermarriage and Social Distance Among U.S.
Immigrants at the Turn of the Century." *American Sociological Review* 96: 405–32.

Park, R.E. and E. Burgess (1969). *Introduction to the Science of Sociology* [1921]. Chicago:
University of Chicago Press.

Porterfield, E. (1982). "Black-American Intermarriage in the United States." *Marriage and
Family Review* 5(1): 17–34.

Portes, A. and R.G. Rumbaut (2001). *Legacies: The Story of the Immigrant Second Generation.*
Berkeley: University of California Press.

Portes, A. and M. Zhou (1993). "The New Second Generation: Segmented Assimilation and Its Variants Among Post-1965 Immigrant Youth." *Annals of the American Academy of Political Sciences* 53: 75–98.

Price, C.A. and J. Zubrzycki (1962). "The Use of Inter-Marriage Statistics as an Index of Assimilation." *Population Studies* 16(1): 58–69.

Qian, Z. (1997). "Breaking the Racial Barriers: Variations in Interracial Marriage Between 1980 and 1990." *Demography* 34(2): 263–76.

Qian, Z. and D.T. Lichter (2001). "Measuring Marital Assimilation: Intermarriage Among Natives and Immigrants." *Social Science Research* 30: 289–312.

Rosenfeld, M.J. (2002). "Measures of Assimilation in the Marriage Market: Mexican Americans 1970–1990." *Journal of Marriage and the Family* 64: 152–62.

Ruggles, S. and Sobek, M. (2004). *Integrated Public Use Microdate Series, Version 3.0.* Minneapolis, MN: Minnesota Population Center.

Sandberg, N., ed. (1973). *Ethnic Identity and Assimilation: The Polish Community.* New York: Praeger.

Wildsmith, E., M.P. Gutmann, and B. Graton (2004). "Assimilation and Intermarriage of U.S. Immigrant Groups, 1880–1990" (Mimeo).

Zhou, M. (1997). "Segmented Assimilation: Issues, Controversies, and Recent Research on the New Second Generation." *International Migration Review* 31(4): 975–1008.

PART IV

ECONOMY AND SOCIETY

CHAPTER SEVENTEEN

Immigrant Social Mobility and the Historian

KENNETH A. SCHERZER

The hope for a better job inextricably links upward mobility to the American dream. The mythology which surrounds it is a source of pride and national self-identity, exemplified by the pabulum of Horatio Alger and other rags-to-riches stories common in popular culture. The dream of success has proven an important lure for immigrants even if real achievements were often modest. This gap between hope and reality has made the study of ethnic differences in wealth and occupation of newcomers and their children an important subject for social historians. Nevertheless, penetrating myths to measure the extent of immigrant mobility has proven both complex and difficult despite nearly four decades of scholarship.

Much of the problem in studying mobility stems from its amorphous nature. More often than not, scholars use mobility to study the social stratification of American society rather than individual behavior, leading some sociologists to call for a return of the individual – the mechanisms of mobility such as social networks and career paths that shape personal choices – to the study of mobility (see Brieger 1990, ch. 1). Still, movement from one job category to another indirectly measures a number of things, ranging from English language skills to intermarriage levels. All these are important measures used by sociologists to compare rates of assimilation in an increasingly industrialized, highly dynamic capitalist economy. Historians have found that pre-industrial traditions, rooted in peasant backgrounds, often kept immigrants from adopting middle-class values of success. Many ethnics traded long-term prospects of improvement for the immediate security of home ownership. Nineteenth-century Irish immigrants sometimes even sacrificed the education of children for the immediate needs of the family economy.

Efforts by historians to examine differences in occupational mobility between immigrant groups have been further complicated by long-term structural changes in the United States. In the late nineteenth and early twentieth centuries, the American economy was based upon heavy industry, which produced numerous low-level manufacturing jobs. By the 1960s, this had been replaced by a service economy with many low-paying service sector jobs at the bottom, well-paid professional employment at the top, but often little in between. Early twenty-first-century trends confirm uneven levels of opportunity among different strata. Furthermore, changes in the labor market – easier to infer than to measure – often stifled levels of mobility regardless of ethnic background. The disappearance of manufacturing jobs in the post-industrial economy and the accompanying expansion of the low-paid service sector have slowed intergenerational mobility, particularly for many Hispanic immigrants. Preferential immigration policy geared toward family reunification and the recruit-ment of highly skilled professionals has produced a bifurcated system of opportunity. Less skilled immigrants who join family members within the United States face bleak prospects for advancement, while educated professionals given preferential admission demonstrate levels of success well above the national average. Finally, in local labor markets, the volume of immigration often depresses prevailing wage levels, under-cutting opportunity for natives and newcomers alike.

Each era of immigration to the United States has had its own ethnic pattern of occupational advancement. In the two decades before the Civil War, the success of German and English immigrants stood in stark contrast with the dire poverty of the famine Irish. Early in the twentieth century, the limited mobility of Poles, Irish, and Italians, who tended to cluster in unskilled and semi-skilled industrial employment, differed markedly from the success of Jewish immigrants following twin paths of petty entrepreneurship and education out of poverty. In postwar America, particularly in the wake of the 1965 Hart–Celler Act which removed 1920s-era immigrant quotas, South Asians, Japanese, Koreans, and Jamaicans reached or surpassed native-born levels of status. By contrast, Mexicans, Central Americans, Puerto Ricans, and Haitians remained mired at the bottom, often for more than two generations. Native-born blacks, a group beyond the scope of this chapter, were the one group for which scholars have found consistently low levels of advancement regardless of period.

Methods Used to Study Historical Mobility

Historians have long used mobility tables to measure changes in employment status between ethnic groups by comparing occupational ranking over successive periods. First developed by sociologists, these tables show shifts between an initial job in America and employment one or more decades later. They can also chart inter-generational mobility by comparing occupational ranks of sons with those of their fathers. This can show the extent to which sons of blue-collar fathers transcended their fathers' rank and whether white-collar fathers were able to pass their status to kin. Advancement in rank also served to indirectly measure whether immigrant groups valued education differently because white-collar positions typically required more schooling than did blue-collar trades.

For all these potential strengths, historians have also discovered problems in trying to use mobility tables. Unlike sociologists who could administer surveys, historians have faced enormous problems gathering data due to incomplete records and changes in definitions of occupational categories used to measure rank. Which best measures past levels of mobility: job rank, rates of home ownership, or estimates of income? More important, can occupational ranking schemes employed by contemporary socio-logists be applied retroactively to the nineteenth century where contemporaries categorized jobs differently?

Since the early 1960s, historical studies of mobility have generally ranked jobs into several broad status categories. Unskilled and semi-skilled manual workers were at the bottom of an occupational pyramid, with a broad collection of skilled blue-collar trades in the middle, followed by a small band of petty-proprietary and white-collar workers further up, culminating in an elite of professionals and businessmen at the apex. Historians generally drew data for mobility tables from manuscript federal censuses supplemented by city directories, each of which had limitations. During the heyday of mobility research, scholars had access to only four censuses containing enough detailed information to study occupation: 1850, 1860, 1870, and 1880 (the 1890 census had been lost and the 1900 schedules were not yet released; today, censuses are available through 1930). And since neither set of records listed actual incomes, historians used contemporary sociological studies to producing rankings which were more presumptive than real.

Ranking occupations proved to be an imprecise science. Did the name of a product listed by a census enumerator under occupation indicate a lowly worker or the owner of a company? Should a lowly-paid teenage clerk be classified as higher status than a better-paid skilled craftsman simply because clerks were white-collar? And was that clerk the boss's son – a manager in training – or yet another poorly-paid teenage office worker? Questions like these suggested limitations in using twentieth-century sociological classifications to rank jobs data collected a century earlier.

Data linkage, the crucial second step in mobility studies, has proven similarly daunting. Measuring changes in occupational status over a worker's lifetime or from one generation to another requires the researcher to trace her subject though subsequent censuses, most often with the assistance of city directories. In this tedious process, researchers faced the nearly insurmountable task of tracing individuals, many of whom had common names. Overcoming this problem by discarding individuals with common names risked introducing bias into the samples because so many of these names happened to belong to Irish immigrants. Only a minority, usually between one-third and one-half, could be traced from one decade to the next, due to death, out-migration, and ambiguity over common names. Census enumerators invariably missed substantial numbers of people. City directories had their own limitations, omitting women, younger workers, and residents of poorer neighborhoods of little interest to the commercial subscribers who purchased these volumes. Poor workers were frequently hostile to directory canvassers and census enumerators, resulting in spectacular undercounts, such as the 1865 New York State Census which showed a 10 percent drop in the New York City population attributable to tax avoidance and draft dodging during the Civil War. (Chronic undercounts among the poor continue to be a problem among modern censuses.) As great as these problems were, the greater difficulty of data linkage without directories predisposed historians to study urban areas at the expense of rural areas and small towns where most Americans resided before 1920 (Knights 1971; Griffen and Griffen 1978; Thernstrom and Knights 1970; Alcorn and Knights 1975; Parkerson 1982; Scherzer 1992).

The Rise and Fall of Mobility History

Despite such methodological problems, few new topics created as much excitement within the field of American social history as did the study of social mobility. And fewer still have faded so totally from attention. Stephan Thernstrom's classic study of Newburyport, Massachusetts promised to open a new era of community studies. However, the torrent of quantitative research which Thernstrom unleashed, instead, "came to a crashing halt in the late seventies, in part due to increasing disenchantment with quantification among historians, in part because the research of social mobility quickly reached a conceptual impasse" (Perlmann and Waldinger 1997, pp. 983–6). Thernstrom's observation (Stave 1977, p. 238) that "I don't think there is, nor do I think there should be, an incredibly glowing future for mobility studies *per se*" came true, but with an irony that he had not anticipated. Social mobility has all but disappeared from the historical literature, relegated to the sociological study of stratification from whence it first emerged and, in rare cases, econometric studies.

The sociological study of mobility was pioneered by Pitirim A. Sorokin in his theoretical work, *Social Mobility*, first published in 1927. Sorokin moved beyond the conventional definition of success as an individual attribute to make vertical mobility a measure of social stratification and the permeability of class boundaries. Yet his definition of mobility was an expansive one, encompassing changes in religion, marital status, or other changes in social characteristics and even lateral changes in employment within a factory. By demonstrating that vertical mobility varied from society to society and over different eras, Sorokin effectively challenged static views of mobility and historicized the study of social structure.

Mobility gained renewed attention during the 1950s when social scientists viewed America's social structure as exceptional compared with Europe. In *Social Mobility in Industrial Society* (1959), coauthored with Reinhard Bendix, Seymour Martin Lipset argued that social mobility – or the perception in America of high levels of mobility – inhibited the formation of class consciousness among American workers, thereby forestalling the development of a socialist movement akin to that found in western Europe (see Lipset and Bendix 1959; Glazer 2002a, 2002b; Kaelble 1986). Although subsequent sociological studies remained inconclusive, the work of Lipset and Bendix, together with an earlier study by W. Lloyd Warner of status mobility in "Yankee City" Newburyport, Massachusetts (Warner and Lunt 1941; Warner and Stole 1945), provided both the intellectual foundations and tempting targets for historians as they, too, began to study social mobility in the 1960s.

Stephan Thernstrom's *Poverty and Progress: Social Mobility in a Nineteenth Century City* (1964) unleashed a veritable flood of quantitative studies of immigrant mobility which, in turn, ignited interest in "bottom-up" studies of working-class communities for American social historians. Undoubtedly, much of the appeal of his study lay, as Thernstrom himself observed on the twentieth anniversary of its publication, in the timing of the book (Thernstrom 1986). With the exception of Merle Curti's study (1959) of frontier Trempealeau County, manuscript censuses, city directories, and property records had been largely overlooked by historians. Thernstrom's examination of mobility in Newburyport, highly critical of Warner, appeared at a time when historical writing was dominated by biographies and political histories. Although his work escaped notice by the leading historical journal (which mentioned it in a brief booknote as a new work of sociology), its appearance on the cusp of important changes in the writing of history soon made it a remarkably influential book. Thernstrom's study of working-class Irish immigrants focused on the lives of ordinary people and its research methodology lent itself to replication for numerous other communities, spurring numerous lesser studies before the wave finally played out.

The synergy between changes in the historical profession, the emerging social-scientific approach, and the simplicity of Thernstrom's quantification made *Poverty and Progress*, in the words of historian Michael Frisch (1986), "excitingly radical and reassuringly traditional in almost every methodological, professional, cultural, and political sense."

In retrospect, much of this appeal may have stemmed from the very modest levels of upward mobility Thernstrom found among sons of Irish laborers drawn from a succession of federal manuscript census schedules between 1850 and 1880. Unskilled workers remained in the same low-status job a decade later by a ratio of two to one; only one in 10 escaped poverty by advancing to a skilled trade. For most, then, middle-class success remained a distant dream. The fact that so many unskilled workers remained common laborers, the difficulty of laborers entering a skilled craft, the inheritance of this occupational disadvantage by sons, and the modest progress after many long decades offered a far more pessimistic picture of social mobility than had Lipset and Bendix. Many parents also sacrificed the education of their children by investing family resources in the short-term security of home ownership.

High levels of geographical mobility in which many unskilled workers left New-buryport compounded this already bleak situation. Early twentieth-century reformers often linked severe social dislocation to rootlessness. Drawing on this argument, Thernstrom argued that occupational failure created a floating proletariat of poor workers who moved from place to place in search of employment. To be sure, other factors besides poverty could have produced high levels of transiency. We now know that other life-cycle characteristics which Thernstrom did not take into account may have distorted his findings. Young low-status men are a more volatile group because of their age. Nevertheless, the disappearance of up to two-thirds of the population from the censuses over the course of a decade suggested that few immigrants remained in stable immigrant neighborhoods long enough to benefit from ethnic benevolent institutions. The Newburyport findings, combined with the results of a larger study of Boston (Thernstrom 1973, p. 41; Thernstrom and Knights 1970; see also Chudacoff 1994), led Thernstrom to conclude that high levels of geographical mobility among "poor people in particular" made cities "a Darwinian jungle, in which those on the upper rungs of the class ladder were most likely to survive to be counted in the future."

Such an assessment clashed with the Pollyannaish view of American class so common in postwar historical writing. Although Thernstrom found enough small hints of mobility to explain the wide acceptance of the Horatio Alger rags-to-riches mythology in the nineteenth century, his findings mainly challenged the "consensus" views of Lipset and Bendix that American class structure was uniquely open compared with the rigid class boundaries of Europe. Thernstrom's rediscovery of class made mobility an important topic within American history. Would the study of social mobility retain its allure if the results were more optimistic?

By 1973, in an authoritative study of Boston spanning the period from 1880 to 1970, Thernstrom substantially revised his findings. Boston data showing that "intergenerational *transmission* of low manual status was less common than upward social mobility," led him to now conclude: "I apparently erred in taking the New-buryport findings as a base line for gauging levels of mobility in nineteenth-century America" (1973, pp. 245–50). Despite erratic patterns of advancement for Irish and

Italians compared to Jewish and English workers, the results were nonetheless encouraging. They showed "a fairly high and relatively constant rate of upward intergenerational mobility, with a very large minority of working-class sons moving up into at least the lower echelons of the white-collar class, and with a clear majority" of poor youths escaping into "skilled trades or a white-collar post." Only black workers and their children failed to show progress (Thernstrom 1973, pp. 112–14, 154–65, 269–71, n. 35).

The next decade brought a number of studies replicating Thernstrom's methodology in one form or another for cities like Milwaukee, Pittsburgh, Detroit, Poughkeepsie, and New York. Their findings were decidedly less sanguine about opportunities for upward mobility in industrial America. A comprehensive review of the literature by John Bodnar concluded that "most immigrants not only began their careers in the lower social and economic levels of the American economy," but also remained far less likely to rise to higher-status jobs than natives. This was true not only for nineteenth-century Irish workers, more than half of whom remained unskilled workers, but also for twentieth-century groups ranging from Poles in Detroit to Mexican immigrants in Los Angeles. On the basis of these studies, Bodnar characterized any expectation for significant upward movement during most immigrants' lifetimes as "unrealistic" (Bodnar 1985, pp. 169–71; see also Conzen 1976; Griffen and Griffen 1978; Zunz 1982; Barton 1975; Bodnar, Weber, and Simon 1982; Kessner 1977; Romo 1983).

Blue-collar backgrounds also handicapped advancement for the children of immigrant fathers. Even having a white-collar father was no guarantee against backsliding. Where Thernstrom saw steady improvement from one generation to the next, Bodnar found progress to be "neither inevitable nor simply a function of time." As often as not, the sons of manual laborers found themselves more likely to "repeat the occupational patterns of their fathers than to rise above them." Smaller industrial cities with a smaller range of employers, like Steelton, Pennsylvania, Poughkeepsie, New York, and Fall River, Massachusetts, had more limited opportunities than cities like Cleveland, Boston, or New York City. Nevertheless, even in major cities, between 70 and 80 percent of immigrant sons whose parents were blue-collar workers and half of all sons remained in the same occupational strata as their parents. For Germans, who were among the most upwardly mobile ethnic groups early in the twentieth century, Bodnar found that "cheaper, factory-produced goods" produced downward mobility for sons (1985, pp. 169–75).

A decade of intense study had not only produced contradictory results, but also demonstrated methodological limitations in the techniques historians had used to examine social mobility. From the outset, incomplete and often biased records, such as savings account registers and property assessments, had limited sources which might have supplemented occupational classification. Now the hierarchical classification of occupations using sociological criteria itself came under increasing scrutiny. In a wide-ranging critique of mobility studies, Howard Chudacoff (1982) – himself a pioneer in the field with a study of Omaha (1972) – listed a number of fundamental problems. These included the misleading nature of occupational titles, the wide variation in pay within even the same job classification, and the artificiality of using the twentieth-century division of blue-collar and white-collar to measure historical status. The use of broadly occupational categories hid meaningful differences in job type. Categories such as "entrepreneurial" ignored business risks that often led to failure instead of success. Nor did most studies adequately address structural concerns such as macro-economic business cycles or differences in employment markets from one community to another. Furthermore, most scholars excluded women because name changes in marriage and the virtual exclusion of women (save for widows) from city directories make them difficult to trace in successive censuses. The absence of gender from mobility studies forced historians to treat mobility in isolation from the operation of the family economy. Inconsistent research methodologies kept historians from placing their findings in a broader context. Perhaps the most damning criticism of historical mobility studies came from James Henretta (1977) who suggested that the ideology of mobility may not have been embraced by many of the subjects historians sought to study. If immigrant workers preferred security to status or dignity and autonomy to consumption, then the entire assumption underpinning the study of mobility threatened to collapse.

The "new labor history," together with a backlash against quantification, finally stemmed the tide of mobility studies in the 1980s. Heavily influenced by the British labor historian E.P. Thompson (1963, p. 9; see also Fitch 1984), the post-Thernstrom generation of American social historians turned from strata to culture when they examined class, embracing Thompson's dictum: "I do not see class as a 'structure', nor even as a 'category', but as something which in fact happens . . . in human relationships." If class were not structural, "The finest meshed sociological net" could not "give us a pure specimen of class, any more than it can give us one of deference or of love." Such a broad rejection was taken up by an entire generation of scholars of the American working class. Sociology was out and the thick description of cultural anthropologist Clifford Geertz replaced mobility tables. Quantification, the much-heralded tool of Thernstrom's generation, now was attacked for being blind to class culture and, by implication, conservative in nature (like the neo-classical economics permeating econometrics). Reeling from ideological attacks from the Left and showing fatigue from the diminishing returns many quantitative historians had felt after their labors, "quantitative social science history collapsed suddenly," in the words of Edward Ayers, "the victim of its own inflated claims, limited method and machinery, and changing academic fashion," leaving a "new generation" defining "itself in opposition to social scientific methods just as energetically as an earlier generation had seen in those methods the best means of writing a truly democratic history" (1999).

The Flowering of Social-Scientific Mobility Studies

Ironically, just as most historians' interest turned away from mobility after the mid-1980s, largely abandoning the field to sociologists or, in one notable case, an economic historian, the methodological sophistication of studies began to improve immensely. These newer social-scientific studies classified occupation with greater precision, employed powerful new multivariate techniques like logit to disentangle factors underlying changes in status, and skillfully melded cultural analysis and oral history with quantitative methodology. The newer studies, which form the basis of the remainder of this chapter, have examined urban–rural differences in mobility rates, improved upon methodological problems in measuring socio-economic status, refined our understanding of structural factors and location in shaping opportunity, and probed the intrinsic definitions of status used by immigrants to define status. Some scholars have looked at mechanisms for advancement by studying the role of high school education in fostering success among different ethnic groups in Somerville, Massachusetts and Providence, Rhode Island. Others have underscored the exceptional success of Jewish immigrants in harnessing petty-entrepreneurship and education towards advancement. Finally, sociologists and historians have begun to understand the operation of opportunity in postwar America, where differential patterns of immigration have intensified inequality within and between different ethnic groups.

Scholars studying pre-Civil War immigrants have examined the complex nature of mobility, tying pre-migration conditions to subsequent success in America as measured by occupation, income, and land-ownership. In one study, Walter Kamphoefner (1987) traced German immigrants from their pre-migration homes in Techlenbur and Lippe-Detmoder in Germany to rural Missouri. Those with the greatest resources prior to migration acquired the largest farmsteads in America, although opportunities to own farms were real even for those of modest means. Consequently, midwestern farm communities offered much better prospects for immigrant success than cities. Rural Germans quickly achieved levels of prosperity rivaling those of native-born farmers, while their urban countrymen fared far worse than natives. German immigrants living in St. Louis were more likely to be young transients with little money or prospects. Many suffered downward mobility as a result of immigrating and only the most highly skilled prospered in their trades. No wonder four out of five immigrants from Lippe traded their old trades for agriculture and many Germans who had settled in cities eventually relocated in the countryside.

Much the same held for Norwegian immigrants from Balestrand once they moved to the upper midwest. Jon Gjerde (1985) found that old country farming experience and community structure translated into advantages over native farmers in a number of ways. Norwegian farmers were more aggressive in acquiring good land and farm animals than were their native-born neighbors. They adjusted to the new agricultural economy which favored wheat production over other crops, and, in time, overcame their tradition of austere living to embrace the bourgeois lifestyle of the successful midwestern farmer. For both Germans and Norwegians, modest successes in establishing farms encouraged chain migration to rural communities and minimized inequality. Taken together, these two studies suggest that most urban-based mobility studies have overlooked the more hopeful reality of rural achievement, a success story all the more important because most nineteenth-century Americans still resided on the farm.

The importance of this urban–rural divide for the antebellum period is further underscored by a recent study by economic historian Joseph P. Ferrie (1999). A sample of 5 percent of males who arrived by ship in America from the United Kingdom and Germany during the period 1840–5 traced in 1850 and 1860 manuscript censuses allowed Ferrie to study where immigrants ultimately settled in America and how they fared. Of those immigrants who arrived in New York City just prior to the 1850 census, nearly two-thirds quickly departed. This was especially true for skilled British workers, nine out of ten of whom left depressed eastern labor markets for the frontier, where wages were higher. Since only two out of five immigrants remained within the New York City vicinity – the commercial classes with the resources to succeed and the very poor, like the Irish, who arrived nearly penniless – Ferrie argued immigrants showed "a deliberateness that suggested the care with which many planned their journeys."

The direction of moves also suggested that high levels of geographical mobility indicated "calculated calibrations to improve immigrants' circumstances" rather than "mere rootlessness." Many initially settled in rural areas "in anticipation of a subsequent move back into an urban area," such as St. Louis and Milwaukee. Immigrants hoped that these newer midwestern cities, unlike cities on the eastern seaboard, would offer greater opportunities. To be sure, the most highly mobile immigrants and natives were also more volatile in terms of occupation than non-movers. Yet over time the gamble paid off. Immigrants were able to add an average of nearly 15 percent to their net wealth for every year they lived in America, thus demonstrating "the reasonableness of the immigrant's decision to come to the United States" (Ferrie 1999, pp. 187–90).

Ferrie's analysis also confirmed the findings of earlier historians on the risks that awaited immigrants in a crowded labor economy. Most new arrivals experienced downward occupational mobility upon arrival, particularly white-collar and skilled workers forced to settle for lower-status work. Only German refugees from the Revolution of 1848 improved their standing, ostensibly because of their exceptional levels of skill. Over time, one-quarter of white-collar and skilled workers suffered declines in rank compared with one-third of unskilled whose rank improved. Ferrie's findings were also consistent with other studies in underscoring ethnic differences in occupational trajectory. The Irish experienced the most difficulty in establishing themselves while German and British immigrants did far better.

Italian immigrants also made rational calculations in coming to America, although their choices often involved helping families at home rather than improving standards of living here. In a comparative analysis of Italian immigrants in Buenos Aires and New York City during the late nineteenth and early twentieth centuries, Samuel L. Baily (1999, pp. 93–120) demonstrates that most initially sought to accumulate a sufficient surplus to send to family members in Italy or to provide for their own return. Italians in both cities largely succeeded in purchasing homes, underwriting mutual aid societies, and sending remittances to overseas relatives. However, differences in prevailing labor markets between Argentina and the United States produced divergent strategies. Greater opportunities for skilled and white-collar workers in Buenos Aires, which was Argentina's commercial and bureaucratic hub, produced greater occupational mobility for South American Italian immigrants than it did for their northern compatriots. They were more likely to invest their surplus earnings in business, homes, school, and formal institutions. By contrast, the New York City economy was primarily commercial and industrial rather than bureaucratic and its labor market mainly created unskilled, semi-skilled, and service jobs. Where immigrants depended upon individual social networks to find jobs in Buenos Aires, New York Italians relied upon *padroni* to channel unskilled laborers to large building projects like the subway. Such limited opportunities translated into an earning strategy which, Baily argues, focused on the short term. With the New York immigrants looking towards an imminent return to Italy rather than investing in community institutions here, the combination of strategy and labor market translated into lower levels of occupational mobility in New York City than in Buenos Aires.

Sociologists who have traced mobility rates from the late nineteenth century through the 1970s observed similarly high levels of upward mobility – well above what Bodnar and other historians had found. Challenging Thernstrom's contention that culture handicapped Irish immigrants when compared to native-born and German workers, Nancy S. Landale and Avery M. Guest (1990, p. 294) argued that "white men over the last century have generally not faced serious barriers to mobility related to generation" or national origin. Although the Irish were over-represented within low-rank blue-collar jobs in 1880, the proportion of Irish white-collar workers rose from 6 percent to 22.1 percent by 1900. Even more broadly, the focus of most historical attention upon the late nineteenth century may have distorted our understanding of mobility. Continuity of jobs between generations was higher a century ago than at later times because many sons grew up on family farms and followed in their father's occupational footsteps as a condition for the inheritance of farm land. An examination of broad trends of intergenerational mobility "indicated an increasing association between origins and destinations from the late 1800s to World War I, a relatively constant opportunity structure between World War I and 1962, and a declining relationship between 1962 and 1973" (Guest, Landale, and McCann 1989, p. 374).

Sociologists also refined measures of socio-economic status, allowing them to employ sophisticated statistical techniques to disentangle the complex factors that underlay ethnic differences. Where historians had grouped occupations into four or five discrete categories that could be analyzed using simple percentage tables, the continuous-scale socioeconomic index (SEI) allowed later researchers to employ multivariate statistical techniques like multiple regression. The resulting studies, although not numerous, have been finer grained. A study by Sharon Sassler and Michael J. White (1997; see also Worrell 2001) utilized a "Public Use Sample" of the 1910 census to study how the family economy and gender differences shaped the way in which immigrants directed resources to their children. Ethnicity turned out to be less important than other factors in determining the occupational rank of never-married sons. The SEI level of a father had the greatest impact on the job attainment of his son, explaining 13 percent of the variation. Although the overall effect of ethnicity on SEI was statistically significant, clear ethnic differences were apparent only for certain groups; Jewish and English Canadian sons scored higher while blacks held lower-status jobs than did other groups.

If sons tended to inherit their father's status regardless of ethnic background, did this pattern also hold for daughters? Sassler and White expected to find two patterns of family strategies. Either a daughter might drop out of school to work for money to further a brother's education or, for ethnic groups which discouraged women from working, a son might be expected to sacrifice his career in order to keep a sister from having to work outside of home. Instead, they found no significant difference between sons and daughters. Larger families strained resources for children regardless of sex. Nonetheless, gender did shape occupational patterns for immigrant daughters in two respects. The gendered labor market limited long-term opportunities for women so that daughters advanced less in their careers than sons. Second, fathers who were committed to remaining in America were more likely to have daughters who worked. Higher levels of house ownership and American citizenship boosted the SEI for daughters more than sons, suggesting that families may have relied upon the earnings of a daughter to raise money for the purchase of a home. This was especially true for more established groups such as Germans than it was for newer immigrants such as Poles.

Sociological studies have also shed light upon the impact of structural factors, such as the local labor market, in shaping employment during the late nineteenth and early twentieth centuries. Emerging cities, such as Los Angeles and San Francisco on the west coast or Atlanta in the south, created more opportunities for immigrants than did older cities in the northeast or midwest – although many gains in these volatile urban economies risked being short-lived (Morawska 1990). Location could have enormous impact on success for immigrants settling in rural areas. Portuguese had lower levels of literacy and occupational status, and had fewer financial resources than did most other European immigrants during the late nineteenth century. Since employment was highly dependent upon migrant networks, those without family connections sometimes ended up as contract labor on Hawaiian sugar plantations where status was little better, as Caucasians, than imported unskilled Asian labor. Most Portuguese sugar plantation laborers remained unskilled and left Hilo once their contracts were finished (Baganha 1991). Single unskilled "policy owner" workers, who labored in the textile mills of Taunton, Massachusetts also remained mired in low-status jobs. Only immigrants to the farming community of Milpitas, California were able transcend skill barriers. They worked as agricultural laborers on the general and dairy farms owned by established Portuguese which served the San Francisco Bay area market. Where only one in 20 of the Hawaii and Taunton immigrants were able to escape unskilled labor, 83 percent of the California household heads themselves became employers or self-employed.

In single industry towns where opportunities were limited and white-collar jobs rare, immigrants constructed their own internal system of stratification. A carefully researched study by Ewa Morawska blended sociological methodology with a keen appreciation of the limitations of structural categories (1985, pp. 222–3, 226–39) to penetrate the " 'intrinsic' " world of ethnic mobility. The eastern central Europeans she studied in Johnstown, Pennsylvania sought rewards not only of income and occupation, but also valued resources of membership in social and political organizations. Stratification existed through lifestyle and culture and had a social meaning that was far richer than conventional categories had suggested. Immigrant residents of the closed factory town created their own "fundamentally classless but non egalitarian system" for a community where the highest-status jobs they encountered might be the ethnic store owners and doctors in their neighborhood. In such a highly localized world, leadership of a fraternal organization or even length of residence within Johnstown became the main measures of social standing, although the importance of wealth in defining rank increased as the community matured. After immigrants gave up their plans of returning to Europe and decided to remain in the United States, social status came to be defined less by occupation, education, or income than by the power to make "others dependent upon one's professional services." Where jobs did define status, oral history interviews showed that immigrants created their own separate rankings which were often at odds with those used by scholars. As might be expected, eastern Europeans and their children ranked semi- and unskilled mill and mine work at the bottom, skilled employment in the middle, and ethnic businessmen at the top. However, many small businesses and ethnic service trades were actually placed *below* skilled blue-collar trades. In nearly all cases, respondents felt that incomes and visible possessions were better measures of status than was occupation.

This internal stratification system continued to operate into the second generation. Between 1915 and 1930, the proportion of ascents into higher-status work barely exceeded that of declines, 53 percent versus 47 percent. Bleak prospects fostered fatalism and a "semicaste" social division. Workers now saved for basic security and to achieve a good life within the boundaries of their working-class ethnic community, not to escape it. Second-generation eastern Europeans sought to improve upon the lives of their fathers by seeking office jobs, skilled trades, or at least mill jobs with better working conditions (Morawska 1985, pp. 264, 282–8; see also Hareven 1982). While a few immigrant sons succeeded – measures of occupational mobility showed 65 percent climbing out of the lowest employment levels – the Great Depression not only put a stop to any further advancement, but also undid much earlier progress. Of those who had escaped low-status jobs after 1915, 45 percent fell in status during the 1930s and few were able to recoup earlier gains until the 1940s. Many sons found themselves little better off than their father had been and only those who inherited family business had any success in escaping the ravages of the Depression.

Paths towards Mobility – Jewish Differences and Education

If social-scientific scholarship refines our understanding of structural and cultural forces in shaping mobility, it also reinforces one key finding of earlier studies: the exceptional levels of upward mobility among East European Jews. Historians may have found little evidence in the United States to support Max Weber's classic formulation concerning the role of Protestantism in fostering entrepreneurship and commercial success. For Jewish immigrants in the late nineteenth and early twentieth centuries, by contrast, the movement into commerce and the professions was nothing short of meteoric. In Boston, Jews were disproportionately represented in white-collar professions from the outset. Although small numbers in Thernstrom's sample weaken its reliability, he found that half of Jews who began as common laborers had advanced out of this category by the end of their career, double the rate of any other group. And where only one in 20 Irish immigrants began in "business for profit," the figure for first-generation Jewish immigrants was 45 percent (Thernstrom 1973, pp. 137, 152; Bodnar 1985, p. 171).

Similar results held for other cities. Thomas Kessner (1977, pp. 124–5) found that two-thirds of Jewish immigrants in New York City had skilled trades upon arrival compared with only one in five for Italians, the largest immigrant cohort at the turn of the twentieth century. Data from the 1905 New York State census showed that Jewish manual workers were 25 percent more likely to move into white-collar jobs within a decade than any other group. Likewise in 1915 Providence, Rhode Island (Perlmann 1988, pp. 132–3, 154–5), fewer than one in four Russian Jewish immigrants started as manual workers employed by others compared to nearly three out of four for Italians and Irish and two out of three for natives. Jews were nearly twice as likely as other immigrants to be classified as professionals and 23.2 percent were proprietors. Even many of the poorest Jewish immigrants were self-employed – one in five among manual laborers – and 22.3 percent worked as peddlers.

Such economic achievement translated into similarly high levels of intergenerational mobility for Russian Jews. New York Jewish children rapidly advanced into white-collar jobs compared with Italian sons, one-quarter of whom remained mired in unskilled employment. Second-generation sons produced SEI scores that were the highest among any group of immigrant children in Providence. The mean occupational level of 1915 Jewish high school graduates was 12 percent higher than groups in 1925 while the gap for 1925 graduates traced to 1935, though narrower, was still 10 percent.

Even controlling for prior parental characteristics associated with success, Jewish sons enjoyed stronger "translation of resources into achievement" in several studies (Model 1988, p. 5). With Jewish immigrants showing higher levels of literacy prior to migration – perhaps out of religious requirements to read prayers and follow Talmudic law – it was not surprising that cultural heritage translated into post-migration educational attainment. Even though Jews who came to America had less religious commitment than those who remained in Europe, they still valued education and this translated into a high "general status of learning and jobs based on it." Jewish students were more likely to enter high school, to pursue more rigorous classical and college preparatory tracks, and, in particular, to graduate.

Despite high levels of crime and low testing on standardized tests during World War I, the first generation of Jewish immigrants aggressively pursued entrepreneurship, even if it meant owning a pushcart. The second generation pursued college education and had attendance rates that were twice those of other groups. By the 1960s, occupation niches based upon education had replaced the garment trades and retailing which attracted Jews in earlier decades (Perlmann 1988; Gold and Phillips 1996; Kessner 1977; Thernstrom 1973). Data from Los Angeles suggest that Jews continue to enjoy higher levels of earnings into the third and fourth generations, trading their traditional ethnic occupational niche for a new and more lucrative one as highly educated professionals and managers (Waldinger and Lichter 1996).

A number of explanations have been offered to explain Jewish success. Much of the difference may stem from the special fit between occupational backgrounds of Jewish immigrants and the economic niches open to them in the United States (Gold and Phillips 1996; see also Morawska 1990). Jews were "more skilled, literate, and familiar with urban life" than other southern and eastern European immigrants, many of whom were impoverished males who merely saw the United States as a temporary sojourn before returning to Europe. As religious refugees, they had no place to which they could return. Second, the presence of family members enhanced this permanence while solidifying social networks in a way that translated into employment. Wives and children formed an important component of home-based manufacturing. High levels of industrial employment prior to migration prepared Jewish immigrants for small industry and they comprised more than twice their proportion of the entire skilled immigrant workforce in 1914. A third factor propelling Jewish mobility was the concentration of Jews in the needle trades, a sector where the cost of setting up a new business was exceptionally low. The flow from sweatshops to petty-entrepreneurship in garment assembly, cigar and cigarette making, and various small manufacturing trades combined with peddling cigarettes to foster essential entrepreneurial skills. Finally, Russian Jews benefited from charitable institutions and industrial niches established by earlier German Jewish immigrants who had arrived before the Civil War.

The experience of Jewish immigrants suggests that paths toward mobility may have more to do with understanding opportunity than differences between ethnic groups. From the early twentieth century, the industrial economy made education the key to better pay. In the nineteenth century, blue-collar workers may have been able to advance to non-manual employment with just a basic grammar school education, but high schools became indispensable for the children of white-collar parents and, increasingly, for the sons of workingmen. Reed Ueda's study (1987, pp. 153–85) of high schools in Somerville, Massachusetts demonstrated how, by 1915, graduating high school doubled the chance of blue-collar sons making it to white-collar employment compared with those having just a grammar school education. Nevertheless, class and ethnic backgrounds remained underlying forces in shaping mobility, slowing ascent for working-class immigrant children. Despite its crucial role in opening the door to better-paying employment, high school remained a luxury for many blue-collar families. While 86 percent of English and Yankee sons who graduated grammar school went on to high school, the figure for blue-collar Irish sons was two-thirds. Ethnicity also shaped the chance of graduating, but in a paradoxical way. Irish children graduated public school less often than did English Canadian or Yankee sons and daughters, but the resources that working-class Irish parents scrounged to invest in sending a child to a Latin high school actually boosted Irish graduation rates above those for other groups.

Joel Perlmann's (1988) study of the impact of schooling upon Irish, Italian, Russian Jewish, and black children in Providence, Rhode Island between 1880 and 1935 offers the most exhaustive examination of how ethnic difference shaped educational rates and occupational achievement. Controlling for difference in family background in terms of father's occupational index, the value of property ownership, the number of siblings in the household, and whether both parents were present, Perlmann was able to disentangle ethnic factors influencing mobility from those based on class. For all groups regardless of background, foreign birth depressed wages and concentrated families in bottom-rung unskilled and semi-skilled jobs. In 1880, Irish workers scored 26.2 out of 100 on an occupational scale, while for Yankees the score was 40.8. Two decades later, Irish and Italian occupations still lagged far behind those of natives with scores of 28.8 and 30.3, respectively. By contrast, Russian Jews outscored other groups in 1915 and 1925.

Nevertheless, socio-economic status was a far better predictor of high school attendance for Providence children than ethnic background. In other words, once Perlmann statistically controlled for class distinctions between immigrants and Yankees, many of the initial ethnic differences also disappeared. With time, occupational advancement also narrowed the gap between the Irish and other groups. Irish families still lagged behind in terms of occupation throughout the period studied, but residual differences in school attendance and graduation rates vanished. Perlmann offered several explanations for this phenomenon: the gradual disappearance of traditional values which favored communal obligations over individual advancement, the growth in literacy levels among subsequent waves of immigrants, the strength of Catholic parochial education, and the growing acceptance of the Irish once they overcame nativist prejudices to occupy a higher political and occupational stratum.

By 1925, Irish children attending high school were more likely to graduate than were Yankee children.

If the Irish were able to show steady progress in overcoming educational difference, albeit at a slower rate than Russian Jews, Italians continued to lag behind, even after controlling for socio-economic background. Italian median occupation scores improved only marginally during the 25-year period studied and school attendance was worse than for other groups for both old-country-born Italians and for their children. Only one-third entered high school in 1933 compared to more than half for other immigrants. Undoubtedly much of this disparity reflected high remigration rates among the Italians, with nearly half returning to Italy in the period prior to 1925. Yet the magnitude of the gap also suggested the importance of pre-migration culture in shaping educational choices for certain immigrants. Italian education rates resembled those of Slavic immigrant groups in other cities, particularly the Poles, leading Perlmann to conclude that shared peasant backgrounds "from preindustrial areas not characterized by any special commitment to literacy" (1988, p. 121) undercut educational attainment and, consequently, mobility levels for decades after immigration.

Post-World War II Mobility and the New Immigrants

World War II marks an important watershed in our understanding of social mobility. For the period before the war, a wealth of documents fueled the abundance of historical studies. After the war, historians have been forced to depend largely upon sociological studies based upon aggregate census data and social surveys. Before the war, attention focused mainly upon European immigrants and their children. After the war, third-generation European-ancestry Americans differed little from native-stock Americans. Most importantly, the elimination of quotas in 1965 has made immigration far more diverse, with workers from a wide range of Asian, Latin American, and African countries superseding traditional European groups.

Recovery from the Depression eroded many earlier ethnic differences. Second- and third-generation immigrants overcame a range of barriers to advancement. Among these were negative stereotypes that defined white identity by excluding southern and eastern Europeans, an anti-immigrant climate which led to harsh Americanization programs in schools, and quotas against admission to higher education for Jews. Working-class children often saw little connection between what they were taught in school and occupational advancement and others rebelled against the parental pressure to advance. Nevertheless, the children of immigrants still benefited from better schooling to advance occupationally (Perlmann and Waldinger 1997). Intermarriage, assimilation, and a broadening definition of what it meant to be an American blurred ethnic difference.

The most comprehensive overviews of ethnic mobility for this period underscore the success of education in raising incomes for the descendants of European immigrants, Asians, and even non-white groups such as West Indians and Asians, to levels often surpassing those of old-stock Anglo-Americans. (Whether the relative success of immigrants was due partly to the decline in status of native-stock Americans as farming declined in rural areas is unclear; see Ueda 1993; Grasmuck and Pessar 1996.) By the 1950s, Chinese, Koreans, and Japanese rapidly moved into the middle class.

In the post-1965 period newer immigrants established occupational niches using retail and grocery stores and following a path to petty-ownership first blazed by Jewish immigrants. Be it Korean greengrocers, drycleaners, and beauty supply stores, Dominican bodegas (grocery stores), or West Indian and Caribbean storefront markets, many pursued entrepreneurship. Other immigrants, such as Haitians, Sudanese, and West Indians, expanded into the service economy, in hotels, as cabdrivers, or in service positions in health-care.

As with earlier waves, postwar immigration continued to foster sharp inequality within US society (Ueda 1993, pp. 92–6). An influx of poor from third world regions heightened class divisions within ethnic communities by bringing in new low-income immigrants from China who were quite different from established middle-class Chinese who had escaped earlier from Chinatowns. The growing middle class of Mexican Americans were also markedly different from undocumented workers. The acceleration of Hispanic migration depressed wages and widened economic inequality "in response to economic resources and conditions, time of arrival, and internal capacity to organize economic gain." Despite the success of some groups, the poverty of many Hispanics increased significantly, particularly among poorly educated Mexicans and Puerto Ricans whose incomes lagged behind. While only 35 percent of native-born Americans worked in secondary sector jobs such as agriculture, services, and light industry, the figure for Mexican immigrants topped 55 percent (Jiobu 1988, pp. 83–90, 94–7; Morawska 1990, p. 201). Some of the low levels of mobility were undoubtedly the result of factors unique to particular groups.

Many Mexicans exported much of their earnings to their home country and, in a pattern reminiscent of early twentieth-century Italians, planned for an ultimate return to Mexico. Puerto Ricans continued to lag behind others throughout the 1970s despite long residence in northeastern cities. The stagnation in income of many Southeast Asians contrasted with the success of South Asians.

What most separates recent from earlier patterns of immigration is the bifurcation of labor in the post-1965 period as a result of federal immigration and refugee policies, as well as a changing labor market. This has produced a striking gulf between remarkably successful professional immigrants on the one hand, and the very poor on the other, both operating within two largely independent labor markets (Portes and Rumbaut 1996, pp. 58–70). Newcomers from Mexico and Central America stand in contrast to those from Asia for whom advantages of medical training and strong middle-class aspirations stand in contrast even to the native-born population. In terms of education levels, the proportion of college graduates among recent immigrants equaled that of the general US population in 1990, but more than one-third had occupations classified as professional and managerial – well above the native average. Immigrants from India, Taiwan, Korea, and China exceeded native-born averages in education while those from Southeast Asia (excluding Vietnam), Haiti, Italy, Central America, and Mexico lagged behind (educational levels for most other groups were near the average for US-born workers). Education differences translated into earnings with the median immigrant household earning $1,800 less than their native counterparts. Ironically, the lowest household income was found among immigrants from the former Soviet Union, an indication less of disadvantage than of smaller household size and a higher proportion of elderly (over 45.8 percent).

Entrepreneurship has become the other main path to success for late twentieth-century immigrants besides education. Just as Jewish immigrants had once depended upon Landsmannschften mutual support institutions to create a commercial base within their community, so have Japanese and Chinese immigrants come to depend upon firms serving co-ethnics. The figures for self-employment, minority firm ownership, and proportion of firms with paid employees have been highest for Koreans, Indians, and Chinese (Portes and Rumbaut 1996, pp. 72–7; Morawska 1990). Even the most impoverished immigrant groups had levels of small business ownership exceeding those of American blacks. Enclave-based employment among Cubans living in Miami ultimately allowed one-fifth to become self-employed, thus achieving higher incomes than those who worked outside in the secondary sector. But this reliance on ethnic communities could have its downside. Internal success produced inequality when small businessmen often exploited co-ethnic employees in the workshops, restaurants, and stores of Chinatowns and Koreatowns.

Self-employment sets Koreans in New York City and Los Angeles apart from other groups. Although most Koreans who came to the United States after 1965 intended to enter white-collar employment, their poor knowledge of English forced many into blue-collar trades (Min 1996, pp. 46–72). There they labored to accumulate sufficient capital to open small businesses. Korean immigrants arriving in the 1980s were better prepared for the difficulties that awaited them and more likely to bring sufficient capital to open their own business. By the 1990s this group had more business per capita than the Chinese and gross receipts from business second only to East Indians, many of whom worked as well-paid physicians. Korean businessmen came to cluster in drycleaning, grocery, nail care, Asian-related goods, and garment trades but also in liquor stores and small groceries located in minority neighborhoods. The middleman function these businesses played in neighborhoods such as south central Los Angeles became a source of considerable tension culminating in the violence directed against them by blacks during the Los Angeles riots of 1992. In this way, lack of preparation for employment in one part of the economy opened up opportunities in another, producing upward mobility but at a considerable cost: more strenuous work than in Korea, dependence upon family members for labor, and operation in dangerous neighborhoods among clientele who were frequently hostile.

Mexicans and Mexican Americans in Los Angeles show no such mobility; for most the income gap between them and the native population has widened (Waldinger 1996; Ortiz 1996; Lopez, Popkin, and Telles 1996). In 1990, 75 percent of Mexican immigrants had not completed high school compared to 65 percent among second-generation Chicanos, and 91 percent for native-born whites who had. Where Anglos in Los Angeles saw their incomes shoot up from $33,700 to $56,180 between 1969 and 1989, a sample of Mexicans who arrived in the 1960s saw their incomes rise only slightly from $17,600 to $23,720. Controlling for differences in education, age, English proficiency, and other background variables cut this gap only by half. Nor did Mexicans draw any advantage from their ethnic community by creating an occupational niche. Instead, Barrios became "mobility traps" where "concentration in an ethnic specialization saturates supply and thus increases the potential for competition with one's own kind" (Waldinger 1996, p. 451). Second-generation earnings levels may have advanced from bottom rank to one notch above that of

African American males, but the gap between whites and Chicanos still widened despite increases in earnings for both groups. The same pattern held for Central American immigrants, with one difference: domestic service replaced agriculture as the principal sector of employment at the bottom.

Conclusion

This brief review of the literature on the history of immigrant social mobility demonstrates an inexorable climb up the social ladder for European descendants despite discrimination and structural constraints such as depressed wages and limited opportunities in factory towns. In nineteenth-century America, escape from eastern cities to midwestern farms provided the greatest opportunity for advancement although most immigrants saw little change in occupational rank during their lifetime. When progress did come, it was their children who benefited, particularly those who came of age after World War II, when the new prosperity finally undid the damage of the Great Depression. By contrast, the prospects for the newer post-1965 immigrant and their children remain decidedly mixed. To be sure, a legal preference for immigrants with strong middle-class backgrounds and high levels of education has brought rapid advancement for the privileged few. Yet the excruciatingly slow advance of Mexicans and Central Americans even during the boom times in the 1980s and 1990s is hardly encouraging. Such slow progress is all the more alarming with census estimates now showing Americans who define themselves as Hispanics having supplanted blacks as the largest minority group (US Census Department 2003). It is too early to tell whether the collapse of the dot.com economy and slow rates of job recovery will produce a long-term disruption of the historical patterns which promised modest progress for newer immigrants, much as they did for Poles, Italians, and Irish early in the last century. Downward mobility for some white Americans might well bring an unexpected convergence with immigrants, both of whom will suffer all the more for having upper-middle-class dreams dashed. In any case, social mobility remains an important topic that demands renewed historical attention, not just the highly suggestive but incomplete sociological and economic scholarship of the last two decades.

REFERENCES

Alcorn, Richard S. and Peter R. Knights (1975). "Most Uncommon Bostonians: A Critique of Stephan Thernstrom's *The Other Bostonians.*" *Historical Methods Newsletter* 8: 98–114.

Ayers, Edward (1999). "The Pasts and Futures of Digital History." http://www.iath. virginia.edu/vcdh/PastsFutures.html (February 1, 2003).

Baganha, Maria Ioannis Benis (1991). "The Social Mobility of Portuguese Immigrants in the United States at the Turn of the Nineteenth [sic] Century." *International Migration Review* 25: 277–302.

Baily, Samuel L. (1999). *Immigrants in the Land of Promise: Italians in Buenos Aires and New York City, 1870–1914.* Ithaca, NY: Cornell University Press.

Barton, Josef (1975). *Peasants and Strangers: Italians. Rumanians. And Slovaks in an American City, 1890–1950.* Cambridge, MA: Harvard University Press.

Bodnar, John (1985). *The Transplanted: A History of Immigrants in Urban America.* Bloomington: University of Illinois Press.

Bodnar, John, Roger Simon, and Michael P. Weber (1982). *Lives of their Own: Blacks, Italians, and Poles in Pittsburgh, 1900–1960.* Urbana: University of Illinois Press.

Brieger, Ronald L. (1990). *Social Mobility and Social Structure.* Cambridge: Cambridge University Press.

Chudacoff, Howard P. (1972). *Mobile Americans: Residential and Social Mobility in Omaha, 1880–1920.* New York: Oxford University Press.

—— (1982). "Success and Security: The Meaning of Social Mobility in America." *Review in American History* 10: 101–12.

—— (1994). "A Reconsideration of Geographical Mobility in American Urban History." *The Virginia Magazine of History and Biography* 102: 501–18.

Conzen, Kathleen Neils (1976). *Immigrant Milwaukee: Accommodation and Community in a Frontier City.* Cambridge, MA: Harvard University Press.

Curti, Merle (1959). *The Making of an American Community: A Case Study of Democracy in a Frontier County.* Stanford, CA: Stanford University Press.

Decker, Peter R. (1978). *Fortunes and Failures: White Collar Mobility in Nineteenth-Century San Francisco.* Cambridge, MA: Harvard University Press.

Edel, Matthew, Elliott D. Sclar, and Daniel Luria (1984). *Shaky Palaces: Homeownership and Social Mobility in Boston's Suburbanization.* New York: Columbia University Press.

Ferrie, Joseph P. (1999). *Yankeys Now: Immigration in the Antebellum United States, 1840–1860.* New York: Oxford University Press.

Fitch, Nancy (1984). "Statistical Fantasies and Historical Facts: History in Crisis and Its Methodological Implications." *Historical Methods* 17: 239–54.

Frisch, Michael (1986). "*Poverty and Progress*: A Paradoxical Legacy." *Social Science History* 10: 15–22.

Gjerde, Jon (1985). *From Peasants to Farmers: The Migration from Balestrand, Norway to the Upper Middle West.* Cambridge: Cambridge University Press.

Glazer, Nathan (2002a). "Lipset's Big Question." *The Public Interest* 148: 111–18.

—— (2002b). "Why Americans Don't Care About Income Inequality." Paper presented at Wiener Inequality and Social Policy Seminar, Kennedy School of Government, Harvard University. http://www.ksg.harvard.edu/inequality/Seminar/Papers/Glazer.pdf (February 11, 2002).

Gold, Steven J. and Bruce Phillips (1996). "Mobility and Continuity among Eastern European Jews." In Silvia Pedraza and Rubén G. Rumbaut, eds., *Origins and Destinies: Immigration, Race, and Ethnicity in America.* Belmont, CA: Wadsworth, pp. 182–94.

Grasmuck, Sherri and Patricia Pessar (1996). "Dominicans in the United States: First- and Second-Generation Settlement, 1960–1990." In Silvia Pedraza and Rubén G. Rumbaut, eds., *Origins and Destinies: Immigration, Race, and Ethnicity in America.* Belmont, CA: Wadsworth, pp. 280–92.

Griffen, Clyde and Sally Griffen (1978). *Natives and Newcomers: The Ordering of Opportunity in Mid-Nineteenth-Century Poughkeepsie.* Cambridge, MA: Harvard University Press.

Guest, Avery M., Nancy S. Landale, and James C. McCann (1989). "Intergenerational Occupational Mobility in the Late 19th Century United States." *Social Forces* 68: 351–78.

Hardy, Melissa A. (1989). "Estimating Selection Effects in Occupational Mobility in a 19th-Century City." *American Sociological Review* 54: 834–43.

Hareven, Tamara K. (1982). *Family Time and Industrial Time: The Relationship between the Family and Work in a New England Industrial Community.* Cambridge: Cambridge University Press.

Henretta, James A. (1977). "The Study of Social Mobility: Ideological Assumption and Conceptual Bias." *Labor History* 18: 164–78.

Hershberg, Theodore (1981). *Philadelphia: Work, Space, Family, and Group Experience in the 19th Century.* New York: Oxford University Press.

Jiobu, Robert M. (1988). *Ethnicity and Assimilation: Blacks, Chinese, Filipinos, Japanese, Koreans, Mexicans, Vietnamese, and Whites.* Albany: State University of New York Press.

Kaelble, Hartmut (1986). *Social Mobility in the 19th and 20th Centuries: Europe and America in Comparative Perspective.* New York: St. Martins Press.

Kamphoefner, Walter D. (1987). *The Westfalians: From Germany to Missouri.* Princeton, NJ: Princeton University Press.

Katz, Michael B. (1975). *The People of Hamilton, Canada West: Family and Class in a Mid-Nineteenth-Century City.* Cambridge, MA: Harvard University Press.

Kessner, Thomas (1977). *The Golden Door: Italian and Jewish Mobility in New York City, 1880–1915.* New York: Oxford University Press.

Knights, Peter R. (1971). *The Plain People of Boston: A Study of City Growth.* New York: Oxford University Press.

Landale, Nancy S. and Avery M. Guest (1990). "Generation, Ethnicity, and Occupational Opportunity in Late 19th Century America." *American Sociological Review* 55: 280–96.

Landale, Nancy S. and Stewart E. Tolnay (1993). "Generation, Ethnicity, and Marriage: Historical Patterns in the Northern United States." *Demography* 30: 103–26.

Lipset, Seymour Martin and Reinhard Bendix (1959). *Social Mobility in Industrial Society.* Berkeley: University of California Press.

Lopez, David E., Eric Popkin, and Edward Telles (1996). "Central Americans: At the Bottom, Struggling to Get Ahead." In Roger Waldinger and Mehdi Bozorgmehr, eds., *Ethnic Los Angeles.* New York: Russell Sage Foundation, pp. 279–304.

Min, Pyong Gap (1996). *Caught in the Middle: Korean Merchants in America's Multiethnic Cities.* Berkeley: University of California Press.

Model, Suzanne W. (1988). "Italian and Jewish Intergenerational Mobility." *Social Science History* 12: 29–51.

Morawska, Ewa (1985). *For Bread with Butter: The Life-Worlds of East Central Europeans in Johnstown, Pennsylvania, 1890–1940.* Cambridge: Cambridge University Press.

—— (1990). "The Sociology and Historiography of Immigration." In Virginia Yans-McLaughlin, ed., *Immigration Reconsidered: History, Sociology, and Politics.* New York: Oxford University Press, pp. 187–238.

Olzak, Susan D. (1989). "Causes of Shifts in Occupational Segregation for the Foreign-Born: Evidence from American Cities, 1870–1880." *Social Forces* 68: 593–620.

Ortiz, Vilma (1996). "The Mexican-Origin Population: Permanent Working Class or Emerging Middle Class." In Roger Waldinger and Mehdi Bozorgmehr, eds., *Ethnic Los Angeles.* New York: Russell Sage Foundation, pp. 249–77.

Parkerson, Donald H. (1982). "How Mobile Were Nineteenth Century Americans?" *Historical Methods* 3: 99–109.

Perlmann, Joel (1988). *Ethnic Differences: Schooling and Social Structure among the Irish, Italians, Jews, and Blacks in an American City, 1880–1935.* Cambridge: Cambridge University Press.

Perlmann, Joel and Roger Waldinger (1997). "Second Generation Decline? Children of Immigrants, Past and Present – A Reconsideration." *The International Migration Review* 31: 983–6.

Portes, Alejandro and Rubén G. Rumbaut (1996). *Immigrant America: A Portrait*, 2nd edn. Berkeley: University of California Press.

Romo, Ricardo (1983). *East Los Angeles: History of a Barrio.* Austin: University of Texas Press.

Sassler, Sharon and Michael J. White (1997). "Ethnicity, Gender, and Social Mobility in 1910." *Social Science History* 21: 321–57.

Scherzer, Kenneth A. (1992). *The Unbounded Community: Neighborhood Life and Social Structure in New York City, 1830–1875.* Durham, NC: Duke University Press.

Sorokin, Pitirim (1927). *Social Mobility.* New York: Harper & Bros.

Stave, Bruce M. (1977). *The Making of Urban History: Historiography through Oral History.* Beverly Hills, CA: Sage.

Thernstrom, Stephan (1964). *Poverty and Progress: Social Mobility in a Nineteenth Century City.* Cambridge, MA: Harvard University Press.

—— (1973). *The Other Bostonians: Poverty and Progress in the American Metropolis, 1880–1970.* Cambridge, MA: Harvard University Press.

—— (1986). "Poverty and Progress Revisited: A Response to Reiss, Frisch, and Pessen." *Social Science History* 10: 33–44.

Thernstrom, Stephan and Peter R. Knights (1970). "Men in Motion: Some Data and Speculations about Urban Population Mobility in Nineteenth-Century America." *Journal of Interdisciplinary History* 1: 7–35.

Thernstrom, Stephan and Richard Sennett, eds. (1969). *Nineteenth Century Cities: Essays in the New Urban History.* New Haven, CT: Yale University Press.

Thompson, E.P. (1963). *The Making of the English Working Class.* New York: Random House.

Ueda, Reed (1987). *Avenues to Adulthood: The Origins of the High School and Social Mobility in an American Suburb.* Cambridge: Cambridge University Press.

Ueda, Reed (1993). *Postwar Immigrant America: A Social History.* Boston: St. Martin's Press.

US Census Department (2003). "Resident Population Estimates of the United States by Sex, Race, and Hispanic or Latino Origin: April 1 2000, July 1 2000, and July 1 2001." National Population Estimates – Characteristics by Sex, Race, and Hispanic or Latino Origin. http://eire.census.gov/popest/data/national/tables/asro/US-EST2001-ASRO-02.php (January 22, 2003).

Waldinger, Roger (1996). "Ethnicity and Opportunity in the Plural City." In Roger Waldinger and Mehdi Bozorgmehr, eds., *Ethnic Los Angeles.* New York: Russell Sage Foundation, pp. 445–70.

Waldinger, Roger and Michael Lichter (1996). "Anglos: Beyond Ethnicity?" In Roger Waldinger and Mehdi Bozorgmehr, eds., *Ethnic Los Angeles.* New York: Russell Sage Foundation, pp. 417–29.

Warner, W. Lloyd and Paul S. Lunt (1941). *The Social Life of a Modern Community.* New Haven, CT: Yale University Press.

Warner, W. Lloyd and Leo Stole (1945). *The Social Systems of American Ethnic Groups.* New Haven, CT: Yale University Press.

Worall, Janet E. (2001). "Labor, Gender, and Generational Change in a Western City." *Western Historical Quarterly* 32: 437–67.

Zunz, Olivier (1982). *The Changing Face of Inequality: Industrial Development and Immigrants in Detroit, 1880–1920.* Chicago: University of Chicago Press.

CHAPTER EIGHTEEN

Labor and Immigration History: First Principles

LEON FINK

Since the maturation of social history in the 1970s, of course, labor and immigration history have regularly overlapped and often informed each other's agendas. A student (in this case, the author) of Herbert Gutman's "new labor history" readily remembers graduate seminar discussions of Handlin, Higham, Yearley, and Greene as core readings (Handlin 1941; Higham 1963; Yearley 1957; Greene 1968). What is more, a few of Gutman's own early students effectively *became* immigrant and ethnic social historians (Yan-McLauglin 1977; Shaw 1976; Gordon 1993). In retrospect, it is perhaps not surprising that the author's own first published book reviews were in the *Journal of Ethnic Studies*, not *Labor History* (Fink 1974, 1976). Both fields, after all, identified movement *across borders* and *to and from the workplace* as central to their research agenda.

On the other hand, the characters, plot, and resolution of the stories told by both sets of historical narrators involved subtle, and sometimes not so subtle, distinctions. Labor history was about work, industrial relations, class conflict, the trade union and its allied political movements, and perhaps working-class culture. Immigration history, correspondingly, covered the act and motivation of migration, ethnic and religious identities of the immigrant community, and the questions of group identity (degrees of assimilation or "Americanization") and economic mobility. In short, if the two fields shared common borders, "crossing over" still left a tangible sense of entering a new and exotic intellectual terrain. Even now, if the gates connecting the one subfield to the other have been thrown open, they still demarcate discrete investigative traditions. So, just what baggage did – and do – those traditions carry? That is the subject of this chapter.

Certainly, a tension between the fields – and their designated historical subjects – was evident earlier on. Indeed, for labor history "founder" John R. Commons, the new immigrant workforce at the turn of the twentieth century represented more threat than opportunity. Jefferson's creed that "all men are created equal," Commons avowed, should be worn lightly when it came to both "Negroes" and the "peasants" of southern and eastern Europe who were now arriving on US shores. The latter, reported Commons, have been reduced to the qualities similar to those of an inferior race that favor despotism and oligarchy rather than democracy. Whether with our public schools, our stirring politics, our ubiquitous newspapers, our common language, and our network of transportation, the children of the European immigrant shall be able to rise to the opportunities unreached by his parents is the largest and deepest problem now pressing upon us. (Commons 1907, pp. 1, 3–4, 10–11)

Commons's nativist and racist streak, of course, was prevalent among many Progressive-era reformers. No doubt, however, his angle of vision, coming as it did through the lens – and perceived interests – of a labor movement rooted in old-stock skilled workers also limited his sympathy and curiosity towards America's immigrant working class.

And what of the worker subject for the founders of immigration history? For orientation Jon Gjerde's recent genealogy of the field is a useful starting point (Gjerde 1999). Gjerde identifies two "foundational" influences on immigration history: the "Chicago school of sociology" with its ecological or behavioralist approach to the study of the human community, and the "ethnic Turnerians" who emphasized a more bottom-up concern for enduring cultural traditions. As potential guides to immigrant *labor* history let us take the two in turn.

In William I. Thomas and Florian Znaniecki's *The Polish Peasant in Europe and America* – the classic representation of the Chicago school – Polish laborers are treated first and foremost as "*group* members," that is, a people or ethnic group who perforce experience the "disorganization" and "demoralization" of a peasantry trans-formed into a new urban proletariat. If less pessimistic than Commons (Thomas and Znaniecki hold out hope that a "cooperative" or voluntary society may ultimately replace the organic social glue of the old peasant community), their analysis of immigrant worker inferiority is not so far removed from that of the Yankee labor historian (Thomas and Znaniecki 1984, p. 289). Even if the new social historians, post-1960s, stressed immigrant agency rather than breakdown, Gjerde convincingly argues that they still betrayed the influence of their environmentalist-minded forebears in their common assumption that immigrants moved from an organic "traditional" society and culture to a "modern" one based on individualistic ambition and voluntary ties (Gjerde 1999, pp. 48–9).

But a more direct and profound intellectual lineage from the Chicago school founders to the contemporary academic field was reflected in the work of Oscar Handlin. In his influential yet controversial book-length essay, *The Uprooted* (1951), Handlin grappled at length with workers and the work process. Revealingly, when Handlin looked back on his celebrated work some 20 years after it first appeared – at a time when a new generation of works in both immigration and labor history had just begun to appear – he avowed that "the great issues connected with labor as a nexus of social relations remain unexploited; and the conclusions sug-gested in *The Uprooted* have therefore scarcely been tested." In particular, with his vantage point on the immigrant workforce, Handlin had meant to contest labor historians' fixation on the "solidarity and unity of the laboring classes," a notion which Handlin suggested had become "fixed in historical thinking through the influence of John R. Commons and his school." Labor history's focus on the army of producers was "too encompassing" in Handlin's retrospective view: his own research, he explained, had led him to conclude that workers' role as consumers was more vital to their aspirations and consciousness than their role as producers. "Any job would do for them," soberly concluded Handlin about an immigrant working class determined to claw its way up the American economic ladder. Handlin had the Commons school pegged wrong in at least two major respects: Commons et al. never assumed worker solidarity and, in fact, were preoccupied with discovering the sources of American exceptionalism (or the very *lack* of such solidarity), and Commons himself specifically emphasized the consumerist element in capitalist development. Still, however clumsily, Handlin had engaged the central currents of labor history thinking in ways subsequently duplicated by few of his immigration history descendants. One senses, moreover, that Handlin's own move away from a "social class" analysis was both a gradual and at least theoretically wrenching experience: "For a considerable period," he allowed in 1973, "I, too, thought in this way, despite the evidence I was gathering" (Handlin 1973, pp. 313, 312, 62–3).

To return to Handlin's texts armed with such subsequent reflection is to reveal a fascinating search for explanatory coherence at the heart of his enterprise. First, there was the undeniable fact of immigrant worker exploitation. "Immigrants made for themselves a role that could have been occupied by no other element in American society – no other was so thoroughly deprived of the opportunity for choice." Or, as he had put it in an earlier volume with but a touch of euphemism: "Therein lay the significance of the Irish in the city's economic life. Before their arrival the rigid labor supply had made industrialization impossible. . . . Capitalists readily admitted that they could not 'obtain good interest for their money, were they deprived of this constant influx of foreign labor'" (Handlin 1941, pp. 87–8). Secondly, as Handlin saw it – drawing on a concept he linked to the "rediscovery of Marx, by existential philosophy, and by widely read novels" – there was "alienation" (Handlin 1973, p. 321). Yet, immigrant worker alienation, as Handlin described it, was even more encompassing than what Marx specified in the distancing of the worker from the worker's product or even in the commodification of labor power. It was also the *anomie* of modern life itself – thus the author's Durkheimian trope of a psychological "uprooting." As Handlin stressed about the insecurity of piecework and unemployment, and the accompanying necessity of both female and child labor: "The degradation lay in the *kind* of work. . . . In all matters the New World made the peasant less a man" (Handlin 1973, pp. 68, 70, 72).

Finally, Handlin was struck by the way the new labor force had – or rather had not – grappled with its lot. With his original research ending in 1865 (the revised version of *Boston's Immigrants* stops in 1880) – and given that *The Uprooted* was more impressionistic essay than historical synthesis – Handlin avoided or ignored all the major upsurges of immigrant workers as "organized labor." He, in turn, wrote about his subjects as if they had never entered upon strategic class-based initiatives – whether as Knights of Labor, AFofL craft unionists, Wobblies, or ramrods of the CIO. Rather, what impressed Handlin was their *lack* of concerted opposition to the new system which had both uprooted and exploited them:

> it did not matter how harsh the immigrants judged their lot. They were inextricably involved in their situation, saw no apparent means of escape, and found no hands

extended to assist them. Through most of this period the labor unions either barred the foreign-born from membership or made no effort to organize them. . . . The unskilled laborers never effectively made their voices heard, never discovered a way to help themselves.

Essentially writing off both workplace or political options of group mobilization for the immigrant working class, Handlin insisted that "mostly, they worked on; after their fashion, they accepted their place." Consigned to an individualistic culture, they learned their lessons and themselves became proprietary individuals. "In the pursuit of this fleeting success, the peasant broke with his past. His constant task here was to transform income, no matter how small, into capital" (Handlin 1973, pp. 73, 74, 75).

Handlin's ambivalent acceptance of the "breakdown" model of immigrant acculturation posed a formidable challenge to subsequent immigrant historians. Hardly a simple celebration of "Americanization," Handlin effectively dismissed both the labor movement and ethnic subcultures as romantic or nostalgic illusions that in practice *did not* really cushion the typical immigrant's journey. In his view, the pain of disorientation and insecurity accompanying immigration marked the necessary historical birthpangs of a new, more worldly individual (Ueda 1990). By the mid-1960s, however, a younger generation of historians, less enamored of free-floating cosmopolitanism as a worthy intellectual ideal, looked back on older ethnic and laboring communities as a source of cultural and political alternatives to the conventions of "mainstream" American history. Thus it was that those whom Gjerde christens the "ethnic Turnerians" were born, taking their lead from Rudolph J. Vecoli's influential 1964 essay, "*Contadini* in Chicago" (Vecoli 1964). More impressed with resiliency of ethnic heritage than its fragility, the post-Handlin "continuity school" has tended to dominate the interpretive field in recent decades.

Within this revisionist literature, John Bodnar's *The Transplanted* (1985) ultimately provided an alternative synthetic template to *The Uprooted*, one heralded in its very title. And, clearly, in immigration history's turn to ethno-community we also enter a very different relationship to labor and working-class history. Bodnar as an "immigration historian" is very much like Herbert Gutman as a "labor historian" – i.e. a community-focused social historian who readily crossed subdisciplinary walls. Drawing on the work of the British social historian, E.P. Thompson, Gutman had criticized a trade union-dominated labor history for "isolating [workers] from their own particular subcultures and from the larger national culture" (Gutman 1977, p. 10). Spearheading the US version of the "new social history" which had come of age in the early 1970s, Gutman nevertheless warned of a tendency towards professional over-specialization, a malady he exemplified with the hypothetical case of an "Irish born Catholic female Fall River Massachusetts textile worker and union organizer involved in the disorderly 1875 strike." Social historians, he suggested, would "carve" such a subject into nine or ten subfields, "wash[ing] out the wholeness that is essential to understanding human behavior" (Gutman 1977, p. xiii). In a provocative research essay, Gutman suggestively linked worker and immigrant history through the encompassing subject of the "work ethic" and "first generation factory workers" – a lens which revealed an underlying continuity of resistance amidst the demographic discontinuity of the American working class. In what other ways Gutman might have pushed such connections we will never know. His own disparate scholarship and premature death rendered Gutman more sage than exemplar of new approaches to the immigrant/labor history mix. But clearly Bodnar had picked up Gutman's call. Indeed, Bodnar's first major work – *Immigration and Industrialization: Ethnicity in an American Mill Town, 1870–1940* (1977) – could readily be classified in either the labor or immigration history camp.

Unlike Handlin, yet so much like other "new labor historians," Bodnar stressed less the fracture than the adaptation and capacity of immigrant workers, defined by both their ethnic and class (or work-centered) ties:

> Steelton's immigrants and migrants were neither tradition-bound peasants nor disillusioned settlers. . . . Transition from preindustrial to industrial society involved a process of accommodation rather than of uprooting. After several decades in the industrial environment, the displaced peasants of southern Europe were neither wandering adrift, embracing traditional American middle-class values, nor living European life-styles. They were creating a new milieu which was a blend of their cultural heritage and emerging working-class status.

"At the confluence of ethnicity and class," Bodnar argued, the Slavic steelworkers he concentrated on – unlike either their Irish and German forebears who achieved measurable individual mobility, or African Americans who were "driven down and out" – secured a measure of security only by collective action through labor solidarity (Bodnar 1977, pp. 152, 154–5).

If his Steelton study concentrated on "competing organizations" – i.e. ethnic, labor, and to a lesser extent religiously based group life – Bodnar had effected a subtle yet important interpretive shift by the time of *The Transplanted*. Still very much preoccupied with the dual influences of labor and immigration history, Bodnar now noticeably veered away from the favored frameworks of each subdiscipline. Rather than emphasize either the "ethnic community" of immigration historians or the "class-in-formation" model of labor historians, Bodnar filtered his treatment of ex-peasants confronting urban-industrial capitalism through the institution of the immigrant family household. As opposed to those, like Handlin, who had invoked the breakdown of the family, Bodnar argued that "new economic structures actually reinforced traditional ways of ordering life and, consequently, contributed to a supportive 'external environment' for capitalism to succeed" (Bodnar 1985, p. 84).

Bodnar's intellectual passage to *The Transplanted* was prefigured by insights drawn from a massive Pennsylvania oral history project presented in *Workers' World: Kinship, Community, and Protest in an Industrial Society, 1900–1940* (1982). Determined to get beyond the "tendency to explain behavior and culture in terms of abstract generalizations and to overlook the reality of individuals attempting to structure their lives in the face of everyday problems," Bodnar's life history interviews determined to capture "the interior of the workers' world." Most notably, this closer interrogation of working-class lives in mill towns, mining regions, and factory districts revealed a persistence, even a strengthening, of the family household bond and authority across the historical experiences of immigration (and subsequent migrations), unemployment, and general job insecurity. In contrast to the work of "[David] Montgomery and other historians [who] have described twentieth-century labor

movements as 'an unprecedented quest' for social power and [workplace] control,"
Bodnar stressed "the complexity of human aspiration and the powerful need to
maintain the family system" amidst the clash between "tradition" and "modern
industrial capitalism." As Bodnar concluded, "during the half-century of industrialization after 1890, a family-oriented culture defined the framework of individual
lives" (Bodnar 1982, pp. 5, 8, 182, 178).

In adapting the message drawn from Pennsylvania ethnics to the entire immigrant
experience, *The Transplanted* reconfigured conventional settings in both immigration and labor history. By redefining the urban ecology as supportive of, rather than
destructive to, cultural continuity, Bodnar neatly reconciled the Chicago environ-
mentalist school with Turnerian culturalist traditions. He also frontally challenged
labor history's focus on protest, politics, and collective struggle. In invoking both
the immigrants' "legacy of organizing activity and union battles" (i.e. a working-
class paradigm) and "one of strong obligations to familial and communal networks
and household economics," Bodnar left little doubt as to which of the two took
historical precedence. Organizing among immigrant workers might succeed to the
extent, consciously or unconsciously, that class-based organizations connected to
family goals: "When the drive for improved conditions and treatment at work was
combined with a quest for household stability, the labor movement was suddenly
riveted to powerful goals which could temporarily transcend ethnic and skill differentials." Such was the immigrant's "pragmatic culture of everyday life," a familial
decision "to deal with capitalism, albeit on their own terms, and to do whatever was
necessary to survive . . . made *before* coming to America" (Bodnar 1985, pp. 114–
15, 210, 116). Effectively, a functionalist, even utilitarian, explanation of immigrant
adaptation – though one based on a calculus of family welfare rather than individual
economic goals – Bodnar had turned Handlin's tragedy of peasant alienation into a
morality tale for cautious, petty proprietors. In Bodnar's project, therefore, what
began as a careful balancing of two historiographical traditions ended as something
else. For its part, labor history, *qua* working-*class* or even work-centered history, is
reduced in such a framework to a relative sideshow. Equally, however, the distinctiveness of particular ethnic experience and the impact of specific Old World tradition on New World behavior also recede before a more universal "sense of realism,
an ability to remain pragmatic in the face of the prevailing American bourgeois
ideology" (Bodnar 1982, p. 168). Perhaps the very reliance on life histories pursued
via individual oral histories, the method which underlay Bodnar's conceptual breakthrough in *Workers' World*, effectively pushed all public and other group endeavors
to the historical backseat as priority was ceded to life trajectories defined by personal, mostly private, struggles.

Apart from the challenge of overarching synthesis, how do recent case studies by
immigration historians handle the worker experience? Let me select three studies of
the Italian American experience – which arguably has produced the single most sophisticated set of studies within American immigration history – by way of example.
Dino Cinel's *From Italy to San Francisco: The Immigrant Experience* (1982) is
surely one of the most subtle portraits of its kind. While carefully testing for both
persistence and discontinuity within the dynamic process of immigrant adaptation,
Cinel counters a purely ecological model of change with the power of Italian regionalism and campanilismo (or localism). People continued to act, in short, according

to a particular small-group logic. In the workplace, for example, fishing persisted as the dominant trade for families from Santa Flavia, while Lorsicans quickly secured a near monopoly on garbage collecting, and Genoese and Luccans eventually split the produce and independent grocery markets between them (Cinel 1982, pp. 258, 147–52, 152, 217).

Still, while Cinel has a great deal to say about occupation and migration across three generations and three decades of immigration, his framework has little to contribute to the classic terrain of labor history. His preoccupation with the economic skill, achievement, and mobility of his subjects does provide interesting evidence about the shift from farming to commercial pursuits, from personal service to manufacturing jobs, and – outside of fishing-related families – the dramatic occupational differences between Italian American sons and Italian fathers (Cinel 1982, pp. 138–47). Such a focus, however appropriate as an index of change or continuity from Old World to New, effectively ignores the question of immigrant socialization as "workers." Indeed, though Cinel admirably treats identity formation among Italian Americans in chapters on "Regionalism" and "From Regionalism to Nationalism" – in the latter of which he emphasizes the symbolic power of Fascism in the immigrant community – identity as affected by workplace or other intercultural sites goes unexplored. Indeed, the only reference to worker associationalism in the book concerns anti-Italian nativism:

> The situation became unmanageable immediately after the turn of the century, as a result of a sudden and artificial increase in the number of yearly arrivals. In the tense atmosphere of labor disputes in San Francisco at the time, two groups had a vested interest in the creation of a large pool of immigrant labor: American businessmen and Italian immigrant entrepreneurs. The Americans had realized that the city's isolated geographical position worked against them, since labor could not easily be imported from other cities to break strikes. Italian labor was the answer. The San Francisco unions, for their part, systematically excluded Italians from membership. (Cinel 1982, p. 223)

While the passage quoted above appears (at least to the labor historian) the perfect prologue to discussion of the actual dynamic of interethnic social relations at work, it proves to be a throwaway line, never pursued given the author's other narrative priorities.

Donna Gabaccia's *Militants and Migrants: Rural Sicilians Become American Workers* (1988) directly picks up the baton that Cinel drops: just how did Italian migration (in this case peasants from the "red town" of Sambuca, Sicily) affect class formation on both sides of the transnational divide? When poor wheat harvests and suppression of peasant revolts affected Sambuca in the 1890s, a mass migration dispersed *paesani* to a complex variety of American settings: from Louisiana sugar-cane cutters and Illinois railway gang laborers, coal miners, and construction workers to Tampa cigar makers and Brooklyn barbers, tradespeople, and garment workers. Among other findings, Gabaccia stresses that worker activism – whether in Sicily or diaspora regions – depended on the admixture of radical artisans with peasant or ex-peasant workers. In the United States greater distance from both *padroni* and socialist leaders made for less politicization (as well as less corruption) in laboring ranks.

Finally, whereas "the policies of the Italian nation-state and the taxes imposed by local government" drove peasants to labor militancy in the home country, "migrants' contact with American politics" (and hence political activism) remained quite limited for many years" (Gabaccia 1988, pp. 112, 120–1, 148).

In short, Gabaccia's "village-outward" approach – with its attention to both structure and agency at either end of the migrant (and reverse migrant) stream – neatly brings into play key factors otherwise missing in assessing worker and immigrant "outcomes" (Gabaccia 1988, p. 2). To be sure, the very intensity of a place-based focus inevitably obscures other themes. Immigration historians will want to know more about the post-migrant generations; labor historians will wonder if, when, and how Italian peasant-workers integrated themselves into a larger workers' world. Even in hinting at the impact of such exogenous and diverse events as the Red Scare, the long-term abandonment of wage earning by immigrant workers' children, cyclical depressions, and Mussolini-era nationalism on Italian American worker militancy suggests the challenge to a community-based interpretive framework (Gabaccia 1988, pp. 147–8).

No work of recent years tackles more comprehensively the diverse questions of immigration and labor historians than Gary R. Mormino and George E. Pozzetta's *The Immigrant World of Ybor City* (1987). The very subtitle – *Italians and Their Latin Neighbors in Tampa, 1885–1985* – testifies to the book's uncommon scope: at once connecting and comparing the core Italian American experience to key immigrant "others," here Spaniards and Cubans, and taking a longitudinal view of ethnic community development over time. In contrast to Gabaccia's "village-outward" approach from the sender community of Sambuca to various receiving communities in the United States, Mormino and Pozzetta adopt what might be called a "city-backwards" approach in tracing various Tampa immigrant groups back to the land, culture, and political moment of dispersal. Taking advantage of the coincidence that the great majority of early Italian arrivals hailed from the single Sicilian village of Santo Stefano, the authors reconstruct the entire cigar-making world of Ybor City with uncommon verve. We begin with an Italian countryside in revolt against landlords and clerics, as led by schoolteacher-agitator Lorenzo Panepinto. Many of the *Stefanisi* who wind up in Tampa cigar factories find a comfortable fit between their own home-grown radicalism and the labor culture of the Spanish and Cuban workers who have preceded them to the trade. Incorporating the tradition, begun in Cuba, of the *lector* (reader) as a sign of skill and independence within the craft, a transnational "Latin" (i.e. Italian- and Spanish-speaking) working class developed a militant tradition in the years before World War I. With their organized strength built around mutual aid societies as well as the Cigarmakers International Union, "after 1905 Ybor City's cigarmakers and their families could expect better health services than almost anyone in Tampa" (Mormino and Pozzetta 1998, pp. 11, 17, 21–38, 97–134, 200).

To be sure, the pursuit of the Ybor City community across the twentieth century to its ethnic and post-industrial demise does not quite match the descriptive sparkle of the formative years. Still, the authors' extended chronological reach does yield dividends. We not only follow the break in the labor community occasioned by World War I, but also the persistence of radicalism occasioned (especially in the Italian community) by the Sacco and Vanzetti case and the rise of fascism. The denouement is clearly reached in the 1960s. Changing demographics – an aging population no longer able to build for the future – urban renewal, and out-migration signal the end of both the power and presence of the local Latin working class (as well as the disappearance of the industry on which it was built) (Mormino and Pozzetta 1998, pp. 143–69, 305–6).

In neatly conjoining the strengths of both labor and immigration history, the authors fail in only two particulars at delivering the vaunted "wholeness" of Ybor City's social-historical experience. First, the culture of labor they present is a virtual male-only edifice. Second – and perhaps more critical for their argument – it notably underplays the race theme in southern "white" working-class life. While the authors mention the impact of a 1967 race riot occasioned by a police shooting of a black youth, they offer little prior context for the subsequent white flight from the Ybor City community. Evidence suggests, however, that some of the coherence of the Latin labor community had always rested on a degree of local race polarization. From the beginning, the authors allow, "open hostility toward blacks deflected some of the nativism and discrimination immigrants commonly encountered elsewhere" (Mormino and Pozzetta 1998, p. 58). And even within the Latino community there is the suggestion of discrimination against Cubans on the basis of skin color (Mormino and Pozzetta 1998, p. 253). The complaint that the authors of this most horizontally and vertically extended version of "immigration histories" have still not done enough to capture the complexity of American "labor history" reveals only the size of the conceptual challenge facing the practitioners of both subdisciplines.

So, how effective has the bridge-building been from the other side of the disciplinary divide? To answer, let us briefly explore three of the most influential of recent labor histories of immigrant working-class communities.

James R. Barrett's *Work and Community in the Jungle: Chicago's Packinghouse Workers, 1894–1922* (1987), like Bodnar, neatly conjoins labor and immigration history, but unlike Bodnar maintains a focus on the immigrant community's *class* challenge to corporate domination. Refuting Upton Sinclair's classic picture of a largely passive, totally victimized industrial serfdom, Barrett stresses human agency in Packingtown both at the workplace and in surrounding back of the yards and adjacent African American neighborhoods. The immigrant family's very search for security (*à la* Bodnar), Barrett suggests, was best realized through *collective* action, which in turn transformed and expanded the inherited culture and consciousness of immigrant workers. A kind of "Americanization from the bottom up," therefore, helped to overcome original ethnic and skill divisions within the workforce, although it was not until the coming of the CIO in the late 1930s that industrial unionism surmounted the ultimate and debilitating race divide among workers. More than most labor histories, in its detailed investigation of immigrant-centered saloons, settlement houses, churches, residency, and home ownership, *Work and Community* ably explores the interior of working-class immigrant socialization. Still, given Barrett's chronologically concentrated and workplace-centered narrative, there are perhaps two major limitations here from the perspective of immigration history. First, we are left to wonder whether the "breakthrough" moment for the packinghouse workers came because of or in spite of their immigrant backgrounds, that is, had they become that much more "Americanized" or were they still drawing creatively on the strength of "ethnic" communal identities? Second, how much of either continuity or a break with "Old World" traditions existed in the initial political dispositions of the Packingtown workers? Here, we are reminded of the advantages (if not the necessity) of Gabaccia's "village-outward" approach (Barrett 1987, p. 138, see also pp. 64–197, 188–231).

Lizabeth Cohen's *Making A New Deal: Industrial Workers in Chicago, 1919–1939* (1990) frontally confronts both questions raised about the Packingtown workers. In an ambitious study not only tackling the central core of industrial Chicago but also stretching in time from the debacle of union defeat in the 1919 steel strike through CIO victory in the late 1930s, Cohen sets up a near-perfect field for relating immigrant socialization ("Americanization") to questions of class formation (worker solidarity). Nor does she shrink from the task. With the advantage of assessing the socialization process across two to three generations, Cohen, in fact, makes such socialization a cornerstone of her argument. The 1919 workers' world, she suggests, was one of geographic and cultural isolates. "Although Irish and German butchers, Slavic laborers, and black newcomers worked together in the packinghouses, at the end of the day they headed home to worlds segregated according to race, skill, and ethnicity" (Cohen 1990, pp. 21, 29). In the intervening years between 1919 and the CIO upheaval, Cohen suggests, ethnic identity became less parochial (as new immigration slackened off), mass culture (in the form of chain stores, movie theaters, and radio stations) created "a second-generation ethnic, working-class culture," and the welfare capitalist policies of large corporations further homogenized the experience and expectations of employees. The crunch, of course, came with the Great Depression. Suddenly, neither corporate nor ethnic leaders could satisfactorily address worker distress; now the slowly-evolving integration of the working class would take political form through the "New Democratic Coalition," and workplace form – despite continuing racial tensions – through the CIO "culture of unity." Cohen's thesis, in short, depends on a cultural argument about what happened to immigrant (and to a lesser extent African American migrant) workers over time. "An important reason why workers of diverse ethnicities and races succeeded in asserting themselves collectively as Democrats and as unionists by the 1930s," she concludes, "was that they had more in common culturally from which to forge alliances" (Cohen 1990, pp. 94–7, 147, 211, 2, 367, 365).

Yet, though subtle in conception and captivating in its explanatory reach, Cohen's "one-class-out-of-many" approach to immigrant socialization disregards the cultivated analytic perspective of new immigration historians. At the chronological front end of her argument, for a start, she does little to reconstruct the cultural or political mindset of the first-generation immigrant workers. We never learn how their own, inherited or adjusted, ideologies connected with that of their adopted country. And this proves a crucial oversight. Assuming a narrow, caste-like outlook for the early ethnic communities, Cohen hardly stops to consider how 90,000 diverse Chicago steelworkers mobilized in 1919 – before welfarism, before mass culture – and almost succeeded *despite* a hostile government and unhelpful craft union structures (Cohen 1990, p. 39). Instead, with shades of Oscar Handlin, Cohen ultimately suggests that the immigrant working-class communities needed to be "broken down" before they could "riseth up." Similarly, welfare capitalism – in the absence of articulation of the workers' own inherited beliefs – must serve here to provide the conceptual ideals and sense of entitlement that a broad-based workers' movement would ultimately rely upon. In short, Cohen's framework – probably the most comprehensive and compelling analysis available for the rise of the twentieth-century labor movement – ignores rather than incorporates the transnational (or "ethnic Turnerian") focus of its sister field. Even asking how a Gabaccia or Mormino might have handled the Chicago story is to raise a host of still-persistent perspectival differences between genres.

The relative diffidence of both labor and immigration history on cultural or "identity" questions (i.e. labor historians do not venture much beyond expressions of class solidarity, while immigration historians rarely extend themselves beyond concern for the second generation) has, in fact, left a hole that race-centered cultural historians and American Studies scholars have recently ventured to fill. Beginning with David Roediger's *Wages of Whiteness: Race and the Making of the American Working Class* (1991) and continuing through an extended series of studies, admittedly focused more on the "perception" of immigrants than the interior of the immigrant or ethnic communities themselves, "critical race" scholars have emphasized an initial pattern of anti-immigrant racialization (in which despised immigrants were regarded as less-than-white by the native-born), followed by a secondary pattern of immigrant-generated racialization (in which immigrants display their "whiteness" by disdainful distance from blacks) (Ignatiev 1995; Brodkin 1998; Foley 1997). The most encompassing overview within this genre is probably Matthew Frye Jacobson's *Whiteness of a Different Color: European Immigrants and the Alchemy of Race* (1998), which neatly demarcates a three-stage chronology of black/white dichotomy (1790–1840), "variegated whiteness" in which some immigrant groups were perceived as non-white (1840–1924), and the Caucasian consensus period, in which diverse nationalities, once excluded, were again accepted under the white umbrella (1920–1965) (Jacobson 1998, pp. 31, 38, 40, 96). Likewise, Barrett and Roediger emphasize the degree to which the long-recognized ethno-racial hierarchy among European immigrant groups encouraged a volatile race-obsessed politics among workers as well as employers seeking an economic advantage (Barrett and Roediger 1997).

While adjoining a rich and long-established literature on immigrant/African American relations in labor history, whiteness scholars distinguish themselves by their emphasis on the protean category of white racial identity (Bernstein 1990; Arnesen 1994; Halpern 1997). Yet, just how to do this has drawn considerable criticism (Arnesen 2001; Kolchin 2002). As Eric Arnesen, most notably, has contended, whiteness historians have been terribly vague about *whose lens* they are borrowing to label immigrant groups as "non-white," "inbetween," or "becoming white": moreover they "tend to depict their composite whites in a fairly one-dimensional manner and to focus exclusively on instances of dramatic [racial] conflict" (Arnesen 2001, pp. 19–21, 23). Even Barrett allows that "the precision of whiteness as a category of analysis has yet to be fully established on the basis of rigorous studies of particular workplaces, unions, and communities" (Barrett 2001, p. 40). We might add that, unlike the best of immigration history, whiteness literature largely stops at the water's edge of the nation's borders: there is little exploration of how American racial identity and taxonomies were influenced by deeply rooted and extensive European forays on the same subject (D'Agostino 2002). If, when, and how an exclusionary white identity came to dominate the assimilationist impulse in

Euro-American communities are questions worth testing; if it is to be convincing, however, and not merely to replace one mono-causal explanation for immigrant working-class behavior with another, such inquiry must be incorporated (as it has not yet been) into the time/space development – and internal differentiation – of the immigrant community.

My point here is simply that "whiteness" – as an explanation for both social identity and community behavior – has, in part, filled a vacuum left by labor- and immigration-focused social historians moored too closely to their original research agendas. Neither, in short, has pushed sufficiently to link class (workplace-based identity) or ethnicity (immigration-based identity) to the longer-term *outcomes* of US political culture, including, obviously, racial subordination, but also such particularisms as the rise of religious-based social movements. Far better that racial – or religious – identity should be taken up in the rich empirical context that we have come to expect from both labor and immigration history in dealing with other aspects of working-class life, than abandoned to all-too-sweeping generalizations based on a few selective texts.

Whatever the self-limitations of the two subfields under review, a couple of recent works offer promising examples of "bridging" operations, felicitously borrowing from multiple subdisciplinary perspectives. One example is found in Gunther Peck's *Reinventing Free Labor: Padrones and Immigrant Workers in the North American West, 1880–1930* (2000). Selecting three dramatically different case studies of *padrone–immigrant* worker relationships – Italians in Canada, Greeks in Utah, and Mexicans on both sides of the Rio Grande – Peck conveys the specificity of each of these three contexts while at the same time making a larger case for the meaning of such examples of coerced labor within a society self-consciously dedicated to the principles of "free labor." Peck convincingly argues for a reassessment of the spatial dimension of "western" socio-economic development. Instead of the "footloose West" of Wobbly lore – where freedom of movement produced a supposedly more liberated, radicalized labor movement – Peck insists that we incorporate a transnational dimension into our understanding of western labor conflicts. His story thus begins with the rehabilitation, in its new capitalist setting, of the older European system of the *padrone* (or labor boss). Modern class relations, he suggests, must take account of not only the workplace itself but also the "prior" relationships which governed the recruitment of labor (in this case what he calls the "commodification of mobility between jobs, between nations, and between cultures"). Finally, by importing from immigration history the concept of a community extended across space, Peck makes new sense of much western labor militancy. It was not so much the "free air" of the west, he suggests, as ties (consecrated through village associations, coffeehouse culture, as well as marriage vows) across borders and great distances that sustained immigrant workers' will to fight and ultimately bring down the *padrone* system. At the same time, he demonstrates, those ties of ethnic identity became more elastic in the heat of battle and in necessary cooperation with "outsiders" (Peck 2000, pp. 224, 160–5).

Peck's conceptual framework neatly combines the main themes of new labor and recent immigration history (and, albeit less successfully, themes from gender studies and critical race theory). That workers "on the move" should be analyzed as part of an intergenerational cultural passage – in short, by the bedrock methods of immigration history – seems perfectly obvious. That we should also test their "moves" in relation to employers and fellow workers – in short, by the yardstick of social class relations well developed in labor history – is surely just as self-evident. In practice, however, accomplishing both tasks in one project proves not so easy. That Peck's book concerns a *particularly mobile* community – i.e. he is not pressed to show extended relations over time between immigrants and persistent worker-citizens – may have helped him square the circle.

Another "crossover" study worth mention is Nancy A. Hewitt's *Southern Discomfort: Women's Activism in Tampa, Florida, 1880s–1920s* (2001). Although conceived from within the precincts of gender and women's history, Hewitt's work casts light on the core themes we have examined above in both immigration and labor history – particularly so, since it re-examines turf previously occupied by Mormino and Pozzetta. More than simply restoring a gender balance for the Ybor City narrative, moreover, Hewitt's emphasis on "women's activism" effectively places her subjects within a well-developed urban and international political history – a context missing not only from Mormino and Pozzetta's account but slighted by most social histories. In particular, Hewitt's standpoint uncovers the fascinating interaction between Tampa–Ybor City Cubans and revolutionaries like José Martí prior to Cuban independence as well as the dramatic defeat of a Cuban-centered federation of anarcho-syndicalist cigar makers by the combined forces of Tampa's "best men" and the American Federation of Labor's Cigar Makers' International Union (Hewitt 2001, pp. 67–136). Hewitt's broader city-wide compass also enables a deep investigation of race and ethnic group conflict and cooperation as well as shifting alliances among middle-class and working-class representatives. To be sure, the same lens that adds precision and breadth to the list of local actors "fuzzes" the broader social-economic picture while also delimiting its time and space (i.e. no sender community analysis) coordinates. Such, inevitably, are the tradeoffs of this enterprise.

On balance, the "wholeness" we desire in "understanding human behavior" will be substantially advanced when immigration historians become more attuned to the power relations and changes in group identity in both sending and receiving communities, and when labor historians give more attention to the processes of labor *recruitment* as well as the sources of worker motivation outside the workplace itself. Even after such conceptual synthesis is accomplished, to be sure, we will want our "whole" history also to reflect a sensitivity to politics, gender, race, etc. – in short to whatever else appeared to *matter* to the people and places we are writing about. In the meantime, the two venerable fields of immigration and labor history will continue to claim our attention as two of the most creative and incisive arenas in contemporary historical scholarship.

NOTE

The author gratefully acknowledges the suggestions and criticisms of Peter D'Agostino, Eric Arnesen, Susan Levine, and Reed Ueda in the preparation of this chapter. He also thanks William Malone, Eric Smith, and Jay Stanek for helping him think through these issues in a 2001 graduate colloquium on "Immigrants in the Global Marketplace."

REFERENCES

Arnesen Eric (1994). *Waterfront Workers of New Orleans: Race, Class, and Politics, 1863–1923*. Urbana: University of Illinois Press.

—— (2001). "Whiteness and the Historians' Imagination." *International Labor and Working-Class History* 60: 3–32.

Barrett, James R. (1987). *Work and Community in the Jungle: Chicago's Packinghouse Workers, 1894–1922*. Urbana: University of Illinois Press.

—— (2001). "Whiteness Studies: Anything Here for Historians of the Working Class?" *International Labor and Working-Class History* 60: 33–42.

Barrett, James R. and David Roediger (1997). "Inbetween Peoples: Race, Nationality and the 'New Immigrant' Working Class." *Journal of American Ethnic History* 15: 3–44.

Bernstein, Iver (1990). *The New York City Draft Riots: Their Significance in American Society and Politics in the Age of the Civil War*. New York: Oxford University Press.

Bodnar, Jon E. (1977). *Immigration and Industrialization: Ethnicity in an American Mill Town, 1870–1940*. Pittsburgh: University of Pittsburgh Press.

—— (1982). *Workers' World: Kinship, Community, and Protest in an Industrial Society, 1900–1940*. Baltimore: Johns Hopkins University Press.

—— (1985). *The Transplanted: A History of Immigrants in Urban America*. Bloomington: Indiana University Press.

Brodkin, Karen (1998). *How Jews Became White Folks and What That Says About Race in America*. New Brunswick: Rutgers University Press.

Cinel, Dino (1982). *From Italy to San Francisco: The Immigrant Experience*. Stanford, CA: Stanford University Press.

Cohen, Lizabeth (1990). *Making A New Deal: Industrial Workers in Chicago, 1919–1939*. New York: Cambridge University Press.

Commons, John R. (1907). *Races and Immigrants in America*. New York: Macmillan.

D'Agostino, Peter (2002). "Craniums, Criminals, and the 'Cursed Race': Italian Anthropology in American Racial Thought, 1861–1924." *Comparative Study of Society and History* (April): 319–43.

Fink, Leon (1974). Review of Allen F. Davis and Mark H. Haller, *The Peoples of Philadelphia, 1790–1940*, and Joseph A. Ryan, ed., *White Ethnics: Life in Working Class America*. *Journal of Ethnic Studies* 2 (Summer): 92–5.

—— (1976). Review of John E. Bodnar, ed., *The Ethnic Experience in Pennsylvania*. *Journal of Ethnic Studies* 3 (Winter): 97–9.

Foley, Neil (1997). *The White Scourge: Mexicans, Blacks, and Poor Whites in Texas Cotton Culture*. Berkeley: University of California Press.

Gabaccia, Donna (1988). *Militants and Migrants: Rural Sicilians Become American Workers*. New Brunswick: Rutgers University Press.

Gjerde, Jon (1999). "New Growth on Old Vines – the State of the Field: The Social History of Immigration to and Ethnicity in the United States." *Journal of American Ethnic History* 18 (Summer): 40–65.

Gordon, Michael A. (1993). *The Orange Riots: Irish Political Violence in New York City, 1870 and 1871*. Ithaca, NY: Cornell University Press.

Greene, Victor R. (1968). *The Slavic Community on Strike; Immigrant Labor in Pennsylvania Anthracite*. Notre Damen IN: University of Notre Dame Press.

Gutman, Herbert G. (1977). *Work, Culture and Society in Industrializing America*. New York: Vintage.

Halpern, Rick (1997). *Down on the Killing Floor: Black and White Workers in Chicago's Packinghouses, 1904–54*. Urbana: University of Illinois Press.

Handlin, Oscar (1941). *Boston's Immigrants, 1790–1865: A Study in Acculturation.* Cambridge, MA: Harvard University Press.

—— (1973). *The Uprooted,* 2nd edn. Boston: Little, Brown.

Hewitt, Nancy A. (2001). *Southern Discomfort: Women's Activism in Tampa, Florida, 1880s–1920s.* Urbana: University of Illinois Press.

Higham, John (1963). *Strangers in the Land: Patterns of American Nativism, 1860–1925.* New York: Atheneum.

Ignatiev, Noel (1995). *How the Irish Became White.* New York: Routledge.

Jacobson, Matthew Frye (1998). *Whiteness of a Different Color: European Immigrants and the Alchemy of Race.* Cambridge, MA: Harvard University Press.

Kolchin, Peter (2002). "Whiteness Studies: The New History of Race in America." *Journal of American History* 89 (June): 154–73.

Mormino, Gary R. and George E. Pozzetta (1998). *The Immigrant World of Ybor City: Italians and Their Latin Neighbors in Tampa, 1885–1985* [1987]. Gainesville: University Press of Florida.

Peck, Gunther (2000). *Reinventing Free Labor: Padrones and Immigrant Workers in the North American West, 1880–1930.* New York: Cambridge University Press.

Roediger, David (1991). *Wages of Whiteness: Race and the Making of the American Working Class.* New York: Verso.

Shaw, Douglas V. (1976). *The Making of an Immigrant City: Ethnic and Cultural Conflict in Jersey City, New Jersey, 1850–1877.* New York: Arno Press.

Thomas, William I. and Florian Znaniecki (1984). *The Polish Peasant in Europe and America* [1927], ed. and abridged by Eli Zaretzsky. Urbana: University of Illinois Press.

Ueda, Reed (1990). "Immigration and the Moral Criticism of American History: The Vision of Oscar Handlin." *Canadian Review of American Studies* 21 (Fall): 183–201.

Vecoli, Rudolph (1964). "*Contadini* in Chicago: A Critique of *The Uprooted.*" *Journal of American History* 51: 404–17.

Yans-McLaughlin, Virginia (1977). *Family and Community: Italian Immigrants in Buffalo, 1880–1930.* Urbana: University of Illinois Press.

Yearley, Clifton K. (1957). *Britons in American Labor: A History of the Influence of the United Kingdom Immigrants on American Labor, 1820–1914.* Baltimore: Johns Hopkins University Press.

CHAPTER NINETEEN

Immigration in the Economy: Development and Enterprise

NIAN-SHENG HUANG

The impact of immigration on economic and business history in the United States has often been recognized as a phenomenon of the nineteenth century, especially during its second half when 15 million immigrants came to America seeking new opportunities generated by industrialization, urbanization, and westward expansion. Immigration patterns, however, began to shape the central institutions of economic development in the colonial era and were involved continuously in the transformation of economic culture. The role of immigration in the economy can thus be profitably studied in a comparative cultural context that is chronologically framed in a long-term perspective.

Four major factors – land, collective belief, labor, and entrepreneurship – played critical roles in shaping the linkages between the economy and immigration. These formative factors underwent different stages of metamorphosis themselves and, as such, constitute the focal points of the following historical discussion.

Land

The imperial economies of colonial North America centered upon land, yet land-owning systems varied significantly from region to region. Soon after the fall of the Aztec empire, Spanish conquistadors installed the *encomienda* system that gave them extensive controls and privileges over the land and its residents. Hernando Cortés, for example, was allowed to own 22 towns and control 23,000 Native Indians as his vassals (Meyer et al. 2003, p. 132). Subjecting Native Indians to treatment as serfs, the encomienda system produced a ruling class in Spanish Mexico with all the characteristics of a landed aristocracy of European birth: inherited wealth, personal loyalty, and high-handed authority. Although the system was discontinued by the early seventeenth century, it was succeeded by the *hacienda* system which was also based on large-scale land holdings conducive to rigid economic stratifications and activities centered on leisure and consumption rather than production in the colonial Spanish Mexican economy (Chevalier 1982).

Locked between the Canadian Shield to the north and the Appalachian Mountains to the south, early French settlements in the St. Lawrence River Valley lacked favorable weather, fertile soil, and potential space for commercial agriculture and expansion. Navigating west along the St. Lawrence River, however, the French colonists had the great advantage of reaching the Great Lakes region years before the English did. The unobstructed Mississippi Valley further invited them to cross the continent as far south as to the Gulf of Mexico in 1684, when Massachusetts Puritans, who had just lost their charter to the crown, were struggling to preserve their government, and when Virginians were still rebuilding their capital Jamestown after rebels led by Nathaniel Bacon had burned it to the ground less than a decade earlier. Yet, the real interest of the French was not tillable lands but animal furs. The vast North American territory became useful to them only when they could find Native Indians who would trade beaver hides, mink pelts, and moose skins. French Canada never became a land of intensive agriculture but remained a trading post through the colonial era.

As was in Old France, "no land was without a seigneur" in the French-controlled St. Lawrence River Valley according to scholars such as Richard C. Harris, and the transplanted seigneurial system established a dominant social pattern in the colony. Seigneurs collected rents from tenants who, in addition to their services to their lords, were also charged for fishing, cutting wood, and using the seigneur's mill. Farming on a piece of long and narrow land within the seigneurial boundaries that could not be further conceded, the *censitaire* was tied to the *roture* as much as his lord to the seigneury. Bound to mutual loyalties and inherited responsibilities, neither had a desire to move out from the domains.

The law made it clear that for anyone who was not an original owner or a direct inheritor of the seigneury, buying or selling a seigneurial estate would be extremely difficult. Once an ancestor's landholding did fall into alien possession, tradition dictated that it would be the highest honor and most important obligation for those descendants to regain ownership and to restore the integrity of family property. By the same token, a seigneur, no matter how downtrodden his financial circumstances might be, would refuse to try his hand in any business or commercial activity that might suggest he had to demean himself to a low profession.

The elites of the British Thirteen Colonies formed in a social system that was not conducive to the support of quasi-feudal economic or political institutions, and rose through a process of social mobility that reflected a dynamic agricultural economy.

Quitrents, a form of payment, substituted for feudal services and obligations in many places in the middle colonies. Dutch patrons, English manor owners, and Quaker proprietors never monopolized or dominated the entire rural land market. Participation in landholding, land investments, and speculations cut across the social structure. The "middling" sort of families were also able to buy land and farm out a living alongside wealthier ones. As part of a relief policy at a time when currency was scarce and the public treasury underfunded, colonial governments granted land to needy individuals and families. Head-rights in the south, giving out acreage per capita, were long-established incentives to encourage immigration in the seventeenth century. Townships and homesteads were granted as early as the 1730s in Massachusetts to compensate wounded soldiers or those survivors who had suffered the loss of family members or relatives during military expeditions.

In the Thirteen Colonies, peopling the land involved settling immigrants (colonists who migrated from Britain and the rest of Europe) as factors for regional development through independent owner-operated farms. An economic and political dynamic sprang from the connection between immigrant settlement and a land policy based on popular and invidualized freeholdership. The availability of land to middle- and small-size owners provided an economic platform that boosted participatory public life. Many a freeholder's pride in property ownership and frequent activity in public affairs stood in sharp contrast to the more limited political involvement of tenant populations in New France to the north, and sharecroppers, day laborers, and *repartimiento* (coerced Native Indian labor) in New Spain to the south.

No sooner had settlers arrived along the Atlantic coast than a great variety of movements seeking new settlements further inland began to spread: Virginians heading to the Piedmont and to the foothills of the Blue Ridge Mountains, the Irish, Scottish, and Germans passing the Jerseys and Pennsylvania to the western country, and thousands more to the Appalachian Mountains, to the Adirondack Mountains, to the Hudson River, to the Catskill Mountains, to the Connecticut River, to Long Island, to the Merrimack River, to the White Mountains, and to the Green Mountains. The Proclamation Line across the Appalachian Mountains drawn by the British government in 1763, which caused much resentment in the colonies, broke down soon after the Revolutionary War. The correlation between land development policy and population movement formed in the colonial era would act as an economic dynamic for territorial expansion that would continue through the nineteenth century. Colonial and early national land policy encouraged immigration and installed immigrant settlers as primary units of farm labor and capital ownership that drove the expansion of an agricultural hinterland for regional development.

Collective Belief

Ever since John Winthrop used the analogy of building a "city upon the hill" in his lay sermon on board the *Arbella* to the New World in 1630, a sense of self-righteousness and glory has become one of the sturdiest underpinnings supporting migration and settlement. As in the biblical exodus from Egypt and settlement in Canaan, Puritan settlers dreamt of establishing a model community that would be a beacon to the Christian world, an inspiration to exemplify religious reform that sustained them in the vicissitudes of the early years of colonization.

In contrast to their Catholic neighbors in Spanish Mexico or French Quebec, the religious zeal of Protestants in the British North American colonies did not lead to a holy crusade to convert the Native Indians into Christians (Egnal 1996; White 1991). Instead they focused their attention on how to exclude the Native Indians from the territories they invaded. A different spiritual seed of colonialism had a far-reaching significance from the very start. Unlike the Spanish colony in Mexico where interracial marriages became commonplace, and unlike the French who actively sought alliance with the Algonquians, the English colonists did not form a bi-racial society with Native Indians. That the English colonies were peopled primarily by incoming immigrants rather than by a mixing with the native population was the basic pattern which would become all the more important for attracting future immigration as time went by. Consider that whereas it took about 170 years to settle the 13 original colonies, two decades after Independence the United States doubled its size by acquiring Louisiana in 1803. The country's size almost doubled again by the end of the Mexican–American War in 1848 when the defeated Mexican government conceded half of its land. The early imperial ambition to build an empire from ocean to ocean quickly came to fruition.

Americans must have felt very special indeed and their resiliency through years of hardship in migration, settlement, and expansion was the result of a missionary conviction of being God's chosen people. The gratifying knowledge that it was God's will that their nation should expand suggested an external application too tempting for many not to oblige. Through the Manifest Destiny of the first half of the nineteenth century as well as the American exceptionalism of the second half, worldly explanations for material progress accommodated divine providence as the ultimate call for continuous advancement.

Paradoxical as it seems, this collective belief in national progress – a popular frame of mind animated by an aspirational idealism or spirit – often had an earthly bent for sanctifying, glorifying, or condemning secular actions (Weiss 1969, p. 19). A good illustration of this idealistic outlook could be found in the painting by John Gast, *American Progress*, which was made popular by the numerous lithographical prints reproduced by George A. Crofutt in his transcontinental tourist guide in the 1870s. As the artifact shows, confidence in both angelical blessings and human progress encouraged a forward movement on earth, not a psychological nostalgia for the distant and illusive past. Looking at this picture, Crofutt said, "What American man, woman, or child, does not feel a heart-throb of exultation as they think of the glorious achievements of PROGRESS since the landing of the Pilgrim Fathers, on stanch old Plymouth Rock!"

American aspirational idealism seldom was separable from practical applications. For many immigrants seeking to become American, America began on a "dream" horizon or imaginary that generated impulses to seek religious sanctuary, political freedom, or economic betterment. America became an idealized and mythic land partly because many immigrants came shaped by this dream imaginary and worked to realize it. Successive waves of immigration perceived this visionary horizon and transmitted it intergenerationally so that it would receive expression in different forms and in renewed contexts.

Seymour Martin Lipset (1990, pp. 67–8) described an almost naïve popular conviction in the United States that although not anyone could become a "winner," everyone was at least entitled to think and behave like one: a forward-looking vision and positive attitude toward achieving progress characterized a popular, living philosophy. These elements were especially valuable qualities for immigrants to possess in this new country where difficult and even hostile conditions often weighed heavily on them. The resiliency and confidence to move on after setbacks and disappointments, and to maintain self-respect and dignity in the face of social barriers, spiritually underscored generations of immigrants, young and old, men and women.

Becoming an American involved adapting to an individualistic norm of behavior that was not only a practical guide but a new inspirationally motivating force. Both the practical and romantic blended into an idealized new identity which transcended tradition, religion, nationality, language, and history. Not a small number of immigrant newcomers felt themselves assuming an exalted and individualized status, detached from ethnic background and any lingering habits from their native language or culture (Antin). Internalizing the spirit and discourse of individualism was a principal rite of passage for immigrants to become Americans, although American-ization was never synonymous with merely adapting to individualism. Newcomers grappled with internalizing the public ethos that individual self-interest was the key to economic betterment. This way of thinking contradicted what most immigrants were taught in their cultural heritage: a discourse of economic duties to family and kin, to communal units, and the ancestral nation. The process of becoming Amer-ican challenged many of those deeply rooted orientations toward collective life.

The segmentation by race or ethnicity of the immigrant population limited the choice and scope of economic activity (Laslett and Lipset 1984). Because migrating ethnic populations created many self-congregated as well as exogenously segregated communities, any form of collaboration and teamwork to promote economic advance-ment had a tendency to originate from a particular segment of the neighborhood, from an enclave. The economic horizon of the first-generation and even second-generation immigrant created a dual adaptation: toward a strong attachment to ethnic identity and collective solidarity, on one hand, and toward an opportunistic ethos of individual rights on the other. The economic psychology of the American immigrant was shaped by a continuous process of sorting through and balancing these polarities.

Labor

Notwithstanding a constant demand for and a frequent shortage of labor beginning in the colonial era, not every immigrant was welcomed as a worker (Nash 1979; Smith 2004). Early authorities on each side of the Atlantic possessed different plans and strategies for recruiting laborers. The British government believed it to be beneficial for all parties that socially marginal people of the mother country were sent to the colonies. Caught between the need for an imported labor force to achieve economic prosperity and the desire for social stability, colonial authorities remained ambivalent about the arrival of such newcomers. Efforts made to encour-age immigration and to select immigrants at the same time shaped a pattern of labor shortages, transiency, rotation, and exclusion that extended from the era of the agricultural economy under colonialism to the industrial revolution of the manu-facturing economy of the United States.

The early stockholders of the Massachusetts Company, for example, screened potential candidates before they sailed and shipped back those they thought to be unfit for the new colony. Propriety in both spiritual life and social behavior certainly played a significant role in those early considerations and Puritan conformity became a benchmark to keep the population in line with the orthodoxy. That Quaker settlers were expelled and executed and that Anne Hutchinson was excommunicated and banished shortly after the colony was established indicated the uncompromising seriousness of the Calvinist theocracy's commitment to preserving the purity and homogeneity of the community.

No sooner had a demand for labor begun to spread in the colonies than many saw the potential profit to be made in linking domestic needs with the international labor market. Merchants, traders, and shipmasters sent agents all over Europe who tried every propaganda scheme to lure the credulous to board ships heading for America. An enormous transatlantic business emerged and some traders' scandalous practices shocked the public. Misrepresentations of the real colonial prospect, fraudulent portrayals of the terms of service, and a hearty consumption of good and bad liquor were among the most convenient tricks to trap unsuspecting people into signing up for the New World. Several months on the high seas, unhealthy sanitary conditions of the merchant ships, and a variety of diseases killed so many passengers who had hoped to join the labor force in the colonies that this deplorable record was exceeded only by that of the more notorious Middle Passage in the slave trade.

As the importation of immigrant labor continued, attempts were made on the receiving end to ensure the moral and financial condition of the new arrivals. In some colonies the acceptance of an immigrant would depend on a deposition to attest his/her moral character and proper behavior, submitted by resident friends or relatives who knew them. Beginning from the 1680s, Massachusetts authorities instituted a surety of £100 for every newly arrived adult, £50 for a child or an elderly person, which would be used as an indemnity against any potential liability to the town treasury in case the person should fall into sickness or poverty. Anyone who could not afford the money or could not find someone else to put up a bond for the same purpose would be denied entry.

No policies, however, could totally prevent poor immigrants, as well as poor internal migrants and transients, from arriving. The office of the overseers of the poor was finally established in many communities to handle the issue of poor relief, while many almshouses, workhouses, houses of correction, hospitals, asylums, and special farms were used to confine the destitute, the sick, the widowed, the orphaned, the aged, and the idle. Realizing the heavy burden of relief and the limits of public funds, colonial authorities found the English relief policies useful and began to institutionalize a similar requirement for residency. The first Massachusetts settlement laws were passed in 1656, which required four months of residence before a person could establish the full legal rights of a resident, including the right to claim public relief. During those four months, the background of the newcomer would be closely scrutinized and any suspicion of a moral or financial nature could cause them to be warned out from the community. Among the earliest colonial laws to distinguish residents from immigrants and non-residents, these regulations clearly indicated that not all outsiders were welcome – their classification alone as non-residents gave them fewer legal rights and protections than residents. The four-month waiting period was later found inadequate and extended to 12 months in a new act in 1690, which remained in effect until 1824. This long-held colonial practice of accepting an outsider only after a lengthy testing period also seemed to have laid a basis for the two-step naturalization process from residency to citizenship in the future United States.

Discrimination against the lower classes of outsiders, non-residents, and aliens reached a new level when they happened to have the wrong accent or religion. People coming from Ireland and the German states were particularly viewed with suspicion. New York and Boston authorities routinely quarantined ships from Palatinate and other poverty- and disease-stricken regions. The perception that ships from those alien lands would be most likely to carry diseases persisted so much that typhus came to be known as "Palatine fever" in these seaport regions in the early 1700s. Nor was anything Catholic viewed favorably in many colonies, especially in the Protestant strongholds in New England. The French Acadians posed a constant threat to the Protestant fishermen and frontiersmen in the northeast who hardly passed a day without fear that not far away across the border a French or papist plot against them was in the making.

Even the first Irish Charitable Society in Boston, founded in 1687, declared that their benefits would not be given to the Catholics; they merely cared about the Scottish and Protestant Irish who emigrated to the colony. When the Irish arrived, many had no other choice but to move on, such as a group of Ulster weavers, coming in 1718, who had to settle in New Hampshire instead of Boston. Twenty years later, all the five Irish families of Lexington were warned out. Equally unwelcome were African blacks, Native Indians, and other racial outsiders. Boston town records repeatedly documented their whereabouts and deportations. The desire to keep all unwanted people out was such that the Boston town meeting, in 1747, appointed two searchers who were authorized to inspect every household to register and report to town authorities any resident strangers.

Poor immigrants continued to arrive and no one could force them out of doors completely. In fact, the willingness of friends and relatives to help them hide was an important factor inducing them to come. Humanitarian organizations sometimes served as a temporary shelter as well. Many refugees from the war-torn frontiers went straight to the almshouses in safe areas, and sick or starving passengers to the asylums as soon as they landed. After a few weeks and sometimes as long as a year, they recuperated and moved on. Rather than stay at the urban centers along the coasts, hundreds preferred to settle in the less populated and mountainous interior where land was available and official interference less frequent.

At a time when the government-controlled "just price" was the rule of the day and when much of business competition was centered on the availability of cheap labor, it all made good sense for employers to acquire help at the lowest cost. A poor, friendless, and unprotected non-resident's first instinct was to accept any offer of work in order to survive, not to bargain for higher wages or better working conditions, since he had few employment options. Employers knew this well and some took advantage of the situation, even coercing and abusing their employees. The law sometimes favored the weaker party. An apprentice could sue a master if he believed he had enough evidence to show that he was badly treated and deserved justice. There were many servants, apprentices, and journeymen who took the risk of running away for personal independence or better pay in other regions.

The stream of runaways, along with worker transiency, exacerbated a chronic shortage in the colonial labor market. Only a continuous influx of new labor from the outside could fill the void they left. Sporadic in nature at first, this rotation of labor gradually formed a general pattern as production and employment expanded during the industrialization of manufacturing. A new group of immigrants would be employed to take the lowest-paid and least-respected jobs if they managed to stay in the urban areas. Replacing the girls of native families in the textile factories at first, for example, the Irish and the French Canadians themselves were later gradually replaced by the Greeks and Poles toward the end of the nineteenth century.

If the early handicraft manufactures began the demand for a rotating supply of immigrant labor, accelerated industrial growth demanded it far more. As in the colonial societies, economic benefit for some, however, might not be socially acceptable to others. When the famine in Ireland and poverty and political instabilities in Europe brought thousands of the downtrodden to America each year, sentiments against foreigners also became more pronounced. In an organized effort to curb immigration, the Know Nothing Party in the 1850s specifically proposed an anti-foreign immigration policy in their party platform. Indeed, the growing demand for cheap immigrant labor was concurrent with widespread social anxieties toward foreign-born workers who might lower general economic conditions. Newspaper cartoons caricatured Jews in stereotyped versions of Shakespeare's Venetian merchant Shylock. Yellow-skinned, pigtailed, and gambling-prone, the Chinese coolies appeared to be beyond any attempt at assimilation. Dennis Kearney and the Workingmen's Party in California in the late 1870s openly declared that "the Chinese must go," and gave voice to a general sentiment in the state. Laborers and small businesses were threatened by the prospect that after the Central Pacific and the Union Pacific Railroads were joined in 1869, thousands of Chinese workers would be dismissed by the railroad companies and return to San Francisco and other communities to compete for low-paying jobs with the native population.

Before the turn of the twentieth century, immigrants from southern and eastern European countries began to greatly outnumber those from northern and western Europe, putting the tolerance and sensitivities of natives to another serious test. The social Darwinist theory of survival of the fittest was invoked to deal with the new immigrants from Europe. Those who feared interracial marriages which might dilute and impair the Anglo-Saxon stock called for stricter immigration controls. An effort was launched to ascertain the correlation of different levels of human intelligence with racial and ethnic categories. A literacy test administered to restrict immigrants seeking entry was passed into law by Congress which also instituted discriminatory national origins admissions quotas based on dubious notions of the inferiority of immigrants from southern and eastern Europe.

As the doors closed against European immigration, Mexican immigration began to emerge as a new and important source of labor. The irrigation revolution of the late nineteenth century turned many regions of the American west into some of the most prosperous agricultural producing regions in the world, especially California. The borders between the United States and Mexico were open to people on both sides who could pay a nominal fee for travel. Mexican farm workers became the backbone of commercialized agriculture production in such states as California, Texas, and Florida. Many who saw the Mexican migrant workers as a drain on public relief funds during the Great Depression advocated and secured their mass repatriation. But World War II presented a different scenario when manpower shortages created by mass conscription induced the federal government to make an agreement with the Mexican government (that lasted until 1964) to allow agricultural workers from Mexico, known as *braceros*, to work temporarily in the United States.

An economy so closely tied to an international labor market has always had a double-edge. Immigrant labor historically played a decisive role in shaping the US economy, especially during its formative stages. Popular opinion often split over the need for immigrant workers. The demand for immigrants from the drive for business competitiveness, on one hand, has been counterposed against popular fears that they caused social complications and expensive welfare policies. Conflicting views over the impact of immigrant labor continued into the post-industrial era when American labor increasingly competed on several fronts on a worldwide stage. In some traditional industries, such as agriculture, residential housing construction, domestic service, and restaurant and food service, immigrant workers filled a growing domestic labor need. The flow of immigrant workers has made these businesses profitable, but it has also generated heated debates over fears that it has been accompanied by the rise of illegal or irregular immigration and by uncontrolled borders.

In newer financial and high-tech industries, multinational corporations have moved plants and offices outside the United States to seek highly specialized and yet less expensive white-collar employees overseas. This so-called "out-sourcing" is a type of reverse immigration: a pattern where jobs "immigrate" to laborers who otherwise might have immigrated to the United States. Just as Nike and Zenith workers found out a few decades ago that their jobs had moved to Southeast Asia and Latin America, employees of AT&T and Oracle are now replaced by operators in foreign countries. The globalization of labor, of which immigration is one component, has brought into collision diverse economic interests and forms of competition at various domestic and international levels. This process has challenged the imagination of public policy makers who seek to coordinate immigration control with job policies and domestic employment protections.

Entrepreneurship

Economic sociologists have observed that immigrant communities tended to produce proportionally more entrepreneurs than the native population.

Federal census data collected between 1880 and 1980 indeed showed that the foreign-born population persistently displayed a higher rate of self-employment than the native-born. What were the reasons to explain this phenomenon? If most immigrants came from less developed regions in the Old World, what factors made them more inclined to pursue independent economic activities in America? Or can it be argued that in spite of the less favorable political and economic situations of their origins, certain cultural characteristics gave immigrants a sharper entrepreneurial edge than natives in the modern competitive environment?

By definition, entrepreneurs are unconventional risk-takers and innovators who are rarely content with the status quo. Immigration was a process of self-selection that recruited people with these qualities. By deciding to leave their homelands and to embark upon a new life in a foreign land, immigrants marked themselves as people who were willing to voyage on a long journey full of uncertainties. To rebuild their lives and to struggle for survival in new surroundings, immigrants had to be risk-takers with a strong determination to control external circumstance. Compared with those natives whose status in their homeland was considered an unquestioned birthright, the immigrants' position in their adopted nation had to be earned and sustained. Unable to take their security for granted, immigrants compensated by controlling their economic environment through self-employment and what some social scientists have described as "self-exploitation." Immigrant small businessmen, for example, often kept their shops open for long hours, closed for fewer holidays, and paid their employees less, many of whom were family members and relatives. Complaints against newcomers, such as those by the English about the Irish, by the Irish and Germans about the Italians and Poles, or by Californians of European descent against Asians and Latinos, repeated the refrain that newly arrived cheap laborers had undermined the conditions of employment. In the early twentieth century, New York City merchants lamented how the artificial flower business used to be dominated by "American" and German workers, "then the Italians and Jews came in and killed it." Historian Thomas Kessner described "One such Italian family, typical of many" (1977, pp. 73–4), whose work pattern aroused such complaints.

> [The family] consisted of a grandmother living with a couple and their four children, aged 4, 3, 2, and one month. The mother and grandmother could not leave the house to work, and it was, of course, illegal for the young children to do so. Nonetheless, all except the father and the two youngest babies made artificial flowers. The three-year-old worked on petals, her older sister, still too young for school, separated stems and dipped them into paste, while the two women placed petals on the stems. One hour's work for the four workers produced a gross of flowers, and these 144 pieces earned them 10 cents. A twelve-hour day earned this team $1.20; a good week $7.00.

The survival strategy of this family was based on using family members as employees, a practice believed to be more trustworthy, reliable, and cost-effective. They, like every new generation of immigrant families, had the willingness to take on the least desirable jobs for longer hours and lower pay, and to "exploit" themselves in terms of taking little compensation in order to wedge themselves into a labor market dominated by predecessor groups. Immigrants transferred the same work attitudes from the labor market into entrepreneurial arenas.

Business opportunities were limited for aspiring ethnic entrepreneurs, who did not have strong financial backing or an established business network to rely on. What they had instead were social-capital assets derived from the distinctive ethnic sociology and cultural solidarity of their communities (Light and Gold 2000). Immigrants often went to and settled in places where they had relatives and friends who were crucial in helping them locate housing, employment, and business opportunities. The Japanese "ko" or the "gye" among the Korean immigrants were rotating credit associations and mutual aid cooperatives. The "hui" (an association or a club) played a similar role in the entrepreneurial activities of Chinese immigrants in the nineteenth and twentieth centuries who came from southern China where there was a long-standing local tradition of the hui. When a person wanted to raise a certain amount of capital beyond his regular family income, he could organize a hui by asking several of his relatives and friends to agree to put up every month a small amount of money to form a common pool of funds. He and other members of the hui would be entitled to draw money from the pool in turn month by month. The arrangement of this organization made it possible for all members of the hui to use the collected sum for conducting business activities without resorting to a commercial bank that charged high interest. As a mutual help organization, the hui was highly dependent on the mutual trust of members. It could function only because it was deeply rooted in the moral traditions of reciprocity recognized by the people of southern China for generations which they brought with them to the United States. Many immigrant business ventures would not have been launched without the financial support derived from this distinctive ethnic mutual help association.

Ethnic entrepreneurs often made headway as they explored opportunities passed by, overlooked, or rejected as unfit for their status by natives. These included domestic service, street and building cleaning, waste recycling, laundry service, restaurant and fast-food service, and gardening. Immigrant entrepreneurs began their inroads into the business world from activities in under-serviced areas that required intensive labor but only produced marginal profits.

Because of the ways ethnic businesses were conducted, those ethnic groups that instrumentally utilized family ties, kinship, and ethnic networking had certain competitive strengths. To a large extent, ethnic entrepreneurs recruited heavily from the co-ethnic community, creating employment opportunities for newly arrived immigrants and reducing costs for employers. Financial support from the ethnic community and patronage from the ethnic neighborhood were also key factors for business success. Immigrants who became successful employers and entrepreneurs depended to a large degree on the reliable and various sets of ethnic resources upon which they were able to draw. A strong sense of intergenerational legacy that came from family ties was a primary motivating force that propelled many first-generation entrepreneurs. They felt a parental duty, a family obligation, to build an economic base that could launch their children and even successive generations to increasingly higher levels of social mobility.

Given the difficult environment in which to initiate any new business, a small margin of advantage had the potential to be crucial for success. The willingness to work long hours and to cut basic costs must have been minimum requirements in the early stage of capital accumulation. Immigrant taxi owner-operators in big cities, for instance, could compete with large firms because many of them reduced their costs by combining their resources to buy a taxi and by taking shifts so that the cab would be on the road 24 hours a day. The willingness and ability to save as much money as possible for future investment would be another important factor. Many an obscure ethnic business was launched without the preliminary prospect of support from a mainstream commercial bank, but an ethnic entrepreneur supported by a familial network practicing thrift and saving developed a decisive edge in the early start-up phase of business.

The changing components of the so-called new immigration after World War II, especially after the 1965 Hart–Celler Act was passed, had a major effect on the profile of entrepreneurship in immigrant communities. This and subsequent laws in the 1970s gave preference in gaining admission to those with valuable skills and talents. Thus, during the post-World War II period, highly trained, educated, and skilled professionals immigrated in unprecedented numbers. The increased size of the new immigrant professional and white-collar class accentuated the roles they played in the economy. "The immigrant imprint is most dramatic in Miami," as Roger Waldinger and his colleagues have pointed out (Waldinger et al. 2000, p. 356), "where a 30-year influx of Cuban refugees has transformed a decaying, stagnant city into a booming economy that some analysts have called the 'capital of Latin America'." Many of those Cuban refugees were from the middle class in Cuba and possessed experience and assets in capitalist ventures. Similarly, many groups from other countries achieved an impressive rate of success in entrepreneurial endeavors because of the extent to which they were trained in business and commerce in their own cultures. Ivan Light and Steven J. Gold have observed that "traditional positions in the occupational hierarchies of their homeland prior to migration" could produce a significant impact on the economic status of many immigrants after their arrival. "For many South Asian migrants," they continued, caste position influences entrepreneurship. Migrants from "commercial cultures," like the Parsis, the Banyas, the money lending Bhatias, the Memons, the Bohras, the Khojas – all Gujarati groups – long dominated trade and commerce in West India and later in East Africa as well. These are precisely the most entrepreneurial of the "South Asians" in Britain and the United States where they reproduced their business expertise overseas much more rapidly than the nonmercantile caste groups could learn them in the first place. (Light and Gold 2000, p. 40)

These examples indicated that unlike many immigrants in the past who needed years of hard work and learning about business to become successful, many new immigrants, largely because of their past experience and background, were able to become middle-class entrepreneurs with greater speed. Immigrants coming to the United States with a college degree in their home country had a particular advantage. Indeed, many who came for postgraduate training started new enterprises in professional fields once they were credentialed. In a single generation, these newcomers became scientists, engineers, medical doctors, lawyers, executives, middle managers, financial advisers, social workers, and other professionals: a socio-economic horizon which in the past had taken at least two generations for members of the same immigrant family to attain.

The globalization of human capital created a pattern of mobility in which migrants seeking to become entrepreneurs had moved many times before settling in the United States. Thus, when Illsoo Kim examined the urban Korean communities, he discovered that "Korean immigrants who entered the United States via Latin American nations were the first to enter the fruit and vegetable business, in 1971." He also pointed out that:

These immigrants had run various businesses in Latin America after having encountered severe difficulties in progressing from the designated agricultural colonies of their original settlements to the metropolitan areas of Latin America. From there they migrated again, to the inner cities of the United States. During the years of uncertain and hostile journeys in foreign countries, they acquired a remarkable business acumen and a special sensitivity to economic opportunities. Furthermore, as we might recall, they were heavily drawn from among the North Korean refugees in South Korea, who constitute a tough-minded, aggressive, and marginal group in South Korean society. It is no wonder that the members of this Latin American contingent first detected economic opportunity in the fruit and vegetable business when they settled in New York City. News of their success quickly spread throughout the Korean community in the area, and new immigrants from South Korea quickly followed them into the business. This economic news also spread to Koreans in Philadelphia, resulting in the emergence of Korean fruit and vegetable enterprises in that city. (Kim 1981, pp. 113–14)

Apparently, a succession of difficult moves by Korean migrants through tough environments in one country after another constituted a preparation in the skills and aptitudes that would be useful in seizing greengrocery opportunities in the United States.

As more immigrants became business owners and entrepreneurs, ethnic businesses became an increasingly important part of the general economy. They shaped new markets for consumer products, housing, schools, medical and health facilities, and banking and financial services.

The operation of ethnic businesses, however, still faced serious problems and limitations. Many operated in decayed high-crime central-city neighborhoods. Tensions between immigrant merchants and locals could lead to confrontations involving prolonged boycotts, walkouts, and negative publicity. Ethnic businessmen also had a hard time breaking into the mainstream market. As a middleman operating between big corporations and local consumers, the ethnic entrepreneur was subject to pricing pressures, high rent and overhead, and tensions within the social surroundings of business operations. Moreover, years of working up to 80 hours per week eventually took an inescapable physical and psychological toll. Those who suffered a status loss as a result of immigration felt they had given up a part of their self-esteem. Small shopkeepers who formerly had been physicians, white-collar professionals, and executives found their proprietorship a small compensation for status decline. Pressure and adversity, however, intensified the tenacious determination of ethnic entrepreneurs.

As she built a career as a newspaper publisher after immigrating to Seattle, Assunta Ng responded, "I don't get discouraged, and I don't take 'No' for an answer."

As the new immigrants of the post-1960s decades worked hard to protect and promote the ethnic economy, scholars also began to notice how skillfully female immigrant entrepreneurs in particular have applied their cultural knowledge to their business activities. As the study by Arlene Dallalfar (1994) has shown, in the Los Angeles area, where the rate of self-employment among Iranian households was as high as 61 percent, Iranian women achieved an impressive degree of participation and leadership in business fields such as travel agencies, financial and legal services, restaurants, real estate, and retailing and wholesaling.

Leila and her husband Saeed owned a small grocery store in Westwood, which was a Mecca for those who loved the amazing varieties of Iranian and Middle Eastern tea, bread, coffee, spices, herbs, and pastry. They not only sold ethnic food to customers but also provided information about ingredients, produce, and recipes. Leila was particularly attentive to each customer's individual tastes and needs, and understood that her knowledge of Iranian customs, rituals, and culinary practices was as valuable as the merchandise she was selling. Indeed, the foods, fruits, and processed sweets the couple provided that were often the centerpieces at many Iranian social events and weddings were available from few other sources.

Converting two rooms in her house for her clothing business, Nadia, whose husband was unable to find a job for a long while, catered to Iranian women by making suits, evening wear, and beaded dresses. Her customers were greeted as friends upon arrival and were offered Turkish coffee and traditional Iranian refreshments. This formality, followed by a social conversation as long as 20 minutes, was a necessary prelude to the business of selling and purchasing. As in Iranian culture, socializing was part of business activity and had to be conducted at the business establishment according to the prerequisites of Iranian customs. Spending no money on advertising, the attention she paid to creating a discrete, cozy, relaxed, and proper atmosphere ensured her reputation among her customers. The success or failure of her business depended heavily on the service and conduct throughout the transaction, which her customers expected from their arrival to the final back-and-forth bargaining over the price of the clothing they chose. A careful application of Iranian cultural and interpersonal practices to the American business context significantly contributed to Leila's and Nadia's successful enterprises. In an era of globalizing economies and migrations, entrepreneurship required an immigrant's cultural knowledge to form the link between communities and commerce.

Conclusion

The influences of immigration on the economic and business history of the United States can effectively be explored by locating these forces in patterns comparative cultural context and in a long-term chronological framework. Different institutions for colonization in Latin America, French Canada, and British North America shaped the subsequent paths each region took over the years. The rapid economic development of the United States in the nineteenth century owed its genesis to the advantageous conditions formed in the basic social structure and value systems established in the colonial era. The industrial expansion from the beginning of the nineteenth century also introduced new patterns of immigration which dramatically enlarged the set of linkages between the economy and ethnic subgroups that promoted overall growth.

Economic change, coupled with immigration, involved cultural adaptation which, as T.H. Breen wrote, "was a continuing series of reciprocal relationships, involving borrowing and resistance, conflict and cooperation, modification and invention" (1984, p. 197). The development of the US economy may be viewed as the long-term outcome of this cultural process as it was reconfigured by successive waves of ethnically differentiated migrations. Generations of immigrants, and their working and commercial experiences within the institutional framework of the United States, exemplified the ever-changing cultural dynamics of a modern globalizing economy.

REFERENCES

Antin, Mary (1912). *The Promised Land*. Boston: Houghton, Mifflin.
Bodnar, John (1992). *Remaking America: Public Memory, Commemoration, and Patriotism in the Twentieth Century*. Princeton, NJ: Princeton University Press.
Breen, T.H. (1984). "Creative Adaptations: Peoples and Cultures." In Jack P. Greene and J.R. Pole, eds., *Colonial British America*. Baltimore: Johns Hopkins University Press, pp. 195–232.
Chevalier, François (1982). *Land and Society in Colonial Mexico: The Great Hacienda* [1963], trans. Alvin Eustis. Berkeley: University of California Press.
Dallalfar, Arlene (1994). "Iranian Women as Immigrant Entrepreneurs." *Gender and Society* 8: 541–61.
Egnal, Marc (1996). *Divergent Paths: How Culture and Institutions Have Shaped North American Growth*. New York: Oxford University Press.
Harris, Richard Colebrook (1988). *The Seigneurial System in Early Canada: A Geographical Study* [1966]. Montreal: McGill-Queen's University Press.
Kessner, Thomas (1977). *The Golden Door: Italian and Jewish Immigrant Mobility in New York City, 1880–1915*. New York: Oxford University Press.
Kim, Illsoo (1981). *New Urban Immigrants: The Korean Community in New York*. Princeton, NJ: Princeton University Press.
Laslett, John H.M. and Seymour Martin Lipset, eds. (1984). *Failure of a Dream? Essays in the History of American Socialism*, rev. edn. Berkeley: University of California Press.

Light, Ivan and Steven J. Gold (2000). *Ethnic Economies.* San Diego, CA: Academic Press.

Light, Ivan, Parminder Bhachu, and Stavros Karagcorgis (1993). "Migration Networks and Immigrant Entrepreneurship." In Ivan Light and Parminder Bhachu, eds., *Immigration and Entrepreneurship.* New Brunswick, NJ: Transaction.

Lincoln, Abraham and Stephen A. Douglas, "Seventh Lincoln-Douglas Debate, Alton, Illinois." (1999). In David E. Shi and Holly A. Mayer, eds., *For the Record: A Documentary History of America.* New York: W.W. Norton, vol. 1, pp. 561–9.

Lipset, Seymour Martin (1990). *Continental Divide: The Values and Institutions of the United States and Canada.* New York: Routledge.

Meyer, Michael C., William L. Sherman, and Susan M. Deeds (2003). *The Course of Mexican History*, 7th edn. New York: Oxford University Press.

Nash, Gary B. (1979). *The Urban Crucible: Social Change, Political Consciousness, and the Origins of the American Revolution.* Cambridge, MA: Harvard University Press.

Paz, Octavio (1985). *The Labyrinth of Solitude* [1961]. New York: Grove Press.

Smith, Billy G., ed. (2004). *Down and Out in Early America.* University Park: Pennsylvania State University Press.

Tocqueville, Alexis de (1969). *Democracy in America.* Garden City, NY: Anchor Books.

Waldinger, Roger, Howard Aldrich, and Robin Ward (2000). "Ethnic Entrepreneurs." In Richard Swedberg, ed., *Entrepreneurship: The Social Science View.* New York: Oxford University Press, pp. 356–88.

Weiss, Richard (1969). *The American Myth of Success: From Horatio Alger to Norman Vincent Peale.* New York: Basic Books.

White, Richard (1991). *The Middle Ground: Indians, Empires, and Republics in the Great Lakes Region, 1650–1815.* Cambridge: Cambridge University Press.

SUGGESTED FURTHER READING

Atack, Jeremy and Peter Passell (1994). *A New Economic View of American History*, 2nd edn. New York: W.W. Norton.

Casson, Mark and Andrew Godley, eds. (2000). *Cultural Factors in Economic Growth.* Berlin: Springer.

Egnal, Marc (1996). *Divergent Paths: How Culture and Institutions Have Shaped North American Growth.* New York: Oxford University Press.

Engerman, Stanley L. and Robert E. Gallman, eds. (1996–2000). *The Cambridge Economic History of the United States* (3 vols.). Cambridge: Cambridge University Press.

Harris, Richard Colebrook (1988). *The Seigneurial System in Early Canada: A Geographical Study* [1966]. Montreal: McGill-Queen's University Press.

Hondagneu-Sotelo, Pierrette, ed. (2003). *Gender and U.S. Immigration: Contemporary Trends.* Berkeley: University of California Press.

Light, Ivan and Steven J. Gold (2000). *Ethnic Economies.* San Diego, CA: Academic Press.

Riding, Alan (2000). *Distant Neighbors: A Portrait of the Mexicans.* New York: Vintage Books.

Thompson, John Herd and Stephen J. Randall (1994). *Canada and the United States: Ambivalent Allies.* Montreal: McGill-Queen's University Press.

White, Richard (1991). *The Middle Ground: Indians, Empires, and Republics in the Great Lakes Region, 1650–1815.* Cambridge: Cambridge University Press.

CHAPTER TWENTY

Immigrants in the American Housing Market

BARRY R. CHISWICK AND PAUL W. MILLER

When immigrants arrive in a country, one of the first things they must do is find somewhere to live, if only temporarily. Many may live with family and friends until they find suitable permanent accommodation. But eventually the great majority of immigrants will establish their own homes. Both immigrants who have been in the United States for some time and the native-born who move either intra-state or inter-state face the same decisions.

In what types of homes do immigrants live? Do they seek to live in large homes? Or small homes? How many own their homes outright? What is the value of the homes immigrants own, or are buying? Do they rent? How much rent do they pay, on average? Do the answers to these questions differ for immigrants compared to the native-born? Do they differ across immigrant groups according to how long they have lived in the United States and the skill levels of the groups, and perhaps even according to other visible indicators, such as ethnicity or language background?

Answers to these questions are essential to understanding the dimensions of the immigrant demand for housing.[1] Since the end of the nineteenth century when social reformer Jacob Riis published *How the Other Half Lives*, his study of tenements and their immigrant residents in New York City, scholars have demonstrated that information on the housing circumstances of immigrants can also provide insights into the important issue of immigrant assimilation. Do the types of homes that immigrants live in vary with duration of residence? If home ownership is viewed as an index of immigrant assimilation, it would be expected that as the immigrants spend more time in the United States the characteristics of their housing circumstances would converge with those of the native-born.[2]

The analysis that follows seeks to provide answers to these questions. It is based on the 2000 US Census of Population, Public Use Microdata Sample, 1 percent sample of the population, limited to persons aged 25 years and older.[3]

Immigrant housing is considered by period of arrival and is contrasted with that of the native-born. As a way of controlling for "permanent income," the discussion is also presented by level of education. Type of home is considered (e.g. mobile home, detached home, apartment, etc.), as is the size of dwelling place (i.e. number of rooms) and the value of dwellings for owners.

The second part of the chapter examines the type of ownership of the individuals' accommodation. The next section studies the types of housing individuals own, and the values and sizes of the homes owned. The types of homes rented by individuals, and the values and sizes of these rental properties are explored in the next section. The last part of the chapter provides a summary and discussion of the findings.

Owning versus Renting

The 2000 Census of Population provides information on the type of ownership of the individuals' accommodation. Four categories are identified: (1) owned with mortgage; (2) owned outright; (3) rented for cash rent; and (4) rented with no cash rent. The last category is intended to capture cases where the accommodation is occupied by a renter, but no cash rent is charged, perhaps in compensation for work done (e.g. caretaker or residence for a clergyman) or as an unrequited income transfer (e.g. letting a relative live rent-free).[4] Of most interest in these data, however, is the distinction between owning and renting (for cash rent), as these may form two separate but interrelated housing markets. By analyzing the characteristics of the constituents of each of these markets, information can be obtained on whether the markets are indeed distinct or integrated.

Table 20.1 presents data on the distributions of the native-born and immigrants across types of ownership in the year 2000. Around one-quarter (24 percent) of the native-born aged 25 years or more own their homes outright. A further 52 percent own but have a mortgage. The remaining one-quarter (24 percent) of the population are renting.[5] In comparison, only around 13 percent of immigrants aged 25 years or more own their homes outright, 43 percent of immigrants have a mortgage on the houses in which they live, while 45 percent of immigrants are living in rented accommodation. Thus, the typical native-born person is more likely to own their home (whether outright or with a mortgage) than the typical foreign-born person.

Table 20.1 Type of home ownership by nativity and duration of residence, persons aged 25 and over, 2000 US Census (percent distribution)

Type of ownership	Native-born	Arrival cohort					Total foreign-born
		1995–2000	1990–4	1985–9	1980–4	Before 1980	
Owned outright	23.98	4.14	5.55	6.42	8.01	23.25	12.58
Owned with mortgage	51.84	24.01	35.90	43.95	50.86	50.20	42.72
Rented for cash rent	22.51	70.27	57.14	48.38	39.79	25.24	43.33
Rented, no cash rent	1.67	1.58	1.41	1.25	1.34	1.31	1.37
Total	100.00	100.00	100.00	100.00	100.00	100.00	100.00

Source: 2000 US Census of Population, Public Use Microdata 1% Sample.

The proportion of immigrants who own their homes outright rises with duration of residence. Indeed, the percentage that own their homes outright is lowest among the most recent immigrants (4 percent, 1995–2000) and is highest among the "before 1980" arrival cohort (23 percent), and this percentage is comparable to that of the native-born (23 percent). If home ownership is taken as an indicator of assimilation, these data show that immigrants essentially catch up with the native-born after several decades of residence in the United States. Similarly, the percentage of the arrival cohort who own with a mortgage rises with duration of residence, from 24 percent for the 1995–2000 cohort to 50 percent for the before 1980 cohort. Conversely, the percentage of the group who rent falls sharply with duration of residence, from around 70 percent among the most recent arrival cohort (1995–2000), to only 25 percent among the oldest arrival cohort (pre-1980 arrivals).[6]

The tendencies towards home ownership may vary according to the characteristics of the individuals. One characteristic that is a very good indicator of success is the level of education. It is well known that the better educated tend to have higher levels of income, lower rates of unemployment, higher occupational prestige, and better English language skills than their less-educated counterparts. Education can be used as a proxy for the individual's permanent earnings or income that will be a major determinant of their demand for housing. Education may be superior to current incomes, which are subject to transitory influences (such as a period of unemployment), as a measure of permanent income.

The threshold level of education used in this presentation is high school graduation: individuals up to and including high school graduates are categorized as having a low level of education; all those above this level are categorized as having a high level of education. Fully 46 percent of the native-born are in the less educated group under this definition, as are 57 percent of the foreign-born.

The better educated are less likely than the less well educated to own their own homes outright. This is the case for both the native-born and the foreign-born. However, more of the highly educated than of the less well educated own their homes with a mortgage. The proportions owning with a mortgage are 60 percent among the native-born for the better educated compared to 42 percent for the less well educated; 50 percent among the foreign-born for the better educated compared to 37 percent for the less well educated. Consequently, among the native-born the less educated are more likely to rent than the highly educated (27 percent renting compared to 22 percent). Among the foreign-born considerably more of the less educated are renting than is the case among the highly educated (49 percent compared to 39 percent).

The changes in home ownership with duration of residence in the United States described for the total foreign-born in Table 20.1 carry over to the separate analyses undertaken for the highly educated and the less educated groups (Tables 20.2 and 20.3). Thus, home ownership rises with duration of residence, and the incidence of renting declines with duration of residence within each education group. In both cases immigrants in the oldest arrival cohort (pre-1980 immigrants) have patterns of home ownership comparable to those of the native-born, though the less well educated have a slightly lower rate of outright ownership than their native-born counterparts. Among the foreign-born, the increase in home ownership with duration of residence is slightly steeper for the better educated than for the less well educated.

Table 20.2 Type of home ownership by nativity and duration of residence, highly educated persons aged 25 and over, 2000 US Census[a] (percent distribution)

| Type of ownership | Native-born | Arrival cohort | | | | | Total foreign-born |
		1995–2000	1990–4	1985–9	1980–4	Before 1980	
Owned outright	18.18	3.49	4.91	5.69	6.99	18.95	10.61
Owned with mortgage	59.81	25.71	43.96	54.26	60.69	59.31	50.40
Rented for cash rent	20.64	69.39	49.89	38.94	31.28	20.77	37.88
Rented, no cash rent	1.37	1.40	1.25	1.11	1.04	0.97	1.12
Total	100.00	100.00	100.00	100.00	100.00	100.00	100.00

(a) Highly educated refers to at least some education beyond high school graduation.

Source: 2000 US Census of Population, Public Use Microdata 1% Sample.

Table 20.3 Type of home ownership by nativity and duration of residence, less well educated persons aged 25 and over, 2000 US Census[a] (percent distribution)

| Type of ownership | Native-born | Arrival cohort | | | | | Total foreign-born |
		1995–2000	1990–4	1985–9	1980–4	Before 1980	
Owned outright	30.79	4.69	5.98	6.88	8.72	26.63	14.05
Owned with mortgage	42.49	22.53	30.36	37.54	44.00	43.02	37.01
Rented for cash rent	24.70	71.03	62.13	54.24	45.72	28.76	47.39
Rented, no cash rent	2.02	1.74	1.52	1.34	1.56	1.59	1.55
Total	100.00	100.00	100.00	100.00	100.00	100.00	100.00

(a) Less well educated refers to those with only a high school diploma or less.

Source: 2000 US Census of Population, Public Use Microdata 1% Sample.

Thus, both the owner housing market and the rental housing market are sizeable. The data presented above show that while some groups (e.g. the native-born and immigrants who have resided in the United States for a long time) are relatively more likely to own their homes, most groups have sizeable proportions in the other ownership categories. The owner-occupied and rental housing markets can obviously be distinguished using characteristics such as educational attainment, birthplace, and duration of residence in the United States of the foreign-born. Further distinctions may be developed in terms of the nature of the homes that the groups own or rent (e.g. large rather than small homes, high value rather than low value). The following sections examine these issues.

Owner-Occupiers: What Do They Own?

Home ownership may imply different things for different people. For some people it may mean they own a large, detached house. For other people it may mean owning a small apartment (coop or condominium) in a high-rise complex. Five major types of housing can be identified: (1) mobile homes or trailers; (2) detached houses; (3) attached houses; (4) a unit in a small block of apartments (defined as 1 to 9 apartments); and (5) a unit in a large block of apartments (defined as 10 or more apartments). While these types of homes can be viewed as separate markets, they will obviously be related in practice to the extent that conditions in one market (e.g. higher prices) will impact on other markets.

The overwhelming majority of the adult native-born (83 percent) live in detached houses (Table 20.4). Eight percent live in mobile homes or trailers, around 5 percent in attached houses, and only 4 percent live in apartments. In comparison, 75 percent of the foreign-born live in detached houses, 4 percent in mobile home or trailers, 9 percent in attached houses, and 12 percent in apartments. Hence, the main distinction between the native-born and the foreign-born is that proportionately more of foreign-born owner-occupiers live in apartments, and proportionately fewer live in detached houses or mobile homes/trailers.

Examination of the data by duration of residence reveals one major pattern. As duration of residence in the United States lengthens, slightly more of the

Table 20.4 Type of building of home owners by nativity and duration of residence, persons aged 25 and over, 2000 US Census (percent distribution)

Type of building[a]	Native-born	Arrival cohort					Total foreign-born
		1995–2000	1990–4	1985–9	1980–4	Before 1980	
Mobile home or trailer	7.87	6.67	6.39	5.12	4.05	3.45	4.39
Detached home	83.31	68.96	70.35	71.98	75.53	77.67	74.96
Attached home	4.64	10.88	10.66	10.70	10.07	7.69	9.08
Unit in small block of apartments	2.62	7.86	8.12	8.56	7.30	7.44	7.69
Unit in large block of apartments	1.45	5.46	4.41	3.62	3.03	3.68	3.82
Other	0.11	0.17	0.07	0.02	0.02	0.07	0.06
Total	100.00	100.00	100.00	100.00	100.00	100.00	100.00

(a) Small block of apartments is defined as between 1 and 9 apartments; large block of apartments is defined as 10 or more apartments.

Source: 2000 US Census of Population, Public Use Microdata 1% Sample.

foreign-born live in detached houses (increasing from 69 percent for those who arrived in 1995–2000 to 78 percent for the pre-1980 arrival cohort). A corresponding smaller proportion live in attached houses as duration increases (from 10.9 percent to 7.7 percent). There is little change with duration of residence in the percentage living in apartments or mobile homes. While the distribution of the older cohorts of the foreign-born across types of homes is more like that of the native-born than is the distribution of the recent arrivals, there is still a marked difference in the types of homes occupied by the owners in each broad birthplace group.

Data on the number of rooms for those who own their home show that the typical home owned by a native-born person has six rooms (median of six, mean of 6.8) (Table 20.5). The typical home owned by a foreign-born person also has six rooms (median of six, mean of 6.0). Hence the striking feature of the data is the similarity of the sizes of the homes owned and occupied by the foreign-born and native-born populations: the homes of the foreign-born are only slightly smaller than those of the native-born.

Members of the older arrival cohorts are more likely to own somewhat larger homes than is the case for members of the more recent arrival cohorts. Thus, the median size of home owned by the foreign-born is five rooms for those who have resided in the United States for up to 15 years, and six rooms for those who have lived in the United States for 15 or more years. Even among the immigrants who arrived in the United States before 1980, however, the typical home that is owned is slightly smaller than that owned by the average native-born person, the mean is 6.2 instead of 6.8 rooms.

Table 20.5 Size of home of home owners by nativity and duration of residence, persons aged 25 and over, 2000 US Census (percent distribution)

Number of rooms in residence	Native-born	Arrival cohort					Total foreign-born
		1995–2000	1990–4	1985–9	1980–4	Before 1980	
One or two	0.81	6.37	6.69	6.18	5.42	3.50	4.78
Three	2.55	15.57	16.01	17.13	16.18	10.04	13.11
Four	7.70	10.76	10.09	9.72	9.02	9.20	9.48
Five	20.40	_19.09_	_19.33_	_18.42_	17.69	18.79	18.67
Six	_24.08_	17.86	18.57	19.23	_19.60_	_20.68_	_19.83_
Seven	18.08	11.89	12.55	12.57	13.90	15.30	14.10
Eight	13.10	9.18	9.20	8.42	9.49	11.10	10.10
Nine +	13.27	9.27	7.55	8.34	8.70	11.37	9.93
Total	100.00	100.00	100.00	100.00	100.00	100.00	100.00
Mean number of rooms	6.77	5.72	5.61	5.65	5.79	6.24	5.97

Notes: Median size category is underlined. To compute the mean, a value of 12 has been assigned to the open-ended upper category of nine or more rooms.

Source: 2000 US Census of Population, Public Use Microdata 1% Sample.

The respondents provided estimates of how much their home (house and lot) would sell for if it were for sale (Table 20.6). The median home value for the native-born in 2000 is in the $100,000 to $149,000 category. Around 14 percent of the native-born own homes valued at less than $50,000, while 9 percent live in homes valued at $300,000 or more. The median home value for the foreign-born is also in the $100,000 to $149,000 bracket. Only 10 percent of the foreign-born own homes valued at less than $50,000, while 15 percent own homes valued at $300,000 or more. The mean values of the homes owned by the native-born and the foreign-born are $156,000 and $198,000, respectively. Thus, despite owning slightly smaller homes, and being more likely to own an apartment rather than a house, the foreign-born own, on average, higher-valued homes than the native-born.

There are at least two main reasons why this pattern might arise. The first is that home values rise over time. Individuals who have recently purchased their homes are more likely to have a higher estimate of the current value of their home than individuals who purchased their homes many years ago, and so must estimate (and most likely undervalue) the current value. Hence, the higher value of the homes owned by the foreign-born may simply reflect more accurate reporting by virtue of the fact that more of them will have recently purchased their homes.

Information on home values by duration of residence among the foreign-born shows that the values of the homes owned by older arrival cohorts exceed those of the more recent arrivals, which is consistent with an immigrant adjustment phenomenon.

Table 20.6　Value of home of home owners by nativity and duration of residence, persons aged 25 and over, 2000 US Census (percent distribution)

| Value of residence ($000) | Native-born | Arrival cohort | | | | | Total foreign-born |
		1995–2000	1990–4	1985–9	1980–4	Before 1980	
Less than $25	4.94	5.39	5.64	4.68	3.94	2.85	3.81
$25–49	8.91	7.19	6.22	6.14	6.23	5.60	5.97
$50–70	10.11	7.19	6.73	7.24	6.71	6.12	6.53
$70–99	19.32	14.64	14.48	14.43	13.85	13.12	13.70
$100–149	22.25	21.20	21.56	20.73	20.51	19.85	20.39
$150–199	13.75	15.68	16.85	18.01	18.38	17.95	17.70
$200–299	11.50	14.88	15.55	15.99	16.47	17.55	16.71
$300+	9.22	13.83	12.97	12.78	13.91	16.96	15.19
Total	100.0	100.0	100.0	100.0	100.0	100.0	100.0
Mean value $000	156.12	185.49	181.36	184.66	191.31	208.85	197.65

Notes: Median value category is underlined. The census microdata files present information on home value in 24 categories. This has been aggregated into the eight categories listed in this table for expositional reasons. The mean has been computed by assigning mid-points to the 23 closed-value intervals recorded in the census microdata file, and a value of $1,500,000 for the open-ended upper interval of $1,000,000 or more.

Source: 2000 US Census Public Use Microdata 1% Sample.

However, even among the recent arrivals, the typical home owned by the foreign-born is of much higher value than that owned by the native-born.

An important reason why the aggregated data for the foreign-born may show a higher mean value of owner-occupied dwellings than for the native-born is associated with the geographic concentration of the foreign-born. Immigrants live disproportionately in states with high home values. California, New York, New Jersey, Illinois, Texas, and Florida are the six states in which the foreign-born are heavily concentrated (see Chapter 14). While these six states account for fully two-thirds of all foreign-born residents in the United States in 2000, only one-third of the native-born live in these six states. Since home prices vary across states, this geographic concentration will impact on the aggregate level data on home ownership. Indeed, the analyses presented in Chiswick and Miller (2003) show that the regional concentration of immigrants is a major contributor to the large differences in home values by nativity.[7]

Finally, it is of interest to examine the links between personal/demographic factors and the characteristics of the homes of owner-occupiers. In order to abstract from the impact of the geographic concentration discussed above, computations were made for California. This is the major immigrant-receiving state: about 30 percent of the foreign-born in the United States in 2000 live in California, in contrast to 10 percent of the native-born.

When data are computed on the value of owner-occupiers' homes in California for the highly educated and less well educated subsets of the population, two main findings emerge (Tables 20.7 and 20.8). First, unlike the data for the aggregate-level analysis, the mean home values for the native-born are about the same as those for the foreign-born for both the better educated ($330,000 vs. $329,000) and the less

Table 20.7 Value of home of home owners by nativity and duration of residence, highly educated persons aged 25 and over living in California, 2000 US Census (percent distribution)

Value of residence ($000)	Native-born	Arrival cohort					Total foreign-born
		1995–2000	1990–4	1985–9	1980–4	Before 1980	
Less than $25	1.11	2.36	1.72	2.03	1.76	0.88	1.39
$25–49	1.30	3.98	2.78	2.75	2.55	1.94	2.39
$50–70	1.60	1.32	0.81	1.61	1.41	1.16	1.24
$70–99	5.83	3.98	4.06	4.90	3.91	4.11	4.18
$100–149	13.77	12.94	11.25	12.58	11.67	11.08	11.54
$150–199	15.64	12.85	16.31	16.79	18.05	16.35	16.48
$200–299	23.26	21.33	24.28	24.24	24.36	23.92	23.91
$300+	37.48	41.24	38.81	35.11	36.28	40.55	38.88
Total	100.0	100.0	100.0	100.0	100.0	100.0	100.0
Mean value $000	330.43	326.02	311.36	303.80	316.24	344.41	328.93

Note: Median value category is underlined.

Source: 2000 US Census of Population, Public Use Microdata 1% Sample.

Table 20.8 Value of home of home owners by nativity and duration of residence, less well educated persons aged 25 and over living in California, 2000 US Census (percent distribution)

| Value of residence ($000) | Native-born | Arrival cohort | | | | | Total foreign-born |
		1995–2000	1990–4	1985–9	1980–4	Before 1980	
Less than $25	3.99	4.71	4.61	3.57	3.11	2.27	3.02
$25–49	3.82	3.71	3.21	4.38	3.19	2.54	3.09
$50–70	4.46	3.89	4.80	4.91	4.17	3.69	4.09
$70–99	12.74	14.19	10.86	15.08	13.12	11.71	12.56
$100–149	20.39	18.84	23.77	25.39	25.12	23.16	23.61
$150–199	19.95	18.28	19.17	22.02	22.90	24.23	22.73
$200–299	18.61	18.94	17.97	13.75	15.81	17.00	16.51
$300+	16.04	17.44	15.61	10.90	12.59	15.40	14.37
Total	100.0	100.0	100.0	100.0	100.0	100.0	100.0
Mean value $000	204.06	210.42	197.92	177.46	189.78	205.96	198.18

Note: Median value category is underlined.

Source: 2000 US Census of Population, Public Use Microdata 1% Sample.

well educated ($204,000 vs. $198,000). This suggests that the regional concentration of immigrants is a major factor in the large differences in home values by nativity in the aggregate data.

There is little difference in California across arrival cohorts for the less well educated in the mean values of the homes, whereas for the better educated there is a difference of around $18,000 (or around 6 percent) between the mean value of the homes owned by members of the most recent (1995–2000) and most distant (before 1980) arrival cohorts, with the latter having the higher value.

These data show, therefore, that factors that are associated with economic success in the United States are associated with larger homes and higher-valued homes for immigrants as well as for the native-born.

Renters: What Do They Rent?

Individuals will rent accommodation for a variety of reasons. For some it is a stepping-stone to home ownership. For others their expected length of stay in a particular location may not be long enough to justify incurring the fixed costs associated with the purchase of a home. Still others may not have sufficient capital to purchase a home even with a mortgage. Finally, others may live in areas where the rental market is thicker or rental prices are lower relative to house prices than elsewhere.

Most of those who rent, rent apartments. Among the native-born renters, around 60 percent are in apartments, with slightly more rental units in small blocks of apartments than in large blocks of apartments (Table 20.9). Around 36 percent are

Table 20.9 Type of building of renters by nativity and duration of residence, persons aged 25 and over, 2000 US Census (percent distribution)

Type of building[a]	Native-born	Arrival cohort					Total foreign-born
		1995–2000	1990–4	1985–9	1980–4	Before 1980	
Mobile home or trailer	4.57	2.63	2.41	2.17	1.94	1.88	2.25
Detached home	29.61	12.34	13.84	17.39	19.62	20.50	16.27
Attached home	6.09	6.09	6.76	7.42	7.46	6.76	6.78
Unit in small block of apartments	32.43	34.50	35.24	34.84	33.64	31.67	33.97
Unit in large block of apartments	27.25	44.39	41.70	38.15	37.30	39.12	40.68
Other	0.06	0.05	0.05	0.04	0.04	0.07	0.05
Total	100.00	100.00	100.00	100.00	100.00	100.00	100.00

(a) Small block of apartments is defined as between 1 and 9 apartments; large block of apartments is defined as 10 or more apartments.

Source: 2000 US Census of Population, Public Use Microdata 1% Sample.

renting houses, and most of these are in the category of "detached houses." Among the foreign-born who rent, 75 percent are in apartments, and the majority of these are renting units in a large block of apartments. Only 23 percent are renting houses, and most of these are detached houses.

Hence, these data show that the foreign-born renters are more likely than native-born renters to rent apartments. They are also relatively more likely to be renting an apartment in a large block rather than in a small block of apartments.

There are variations in the distribution of renters across types of buildings among the various immigrant arrival cohorts. Immigrants are more likely to rent a detached home as the duration of residence increases. While only 12 percent among the most recent arrival cohort (1995–2000) rent detached houses, this percentage increases to 21 percent among the most distant arrival cohort (before 1980). On the other hand, the tendency to rent in a large block of apartments decreases with the duration of residence: this is given by the drop in the percentages between the most recent cohort (1995–2000) and the most distant cohort (before 1980) from 44 percent to 39 percent.

Rental dwellings are smaller than owner-occupied homes. On average there are 4.4 rooms for rental properties among the native-born compared to 6.8 rooms for owner-occupied properties; 3.5 rooms for rental properties among the foreign-born compared to 6.0 rooms for owner-occupied properties (Table 20.10). This is linked to the greater prevalence of apartments in the rental market.

Comparison of the number of rooms in rental properties for the native-born and foreign-born reveals that the native-born rent, on average, properties with one extra room compared to the foreign-born (median of four rooms and mean of 4.4 for the

Table 20.10 Size of home of renters by nativity and duration of residence, persons aged 25 and over, 2000 US Census (percent distribution)

Number of rooms in residence	Native-born	Arrival cohort					Total foreign-born
		1995–2000	1990–4	1985–9	1980–4	Before 1980	
One or two	11.29	34.09	34.55	32.93	31.60	25.60	31.77
Three	17.82	22.27	22.95	22.33	22.13	22.22	22.39
Four	26.86	22.70	21.29	21.39	21.02	22.82	22.00
Five	22.32	11.98	13.70	13.92	14.44	16.43	13.98
Six	12.43	5.22	4.73	5.88	6.04	7.54	5.86
Seven	5.13	1.99	1.67	1.98	2.72	3.01	2.24
Eight	2.52	0.97	0.59	0.98	1.27	1.35	1.02
Nine +	1.64	0.78	0.51	0.58	0.79	1.04	0.75
Total	100.00	100.00	100.00	100.00	100.00	100.00	100.00
Mean number of rooms	4.42	3.37	3.32	3.41	3.51	3.72	3.46

Note: Median size category is underlined.

Source: 2000 US Census of Population, Public Use Microdata 1% Sample.

native-born; median of three rooms and mean of 3.5 for the foreign-born). This difference is also linked to the greater prevalence of apartments compared to houses in the rental market for the foreign-born compared to the native-born.

There is a tendency for the mean size of home of the foreign-born to increase with duration of residence in the United States. Even among the cohort of immigrants who arrived in the United States before 1980, however, the mean size of rental accommodation (3.7 rooms) is smaller than that among the native-born (4.4 rooms). Interpretation of these data from the perspective of immigrant adjustment is complicated by the pronounced switch from rental accommodation to owner-occupied accommodation with duration of residence, as shown in Table 20.1.

The median monthly rent paid by the native-born is $500 to $699 (mean of $597) and for the foreign-born it is also $500 to $699 (mean of $680) (Table 20.11). Recent arrivals pay the highest rent, around $726 per month on average.

These data appear to tell an alarming story: on average across the United States immigrants rent smaller homes than those rented by the native-born and pay much higher rents. Further analysis of these data by state of residence (see Chiswick and Miller 2003) indicates considerable state-by-state differences. Much of the rental price difference is due to immigrants being more likely to live in high rental price states. Restricting the analysis to California provides standardization for the location factors, and splitting the sample into those with a high school degree or less and those with more schooling controls for education, a measure of permanent income.

The better educated in California pay higher rents, on average, than the less well educated ($983 per month compared to $694 per month for the native-born; $946 per month compared to $651 per month for the foreign-born) (Tables 20.12 and

Table 20.11 Monthly rent paid by renters by nativity and duration of residence, persons aged 25 and over, 2000 US Census (percent distribution)

Monthly rent paid ($)	Native-born	Arrival cohort					Total foreign-born
		1995–2000	1990–4	1985–9	1980–4	Before 1980	
Less than $300	16.94	6.07	7.61	7.54	8.81	11.87	8.29
$300–399	13.66	8.81	9.04	9.31	9.16	9.05	9.04
$400–499	15.40	13.71	13.01	13.51	12.95	13.16	13.31
$500–699	26.57	32.32	34.04	32.60	32.74	29.68	32.19
$700–899	14.15	19.71	21.26	22.23	20.29	18.48	20.26
$900+	13.28	19.38	15.03	14.80	16.05	17.76	16.91
Total	100.0	100.0	100.0	100.0	100.0	100.0	100.0
Mean rent ($)	596.91	726.04	656.18	655.28	662.90	675.81	680.16

Note: Median rent category is underlined.

Source: 2000 US Census of Population, Public Use Microdata 1% Sample.

Table 20.12 Monthly rent paid by renters by nativity and duration of residence, highly educated persons aged 25 and over living in California, 2000 US Census (percent distribution)

Monthly rent paid ($)	Native-born	Arrival cohort					Total foreign-born
		1995–2000	1990–4	1985–9	1980–4	Before 1980	
Less than $300	3.20	2.17	4.03	2.51	2.94	3.87	3.10
$300–399	3.66	2.86	3.47	3.84	4.15	3.90	3.57
$400–499	6.77	5.44	5.38	5.95	7.53	7.91	6.40
$500–699	22.51	20.30	26.94	27.58	23.82	23.16	23.97
$700–899	22.71	19.10	24.00	26.32	24.88	21.00	22.49
$900+	41.16	50.13	36.18	33.80	36.67	40.16	40.47
Total	100.0	100.0	100.0	100.0	100.0	100.0	100.0
Mean rent ($)	982.98	1076.34	858.80	873.04	902.06	949.49	946.21

Note: Median rent category is underlined.

Source: 2000 US Census of Population, Public Use Microdata 1% Sample.

20.13). The foreign-born in California pay slightly lower rents than the native-born, both among the highly educated and the less well educated. The difference by nativity is, however, only around $30 to $40 for each level of education. This compares with a difference of around $122 for the data for California aggregated across all levels of education. Analysis which uses finer categorizations of level of education would result in further erosion of the differential evident in the aggregate-level data in the mean rents paid by the native-born and the foreign-born.

Table 20.13 Monthly rent paid by renters by nativity and duration of residence, less well educated persons aged 25 and over living in California, 2000 US Census (percent distribution)

Monthly rent paid ($)	Native-born	Arrival cohort					Total foreign-born
		1995–2000	1990–4	1985–9	1980–4	Before 1980	
Less than $300	8.98	4.98	5.18	5.76	6.97	9.69	6.67
$300–399	7.95	9.70	9.03	8.62	8.91	8.55	8.90
$400–499	12.34	12.86	14.26	14.74	14.20	13.40	13.94
$500–699	30.31	34.80	36.88	36.90	36.31	34.25	35.84
$700–899	20.21	19.15	20.14	20.79	19.95	19.56	19.97
$900+	20.22	18.51	14.51	13.19	13.67	14.54	14.67
Total	100.0	100.0	100.0	100.0	100.0	100.0	100.0
Mean rent ($)	694.24	692.29	652.57	641.15	641.68	641.22	651.31

Note: Median rent category is underlined.

Source: 2000 US Census of Population, Public Use Microdata 1% Sample.

Summary and Discussion

Immigrants are more likely to rent their dwelling place than the native-born, who mostly own their homes outright or with a mortgage. While 45 percent of immigrants are found to live in rental properties, only one-quarter of the native-born are renting. Analysis conducted by arrival cohort shows that the percentage of immigrants who own their homes outright rises with duration of residence, with the earliest arrival cohort (pre-1980) having a pattern of home ownership comparable to that of the native-born. Hence, where home ownership is viewed as a measure of assimilation, there is convergence between the foreign-born and the native-born after several decades of residence in the United States.

Education can serve as a proxy for the individuals' permanent income. The better-educated foreign-born are more likely to own their homes with a mortgage than the less well educated. However, the less well educated foreign-born are more inclined to own their homes outright. Nonetheless, the better educated experience steeper changes in home ownership than the less well educated as the duration of residence increases.

As for the types of homes owned, the foreign-born are more likely to purchase apartments (12 percent) than the native-born (4 percent), whereas more of the native-born live in detached houses (83 percent) than is the case among immigrants (75 percent). However, slightly more of the foreign-born live in detached houses as duration of residence lengthens. It is also found that the home sizes of the foreign-born are slightly smaller than among the native-born, yet, on average, they have homes of higher value.

Disaggregated analyses of the immigrants in California (the major immigrant-receiving state) are conducted to examine the links between personal/demographic factors and decisions on home ownership. The results indicate that while home values in California are much higher than the national average, the patterns established for the national aggregates generally carry over to the analyses for California. Thus the better educated own larger homes and properties of higher value than the less well educated for both the native-born and the foreign-born. Moreover, among the foreign-born, the size of home increases more with duration of residence for the better educated than for the less well educated. However, while the values of the homes among the better educated rise with duration of residence, there is little variation in home values by duration of residence among the less well educated in California.

Analyses on renters' decision show that the foreign-born renters are more likely to rent apartments than houses as compared to the native-born renters. It is also found that immigrants tend to shift to renting detached houses as their duration of residence in the United States increases. The rental properties of the foreign-born are smaller than those of the native-born by about one room on average. In addition, the foreign-born are found to pay higher rents than the native-born, with the most recent arrivals paying the highest rents. Separate analyses on California, however, show that the better educated pay higher rents than the less well educated for both the native-born and the foreign-born, and that there is little difference in rents by nativity when one looks within California by education level.

These analyses point to a diverse range of issues on immigrant housing where further research is needed. One is the "own versus rent" decision, including changes in immigrants' tenure type with duration of residence. While this type of study is best conducted using longitudinal data, study of cross-sectional data sets will yield valuable information.[8] Separate analysis for the major immigrant-receiving states, or analyses using state fixed effects, needs to be undertaken, and findings for the various states need to be compared and any differences explained.

The study of immigrants' housing choice should pay particular attention to the differences across racial and ethnic groups. The immigrants from Asia, who comprise the most recent waves of migration to the United States, should certainly be a focus for such research. Hispanic immigrants, who tend to be low-skilled, and have relatively unfavorable labor market outcomes, are another group that should provide a focus for research.

The nexus between labor market outcomes and housing decisions should also be examined. An interesting avenue for research would be to develop a concept for the immigrant housing market analogous to the "immigrant catch-up" concept that has a central place in most discussions of immigrant labor market performance (see Chiswick 1978). Integrating labor market concepts and models of immigrant assimilation with decisions in the housing market is a promising direction for future research.

Moreover, the types of homes that immigrants demand can also be analyzed further. The census data contain considerable detail on the characteristics of houses. When combined with the information on home prices (for owner-occupiers) and rentals (for renters), and housing characteristics, using a "hedonic price" approach it would be possible to determine the implicit prices that natives and immigrants pay for the various characteristics. Whether these prices differ, other variables being the same, between immigrants and the native-born, in the ownership and in the rental markets, is of interest.[9]

Finally, the study of immigrant housing might be extended to link mortgage and rent payments to household incomes. This type of approach provides insights into so-called "housing stress." Junankar, Pope, Kapuscinski, Ma, and Mudd (1993), in a study of immigrant housing in Australia, define an income unit in "housing stress" where its gross weekly income is in the lowest 40 percent of the distribution, and the cost of the housing unit, as a proportion of income, is in the top 30 percent of the distribution. Indices of housing stress can be computed for demographic groups (defined, for example, by birthplace and skill level) and for various locations. They could also be computed for immigrants in the various arrival cohorts to examine the extent of disadvantage incurred by recent arrivals compared to longer-term residents.

The study of these issues has the potential to enrich our understanding of decision making in relation to the most important asset for most Americans – the family home. It also has the potential to inform on the links between the housing and labor markets, and on immigrant assimilation into American society. Such study will help identify patterns of success and failure among immigrants and the native-born, and provide a better basis for policy making regarding immigration in both the housing and labor markets.

NOTES

We thank Derby Voon for research assistance. Chiswick acknowledges research support from the Institute of Government and Public Affairs, University of Illinois. Miller acknowledges financial assistance from the Australian Research Council.

1   For assessment of the research on the demand for housing see, for example, Arnott 1987, Olsen 1987, and Sheppard 1999.
2   This would be analogous to the labor market assimilation of immigrants. See, for example, Chiswick 2005.
3   In constructing this profile of immigrants' demand for housing, immigrant location is taken as given. For a parallel analysis of immigrant location see Chapter 14.
4   Only about 1.7 percent of the native-born and 1.4 percent of the foreign-born live rent-free.
5   The issues involved in the "own versus rent" decision are outlined in Anstie, Findlay, and Harper (1983). Whether a person should own or rent depends on a range of circumstances, including the length of time they expect to live in the particular location, the rate at which they can borrow money, and the amount of assets that they have. Owning is not the optimal decision for everyone.
6   This pattern of change in immigrants' housing tenure choice with duration of residence in the United States is remarkably similar to that for Australia reported by Junankar, Pope, Kapuscinski, Ma, and Mudd (1993).
7   The extent of the regional differences in home values is evident from the information presented in appendix tables available from the authors upon request.
8   The work by Coulson (1999) and Painter, Gabriel, and Myers (2001) provides an excellent starting point.
9   The real estate literature provides a number of promising models that could be applied in this type of analysis. Junankar, Pope, Kapuscinski, Ma, and Mudd (1993, appendix 2) provide an overview.

REFERENCES

Anstie, R., C. Findlay, and I. Harper (1983). "The Impact of Inflation and Taxation on Tenure Choice and the Redistributive Effects of Home-Mortgage Interest Rate Regulation." *Economic Record* 59(165): 105–10.

Arnott, Richard (1987). "Economic Theory and Housing." In Edwin S. Mills, ed., *Handbook of Regional and Urban Economics*, Vol. II. Oxford, Eng.: Elsevier Science, pp. 959–88.

Chiswick, Barry R. (1978). "The Effect of Americanization on the Earnings of Foreign-Born Men." *Journal of Political Economy* 86(5): 897–922.

Chiswick, Barry R. and P.W. Miller (2003). "Issue Paper on the Impact of Immigration for Housing." In *Issue Papers on Demographic Trends Important to Housing*, Office of Policy Development and Research, US Department of Housing and Urban Development, pp. 1–77.

Coulson, N. Edward (1999). "Why Are Hispanic- and Asian-American Homeownership Rates So Low? Immigration and Other Factors." *Journal of Urban Economics* 45(2): 209–27.

Junankar, P.N., D. Pope, C. Kapuscinski, G. Ma, and W. Mudd (1993). *Recent Immigrants and Housing*. Canberra: Australian Government Publishing Service.

Olsen, Edgar O. (1987). "The Demand and Supply of Housing Service: A Critical Survey of the Empirical Literature." In Edwin S. Mills, ed., *Handbook of Regional and Urban Economics*, Vol. II. Oxford, Eng.: Elsevier Science, pp. 989–1022.

Painter, G., S. Gabriel, and D. Myers (2001). "Race, Immigrant Status, and Housing Tenure Choice." *Journal of Urban Economics* 49(1): 150–67.

Riis, Jacob (1890). *How the Other Half Lives: Studies Among the Tenements of New York*. New York: Charles Scribner's Sons.

Sheppard, Stephen (1999). "Hedonic Analysis of Housing Markets." In E.S. Mills and P. Cheshire, eds., *Handbook of Regional and Urban Economics*. Oxford, Eng.: Elsevier Science, pp. 1595–635.

Part V

Culture and Community

CHAPTER TWENTY-ONE

Immigration and American Diversity: Food for Thought

DONNA R. GABACCIA

One evening in 1995, friends visiting me from Germany requested a barbecue meal. Perhaps they had tired of my family's eclectic, Americanized Italian diet, which we supplemented with recipes borrowed over the years to create low-fat, vegetarian, and Chinese- or Mexican-style alternatives. No, they insisted, they just wanted to try soul food – which they had learned to love in Buffalo and Chicago – in its original homeland. Wasn't barbecue best eaten in simple restaurants in the American south? Indeed, there were many barbecue restaurants in my then-hometown of Charlotte, North Carolina; they were wildly popular with my students; my future colleagues had taken me to one when I had interviewed for my first job in the south, perhaps hoping to introduce an ignorant Yankee to an unfamiliar local food.

Eating barbecue with my friends led quickly to discussions about cultural diversity. When we arrived at the restaurant, I learned to my surprise that they were expecting to eat beef ribs. What they received instead was one version of North Carolina barbecue – tangy pulled pork. Fortunately, they were adventurous eaters and they tackled their plates with enthusiasm. Meanwhile I focused on another intriguing menu item, called spicy potatoes. The waitress informed me these were Greek potatoes and that the owner and chef was a Greek immigrant. I enjoyed the potatoes, although I did not find them spicy. Later that evening we all went home well-fed. And quite thoughtful.

This story may make you hunger for ribs, pork, or spicy potatoes, but that is not why I tell it. Rather, my goal is to encourage you to ponder what we mean when we say an experience provides "food for thought." Loosely interpreting Lévi-Strauss (1962, p. 128), many scholars insist that food is "good to think." What kinds of thoughts went through your head as you read about our simple barbecue meal? Did you wonder why barbecue was different in Charlotte and Chicago? Were you surprised (as I was) to find spicy potatoes at a barbecue restaurant? (If you regularly eat barbecue spaghetti in Memphis, perhaps you were not surprised at all.) When you learned the cook was a Greek, did his barbecue still qualify in your mind as authentic soul food? As southern cuisine? Thinking about simple foods leads straight to major themes in American history – in this case, immigration, regionalism, and cultural amalgamation.

The choices people make about eating are rarely trivial or accidental. Food is a central concern of human beings in all times and in all places. In part that is because the production, processing, marketing, preparation, and eating of food are time-consuming human activities, whether among the hunters, gatherers, and corn-cultivators of pre-Columbian America or in a post-industrial society such as the United States today. The production, processing, and marketing of foods reveal relations of power between socio-economic classes and among members of distinctive castes, classes, genders, and ethnic groups. Similarly, domestic activities such as cooking and eating reflect intimate social relations and the distribution of power by age, gender, and status within families and communities. What, when, how, and with whom people eat tells us much about their most fundamental cultural and religious assumptions. Political decisions and laws can ban certain foods or regulate the production and marketing of others. For centuries, people have also sensed a close connection between food and identity, proclaiming, "Man is what he eats" (a senti-ment attributed to the German philosopher Ludwig Feuerbach) or "Tell me what you eat, and I will tell you who you are" (a saying attributed to the French jurist and gastronome Anthelme Brillat-Savarin). To write about food, scholars hunt out, gather, and digest information about environment, agriculture, business, industry, markets, culture, family, and religion. Needless to say, the study of food is a multidisciplinary endeavor (Camp 1989).

Yet only quite recently has historical study of eating (sometimes called culinary history) or of food-related human habits (often called foodways) become a popular way to think about the United States as a nation of immigrants. Most of these studies – on which I draw heavily for the second and third parts of this chapter – focus on the late nineteenth and twentieth centuries. For some authors, the trans-formation of immigrants' food habits represents a form of Americanization that is nevertheless distinct from assimilation because it produces many culturally distinctive styles rather than a single Anglo or British style of cooking and eating (Shenton, Pellegrini, Brown, Shenker, and Wood, 1971; Levenstein 1988, p. 108; Diner 2001; Inness 2001). Others instead show the arrival of newcomers in North America transforming the foodways of natives, reversing the usual narrative of immigration history (Pillsbury 1998, ch. 7; Gabaccia 1998). Most hotly debated, however, is the question of whether or not there is an American national cuisine. Some deny its existence (Mintz 1996, p. 95). But others insist that the evolving yet also persisting multi-ethnic regional foodways of this country are themselves distinctively American (Hess and Hess 1989, pp. 333–7; Brown and Mussell 1984, pp. 5–6) or they point to mass-manufactured, commercial, or "fast foods" as the country's national dishes (Boorstin 1973, ch. 35; Hogan 1997, p. 1; Schlosser 2001). My own preference has been to explore foodways as a story of mixing and blending in communities and markets as shoppers, cooks, and eaters have combined commercially invented foods with traditional elements of many regional and national cuisines.

Culinary history thus mirrors closely our general understandings of the United States as either a melting pot that transforms immigrants, a mosaic of separate ethnic traditions, or a mestizo nation that blends and mixes many traditions in new or distinctive American forms. All versions of culinary history agree on one point, however: in none is compulsion or conflict the most important engine of culinary change. Changes in the way people eat may be accompanied by feelings of sadness or loss and many people seek comfort in the familiar foods of their childhood or in preserving or reviving the recipes they believe their ancestors preferred. But these same people are – as cooks and as eaters – usually motivated to change their diet voluntarily by the pleasures they take in novelty and because of their curiosity and creativity. This tendency to seek comfort in the familiar while simultaneously desiring new culinary experience produces distinctive foodways in the United States but it is by no means unique to this country and can be found almost everywhere in the world. In the United States, it has produced the culinary equivalent of many jazz performances in many regions – particular forms of creative expression produced in particular places for enjoyment nationwide.

It may well be that food – along with dance, music, sports, and some other forms of pleasurable, yet also commercialized, activities – provides arenas where particularly rapid cultural accommodations between natives and newcomers can occur. Food and dance have generally provided folkloric and often stereotypical ways for immigrants to represent their cultures to Americans in positive ways and in ways that Americans can respond to positively as non-threatening. But while theories of cultural assimilation generally suggest it is immigrants alone who change or adapt to American culture, food exchanges instead reveal a long history of natives changing their eating habits in response to the newcomers. In our own times, tasting a new food is rendered reassuring by well-established rituals of eating in an immigrant-run restaurant or wordlessly exchanging cash for groceries in an immigrant neighborhood store. Eating together has a long history of symbolizing peaceful acceptance among peoples of differing cultures; it is also a decidedly less threatening activity to buy a new food for lunch from an immigrant food vendor than to invite her family into your home or to discover that your son or daughter intends to marry one of her children.

Students of culinary history often assume that Americans' interest in sampling foreign or exotic food is a modern fad, limited to educated Americans and facilitated by a recent era of intensive globalization. This chapter instead documents recurring food exchanges among newcomers and natives during three great waves of migration to North America. Modern scholars call the first of these migrations (1500–1760) the Columbian exchange. The second period of important culinary exchange was the century (1830–1930) of the so-called mass migrations. We are still in the midst of the third of these exchanges, the product of immigration's new growth after 1965. While all three migrations shaped many other nations, too (as anyone who has sampled pizza at a Turkish kebab shop in Germany or Australia knows), the United States has received a decidedly more diverse selection of the world's migrants than many other countries.

The long history of international migration to the United States shows that food exchanges are nothing new. Most occurred in the mundane places – stores, fields, factories, kitchens – where ordinary people worked, shopped, and ate. Newcomers have been so intimately involved in production, processing, and marketing of foods that natives have been adopting their foods almost continuously since 1500. And for centuries, too, newly arrived producers and consumers have learned to eat strange foods common to North America or popular among its natives. The considerable diversity of individual, family, and regional eating habits that we see in the United States is the product of these exchanges. That diversity continues to challenge standardized and mass-produced foods in defining what is American, and national, in American foodways. There may be no national American cuisine, but soul food, Chicago pizza or Tex-Mex chili are just as distinctively American – true icons of the nation – as are mass-produced McDonald's hamburgers or Coca-Cola. And they are just as widely eaten, throughout the United States. That, after all, is why my tourist friends were so eager to sample them during their vacation. Eating was one more way for them to "experience America."

Columbian Cooking

Elementary school students once learned that European empire-builders and explorers linked old and new worlds as they searched for Glory, God and Gold. Culinary historians more often emphasize Europeans' lust for the spices of Asia and for the sugar that – first brought to the Mediterranean from the Arab world and then carried to the Atlantic islands – initiated the transatlantic slave trade (Mintz 1985). For 300 years, the introduction of European animals and crops – notably wheat, fruit trees, horses, chickens, and pigs – to the new world, and the global transportation of new world potatoes, corn, peppers, tomatoes, and potatoes (Coe 1994) transformed foodways everywhere on the planet (Crosby 1972). While it would be incorrect to ignore the passion and violence with which natives and newcomers battled for control of North American soil and water (the source of so much of their food), or the inhumanity with which European slave traders transported Africans to the new world to raise sugar, the complete conquest of one culinary tradition by another was not the usual outcome of the Columbian exchange. If that were the case, few North Americans would eat corn, while indigenous Americans would have abandoned turkeys, popcorn, and hominy for roast beef, cheese, and wheat. In the sixteenth century human beings still raised and processed much of their own food, giving natives clear advantages even during conquest: they knew the plants, animals, and climatological and natural peculiarities of North America as newcomers did not. British, Dutch, French, and Spanish empire-builders were far from their own fields, lakes, and forests; they could scarcely feed themselves with food transported by sailing ships across the vast Atlantic Ocean.

North America had long been a culinary mosaic, in large part because of its vast diversity of eco-systems. The humans who first migrated to North America from Asia had provisioned themselves by gathering local vegetables, roots, and fruits and hunting large game animals; mammoths and tigers probably became extinct as human populations increased. Six millennia before Europeans arrived in North America, corn cultivation had spread with empire-builders and traders from the early civilization of central Mexico. By 1500, corn had reached its climatological limits but it had done so without unifying eating habits into a common continental cuisine (Weatherford 1991, ch. 9). In the southwest, large villages of settled agriculturalists raised surpluses of corn in the encircling fields, processing and cooking the grain in many ways, and irrigating their fields where necessary. North of the Colorado River and eastward on the Great Plains, temperatures were too cold or rainfall too undependable for corn cultivation. On the Plains, natives hunted bison and other large game and engaged in long-distance migrations in order to obtain corn in the southwest or in the Mississippi Valley, where settled agriculture also produced large and dense settlements of mound builders. In both the northeastern and southeastern woodlands, most natives migrated seasonally between patches of cleared forest, where they cultivated corn, and the forests or coastal regions where they hunted game, collected shellfish, and gathered vegetable foods. Almost everywhere, cultivation of corn and the gathering of plant foods were women's tasks; men specialized in hunting and fishing. Women processed and cooked most food for immediate consumption, and many groups had well-developed rituals for distributing and eating large quantities of meat when hunters killed it. Surpluses and storage of corn, fish, and meat were limited, but long-distance trade in corn was common. Trade routes had not, however, penetrated the Rocky Mountains; on the west coast, small tribal groups in California managed large oak forests (eating acorn meal) or (in the northwest) traveled seasonally to fishing camps to supplement diets of berries, other fruits, nuts, and roots.

The invasion of North America by explorers representing many European empires guaranteed that North American foodways remained diverse. Merchants, artisans, farmers, and clerics from France, England, Scotland, and the Netherlands shared roughly similar diets. Wheaten bread, while increasingly popular among the wealthiest urban dwellers, had not yet replaced dark peasant breads of rye, oatmeal, and barley. All enjoyed dairy products – cheese, butter, milk – eggs, beers and ales of fermented grain, and thick soups of beans, pulses, and small amounts of meat, with the English showing a marked preference for beef over chicken and pork. The diet of the Spanish was instead rooted in the Mediterranean. They, too, ate cheese, eggs, and chicken, but even the poor ate them with bread made from wheat; their cooking fat was oil pressed from olives; their preferred drink was wine; and they ate more lamb, goat, and mutton than beef (Pilcher 1998, pp. 28–30). What European newcomers shared, bringing them into sharp conflict with native food producers, was their organization of agriculture on privately owned land. Hunting was the privilege of land-owning nobles in Europe, where the much poorer peasants ate only domesticated animals and raised crop surpluses for sale to their much wealthier and urban neighbors.

By the time Spanish invaders reached New Mexico, many Spanish-origin soldiers and priests had already adopted central Mexican food customs – notably their taste for corn and hot, pungent peppers. In the American southwest, their main challenge was to coerce natives to deliver corn surpluses and to raise wheat for their missions and forts. Delivering grain surpluses did not require a fundamental rearrangement of native agriculture, but cultural resistance to Spanish rule and religious conversion sparked successful rebellions. By the eighteenth century, however, natives and newcomers were almost equally dependent on European pigs and sheep for meat and fats (Pilcher 2001). Both ate corn (in the form of flat breads and stews) and wheat (as bread or sweetened baked goods). European fruits were popular with both, too. Natives who had begun to herd goats and sheep had learned to drink milk and make cheese from it. Unlike the natives of central Mexico, who continued to form flat breads (tortillas) of corn masa, natives in the American southwest and northern Mexico often made them with wheat. For native groups on the Great Plains, the invasion by Spaniards and Mexican creoles instead meant adoption of the horse, which allowed them to hunt bison more effectively. It also made them more effective warriors, allowing them to raid the food supplies of the more sedentary cultivators and herders.

On the east coast of North America, newcomers met natives accustomed to migrating seasonally in order to cultivate corn fields, hunt, fish, and gather in the forests of the region. Since the numbers of European settlers in the east grew so rapidly, and the settlers wished to own the land they cultivated, pitched battles and bloodshed accompanied struggles between natives and newcomers for the land that fed them both. British empire-builders encouraged natives to settle in villages hoping they would then produce surpluses (of fish, rice, corn, or meat) for export to the sugar-raising islands of the Caribbean. Alternatively, they looked to natives to provide the animal skins that might fetch a good price among Europe's consumers. Despite these rough similarities, however, regional differences in culinary exchange emerged quickly on the east coast and were apparent already by the eighteenth century.

New England deserved its name, for settlers from England dominated there and soon constrained dwindling native populations to abandon their wandering to hunt and gather. But even in New England, newcomers could not easily transplant their ideal English foodways unchanged to a new environment. Try though settlers did, New England never produced dependable wheat harvests. New Englanders purchased Indian corn and learned to cultivate, grind, and eat it as bread, generally by mixing it with rye flour. Native beans replaced European ones, and pork was added to them, creating baked beans. English women transformed pumpkins into pies, corn into Indian pudding, and cranberries into sauces by applying English cooking techniques to native ingredients. The British successfully introduced their domestic animals, and creative cooks in New France and New England added milk and cream to native stews of shellfish, producing clam chowder (Simmons 1984, p. xviii). As natives were confined to sedentary village life, they added chicken and pork to their own cooking pots even as the English developed a taste for deer and turkey meat and learned from natives how to transform the sap of maple trees into a sweet syrup. Europeans made and fermented cider from apples in great quantities, but – more dependent on corn than their European ancestors – they brewed far less beer and ale; rum made from the sugar raised in the Caribbean replaced these traditional drinks, and became an important item in Europeans' trade with natives, exchanged for furs, skins, and corn.

Further south, the warm, coastal areas of the southern Atlantic coast promised far better opportunities to create agricultural surpluses for export. Focused on commercial agriculture, developers of early Virginia and Carolina plantations turned to natives who not only extended corn cultivation to sell but transformed their annual hunts of deer meat into an important export trade, exchanging skins for Europeans' rum, cooking pots, and weapons. Extensive commerce facilitated natives' adoption of European domestic animals, notably the pig and the chicken. As in New England, wheat would not grow dependably in a humid climate and Europeans in the south adopted corn with even greater enthusiasm. By the 1700s, European settlers had assembled a workforce of indentured Europeans and enslaved Africans who could both feed themselves and raise tobacco, indigo, or rice for export. They were unsuccessful in introducing European grapes or in transforming native grapes into a palatable wine, however; aping the life of the English gentry, they imported wine from across the Atlantic or drank rum instead. The consumption of milk, cream, and cheese probably declined because milk spoiled so easily in the heat; pigs – prolific because able to digest almost any source of food – soon became more common than cattle or cows (Taylor 1982, pp. 22–6). Europeans also adopted foods from Africa (or brought to North America from Africa after being introduced there from Spanish and Portuguese America) – rice, yams, groundnuts, sesame, fritters, and hot peppers (Carney 2001).

In the temperate, rich valleys of the middle Atlantic region, Germans, dissenting British Quakers and Anabaptists, Dutch and Swedish settlers quickly generated surpluses of wheat, salt pork, and dairy products on their much smaller farms; they exported food to southern plantations, to the sugar-growing British Caribbean islands and to rocky New England. Both the so-called Pennsylvania Dutch (German-speakers) and the Dutch of New York enjoyed diets that were richer than those of their New England neighbors but also less influenced by European aristocratic customs than the meals of the southern plantation owners. Furthermore, political did not translate automatically into culinary hegemony. Dutch cookies and German sausage survived and flourished under British rule because food preparation (like use of the German and Dutch languages) was an element of private family life (Rose 1989; Weaver 1982). By contrast, in the frontier regions of this area and the upland south, Scottish and Irish settlers typically ate a diet little different from that of their native American neighbors. Europeans hunted, fished, and cultivated shifting patches of corn, which they also prepared in native fashion. They even borrowed the bear-grease flavoring favored by natives of the southeastern mountains (Taylor 1985, pp. 5–6).

In colonial America, humans grew and processed most of their own food and commercial purveyors of food and drink were limited to a few cities and to rural taverns serving travelers. Food exchanges were a common form of cross-cultural interaction well before the American food supply was transformed by mass production for mass markets. Native foods prevailed on the frontiers of European settlement and corn remained important even as private property and European settled agriculture replaced seasonal migrations as the main form of provisioning. The mingling of Europeans' meat with natives' corn and pumpkin occurred in somewhat different forms in the cooking pots of natives and newcomers alike. Environment, climate, and invasion by many empires guaranteed that North American foodways remained regional: contrasts between the foodways of the northern European east coast and the Spanish and native southwest were particularly sharp. Regional diversity would persist into the nineteenth and twentieth centuries largely because new waves of migration would repeatedly neutralize the potentially homogenizing effects of commercialization and industrialization of food production.

Production and Consumption of Food During the Mass Migrations, 1830–1930

The century between 1830 and 1930 was a tumultuous one, now often understood as the take-off phase of what we today call globalization. In a single century, more than 35 million foreigners entered the United States, and a substantial majority of them remained as permanently settled immigrants. In the first three-quarters of the nineteenth century, they came in large numbers from Germany, Ireland, Canada, Great Britain, the Netherlands, and Scandinavia. The much smaller group of Chinese probably attracted the greatest attention for their habits of dress and cooking and their appearance. By the early twentieth century, Italians, along with Jews and Polish Catholics and Orthodox Christians from southern, central, and eastern Europe, formed the largest groups of newcomers, while Japanese, Koreans, and a growing migration from Mexico struck social Darwinist natives of the country as even more threatening. Over the course of the century, the largest groups of immigrants settled in east and west coast cities, but substantial numbers also farmed or lived in the small market towns of the midwestern and Great Plains states. Still others took seasonal jobs in the southwest and west. Both before and after the Civil War, aside from a few large cities, immigrants almost completely bypassed the south.

With foreigners making up almost 15 percent of the US population, immigrants were involved in every area of American life. Immigration from abroad made possible the expansion of the United States through treaty and warfare. In 1830 the country's population had been divided between the declining family farmers and growing merchant-dominated cities of the east, and the slave-driven plantations of the American south. Migration westward tipped the balance toward a free labor economy. In the 1830s, too, most Americans – whether black or white, free or slave, newcomer or native – still raised, processed, preserved, and prepared most of the foods they consumed. One hundred years later, by contrast, the typical American was a city-dweller and a wage-earning consumer of foods transported over very long distances. Shifting populations of farm workers on large-business farms raised their food, as the numbers of family farmers had fallen steadily after 1890. Meat, vegetables, and grains raised in the west, midwest, and southwest traveled first to corporate, large-scale processors that canned, butchered, packaged, and then shipped them first to wholesalers and then through a series of retail merchants to the markets, grocery stores, and pushcarts where urban consumers waited (Cummings 1940; Boorstin 1973). As family farmers, agricultural workers, developers of food industries, retailers, and shoppers, immigrants were active at every point along this increasingly long, complex chain of food provisioning. Thanks to a spate of recent studies (Levenstein 1988, 1993; Gabaccia 1998; Pillsbury 1998; Diner 2001) we now better under-stand the important culinary transformations of this important era of immigration.

Family Farmers

Like natives, farmers with foreign roots produced food under rapidly changing conditions as the century progressed. In the midwest before, during, and just after the Civil War, large numbers of German, British, Dutch, and Scandinavian farmers hoped to renew familiar, rural ways of lives and to re-establish in the new world patrimonies they had often been denied in land-pressed Europe. While some traveled directly to frontier areas such as Wisconsin, Missouri, Texas, and Minnesota, many more moved into older farming districts in Iowa, Ohio, and Michigan, as these were abandoned by natives. Americans often commented on the tidy appearance of the ground on German, Dutch, and Scandinavian farms, and noted their preference for growing fruits and vegetables, and raising a variety of animals to provide meat and milk, rather than purchasing food and concentrating on the cultivation of a single, cash crop (Conzen 1990). In Texas, farmers like Elise Waerenskold went to great lengths to bring or import seeds and even saplings in order to raise crops they had known at home but could not find in the United States – in her case rutabagas and special varieties of pears and apples. Germans and Danes often specialized in dairy and cheese-making and they were more likely to fodder their animals through the winter to guarantee a steady supply of milk which natives more often did without. The division of labor in German farm families was also distinctive: German girls and women both plowed and harvested, working in the fields alongside men, although (much like American women who avoided field work) they also usually had responsibility for large kitchen gardens that fed their families, while men assumed responsibility for marketing agricultural surpluses such as hogs, wheat, or corn (Pickle 1996, p. 185).

Most children growing up on immigrant family farms remembered eating solid, if sometimes monotonous, and calorie-rich diets that contained reminders of the family's European origins. German one-meal dishes simmered all day on the stove while women worked outside; some gradually evolved into the casseroles that became icons of midwestern, rural, farm eating. Czech pancakes with cottage cheese or fruit preserves or sauerkraut with dumplings made immigrant family meals noticeably different from those of farmers with roots in New England (who still ate pies and beans) or in the upper south (with its preference for cornbread and fried meats). Germans introduced hops and the small dark grains they used for bread-making; they planted them along with wheat and corn, and they experimented with the brewing of beer. While many immigrants planted grapes in hopes of producing home-made wines, natives increasingly looked askance at their efforts as morally suspect. Still, change, borrowing, and creativity were to be found everywhere, even before the Civil War. In Texas and Oklahoma, beef soon competed with pork and chicken as the preferred meat. Whether it was Germans (with their knowledge of pounding, breading, and frying pork or veal into wienerschnitzel) or southerners (with their traditions of breading and frying chicken) who first took a Texas beefsteak and transformed it into a chicken-fried steak, both Germans and natives soon ate the dish with the pan gravy typical of southern cooking. Church suppers and fund-raisers introduced the specialties of one group – whether yeast breads, sauerkraut, or the Norwegian's lutefisk (reconstituted dried fish) – to neighbors of differing backgrounds (Gabaccia 1998, pp. 142–3).

Commercial Farming

After the Civil War, family farmers and ambitious businessmen of both native and recent foreign birth responded to rapid urban population growth by experimenting with mass cultivation of wheat on the Great Plains. Vast cattle drives to towns like Wichita and Kansas City funneled millions of tons of beef into a new, and increasingly national, system of meat distribution. Family homesteaders in the upper midwest and the drier portions of the Great Plains found that prices for the wheat they raised and transported by railroad soon dropped, threatening their ability to make mortgage payments on their land. As millions of family farmers left the land and the numbers of eastern consumers burgeoned, farming became big business. But only those with significant capital could succeed in the large-scale commercial farming. Vast, new business farms employed seasonal wage-earners and agricultural equipment to speed production and to reduce the costs of delivering wheat to milling centers such as Minneapolis.

On the Pacific side of the Rocky Mountains, too, the railroad linkage of east and west after 1869 opened possibilities for large-scale investment in the production of food for consumers and workers far away. And in Hawaii, American investors followed a somewhat similar trajectory in developing new fruit and sugar plantations on lands they would soon claim for the nation. In both places, significant numbers of foreigners as well as natives developed agribusinesses, often introducing new crops (rice, broccoli, Napa cabbage, new wine grapes) or perfecting the cultivation of older ones. The most successful of large-scale western producers was arguably Giuseppe DiGiorgio, a Sicilian immigrant who had never worked in the fields but had begun his business career as a retailer and wholesaler (Gabaccia 1997/8, pp. 10–12). California also saw several generations of immigrants develop successful grape-growing and wine-making enterprises. The earliest endeavors were in the hands of the Franciscan missionaries who had arrived from Europe and from central Mexico in the late 1700s and early 1800s; eager to produce for the big-spending, hard-drinking miners of the gold rush era of the 1850s, German immigrants extended the planting of vineyards to northern California, closer to San Francisco. In the early years of the twentieth century Italian, Slovenian, Swiss, and new German immigrants revived and replaced vines that had fallen to a phylloxera infestation, and began to grow red as well as white grape varieties. California had Chinese potato "kings" while Japanese monopolized the growing of peas and strawberries.

In addition, significant numbers of Japanese, Chinese, and European immigrant workers succeeded in becoming tenant and small landowning "truck" farmers by concentrating on the intensive cultivation of fruits and vegetables for sale to nearby urban markets. In the west, Japanese growers organized cooperatives to sell their crops collectively; in the midwest, German, Scandinavian, and Finnish immigrants also organized producer cooperatives that sold grain, cream, milk, and cheese to wholesalers and negotiated special freight rates for their products. In somewhat similar fashion, San Francisco's fishing and shrimp-drying industries were largely in the hands of immigrants from China and Italy.

Far outnumbering immigrant potato kings or truck farmers, however, were the low-paid and seasonal workers employed by western agribusinesses. Gangs of Chinese, Japanese, Korean, Italian, Portuguese, and Slovenian immigrants, typically working under a labor contractor, found employment on the large farms that specialized in citrus fruit, grapes, or vegetables raised for long-distance shipping. Large owners such as Giuseppe DiGiorgio built separate camps where each nationality had its own cook and lived semi-segregated from others. After 1890, when American investment created railroads reaching deep into central and western Mexico, and even more after the 1910 Mexican revolution, Mexicans began to replace Europeans and Asians as agricultural laborers. Between 1917 and 1929, the restriction on immigration from southern and eastern Europe and the exclusion of immigrants from Asia hastened this transition.

Immigrants in Food Industries

To a considerable degree, it was urban and immigrant consumers who fueled demand for the mass-produced foodstuffs of the west. Transcontinental railroads could carry tons of material but organizing the mass transportation of perishable foods over vast distances was nevertheless a daunting challenge. It was prohibitively expensive to transport living animals to thousands of urban slaughterhouses or whole grains to thousands of urban mills; it was even riskier to ship highly perishable fresh fruits and vegetables across the continent. Nor were growers in California simply large-scale truck farmers who knew the tastes of and could sell directly to the culturally diverse immigrant consumers of eastern cities. Vast new industries to bottle, can, preserve, dry, mill, slaughter, package, and prepare foodstuffs, along with new systems for wholesaling and retailing fresh and processed foods, became important as they connected agribusinesses and consumers separated by thousands of miles.

The development of American food industries, much like other arenas of American life in the nineteenth century, was sharply segmented by race and culture. Social prejudice, limited access to capital and credit, and legal impediments and prohibitions combined to exclude African Americans (along with most Japanese and Chinese immigrants) from success as either investors or operators of large food businesses. By contrast, foreigners from central, southern and eastern Europe were actually better represented as large-scale entrepreneurs in food production than in any other major industry. Nevertheless, food industries remained fairly sharply divided between those developed by natives and those dominated by the foreign-born (Gabaccia 2002).

Foreigners almost completely dominated the production of alcoholic beverages as investors, managers, and as workers. This is scarcely surprising in a country where Protestant natives increasingly associated moral rectitude with abstinence from alcohol consumption. German brewers developed family businesses into corporate dynasties in New York, St. Louis, Chicago, and Milwaukee as they modified traditional manufacturing processes and bottled lager beers for shipment all over the United States and eventually also abroad (Schneider 1990, p. 189). Immigrants in California not only planted vineyards but, beginning with Agostin Haraszthy in the 1850s, began to experiment with production of wine on a scale unknown in Europe (McGinty 1998). Haraszthy employed large numbers of immigrants (many of them Chinese) to build huge underground aging vats and to tend his vineyards. Later in the century, Italian winemakers organized separately from the older American winemakers, many of whom were Germans or their children. The Italian Swiss cooperative colony and other Italian winemakers also began to produce Chianti-style red wines, bottling them in traditional, straw-wrapped bottles, whereas most of California's earlier wine growers had specialized in the production of sweeter white dessert wines. These early experiments with large-scale, industrial modes of production shipped large quantities of wine to east coast immigrant drinkers well before the creation of a University of California enology department dedicated to technical training of wine chemists.

As one might predict, immigrants also dominated the import trade. Food imports from countries such as Italy and China soared with immigration, and Italian economists argued that migration offered good opportunities for Italian shippers, along with businessmen dealing in wine, canned tomatoes, cheese, and olive oil, to build trade empires rivaling those of the Venetians and Genovese of the Middle Ages (Cinotto 2001, pp. 324–7). Giuseppe DiGiorgio began his business career as a small-scale importer of Sicilian lemons. Importers also experimented with large-scale export to their homelands – for example, export of dried California shrimp to China.

In rather sharp contrast, few foreigners succeeded in developing large-scale canning and preserving industries. The second-generation German, Pittsburgh's H.J. Heinz, was arguably the most successful and innovative of the otherwise almost thoroughly native group of fruit and vegetable processors. Like other canners and preservers of vegetables, fruits, and fish, Heinz hired largely female and foreign-born workers. This was also the case in Minneapolis, which became a center for the milling of the millions of tons of wheat grown on the Great Plains into white flour. Natives – many of them with roots in New England – developed this industry too. And in Michigan, the manufacturing of new, ready-to-eat-breakfast cereals from grains was also in native hands. Like ketchup and other industrial foods such as canned and condensed milk, and white breads, Kellogg and Post touted their breakfast cereals to consumers as dependable, sanitary, healthful, and of an absolutely predictable standard.

Both natives and newcomers invested in and became prominent as developers of meat-processing, baking, and wholesale as major industries. Irish and German immigrants numbered among the hog butchers and beef packagers who made the slaughter and salting of pigs (before the Civil War) and (after the war) the slaughter and packing of pre-cut beef for shipping in refrigerated cars one of the country's 10 largest industries. By 1910, 80 percent of all workers in the meat-packing plants of Chicago were immigrants (Barrett 1987, p. 39). German and central European immigrants also played a role in the development of the country's first large cracker and bread bakeries and in the mass manufacture of the yeast used in those bakeries. Both of these industries, too, hired large immigrant workforces. Before he became a grower, Giuseppe DiGiorgio had succeeded as a wholesaler, developing an auction house system (modeled on European precedents) for delivering fresh produce to eastern cities. DiGiorgio then worked backwards to supply his own auction system with fruit and vegetables grown on his own farms. Other immigrants developed the early regional supermarkets that would eventually replace both urban central markets and DiGiorgio's auction houses as the most important nationwide system of wholesaling. It is probable that foreigners succeeded in wholesaling, baking, and butchering because of their considerable importance as retailers of food to local communities. Smaller and local retail businesses trained individual entrepreneurs in the ways of American business and provided a ready network for wholesalers of similar background. Certainly this was the case for DiGiorgio who had first arrived in America with a shipment of his father's lemons to be sold in Baltimore.

Immigrant Retailers; Immigrant Consumers

The small-scale retailing of food to multi-ethnic consumers in American cities was one of the most important employment niches, and one of the most common routes to modest economic mobility, for immigrants of many backgrounds (Kraut 1983). For every business leader of a food industry, there were thousands of immigrant grocers, saloon-keepers, candy-sellers, and restaurateurs. An explanation for this concentration is not hard to find. Consumers of recent foreign origin – immigrants and their children – dominated the populations of most American cities in the early years of the twentieth century, forming anywhere from about one-third to almost half of all urban dwellers. Who knew the tastes, customs, and prejudices of such consumers better than entrepreneurs of their own backgrounds?

Still, immigrants' special knowledge of immigrant consumers cannot completely explain the development of quite distinctive ethnic niches in particular branches of retailing. In the 1850s, Protestant and Catholic Germans opened restaurants and groceries while German-speaking Jews specialized in dry goods. Later in the century there were many more Italian, Chinese, and Mexican than Polish, Japanese, or eastern European Jewish restaurants relative to populations of immigrant consumers. (This may reflect the fact that single men – the most likely customers for restaurant meals when far from home – dominated in the former groups, while gender-balanced migrations and family groups were more common among the latter.) Greeks specialized in the retailing of candy and ice-cream, and (somewhat later) in lunch-wagons and diners, Italians in the marketing of fruit and vegetables. Similarly, some immigrant neighborhoods had many saloons, while others had almost as many tea- and coffee-houses. Some had many meat and poultry stores, others more small bakeries and pastry shops. In part, this clustering of immigrants in particular forms of retailing reflected a kind of chain migration into business. A single early restaurateur who hired relatives or other immigrants from his hometown as kitchen help and waiters quickly trained a new generation of entrepreneurs: after gaining expertise in business and sometimes even borrowing money from their former employers, they opened similar businesses. Many retail businesses provided employment for entire families: in a German saloon, Japanese hotel dining room, or Jewish delicatessen, the wife and mother prepared foods for a free lunch or counter treats in the nearby (or even attached) family apartment. She might also tend the counter or bar during hours when her husband worked away from home. In immigrant restaurants, women frequently operated the cash register while men cooked and waited on tables. Children, too, waited on tables, served customers, or ran errands for their parents' grocery stores. Literally growing up in a business, and thus familiar with small-scale business practices from an early age, many immigrant children followed in their parents' footsteps into careers as food retailers, reproducing the economic niches the immigrant generation had created (Gabaccia 1998, pp. 84–6).

Immigrant retailers delivered to immigrant consumers both the bounty of American agribusinesses and the familiar and sometimes imported products of their original homelands. For everyday meals, most immigrant wives and mothers, along with the cooks responsible for feeding boarding-house or gang labor clientele, served up fare familiar from the old world, altered as income, the availability of ingredients, and creativity dictated. Polish, German, and Irish immigrants continued to eat large quantities of potatoes while Chinese railroad-builders and laundrymen preferred rice. Food habits learned early in life, even before children learned to speak, were rarely abandoned completely in later life. And children raised in immigrant families – like most humans – associated the foods of their childhood with security, comfort, and their mothers: in times of stress they preferred to eat familiar foods even after otherwise substantially changing their eating habits.

Catholic and Jewish religious principles strengthened culinary continuities for some groups. Catholic Christians continued to seek fish or vegetarian fare on Fridays and during Lent. Orthodox Christians maintained even more extensive taboos (against eggs, oil, and other ingredients) during lengthier fast periods. Jews who attempted to follow the rules of kashrut, which required ritually slaughtered meats and the strict separation of milk and meat products at mealtimes, faced the largest challenges to maintaining culinary purity in their diet, for in the United States lard was the most common cooking fat, and meat was generally slaughtered far away and by

Christian butchers. Jewish immigrants typically paid higher prices for their meat than other poor Americans in order to obtain products they were sure met their standards for ritual purity (Diner 2001, pp. 180–2). Even relatively poor immigrants willingly purchased relatively expensive imported goods – from olive oil and pasta to soy sauce and dried mushrooms – in order to obtain familiar ingredients.

The continuation or elaboration of eating habits rooted in other lands contributed to a rudimentary sense of fellow feeling among immigrant neighbors, reinforced by the fact that they were also more likely to shop together in stores operated by their fellow countrymen than they were to seek out the first chain stores that had begun to open (albeit typically outside immigrant neighborhoods) by the 1920s. But even this symbolic connection of food to American ethnicity was far more pronounced among Jews, Germans, and Italians, for example, than it was among the Irish or Poles (Diner 2001, pp. 222–3). In some communities, grocery stores, restaurants, and cafés – much like saloons for Germans before them – were literally centers of community life, where neighbors met to socialize and gossip in their own language and among their own kind. For the Irish, drinking their own darker brews and whiskies in the equivalent of old world public houses may have provided a sense of communalism as much as a shared meal of potatoes, porridge, or cabbage.

Immigrant Retailers and Cross-Cultural Exchange

Despite significant continuities in immigrants' foodways, it would be mistaken to exaggerate the conservatism of the newcomers or their isolation from other American consumers or from the changes sweeping the American food chain. In school, the children of immigrants learned about Thanksgiving turkeys (Pleck 2000, pp. 27–9) or, more negatively, felt embarrassed about their home-packed lunches of outsize sandwiches on home-baked breads. By the early twentieth century, immigrant girls generally received rudimentary introductions to cookery in home economics classes. Nurses, teachers, and settlement house workers urged Japanese and Italian children and their mothers to adopt the northern European custom of having children continue to drink milk for many years. Under such pressure, and unlike many of their parents, children sometimes viewed white bread and canned fruits as superior to the soups, vegetables, or pickles served up by their mothers and concocted from ingredients purchased in corner groceries. By the 1920s, food producers were also learning how to tailor advertising for immigrant consumers, and even publishing brochures of recipes for them in their native languages: Crisco manufacturers, for example, boasted that Jews had been waiting centuries for their product (which – as a vegetable oil – could be safely used with both milk and meat meals, and did not violate the prohibitions against kashrut as did the pork product, and hitherto preferred American fat, lard (Gabaccia 1998, p. 163)).

The sheer bounty of American food markets and the relatively low cost of food in the United States allowed many immigrants with recent memories of scanty or (more often) monotonous diets to change, increase, and improve the foods they ate, although often following old world tastes in making their selections. Ingredients – pasta, beef or fish, pastries, wine, coffee – that had in their homelands been limited to Sabbath or feast-day meals now appeared almost daily on the table. Women of many immigrant groups devoted more time to food preparation than they had in their homeland, as all immigrant groups increased the amounts of meat (especially beef), sugar, white flour, coffee or tea, wine or beer, and prepared snacks, sweets, and ice-cream (generally purchased outside the home) consumed. Experimentation with once-scarce or prohibitively expensive but now readily available ingredients also became a source of domestic culinary experimentation: meat balls, made from the readily available ground American beef, found their way into southern Italian tomato sauces; earlier, the addition of meat to a Cantonese mixture of stir-fried vegetables and noodles had produced the dish of chow mein.

Nor was culinary transformation in the marketplace or kitchen limited to immigrant consumers. Immigrant communities were often so divided (by home region, class, or conflicting religious, political, or familial alliances), and so roiled by constant population turnover, that strictly immigrant clienteles could not generate dependable incomes even for relatively small businesses. Whether they hawked food from pushcarts, corner candy stores, small groceries, or tiny "mom and pop" restaurants, immigrant and native businessmen alike saw expansion as the key to success. Expansion required immigrant entrepreneurs to attract a wider circle of shoppers, including immigrant near neighbors of other backgrounds and, ultimately, long-time and firmly middle-class, native eaters.

Immigrant entrepreneurs' search for new customers extended across the socio-economic and ethnic range of urban America where both immigrant workers and wealthier consumers clustered. Beginning in the middle years of the nineteenth century, some highly trained immigrant hoteliers, chefs, and restaurateurs, such as Giovanni and Lorenzo DelMonico in New York, had built large businesses by marketing the leisure-time and recreational perquisites of European styles of dining and relaxation – replete with French menus and imported wines – to upwardly mobile Americans. In the years around the turn of the century, Italian restaurants in New York's Greenwich and San Francisco's North Beach attracted rebellious young American consumers who called themselves Bohemians. Bohemians found more than physical sustenance in inexpensive meals of spaghetti alla bolognese, washed down by "dago red" (wine), served up by singing waiters with foreign accents, and accented by the chef's or owner's philosophical thoughts on life and culture. They believed they found also a pleasure-loving antithesis to the staid, cerebral, and moralizing Victorian culture they were trying to reject.

On a much humbler level, German brewers in the years bracketing the Civil War had succeeded in attracting a wide and multi-ethnic clientele for their new, light, and effervescent lager beers. They found customers even in those parts of the country – rural areas, the American south – where cultural and religious hostility to alcohol consumption seemed particularly intense. By the late nineteenth century, small merchants in Chinatown survived by marketing initially exotic foods to tourists curious to visit the Chinatowns created by residential discrimination. Newer immigrant neighbors also discovered a taste for chow mein in Chinese restaurants: Jewish immigrants in New York recall eating Chinese food as one of the low-cost pleasures of urban life, bringing with it a sense of adventure and cosmopolitanism outside ghetto communities. For humbler consumers, too, smaller treats in the form of foods served from street pushcarts, at saloon free lunch counters, or from early lunch cars and diners – including pastrami sandwiches, hot dogs, red hots, and even hot tamales – provided comparable, if smaller and inexpensive, doses of pleasure and excitement in the midst of a routine workday. By the 1920s, tourists and urban neighbors who had tried such foreign foods on excursions to these foreign lands close to home (as they were sometimes advertised by local Chambers of Commerce with full support from foreign-born merchants) were trying to cook the dishes they had eaten there themselves. Ladies magazines aimed at the national market of middle-class American housewives included recipes for German, Italian, and Chinese dishes, noting how they could vary monotonous diets and add a note of novelty and pleasure to familiar meals.

Cross-cultural exchanges in the marketplace were not random, however. Rarely did Americans willingly or knowingly taste, or adopt, immigrant dishes that included organ meats or offal. Natives definitely preferred hot dogs to blutwurst (made with blood and fat) and chili with beef and beans to menudo (made with tripe). Immigrants' incorporation of foods was equally selective. While willing to pay high prices for a few familiar food items, immigrants initially did not as often as natives purchase the comparatively expensive manufactured and processed foods pouring from the new food industries of the country. Immigrants accustomed to home-baked or bakery breads, or the dark breads of central and eastern Europe, initially turned up their noses at the highly processed white American flour and white American bread. Male newcomers in particular attributed natives' consumption of processed foods to the laziness of American women who – they claimed – were too busy with social activities and volunteer work to care for their homes and children properly as newcomer women did. Women immigrants who prided themselves on their culinary skills as breadgivers had their own reasons for rejecting vegetables, fruits, or meats from cans.

Across a century of the mass migrations, the dynamics of cultural exchange may have intensified with the commercialization of food production and the rise of the modern food consumer, but they were not fundamentally altered by them. Few Americans today remember the culinary experimentalism of the age of the mass migrations; they think of the past as far removed from our own era of innovative, adventurous, or purportedly post-modern eating. This sense of a sharp break from the past reflects less the absence of past experimentalism than it does the sharp declines in immigration from Asia and Europe in the middle years of the century. In 1924 the United States passed draconian immigration restrictions; the number of newcomers waned and reached its nadir during the Great Depression and World War II. While new immigrants from Mexico and Puerto Rico, and southerners, both black and white, brought new tastes to northeastern and western American cities during this period, the influx of foods from across the oceans faltered. Even when immigration revived slowly in the immediate postwar years, restrictive and racist immigration laws, along with heightened Cold War concerns about security, kept the total numbers of newcomers much lower than in the early years of the century. And by 1965, when immigration law again changed, opening the door to modest increases in immigration, the amalgamation of Asian, European, and native foods was so far advanced that it seemed unworthy of note; indeed it had been almost completely forgotten. Nevertheless, much as in the much earlier era of the Columbian exchanges, the increasingly commercialized culinary exchanges of the mass migrations century had again substantially transformed the eating habits of all.

New Immigrants, New Ingredients, a New Century

In 1965, shortly after civil rights legislation eliminated institutionalized racism in American public life, the US Congress passed a law to eliminate racism in the country's immigration policy. Although the new law raised modestly the total numbers to be allowed into the country, its purpose was to select immigrants on new grounds, and to give the chosen few access to visas through a complex preference system. The numbers of immigrants entering the country increased after 1965 and began to draw considerable comment by the 1980s. Most observers commented on a striking change that quickly occurred in immigrants' origins. Congressmen had expected the 1965 law to facilitate the entry of formerly restricted groups from southern and eastern Europe; in fact, the largest groups of newcomers now originated in the Caribbean, Latin America, and Asia – regions that also had long histories of migration to the United States. Increasing numbers now also came from areas that in the past had sent few to the United States – notably the Middle East and Africa. Less commented upon was the fact that almost one-third of the new immigrants were well-educated professionals – many of them English-speaking, and sometimes also American-educated – who had been prosperous members of the elite of their homelands. Nor were immigrant origins alone changing after 1965. Newcomers now entered a country that insisted on toleration for multicultural diversity rather than mounting campaigns to eliminate cultural difference.

Today, as in the past, immigrants can be found almost everywhere along the complex food chain required to provision a post-industrial society. The near-collapse of family farming and the rise of corporate forms of management in food industries, however, leave today's immigrants more concentrated than during the mass migrations in low-level wage-earning positions. Still, immigrant retailers and restaurateurs continue to function as important mediators in a new round of cultural exchanges And these exchanges – as in the past – are transforming the eating habits of newcomers and natives alike.

The large-scale cultivation of fruit and vegetables for urban consumers continues to depend heavily on workers newly arrived from abroad. Immigrants from the Caribbean and Central America plant, prune, and harvest the orchards of Florida and the apple orchards of New Hampshire (Hahamovitch 1997, pp. 200–1). In the southwest, agricultural workers born in Mexico, Asia, and Europe were temporarily challenged in the 1930s by native workers called Okies and Arkies (poor, displaced farmers from the dustbowls of Oklahoma and Arkansas); for 20 years after World War II, however, Mexicans were recruited as seasonal and temporary agricultural laborers under the Bracero Program (Calavita 1992), and they continue to dominate this work today, especially in the west. Large growers in the southwest and Florida regularly petition Congress to guarantee the survival of special visa programs that allow workers from Mexico, Central America, and the Caribbean to enter the country temporarily as harvest laborers but that also require them to return home again at the end of their contracts.

Truck farming has not completely disappeared from the chain of American food provisioning and for some immigrants it continues to provide an escape from agricultural wage-earning into tenant farming or even land ownership. Both the popularity of upscale restaurants and the desire of wealthy Americans for fresh and often organic produce have created improved opportunities for small-scale producers who market their own products to select restaurateurs, food markets, and consumers. Often, however, it is natives and not recent newcomers who enjoy the easiest connections and who best understand the culinary preferences of upscale restaurants such as Alice Water's Chez Pannisse in Berkeley. These new small-scale producers are more accurately characterized as boutique than as family or truck farmers.

More commonly, immigrants who escape agricultural labor find more permanent employment in food processing plants. The relocation of American meat packing and processing from older so-called rustbelt sites such as Chicago, Cincinnati, and Buffalo to newer locations in the sunbelt (which stretches from the Carolinas to California) has attracted new immigrant workers even to areas (especially in the southeast) where few newcomers ventured in the past. Chicken processing plants in North Carolina and in Arkansas employ large numbers of Mexicans, Asian refugees, and Caribbean workers; there, immigrants work alongside native women and black and white men displaced by the decline of local textile industries or the collapse of family farming enterprises (Fink 2003, pp. 17–21). Unfortunately, too, these newer workplaces often reproduce the nightmare working conditions of the old meatpacking jungles of Chicago, as the nation discovered when 25 workers died in a fire in a processing plant that locked in its workers during each daily shift in Hamlet, North Carolina.

Despite this apparent continuity, a century of corporatization and consolidation in American food industries has changed immigrants' place in them; few immigrants are now found among industry leaders as they were in the past. The transition from individual proprietorship, partnership, and family-owned and -managed businesses was, of course, already well under way during the mass migrations. Beginning in the 1920s a few very large food corporations emerged as corporations consolidated, and these have diversified over the past 80 years by buying up many smaller companies and brand names. The scale of food production and trade has also increased remarkably although several counter-trends – including franchising and artisanal or boutique, specialized production of high-quality foods and drinks for wealthy consumers – can also be noted. Opportunities to transform small, family-run enterprises into leading corporations have declined, and the path to corporate leadership now more typically begins in MBA programs than on the shop floor or behind the sales counter in a smaller enterprise. Both changes help to guarantee that natives more completely dominate American food industries today and that niches for foreigners in food industries have contracted.

Significantly, foreigners no longer dominate the production of wine, beer, or spirits; immigrants' alcohol niche in food industries has almost disappeared (Gabaccia 2002). Its disappearance reflects the growth of a large population of native consumers of alcoholic beverages which blurs the once-sharp line separating rural, Protestant teetotalers from urban consumers of recent foreign origin. Ironically, perhaps, prohibition contributed to this change. Many immigrant wine and beer producers did not survive the collapse of a legal market for their wares between 1919 and 1933, and corporate managers or new investors, sometimes with the assistance of younger generations of the founding family, had to rebuild both industries in the very hostile environment of depression and war in the 1930 and 1940s. True, some major American breweries (for example, Busch) and even more California wineries (for example, Gallo) remain in the hands, and in a few cases the management, of the descendants of German or Italian immigrant brewers and vintners. Equally true, natives from the so-called Protestant Bible Belt (rural southern and midwestern areas; see Sack 2001), and recent converts to the evangelical and Pentecostal Protestant churches that grew rapidly during yet another period of revivalism in the 1970s and 1980s, still pride themselves on their abstinence from alcoholic beverages. Overall, however, American consumers after World War II exhibited not only a revived thirst for beer but a sharply increased interest in domestically produced wines. By the 1970s and 1980s natives were investing in smaller-scale breweries, vineyards, and wineries and beginning to produce high-quality vintages to challenge European imports. These boutique enterprises, too, were often owned and operated by long-time natives who sought to produce the kind of idiosyncratic and complex flavors that beer bottling, and the sale of jug wines, by an earlier generation of immigrant entrepreneurs had removed through standardization and mass production. Like boutique farmers, furthermore, these new small-scale producers marketed their products not to new working-class immigrants but to well-heeled natives, along with their elite and often cosmopolitan immigrant counterparts.

A few immigrants have built successful new businesses in economic sectors they once dominated. Tom Carvel and his Carvel Ice Cream chain provides just one early example of a twentieth-century immigrant succeeding in a niche – in this case confectionery – already dominated by immigrants, in this case, Greeks and Italians. In the import industry, too, the Unanue family founded Goya food products in 1936; Goya is now the largest Hispanic-owned company in the United States, employing 2,000 people worldwide. While its managers are now native-born members of the family, the company still sells identifiably Latin and Hispanic foods to a clientele that includes Spanish-speaking new immigrants from Mexico, the Caribbean, and South America along with native consumers who want to add Latin flavors to their own diet (Gabaccia 1998, p. 166). Today, Mexican and Mexican American manufacturers of tortillas such as Azteca (in Illinois) and Rudy's (in Dallas) are also very big businesses that are still owned and managed by their founders and their children and grandchildren (Pilcher 2001).

In most cases, however, large-scale producers and retailers of the foods we know have immigrant roots are not under the ownership or management of immigrant founders or their direct descendants. A quick survey of the major producers of salsa, pizza, or chow mein noodles reveals that none are in the hands of immigrants, nor are their corporate managers of Mexican, Italian, or Chinese descent. Pizza Hut was not founded by Italians, nor was Taco Bell founded by Mexican Americans. Frequently companies and brands founded by earlier immigrant entrepreneurs – whether Lenders' bagels or Progresso's sauces – have been purchased by major American food corporations such as General Foods, Coca-Cola, Kraft, Beatrice, or Phillip-Morris. The largest American food conglomerates continue to look for businesses that grow and succeed by selling to immigrant or minority consumers; Azteca, for example, was briefly owned by Pillsbury in the 1980s before Arthur Velazquez (one of its founders, and himself an MBA) bought it back again (http://www.google.com/search?hl=en&lr=&ie=UTF-8&oe=UTF-8&q=azteca+pillsbury). Even in food retailing, many shareholder-owned, large-scale and corporate restaurant and grocery chains now market products associated with the foodways of many newer immigrant groups.

The so-called international aisle in large grocery stores and restaurant chains such as the Olive Garden actually compete with immigrant entrepreneurs for the food dollars of recently arrived immigrants, especially the more prosperous among them. And in the case of tortillas, Mexican American and immigrant manufacturers find they must also compete with the huge Mexican food conglomerate Maseca which exports its Mission brand tortillas to the United States.

Nevertheless, the small-scale retailing of food remains an important economic niche for immigrants in American food industries. Small businesses operated by recent immigrants continue to cater to Indian, Vietnamese, Mexican, Ethiopian, Jamaican, and other immigrant food-buyers. Mexican, Latino, and Hispanic grocery stores, bakeries, butcher shops, and small restaurants appear wherever large numbers of Spanish-speakers find jobs in construction, agriculture, or industry. In the east their products may be aimed at Dominican, Puerto Rican, Cuban, and other island peoples from the Caribbean, whereas in Los Angeles they more often sell the products of Mexico and the rest of Central America. Other small stores know, and cater to, the special food preferences and taboos of Muslim or Hindu consumers from south and west Asia. In some cases, entrepreneurs from China, Vietnam, Cambodia, or the Philippines offer a range of products, intending to capture a pan-Asian range of shoppers from diverse backgrounds. It is a rare American city that does not have one or more grocery stores catering to recent immigrants (Gabaccia 1998, ch. 8).

As in the past, too, these small retailers find a broader clientele among native customers, often across the socio-economic spectrum. For example, in many American cities, immigrant Koreans dominate the retailing of fresh produce or greengroceries: natives, long-time Americans, and recent arrivals all shop for cherries, apples, leeks, onions, and potatoes – not kim chee – at the typical Korean market. In inner-city ghettoes, occasional violent confrontations between low-income consumers and new immigrant retailers, often unversed in American racial etiquette or its many regional variations, have produced headlines. Immigrant restaurateurs also seem particularly savvy in attracting sophisticated, well-traveled, or merely adventurous American consumers willing to seek close to home tastes they first encountered on a vacation abroad. Typically, a bicultural and bilingual immigrant staff in these small businesses stands willing and able to explain meal choices, or a grocery store advertises its products in two languages and organizes its wares in ways that natives understand or find familiar (e.g. self-service, check-out counter, sale items, etc.). Ethiopian, Thai, Mexican, Central American, Vietnamese, and Cuban restaurants have introduced American diners to a wide range of new food items and tastes. And survey data suggest that considerable numbers of American consumers, having tried new dishes in immigrant restaurants, often search their supermarket and bookstore aisles for the recipes and ingredients that allow them to reproduce, and then to alter, these new tastes in their home kitchens. According to food columnists, even sushi is now being produced regularly in homes in the American midwest (Morrow 2003), where American cooks add mango, cilantro, and mint and even experiment with "meat and potatoes" maki.

As in the nineteenth century, too, it is immigrant chefs who play a special role in providing sophisticated and purportedly authentic or creatively global dishes for wealthy diners in many urban fine restaurants. The growing importance of culinary knowledge as a marker of class status in the United States since the 1980s means that French, German, Japanese, Chinese, Mexican, or Italian immigrant chefs can not only gain a following for their kitchen creativity but earn a very good income and sometimes even celebrity status by doing so. Still, the sophisticated diners who enjoy fusion meals at restaurants with names such as "Ciao Mein" (Italian/Asian in Hawaii) or who sample Nuevo Latino foods in Miami or Pacific Rim foods (California/Asia blends) in Seattle might be surprised to walk into the kitchens of such restaurants and discover that most of the rest of the kitchen staff also speak Spanish.

Restaurants and grocery stores thus remain important sites of cross-cultural exchange at the start of the twenty-first century. And despite the fact that the United States now celebrates its tolerance for cultural diversity, and hesitates to campaign negatively to change the eating habits of newcomers, recent immigrants to the United States show few signs that they will be more conservative in their eating habits than earlier arrivals. Of course, immigrants from Vietnam and Ethiopia do not immediately abandon familiar tastes and preferences when they enter the United States. Many note that, for example, for adopted children, foods of their homelands – whether sticky rice, enchiladas, or njera – can provide comfort during the period of considerable and stressful cultural adjustment that migration and the learning of English still require (http://www.famcam.org/ngasha_book.html). Much like their predecessors, however, today's immigrants are selectively incorporating the ingredients of local grocery stores and the dishes of their neighbors, and transforming their own diets in the process. Mexican immigrants' shopping baskets include soft drinks and ground beef, as well as masa and corn husks (for making tamales at home) and corn or flour tortillas. Children and teenagers in immigrant families seem particularly attracted to American fast food. Working mothers in immigrant families face many of the same challenges in preparing food daily as do working women in all American families: purchasing prepared foods and meals not only supports immigrant businesses offering traditional fare, but leads to experimentation with microwave meals and ready-to-eat products such as breakfast cereals and frozen pizzas. Immigrants also seem to face another challenge common to natives: incorporating outsize fast-food snacks, sugary sweets and soft drinks and more meat and milk into their diets usually means weight gain along with predictable health problems such as heart disease and adult-onset diabetes.

Today's immigrants – along with their children and grandchildren – can be expected to shape the American foodways of the twenty-first century in predictable ways. Despite the supposed threat of McDonaldization to the diverse life and eating habits of the world (Ritzer 1993), diversity in ethnic and regional foodways is likely to persist, and both are also likely to alter the foods delivered by corporate mass-producers in the years ahead. In Hawaii, New York, Los Angeles, Miami, and even in the small towns of North and South Carolina, immigrants are again tossing their own ingredients and cooking techniques into much older regional melting pots. In Miami, Cuban sandwiches, and in California fish tacos with coleslaw represent new regional, and still distinctively American, inventions; in New York, it is the spices of India that find their way into pizza, while in California, the Mayan Pizza with Mexican flavors and accompaniments predicts the persistence of culinary regionalism well into the future. Advocates of healthier "light" eating have even urged web browsers to try black-eyed peas and Chinese greens over rice (http://www.healthwell.com/deliciouskitchen/recipes/peaschinesegreens.cfm?key=21). Often too, these new regional dishes incorporate corporate products, as does the Hawaiian dish of musubi. In this dish, a cube of Japanese rice, wrapped in seaweed, is topped with a corporate canned meat product – Spam – that is widely loved throughout the islands (http://alohaworld.com/ono/recipes/spammusubi.htm). And in California, Japanese tourists now regard eating a California roll (avocado, imitation crab, compressed pollock, and cucumber) as a kind of travelers' rite of passage. Corporate marketers' enthusiasm for identifying consumer niches demographically by income, education, ethnicity, and race (Halter 2000, pp. 5–6) ignores this new round of hybridization but there is little reason to believe that American diets will not change as much in the next century as they did in the past one. Many of those changes will again emerge directly from immigration and from food exchanges occurring in today's restaurants, groceries, and kitchens.

Culinary Nation-Building

Many of the foods discussed in this chapter are distinctively American and so widely and ubiquitously eaten in the United States (but almost nowhere else) that they might be considered national dishes as well. Why then do most scholars nevertheless insist that the United States remains a nation without a national cuisine? To a considerable extent, the problem lies with the term cuisine. While a dictionary defines cuisine simply as "a characteristic manner or style of preparing food" – for example, as the distinctive foodways of a cultural group – anthropologists since Jack Goody (1982) have instead typically reserved the term cuisine for those styles of cooking that become codified and fixed by professional cooks and accepted as the fine dining tradition of the nation by elite eaters. Cuisine is thus intimately associated with sharp class differences: professional chefs create cuisine not only by preparing meals for discerning eaters of their society's elite, political, or ruling classes but by codifying and fixing a particular range of dishes, particular preparation techniques, and particular tastes as characteristic of that group. They then assure the reproduction of a cuisine by writing recipes, cookbooks, and dining manuals that establish boundaries between those foods and practices within and outside the cuisine. In the United States, corporate or commercial, regional, and immigrant influences on foodways have all worked against such codification.

Before 1776, there was, of course, no American nation and there could be no national cuisine. The natives of North America did not call themselves Americans, although the European invaders sometimes did. As the colonials of European descent claimed the term American for themselves, their concern with culinary nation-building remained surprisingly limited. As far as we know, the founding fathers of the United States did not worry much about creating a national cuisine. Indeed in a country with a federal system of government, where individual, local, and state rights, along with the right to religious diversity, were often jealously guarded, and where sectional conflicts between north and south persisted even after the Civil War, it would have been surprising if a national cuisine had emerged from regional colonial foodways. Furthermore, the down-to-earth republican aspirations of political leaders in Washington, Albany, or Richmond discouraged the development of a formal or codified "court" cuisine of the type emerging in many European capitals in the late eighteenth and early nineteenth centuries.

The publication now regarded by scholars as the first American cookbook (written in Connecticut by Amelia Simmons, in reprint (1984)) is American largely because it was printed in the new world for English-speaking readers (rather than being imported from England) and because it used ingredients – for example, corn and pumpkin – and techniques (for example, wood ash for leavening gingerbread) borrowed from the natives of North America. A quick comparison of Amelia Simmons's recipes to those in the collection of a southern plantation owner such as Harriott Horry (see Hooker 1990) confirms the importance of regional culinary variations in the new republic. Simmons's recipes represented only the foods of common, urban New Englanders, not those of the southeast or upper midwest. Horry's elite recipes might have become the basis for a regional cuisine, but the slave cooks on her plantations were not in a position – lacking both literacy and independence – to codify it as such. Only foreign visitors seemed willing to proclaim on the subject of American food or to find in the United States distinctive national foodways. To do so they noted how American eating habits differed from those of Europe, and they generally noted the ubiquitous prevalence of corn and hog meat, the use of corn liquor, cider, or rum instead of ale and beer or wine, and preferences for great quantities of food, often simply (or, many claimed, "badly") cooked and also very hastily consumed. None saw in American foodways a distinctive national cuisine; the way Americans ate seemed both too lowly and too unrefined to qualify as that (for example, Taylor 1982, pp. 70–1).

By the late nineteenth century, the foods we now label ethnic – especially those introduced by immigrants – became discernible alongside the corporate foods mass-produced for a national market. The spread of both kinds of food seemed to have challenged a group of elite, native-born women – largely from New England and New York – to attempt for the first time to define and to codify an American national cuisine. To a surprising degree, and especially in the textbooks of home economists and the campaigns of temperance and prohibition reformers, culinary nationalists urged the poor women of the American south, the farmwives and native Americans of the west, and the immigrant women of northern cities to adopt the foods and purportedly abstemious eating habits of colonial New England – oatmeal and milk breakfasts, codfish cakes, white sauces, broths made with lamb and barley, and corn puddings (Levenstein 1988, pp. 103–4). Their emphasis was not on taste and refinement – those seeking fine dining in this era instead opted for French cuisine served by immigrant chefs in the new restaurants and grand hotels that became a focus of *haute bourgeois* life – but rather on health, simplicity, and financial restraint. In particular, female reformers admonished natives and newcomers alike to reject as un-American and expensive the supposed poisons of alcohol and of strange, sugary, or cheap street snacks hawked by immigrant retailers. Reformers also rejected the canned meats of Chicago's jungles, along with canned fruit and vegetables and even ready-to-eat cold breakfast cereals as too expensive or low-quality for a poor family's diet. Reformers assessed the degree to which immigrant women adopted codfish and corncakes, not ground beef or canned beans, as signs of immigrants' assimilation: a family still eating sauerkraut, could be labeled "not yet Americanized" (Gabaccia 1998, p. 123). While the daughters of immigrants clearly incorporated some elements of the reformer's ideal of American cuisine into their family kitchens, codfish and corn pudding did not replace dishes rooted in their homelands or prevent women from adding new mass-produced ingredients pouring from American food factories. In short, reformers failed to create an American cuisine during the years of the mass migrations. Wealthy Americans who strayed from French cuisine were more likely to sample immigrant fare as *bon vivant* Bohemians than return to the diets of colonial New England.

Immigrants of the mass migrations era defined American food differently from the reformers, although they too distinguished between American and their own foodways. For Mary Antin newly arrived from a Jewish Russian ghetto, as for many immigrants, introduction to American food took the form of an early eating experience with canned foods, mass-produced loaves of white bread, or with the tropical bananas that were not widely available in Europe (Gabaccia 1998, p. 36). For immigrants, as for many poor consumers in the south and midwest, Heinz and his "57 varieties" – for example, ketchup or baked beans – Gold Medal Flour, and breakfast cereals defined as American those foods that were mass-produced and sold in a jar or a can. Today, too, people around the world identify similar, simple products of American food industries – from canned goods to fast foods – as the single most important expression of American culinary genius. But none would argue that these products, when taken together, constitute a cuisine. They are both too accessible and their tastes are too standardized and dependable to qualify as cuisine.

Nor did a cuisine emerge in the half-century between immigrant restriction and the revival of immigration after 1965. As late as the 1930s, organizers of the WPA Federal Writers' Project "America Eats" lectured state coordinators that they would not accept essays on dishes of recent immigrant origin or include in their publication descriptions of the latest corporate food fads, such as hamburgers, hotdogs, or "Suzi-Q" fried potatoes (Gabaccia 1998, p. 143). At least in Washington, definitions of American food apparently still rested on the regional hybrids of the colonial era broadened beyond New England to include the humble foods of the southeast, southwest, Florida, and the western frontiers. Even as writers for the Federal Project explored regional traditions, these regional hybrids were changing in response to culinary exchanges and the incorporation of new immigrant ingredients. By the 1950s, travelers – much like my German visitors in 1995 – wanted to sample New York's bagels with cream cheese, Philadelphia's hoagies, New Bedford's chow mein sandwiches, Chicago's deep dish pizza, or Cincinnati's distinctive chili blend of beans, spaghetti, and the spices of the eastern Mediterranean. All these new regional dishes blended the ingredients and tastes of immigrant cultures. None could be found on the tables of fine restaurants, where French or so-called continental (European) cuisine still prevailed.

During the prosperous postwar years, ever larger numbers of Americans ate ever more of the mass-produced and standardized products of the country's food industries: east, south, west, and north, Americans of diverse backgrounds purchased and ate vast quantities of ketchup on hamburgers and hotdogs and enjoyed Coca-Cola, canned beans, breakfast cereals, soft, white bread, a dizzying array of chocolate and nut candy snacks, and jello desserts. By then, so many Americans were eating ethnic foods, that mass-production of these foods by large food conglomerates threatened to sever even memory of spaghetti, pizza, bagels, sauerkraut, fortune cookies, kosher hot dogs, or tortilla chips as products of the immigrant communities and immigrant food businesses. The line dividing American from immigrant foods seemed to disappear as ethnic foods found their way into corporate food industries, rendering almost invisible the century of culinary exchanges that preceded them. Ethnic food in cans or the frozen food counter were all simple, inexpensive, and accessible to all; they did not generate a cuisine, nor were they ever celebrated by chefs as American fine dining. On the contrary, intellectuals more often castigated them as abominations (Gabaccia 1998, p. 2).

The arrival of new immigrants after 1965, and the celebration of the United States as a multicultural mosaic of many cultures, did result in the codification of ethnic cuisines, in the form of dozens of cookbooks generated by municipal, corporate, and federal food festivals (Gabaccia 1998, p. 187). Yet this occurred at a time when fewer and fewer Americans limited their food consumption to ingredients or dishes from any one cultural tradition, let alone to the cultural choices of their immediate ancestors. Community cookbooks instead revealed the eclectic mixes of ethnic traditions, blended in idiosyncratic ways by members of churches, synagogues, and community organizations in various parts of the country. By the time mass-produced, bottled salsa replaced ketchup as the best-selling condiment in the 1980s, Americans seemed about to forget even that salsa had origins in Mexico. And when American corporations began exporting pizza, bagels, and tacos abroad, foreign consumers, too, came to see these foods as American, forgetting their ethnic origins among immigrants and foreigners. Israelis buying bagels, for example, believed they were eating an American, not a Jewish, dish. Whether at home or abroad, however, no one was likely to view the humble and ubiquitous bagels, ketchup, and pizza as definers of an American cuisine.

Tensions between ethnic and regional foods on the one hand and corporate foods on the other are nevertheless still visible in American life in recent years. Spurred on by counter-cultural critiques of American food industries, and of the taste and quality of the foods they produced (Belasco 1989, pp. 50–4), more American consumers began to express interest in again finding ethnic foods they deemed authentic – that is, untouched by the corporate chemist or packaging of mass marketing. Ironically, consumers seeking more authentic versions of the foods that they had eaten abroad or that they believed their grandparents had enjoyed in a simpler time began patronizing smaller restaurants and seeking ingredients in ethnic groceries, many of them opened by newer immigrants. In some cases – as in the pizza parlors of western Connecticut or in the barbecue restaurant I described at the beginning of this chapter – authentic ethnic food was then dished up by cooks and entrepreneurs who were completely unconnected culturally to the people who had introduced it to American diners in the first place (Gabaccia 1998, pp. 197–8).

At times, then, American food has meant simply whatever natives enjoyed eating and newcomers did not. It has meant foods eaten only in the United States, or more commonly here than elsewhere in the world. (Corn, for example, continues to be eaten more extensively in Peru, Mexico, and the United States than in any European or Asian country.) The dishes of the American southeast, southwest, and upper midwest – whether barbecue, pasties with rutabagas and ground beef, or chili con carne – were invented in the United States and are as authentically American as is Chicago's deep dish pizza (invented by a Texan newly arrived in the city in the 1940s) or spaghetti with meatballs – a dish developed by Italian immigrants in American cities and never cooked in Italy. Our national dishes might best be considered those that have been eaten generally, by many persons, and everywhere throughout the country. And, again, many foods – some ethnic or regional in origin and others mass-produced and standardized – meet that qualification. Spaghetti is consumed as widely throughout the United States as is Coca-Cola. Perhaps this is why critics of globalization and of the spread of McDonald's, Pizza Hut, and Taco Bell around the word fear they will result in a general Americanization of world foodways and the destruction of other national cuisines. In fact, however, most studies show that these mass purveyors of standardized foods usually must adjust the offerings and tastes on their menus in order to please local consumer desires (Watson 1997).

Labeling a food American or national is not enough to create a national, American cuisine recognized at home or abroad. Nor is regionalism alone a satisfactory explanation for the absence of an American cuisine: regional variations in cooking are quite marked also in France or China without preventing their national cuisines from being canonized and celebrated at home and throughout the world. What the United States has lacked has been a close relationship between wealthy, politically powerful, and self-consciously American diners and chefs who work with ingredients, concepts, and tastes that are clearly American and national. Hamburger is still not *haute cuisine*. In the past two decades, chefs experimenting creatively with the local products of boutique farms, wineries, breweries, and dairies have begun to invent American, nuevo or new regional American cuisines for well-heeled diners, usually labeled as yuppies (Young Urban Professionals). Almost every American city now boasts menus and local newspaper food pages that examine the special tastes of American foods, combined in imaginative ways with the culinary traditions of the country's many regions and many American ethnic groups. Whether such experiments will coalesce into an American cuisine in the century ahead cannot be known and may depend more on class-formation than on the dynamics of the food marketplace. If it does, however, it will probably not much change the everyday eating habits of Americans. We can expect instead that the eclectic blending of old, new, commercial, and ethnic, will continue to distinguish American national foodways from American cuisine well into the future. New ingredients have again been tossed into the American food chain and we – native and newcomer alike – are all still busy eating from the melting pot.

REFERENCES

Barrett, James (1987). *Work and Community in the Jungle: Chicago's Packinghouse Workers, 1894–1922*. Urbana: University of Illinois Press.

Belasco, Warren (1989). *Appetite for Change: How the Counterculture Took on the Food Industry, 1966–1988*. New York: Pantheon Books.

Belasco, Warren and Philip Scranton, eds. (2002). *Food Nations: Selling Taste in Consumer Societies*. New York: Routledge.

Bentley, Amy (1998). *Eating for Victory: Food Rationing and the Politics of Domesticity*. Urbana: University of Illinois Press.

Boorstin, Daniel (1973). *The Americans: The Democratic Experience*. New York: Random House.

Brown, Linda Keller and Kay Mussell, eds. (1984). *Ethnic and Regional Foodways in the United States: The Performance of Group Identity*. Knoxville: University of Tennessee Press.

Calavita, Kitty (1992). *Inside the State: The Bracero Program, Immigration, and the I.N.S.* New York: Routledge.

Camp, Charles (1989). *American Foodways: What, When, Why, and How we Eat in America.* Little Rock, AR: August House.

Carney, Judith (2001). *Black Rice: The African Origins of Rice Cultivation in the Americas.* Cambridge, MA: Harvard University Press.

Cinotto, Simone (2001). *Una famiglia che mangia insieme: Cibo ed ethnicità nella comunità italoamericana di New York, 1920–1940 (A Family that Eats Together: Food and Ethnicity in the Italian American Community of New York, 1920–1940).* Torino: Otto Editrice.

Coe, Sophie D. (1994). *America's First Cuisines.* Austin: University of Texas Press.

Conzen, Kathleen (1990). "Immigrants in Nineteenth-Century Agricultural History." In Louis Ferleger, ed., *Agriculture and National Development: Views on the Nineteenth Century.* Ames: Iowa State University Press, pp. 303–42.

Crosby, Alfred W. (1972). *The Columbian Exchange: Biological and Cultural Consequences of 1492.* Westport, CT: Greenwood.

Cummings, Richard (1940). *The American and His Food.* Chicago: University of Chicago Press.

Diner, Hasia R. (2001). *Hungering for America: Italian, Irish, and Jewish Foodways in the Age of Migration.* Cambridge, MA: Harvard University Press.

Fink, Leon (2003). *The Maya of Morganton: Work and Community in the Nuevo New South.* Chapel Hill: University of North Carolina Press.

Gabaccia, Donna R. (1997/8). "Ethnicity in the Business World: Italians in American Food Industries." *The Italian American Review* 6(2): 1–19.

—— (1998). *We Are What We Eat: Ethnic Food and the Making of Americans.* Cambridge, MA: Harvard University Press.

—— (2002). "As American as Budweiser and Pickles? Nation-Building in American Food Industries." In Warren Belasco and Philip Scranton, eds., *Food Nations: Selling Taste in Consumer Societies.* New York: Routledge, pp. 175–93.

Gonzalez, Gilbert G. (1994). *Labor and Community: Mexican Citrus Worker Villages in a Southern California County, 1900–1950.* Urbana: University of Illinois Press.

Goody, Jack (1982). *Cooking, Cuisine, and Class: A Study in Comparative Sociology.* New York: Cambridge University Press.

Hahamovitch, Cindy (1997). *The Fruits of their Labor: Atlantic Coast Farmworkers and the Making of Migrant Poverty, 1870–1945.* Chapel Hill: University of North Carolina Press.

Halter, Marilyn (2000). *Shopping for Identity: The Marketing of Ethnicity.* New York: Schocken Books.

Hess, John L. and Karen Hess (1989). *The Taste of America.* Columbia: University of South Carolina Press.

Hogan, David Gerard (1997). *Selling 'Em by the Sack: White Castle and the Creation of American Food.* New York: New York University Press.

Hooker, Richard J., ed. (1990). *A Colonial Plantation Cookbook: The Recipe Book of Harriott Pinckney Horry, 1770.* Columbia: University of South Carolina Press.

Inness, Sherrie A. (2001). *Pilaf, Pozole, and Pad Thai: American Women and Ethnic Food.* Amherst: University of Massachusetts Press.

Kraut, Alan (1983). "The Butcher, the Baker, the Pushcart Peddler: Jewish Foodways and Entrepreneurial Opportunity in the East European Immigrant Community." *Journal of American Culture* 6 (Winter): 71–83.

Laudan, Rachel (1996). *The Food of Paradise: Exploring Hawaii's Culinary Heritage.* Honolulu: University of Hawaii Press.

Levenstein, Harvey A. (1988). *Revolution at the Table: The Transformation of the American Diet.* New York: Oxford University Press.

—— (1993). *Paradox of Plenty: A Social History of Eating in Modern America*. New York: Oxford University Press.

Lévi-Strauss, Claude (1962). *Le totemisme aujourd'hui*. Paris: Presses universitaires de France.

McGinty, Brian (1998). *Strong Wine: The Life and Legend of Agostin Haraszthy*. Stanford, CA: Stanford University Press.

Mintz, Sidney W. (1985). *Sweetness and Power: The Place of Sugar in Modern History*. New York: Viking.

—— (1996). *Tasting Food, Tasting Freedom: Excursions into Eating, Culture, and the Past*. Boston: Beacon Press.

Morrow, Jack (2003). "Sushi – Big Time." *New York Press* 13(49) (http://www.nypress.com/).

Nathan, Joan (1994). *Jewish Cooking in America*. New York: Knopf.

Pickle, Linda Schelbitzki (1996). *Contented among Strangers: Rural German-speaking Women and their Families in the Nineteenth-century Midwest*. Urbana: University of Illinois Press.

Pilcher, Jeffrey M. (1998). *Que vivan los Tamales! Food and the Making of Mexican Identity*. Albuquerque: University of New Mexico Press.

—— (2001). "Tex-Mex, Cal-Mex, New Mex, or Whose Mex? Notes on the Historical Geography of Southwestern Cuisine." *Journal of the Southwest* 43(4): 659–79.

Pillsbury, Richard (1998). *No Foreign Food: The American Diet in Time and Place*. Boulder, CO: Westview Press.

Pleck, Elizabeth (2000). *Celebrating the Family: Ethnicity, Consumer Culture, and Family Rituals*. Cambridge, MA: Harvard University Press.

Ritzer, George (1993). *The McDonaldization of Society: An Investigation into the Changing Character of Contemporary Social Life*. Newbury Park, CA: Pine Forge Press.

Rose, Peter G. (1989). *The Sensible Cook: Dutch Foodways in the Old and New World*. Syracuse, NY: Syracuse University Press.

Sack, Daniel (2001). *Whitebread Protestants: Food and Religion in American Culture*. New York: St. Martin's Press.

Schneider, Dorothee (1990). "The German Brewery Workers of New York City in the Late 19th Century." In Robert Asher and Charles Stephenson, eds., *Labor Divided: Race and Ethnicity in the American Working Class*. Albany: State University of New York Press.

Scholosser, Eric (2001). *Fast Food Nation*. New York: HarperCollins.

Shenton, James P., Angelo M. Pellegrini, Dale Brown, Israel Shenker, and Peter Wood (1971). *American Cooking: The Melting Pot*. New York: Time-Life Books.

Simmons, Amelia (1984). *The First American Cookbook*. New York: Dover Press.

Taylor, Joe Gray (1982). *Eating, Drinking, and Visiting in the South*. Baton Rouge: Louisiana State University Press.

Watson, James L., ed. (1997). *Golden Arches East: McDonald's in East Asia*. Stanford, CA: Stanford University Press.

Weatherford, Jack (1991). *Native Roots: How the Indians Enriched America*. New York: Crown Books.

Weaver, William Woys, ed. (1982). *A Quaker Woman's Cookbook: The Domestic Cookery of Elizabeth Ellicott Lea*. Philadelphia: University of Pennsylvania Press.

Witt, Doris (1999). *Black Hunger: Food and the Politics of U.S. Identity*. New York: Oxford University Press.

Wu, Frank H. (2002). *Yellow: Race in America Beyond Black and White*. New York: Basic Books.

CHAPTER TWENTY-TWO

Immigration and Language

NANCY C. CARNEVALE

Issues of language have been and continue to be a central feature of immigrant life in America. This is arguably the case even for immigrants from English-speaking countries who first encounter the American vernacular upon arrival. Much of what we typically associate with immigrant life, including immigrant/ethnic enclaves and generational divisions within immigrant families, is in large measure attributable to language. Language has been the site of cultural as well as political battles dating back to the era of contact when, as one Native American author reminds us, English became America's "second tongue" (Spack 2002).

Language is critical to the creation of individual and group subjectivity. It is through language that we construct our experience and in turn it is language that expresses and reflects that experience. Language is never merely a form of communication; it is the means through which we perceive and understand the world as well as the medium through which we present ourselves in a social context. Language defines the self and its relationship to others. As one linguist notes, "Language . . . is more than a tool for communication of facts between two or more persons. It is the most salient way we have of establishing and advertising our social identities . . . the way we use language is more complex and meaningful than any single fact about our bodies" (Lippi-Green 1997, p. 5).

The writings of immigrant and ethnic Americans themselves confirm the central role that language has played in their experiences of America. The link between identity and language, the way immigrants experience language shift, and the emotional dislocations caused by it are evident in these works. The following are excerpts from English language works, although it is important to recognize that immigrants and ethnics have contributed numerous works to American literature in their own languages as well as in English, sometimes incorporating two or more languages (Sollors 1998, p. 7).

In *Lost in Translation*, Eva Hoffman describes the transition she made while still a child from her native Polish to Canadian English in the post-World War II era as a process of becoming increasingly distanced from words and what they represent: "the problem is that the signifier has become severed from the signified. The words I learn now don't stand for things in the same unquestioned way they did in my native tongue." She explains, for example, how the word "river" in Polish, "a vital sound, energized with the essence of riverhood," becomes in English an empty word, "a word without an aura. It has no accumulated associations for me.... It does not evoke" (Hoffman 1989, p. 106). In the acquired language, words become devoid of the seemingly "natural" meanings they held in the native language.

Hoffman's memoir also grapples with issues of public and private symbolized by the two languages in which she has lived her life. The receipt of the present of a diary as an adolescent forces her to confront directly the issue of which language best represents her interior world. She chooses English, the language of the present, even though the use of this public language results in a certain distancing from her own self, to the extent that she finds herself unable to use the pronoun "I" but must resort to "you." Rather than write about her innermost feelings as befits a teenager confiding to a diary, in English she feels that she can only write as a detached observer.

The public/private split created by living in two languages is a theme that crosses different ethnicities and historical periods. Writing of his youth in a Jewish enclave in the South Bronx during the interwar years, Sherwin Nuland describes the Yiddish spoken by his grandmother as "the sound of home. It was the language that Jews have for centuries called mammaloschen, the tongue spoken by mothers" (Nuland 2003, p. 18). Indeed, psychoanalysts have drawn the connection between language and the mother. Speaking is the means through which one maintains a connection to the mother – by using the "mother tongue" – or separates from her by adopting a foreign language. The difficulty some have in adopting a new language may stem from issues of separation from the mother (Grinberg and Grinberg 1989, p. 106).

Richard Rodriguez's *Hunger of Memory* also grapples with the separation of public and private according to language use along with the difficulties of translating the self into another language. His description of the boyhood experience of his grandmother calling to him in Spanish in the presence of an American friend illustrates these issues:

He wanted to know what she had said. I started to tell him, to say – to translate her Spanish words into English. The problem was, however, that though I knew how to translate exactly *what* she had told me, I realized that any translation would distort the deepest meaning of her message: It had been directed only to me. This message of intimacy could never be translated because it was not *in* the words she had used but passed *through* them. So any translation would have seemed wrong; her words would have been stripped of an essential meaning. (Rodriguez 1981, pp. 30–1)

Spanish was for the young Rodriguez the language of home and intimacy. In contrasting his parents' use of Spanish and English, he writes: "The language of their Mexican past sounded in counterpoint to the English of public society. The words would come quickly, with ease. Conveyed through those sounds was the pleasing, soothing, consoling reminder of being at home" (Rodriguez 1981, p. 13). Just as Spanish symbolized the intimacy of family life, English came to embody the public world of achievement and, with it, greater isolation. Rodriguez seems to have been unable to move easily between the public and private worlds symbolized by English and Spanish. Once he mastered English, Rodriguez could not return to Spanish – or to his family. As he explains, "A powerful guilt blocked my spoken words . . . I'd know the words I wanted to say, but I couldn't manage to say them.

I would try to speak, but everything I said seemed to me horribly anglicized" (Rodriguez 1981, p. 13). While Rodriguez situates his discussion of language within the context of intimacy, he is also describing the inability of his Spanish language self and relationships to survive the translation into the larger English-speaking world outside of his home. Hoffman is more cognizant of what is involved in the wholesale adoption of another language, in her case as for Rodriguez the public language of English: "This language is beginning to invent another me" (Hoffman 1989, p. 121).

On a day-to-day level, second-generation children often assume responsibilities beyond their years due to a greater facility with English than their parents. Esmeralda Santiago writes of her visits to the welfare office to translate for her Puerto Rican mother: "I was always afraid that if I said something wrong, if I mispronounced a word or used the wrong tense, the social workers would say no, and we might be evicted from our apartment . . ." (Santiago 1993, p. 249). Along with adult responsibilities sometimes came a sense of superiority over parents who were infantilized by their linguistic dependence on their children. In her novel, *The Translator*, Suki Kim captures the frustration of a Korean immigrant who has to rely on his daughter to translate for him:

> He was certain that if he could speak the language he would resolve all matters with a quick phone call. He seemed to resent Grace for relating to him what he did not want to hear, that the debts must be paid instantly. . . . But most of all, he seemed angry at his own powerlessness. The ordeal of having to rely on his young daughter for such basic functions humiliated him. He never seemed to forget that humiliation. (Kim 2003, pp. 108–9)

The ambivalence about living in a new world and a new language is sometimes encapsulated in the process of taking on an American name. The author Chang-Rae Lee describes the experience for his mother and himself of selecting an American name in anticipation of his entering the first grade. Beyond learning English ("at all costs he must learn English, and with a good accent"),

> Next, the boy would need an American name. This was more difficult for her, because all those funny-sounding names held no meaning for her, no nuance or significance. An old astrologer who consulted ancient charts and equations had chosen my Korean name, matching the exact time of my birth on this day, of this month, of that Year of the Snake, with certain characters, to arrive at the most auspicious of combinations. But here in America she had to leave the crucial naming to me . . . for weeks I couldn't decide between Greg and Peter and Bobby. But Greg and Peter and Bobby really weren't like me. . . ." (Watkins-Goffman 2001, p. 90)

The selection of an American name extends the emptiness of the signifier to the individual him or herself, suggesting the impossibility of retaining one's pre-migration or native language identity in English.

In *Mount Allegro*, an autobiographical novel of Italian immigrant life in the early decades of the twentieth century, Jerre Mangione reveals the way that language delineated his life into two separate worlds, echoing the distinction that Hoffman and Rodriguez explicitly draw between the private and public worlds mirrored in language. Of all of the differences between the Italian world of the home and the American world outside, writes Mangione, "The difference that pained me most was that of language, probably because I was aware of it most often" (Mangione 1972, p. 50). Unlike Rodriguez's family which, at the behest of the Catholic nuns who were his teachers, stopped requiring Rodriguez to speak Spanish at home, Mangione's mother insisted that her children only address her in Italian although she took pride in their ability to speak English. Conflict manifested through embarrassment and arose for Mangione only when his two linguistic universes and the two distinct parts of his life that they represented collided, such as when his mother called to him in Italian while he was playing in the street with his non-Italian friends.

Yet even within his own home, Mangione experienced a split with regard to language, for he realized early on that "the language we called Italian and spoke at home was not Italian. It was a Sicilian dialect which only Sicilians could understand." As a second-generation child, Mangione manifested an acute sensitivity to the regional differences of Italian and the implications for their use: "Proper Italian sounded like the melody of church bells and it was fresh and delicate compared to the earthy sounds of the dialect we spoke." Mangione goes on to note that he found it "hard to understand how two persons could carry on an honest conversation in a language so fancy" (Mangione 1972, p. 51). For the second generation, differences between dialects spoken with familiars and standard versions of their own languages may complicate their experience of language.

A common although little discussed phenomenon among very young second-generation children is the inability to distinguish between the two (or more) languages spoken in the home. Anthropologist Norma Gonzalez writes of her own experience communicating with her Spanish-speaking grandmother:

> I was convinced that what was intelligible to me was intelligible to her because somehow we understood and communicated. Languages had blurred, and it was difficult to disentangle where one left off and another began. There was no boundedness to language, no readily identifiable edges that could be marked off. There was only communication, however and whenever it took place. How often have I heard of Latino adults who as children were admonished to speak only English in the school grounds and their unspoken dread that somehow they would not be able to tell the difference. (Gonzalez 2001, pp. 49–50)

Unlike the first- and second-generation authors cited above, many first-generation immigrants were not able to make a complete transition from one language to another. Immigrants past and present have instead relied on their own distinctive idioms that reflected and articulated the immigrants' new lives in America. By the turn of the twentieth century, for example, Italian immigrants had created a creole which consisted of Italian dialects, English, and Italianized English words, which has been referred to as "Italglish" or "Italo-Americanese." This form of speech, far more common than actual knowledge of standard English, was understood by Italian immigrants across the country although regional variations existed. Californian Italian Americans used words that reflected differences in their local American environments as well as the fact that most of them originated from the northern provinces of Italy as opposed to the southern Italians who made up the bulk of the Italian population on the east coast. Yiddish underwent a similar transformation in the early years of the century although the Yiddish case is unique in that the Jewish community actively debated the changes to the language as they were occurring, demonstrating an appreciation of the relationship between language and culture that has not always been evident with other immigrant/ethnic groups. These hybrid languages often encompassed elements from non-English-language-speaking immigrants encountered for the first time in America. Nuland describes his father's speech as:

> a self-constructed English pronounced in a way that emanated from no one's lips but his, a particularistic accent that is better described as having been Yiddishoid than Yiddish, infiltrated as it was with the speech mannerisms of the Italian-born garment workers with whom he toiled in the sweatshops . . . I have never heard anyone speak that way, either in terms of pronunciation or sentence structure. (Nuland 2003, p. 10)

More recently, "Spanglish" has become widely recognized, if not necessarily accepted, as the language of many immigrants in the United States from Spanish-speaking countries.

Although the blending of immigrant and host languages followed similar patterns, there are important differences in the histories and particularly in the reception of these immigrant idioms by Americans. While Yiddish incorporated English in various ways, for reasons unique to the Yiddish language American English borrowed from it as well, a reciprocity which did not occur to the same degree with Italian languages, for example, that were being spoken at the same time. Yiddish is arguably the most embedded language in American English, with widely known borrowings, such as "maven" and "schmuck," as well as recognizable speaking patterns and styles of speech (Dillard 1985, pp. 103–4). This has lent Yiddish a certain degree of acceptance through familiarity, at least in major urban centers such as New York. But borrowings from immigrant languages are a common phenomenon that predates the age of migration. They have significantly expanded American English, in the process helping to define and express American life. "Yankee" and "dollar," for example, are both derived from the Dutch who were a strong presence in early New York. More profound was the influence of the speech patterns of the descendants of African slaves on the speech of southern whites, an influence that extended to the plantation owners (Dillard 1985).

Language and National Identity in American History

The history of language in America – English as well as other languages – is interwoven with the struggle to create a national identity which, given the racial dynamics of American history, has itself been a raced identity, at different times implicitly or explicitly so. Beginning with early English colonists who eventually came to view Native American languages as inferior, language has been used as a means of asserting political and cultural domination. Conceptions about the national language and non-English languages have changed over time, often reflecting social and cultural anxieties regarding newcomers.

English became the language of the country by sheer force of numbers. Although French and Spanish colonizers brought their own languages, to current-day Louisiana and the southwest respectively, the English colonies were far more numerous. According to one historian (Gray 1999) in the early years of contact between colonists and Native Americans, language itself initially carried no connotations of racial inferiority. Early colonists did, however, believe that the English language was the only way to convert Native Americans to Christianity and thus redeem them from their "savage" state. Beginning in the eighteenth century, language and nationhood became explicitly linked in the thinking of Romantic philosophers led by Herder. This was the underpinning for the association of different languages with the concepts of civilized and uncivilized that were thought to reflect the level of development of a people. Thus, the denigrated languages of Native Americans became further evidence of their supposed barbarism.

Already in the 1600s, missionary schools were established which began receiving government aid once the United States were formed, anticipating a formal "English-only" education reform movement for Native Americans which was instituted following the Civil War, just as settlers were increasingly moving westward and encroaching on native lands. This policy dominated linguistic relations between whites and Native Americans until 1934 when the Indian Reorganization Act was passed, allowing for tribal self-government and the renewal of Native American languages, legislation that was not fully implemented until 1990 with the passage of the Native American Languages Act (Spack 2002).

Language was an instrument of domination in the slave system as well as in the case of Native Americans. Beginning with their capture, slave traders separated African slaves according to their language groups in an attempt to thwart any uprisings. Once in the New World, slave owners punished any who were caught speaking African languages, in at least a few cases by removing their tongues. The struggle of slaves to become literate in English in the face of intense opposition by slaveholders is well known, however; slaveholders jealously guarded their linguistic privilege, opposing efforts by slaves to acquire more than a rudimentary ability to speak English. As one scholar notes, "control over language use was an integral part of the system of racial domination that developed in and from slavery" (Schmidt 2000, p. 108).

Early Americans including Noah Webster and John Adams believed that language held a central place in the creation of the United States and the formation of a national identity. By creating a distinctively American language, they and others believed Americans could more readily distinguish themselves from the British and establish a new nation. Noah Webster's near fanatic devotion to perpetuating a standardized spoken and written form of American English was an expression of this desire for linguistic unity as a precursor to the formation of a national identity, as was John Adams's proposal to establish a national language academy to enshrine English as the national language. Although not widely debated at the time, there was post-revolutionary discussion of adopting entirely different languages such as French or even ancient Greek or Hebrew in order to further distance Americans from the British (Heath 1981; Shell 1993).

Even though English was the predominant language, early America was linguistically diverse. According to the 1790 census, one in four Americans did not speak English as a first language, representing 902,000 people out of a total population of 4 million (independent of Native Americans). Advertisements for runaway indentured servants and slaves between 1725 and 1775 provide some sense of just how many languages were commonly spoken. According to the ads, the runaways spoke a number of languages including Dutch, French, Welsh, and Irish in addition to their own native languages (Lepore 2002, p. 28). In perhaps the most striking example of the tenuous sway of English in early America, German was the first language of as many as two-thirds of Pennsylvanians. In total, some 45,000 German immigrants populated the colonies by 1745 (Dillard 1985, p. 96). Indeed, Benjamin Franklin complained bitterly about the preponderance of German language newspapers, legal documents, and street signs and was no doubt equally infuriated, as we can assume others were, by the German language versions of the Constitution and the Articles of Confederation that were in circulation. German as well as French language schools abounded and many Americans attended non-English church services and/or read foreign language newspapers. Nevertheless, despite the significant percentage of non-English speakers in early America, the ideas of Webster and others were largely a reaction to British colonial rule rather than the number of non-English speakers in the newly independent United States (Lepore 2002, pp. 28–9).

While disputes regarding the Spanish language are generally perceived as a recent phenomenon, there is a long history of conflict and some tolerance for the Spanish language in the United States. From the annexation of New Mexico in 1848 up until statehood was granted in 1912, Spanish coexisted with (and in some situations superseded) English in the administration of the territory due to the predominance of Spanish speakers, although the 1848 Treaty of Guadalupe Hidalgo that formalized the annexation of the area was understood at the time as ensuring protection for the culture of the native-born population, a protection that was interpreted as extending to language rights. Spanish was widely used despite the fact that the "Anglos" who had immigrated to the area held a disproportionate share of political power in the territory. Court proceedings, legal documents, and official notices all employed both languages. In the early territorial phase, classes at most public schools were conducted entirely in Spanish while others offered bilingual education, with the smallest percentage reserved for English-only schools (Conklin and Lourie 1983, p. 67; Kloss 1977, 129–34). Statehood, however, was delayed until 1912 when English speakers finally came to outnumber Spanish speakers. Spanish then began to lose its stature and to decline in public use despite the large numbers of Spanish speakers that remained in the new state and the official language rights guaranteed by the new state constitution on a "trial basis" and renewed twice thereafter in 1931 and 1943.

While were largely tolerated and at times even Flourished in the U.S., paticularly in the nineteenth century, non-English languages (with the exception of Native American languages) is part of the national history, this changed dramatically with the advent of a large non-northern European immigration stream. This mass arrival of immigrants who did not appear to fit easily into existing racial categories raised new questions regarding race and its relationship to language and ultimately to definitions of Americanism.

The "new immigrants" consisted of southern and eastern Europeans who were seen as differing noticeably in appearance and customs from the northern European immigrants who preceded them. Their large numbers – over 12 million between 1901 and 1920 – and concentration in urban centers made this migration more visible than those in the past. Bolstered by the intellectual currents of Anglo-Saxonism and scientific racialism that had swept Europe and America earlier in the century and had filtered down into American society at large, these southern Italians, Poles, Russian Jews, and other immigrant groups were widely perceived as racially ambiguous and as such inferior to native-born Americans. Some race theorists and social scientists believed that language was related to race, even though this relationship was never precisely defined and often contradictory. Anglo-Saxon superiority was associated with the English language itself, considered by some to be the highest form of speech. While English was thus elevated in status, the languages of the new immigrants – and their speakers – were devalued. The explosion of intelligence testing beginning with tests conducted on immigrant recruits during World War I reflects then contemporary ideas regarding immigrant languages. The tests found that southern and eastern Europeans had low intelligence due to hereditary inferiority that included foreign language usage (Portes and Rumbaut 2001, p. 115).

Beginning in the late nineteenth century, laws were enacted that linked linguistic ability with full participation in American life and later with entry into the country. This legislation reflects in part the special resonance that literacy and the English language held in this period and, in the case of restrictionist legislation, the uncertainty that existed regarding the possibility of racial assimilation of the newcomers. In the 1880s and 1890s, individual states began enacting voting laws that required English literacy, although some had instituted similar legislation as far back as the 1850s. In 1906, for the first time in the history of the nation, prospective citizens were required to pass a nominal English test in order to become naturalized. In 1917, a literacy test to restrict entrance to the country was introduced following three previous attempts in the 20 years prior to that. Although the new immigrants were not named in the legislation, their relatively high levels of illiteracy along with the discussions surrounding the bill make it clear that the literacy test was aimed at limiting the immigration of the "illiterate races," as the newcomers were referred to in Congressional testimony surrounding the bill, largely because restrictionists doubted their ability to assimilate into American society. The content of the literacy test changed over time, but immigrants were essentially required to read a passage in their own language or dialect and demonstrate comprehension of it. Literacy was used to demonstrate the capacity to acquire English and the superior traits associated with the "English-speaking races." Important voices of opposition to the renowned anthropologist Franz Boas, who denounced any notion of linguistic and racial hierachy (Carnevale 2000a).

American entry into World War I and the related hysteria over national loyalties heightened nativist sentiment and gave rise to the ideal of "100 percent Americanism" which entailed a rejection of all things foreign. The use of immigrant languages in any form was a particular target of anti-immigrant activity in this period. Local ordinances were enacted mandating that foreigners use English when in public. No group was more affected by the backlash against foreign languages in this period than German Americans. Although the bulk of German immigration preceded and was eclipsed by the immigrants of the turn of the twentieth century, at the time of the war, Germans were a large and well-organized group and the German language was widely spoken and read in German communities across the country. With American entry into the war, the public use of German in any context was strongly discouraged by official actions as well as an overzealous public. In some cases, for example, vigilantes painted the windows of the homes of German immigrants yellow or covered them with notices indicating that the inhabitants of the house spoke German or read German language newspapers. German street and town names were changed, organizations with German names were pressured into changing them, and German words that had entered American English were substituted with English equivalents, such as "liberty cabbage" for sauerkraut. The number of German language periodicals declined dramatically, German language books were taken off the shelves of public libraries and, in some cases, publicly burned. A large network of German language schools was wiped out and German was dropped from curricula in schools across the country, from the elementary to the college level, sometimes in response to student boycotts (Wittke 1936). While some localities issued formal laws prohibiting the use of German, much of the decline in the language can be attributed to self-censorship within an era of pervasive and vociferous hostility.

The Americanization movement which peaked in the 1920s brought the public and private sectors of the country together in a massive effort to assimilate immigrants, in large part through English language acquisition. The importance of the English language to Americanization was captured in the slogan, "One language, one country, one flag." The Bureau of Naturalization, the forerunner of the Immigration and Naturalization Service, along with the Office of Education, coordinated efforts throughout the country to Americanize immigrants through English language instruction. English courses were provided at adult evening schools, and by employers on the job, some of whom even made night school compulsory for immigrants. Still others offered monetary incentives to workers or compensatory time to learn English. Settlement houses and other social work organizations encouraged immigrants to learn English. English was even taught to some immigrants in their homes – by their own children. Public School 62 in New York City conducted an experiment in "home teaching" whereby second-generation children would teach their "foreign-language parent" how to speak, read, and write English for 15 minutes each day. The degree to which immigrants experienced pressure to learn English is reflected in a 1918 New York State law which mandated all minors aged 16–21 who could not speak English to enroll in adult classes to complete at least the fifth grade.

The dominant society's concern with language was reflected in a preoccupation with the proper usage of English. Fears regarding the degradation of the "American stock" through the introduction of racially inferior immigrants were reflected in concerns that the English language was becoming debased by foreign speakers. As Bailey (1991) notes, concerns about linguistic purity usually arise during periods of national stress which, in this case, took the form of a massive influx of immigrants. At the same time, second-generation children were required to learn and use proper English in order to gain full entry into American society, as the pedagogical practices of the New York City public schools demonstrate. Educators and school administrators placed a premium on instructing immigrant children in how to speak, read, and write English. Indeed, civics was subsumed under the study of English. As one historian of education has noted, "Linguistic transformation was central to making Americans out of immigrants," and the public schools were instrumental in this transformation (Brumberg 1986, p. 6). Yet merely learning English was not enough. The language had to be learned correctly to avoid its debasement by foreign speakers. Deviations in usage were not tolerated. Teachers with any trace of a foreign accent were not permitted to teach courses in English. As late as 1931, educators still saw themselves combating "those tendencies which in a cosmopolitan city like New York tend to debase accepted usage and to inject into English speech foreignisms of pronunciation and intonation" (Carnevale 2000a, p. 77).

World War II marked another period of linguistic intolerance, particularly for those immigrants from countries that were at war with the United States. The wartime imperative for cultural unity created an atmosphere that encouraged all ethnolinguistic minorities to suppress their cultural distinctiveness in exchange for entering the American mainstream. The text of a contemporary cartoon captures the predominant attitude toward "enemy languages": above caricatures of the Japanese, Italian, and German leaders appears the caption "Don't speak the enemy's language."

The German language, already gravely affected by the anti-German sentiment of World War I, was effectively finished off as a major language group by the war's end, with the exception of some religious groups, such as the Old Order Amish who continued to use it and the Pennsylvania Dutch who continued to speak a heavily Germanized English. The use of the Italian language declined markedly in this period. The experience of Italian Americans in the war years provides an example of how intentional and unintentional pressures during times of particular national stress can combine to restrict foreign language usage.

Soon after Pearl Harbor, some 600,000 Italian nationals were declared "enemy aliens," initiating a period of close scrutiny. Italian language usage was considered suspect by government authorities such as the Federal Bureau of Investigation which inspected Italian American homes and monitored their institutions and publications. The use of Italian in any context – familial, business, or social, whether written or spoken – raised suspicions of a disloyal "fifth column." Italian Americans quickly grasped this pervasive sensibility. Individual Italian Americans denied knowledge of the Italian language (sometimes falsely). Some Americanized their names. Parents declined to teach Italian to their children and shopkeepers placed signs in their windows declaring "No Italian spoken for the duration of the war." With US entry into the war, two-thirds of New York City high schools and colleges where Italian had previously been taught stopped offering the language. Enrollment in the remaining programs, which had previously consisted largely of second-generation Italian Americans, declined precipitously and never recovered. The publication of Italian language periodicals dropped by 40 percent in the 1940s. Similarly, Italian radio broadcasts declined in terms of the number of programs and the extent of their reach. While Italian language usage, like German, would likely have decreased over time in any case, the war heightened American suspicion of foreign language use and hastened language shift (Carnevale 2003).

The post-World War II era's emphasis on submerging cultural differences gave way to a national change in attitudes towards immigrants/ethnics and language, beginning in the1960s. Although designed to protect southern blacks, the Voting Rights Act of 1965, which finally barred discrimination based on language and education, signaled a period of liberalization in English language requirements for participation in American political life. In January 1968, Congress passed the Bilingual Education Act as part of the Elementary and Secondary Education Amendments of 1967. The goal of the legislation was to provide bilingual education, primarily to Spanish-speaking children in the southwest, New York, and Florida, but also to other non-English-speaking students in order to help them learn English. Legislators argued that by learning English early, these children could overcome the linguistic barriers to economic and social advancement. Although the ultimate aim of the legislation was for the children to learn English rather than to retain their native languages, the willingness of the legislators to fund bilingual instruction reflected a new receptivity – or at least a diminished hostility – towards foreign languages, even if legislators were largely motivated by the prospect of immigrant votes.

From the beginning, the act was woefully underfunded, suggesting a less than universally enthusiastic response, at least on the presidential level. Initially, legislators called for $30 million to fund bilingual education programs beginning with fiscal year 1969, but President Johnson finally agreed to a mere $7.5 million. Still, the legislation paved the way for immigrants and ethnics to claim the right to their native languages.

The 1974 Lau v. Nichols case significantly expanded the scope of the Bilingual Education Act. As a result of the lawsuit, local school boards were required to provide bilingual education to any foreign-speaking population of 20 or more children, regardless of whether or not state or federal funds were available. This landmark decision contributed to the enactment of the 1974 amendments to the Bilingual Education Act, essentially expanding federal support for bilingual education. Significantly, although bilingual education was still meant to be transitional, the new legislation did not preclude the possibility of establishing programs designed to maintain native languages and cultures. A second set of amendments in 1978 further elaborating the bilingual education program demonstrated the continuing interest in and support for bilingual education. Nor was the federal government alone in proposing bilingual education programs. Forty states followed suit, including such unlikely candidates as Alabama, Arkansas, and Nebraska, either mandating or allowing bilingual education. Most of the states emphasized the transitional nature of the programs. By 1980, the overall federal budget for bilingual education programs totaled $167 million. Over 300,000 children were enrolled in such programs nationwide and a number of new federal agencies, such as the Office of Bilingual Education and Minority Languages Affairs within the Department of Education, had been formed.

The Bilingual Education Act and subsequent amendments were passed against the backdrop of the liberalization of immigration laws through the 1965 amendment to the McCarran–Walter Act of 1952. This immigration legislation did away with selection according to race or ancestry, opening the way for a new wave of immigration comprised mainly of immigrants from outside of Europe, particularly from Latin America, Asia, and the Carribean.

The ethnic revival of the 1960s and 1970s also formed a significant part of the context in which bilingual education developed. In this period, ethnic Americans began to assert cultural identities which included languages. This reassertion of ethnic pride undoubtedly contributed to a more linguistically permissive environment in the United States. Although Spanish-speaking children were the overwhelming beneficiaries of bilingual education programs, other ethnic groups took advantage of the legislation as well. In New York, for example, bilingual programs for Italian children flourished in the 1970s.

While the legislation and the assertion of ethnicity of the 1960s and 1970s have ushered in and reflected a new era of tolerance for immigrant languages, some

Americans have resisted these changes. Bilingual education has been and continues to be a lightning rod for American attitudes toward immigrants and language. The attempts to make English the official national language during the 1980s and 1990s – at the height of the latest mass wave of immigration – along with recent efforts to dismantle bilingual education programs, are indicative of the degree to which language and national membership remain linked. During the late 1980s and early 1990s, 23 states passed measures making English the official state language when Congress resisted repeated attempts to pass a constitutional amendment in the same period. Although most of these laws were not enforced, in a few states the measure was more actively applied. In Arizona, for example, where an English-only law was narrowly passed by voters in a referendum, welfare workers and state park rangers were required to give information in English, regardless of whether they were capable of assisting non-English speakers in their own languages. The law was later declared unconstitutional by the Arizona Supreme Court, the first English-only law to be overturned since the 1920s.

In 1996, HR bill 123, which sought to make English the official language of the United States, was approved by the House of Representatives but was later defeated in the Senate. House Speaker Newt Gingrich expressed the concerns of the Republican backers of the 1996 measure during what was described as an "emotional debate" which lasted almost six hours: "Is there a thing we call American? Is it unique? It is vital historically to assert and establish that English is the common language at the heart of our civilization." Yet, as Democratic opponents of the bill pointed out, 97 percent of Americans speak English well and less than 1 percent of federal documents are printed in any other language. Just as in the early years of the twentieth century, the English only movement arose in response to a specific immigration stream, in this case mainly Spanish speakers whose sheer numbers raised fears of a linguistic/cultural threat. Today, legislation similar to the 1996 measure is pending in Congress and individual states continue to pass statutes recognizing English as the state language.

Language issues surfaced in the 1990s in other contexts. In 1996, the Oakland School Board set off a nationwide debate on Ebonics, currently known as African American Vernacular English (AAVE), when they formally recognized it as a language and asked for funding for bilingual education in an effort to better teach standard American English to the largely African American school body. Critics of the ruling, including many African Americans, contended that what was more accurately described as a linguistic style had been elevated to the status of a distinct language, but some scholars contend that AAVE has its own structure and is systematic; it is "not the random and careless speech which many mistakenly assume it to be" (Mufwene, Rickford, Bailey, and Baugh 1998, p. 2). Features of AAVE can be found in the speech of between 60 and 80 percent of African Americans (Johnson 2000, p. 141).

Bilingual education again became a topic of intense debate in the 1990s, culminating in 1998 with California's controversial decision to do away with bilingual education after years of maintaining one of the most extensive programs in the nation. The opponents of bilingual education included Hispanic Americans who felt that their children were disadvantaged by these programs which, they claim, fail to teach their children English. It is noteworthy that the continuing debates over whether to make English the official language and whether to maintain bilingual education programs took place at a time when the ethos of multiculturalism pervaded college campuses and led to intense debates at all levels of society regarding the meaning of being American. Yet, Spanish notwithstanding, language does not form a significant part of the current understanding of multiculturalism (Sollors 1998, p. 4).

For the dominant culture in the United States, the desire to have immigrants and their children speak English at the expense of their own native languages remains a part of the nation's ongoing struggle to define itself, to stake out the figurative borders of America. The link between language and full membership in American society, however, remains a contested one. That attention to language issues is most intense during times of national crisis such as war and periods of mass immigration suggests that language is also a key area for the expression of cultural anxieties and insecurities.

Interdisciplinary Perspectives on Language and Ethnicity

A number of disciplines consider the relationship of language to immigrants and ethnicity, resulting in a significant degree of overlap between fields, particularly those of sociolinguistics and linguistic anthropology. Since it is somewhat artificial to separate them and difficult to summarize such a large and diverse body of literature here, the following discussion highlights the major interdisciplinary insights and areas of inquiry into language and ethnicity.

Underlying the analysis of language and ethnicity is an understanding of the strong tie between language and ethnic identity. As a sign system, language signifies ethnicity and functions as a medium to transmit culture and ethnicity. On a subjective level, language is experienced as constitutive of both the individual and the larger group culture. That is, native speakers of minority languages often consider language as an "essential or inborn (therefore 'essentialist') characteristic of 'the people'" (Fishman 1999, p. 160). The ethnic language is not always essential to the transmission or maintenance of ethnic identity and culture. Even if not actively used, language can serve a symbolic function in transmitting ethnicity. Nor do all ethnic groups in the United States or elsewhere experience the link between language and ethnic identity to the same degree. Social and historical circumstances condition the degree to which ethnic groups connect the two. Religion is far more central to Jewish ethnicity, for example, than language.

Much of the work on language and immigrants has examined the relationship between language and ethnicity through language shift, language maintenance, and bilingualism. *Language shift* is a commonly used measure of the degree of assimilation. Indeed, language has been described as "the best single pattern of cultural change and an early indicator of social assimilation" (Lopez 1999, p. 221). The prevailing sociological/sociolinguistic model of language shift is one of generational change leading from acculturation to assimilation. The first generation uses the native language almost exclusively with only a rudimentary knowledge of English; the second generation is bilingual to various degrees, with at least the ability to understand and perhaps even to speak the language of their parents. This group experiences a complete language shift to English by the time they reach adulthood if not sooner although private usage of the native tongue in the household of origin may persist. By the third generation, the native language is lost since the second-generation parents speak English at home, although interest in the language on the part of the third generation may resurface as part of an attempt to construct a symbolic ethnic identity (Fishman 1989; Veltman 1983). This model is used to explain the fate of European languages in America from the wave of immigrants at the turn of the twentieth century as well as the linguistic experience of more recent immigrant groups including Spanish-speaking and Asian language groups. The relatively rapid and complete shift to English is attributed to the economic and social advantages that accrue to English speakers, along with the pervasive association of English with the dominant American culture, and the clearly elevated status that English enjoys above all other languages. Another outcome besides language shift is the creation of hybrid languages noted above. Some scholars question the stability of Spanglish and similar hybrids and so object to the designation "language," preferring instead to discuss this in terms of a transitional phenomenon *en route* to language shift.

Given the rapidity of language shift, *language maintenance* in America has historically been particularly difficult. The overwhelming dominance of English in all areas of American life and the general lack of interest, both culturally and politically, in promoting other languages combine to account for the difficulty in maintaining minority languages. Language shift is facilitated by the immigrant group itself within the American context. The implicitly high economic and cultural status of English leads foreign language speakers to positively evaluate English language speakers within their own communities. Thus, the immigrant/ethnic family itself assures the transmission of the dominant language as English speakers within the family gain higher status for their facility with English. As more and more English speakers within the immigrant/ethnic community are rewarded by their own communities for their language facility, the language of origin becomes superfluous (Fishman 1989, p. 206).

Linguistic anthropologists and others have focused attention to a greater degree on the ideological dimensions of language usage and how power is exercised through language to explain phenomena like language shift and language maintenance. Since it is through the control of language that access to resources is limited and institutional power maintained, language can be seen as a kind of "symbolic capital," an asset which can be transformed into social and economic capital. Through "symbolic domination," the dominant language comes to appear is inherently superior when in fact it receives its legitimation through the state and in particular through the educational system (Bourdieu 1985, 1977). Linguistic minorities and the working class internalize this belief to the point where the superiority of the dominant language becomes unquestionable. Indeed, language shift could not occur so readily nor would language maintenance be so difficult if it were only a matter of the social and economic rewards theoretically available to English language speakers in the United States. Rather, it is the *language ideologies* – broadly defined as the meanings and values assigned to language – that play the decisive role in determining whether language shift or language maintenance will take place. The individual is impacted by the social forces that affect language shift and language maintenance through the ideologies that have accrued to a given language and that contribute to the perception of one language as devalued and another as dominant (Woolard 1998).

There are situations in which language maintenance is more likely. In religious communities in which language and religious practices are closely tied, such as among the Amish or those socially and economically isolated communities such as Native American reservations where language maintenance is also a matter of cultural survival, original languages are more likely to be maintained. Language communities that contain high concentrations of foreign language speakers who are also relatively isolated can lead to higher than average levels of language maintenance, as is the case in certain contemporary Spanish-speaking communities. In general, a steady influx of new arrivals is the most likely source of language maintenance.

Bilingualism is largely a phenomenon of the second generation although in some sense this is a misnomer because in the United States bilingualism is more of a transitional phenomenon on the way to English monolingualism. Indeed, the rates of language loss in the United States far surpass those of other countries. According to one study, the language loss that occurs in just one generation in America would take 350 years in the average nation (Hakuta 1986, p. 167). The historical circumstances upon entering the United States along with the linguistic history of the country of origin can lead to different rates of bilingualism. Sociologists have found, for example, that differences do exist between ethnic groups, with Spanish speakers having higher rates of bilingualism than Asian language speakers, for example (Lopez 1999, pp. 216–18). Contrary to popular perception, however, Spanish language shift is proceeding at a rate comparable to if not greater than that experienced by earlier immigrants (Gonzalez 2001, p. 177). It is important to keep in mind that there are tremendous differences within language groups as well as between them. Spanish speakers from Central American countries that have had a traumatic recent history, such as Nicaragua and El Salvador, display a willingness to abandon their language along with other cultural markers that forms a distinct contrast to other Latino groups. Another factor in accounting for different experiences of bilingualism and language maintenance is the assertion of ethnic pride, which is evident today in certain Spanish-speaking groups such as Mexican Americans (Chicanos), and African Americans. Distinctive language usage for these groups has become a way to assert ethnicity and insider status in an effort to wrest control of negative stereotypes from the dominant culture. In the case of African Americans whose culture including speech has become such a central feature of American popular music and culture, using AAVE in certain contexts is a way to assume a positive social/ethnic identity. Unlike the earlier waves of immigration at the turn of the twentieth century, more recent arrivals are not necessarily from lower socioeconomic backgrounds. Highly educated and skilled immigrants who come to the United States already fluent in English – from the Philippines or India, for example – are less likely to feel that their children must give up their language of origin to assimilate and may actively encourage bilingualism.

A phenomenon related to bilingualism that is the subject of much of the work on language and immigrants is *code-switching*, which is the use of elements of two languages (the minority and majority tongue or a standard version of a language and a dialect) in the same linguistic event. This behavior functions, among other ways, to assert a specific identity, to signal in-group status, or to position oneself in a particular way with relation to the addressee. Second-generation ethnic Americans are most likely to have the ability to use elements of both English and the language of their parents, even if they are not fluent in the latter. Sometimes it is an imperfect knowledge of the parental language that requires code-switching to English to express concepts that may or may not be unique to the American context but that the speaker cannot otherwise convey. In some cases, it is precisely those with a mastery of both languages who integrate them with great verbal dexterity. In the case of the first generation who may have limited fluency in English, code-switching allows them to claim some knowledge of and the attendant status associated with the dominant language. Code-switching provides evidence of the dual worlds that immigrants and the second generation in particular occupy.

Research on the evaluation of accents has direct relevance for the study of immigrants and language. Studies have confirmed that speakers with foreign accents are evaluated depending upon the listener's attitudes toward the perceived group, region, or country to which the speaker is presumed to belong. Speakers with high-status accents – French, for example, due to its high-culture associations – are evaluated more positively than those with low-status accents. How accents come to be privileged or devalued is a function of historical context. For example, although one could argue that few countries have as rich a cultural legacy as Italy, the fact that the United States is home to the descendants of millions of immigrants from southern Italy who were initially associated with poverty, illiteracy, and criminality has given speakers with an Italian accent a comparatively lower status in America. Attitudes and behaviors towards linguistically distinct speakers are influenced by the attributions given to a language. Speakers respond accordingly, by for example manipulating their use of high-status accents to benefit from their privileged position (Jones 2001). Often it is the speakers from non-white groups whose accents are devalued, providing a basis for denying social, economic, and other forms of access to the dominant language group society (Lippi-Green 1997). These insights regarding accents are useful in considering the ways in which host societies react to foreign language speakers and immigrant communities in general as well as how immigrants evaluate their own members.

While not a direct outgrowth of the study of language and immigrants, certain concepts related to language are particularly applicable to this subject. The relationship of language to thought and culture is an area of study that applies directly to bilinguals. Linguistic relativism, which is associated with the anthropologists Edward Sapir and Franz Boas and the linguist Benjamin Lee Whorf, holds that cultural knowledge is bounded to varying degrees by language. Whorf went even further in proposing linguistic determinism, that is, that language actually shapes thought. Together, these two propositions constitute the Whorfian hypothesis that maintains that each language creates different forms of thought and general worldview for their speakers. The implications of the Whorfian hypothesis for understanding the experience of the bilingual immigrant or ethnic are intriguing. Although the degree to which thought affects culture continues to be debated, at a minimum we can surmise that immigrants and ethnics with access to two or more languages have a larger frame of reference for conceptualizing their experience. Other linguistic and psychological theories of language place less emphasis on its effect on thought, and psychological studies of the mental worlds of bilinguals have been inconclusive.

There are marked differences between men and women with regard to language usage, with implications for the study of immigrants and language. Women are more likely than men to learn the standard form of speech as a means of social elevation. But studies of lower-class women also indicate that women are often assigned or assume the dual function of elevating themselves through use of the standard language as well as maintaining the traditional forms of the culture including local dialects (Cameron 1992). The ambivalence of the immigrants over the necessity of learning English and their loyalty to their traditional languages – and what each of these positions implies for identity – is sometimes projected onto women.

Future Directions in the Study of Language and Immigrants in America

The subject of language and immigrants has mainly been the purview of scholars outside of the field of history. While the various social-scientific approaches acknowledge the importance of historical specificity, these studies do not by and large provide substantive historical analysis. Typically, those historians who have approached the topic have considered English language acquisition as an index of assimilation or seen language maintenance as a measure of the persistence of ethnicity. These assumptions have limited findings and restricted other lines of inquiry. For example, the lack of facility in the language of the immigrant generation is not necessarily a marker of cultural assimilation. Recent data based on interviews with second-generation youth indicate that even in the absence of knowledge of the parental language, the second generation can identify with its national or pan-national group of origin (i.e. Mexican American or Hispanic/Latino). The way these youths self-identify was found to have more to do with perceived discrimination or limitations to opportunities for social and economic mobility than with whether or not they speak the language of their parents (Rumbaut 1999, pp. 183–5, 190–1). Nor is language fluency coterminous with a native sensibility or understanding of a given culture. Second-generation youth with limited fluency in the parental language nevertheless can have a direct knowledge of and identification with that culture (Bialystok and Hakuta 1994).

A broader historical approach, even when applied to traditional contexts for the examination of language and immigrants/ethnics, can lead to different questions for investigation and subsequently new conclusions. For example, a recent study of language maintenance among second-generation European American children in the early years of the twentieth century discovered that these high-school-aged children and their immigrant parents largely rejected the opportunity to study their own languages in the public schools, not because they had realized complete language shift, but because they opposed the totalizing ethnic identities represented by the standard version of those languages taught in the schools when their own identities were rooted in local/regional identities reflected in dialects (Zimmerman 2002).

Many other areas of investigation remain to be explored. More work needs to be done on the intellectual history of English in America along with the political and social history of how the English language has been deployed, by whom, and for what ends. Recent studies of Native Americans have considered these issues (Gray 1999; Spack 2002), but they obviously have great relevance for immigration scholars. Examination of when and in what context language use becomes contested can be particularly fruitful. A study of how the Midwestern accent came to be accepted as the standard in American speech, for example, situates that development within the country's fears of linguistic contamination by the mass immigration of southern and eastern Europeans in the early years of the twentieth century. Contrary to the pattern of most other nations, it was not the speech pattern of the great industrial and cultural centers – in the American case, the eastern seaboard cities – that became the model of standard American speech, but rather that of the heartland which was associated with a "Nordic" type as opposed to the new immigrants who were flocking to New York and Boston (Bonfiglio 2002). The English language performs metaphorical as well as practical functions in American life. Attention to the meanings attached to English at different historical moments can provide insights into the construction of national identity, an identity that involves issues of race, gender, and class, all of which are informed at different times and to different degrees by the popular sensibilities regarding the (*de facto*) national language.

Approaching language and immigrants from the perspective of the immigrant creates the possibility of accessing immigrant subjectivity, and in particular the emotional worlds of immigrants that are encoded in language. By looking at language – the languages spoken, to whom and under what circumstances, immigrant attitudes towards their languages and English, etc. – we can gain a better understanding of how immigrants experienced life in America as well as how they constructed their identities. Greater attention to language can provide access to the nuances of identity construction that are otherwise not captured. For example, according to Bailey (2002), dark-skinned Dominicans are more apt to identify themselves according to language than race, contrary to the American understanding that race trumps all other categories of identification. Studies comparing the linguistic experiences of different ethnic groups in varying historical periods are necessary to determine how they differ and what might account for those differences, such as distinct linguistic histories in the country of origin.

One central handicap to the study of language and immigrants has been the limited sources for older immigrant groups. The focus in linguistic anthropology and critical theory in recent years on how language reproduces relations of power and culture suggests greater possibilities for approaching the subject of language and immigrants using different types of source material. Ethnic identities that seem natural and constant are in fact continually in flux and are reproduced through language as part of social interactions that include other practices as well (food, clothing, etc.). The fluidity of social identities belies the popular understanding of culture as homogeneous and consistent. Thus, in a very real sense, immigrants constitute their ethnicity in their individual performance of everyday interactions that occur through language. Examining the linguistic practices of immigrants can shed new light on issues of language both by providing an opportunity to analyze language and by creating new possibilities for archival sources. Transcripts of court cases and other formal encounters between immigrant and dominant culture, song lyrics from ethnic theater, oral histories, the largely un-mined store of writings in immigrant languages in works of fiction and non-fiction (Shell and Sollors 2000), all of these allow for the study of language and immigrants beyond issues of language shift and language maintenance.

The issue of power as it is exercised through language, whether on the institutional or the individual level, is particularly important. Along with the need to trace the changing language ideologies specific to English and various immigrant languages in America, and their impact, linguistic interactions on an individual level provide another area for study. Linguistic interactions often involve inequalities of power and this is especially so with immigrants. Immigrants have encountered and continue to encounter the dominant culture through official representatives at many points in their sojourn in the United States, from the moment of arrival onwards. These contacts, which certainly involve elements of power and domination, are of course negotiated through language. Similarly, relations of power within immigrant groups – between men and women, between the generations, between new arrivals and more established immigrants – are also exercised through language, with certain elements of the population able to wield greater control through their knowledge of English and/or standard versions of national languages as opposed to dialects more commonly spoken.

The study of language and immigrants requires an interdisciplinary approach within a historical framework that is already evident in recent work in this field. Such an approach promises to provide the most comprehensive and multifaceted understanding of language in American immigrant and national life.

REFERENCES

Bailey, Benjamin H. (2002). *Language, Race, and Negotiation of Identity: A Study of Dominican Americans*. New York: LFB Scholarly Publishing.

Bailey, Richard W. (1991). *Images of English: A Cultural History of the Language*. Ann Arbor: University of Michigan Press.

Bialystok, Ellen and Kenji Hakuta (1994). *In Other Words: The Science and Psychology of Second-Language Acquisition*. New York: Basic Books.

Bonfiglio, Thomas Paul (2002). *Race and the Rise of Standard American*. Berlin, NY: Mouton de Gruyter.

Bourdieu, Pierre (1985). *Outline of a Theory of Practice* [1977]. Cambridge: Cambridge University Press.

Brumberg, Stephen (1986). *Going to America, Going to School: The Jewish Immigrant Encounter in Turn-of-the-Century New York City*. New York: Praeger.

Cameron, Deborah, ed. (1992). *Feminism and Linguistic Theory*, 2nd edn. New York: St. Martin's Press.

Carnevale, Nancy C. (2000a). "Language, Race, and the New Immigrants: The Example of Southern Italians." In Nancy Foner, Ruben G. Rumbaut, and Steven J. Gold, eds., *Immigration Research for a New Century: Multidisciplinary Perspectives*. New York: Russell Sage Foundation.

—— (2000b). "Living in Translation: Language and Italian Immigrants in the U.S., 1890–1945." Diss., Rutgers University, Ann Arbor, MI: UMI.

—— (2003). "'No Italian Spoken for the Duration of the War': Language, Ethnic Identity, and Cultural Pluralism in the World War II Years." *Journal of American Ethnic History* (Winter): 3–33.

Conklin, Nancy Faires and Margaret A. Lourie (1983). *A Host of Tongues: Language Communities in the United States*. New York: Free Press.

Dillard, J.L. (1985). *Toward a Social History of American English*. New York: Mouton.

Fishman, Joshua, ed. (1989). *Language and Ethnicity in Minority Sociolinguistic Perspective*. Philadelphia: Multilingual Matters.

—— (1999). *Handbook of Language and Ethnicity*. New York: Oxford University Press.

Gonzalez, Norma (2001). *I Am My Language: Discourses of Women and Children in the +Borderlands*. Tucson: University of Arizona Press.

Gray, Edward G. (1999). *New Babel: Languages and Nations in Early America*. Princeton, NJ: Princeton University Press.

Grinberg, Leon and Rebecca Grinberg (1989). *Psychoanalytic Perspectives on Migration and Exile*. New Haven, CT: Yale University Press.

Hakuta, Kenji: (1986). *Mirror of Language: The Debate on Bilingualism*. New York: Basic Books.

Hoffman, Eva (1989). *Lost in Translation: A Life in a New Language*. New York: E.P. Dutton.

Johnson, Fern L. (2000). *Speaking Culturally: Language Diversity in the United States*. Thousand Oaks, CA: Sage.

Jones, Katherine W. (2001). *Accent on Privilege: English Identities and Anglophilia in the U.S.* Philadelphia: Temple University Press.

Kim, Suki (2003). *The Interpreter*. New York: Farrar, Straus & Giroux.

Kloss, Heinz (1977). *The American Bilingual Tradition*. Rowley, MA: Newbury House.

Lepore, Jill (2002). *A is for American: Letters and Other Characters in the Newly United States*. New York: Alfred A. Knopf.

Lippi-Green, Rosina (1997). *English with an Accent: Language, Ideology, and Discrimination in the United States*. London: Routledge.

Lopez, David E. (1999). "Social and Linguistic Aspects of Assimilation Today." In Charles Hirschman, Philip Kasinitz, and Josh DeWind, eds., *The Handbook of International Migration: The American Experience*. New York: Russell Sage Foundation.

Mangione, Jerre (1972). *Mount Allegro* [1942], 2nd edn. New York: Crown.

Mufwene, Salikoko S., John R. Rickford, Guy Bailey, and John Baugh, eds. (1998). *African-American English: Structure, History, and Use*. London and New York: Routledge.

Nuland, Sherwin B. (2003). *Lost in America: A Journey with My Father*. New York: Alfred A. Knopf.

Portes, Alejandro and Ruben G. Rumbaut (2001). *Legacies: The Story of the Immigrant Second Generation*. Berkeley: University of California Press; New York: Russell Sage Foundation.

Rodriguez, Richard (1981). *Hunger of Memory: The Education of Richard Rodriguez*. Boston: David R. Godine.

Rumbaut, Ruben (1999). "Assimilation and Its Discontents: Ironies and Paradoxes." In Charles Hirschman, Philip Kasinitz, and Josh DeWind, eds., *The Handbook of International Migration: The American Experience*. New York: Russell Sage Foundation.

Santiago, Esmeralda (1993). *When I Was Puerto Rican*. New York: Vintage Books.

Schmidt, Ronald, Sr. (2000). *Language Policy and Identity Politics in the United States*. Philadelphia: Temple University Press.

Shell, Marc (1993). "The Politics of Language Diversity." *Critical Inquiry* (Autumn): 103–27.

Shell, Marc and Werner Sollors, eds. (2000). *The Multilingual Anthology of American Literature: A Reader of Original Texts with English Translations*. New York: New York University Press.

Sollors, Werner, ed. (1998). *Multilingual America: Transnationalism, Ethnicity, and the Languages of American Literature*. New York: New York University Press.

Spack, Ruth (2002). *America's Second Tongue: American Indian Education and the Ownership of English, 1600–1900*. Lincoln: University of Nebraska Press.

Veltman, Calvin (1983). *Language Shift in the United States*. Berlin, NY: Mouton.

Watkins-Goffman, Linda (2001). *Lives in Two Languages: An Exploration of Identity and Culture*. Ann Arbor: University of Michigan Press.

Wittke, Carl (1936). *German-Americans and the World War*. Columbus, OH: Ohio State Archeological and Historical Society.

Woolard, Kathryn A. (1998). "Introduction: Language Ideology as a Field of Inquiry." In Bambi B. Schieffelin, Kathryn A. Woolard, and Paul V. Kroskrity, eds., *Language Ideologies: Practice and Theory*. New York: Oxford University Press, pp. 3–50.

Zimmerman, Jonathan (2002). "Ethnics Against Ethnicity: European Immigrants and Foreign-Language Instruction, 1890–1940." *Journal of American History* 88(4): 1383–404.

SUGGESTED FURTHER READING

Amati-Mehler, Jacqueline, Simona Argentieri, and Jorge Canestri (1993). *The Babel of the Unconscious: Mother Tongue and Foreign Languages in the Psychoanalytic Dimension*. Madison, CT: International Universities Press.

Bailey, Benjamin (2001). "Language." In James Ciment, ed., *Encyclopedia of American Immigration*. Armonk, NY: M.E. Sharpe, pp. 810–19.

Crawford, James (1992). *Language Loyalties: A Source Book on the Official Language Controversy*. Chicago: University of Chicago Press.

Ferguson, Charles A. and Shirley Brice Heath, eds. (1981). *Language in the USA*. Cambridge, Eng.: Cambridge University Press.

Finegan, Edward and John Rickford, eds. (2004). *Language in the USA: Themes for the Twenty-first Century*. Cambridge, Eng.: Cambridge University Press.

Fishman, Joshua A. (1966). *Language Loyalty in the United States*. The Hague: Mouton.

Gal, Susan (1989). "Language and Political Economy." *Annual Review in Anthropology* 18: 345–67.

Giles, Howard and W. Peter Robinson, eds. (1990). *Handbook of Language and Social Psychology*. Chichester: John Wiley.

Leibowitz, Arnold H. (1984). "The Official Character of Language in the United States: Literacy Requirements for Immigration, Citizenship, and Entrance into American Life." *Aztlan* 15(1): 25–70.

McCrum, Robert, William Cran, and Robert MacNeil (1986). *The Story of English*. New York: Viking/Elisabeth Sifton Books.

Morales, ed. (2002). *Living in Spanglish: The Search for Latino Identity in America*. New York: St. Martin's Press.

Stavans, Ilan (2003). Spanglish: *The Making of a New American Language*. New York: Rayo.

Van Horne, Winston A. and Thomas V. Tonnesen, eds. (1987). *Ethnicity and Language*. (Ethnicity and Public Policy Series, Vol. VI.) Madison: University of Wisconsin System Institute on Race and Ethnicity.

Zentella, Ana Celia (1997). *Growing up Bilingual: Puerto Rican Children in New York*. Oxford: Blackwell.

CHAPTER TWENTY-THREE

Immigration and Education in the United States

PAULA S. FASS

Education has been central to immigrant experience in the United States and funda-mental to the creation of the American nation. Education broadly understood is the whole manner in which the young are inducted into the society and enculturated to its norms, habits, and values. For the children of immigrants, this could be a very complex and conflicted process which involved a variety of sometimes competing formal and informal institutions and organizations – family and other relatives, church, work, peers, sports, clubs, and, in the modern period, expressions of popular entertainment, such as music, movies, television, the internet, and mall culture. For the purposes of this chapter, however, our attention will be limited to the education of immigrants at and through school and will address these other matters only as they intersect with schooling.

Similarly, it can be argued that all European and African migrants to those parts of North America during the seventeenth and eighteenth centuries which became the United States were immigrants. This would include the colonizers of Spanish and French America, and African slaves, as well as the British settlers of the east coast. I will not be using this expansive definition in this chapter, but will instead restrict myself to those peoples who freely came to the United States after the establishment of the union articulated by the Constitution in 1789. This is not intended to deny the immigrant nature of those early settlers. It is rather to clarify the ways in which schooling, which did not exist as a nation-building enterprise until after the formation of the permanent union, was clearly an expression of national goals and purposes. Indeed, in the American context, schooling and immigration are two profoundly interconnected elements in the process of creating a nation that, unlike many other societies, could not draw upon common history and memory, rituals, or language toward this end.

The absence of homogeneity in population, experience, and social habits was from the beginning an American characteristic, related to the unsystematic manner in which the British North American colonies were settled. Benjamin Rush had this in mind in 1786, on the eve of the formation of the permanent American union, when he proposed that schools, "by producing one general, and uniform system of educa-tion," would make Americans "more homogeneous," and "fit them for uniform and peaceable government" (Handlin 1982, p. 8). Rush's insight, based on already existing experience, would subsequently govern school development as immigration became a serious and important component of the rapid national expansion in the nineteenth century. Indeed, during the nineteenth century America became at once much more heterogeneous as immigrants from three continents – Europe, Asia, and Latin America – reached its shores, and ever more devoted to schooling as a necessary component of nation-building. These two were vitally connected, something often obscured by the fact that American schools are locally based with their regulation within the domain of state power. This relationship is also complicated since schools were not created simply as a result of immigration. Nevertheless, the ways schools developed and their strategic importance at particular times are inseparable from immigration and its powerful contribution to American nationality.

This intertwined development would continue throughout the twentieth century and assume a more urgent economic dimension as schooling became more manifestly bound up in the achievement of social success. It is for this reason that as the twenty-first century unfolds the issue of schooling remains ineluctably connected to the continuing reality of immigration and its ever wider population sources. American nationhood is obviously more institutionalized and empowered in the twenty-first century than it was in 1850, but it remains culturally malleable and open-ended as the nature of America's population evolves and as America's role in the world is redefined. It is for this reason, too, that when Americans seek to address the cultural, economic, or social issues that successive immigrations have raised they have looked to the schools for assistance. Many of these issues – above all the identity, allegiance, and future of the second generation – have remained the same. Others have changed, but over the course of almost two centuries, ever wider and higher reaches of schooling – first "common" primary schools (1830 to 1880), then secondary education in high schools (c. 1890 to 1950), and then finally colleges and universities (c. 1960 to the present) – have been looked to and enlisted in this effort. While America is not unique in this upward expansion of educational resources, which is common to advanced societies, it has been historically the leader in this educational democratization, a leadership fundamentally connected to its early and steady exposure to issues introduced by immigration. Just as the Constitution propelled American imperial expansion into a continent while permitting the incorporation of incoming states on the same terms as the original colonies that thus together constituted the American realm politically, so has schooling provided the institutional mechanism through which the nation constitutes itself socially in the context of an almost continuous but ever changing immigration. While schooling has been under continuous pressure toward this end, its history can best be described and understood by examining three stages in its evolution from the early republic through the early twenty-first century.

Creating the Civic Realm: Education and Immigration in the Nineteenth Century

When the Constitution was adopted in 1789, the young republic's population had not yet reached 4 million. By the end of a century of explosive development and expansion, it was close to 75 million. Immigration contributed significantly to that growth. During the same period, schooling grew from an irregular, unsystematic, congeries of *ad hoc* arrangements that were privately funded, publicly supported, or provided through charity, into an elaborate state-sponsored system that affected practically every child in America in some form of elementary instruction. The great majority of those students attended free public elementary schools that were then seen as an expression of a vibrant American democracy. The system had also developed many upper and lower branches, including secondary education in public high schools and a network of state universities underwritten by national land grant legislation (the Morrill Act in 1862), as well as new public kindergartens for pre-school children. For most of the nineteenth century, the central public policy issues looked to the lower levels of schooling. A much smaller parallel system of parochial (largely Catholic) schools was by then also quite vigorous and significant.

Immigrants were deeply involved in this vast growth of schooling. Their experience needs to be understood from two perspectives: how the schools developed in response to issues relating to immigrants; and how immigrants experienced the schools. This dual axis of interaction was complex and multivalent, not only because the issues meandered over a long nineteenth-century history, but because different groups in different places, not to say different individuals, could have quite divergent relationships and experiences with public education. During this century of national self-definition, schooling became an important expression of the development of state authority as the American nation and economy grew. Many prominent historians have pointed out that early nineteenth-century schooling in the United States intersected in important ways with the growth of industry and the need for a disciplined, well-socialized labor force which the schools could provide. And certainly schooling permitted public oversight of the habits and manners of the young. Nevertheless, schooling itself should not be exaggerated either as an ingredient in that economic development or as an individual means for success. Indeed, schooling throughout most of the first century of American life expressed republican ideals of citizenship far more than it trained in skills necessary to either the individual or the society. By the end of the century those skills and the knowledge that schooling could provide became more significant and more advanced schooling was required; schooling consequently grew in importance and moved to the center of policy discussions.

In the early years of the nation, much was said about the importance of schooling as an essential for republican life, not least by Thomas Jefferson who proposed a system of graduated merit-based selection and advancement together with rudimentary training for the entire population; and his vision has remained resonant through much of American history. But very little was actually done. American students, the children of immigrants among them, were schooled in either private or publicly supported institutions in most of the states, although the new western areas often lacked adequate facilities of any kind and were frequently traversed by zealous missionaries who advocated for schools. The immigrants to the early republic were mostly British, like those who dominated the peopling of the coastal colonies, and their education culturally and socially fell into familiar patterns. A small educated elite graduated from colleges and were highly educated in a classical format. But most Americans were literate and their knowledge and skills grew from a familiar complex of institutions – family, work, church, augmented by rudimentary formal instruction. This changed in important ways starting in the 1830s. The period from 1830 to

1860 was coincident with the first large and significant wave of immigrants to arrive into the United States, and it also saw the development of a market economy and the earliest systems of factory manufacture. It was in this context that the ideal of a public common school first took root in the United States, and it grew alongside other schemes that valued commitment to public improvements. That common school ideal was based on a "republican style" of education, which Lawrence Cremin has summarized as composed of four commitments:

> that education was crucial to the vitality of the Republic; that a proper republican education consisted of the diffusion of knowledge, the nurturance of virtue (including patriotic civility), and the cultivation of learning; that schools and colleges were the best agencies for providing a proper republican education . . . that the most effective means of obtaining the requisite number and kind of schools and colleges was through some system tied to the polity. (Cremin 1980, p. 148)

During these middle decades of the nineteenth century, educational development moved vigorously along all these routes. It established a host of academies and colleges for advanced instruction. It became a system tied to the state. But, most spectacularly, it grew by expanding to larger proportions of the population, a population now strongly augmented by the migration of Irish, German, and Scandinavian immigrants whose cultural education could no longer be taken for granted. Immigrants were also believed to bring poverty and crime. In 1830, 35 percent of the population of those aged 5–19 were enrolled in school. This grew to 38.4 percent in 1840, 50.4 percent in 1850, and then to 57.7 percent in 1860. In 1870, after the Civil War, 61.1 percent of this large age group of American youth broadly conceived were enrolled in school. Enrollment should not be confused with attendance, but the very rapid growth testifies to the state's ability to enforce schooling as something for which children were required at least to register. By then the schools had been transformed from a hodgepodge of forms, types, and variously financed institutions into a systematic education system that was publicly funded and publicly supervised. A common school regime, for which Horace Mann is remembered as a pioneer and toward which goal he had created an active reform society in the 1830s, was an ideal described by Mann in a host of his reports and writings as an American necessity. By the last third of the nineteenth century, it had largely come into being. Mann had sought three things: to make a single school the common environment for all groups and classes so that the schools would "obliterate factitious distinctions in society" (Kaestle 1983, p. 91); that they be financed through public taxation; and that they be centrally overseen in each state. For the most part, the schools that had developed in the north and the west had accomplished all three by this time. After the Civil War, southern schools, which had lagged behind, were also slowly brought onto this path.

For most immigrants, this meant that schools were an arena in which their children now learned American ways for at least the 3 to 4 years of (sometimes irregular) attendance required of them. After the Civil War most states created laws that more effectively enforced attendance. While the importance of schooling for success in the nineteenth century should not be exaggerated, its significance as a means of creating an American identity cannot be too much underscored. Although there were a variety of exceptions, this meant that most children were instructed in the use of the English language, provided with a basic literacy, and required to see themselves as part of an American civic enterprise. Above all, they were exposed to a social institution not within their parents' control. The school as a source of alternative authority, rooted in an American identity, and as an instrument of specific and latent instruction – a school "common" to all – was a powerful means by which the second generation (and less frequently younger members of the first generation) came to recognize how their experience differed from that of their parents. In this sense, the school's role was very different from that of other institutions such as the variously denominated churches, or the workplace with which the children of immigrants in the nineteenth century were all too familiar. Work was the means for survival and the potential route for success. And immigrants and their children trod the same path, with the children more often than not making these two things possible through their contributions to the family purse. School was the realm of childhood. In this arena, the child's separate fate and distinct destiny were inscribed.

The commitment to childhood as a special time and to schooling developed together in the nineteenth century. Both grew from a belief in an individualizing destiny. Childhood was romanticized in the nineteenth century and, as the century progressed, reformers sought more and more to protect and extend its length. For immigrant children, this often resulted in considerable conflict as the goals of parents and those of the culture stood on different grounds. The American version did not always win, since so many factors affected how children related to this divergent authority. Still, the very existence of a conflict was already a victory for 'an American identity that the schools always brought with them – since schooling breached the continuity of culture that the immigrant habits tried to preserve. In addition, language, habits, and beliefs were deeply part of the routines of schooling. Habits of order, punctuality, and cleanliness were often required and not infrequently used as a means of rebuke to homes where these practices were as foreign as the more explicitly "Protestant" values to which they were attached. For German Catholics and for the Irish who made up a large proportion of the mid-nineteenth-century immigrants, this introduced a number of issues of control which were only partially resolved.

Immigrants were, for the most part, not eager to give over authority regarding their children to the schools. Neither were the faith communities to which they subscribed happy to see their community's future confessional identities altered. Throughout the first half of the nineteenth century, despite the protestations of school reformers such as Mann and Frederick A.P. Barnard that the education they envisaged was entirely secular, many immigrant spokesmen saw behind its face a Protestant vision. Thus, despite the general victory of the "common school," immigrants fought for the survival of different kinds of school, which, by the late nineteenth century, continued to serve the specific needs of immigrants and their children. The midwest especially became the site of innumerable German language schools, some of them receiving state support, where continuity between generations could be maintained. Some of these schools provided hardly any English instruction, but taught history and mathematics as well as literacy in German. More encouraged learning in two languages, with German language, history, and culture taught alongside the more conventional subjects. Innumerable small towns as well as large cities such as Milwaukee and St. Louis, in Missouri, Wisconsin, and Iowa were homes to this compromise between national and immigrant cultural goals. Most of these schools would disappear by the end of the century, strangled by increasing nativist sentiment and laws such as the 1889 Bennet Law in Wisconsin.

More lasting, but with its roots in related issues, were the parochial school systems established by the Catholic Church to serve immigrant communities in cities throughout the country. The controversy with the Catholic Church broke into the public arena almost as soon as the public schools became part of the agenda, most notably in New York City where Bishop John Hughes debated with public school advocates over the legitimacy of alternative schools and for a share of the public purse. This debate was not marginal since Governor William H. Seward took the side of the parochial school advocates. His inaugural address in 1840 made clear how much was at stake in immigrant schooling:

> The children of foreigners found in great numbers in our populous cities and towns . . . are too often deprived of the advantages of our system of public education, in consequences of prejudices arising from difference of language or religion. It ought never to be forgotten that the public welfare is as deeply concerned in their education as in that of our own children. I do not hesitate, therefore, to recommend the establishment of schools in which they may be instructed by teachers speaking the same language with themselves and professing the same faith. . . . Since we have opened our country and all its fullness to the oppressed of every nation, we should evince wisdom equal to our generosity by qualifying their children for the high responsibilities of citizenship. (Cremin 1980, p. 167)

In the end, the parochial schools did not win access to public funds, but they did achieve a grudging acknowledgment of their role in the schooling of immigrant children. These schools took a long time to develop, but by the 1880s and 1890s they were serving sizable portions (about 9 percent and often far more in specific places like Chicago) of a now growing number of children of foreign-born parents and an ever larger group of Catholics and others who chose a separate religious education for their children. By then, the change in the sources of immigration had become even greater, taking in larger and larger circles of non-Protestant Europe as the powerful forces of agricultural displacement and industrialization attracted a more diverse pool of immigrants to the United States.

It is worth noting that the concern of school planners with immigrant children was almost exclusively confined to the children of white migrants of European descent who were seen as potential citizens and republican constituents. The children of the small migration from Asia that started in the middle of the nineteenth century, and was soon halted, were hardly a great concern. The schooling of African Americans was a wholly different matter. Almost all slave children were excluded from schools, and teaching them had become illegal throughout the south by mid-century. Free blacks in the north were sometimes schooled together with whites in common schools, and at other times placed in segregated Negro schools. Neither Africans nor Asians were, through much of the nineteenth century, a fundamental consideration in the evolving school regime, although freedmen and their children became the objects of elaborate, though temporary, schooling efforts modeled on the ideal of republican preparation for citizenship during Reconstruction, through the Freedman's Bureau.

The non-English speaking or non-public schools are an important reminder that the schooling of immigrants has never been uniform, not during the common school era and not later as schooling took on new purposes and new power. American education remained locally financed and controlled and without central guidance, and different kinds of schools existed to serve its diverse population. At the same time, the existence of alternative schools was also a sign that the state now had the power to command that the young be schooled formally, and this power called forth imaginative compromises within the immigrant community as well as in American political ideas. These local community solutions to the potential for conflict over the second generation were overwhelmingly composed on American grounds, however. That would become clearer by the late nineteenth century as schooling became more important as an ingredient for successful negotiation of the American economy, and when the, by then, large Catholic school system eagerly sought to imitate the innovations of the public schools in order to maintain the allegiance of its constituents. The immigrant-based non-public schools were always that – a response to the growing power of the state and the national identity that schooling had come to represent in the nineteenth century.

New Purposes, New Means, and New Students

In the late nineteenth and early twentieth centuries, schooling became a much more ambitious enterprise, more crucial to America's position as a growing world power, and a more significant feature of individual success and achievement. The nineteenth-century industrial transformation had by then created a corporate and commercial white-collar world that required higher levels of literacy and business know-how. So too, developments in industry made more refined mechanical, metallurgical, and engineering skills an asset. Even agriculture which had been the common coin of the realm was transformed into a business where higher levels of schooling paid. In the professions – law, medicine, architecture – new requirements and certifications replaced a previously *laissez-faire* situation in which casually reading law or practicing medicine in one of several ways had been a sufficient form of training. Schooling to which some Americans had always looked for avenues to prominence became more central to status and mobility and a necessary means for acquiring the training, diplomas, and social skills required for economic success. And schooling also became a form of licensing as diplomas and degrees became requirements for placement or certification. At the same time, low-level industrial jobs, increasingly dependent on machines and machine processes, remained hungry for brute labor, a hunger that made America a golden portal for immigration. Thus the period saw two related movements meeting at the schoolhouse door – the drive for more and better schooling, and the new millions of immigrant children brought to or born in America whom the schools needed to incorporate into the nation.

The meeting was both fortuitous and uncomfortable. The need for skills and the presence of larger pools of greater varieties of immigrants (Poles, Magyars, Russian and Austrian Jews, Slovaks, Croats, Italians, Syrians, Greeks, Armenians) created significant pressures on the schools both to lengthen the time students spent in school, so that a few years' training in elementary school became inadequate, and to increase the rigor and organization of classroom learning. By the 1880s, bureaucratic drives had already made the school grade and school hierarchy important in primary schools in immigrant-swollen cities. By the end of the century, the old public high school was transformed toward these ends and in the early twentieth century the new junior high school was created. Newer curricula emphasizing modern languages, science, and math rapidly superseded the older emphasis on classical languages and recitation for the academically inclined and college-bound. Older students, kept in school by increasing age-of-attendance requirements and the desire for advancement, forced high schools to deal with students who were neither academically inclined nor headed for college. For them, school leaders and reformers began to design more practical courses of instruction in commercial or mechanical arts, or they expanded high school offerings through a watered-down version of the rigorous academic course. In the late nineteenth century, some cities, like Somerville, Massachusetts, maintained two high schools – one with a Latin-based curriculum for the college-bound and a newer school for those with non-college aspirations. The many students who saw secondary schooling as an avenue to commercial and clerical success quickly made the latter school eclipse the former in size and educational importance. By the second decade of the twentieth century, these multiple tracks became increasingly familiar as alternatives in the new comprehensive high schools that sprouted in cities of every size in all parts of the nation, and even in rural places as the move toward school consolidation took over the countryside.

Immigration fed this process. As the number of immigrants moved past a million a year in the early decades of the twentieth century, and as their parents moved into the steel mills, meatpacking plants, construction sites, sweatshops, and vegetable stands of the major cities, the children found themselves in the newly invigorated and ambitious schools. School officials, eager for the growth of their own enterprises, welcomed them and were challenged and sometimes overwhelmed by the problems they brought: disease and bad teeth; inadequate English language skills and behavior problems; and the irregular attendance that resulted from these problems and their parents' need for their assistance at home. The problems of poverty and displacement that the immigrant children brought were huge, but they were problems whose solutions would make an important contribution to school growth. During the first three decades of the twentieth century, schools at all levels, but especially high schools and junior high schools, evolved as modern institutions in good part in response to these issues. Gymnasiums and nursing staffs, truancy departments and free lunch programs in new cafeterias, guidance clinics and academic testing – all became part of the vast institutional development of the school as a social institution and of the bureaucratization of school systems.

Only a few immigrant children initially went beyond the elementary school in the early years of the twentieth century, and those few were ethnically differentiated: far more Jews than Italians in the eastern cities, more Magyars and Czechs than Poles or Slovaks in the midwest, more Japanese than Mexicans in the west. Many immigrant parents were simply baffled by the idea of physically grown children wasting their time in school when they could be helping their mothers at home or working alongside their fathers for the good of the family. As one Italian mother noted in exasperation at efforts to keep her adolescent children in school, "When girls at 13 or 14 wasted good time in school, it simply made us regret coming to America" (Lassonde 1998: 52) But the requirements stayed in place.

American views about children were increasingly at variance with those of many of the more traditional societies from which immigrants came. Adolescence, newly enshrined as a stage of life by G. Stanley Hall, was attached to childhood in American views as a period of transitional development and of social vulnerability. From the view of socialization, now widely adopted in the reform-minded schools, these were still tender years, which could make the difference between an effectively integrated adulthood and a maladjusted and socially dangerous one. Keeping adolescents in school, and especially the children of immigrants for whom the rocky transition between child and adult could lead to antisocial gang behavior, sexual precocity, and a later life of crime, became all the more desirable and even necessary. Finding ways to occupy their time effectively so they could be kept there longer became a challenge.

By the 1920s the trickle into secondary schools that had begun earlier in the century became a flood of new high school enrollments, now often made up of the children of immigrants. The numbers tell the story well. In Providence, Rhode Island in 1925, almost 70 percent of all children of Russian Jews had entered high school; so had more than 73 percent of the children of Irish immigrants; and even 33 percent of the children of the much more reluctant Italians. The Jews did best in graduating (66 percent), but almost one-half of the Italians who entered were also graduating at mid-decade. It is likely that had Providence contained a significant number of students of Slavic background, their presence in high school would have been lower. But even then no fewer than 10 percent of Polish students would have likely graduated at this point, based on evidence from other cities.

The school people had succeeded and they had built ever larger and more imposing buildings as a sign of that success. In many places, the high school became the biggest building in town, an anchoring symbol of modern democracy and economic opportunity. But, in those buildings, the immigrant children often led lives apart from the children of the native-born, while their destinies also diverged. High schools held out promises which were not always fulfilled since the vast expansion of schooling in the upper grades that took place in the context of immigration had been so rationalized and adapted to perceived student needs and skills that students in a comprehensive high school could have very different experiences and destinations.

Desirable as their presence might be for school expansion, and necessary as it was perceived to be for purposes of socialization, the children of immigrants created problems in the schools and for their new programs. These problems were more and more viewed as matters of academic aptitude, rather than of home preparation or personal motivation. This perspective was underwritten by a growing commitment in American intellectual life to viewing differences among immigrants as biologically determined and to defining ethnic groups in racial terms. At the turn of the century, the problem of immigrant adaptation and poverty was usually understood by reformers, such as settlement house workers, as a result of environmental factors and subject to improvement. But by the second decade immigrant issues were often reimagined as an intransigent effect of race, and the experience of World War I, which increased national xenophobia, tended to confirm this perspective. So did the use of mental tests for intelligence during the war and the resulting reading of differences in scores as evidence for permanent group patterns of performance.

These same tests were adapted after the war by school systems across the country, which used them to sift the growing number of students into categories of higher or lesser potential for educated achievement. The extensive use of the "intelligence quotient" or IQ as it was now called, developed by Stanford psychologist Lewis Terman, and interpreted by him as a stable and dependable measure of learning ability (native intelligence), increased the efficiency of the schools in allocating students to the different tracks they had been developing for the comprehensive high school. During the war, the army tests had already made clear that the "new immigrant" groups, whose numbers had surpassed those of the older British, German, and Scandinavian groups sometime in the late nineteenth century, were consistently scoring lower on these tests than native groups and the so-called older immigrants. And school officials were certainly not surprised when this proved to be the case for IQ tests as well. The IQ tests were a simple solution to a complex problem – how to arrange schools rationally so that all students could benefit to some degree and stay at school longer, at the same time that teaching these ever larger numbers could be organized not around the individual but around ability groups. The IQ could also rationalize different paths in life and different educational outcomes at a time when schooling was becoming more closely identified with social success.

As a result, the vast expansion of secondary education and increased attendance of immigrants was an ambiguous democratic triumph. It certainly permitted some individuals to succeed in the terms of special merit that Jefferson would have approved. But it meant that for many students who were channeled into lesser programs going to high school was far more a social experience than an academic challenge. The expanding American economy through most of the first half of the twentieth century was able to find comfortable places for these students, but the places they achieved hardly carried either the same status or the same potential rewards as awaited those who were channeled further into the colleges, the learned professions, and executive suites. The memory of this differentiation would last and was renewed during the second half of the twentieth century when high school attendance or even graduation would no longer provide the place in the economy it once had.

If the high school distributed its academic resources and rewards differentially among the children of immigrants and natives, its social life was just as complex. Between the 1920s and 1945, a period when all immigration was reduced and immigration from eastern and southern Europe (the new immigration) practically ceased, the high schools became important arenas of Americanizing experience for the second and third generations, the children and grandchildren of those who had come earlier in the century. It was here, in the new cauldron of American life that had become a kind of adolescent rite-of-passage, that the ethnic complexity of America was most often brought home. In most big cities, high schools could vary a great deal, some containing few ethnics, while others included a rich assortment of different groups. In New York – the premier immigrant city – these variations meant that social experiences differed a great deal. In New York, the highly selective Bronx High School of Science was composed overwhelmingly of one ethnic group – Jews. So was the very different Seward Park High School on the poor Lower East Side of New York. But at others, such as Evander Childs High School in the Bronx or George Washington High School in Manhattan, Italians, Irish, and Jews, and usually a few blacks, competed for prominence in extracurricular activities, prizing posts as newspaper editors and election to president of the student body as much and sometimes more than academic honors. This competition often had ethnic dimensions. Even in activities where students did not compete, such as science clubs and glee clubs, they tended to make ethnically different choices that indicated that they were largely selecting their associations according to ethnic groups. Despite the emphasis on immigrant socialization through public schooling, neither school organizers, nor principals and teachers could control the real social distinctions and forms of identity that long years of schooling encouraged among adolescents. Unlike elementary school students, those in high school were both more fully attuned to social nuance and more aware of its importance to them as they prepared to assume adult roles. Caught between the older world of their parents and the new world designed by the schools, they created a third way that was ethnically conscious within the schools. This rich social life drew them together with others with similar backgrounds, problems, and needs. Leonard Covello, the Principal of Benjamin Franklin High School in the Bronx, who wrote an important book on the second-generation experience, understood this in his own life and among the students he observed: "here in America we began to understand . . . that there was a chance that another world existed beyond the tenements in which we lived and that it was just possible to reach out into that world and one day become part of it." That world could be reached through the school. But in the school, it could be imagined only with the help of others like oneself: "Whatever problems we had at school or in the street, we never took up with our parents. These were our personal problems to be shared only by companions who knew and were conditioned by the same experience" (Covello and D'Agastino 1958, pp. 39, 47).

If the public high school was one place where this experience could be shared with others who led similar lives, another was the parochial high school. Although the Catholic Church's efforts to educate the children of immigrants were heavily concentrated at the lower levels of schooling, it became apparent early in the century that the secular success of its congregants would increasingly hinge on further and higher schooling. Impelled by the Third Plenary Council in Baltimore (1884) to create secondary institutions, the Catholic hierarchy in most large cities began to build diocesan schools. This was a slow and costly process. In 1922 there were still only 35 such schools in the whole country. But, by 1947 there were 150 and the number continued to grow. The diocesan high school would allow the children of poor Catholics to reach higher without having to compromise their religious instruction or be forced into contact with students of very different backgrounds. Private Catholic academies had made this available through various religious orders to wealthier Catholics. It was the expansion of the diocesan high schools in the twentieth century that made it available to the Catholic masses. In these schools, secular subjects could be more safely taught by the religious teaching orders while home languages were maintained in religious subjects. Kept closer to home in all these ways, the Catholic high school nevertheless provided immigrant families with ways to allow their children to make social and economic progress in American life. This was a lesson that the Catholic hierarchy and Catholic parents also incorporated into the rapid development in the twentieth century of Catholic institutions of higher education, from Duquesne University in Pittsburgh to Catholic University in Washington, DC.

Religion was only one piece of the immigrant background sometimes challenged by the public school that could be retained in parochial high schools of all kinds,

Catholic, Jewish, as well as Lutheran. Other aspects of culture, such as holiday celebrations, foreign languages not taught in the public schools, views of authority, and intra-group dating that maintained marital endogamy were also more easily safeguarded in this way. No matter how much students might stay with others like themselves, the public schools tended to expose students to a greater variety of culturally acceptable forms and more challenges to a uniform self-identity. Those parents who chose religious schooling understood this well.

It was less possible to protect the young from the growing influence of popular culture with its strong homogenizing and Americanizing trends as the twentieth century progressed. Music, clothing, movies, teen magazines, slang, dating patterns – these were all ways in which the young became another estate in America and through which immigrant youth especially learned to adapt and become more like their peers from other ethnic and native groups. While parochial schools could try to impede this trend through the use of school uniforms and the blacklisting of movies and books, they could hardly stop it completely. And popular culture became an important component of the learning process by which the second generation became part of the American scene.

By the time of World War II and immediately after, many of the challenges which had once defined the agenda of school expansion had jelled into institutional form, most significantly in the guise of the American public high school and its parochial school variants. Attached to these institutions were all kinds of social trends that became associated with youth culture in twentieth-century America. By then, too, most immigrant groups had adapted to this new central American institution, while their young had used it to achieve a sense of themselves as American youth, still connected to ethnic groups and ethnic friends in school and out, but also very much part of a wider and expanding definition of American culture.

Youth culture was only one of the issues the high school had brought to the fore. The other was social mobility. In the nineteenth century schooling had served a few toward this end, but the overwhelming majority of Americans, including immigrants, carved out their place through the expanding American economy. This began to change in the late nineteenth century as certification and licensing made more education necessary to success. The effects were already clear when high schools tracked students with the understanding that high school success was related to success later in life. But this association was still somewhat muted since high school graduation in and of itself was still a significant marker and a desirable achievement. This changed by the end of World War II. The strong modern association between education and social place had started to overwhelm other ways in which status could be achieved in modern society, at least for the vast majority not born to money or social position.

As we have seen, each major new current of immigration had contributed to the alteration of schooling and its purposes. In the early nineteenth century, problems of republican citizenship had empowered the schools to prepare the immigrants of the mid-century for their roles in the commonwealth. In the early twentieth century immigration had transformed the schools into large, comprehensive social environments that were to compensate for the problems of immigrant groups while selectively preparing their children for the new economy. By the second half of the twentieth century, the role of schooling had become demonstrable and urgent for economic success. In that context, Americans looked ever upward as they sought to ensure that immigrants became successful Americans.

The Newest Immigration: Reaching Higher

The differential educational attainments and social mobility of the children of immigrants in the first half of the twentieth century resulted from cultural and economic differences among the groups as well as school policies. Thus Jewish students tended to go further in school than Poles for a variety of reasons relating to their parents' initial literacy, economic circumstances and ambitions, and the role of learning and achievement values. The Irish had used the parochial school system to much better effect than had the Italians because of their closer identification with the American Catholic Church and its hierarchy as well as their drive for social position in America. School policies, as we have seen, often distinguished among students during their academic lives, facilitating or obstructing the potentials of some through limits imposed by testing or tracking. And almost everywhere, neighborhood poverty took its toll on school attendance and the provision of adequate educational facilities, while home conditions made learning more or less possible. In higher education, quotas had been imposed on Jewish students in the first half of the century in professional schools (especially medicine) as well as in selective colleges, such as the Ivy League (most notoriously at Harvard and Dartmouth), because Jews were seen as overreaching their place or insufficiently refined for the high status these schools and achievements signaled. But these differences were the results of policies made at the local level or the toll of social discrimination.

Not until World War II, however, did the federal government discover the enormous national stake in schooling. The huge call-up of troops and the allocation of duties and responsibilities by skill and school level, as well as the painful recognition of the cost of illiteracy in a modern technology-driven army, were one part of this discovery. This led to an unprecedented extension of in-service literacy training during the war, training in mechanical skills, and higher levels of learning at university campuses for hundreds of thousands of men as the army helped create the manpower it needed. After the war, the experience resulted in the provision of further schooling for millions as part of the package of GI benefits. For the first time in history, the federal government was beginning to deploy its resources toward educating the American people.

Another critical result of the war experience was the recognition that investment in research and training at the very highest levels in science, math, and engineering, as well as in foreign languages, was a matter of national security. Americans had won the war not only because soldiers fought on the battlefields, but because scientists and professors who gathered on mountain tops and in laboratories developed new knowledge – in sonar and radar, in atomic weaponry, and in code-breaking. This experience had huge consequences for the postwar world as the government looked to the colleges and universities for the creation of new knowledge. National security matters were further brought home during the Cold War when the Soviet Union launched the first earth-orbiting satellite, Sputnik (1957), and then sent a man into space.

The consequences of these dual discoveries of the national stake in education were at first muted for immigrants and their children because immigration was not much of an issue until the major changes introduced by the reform legislation of the mid-1960s. Until then, the immigration policies of restriction of the 1920s were still in place, somewhat adapted at various points to accommodate postwar and Soviet-era refugees from Europe, including Jews, Germans, immigrants from the Baltic states and other eastern European countries.

This changed dramatically in the 1960s for three reasons. First, the levels of schooling required for success had shifted steadily upward. From the mid-1950s, informed by the experience of the war and subsequent Cold War, and the expansion created in higher education by the GI bill, college-going became a newly democratized objective, desirable for the nation's development and increasingly necessary to the maintenance or fulfillment of middle-class status. High school graduation was, for more and more Americans, no longer sufficient as a goal for their children. This view was encouraged by government policies as federal moneys poured into universities and other institutions of higher education from a multitude of agencies and departments to encourage research, which, in turn, expanded facilities and faculty. Second, the sources of immigration had begun to shift very notably and vigorously with the new legislation of the 1960s. American immigration issues had, until then, been overwhelmingly about European immigrants. The initial entrance of Asians in the nineteenth century had been successfully stanched by the first restrictive immigration policies in American history that targeted particular groups. The immigration of Mexicans had a different policy history but the same consequences since Mexicans had been largely treated as temporary workers rather than immigrants. Despite the long experience with Mexicans in the southwest, where communities had existed since the nineteenth-century American expansion westward, the racializing of this brown population and its relegation to a largely transient agricultural labor force had made their schooling a local inconvenience rather than a central policy focus among educators. This now changed in dramatic ways as family reunification and the change in quota policies brought Asians and Latinos (including Cuban refugees) in large numbers to the United States. Finally, the civil rights legislation and temper of the 1960s brought matters of race to the forefront of social and political awareness. And it raised questions about equity, fairness, access, and mobility for groups hitherto marginalized, African Americans especially, but gradually other groups as well.

In the last 30 years of the twentieth century, this potent mixture once again brought issues relating to immigrants onto the educational agenda to become for the first time subjects for policy at the highest level of government. These issues of race, fairness, and higher education continue to reverberate into the twenty-first century. In addition, considerable numbers among the newest immigrants arrived with many of the problems of poverty, language, and conflicts in socialization and identity that had been part of the agenda of the schools since the late nineteenth century. Whether they came from isolated Vietnamese villages or large Latin American cities, the immigration of the late twentieth century brought children whose needs for basic schooling in citizenship were no less than those of the mid-nineteenth-century Irish and whose needs for socialization were similar to those of the early twentieth-century Italians who preceded them. It could be argued that the most significant distinction between this newest immigration and the old was less a matter of race (after all the European groups had been described as races in the early twentieth century) than the result of the even greater range of dissimilarity in past experience that they brought with them, coming now from all parts of the known world. America was becoming, both abroad and at home, a global empire as people from everywhere created a population complexity probably never before seen in human society. Thus, older problems and more extreme heterogeneity now came together with newer concerns about civil rights in an elevated educational context and a much higher level of federal government attention to the education of its citizenry.

Questions about policy now affected schools at all levels and all immigrant and racial groups. Many of them were not new in the American context: among them questions of social services at school, high school ethnic particularism, and differential graduation rates. Others were genuinely innovative – above all, affirmative action policies and federal mandates for local education. Some were more extreme versions of issues that had already appeared in earlier dialogues over schooling, such as bilingual education and the teaching of special ethnic subject matters.

Preschool education also falls into this last category. In the late nineteenth and early twentieth centuries, kindergarten advocates and teachers had adopted ideals of play with an almost missionary zeal, hoping to provide the children of the poor with a protected arena in which they could develop without the requirements of didactic instruction. Many denominations and settlements adopted kindergartens as part of the extension of social services to poor immigrants. Kindergartens emphasized socialization and expression and were meant to provide a few hours of elevated culture and beauty away from dreary home conditions. As an added benefit, they relieved overstressed mothers of their childcare obligations for a precious few hours. Kindergartens for those aged 5–6, before compulsory schooling kicked in, were expensive and only gradually incorporated into the normal public school regime over the course of the twentieth century. When they were, they became an arena for learning readiness rather than play, for the development of motor, memory, and behavioral skills to prepare children for more formal instruction.

It was this learning readiness that was central to the incorporation of new public preschool programs like Head Start which developed from Lyndon Johnson's Great Society Programs in the 1960s. Growing from the era of civil rights, preschool became less a matter of protection than of preparation, and such programs were intended to compensate for inadequate home environments and to even out the disadvantages that some children brought with them to school. This was very much in line with the new emphasis on education as a means to correct social inequities that was common to the period. Concerned to address issues of inner-city poverty, especially that of children in African American communities, and to counteract its baneful effects, preschool and early childhood programs were adopted for their potential to care for and prepare children of the new and often very poor immigrants from Mexico, Latin America, and post-Vietnam-War Asia. When other features of the Johnson "War on Poverty" were disassembled, this program was kept alive and expanded because it was a useful federal intervention in issues related to adequate preparation for schooling.

Much more contentious was the federally mandated bilingual education that resulted from both legislation and court decisions in the 1960s and 1970s (Lau v. Nichols 1974). This legislation also resulted from the new attitudes and views of the civil rights era, especially as Mexican Americans followed in the path of African Americans in demanding community self-determination and ethnic pride. Its advocates urged that children not be deprived of their home language and its associated culture. As Herschel T. Manual testified in hearings in 1967 in the United States Senate which was preparing to pass the first Bilingual Education Act (1968): "Although English is a basic necessity for the non-English-speaking child, as [for] every child, his native language should not be lightly cast aside. The home language of the child is an individual and community asset which the school should help develop from the child's first enrollment" (Cordasco 1976, p. xvi). This emphasis on genuine bilingualism not just as a practical means toward English acquisition but as a resource for community and group identity was not new. The Germans had acted very much in the same way in the nineteenth century and used their political leverage in heavily German-populated communities in the midwest. But it was new in the twentieth-century context, during which two world wars had created considerable fear and concern about sub-community maintenance. Throughout the century, the acquisition of English had been assumed as a byproduct of ever more vigorously enforced school attendance laws while socialization to a variety of American ways had been an objective. As a result, when the issue was reintroduced in the late 1960s, bilingual education was a subject of much contention. In many communities, despite federal financial assistance, it seriously raised educational costs when many different language communities had to be served often within the same school or school district. As with all new federal mandates, it also necessitated accounting and compliance procedures that were often resented by schools and local officials. Nevertheless, through most of the 1970s, 1980s, and 1990s, in the big cities that were home to diverse groups the children of immigrants from China, Mexico, Vietnam, Cambodia, and many other places were often offered instruction in basic subjects in their native language at public expense. This trend has only now begun to decline, most significantly in California and Washington State because of popular referenda that have registered the view that such instruction is an impediment to English acquisition. In California, bilingual education, except as a temporary stopgap, has now been suspended. And in New York City, growing protest and unhappiness on the part of Spanish-speaking parents at the inadequate progress of their children in acquiring English-language confidence is putting that city's bilingual program in dispute.

Bilingualism is closely related to another issue that is both new and old in the public schools – ethnic cohesiveness. Many schools, especially high schools, are today seen as arenas marked by a nearly complete separation between students from different ethnic backgrounds even when they study side-by-side in the classroom. In the 1930s and 1940s it was not at all uncommon for students in high schools to associate largely with those like them, hanging out together in cafeterias and choosing the same extracurricular activities. But this was always done within a setting that emphasized integration and in many cases banned the speaking of foreign languages in the schools. The realm of extracurricular activities was imagined to be a continuation of the common school ideal and a stimulus to active democratic participation in the multi-tracked high schools. One advocate of these activities noted that they were:

> The one place where democratic ideals and objectives may function in a natural matrix. . . . Whether a student is notably dull, studious, rich, poor, handsome, or ugly

he should have an equal opportunity to be a member of a school organization which ought under all circumstances to be organized upon a basis of democratic society. (Fass 1989, pp. 76–7)

By the 1970s and 1980s, however, this view became suspect as unwelcome pressure toward assimilation and was rejected as tending toward Anglo-conformity. Instead, school life often became a battleground among different groups. In one survey, "frequent fights between race-ethnic groups" were seen as the most significant factor making students feel unsafe at school (Portes and Rumbaut 2001, p. 203). In many colleges, students not only associated by ethnic group but were allowed to live in separate dormitories and found a curriculum newly enriched with a variety of courses which permitted continuous identification with various ethnic cultures. All this was aggravated by the end of the century by the growing re-segregation of schools, especially in places with large Latino populations, a trend that eroded the efforts begun after the great victory for integration and civil rights marked by the Brown v. Board of Education decision in 1954. Americanization efforts that had been very close to the surface in the early twentieth century, no matter what their success, were largely buried by the end of the century. As diversity became a byline of American culture, subgroup identity seemed less of a direct challenge. Indeed, the imposition of cultural uniformity by schools was viewed in the late twentieth century as unworthy of a democratic multicultural society.

Except in one area. In matters relating to material success and opportunity, the schools have more than ever been enlisted in the project of immigrant incorporation. If in the nineteenth century the polity was considered the heart of American citizenship and in the early twentieth century social and cultural habits were seen as the core of an American identity, by the late twentieth century Americans began to embrace a more pluralistic cultural vision. Instead of an older emphasis on political participation or cultural unity, social policies substituted active and contented economic activity as the mainstay of social solidarity. While this economic and consumer emphasis was already solidly in place in the much more culturally homogeneous 1950s (and anticipated even in 1850), it was amplified by the commitments of the civil rights era that followed. At a time when multiplicity in cultural tastes and lifestyle choices dominated approved social perspectives, equal access to economic resources became the dominant objective in a consumer-based society.

In the second half of the twentieth century, the mobility that had been offered as a byproduct of schooling in the early twentieth century became the *sine qua non* of a successfully functioning school system. This was in part the result of the growing importance of consumerism to the American economy, and the close identification between the acquisition of material symbols of success and social worth. In this context, college-going and its economic placement value became a necessity. By the 1980s, these patterns were deeply etched, making competition in and through schooling a central focus of social policy. In fact, the findings of various studies, such as the 1983 report, "A Nation at Risk," that American schoolchildren were not holding their own compared with students elsewhere became the subject of national policy concern. Affirmative action, initially a strategy for the better integration of African Americans into American institutions of all kinds, including higher education, became a football in this process.

Certainly not all of the new immigrant groups were either included in or needed the extra boost that affirmative action policies in college admissions offered. The huge diversity of immigration since the 1960s had included groups such as the Chinese and Koreans who were extremely successful academic performers and whose college-going rates were higher than those of natives. Some groups, such as Indians from South Asia, came from families whose educational and skill levels were already very high and who encouraged their children's achievement. And globalization was making the presence of bi-national students from Asian societies familiar at colleges and universities throughout America. These groups were, like the Jews before them, soon to be found in very large numbers at institutions of higher education, especially in California. But, other groups prominent in the new migration, such as Mexicans and the Hmong people of Indochina, came from cultural backgrounds in which education was not highly emphasized and from homes that were marked by material deprivation. During the 1980s these groups were increasingly included in affirmative action policies at schools that began to provide some extra advantage in the admissions process to those who had succeeded against the odds. Often these policies were seen as a means to increase racial diversity at college, since most of the people joined African Americans and Native Americans in being described as people of color. This coalition has become a new feature of life at institutions of higher education, where it has also often been accompanied by various efforts to increase the diversity of faculty and the subjects of study to help inscribe the multicultural perspective into the university curriculum. The California colleges and universities, among them the University of California and Stanford University, have led in these efforts.

Since the new immigration is enormously diverse, that perspective has not always been welcomed by other groups, such as the Koreans, whose ascent has been unassisted and self-motivated. As in the past, the experience of different groups, and of different individuals, has hardly been uniform and the issues remain contentious and complex. As of this writing, affirmative action has been upheld as a result of two divergent decisions by the United States Supreme Court in 2003, both resulting from admissions policies at the University of Michigan. In the first, Gratz et al. v. Bollinger et al., the court rejected the automatic recalculation of admissions requirements that the university had used in evaluating applications by minority candidates and called for a much more individual approach to the admission of undergraduate students. The second, Grutter v. Bolinger et al., upheld the carefully framed concept of affirmative action that had been introduced in the landmark Bakke decision in 1978, a decision that rejected a numerical quota but allowed the University of California to take race into account in admissions (Bakke v. University of California). In judging that the University of Michigan Law School could continue to include race among its admissions criteria the court clarified its position which had been under dispute in various subsequent federal court rulings and by popular referenda (ballot propositions) in California and Texas in the 1990s.

The best recent study of the long-term consequences of affirmative action, a study by two past Ivy League university presidents, Derek Bok and William Bowen, suggests that affirmative action policy operates successfully in creating a more diverse college-educated professional group among those previously deprived. The graduation rates of those who came to college with an extra boost differed hardly at all from those who did not and they have now become an anchor of a new diverse middle class. From the point of view of social policy, affirmative action has created a more fully incorporative society. The study confirms the larger social issues which underlie the federal government's growing role in educational issues. At the same time, from the point of view of competing students eager for the benefits that entry to the very best schools and professional programs can provide in a highly competitive educational marketplace, issues of personal injustice and unequal treatment are often keenly felt.

While these matters have dominated education at the top, the question of education lower down and its relationship both to successful social and economic integration and to affirmative action has remained a powerful political issue. In California, among other places, the children of Mexican immigrants continue to graduate from high school at much lower rates than others, and only about half make it through. This has been a concern at all levels of policy in the state. But the issues have now developed a national face. Indeed, for the first time in American history, presidential candidates have developed educational proposals as among their primary campaign themes, most recently in President George W. Bush's "Leave No Child Behind" campaign. Bush, a former governor of the state of Texas, a state with a very large Mexican American population, has understood that the successful schooling of the newest immigrants as a matter of both politics and equity is a fundamental national objective. Part of this effort resulted in a renewal of demands that national standards and tests be used to make sure that all children are receiving a basic education that will fit them for participation in a modern, technologically driven, and globally competitive economy. As in the past, the children of immigrants are very much in the minds of those who have launched this campaign, as they are in the minds of those who oppose it as a shallow and inadequate response to a significant problem. The schooling of immigrants has finally been elevated from the local to the national level at a time when schooling at all levels from preschool to professional is a subject of national policy and debate.

Since the first half-century of American life, schooling and immigration have been fundamental matters in national self-definition. While the issues were first dealt with at a fairly rudimentary level and involved largely local commitments, the last 150 years have seen the two become more and more central to American culture, politics, and economic life. Today the question of schooling as it relates to a society still being redefined by immigration is a fundamental one, from the lowest to the highest levels of politics and policy. It also remains an issue close to the heart of every immigrant family eager to keep its children close to their roots in a different past while propelling them onto the road to American success.

REFERENCES

Alba, Richard and Victor Nee (2003). *Remaking the American Mainstream: Assimilation and Contemporary Immigration.* Cambridge, MA: Harvard University Press.
Berg, Ellen (2004). "Citizens in the Republic: Immigrants and American Kindergartens, 1880–1920." PhD diss., University of California at Berkeley.

Bodnar, John (1982). "Schooling and the Slavic-American Family, 1900–1940." In Bernard J. Weiss, ed., *American Education and the European Immigrant*. Urbana: University of Illinois Press.

Bowen, William G., and Derek Bok (1998). *The Shape of the River: Long-Term Consequences of Considering Race in College and University Admissions*. Princeton, NJ: Princeton University Press.

Brilliant, Mark (forthcoming). *Color Lines: Civil Rights Struggles on America's Racial Frontier, 1945–1975*. New York: Oxford University Press.

Caplan, Nathan, John K. Whitmore, and Marcella H. Choy (1989). *The Boat People and Achievement in America: A Study of Family Life, Hard Work, and Cultural Values*. Ann Arbor, MI: University of Michigan Press.

Cordasco, Francesco (1976). *Bilingual Schooling in the United States: A Sourcebook for Educational Personnel*. New York: McGraw-Hill.

Covello, Leonard (1967). *The Social Background of the Italo-American Child: A Study of the Southern Italian Family Moresa and Their Effect on the School Situation in Italy and America*, ed. Francesco Cordasco. Leiden: Brill.

Covello, Leonard, with Guido D'Agostino (1958). *The Heart is a Teacher*. New York: McGraw-Hill

Cremin, Lawrence (1980). *American Education: The National Experience, 1783–1876*. New York: Harper.

Daniels, Roger (1990). *Coming to America: A History of Immigration and Ethnicity in American Life*. New York: HarperCollins.

Dinnerstein, Leonard (1982). "Education and Advancement of American Jews." In Bernard J. Weiss, ed., *American Education and the European Immigrant, 1840–1940*. Urbana: University of Illinois Press.

Fass, Paula S. (1989). *Outside In: Minorities and the Transformation of American Education*. New York: Oxford University Press.

Freedman, Samuel G. (2004). "Latino Parents Decry Bilingual Programs." *The New York Times*, July 14, p. A21.

Handlin, Oscar (1982). "Education and the European Immigrant, 1820–1920." In Bernard J. Weiss, ed., *American Education and the European Immigrant, 1840–1940*. Urbana: University of Illinois Press.

Jefferson, Thomas (1954). *Notes on the State of Virginia*, ed. William Peden. New York: Norton.

Kaestle, Carl F. (1983). *Pillars of the Republic: Common Schools and American Society, 1780–1860*. New York: Hill and Wang.

Katz, Michael B. (1987). *Reconstructing American Education*. Cambridge, MA: Harvard University Press.

Lassonde, Stephen (1996). "Learning and Earning: Schooling, Juvenile Employment, and the Early Life Course in Late Nineteenth-Century New Haven." *Journal of Social History* 29 (Summer): 839–70.

—— (1998). "Should I Go, Or Should I Stay? Adolescence, School Attainment, and Parent–Child Relations in Italian Immigrant Families of New Haven, 1900–1940." *History of Education Quarterly* 38 (Spring 1998): 37–60.

—— (2005). *Learning to Forget: Schooling and Social Life in New Haven's Working Class, 1870–1940*. New Haven: Yale University Press, 2005.

Olneck, Michael and Michael Lazerson (1978). "The School Achievement of Immigrant Children, 1890–1930." *History of Education Quarterly* 18 (Fall): 227–70.

Perlmann, Joel (1988). *Ethnic Differences: Schooling and Social Structure Among the Irish, Italians, Jews and Blacks in an American City, 1880–1935*. Cambridge, Eng.: Cambridge University Press.

Portes, Alejandro and Rubén G. Rumbaut (2001). *Legacies: The Story of the Immigrant Second Generation*. Berkeley: University of California Press.

Rumbaut, Rubén G. (1999). "The Immigrant Experience for Families and Children." Congressional Seminar, June 4, 1998, Spivak Program in Applied Social Research and Social Policy, American Sociological Association, Washington, DC.

Sanders, James W. (1977). *The Education of an Urban Minority: Catholics in Chicago, 1833–1965*. New York: Oxford University Press.

Suárez-Orozco, Marcelo M., Carola Suárez-Orozco, and Désiree Qin-Hilliard (2001). *Interdisciplinary Perspectives on the New Immigration, Vol. 5: The New Immigrant and American Schools*. New York: Routledge.

Tyack, David B. (1974). *The One Best System: A History of American Urban Education*. Cambridge, MA: Harvard University Press.

—— (2003). *Seeking Common Ground: Public Schools in a Diverse Society*. Cambridge, MA: Harvard University Press.

Ueda, Reed (1987). *Avenues to Adulthood: The Origins of the High School and Social Mobility in an American Suburb*. Cambridge, Eng.: Cambridge University Press.

—— (1994). *Postwar Immigrant America: A Social History*. Bedford Books/St. Martin's Press.

Weinstein, Rhona S. (2002). *Reaching Higher: The Power of Expectations in Schooling*. Cambridge, MA: Harvard University Press.

CHAPTER TWENTY-FOUR

Religion and Ethnicity

JOHN MCCLYMER

This chapter tackles a very large but understudied set of questions. In the literature of case studies of immigrant groups only a handful pay close attention to religion. Relying to a considerable extent upon a study of Worcester, Massachusetts, this chapter emphasizes the experiences of European groups in northern cities between the 1870s and the 1920s, although it does also consider experiences of present-day immigrants. Rather than attempting a broad synthesis, the chapter sketches several dimensions of the topic, frames questions for research, and formulates very tentative suggestions about how to begin answering them.

One way to begin is to look at "lived religion" – the phrase is Robert Orsi's whose *The Madonna of 115th Street* "approaches all religion as lived experience, theology no less than lighting a candle. . . ." How did the ways in which immigrants and their descendants actually practice their religions influence their lives? Was faith a support in times of crisis, as they so often claimed? Beyond the impact of belief upon experience is the matter of religion's contribution to increasing the density of community life. Believers did more than attend services. They joined sports teams, played in orchestras, acted in local theatre productions, attended dances, competed in basketball leagues, all under the sponsorship of a church or temple. They also looked to community needs. They raised money for causes of all sorts, volunteered their time and energy, and, in the process, became important people in their communities. In this and other ways religion was a crucial component in acculturation and assimilation. The children who attended parochial schools learned about American history as filtered through a specific ethnic and religious sensibility. They learned too that their chances in life would depend on how their group was perceived, and not only by Yankees but also by other religious and ethnic communities.

Anti-Catholicism and, to a lesser degree, anti-Semitism were crucial determinants of how immigrants and their children were welcomed. Despite the classic works of Ray Allen Billington and John Higham, anti-Catholicism is often ignored in the secondary literature. And the way in which it played into relations among immigrant groups is almost never considered. Also left largely unexplored to date is the impact of religion in the emerging popular culture and mass media, both in terms of the roles of religious organizations such as the Catholic Legion of Decency and in terms of the portrayals of religious characters and rituals, as with Yom Kippur in *The Jazz Singer*. Worcester, Massachusetts in the last quarter of the nineteenth century provides vivid glimpses into several of these dimensions of the influence of religion on the immigrant experience.

Religion and the Ethnic Experience in the "Heart of the Commonwealth"

"The French Canadian loves his church and is loyal to it," Carroll D. Wright wrote in his 1881 *Report* for the Massachusetts Bureau of the Statistics of Labor. Wright had held a hearing on their situation at the insistence of the French Canadians. They were outraged because, in his 1880 *Report*, he had disparaged them as "the Chinese of the eastern states." They were, he wrote, a "horde of industrial invaders" who cared "nothing for our institutions." The hearing caused him to change his mind. He concluded that the Canadians' complete assimilation with the American people was but a question of time.

It was their love of their church that made their assimilation inevitable, Wright concluded. Priests came from Canada, initially as missionaries, and established parishes. Canadians gathered around them, and the missionaries became pastors. Eager to see their flocks "grow and prosper," the priests urged parishioners to acquire property and take out citizenship papers. The parishes then built convents, schools, orphanages, hospitals. They sponsored literary associations, choruses, orchestras, drama societies, and sports teams in addition to sodalities and other religious clubs. The density of community life, focused upon the local church, struck most, as it had Wright at first, as an insistence "upon preserving a distinct national existence within the Republic." That is also how the Canadians themselves viewed it. Worcester editor Ferdinand Gagnon wrote in 1872 that his compatriots in New England "make up a separate society."

> They have formed their own nation. . . . All they have in common with Americans is material interests; beyond that an abyss separates them and their sole concern is to make this abyss impassable. Their true country is Lower Canada.

Not so, Wright concluded. Their efforts to set themselves apart, with parochial schools, French language newspapers, and other Canadian institutions, created more numerous and deeper connections to their new homes. The result, Wright wrote, was that Canadians found "themselves more attached to the new [land] than to the old." In 1901 the Rev. Jules Graton, pastor of St. Joseph's Church in the "French Hill" section of Worcester spelled out some of the underlying logic of this process to the Ward Three Naturalization Club of which he was chaplain. In the early years of the "colony" in Worcester, Canadians were "lost."

> We watched citizens meeting to deliberate upon matters of municipal interest, where they could pass measures that would endanger our political or religious advancement, and we had no voice. . . . We knew no road but the road to the factory, and we had no place to act but in manufacturing . . . we lived in a lethargy that was capable of bringing us to our death.

How long have you been getting any consideration? Since you've been voting. In the past no one knew you, but today when they meet you, they salute you, they even know your name, and they smile at you, because you have become something, because they need you.

L'Abbé T.A. Chandonnet, a missionary priest from Quebec who spent several months preaching at Notre-Dame-Des-Canadiens parish in Worcester, Massachusetts, explained the local church's importance in his history of that congregation. In Canada, the government provided funding, but here a parish is "an achievement." It required "heroic" sacrifices from people who had little to spare. The parish proved their love of their religion, he wrote, and their cultural loyalties. Within their own church, they could hear the Gospel preached in French by a fellow *Canadien*. They could practice *Quebeçois* customs, midnight Mass on Christmas Eve, for example. And their children could learn both the catechism and "proper French." Public examinations on the catechism became important events. Each child required new clothes for the occasion. All the parents turned out to watch. Their children's ability to answer correctly, wrote Chandonnet, proved to parents that they were growing up both Catholic and French Canadian.

Immigrants used their churches, starting with the actual buildings, to proclaim their own worthiness. The second French Canadian church in Worcester, St. Joseph's, rose directly across the street from the Irish St. Stephen's. St. Joseph's was larger, and not by accident. Its cathedral-like expanse made a statement and one directed at the Irish and other Catholic groups more than towards the Yankees. A walking tour of the South Side of Chicago would show the same phenomenon. As ethnic groups moved into the area, they set about building national parishes. Most made it a point of honor to ensure their church would be grander than those that preceded it.

Open expressions of group pride, the buildings can also tell us something important about acculturation, namely that we need to widen our study of it beyond the relations between the host culture and a particular ethnic community. Immigrants sought to find their way into a plural society. In doing so they engaged in what Charles Estus, Sr. and I have called "cultural triangulation." In defining their place in the new land they looked to their own cultural traditions, to the host culture, and to other immigrant groups. Religion was a key component in this process. A Worcester example can serve.

In November of 1888, 600 Swedes marched from the Second Swedish Methodist Church through a snowstorm to a temperance rally at Mechanics Hall where the keynote speaker, US Senator George Frisbie Hoar, hailed as "one of the best omens to the city . . . the coming to us in large numbers of brethren of Scandinavian birth." In the same speech he bemoaned "the great addiction to drink" of "our Irish brethren." Hoar concluded by welcoming the Swedes to the ranks of those who sought each year to pass a referendum banning the licensing of saloons. John Corneli, speaking for his fellow Swedes, indicated that they understood the terms of their welcome. He began with a boast: "The Swedish people are all Protestants." Further, "in this city you will not find a saloon that is run by a Scandinavian, nor one who acts as a tail to one kept by a Frenchman, Irishman, or German." This gained him an enthusiastic round of applause. Yet Corneli and company had marched past Martin Trulson's saloon on their way to the rally. It was directly across the street from the church. And, at least among themselves, Swedes candidly acknowledged that all too many of their countrymen shared the "great addiction to drink" of the Irish.

Less important than the veracity of Corneli's boast was his pledge that "the American people . . . will find that we will not antagonize" their "principles." Swedes would demonstrate, that is, both their attachment to "American" values and the differences between themselves and the Catholic immigrant groups in the city. The Irish reliably voted Democratic. Swedes flocked to Senator Hoar's Republican Party. The Irish voted against the licensing referendum, despite the activities of the Fr. Matthews, as the members of the Catholic temperance societies were called. The Swedes voted for the referendum, despite the convictions of the Lutherans in their midst that the moderate use of alcohol was permissible.

Swedes and Yankees would forge what Kenneth J. Moynihan (1989) has called a "Protestant Partnership." The first Swedes to build a church in Worcester were Methodists. Their Yankee co-religionists generously helped out. One of the first pastors noted in his diary that when the congregation wanted a bell, all they had to pay for was the rope. Swedish Congregationalists and other dissenters had similar experiences. Yankee churches raised funds to help them get started. Swedish Lutherans were the last denomination to build a church. This was because, on the advice of the Bishop of Sweden, they initially attended Episcopal services. There they encountered a welcome so warm that they waited almost a full generation before erecting a church of their own.

These connections to the Yankee community spurred rivalries and ethnic hatreds with other ethnic groups. Catholic and Jewish immigrants not only received no help from the Yankees in building their churches and synagogues but also recognized that the Yankees would discriminate against them because of their faith. Yet, as Wright recognized, their success in building communities centered on church and *shul* did not shut them off from American life. Wright's insight did not become conventional wisdom, however, even after W.I. Thomas and Florian Znaniecki developed it in great detail in their classic *The Polish Peasant in Europe and America* (1918–20). This is perhaps because they wrote about Catholic groups. Applied to Protestant groups, Wright's views were conventional wisdom. Hence the willingness of Yankee Protestants to help build foreign language churches in Worcester.

Swedes and other Protestant immigrant groups claimed a fundamental affinity for American culture. Catholics claimed a fundamental commitment to American political ideals which they carefully distinguished from Yankee customs and values. So did Jews. Some Orthodox Jews recognized profound dissonances between their faith and American culture. Particular groups, such as the Hasidim, solved this by living in a self-imposed quarantine. They joined the Mennonites in establishing distinctive and homogeneous communities. For the most part, however, Wright's paradigm held. Efforts to create Little Canadas or Little Italys mediated but did not impede assimilation.

Lived Religion

Despite the evident importance immigrants and their children attached to religion, and the acclaim Thomas and Znaniecki received for exploring the manifold ways in which parish life shaped the immigrant experience, most scholars have largely downplayed the role of religion when they have not ignored it altogether. A conspicuous exception is Robert Orsi who begins his *The Madonna of 115th Street: Faith and Community in Italian Harlem, 1880–1950* (1985) with a detailed description of the annual *festa* which began on July 16 and went on for several days. At its heart was the great procession in which all participated and during which the faithful would carry enormous candles, some weighing 50 or 60 pounds, often shaped as legs, arms, and other body parts. The idea was to honor the precise way in which the Virgin had interceded to help them regain their health. When they reached the steps of the church from which the procession would proceed, "penitents crawled up the steps on their hands and knees, some of them dragging their tongues along the stone." Orsi continues:

> The questions we must now ask are: What did this devotion mean to the immigrants and their children in the new land? What role did it play in the history of East Harlem? How could this devotion not only survive the sea change but take on a new and powerful life in New York City? What does the devotion reveal about the immigrants' values and hopes? What does it teach us about the nature of their religious faith?

Life in America placed enormous strain upon the traditional southern Italian family and especially upon mothers who were expected to hold the family together and to pass on to the next generation core values of loyalty to blood and respect for elders. Overwhelmed by familial cares, they turned to the Madonna, writing letters to her in which they spelled out their anxieties and prayed for her intercession. The letters provide a rich source of first person narrative about daily life in the community.

Orsi makes a compelling case for the importance of "lived religion" in addressing his questions; he also demonstrates the value of parish records for the study of ethnic communities. Nonetheless his questions remain peripheral to most scholarly discussions of ethnic life; and parish records remain grossly undervalued and underused. There is, for example, a scholarly debate going on about the portrayal of the Day of Atonement in *The Jazz Singer* but not about the role of this most solemn religious event in Jewish life in the decades of the great migration from eastern Europe. Irving Howe wrote in *World of Our Fathers: The Journey of the East European Jews to America and the Life They Found and Made* (1976) that Yom Kippur had "so sacred a resonance" that immigrants "felt that to go [to *shul*] then was to confirm one's identity as a Jew." How did the Day of Atonement ceremonies and prayers shape that identity? How did they enable immigrants to express the sense of loss they experienced in a new and secular world? How did they help them express their hopes? Howe did not attempt to answer any of these questions. There is a vital, fascinating literature still to be written that will take up these questions and analogous ones for other groups.

Religion and the Density of Community Life

Pastors and rabbis openly acknowledged that ethnic groups competed with each other – for jobs, for housing, and for respect. Immigrants had to accept whatever jobs they could find, live in whatever dwelling they could afford. Respect too did not come easily. Others mocked and disparaged one's group and, by extension, oneself. As Thomas and Znaniecki showed, the parish community could soften the blow. Trooping off to work in the stockyards or the steel mills, one was just another

Polack. Inside *Polania* one was respected. One might be president of a society, coach of a team, soloist in the choir. One might play a lead in the annual drama club presentation. A look at parish newsletters shows how varied church organizations were. And how duplicative. The reason, Thomas and Znaniecki argued, was to make certain that there were enough places of honor to go around. Anyone willing to put in the time could be a somebody in the community.

Timothy Meagher's (2001) work on the Irish in Worcester deepens our under-standing of the churches' role in building ethnic communities. Parishes, he shows, directly fostered upward mobility. There was a strong correlation between membership in their temperance societies and occupational success. Membership signaled one's reliability and ambition. It also brought contacts with already successful parishioners. Politicians, lawyers, doctors, opticians, morticians, the whole middle class including the saloon keepers maintained a highly visible connection to their local parish. The parish was a core building block of their success. So was the College of the Holy Cross. It trained a portion of the next generation to become professionals, a role played by the much smaller Assumption College for French Canadians in the city.

While often rivals, the Irish and French Canadians could cooperate as Catholics. Spurned by Worcester's Yankee-dominated banks, they pooled their resources to found Bay State Bank. It provided both groups with mortgages and other financial services and with white-collar jobs as tellers and bookkeepers. Similarly, when City and Memorial Hospitals refused admitting privileges to Irish and French Canadian physicians, Catholics created St. Vincent's Hospital. French Canadians took the lead in erecting the St. Francis Home for the Aged but received active Irish support. Cemeteries were a different matter. Each group had its own.

What this meant was that immigrants and their children could live much of their lives in an Irish or French Canadian or Polish subculture within a larger American Catholic subculture. They gave birth in a Catholic hospital where the attending physician was a member of their own parish, sent their children off to a parochial school, played sports in church leagues, went to dances in the parish hall, marked small and major events with church rituals – baptisms, marriages, funerals – and determined what movies to see from the ratings of the Legion of Decency. Jewish immigrants built similar institutions – hospitals, orphanages, charitable associations, yeshivas, and synagogues. Religious services also defined key moments in their lives. And, as with Catholics, they lived within a Jewish American subculture. Jews might divide among Reform, Conservative, and Orthodox or between German and eastern European, but they all shared a Jewish identity. So too, Catholic ethnic groups could be bitter rivals but all acknowledged a Catholic identity.

Protestant immigrants, such as Worcester's Swedes, had their own subculture as well. Fairlawn was their hospital; Commerce Bank grew out of their Skandia Credit Union; the Lutheran Home cared for their elderly. Their churches sponsored just as many organizations, fielded as many sports teams, hosted as many events. The Lucia Fest packed their churches every December. The key difference, however, was that Swedes lived within a larger American Protestant subculture, one that included Yankees and that claimed to be *the* American culture.

Will Herberg's classic *Protestant, Catholic, Jew* (1955) first articulated the notion that America was not a single "melting pot" but rather three separate pots. Americans had to be religious to be fully accepted by their fellow citizens, he argued, but it no longer mattered which religion one followed. I follow Herberg's overall analysis here, but I have several reservations. One is that these subcultures developed over a much longer period of time than Herberg thought. A second is that it does matter to which religion one belongs – Protestantism was, and remains, normative. Another is that we can no longer think in terms of three major religious traditions. A new immigration from Asia, the Pacific, Africa, and the Middle East is bringing with it new religions.

Religion and Acculturation/Assimilation

First a word about words. Following Milton Gordon (1964), I use acculturation to describe how immigrants adopt American ways. Assimilation describes how they find their way into coherent niches in American society. In using either term we must be careful to avoid several misleading assumptions. The first is that either is a zero-sum process, namely that the more American one became, the less ethnic one necessarily was. Starting with religion, immigrants insisted upon an additive model. There was an American civic religion that many deeply mistrusted because of its clear Protestant bias, as manifested, for example, in the YMCAs and YWCAs. This distrust sometimes took institutional form as in the case of the Catholic Youth Organization (CYO). The principal purpose of the CYO was to keep Catholic children away from the YMCAs and YWCAs.

Another assumption, briefly mentioned above, is that immigrants focused primarily upon the host society. Immigrants knew they were making their way in a society which was often intolerant and which judged them by their accents, their last names, and their religion. They knew that they were in open competition with members of other nationalities. "America does not consist of groups," Woodrow Wilson told an audience of newly naturalized citizens in 1916. "Anyone who thinks of himself as a member of a group is not a true American." Immigrants knew better. Acculturation and assimilation meant more than learning American ways or coming to appreciate American ideals. They meant gaining acceptance for one's own group, both one's specific nationality and the larger Catholic or Jewish community. Protestants did not have this same concern since the host society was already Protestant.

A substantial literature examines the roles of secular agencies, often Yankee-led and funded, in immigrant communities. Studies of settlement houses are especially numerous. The YMCA and YWCA have also attracted attention. What these studies acknowledge only in passing is that these agencies were in direct competition with parishes and synagogues. Nowhere was this sharper than in their claims to be Americanizing agencies. The churches made the same claim. But they meant something quite different.

Both settlement workers and ethnic clerics shared a deep concern about the dangers American culture posed for immigrants and their children. One can hear it in a sermon on the benefits of "mediocrity" given by Father Jean-Baptiste Primeau as recorded in L'Abbé Chandonnet's history. Poverty tempted one to crime and to alcohol as a refuge from suffering, he told parishioners at Notre-Dame. But wealth had its own dangers. It led to the Yankee Protestant world and to apostasy. It led to a concern with fashion and worldly goods. It was a "happy mediocrity" which preserved faith and accomplished great things. Jane Addams did not regard the Yankee Protestant culture as a threat. Hull House existed to bring a secularized version of it to its neighbors. But she did express concern with the commercial "places" – in

Chicago, she wrote, "we just say places" – springing up to meet the "working girl's" and her male counterpart's desire for pleasure. Dance halls headed her list of menaces followed by saloons, movie theatres, amusement parks, and the cheaper kinds of vaudeville. Hull House and other settlements along with the YMCA and YWCA made concerted efforts to provide safe alternatives. And thousands and thousands of immigrants and their children availed themselves of the opportunities they offered.

Millions flocked to parish-sponsored competing programs. There they encountered the churches' and synagogues' myriad Americanization efforts, efforts ignored in the large literature on Americanization. Clergy typically sought to contain the allure of American popular culture even as they insisted upon the intense patriotism of the ethnic group. At dances, for example, there were American popular songs and dance steps and also songs and dances from the Old Country. There were also chaperones and strict rules against drinking. In the church leagues immigrants and their children played American sports such as baseball and basketball but they played against other ethnic parish teams. Would Our Lady of Mount Carmel beat St. Patrick's for the championship? Group pride was at stake. Once again we see the additive model and cultural triangulation in operation.

We can see it too in such overt expressions of ethnic pride as St. Patrick's Day or Saint Jean Baptiste Day or Midsommar. Most festivals honored a saint. Even when they did not, church groups provided many of the floats and most of the marchers. Clergy occupied special places of honor. So did American flags and other patriotic symbols. The implicit claim was that one's own group made the best Americans. Nor were Americans the sole audience. Each nationality wanted to have the most impressive parade, the biggest floats, the largest crowd of onlookers. Swedish newspapers in Worcester, for example, annually bemoaned the size of the St. Patrick's Day parade. For years differences over temperance prevented the city's Swedes from creating a grand Swedish festival, as "drys" refused to attend any event at which alcohol was served. Religious beliefs could divide as well as unite.

Parish minstrel shows provide another example of triangulation. They not only introduced immigrants to traditional American racism, songs, dances, and jokes. They also provided opportunities to make fun of other ethnics and of Yankee Protestants. In 1906 the minstrels of St. John's High School in Worcester mocked Germans in one number and Native Americans in another. This stands in stark contrast to programs at Hull House where each group could depend upon receiving the utmost respect.

Anti-Catholicism and Anti-Semitism

In 1854 a handwritten "platform" of the Native American Party circulated in Massachusetts. Among its planks were the following:

4. War to the hilt, on political Romanism
7. Hostility to all Papal influences, when brought to bear against the Republic
10. The amplest protection to Protestant Interests
14. Eternal enmity to all who attempt to carry out the principles of a Foreign Church or State.

In addition to being a high-water mark of anti-Catholicism, the 1850s also witnessed the triumph of the Maine Law, from New England, where all six states prohibited the sale of alcohol, to New York, to the Nebraska Territory, to Texas. This is not coincidence. Prohibition would triumph again, in 1919, and the 1920s would be marked by equally intense anti-Catholicism. Millions joined the Ku Klux Klan. Millions more shared the Klan's hostility to Catholicism. William Robinson Pattangall, defeated Democratic candidate for governor of Maine in 1924, ran on a platform sharply critical of the Klan. He later admitted that he had seriously under-estimated the salience of anti-Catholicism. "I did not even know it [hatred from 'the long-dead days of the religious wars'] existed, did not realize at all how persistent such a hatred could be when there was nothing to excite it" except "the Klan's brilliant incendiarism." Yet Pattangall himself stated in a 1925 article in *The Forum* that the Klan's "complaints made against the Catholics and foreign-born are very largely true." More specifically:

> The most valid of all the charges the Klan brings against the Roman hierarchy is that secretly it does not accept the American principle of the separation of church and state, but furtively goes into politics *as a church* and attempts to use its spiritual hold on its members as a means for political control.

The Forum had, in its preceding issue, in August 1924, sponsored an "impartial discussion of the Americanism of the Roman Catholic Church," and its reporter who most frequently wrote critically about the Ku Klux Klan, Stanley Frost, warned in the June 1928 issue that Al Smith's "inevitable" defeat, should he gain the Democratic nomination, would likely lead to the creation of a "Catholic Party" modeled on those of Europe. Similar discussions of the "Catholic influence" upon American politics filled the newspapers and magazines of the 1920s.

Thanks to Ray Allen Billington, the salience of anti-Catholicism for understanding the Know Nothings is clear. Its importance for temperance reform, however, is largely overlooked. Henry S. Clubb, secretary of the Maine Law Statistical Society, an organization dedicated to documenting the effect of prohibition, wrote in his *The Maine Liquor Law: Its Origin, History, and Results, Including A Life of Hon. Neal Dow* (1856):

> Perhaps there is no more difficult class to control than the Germans, and next to them the Irish, who form combinations among their respective countrymen to evade the law, and to defeat the ends of justice by either refusing to give evidence or swearing falsely. This is the case in many parts of Worcester County; but the more stringent law just passed [by the newly elected Know Nothings] is expected to reach even these difficult cases.

Both the Maine Law and the Volstead Act were Protestant reforms, attempts to impose evangelical beliefs upon recalcitrant newcomers. Although much studied, scholars have yet to appreciate the temperance movement's importance in the shaping of American culture. For a full century, from the 1830s through the repeal of pro-hibition in 1933, temperance was by far the most popular reform movement as well as the most divisive. Its appeal to Protestants who also supported the Know Nothings in the 1850s and the Klan in the 1920s is a clue scholars have yet to investigate.

Historians of the 1920s, including historians of the Ku Klux Klan, pay little heed to anti-Catholicism and only slightly more to anti-Semitism. Gary Gerstle, for example, devotes a chapter to the 1920s in his *American Crucible: Race and Nation in the Twentieth Century* (2001). It was a decade of nativist triumph, of "racial nationalism," he writes. Yet Gerstle does not discuss the impact of anti-Catholicism, does not even mention Al Smith's campaign for the presidency. Over 36 million people voted in 1928, 13 million more than in 1924. This was an increase of more than 56 percent. As a result, despite the Hoover landslide, Smith got twice as many votes as the 1924 Democratic candidate, John W. Davis. In fact, Smith captured almost as many votes as Coolidge had in 1924. Why, we need to ask, did Smith partisans turn out in record numbers even though their candidate's defeat was a sure thing. His total was 8 million higher than Davis's. Why did Hoover voters turn out in such large numbers when his victory was an equally sure thing? His total was 6 million higher than Coolidge's. This was an increase of 40 percent. The short answer is that this race produced a level of passion rarely seen in American politics. Religion fueled that passion.

Gerstle does discuss, at length, the Immigration Restriction Act of 1924 but only in terms of racism. This is overly simple. Quotas under the law were directly tied to nationality groups. But it did not escape anyone's notice at the time that the quotas discriminated against Jews, Catholics, and Greek and Russian Orthodox believers. The only Catholic nation with a quota comparable to those for Great Britain, Germany, and the Scandinavian countries was the Irish Free State. Norway's quota (6,453) dwarfed Hungary's (473); Sweden's (9,561) was more than four times larger than Russia's (2,248). Racial and religious categories overlapped so strikingly that in proscribing immigrants from eastern and southern Europe one automatically reduced immigration by non-Protestants. In addition, the neo-Lamarckian ideas espoused by eugenicists and other advocates of restriction linked religion and race. Lamarck had theorized that acquired characteristics could be inherited. In the eugenics-inspired version of Lamarck's ideas Catholic countries bred a certain type of person, one easily dominated by authority. It was a characteristic acquired by obedience to an authoritarian church and passed on to each new generation. So too with Jews. Hiram Wesley Evans, Imperial Grand Wizard of the Ku Klux Klan, explained to an audience at the Texas State Fair in 1923 that Jews could not become real Americans. Centuries of persecution had ingrained in them a congenital inability to feel patriotism. No Jew, no matter if he and his descendants lived in the United States for a thousand years, could experience the sentiments of love for his new country that an immigrant from Britain might feel within a year. This was a large part of "the menace of modern immigration."

Religion in the Emerging Popular Culture of the Twentieth Century

Henry Ford actively stirred up anti-Semitic sentiments, first by subsidizing the translation of "The Protocols of the Elders of Zion" and then by publishing *The International Jew: The World's Foremost Problem* (1922). In it he deplores how "Jewish Jazz" was "becoming our national music."

> The people are fed from day to day on the moron suggestiveness that flows in a slimy flood out of "Tin Pan Alley," the head factory of filth in New York which is populated

by the "Abies," the "Izzies," and the "Moes" who make up the composing staffs of the various institutions.

Ford was equally appalled by the Jewish control of the movie studios. "The motion picture influence of the United States, of the whole world, is exclusively under the control, moral and financial, of the Jewish manipulators of the public mind."

Ford's fears of an international Jewish conspiracy were delusional. But Jewish immigrants and their children did do much to shape popular culture during the first half of the twentieth century. A joke of the era went that Americans could not have a holiday without an Irving Berlin song. If Jews wrote much of the popular music, Jews (Al Jolson, Fanny Brice) and Catholics (Bing Crosby, Frank Sinatra) also sang much of it. Jews and Catholics (Gallagher and Sheen, Burns and Allen, Eddie Cantor, Jimmy Durante) wrote and told many of the jokes. And Jews did control production of most of the nation's movies.

In some cases – *The Jazz Singer* (1927) and *Going My Way* (1944) are examples – films dealt directly with the religious experiences of first- and second-generation immigrants. In *The Jazz Singer* Al Jolson played a cantor's son who runs away from home when forbidden to sing "American" songs. The song that most provokes his father's wrath is Irving Berlin's "Blue Skies," a cinematic response to Henry Ford's denunciations. At the heart of the film is the conflict between Judaism and American popular culture. Jolson's character must choose either to sing the *Kol Nidre* on the Day of Atonement or to star in a Broadway revue. He can be either Jakie Rabinowitz, the cantor's boy, or Jack Robin, the jazz singer. In the end, he chooses to be a Jew. His father's dying words, spoken while Jakie sings in the synagogue across the street, are "We have our boy again." Of course, Jakie also gets to star on Broadway as Jack, and the film closes with Jolson performing "Mammy" in blackface to his mother in the audience.

Much has been written about the use of blackface. This preoccupation has had the unfortunate effect of diverting attention from the movie's loving depiction of Jewish religious rites. Cantor Rabinowitz is stubborn as well as blind to the joys of American popular culture but the film endorses his love for sacred music. Jakie/Jack, however much he loves "jazzy" tunes, is still haunted by the beauties of religious song. In Chicago, where he is performing in vaudeville, he attends a concert of Jewish sacred music and flashes back to memories of his father in the synagogue. When forced to choose, he picks his religion. His subsequent success vindicates his choice and affirms that Jews are as American as minstrelsy.

Few other films depicted Jewish religious practices but many dealt with Catholicism. The priest, as played by Bing Crosby in *Going My Way* (1944), Spencer Tracy in *Boy's Town* (1938), or Pat O'Brien in *Angels With Dirty Faces* (1938), became a heroic figure in the movies of the 1930s and 1940s. *Going My Way*, written and directed by Irish Catholic Leo McCarey and starring Irish Catholic Bing Crosby and co-starring Irish Catholic Barry Fitzgerald, all of whom won Oscars, tells the story of Father Chuck O'Malley. Father O'Malley initially displeases the elderly pastor (Fitzgerald) with his fondness for attending baseball games and going fishing but soon wins him over, and the rest of the parish, by turning street gangs into a choir, fixing the church's financial problems, and arranging for a trip back to Ireland for the pastor. Audiences fell in love with Father O'Malley. *Going My Way* was the highest grossing film of 1944, and *The Bells of St. Mary* brought Father O'Malley back the next year in a highly successful sequel. What Crosby's lovable character does is make the parish work. The films' message is that you can bring all of your troubles to church and find solutions. Or, as Father O'Malley tells a nun played by Ingrid Bergman in *The Bells of St. Mary*, if you have a problem, "just dial O for O'Malley."

Hollywood's sympathetic treatment of Catholicism in so many films reflected the considerable power wielded by the Church over the industry. The story of how Catholic pressure forced studio executives to adopt the Production Code of 1934 is well known. Numerous other groups, including many Protestant churches, also had wanted the industry to eliminate explicit references to sex and to ban nudity on screen. What made the difference was that millions of Catholics took an oath annually at Mass to heed the classifications of the Legion of Decency. The Legion rated every film. Catholics promised not to go to see any classed as "objectionable in part" or as "condemned." Either rating spelled box office trouble. The studios therefore made sure that their own Code conformed to the Legion's standards.

Where Hollywood led, radio and television would soon follow. Media censorship had a distinct Catholic tone, and no one dared produce anything that the Church might take amiss. This too constituted acculturation, albeit not of the sort imagined by those historians who bemoan the influence of the movies and mass media generally in homogenizing American culture at the expense of ethnicity. In this instance we need to set Antonio Gramsci and theories of cultural hegemony aside. This is a case of second- and third-generation Catholics imposing their moral values upon the culture generally.

Irving Berlin could not impose; he had to charm. But he did put his stamp upon the popular culture in ways we are only beginning to recognize. One was to sentimentalize and secularize traditional Christian holy days. In *Holiday Inn*, the movie in which Crosby introduced "White Christmas," Berlin seamlessly wove together Christmas with St. Valentine's Day and the Fourth of July as holidays all Americans could celebrate equally. The climax of *Easter Parade*, for which Berlin wrote the title song, featured Fred Astaire and Judy Garland walking down Fifth Avenue, she in her "Easter bonnet" and both so well dressed that newspaper photographers rushed to take their picture. If they passed St. Patrick's Cathedral, they did not stop to attend mass. "White Christmas" continues to influence the way we celebrate the holiday. "God Bless America," introduced by and long associated with Irish Catholic singer Kate Smith, is Berlin's one explicitly religious song. It has become an unofficial anthem. "One cannot have a holiday without a Berlin song" was not just a joke. It was a statement of fact.

Given the ferocity of anti-Catholicism in the 1920s and the rising hostility to Jews through the 1930s, both the sympathetic portrayals of Catholics and Jews in the mass media and the secularizing of Christian holy days were important counterweights. They undermined the notion that the United States was a Protestant country. They enabled first- and second-generation immigrants to see themselves as actively contributing to the culture they were entering. If we could understand how central anti-Catholicism was in American life, we could begin to ask how and why it has diminished to such a remarkable extent. We could say, as Chandonnet did of the building of a parish, that toleration is an achievement.

A New Pluralism?

It is an achievement that grows ever more complex, as Diana L. Eck's *A New Religious America* (2001) explores. In large measure because of the change in immigration laws in the 1960s which permitted previously prohibited groups to enter the United States, Islam, Hinduism, and Buddhism are all growing rapidly. There were as many Muslims as Jews in the United States in 2000; soon there will be substantially more. Some, such as Samuel P. Huntington (2004), are voicing a new nativism. America's "core culture," Huntington insists, is Christian. It can accommodate Jews and Catholics but not Muslims, Buddhists, or Hindus. Their religious traditions and values are too different. This is not a matter of the Hindu prohibition against eating beef or the Muslim use of Friday as the Sabbath or the Buddhist quest for Nirvana rather than Paradise, according to Huntington. It is that the entire complex of beliefs, values, and practices threatens to undermine the American "core."

In many ways this new nativism rehearses earlier arguments against Catholics and Jews. For example, in the 1890s Worcester's Protestants rallied to the cause of high school principal Alfred S. Roe when he was reprimanded for giving special privileges to Protestant pupils. They succeeded in electing a school committee committed to firing the superintendent. Roe went on to a career in the state legislature. He was standing up for the Yankee Protestants, the class which "forms the foundation of New England's character, determines her purposes, and makes and maintains her reputation," and does so "without the intervention of priest, king, or noble."

The new pluralism is complicated, moreover, by the ongoing war against terrorism launched by the United States after the attacks of September 11, 2001, and by the long history of racial discrimination. All of the suicide bombers were radical Islamists, followers of Osama bin Laden. All believed they were doing Allah's bidding in crashing aircraft into the World Trade Center and the Pentagon. The American government, beginning with President George W. Bush, has repeatedly proclaimed that the war on terror is not a war against Islam. But the enemies it has chosen to strike are Muslim. The Taliban regime in Afghanistan sheltered bin Laden and his followers and endorsed his holy war against the United States and the West. The Saddam Hussein regime in Iraq was thoroughly secular. But the occupation of that country gave rise to a number of groups animated by religious belief who proclaimed their hostility to the United States.

This enormously complicates the lives of American Muslims who must constantly defend their religion from criticism and who must constantly profess their own loyalty. This task is all the more difficult because Islam, like Catholicism, rejects the separation of church and state in principle. The Koran, believers insist, provides *the* guide to the whole of life. Law, therefore, must respect Koranic regulations and rest upon Koranic principles. American Muslims, like Catholics before them, have to demonstrate that they nonetheless accept American law, even when it prohibits what the Koran permits (polygamy, for example) or permits what the Koran prohibits (alcohol, for example).

Hindus and Buddhists do not face these problems, at least not to the same extent. They do, however, share the problem of finding ways of practicing their religion in an American context. Eck's study suggests how each community is meeting this challenge. Muslim temples sponsor Scout troops, for example, and for the same reasons that Catholic parishes and Jewish synagogues do. Their children want to participate in American activities; parents and clergy want to make sure that tradition is respected. And so Muslim scouts promise fidelity to Allah and to country. On July 31, 2004 Worcester's Muslims announced plans for a new mosque, and the city's only daily put the story on page one. It detailed that this was to be "far more" than a place of worship. It would have a gymnasium for sports teams; it would have classrooms; it would have facilities for providing assistance to the elderly. It would, the story reassured, operate like the Catholic parishes, Jewish temples, and Protestant churches its readers were already familiar with.

How racist stereotypes will play out in the experiences of Muslims, Buddhists, and Hindus remains to be seen. Japanese and Chinese immigrants encountered venomous hostility, exclusion, and discrimination, culminating in the "relocation" of first- and second-generation Japanese Americans living on the west coast during World War II. Later, they became "model" minorities. Chinese temples in American cities have become tourist attractions. Time alone will tell if new immigrants from Asia, the Pacific, Africa, and the Middle East will have to pass through the same travails.

Conclusion

Historians routinely label Thomas and Znaniecki's *The Polish Peasant in Europe and America* a classic and cite its treatment of the Polish community in Chicago as a model. Few adopt the model in their own research, however. The monographs dealing with one group or another in one city or another form a large and growing literature. Only a handful use parish records, church newsletters, or similar sources even though these are the very materials Thomas used to construct his portrait of Chicago's *Polonia*. The same is true of Robert Orsi's work on Italian Harlem. We hail it as a classic but do not adopt its focus on religion as lived experience. What of Higham's *Strangers in the Land*, perhaps the most admired work in the entire literature? Has it spawned monographs that examine anti-Catholicism? There is Daniel L. Kinzer's *An Episode in Anti-Catholicism: The American Protective Association* (1964) and Linda Gordon's *The Great Arizona Orphan Abduction* (1999), but not much in between.

Indeed it is not too much to say that we pay little attention to religion at all. This chapter attempts to demonstrate that religion was, and remains, a central dimension of the immigrant experience, one that influences every other aspect of that experience. It supplied a frame through which immigrants and their descendants made sense of their new world; it spoke to their need to find hope and solace; it became the focal point of their efforts to build communities; it mediated their adoption of American ways; it assisted their efforts to become citizens and to rise economically; it channeled their rivalries. It is long past time that we started taking it seriously.

REFERENCES

Billington, Ray Allen (1938). *The Protestant Crusade, 1800–1860: A Study of the Origins of American Nativism*. New York: Macmillan.
Chandonnet, L'Abbé T.A. (1872). *Notre-Dame-Des-Canadiens et Les Canadiens aux Etats-Unis*. Montreal: Debarats.

Clubb, Henry S. (1856). *The Maine Liquor Law: Its Origin, History, and Results, Including A Life of Hon. Neal Dow.* New York: Fowler and Wells.

Eck, Diana L. (2001). *A New Religious America: How a "Christian Country" Has Now Become the World's Most Religiously Diverse Nation.* San Francisco: Harper.

Estus, Charles W., Sr. and John F. McClymer (1994). *Gå till Amerika: The Swedish Creation of an Ethnic Identity for Worcester, Massachusetts.* Worcester, MA: Worcester Historical Museum.

—— (1995). "Guest Editors' Introduction: The Swedish Experience in Worcester, Massachusetts." *The Swedish-American Historical Quarterly* 46 (January): 3–7.

Estus, Charles W., Kevin Hickey, and Kenneth J. Moynihan (1993). "The Importance of Being Protestant: The Swedish Role in Worcester, Massachusetts." In Ulf Beïjbom, ed., *Swedes in America: Intercultural and Interethnic Perspectives on Contemporary Research.* Växjö, Sweden: Emigrant Institute.

Ford, Henry (1922). *The International Jew: The World's Foremost Problem.* Dearborn, MI: The Dearborn Independent.

Gerstle, Gary (2001). *American Crucible: Race and Nation in the Twentieth Century.* Princeton, NJ: Princeton University Press.

Gordon, Linda (1999). *The Great Arizona Orphan Abduction.* Cambridge, MA: Harvard University Press.

Gordon, Milton M. (1964). *Assimilation in American Life: The Role of Race, Religion, and National Origins.* New York: Oxford University Press.

Herberg, Will (1955). *Protestant, Catholic, Jew: An Essay in Religious Sociology.* Garden City, NY: Doubleday.

Higham, John (1955). *Strangers in the Land: Patterns of American Nativism, 1860–1925.* New Brunswick, NJ: Rutgers University Press.

Howe, Irving (1976). *World of Our Fathers: The Journey of the Eastern European Jews to America and the Life They Found and Made.* New York: Simon & Schuster.

Huntington, Samuel P. (2004). *Who Are We? Challenges to America's Identity.* New York: Simon & Schuster.

Kinzer, Daniel L. (1964). *An Episode in Anti-Catholicism: The American Protective Association.* Seattle: University of Washington Press.

McClymer, John F. (2000). "Symbolic Rivalries among Yankees, Swedes, and Irish in Worcester, Mass., 1880–1920: Ethnicity and Assimilation as Forms of Cultural Triangulation." In Harald Runblom, ed., *Migrants and the Homeland: Images, Symbols, and Realities* (Uppsala Multiethnic Papers 44). Uppsala: University of Uppsala.

—— (2003). "Un Dimsdale Canadien: Curé and Community in Late-Nineteenth-Century Worcester." In Reed Ueda and Conrad Edick Wright, eds., *Faces of Community: Immigrant Massachusetts, 1860–2000.* Boston: Massachusetts Historical Society.

Meagher, Timothy J. (2001). *Inventing Irish America: Generation, Class, and Ethnic Identity in a New England City, 1880–1928.* Notre Dame, IN: University of Notre Dame Press.

Moynihan, Kenneth J. (1989). "Swedes and Yankees in Worcaster Politics: A Protestant Partnership." *The Swedish-American Historical Quarterly* 40: 23–34.

Orsi, Robert A. (2002). *The Madonna of 115th Street: Faith and Community in Italian Harlem, 1880–1950* [1985], rev. edn. New Haven, CT: Yale University Press.

Patangall, William Robinson (1925). "Is the Ku Klux [Klan] un-American." *The Forum* September: 321–32.

Thomas, W.I. and Florian Znaniecki, (1918–20). *The Polish Peasant in Europe and America.* Boston: R.G. Badger. (There have been many subsequent editions.)

Wright, Carroll D. (1880 and 1881). *Report of the Massachusetts Bureau of the Statistics of Labor.* Boston.

Chapter Twenty-Five

Mutual Aid Societies and Fraternal Orders

Daniel Soyer

Local mutual aid societies and national multi-branch fraternal orders have touched the lives of more immigrants over the last century and a half than has any other institution, with the possible exception of the church. This was especially true in the decades around the turn of the twentieth century, when they provided millions of individuals and families with important material benefits unavailable from any other source. But such organizations continued to play an important role in both old and new immigrant communities at the turn of the twenty-first century as well. Mutual aid societies and fraternal orders are thus an important subject in their own right for anyone interested in the ways in which immigrants constructed their communities.

Because mutual aid and fraternal societies were so widespread, and because they were created and led by immigrants themselves, they are also very useful as lenses on some of the larger issues in immigration history. For one thing, they provide a window on the formation of ethnic identity since they expressed their members' multileveled sense of identification with towns or regions of origin, home countries, linguistic groups, and the United States. Moreover, mutual aid societies and fraternal orders often embodied religious and political divisions within ethnic communities. And yet, even as they revealed all sorts of distinctions within ethnic populations, the societies also helped construct broader ethnic communities and identities. Further, scholars concerned with the degree to which immigrants have preserved their cultures in America (or, conversely, have adopted American ways) have argued over whether the societies represent continuations of similar old-country organizations or adaptations of American forms. Likewise, since the societies provided important material benefits to their members, including, in some cases, low-cost loans, they may help to explain rates of social and economic mobility. Finally, given the societies' role in providing benefits to members' families, they often consisted primarily or exclusively of family bread-winners (mainly men), and thus reflected gender roles within families and cultures.

Studies of immigrant mutual aid societies and fraternal orders fall into several categories. Some studies focus on the societies themselves, generally within the context of one ethnic community (Hernandez 1983; Soyer 1997). These works demonstrate how the societies functioned and what they meant to their members. A related category consists of histories of individual fraternal orders commissioned by the orders themselves to mark their anniversaries. A few of these studies meet high scholarly standards (Pienkos 1990; Kuropas 1996; Kaufman 1982). Another group of studies approaches the topic from the opposite angle, placing the societies squarely at the center of particular ethnic communities. These works show how mutual aid societies and fraternals helped to build communal infrastructures (Alexander 1987; Barton 1975; Mormino and Pozzetta 1987; Emmons 1989). Other histories of particular ethnic communities include sections or chapters on societies. Finally, many articles on ethnic mutual aid societies and fraternal lodges can also be found in ethnic and local historical journals. Though these pieces sometimes have an anti-quarian rather than analytical approach, they can be good sources of information on societies on the local level.

Societies and Orders

Distinguishing between mutual aid societies and fraternal orders is helpful, though in practice the two types of organization overlapped considerably and shared a common culture. A mutual aid society was a local organization that provided its members with certain material benefits as well as a venue for informal socializing and formal leisure activities. Immigrants have been forming such organizations since the colonial period, but their heyday was probably during the century of mass immigration that lasted from the early nineteenth through the early twentieth centuries. Mutual aid societies generally had formal constitutions and bylaws that more or less followed a standard format. Their meetings often involved some degree of ritual, though this was usually relatively simple, consisting of a few passwords, hand signals, and formulaic pronouncements. Mutual aid societies, whose members might number in the single digits or in the hundreds, were perhaps the most basic of all ethnic communal organizations, often arising at an early stage in the establishment of a local colony. Whatever language the members spoke, they frequently referred to their organization using the English word "society." More generically, they fall under the category of "fraternal" organizations.

A fraternal order consisted of multiple branches, often termed "lodges." While these lodges functioned in much the same way as the local societies, they were subordinate in many ways to the national order. For example, the order set the level of benefits to which members were entitled as well as the dues that they had to pay. The order also administered these benefits, which were generally superior to those offered by the local societies. Influenced by such orders as the Masons and Odd Fellows, ethnic fraternal orders, which began to be formed in the 1840s, developed rituals that were sometimes more elaborate than those of the local societies. Like the benefits, these rituals were established at the order level and followed by the local lodges. The lodges sometimes started as independent societies before affiliating with the larger orders, which numbered their members in the tens or hundreds of thousands. In common parlance, the orders were also "fraternals" or "societies."

Mutual Aid and Benefits

Both local societies and fraternal orders offered mutual aid to their members. While societies and orders might also give charity to needy members of their larger communities, the distinction between mutual assistance and charity remains crucial.

The essential difference is that charitable aid flowed from those who had the resources to those who did not. Charity thus erected a class and power hierarchy between donors and recipients, even when both sides were members of the same ethnic group. Mutual aid, on the other hand, flowed back and forth among equals who had pooled their resources. Taking aid from one's society "brothers" or "sisters" did not carry the same stigma as charity because it was assumed that today's recipient was tomorrow's donor. Mutual aid thus followed an ethos of egalitarianism, democracy, and independence. Being a member of a society showed that an immigrant was self-reliant rather than dependent.

Society benefits helped working-class immigrants deal with the common crises of unemployment, illness, and death, and were especially important in the era before the enactment of government social security programs. When a worker took sick at the beginning of the last century, the greatest cost to him and his family lay not in the medical care he received but in the wages he lost because of missed work. Most societies and lodges therefore provided their sick and injured members with a portion of their weekly income for up to a certain number of weeks. While benefits generally did not equal a worker's average weekly income, they did help make up for the loss. To claim his benefits, the sick member reported his illness to the society, which then dispatched a committee to visit him. The committee served two purposes: first, it offered fraternal comfort to the patient; second, it made sure that he really was too ill to work. When the committee reported favorably, benefits usually began in the second week of illness.

Many societies and lodges also hired a doctor to treat the members and their families throughout the year for free or for a nominal fee. The American Medical Association (AMA) and its local affiliates severely condemned this "contract practice" and even boycotted the "society" or "lodge doctors" who engaged in it. Societies elected their doctors at meetings just like any other officer, and the medical societies argued that this rewarded good politicians over good practitioners. The doctors further claimed that overworked, often underqualified, society doctors offered care inferior to that provided by doctors who received the preferred "fee for service." But the real issue may have been the power that the immigrant lodges and societies exercised over the doctors they hired and fired at will. When their guard was down, writers in the medical journals said as much, complaining of the deference that doctors were forced to show toward the workers and shopkeepers who made up the societies and lodges. The societies, for their part, defended the practice as a way to provide low-cost medical care to their members, and vigorously exercised their power to replace physicians who did not please them. Despite the AMA's opposition, many doctors, especially those who were immigrants themselves, found contract medicine useful as well, since it helped them build a patient base.

When a member died, the society helped with the funeral, supplying the hearse and a carriage or two, and, perhaps more importantly, guaranteeing a turnout. Many immigrants wanted to avoid being buried by strangers when they died. This desire had as much to do with the dread of anonymity in death as it did with the fear that religious requirements or customs would be ignored. The societies responded by requiring that members attend the funerals of deceased brothers and sisters, and by maintaining their own cemetery plots where members could be buried among their friends and compatriots.

Societies and lodges also offered a form of life insurance to a deceased member's survivors. In local mutual aid societies the amount the family received usually depended on the number of members in the society. When a member died, his surviving fellows would be assessed a dollar each to provide the death benefit. Thus, the larger the society, the better the benefit. Larger fraternal orders generally mandated a larger fixed benefit of $500 or $1,000, with the burden spread over the entire larger national membership.

The larger benefits paid by fraternal orders made them attractive, but the method by which these benefits were financed produced instability in the orders. Each quarter, members were assessed a sum calculated to equal the amount paid out in death benefits the previous quarter. All members, regardless of age, paid the same amount, and few orders kept adequate reserves. The problem was that as the membership aged the death rate increased and so did the cost of belonging to the order. Younger members began to drop out, feeling that they were bearing a disproportionate share of the burden, and it became harder to recruit replacements. The membership began to shrink, further increasing the cost per remaining member. Eventually, the order was forced to pay out more than it was taking in, and this led to the collapse of many orders.

By the turn of the century, fraternal reformers were calling for the use of actuarially sound insurance rates graded by age. Many fraternal activists resisted, viewing differential rates as a violation of the fraternal principles of brotherhood and equality. In some orders, the battle over reform lasted for years. But by the 1920s, those that continued to thrive had adopted some form of actuarially sound insurance practices.

Societies supplied other benefits as well. Some, for example, mandated lump-sum payments for specified disabilities. Some provided their members with interest-free or low-cost loans. Some helped members find employment. Societies also took up the cases of members needing relief for a variety of reasons not specified in the bylaws and offered relief on an *ad hoc* basis. Finally, some societies, and especially larger fraternal orders, sponsored such institutions as hospitals, sanitaria, orphanages, and old-age homes, at which their members received priority in placement and treatment at reduced rates.

Besides these material benefits, societies provided their immigrant members with an array of intangible non-material benefits. These included the opportunity to receive the sort of honors and recognition that would have been otherwise unavailable to working-class and lower middle-class immigrants. Members conferred honors on each other for selling the most tickets to the annual theater party or picnic, for serving as an officer with distinction, or for recruiting the most new members. Recognition took the form of special resolutions at meetings, plaques, trophies, medals, and advertisements in ethnic newspapers. The societies democratized the conferral of honors not only by offering them to people who would otherwise have been unlikely to receive them in either the old world or the new, but also by giving the majority the right to grant them.

The societies also created an arena for socializing in both formal and informal settings. Members gathered weekly, bi-weekly, or monthly for formal society meetings that followed a fixed order of business. But the formal agenda did not include the card playing, beer drinking, smoking, impromptu debates, and general conviviality that went on both before and after the regular meeting. Outside of meetings, the society calendar was punctuated by a round of recreational events including picnics in the summer, and balls and theater parties in the winter. At these events, members, their families, and friends who had bought tickets escaped from their workaday world and enjoyed themselves amid the pleasant surroundings of an elegant hall or the rural countryside. Not only did these events offer the members a good time, but they raised the visibility and prestige of the society and brought in some money as well. The affairs also benefited specific causes, such as aid to the homeland. It should also be noted that in patronizing the ethnic theater the societies played an important role in supporting foreign language culture in the United States.

Indeed, many societies considered the spiritual, cultural, and moral uplift of their members to be at the core of their mission. Their educational and cultural activities had a consciously dual purpose: to preserve the ethnic language and culture, and, at the same time, to acquaint the immigrants with the American mainstream. Accordingly, they sponsored lectures and classes on current events, literary topics, English language, and both American history and the history of their respective homelands. The orders also promoted ethnic culture by sponsoring theater groups, choruses, and music ensembles, often using "typical" ethnic instruments.

In providing their members with an element of basic social security, the societies played an inherently political role, but scholars have differed over the content of the politics. Some scholars argue that the societies represented a radical alternative to the market economy and its individualistic ethos, pointing out, in sociologist Susan Greenbaum's words, that the societies constituted a form of "economic collectivism" in which the "terms of exchange are designed to be generous, not exploitative." Further, as Greenbaum argues, the organizations were "designed to shield the members from the competitive exploitation" of the capitalist economy in which the members generally occupied the lower ranks (Greenbaum 1991, p. 97, 1993).

Indeed, as largely working-class institutions, immigrant mutual aid societies and fraternal lodges often supported strikes and union organization drives. Some societies banned strikebreakers from membership or offered their members strike benefits. On occasion, unions even emerged out of mutual aid associations. At the very least the societies taught their members the organizational skills and the ethos of solidarity necessary to run a local union as well. As one Chicago employer is said to have commented in the 1920s: "The Mexicans have societies, and of course, if they organize one way, it is but a step to organize another way" (Taylor 1970; 1928, vol. 1, p. 121). The high point of fraternal support for unionization drives came in 1936, when the Congress of Industrial Organizations (CIO) enlisted lodge support in its drive to organize the steel industry. Some 20 fraternal orders, among them some of the largest East European orders, responded and played a crucial role in cultivating community support for the CIO drive.

One of the orders that played an important part in support of the CIO drive was the International Workers Order (IWO), the prime example of a fraternal organization with an explicitly anti-capitalist ideology. Founded in 1930 and led by Communists, the IWO was unabashedly pro-Soviet and followed the party line in all matters. It was also unique in that, though it began as a Jewish group, it quickly became a multi-ethnic order in which 15 immigrant groups, plus native blacks and whites, operated their own sections while sharing membership in the parent organization.

Founded at the outset of the Depression, the IWO thrived during the 1930s (when other fraternals were shrinking), partly by absorbing smaller radical ethnic orders, and partly by recruiting aggressively. Membership peaked in 1947 at 184,000 before falling as the order came under attack during the McCarthy period.

But the orders sometimes played a conservative role as well. Some fraternals, especially explicitly Roman Catholic ones, were outspoken in their anti-Socialism. Even in their support of working-class and union struggles, fraternals did not necessarily have radical aims. In Butte, Montana, for example, David Emmons has argued, local lodges of the Ancient Order of Hibernians and Clan na Gael, two Irish orders, were overwhelmingly working class and sometimes worked with the copper miners' unions to maintain conditions and wages in the mines. Nevertheless, the fraternals' chief interests were basically conservative: neither upward mobility nor radical social transformation, but the guarantee of steady work at wages high enough to maintain a middle-class standard of living for the more stable elements of the community. In pursuit of these aims, the fraternals brought their working-class Irish members together with Irish employers, often to the exclusion of non-Irish or even transient Irish workers (Emmons 1989).

Moreover, historian David Beito (2000) argues that the orders, ethnic and non-ethnic, offered a viable alternative to the social welfare state. They not only allowed their members to avoid the stigma of dependence on public support, but also constructed dense social networks that stabilized even poor communities and helped them avoid social pathology, and taught their members such traditional values as thrift and personal responsibility. As Beito points out, *all* societies policed their members' behavior, an important point because many historians have criticized middle- and upper-class social workers for imposing their values on working-class immigrant clients in a humiliating effort to maintain elite social control. Society constitutions and bylaws demonstrate, however, that immigrant organizations excluded from membership those deemed not to have the proper character, and withheld benefits from those with "immoral diseases," those who drank excessively, or those caught malingering. It turns out that in this respect the immigrants shared the "bourgeois" values of the Anglo elites.

Even the collectivism of the mutual aid societies could help immigrant members succeed in the capitalist economy, especially by providing free or low-interest credit. Chinese and Japanese immigrants, for example, formed rotating credit associations, in which members pooled resources and took turns using the proceeds to open small businesses. These associations were especially important in an era when most "mainstream" banks would not do business with stigmatized immigrant communities, and when immigrant banks were largely unstable and incompetent. Indeed, the rotating credit associations offered a very attractive low-cost and relatively secure alternative to bank loans (Light 1972).

Were immigrant mutual aid societies and fraternal orders radical or conservative? The answer is both. Because the societies were the most basic form of immigrant association, they spanned the ideological spectrum and embodied all the political differences within immigrant communities. Although the proportions differed from group to group, it would have been a rare ethnic community that did not include both radical and conservative organizations, each with its own interpretation of the common values of mutual aid and fraternal solidarity.

Fraternalism and Gender

Although women's and mixed societies certainly existed, most immigrant mutual aid societies and fraternal orders were open only to men, a policy closely connected to their mutual aid function. Not for nothing was one Italian society in Utica, New York, called the Societá Capi dei Famigli Italo-Americana di Mutuo Soccorso (Italian-American Society of Heads of Families for Mutual Aid) (Briggs 1978, p. 142).

Men argued that they joined the societies as a necessary part of their role as primary breadwinners for their families. It was through the societies, they claimed, that they provided their families with insurance against their loss of livelihood. Accordingly, the benefit structures of most orders and societies – even those that did officially accept female members – reflected the needs and rhythms of men's work lives and assumed traditional patriarchal family relationships (McCune 2002, pp. 590–1). Indeed, although men's participation in the societies drew them out of the home and sometimes therefore created tensions within the family, this participation could also be seen as consistent with men's familial roles. Women's organizational activities, by contrast, might be seen as in *competition* with their proper roles; in the words of historian Judith Smith, they "not so much . . . extended kin ties as . . . rivaled them" (1985, p. 143).

Even fraternal orders like the Jewish Socialist Workmen's Circle, which officially recognized women's equality and allowed them membership, had a hard time integrating them fully into organizational life. Women with children found it difficult to attend meetings, and many women simply felt unwelcome in the largely male branches. Over the years the Workmen's Circle experimented with a variety of separate units for women, including special branches that offered no benefits, or that carried benefits at lower levels (and lower cost) than those offered to men. The debate often centered on whether women were more often sick than men, and therefore carried more of an insurance risk, or whether "women's diseases" should be covered. Eventually, the order covered all diseases, but excluded pregnancy and childbirth from benefits. Only in the 1920s did women carve out a place in the order, concentrating their energies on "educational, cultural and social welfare initiatives" (McCune 2002, p. 594).

Of course, many women joined auxiliaries of the men's groups. These auxiliaries carried out social activities, often in conjunction with their "brother" societies, but they tended to offer fewer, if any, benefits to members. Instead, they concentrated on charitable giving, often for the old home.

One interesting exception to the rule was the Polish Women's Alliance (PWA), founded in 1898. The PWA, which had 23,000 members in 1917, sought to reconcile a public role for women with their private responsibilities. It advocated a feminist agenda, actively campaigning against domestic abuse and child labor, and supporting temperance and women's suffrage. In addition to the standard benefits it offered its members a women's reading room, ran Polish language schools and summer camps for children, and provided vocational instruction to girls. By its very existence, moreover, it forced the two largest Polish fraternals – the Polish National Alliance and the Polish Roman Catholic Union – to admit women and allow them an active role. After World War I, however, the PWA turned away from its feminist stance and began to emphasize Polish nationalism and women's responsibility for maintaining Polish culture in America.

Ritual

Following the pattern set by Anglo-American fraternal culture, meetings of immigrant mutual aid societies and fraternal lodges featured such ritualistic elements as secret passwords, hand signals, and opening and closing ceremonies. Lodges of fraternal orders, especially, carried out elaborate and dramatic initiation rituals modeled on those of the Masons, Odd Fellows, and other fraternal orders that were widely popular among American men in the second half of the nineteenth century. In most cases, these sorts of rituals had been virtually unknown to the immigrants in the old country, and their adoption of them in their new home demonstrates the extent to which "mainstream" American culture permeated ethnic cultures as they separated from the cultures of the immigrants' countries of origin.

Anthropologists point out that initiation rituals serve, among other things, to ease transitions from one status to another. For immigrants, fraternal ritual often served to reconcile a sense of identification with their places and cultures of origin with an equally intense desire to integrate into American life. The fraternal form, so quintessentially American at the time, but so malleable in its content, seemed a perfect medium for this task. Through their lodge rituals, whose explicit message was often one of loyalty to ethnic tradition, immigrants were in fact inventing new traditions suited to life in America. The Clan na Gael's ritual, for example, stressed Irish nationalism and Irish identity, but in a way that new arrivals from Ireland found utterly foreign.

Ritual elements found their way into immigrant communities through individuals with experience in Masonic and other mainstream orders. For example, James Sheedy, a Mason, Odd Fellow, and Pythian, wrote the ritual for the Clan na Gael. Similarly, several of the founders of the German-Jewish B'nai B'rith had been Masons or Odd Fellows. In some cases, immigrants joined foreign language lodges of general fraternal orders. Thus, Germans established lodges of the Improved Order of Red Men and the Knights of Pythias, but when these orders grew less amenable to the German presence, they left to form the Independent Order of Red Men and the Improved Order, Knights of Pythias, respectively. These new orders retained the old rituals (in the Red Men's case, based on pseudo-Indian lore), but performed them in the German language. Other German orders took Germanic lore as their theme: the Orden der Hermanns Soehne (Order of Sons of Hermann), the largest German order, with 90,000 members in 1896, adopted the "ancient Teutonic warrior" as its model, while the German Order of the Harugari took its name from legendary ancient Germanic tribes.

Many Catholic immigrants joined fraternal orders despite their church's vehement opposition to secret societies. The church suspected many secret orders of having subversive goals, and specifically objected to the practice of pledging loyalty to principles that the initiates had yet to learn, and to secrecy that might prevent them from being open with their confessors. But Catholic men developed their own orders and rituals, which they defended by posing them as an alternative to the Masons and other anti-Catholic orders. Irish immigrants, for example, formed the Ancient Order of Hibernians as well as the Clan na Gael. The most prominent Catholic order was the Knights of Columbus, whose ritual explicitly attempted to reconcile Americanism with Catholicism.

How American Were the Fraternals?

The adoption by immigrant fraternal orders of American-style fraternal ritual seems to indicate that the orders, as well as independent mutual aid societies, were more akin to American organizational forms than to those found in the immigrants' countries of origin. This is what Oscar Handlin argued in his seminal work, *The Uprooted* (1951). Handlin's immigrants had been stripped of their cultural heritages in the process of migration, and their formation of mutual aid societies was a step in their reorientation toward life in America. The societies, Handlin wrote, "were not vestiges of any European forms." Rather, they were a very American phenomenon, "voluntary, autonomous combinations, free of the state and all on an equal footing" (1951, p. 185).

In the 1970s, however, social historians reacted against the "Handlin thesis," arguing instead that immigrants retained more of their premigration cultures than had previously been thought. Applied to immigrant societies, this meant that the American organizations were directly related to associations common in the old world cultures from which the immigrants had come. Scholars have pointed to the Croatian *zadruga* ("communal family structure") and *Molba* (a system by which friends and family rendered each other aid during harvest time in exchange for food and drink) as precedents for Croatian immigrant societies in the United States. They show that the priestly "blessing of the banners" was a common practice in Slovak societies in the United States, as it was in the guilds of Slovakia (Bodnar 1981, p. 5, 1985, pp. 121–2). In some cases there appears to have been a direct and conscious connection between old world and new world associations. In Cleveland, an Italian society, the Sons of Labor, bore the same name as a society in the members' hometown. Moreover, the secretary of the Cleveland association was the son of the secretary of the group in Italy. All of the members of another Cleveland Italian society, the San Nicoló Society, had belonged to, or were sons of those who belonged to, an agricultural association in San Nicoló, and some even maintained their membership in the hometown organization (Barton 1975, p. 60).

Still, disagreements among historians who study the same ethnic group make it difficult to judge whether the societies should be viewed primarily as elements of continuity or as American innovations. For example, while M. Mark Stolarik (1980, 1996) has generally stressed Slovaks' extensive premigration experience with mutual aid associations, June Alexander (1987) argues that Slovaks in the United States "did not model their fraternal societies after premigration institutions." She quotes one fraternal activist, who wrote in 1903, "America has trained us . . . for fraternal life. Our old country is very poor in this sphere and especially the common people, of which our colony . . . consists, have no conception of mutual aid societies" (Alexander 1987, pp. 17–18). Likewise, John Briggs has contended that mutual aid societies in southern Italy and Sicily "proliferated in the last quarter of the nineteenth," and that the founders of similar societies in America had often come into contact with these organizations before their departure from home (1978, p. 17). But Dino Cinel (1981) and Humberto Nelli (1970) disagree, arguing that the societies in Italy either reached a different social stratum than emigrated or had a fundamentally different character from the association in the United States. These scholars contend that the similarity among the organizations of various immigrant groups makes it more likely that they were influenced by each other, as well as by native-born American groups, than by home-country precedents.

The structure, workings, and activities of East European Jewish immigrant societies were clearly far more American than not. For one thing, the structure of the Jewish societies tended to resemble those of other immigrant groups, and those of native-born Americans, black and white, very closely. Their constitutions and bylaws, celebrated overtly American values: democracy, equality, voluntarism, and independence. Yiddish language manuals which instructed immigrants on how to found and run a society very explicitly linked the societies' democratic ethos and structure to the American form of republican government. This is not to say that the immigrants came to the United States without organizational experience. But, at least among the Jews, traditional communal associations in eastern Europe operated differently from those established here.

Tellingly, those mutual aid organizations that did exist in the immigrants' countries of origin were often new developments in the late nineteenth century, as the areas of emigration were absorbed into the international capitalist economy. In a way, they responded to the same problems and stresses as did the American societies.

Fraternals and "Ethnicization"

By combining aspects of old world and new world culture, immigrant fraternal organizations participated in the process of "ethnicization," the elaboration of an American ethnic identity distinct at once from those of the Anglo-American mainstream and the societies left behind. In many cases, immigrants arrived thinking of themselves more as natives of a particular village or region than as members of a larger nation. Only in the United States did they come to think of themselves as "Italians" or "Poles." Indeed, the fraternal societies clearly manifested regional divisions among the immigrants. Many independent societies and individual lodges were organized by immigrants who shared a town or region of origin. These hometown associations were formal manifestations of the migration "chains" by which relatives, friends, and fellow townspeople followed each other to the United States. Organizations typically carried the names of the hometown: the Kalushiner Benevolent Association (Jewish immigrants from Kalushin), the Sant'Agata Workers' Society (Italian immigrants from Sant'Agata). Here they banded together, ironically carrying out many of their self-Americanizing activities among familiar faces from home.

The societies further divided along religious, political, and other lines. Sometimes even a small town might be represented by a number of societies representing religious and non-religious, or radical and conservative compatriots. Even hometown associations, then, did not simply arise spontaneously from the migration process or premigration organic relationships. Rather, they embodied all of the divisions within a given community.

Societies often became the nuclei of religious congregations, establishing churches, synagogues, and churches. In one unusual case, a mutual benefit society, the Filipino Federation of America (founded 1925), actually evolved into a new religious sect which today continues to have a small but active presence not only in Filipino communities in the United States, but in the Philippines as well. More typically, Catholic societies were sometimes organized by parish priests, but also often predated the parish to which they became attached. In fact, mutual aid associations often played a pivotal role in founding nationality parishes – petitioning bishops, raising money for buildings, and recruiting priests from the old country. Sometimes they even forced the issue by building churches before receiving official approval. Even after parishes were opened there was sometimes friction between an assertive lay leadership based in the societies, the ethnic clergy accustomed to traditional old world deference, and the American hierarchy.

When local societies combined to form larger fraternal orders, they transcended old country regionalism, but not religious and political divisions. Slovaks, for example, founded the National Slovak Society (1890, secular), the First Catholic Slovak Union (1890, Roman Catholic), the Slovak Evangelical Union (1893, Lutheran), the Slovak Calvinist Union (1901), and the Slovak Workers' Society (1915, Socialist). The politics of religion played an especially important role in the Polish community, where the anti-clerical, nationalist Polish National Alliance (PNA) contended with the Polish Roman Catholic Union, which had been founded by priests and remained closely allied with the church. Most PNA members were also loyal Catholics, but their organization put Polish national identity and the cause of Polish nationalism before religion and favored lay over clerical leadership.

Building Blocks of Community

Mutual aid societies and fraternal orders became the leading organizations in many communities. Their halls were the central meeting places for all sorts of ethnic organizations. Their leaders were recognized as the premier communal leaders and sometimes went on to political careers as well. They supported numerous institutions, charities, and central communal bodies, and defended the reputation of their respective ethnic groups. Indeed, the first step in ethnic consolidation often took place when the myriad of hometown associations and other small groups joined together to form the larger fraternal orders.

Fraternal societies and lodges sponsored such community-wide events as picnics and parades that helped solidify ethnic solidarity. In some cases, these events commemorated important moments in the history of the old country, in others they called for recognition of the group's contributions to America. Often, they promoted ethnic or regional folklore. Together, such events constituted a public show of strength that demonstrated to both insiders and outsiders that the ethnic group in question had a powerful and permanent presence in America. They thus contributed to the fraternals' mission to promote the good name of their respective ethnic groups and to counter derogatory images.

The fraternal effort to defend the rights and reputation of their respective ethnic groups sometimes took on a more explicit character. For example, B'nai B'rith formed its Anti-Defamation League in 1914 in the wake of the Leo Frank lynching, to counter anti-Semitism. The Mexican American Alianza Hispano-Americana formed in 1894 in response to Anglo-American efforts to oust Mexicans from politics in the southwest. Over the years it was involved in much civil rights litigation, and in 1911, together with a number of other mutual aid societies and fraternal orders, sponsored the Primer Congresso Mexicanista in Texas to fight discrimination and anti-Mexican violence.

As documented by Mormino and Pozzetta, Ybor City, Florida was one place where mutual aid societies "assumed roles of remarkable responsibility, size, and humanity" (1987, p. 5). There such societies as El Centro Español, El Centro Asturiano, El Circulo Cubano, and L'Unione Italiana built "magnificent" club-houses which included large auditoriums, gymnasiums, cantinas, and bowling alleys. Men gathered daily at the clubhouses after dinner to socialize and play dominoes and cards, and the centers thus helped to establish the societies as the leading institutions of the community, far surpassing the church in influence. As one immig-rant thought when he saw the headquarters of L'Unione Italiana, "My God, in Sicilia only the church and counts build such a monument" (Mormino and Pozzetta 1987, p. 193). El Centro Asturiano and El Centro Español also built hospitals which served members and non-members alike.

While Ybor City was unique in the degree to which societies dominated the local scene, the types of institutions built by the societies there were not unusual. In Cleveland, for example, the Slovenian National Home was home to a hundred fraternal, political, and social groups, and housed a library, gymnasium, meeting rooms, and an auditorium. Such halls not only impressed members of the group that owned them, but others as well. As one Slovenian fraternal organ commented on the dedication of the Slovenian hall in Barburton, Ohio, "A hall in the settlement notifies members of other ethnic groups that Slovenes are people of culture" (Sulič 1996, p. 48). It was partly because of its recognition of the fraternal hall as an important local gathering place that the CIO made such an effort to enlist fraternals in its organizing drives of the late 1930s.

Likewise, the Ybor City societies were not the only ones to establish institutions that, in some cases, outlasted their sponsoring organizations. In New York City, the Federation of Galician and Bucovinean Jews of America, which brought together hundreds of small hometown associations, established Mount Moriah Hospital. Other organizations sponsored sanitaria, orphanages, and schools. The PNA opened Alliance College as a preparatory school in 1911, transforming it into a four-year college in 1948.

Fraternals gave rise to a leadership class whose influence extended beyond their home organizations. While most of the society and lodge members were workers, the leaders were often drawn from the middle class and had the linguistic and other skills to serve as mediators between the immigrants and the broader society. These leaders, who had often started out as laborers, were skilled workers, foremen, shop and saloon keepers, professionals, white-collar workers, and, sometimes, priests. The large fraternal orders themselves offered an avenue of mobility as they professionalized and added more paid staff and leadership positions. Some leaders used their fraternal connections to promote their businesses, while others used them as springboards to elective office. At the very least, they achieved recognition as spokespeople for their ethnic communities.

Fraternals and Transnationalism

Even as fraternals promoted immigrants' adjustment to American life, they also pro-moted ongoing active interaction with their countries of origin – what social scient-ists call "transnationalism." Divisions within home-country nationalist movements sometimes defined the differences among ethnic fraternals in the United States. For example, while the Ancient Order of Hibernians represented the segment of Irish nationalist opinion that supported the acquisition of home rule through parliamentary means, the Clan na Gael supported the use of force to attain complete independence. Both organizations raised thousands of dollars through the years to support the nationalist movement in Ireland. Likewise, much of the internal politics of the PNA involved clashes between the supporters of the National Democratic and Socialist parties in Poland. The PNA devoted tremendous resources to helping Poland gain its independence, even helping to recruit men from American *Polonia* to fight in the Polish army. Societies also sent many relief dollars to their respective home countries, especially during and after World War I.

Fraternals encouraged their members to visit their countries of origin. Some visits were connected with relief efforts, carried out by special organizational delegates bearing aid money for individuals and institutions in their old hometowns. Other visits were recreational and personal: the Verhovay Sickness Aid Association offered trips to Hungary as prizes during recruitment campaigns. Beginning in the interwar years, some governments cultivated the allegiance of their emigrants with the cooperation of the fraternals. The Verhovay Association thus sent delegates to the 1929 World Congress of Hungarians in Budapest (Puskas 1996). Likewise, the PNA had representatives at the World Union of Poles from Abroad that met in 1930. After World War II, the Croatian Fraternal Union organized a number of trips to Croatia, and collaborated on record and film projects with Croatian companies.

Significantly, the fraternals' transnationalism did not detract from their commitment to life in America. True, a trip to the old homeland or hometown might reawaken old affinities and help reinforce a living connection between those who left and those who stayed. But a comparison of conditions in the United States and the old home might also confirm in the minds of the emigrants that they had made the right decision in leaving. Tellingly, even as its delegates attended the World Union of Poles from Abroad, the PNA refused to subordinate itself to Polish leadership, proclaiming that American *Polonia* was not a "Polish colony" but "a component part of the great American nation" (Bukowczyk 1987, p. 70).

Fraternals as "Non-Voluntary Associations"

Mutual aid societies and fraternal organizations fall under the category of "voluntary associations." The fact that only in some cases did a majority of eligible members in a given community actually join a society points to their voluntary nature. But in at least one anomalous case of a group radically excluded from entry into American society – that of the Chinese – societies served as a quasi-governmental power that asserted its authority over nearly all immigrants, whether they liked it or not.

The Chinese community, which remained predominantly male until after World War II, evolved a complex structure that included a variety of societies based on overlapping categories of surname, clan, dialect, and place of origin. These organizations helped immigrants gain employment, ran boarding houses for their bachelor members, provided loans, and arranged funerals. The regional associations combined to form the Chinese Consolidated Benevolent Association (CCBA, also known as the Chinese Six Companies), which also offered certain services, including shipment of remains of deceased immigrants to China. Dominated by the merchant elite, the CCBA dominated most Chinatowns and served as the "principal representative of the Chinese community to non-Chinese Americans" (Ma 1991, p. 150). Besides these official bodies, secret societies known as "triads" ran smuggling, gambling, and prostitution operations and constituted an alternative center of power.

The exclusion of Chinese from American life strongly influenced the Chinese community's organizational structure. Strikingly, Chinese immigrant organizations in the United States more closely resembled similar groups elsewhere in the Chinese diaspora than they did Anglo-American or other immigrant organizations. The centralized CCBA originated in San Francisco and the CCBAs in such Chinatowns as those in Los Angeles and New York were essentially branches of the main organization. CCBA representatives met newly arriving immigrants at the docks and enrolled them in their appropriate association. Because they lacked families, the immigrants were even more dependent on the associations and the CCBA than other immigrants were on their organizations.

Moreover, because American politicians ignored the Chinese, who were excluded from citizenship, the CCBA had an unusual amount of autonomy in running communal affairs. It controlled jobs within Chinatown and contract labor outside, levied occasional assessments on Chinatown residents, and regulated Chinatown businesses. Legally, of course, these regulations and assessments were voluntary. But resisters to CCBA authority faced "civil death" in Chinatown, losing access to necessary legal aid, social services, credit, and physical protection. The CCBA further enforced its power by controlling the ability of individuals to return to China, at first through arrangements with shipping lines, and later by legal harassment of would-be return migrants (Lyman 1986).

Fraternals in Transition, 1920s to 1940s

After World War I, immigrant mutual aid societies and fraternal orders confronted a series of challenges that signaled an end to their period of growth among the groups of the so-called "new immigration" of the late nineteenth and early twentieth centuries. Primary among these challenges was the enactment beginning in 1921 of a series of laws severely restricting immigration to the United States. Immigration restriction meant that the societies would no longer be able to count on an influx of new arrivals to replenish their ranks. They needed instead to hold on to old members and, more importantly, recruit new ones from among the ethnic population already in the country. Women began to play an ever more active role in mixed organizations, and many societies made an effort to attract the members' American-born children. Ironically, both the prosperity of the 1920s and the Great Depression of the 1930s put additional pressures on the fraternals. Nevertheless, they continued to play an important role in their communities, and the beginning of their decline was often more apparent in retrospect than at the time.

After World War I, the fraternals faced increased competition in the provision of both their material and their cultural benefits. Commercial insurance companies began to offer low-cost "industrial" life insurance that compared favorably to the fraternals' death benefits. Some employers also offered insurance benefits, often in a conscious attempt to wean their workers away from independent organizations that might, in times of industrial conflict, provide support for unionization efforts. Over-all, as the insurance business increased in the 1920s, the fraternal sector remained steady, losing the new business to commercial companies. Then, too, fraternal ritual and other activities – ethnic and non-ethnic – began to lose their appeal with the rise of the movies, radio, and other commercial entertainments.

The realization that they would have to attract the second generation to survive organizationally dovetailed with the societies' proclaimed goal of preserving the ethnic culture. Small independent mutual aid societies, especially those based on old-country places of origin, were less flexible and therefore less likely to gain a significant foothold among the American-born generation. The larger fraternal orders, on the other hand, had more resources, and more organizational flexibility in creating special departments suited to the youth. Thus, the 1920s and 1930s saw the rise of fraternal-sponsored schools that taught children the ethnic language and culture; publications in English and the native language aimed at children, youth, and young adults; English-speaking branches; scouting movements; and, especially, sports teams. Combined with aggressive recruitment campaigns, these sorts of activities helped some orders thrive through the interwar era.

Nevertheless, the Depression impacted severely on all of the societies, as claims on their resources rose even as many members fell behind in their dues payments. Even though many societies tried to help those in need to maintain their memberships, many dropped out and membership levels dropped. The crisis in some orders was exacerbated by the fact that their reserve funds were tied up in mortgages they had offered to help their members buy houses. As many members defaulted on their mortgages, the orders were left with property that they could not sell. This was apparently especially a problem among the Polish orders: both the PWA and the PNA had over 80 percent of their assets in mortgages. Some organizations folded, though most of the large orders weathered the storm. The cure to the disease of the Depression also hurt the societies in the long run, as social security and other government programs replaced fraternal benefits.

After World War II

The decades after World War II intensified the challenges faced by the societies. The older European groups began a seemingly inexorable decline, though some staved off the reckoning until the 1970s, because they were more successful in attracting the second generation, because of especially aggressive recruitment drives, because of mergers with other societies, or because a small trickle of immigrants continued to arrive from the old country. Even among those ethnic groups whose presence has grown since the liberalization of immigration laws in 1965 – notably the Chinese, Mexicans, and West Indians – old-style mutual aid and fraternal associations did not reap the benefits as younger immigrants turned to other forms of organization. Finally, in the presence of extensive government-sponsored benefit programs, the very meaning of "mutual aid" has changed.

Abetted by the GI bill, many children of the turn-of-the-century European immig-rants moved into the middle class after World War II. Widespread suburbanization led to the decline of the old ethnic neighborhoods, and so to the decline of the fraternal halls. Moreover, as white-collar employees, these middle-class ethnics had their insurance needs met through employer-sponsored programs or by commercial insurance carriers. Affiliation with an ethnic order no longer seemed quite so natural to third-generation Americans for whom ethnicity was largely symbolic. Memberships aged.

Meanwhile, some fraternal orders attempted to shore up their financial condition by aggressively marketing insurance to wider audiences. To some extent this was successful, but it came at the cost of the organizations' fraternal nature. The Slovenian Mutual Benefit Society even changed its name to the American Mutual Life Association in 1966 in an attempt to draw the American-born and non-Slovenes. The fate of the Verhovay Association reveals the conflicting impulses of some ethnic fraternalists as they tried to find a way to save their organizations. In 1955 the Verhovay Association merged with the Rákóczi Association, another Hungarian group, to form the William Penn Fraternal Association. Over the years it operated more and more like a commercial insurance agency, until in 1971 it dropped the word "fraternal" from its title altogether. Despite a revival of Hungarian feeling in the organization in the 1970s it merged in 1983 with the Catholic Knights of St. George, a formerly German order that was being forced out of business by the Pennsylvania State Insurance Department. As late as 1987, though, all the Germans were ousted from the association's management and the remaining members proclaimed their undying Hungarianness (Puskas 1996).

Other groups with a long presence in the United States, and a long tradition of mutual aid and fraternal societies, have been transformed by massive influxes of new immigrants since the mid-1960s. The Chinese community, for example, once small, mostly male, and mostly Cantonese, is now large and diverse, including immigrants from other parts of mainland China, Hong Kong, Taiwan, and overseas population centers as well. This transformation has led to a proliferation of new organizations: in the 1970s, there were perhaps 900 Chinese organizations in the United States. By the 1990s there were 969 in San Francisco alone. Not only did Chinese organizations divide in a more complex way according to their members' places of origin, but according to politics as well, with some supporting and others opposing the People's Republic. The new organizations challenged the old hierarchy and the hegemony of the CCBA (Lai 1996).

The recent wave of immigration has also changed the organizational structure of the West Indian community in New York. In the late nineteenth and early twentieth centuries, West Indian immigrants to New York founded a large number of mutual aid societies. These associations, usually named for the home island of the members, not only provided vital material benefits to their members, but offered them an important recreational outlet, and a measure of prestige as well. But, while the older societies continue to function, newer immigrants have tended to view them as insular and old-fashioned. The recent arrivals have formed their own organizations, which resemble in some ways the old societies, except that they downplay mutual aid, and are instead "aggressively" social (Kasinitz 1992, p. 120). Many also take a more active political role. To the extent that newer organizations assist their members materially, it tends to be by serving as a clearing house for information on jobs, government benefits, and other external resources.

Similar changes have taken place among Mexicans. True, in the 1980s, Jose Amaro Hernandez (1983) found one organization, the Sociedad Progresista Mexicana, still functioning as it had for decades. At the time he investigated it, the society had 9,000 male and female members, mostly couples, in 68 lodges in California. The members, mostly manual workers, met regularly, maintaining the custom of pass-words and rituals, including a pledge of allegiance to the flags of Mexico and the United States. But there were troubling signs for the society. More than half of the members were in their sixties or older. And the $500 death benefit, the maximum allowed by California law, was hardly enough to attract younger members. A more successful model, at least until it was undermined by a divisive Marxist-Leninist takeover, was the Centro de Acción Social Autónomo (CASA, founded 1969), which at its peak enrolled 4,000 members. But although it considered itself to be following in the tradition of the "mutualistas," most members were passive consumers of services offered by professionals rather than active participants.

The chief difference between recent immigrant societies and their earlier coun-terparts lies in the way they provide benefits. Death and sick benefits, once the mainstays of mutual aid, are now less important, though some groups still help with burial. On the other hand, assisting immigrants negotiate state bureaucracies, and helping them prepare for jobs, have become more important. The Southern California Fukienese Association, for example, provided help with social security matters, assistance with learning bus routes, adult and children's schools, job train-ing, help filling out forms, "emergency relief for the needy," scholarships, and a club house (Lai 1996, p. 43).

Moreover, while early mutual aid societies were mostly run by lay people, today's self-help groups often have professional staffs and, sometimes, outside funding. In the1970s and 1980s, government policy encouraged the formation of "mutual assistance associations" in the hope that they would help refugees avoid public assistance. With the help of federal funding more than 1,200 such associations were formed. Their services included assistance in securing employment, English instruction, and "culturally sensitive forms of counseling." The programs' success, however, had a lot to do with the previous history of the ethnic groups involved. East European refugees were able to tap into well-established and extensive ethnic networks and thereby avoid public assistance much more easily than were Southeast Asians, whose communities did not have deep roots (Majka and Mullan 2002).

Conclusions

Since at least the mid-nineteenth century, mutual aid societies and fraternal orders have played a central role in immigrant life as providers of vital material benefits, recreational activities, and a venue for formal and informal socializing. They have expressed their members' most particular identities as natives of a particular region or town, and as believers in a particular religious or political creed. But they have also helped to construct larger ethnic communities that transcended those minute divisions. While they have consciously promoted ethnic cultures and maintained ties with the members' countries of origin, they have also helped their members to adjust to American conditions and their ethnic groups to exert influence in the larger society. The fact that most societies from a wide variety of ethnic groups have shared the same basic structure and mode of operation points toward their American origin and inspiration. But, each immigrant group has suffused its societies with its particular sensibility, so that if one were to walk into a lodge room on meeting night there would be little doubt to which ethnicity those present belonged.

Cultural styles and material needs change. The societies formed by immigrants in the nineteenth and early twentieth centuries adopted the organizational culture of the fraternal lodge so prevalent in the general society at the time. Their benefits were fitted to the needs of workers of the industrial age, at a time when other sources of social security were few. Immigrants in the late twentieth and early twenty-first centuries looked to different models and had different material needs. Their societies were much more likely to help them negotiate state and private bureaucracies. Nevertheless, much remained the same. Immigrants banded together in societies to help one another find a place for themselves in their new home even as they continued to remember the old.

REFERENCES

Alexander, June Granatir (1987). *The Immigrant Church and Community: Pittsburgh's Slovak Catholics and Lutherans, 1880–1915*. Pittsburgh: University of Pittsburgh Press.

Barton, Josef (1975). *Peasants and Strangers: Italians, Rumanians, and Slovaks in an American City, 1890–1950*. Cambridge, MA: Harvard University Press.

Beito, David (2000). *From Mutual Aid to the Welfare State: Fraternal Societies and Social Services, 1890–1967*. Chapel Hill: University of North Carolina Press.

Bodnar, John (1981). "Ethnic Fraternal Benefit Associations: Their Historical Development, Character, and Significance." In *Records of Ethnic Fraternal Benevolent Associations in the United States: Essays and Inventories*. St. Paul, MN: Immigration History Research Center, pp. 5–14.

—— (1985). *The Transplanted: A History of Immigrants in Urban America*. Bloomington: Indiana University Press.

Briggs, John (1978). *An Italian Passage: Immigrants in Three American Cities*. New Haven, CT: Yale University Press.

Bukowczyk, John J. (1987). *And My Children Did Not Know Me: A History of Polish Americans*. Bloomington: University of Indiana Press.

Cinel, Dino (1981). "Between Change and Continuity: Regionalism among Immigrants from the Italian Northwest." *Journal of Ethnic Studies* 9: 19–36.

Emmons, David (1989). *The Butte Irish: Class and Ethnicity in an American Mining Town, 1875–1925*. Urbana: University of Illinois Press.

Greenbaum, Susan (1991). "A Comparison of African-American and Euro-American Mutual Aid Societies in 19th Century America." *Journal of Ethnic Studies* 19 (Fall): 95–119.

—— (1993). "Economic Cooperation among Urban Industrial Workers: Rationality and Community in an Afro-Cuban Mutual Aid Society, 1904–1927." *Social Science History* 17 (Summer): 173–93.

Handlin, Oscar (1951). *The Uprooted: The Epic Story of the Great Migrations that Made the American People*. Boston: Little, Brown.

Hernandez, Jose Amaro (1983). *Mutual Aid for Survival: The Case of the Mexican American*. Malabar, FL: Robert Krieger.

Kasinitz, Philip (1992). *Caribbean New York: Black Immigrants and the Politics of Race*. Ithaca, NY: Cornell University Press.

Kauffman, Christopher (1982). *Faith and Fraternalism: The History of the Knights of Columbus, 1882–1982*. New York: Harper & Row.

Kuropas, Myron B. (1996). *Ukrainian-American Citadel: The First One Hundred Years of the Ukrainian National Association*. Boulder, CO: East European Monographs.

Lai, Him Mark (1996). "Chinese Organizations in America Based on Locality of Origin and/or Dialect-Group Affiliation, 1940s–1990s." *Chinese America: History and Perspectives*, Vol. II, San Francisco: Chinese Historical Society of America, 1996, pp. 19–92.

Light, Ivan (1972). *Ethnic Enterprise in America: Business and Welfare among Chinese, Japanese, and Blacks*. Berkeley: University of California Press.

Lyman, Stanford (1986). *Chinatown and Little Tokyo: Power, Conflict, and Community among Chinese and Japanese Immigrants*. Millwood, NY: Associated Faculty Press.

Ma, L. Eve Armentrout (1991). "Chinatown Organizations and the Anti-Chinese Movement, 1882–1914." In *Entry Denied: Exclusion and the Chinese Community in America, 1882–1943*. Philadelphia: Temple University Press, pp. 147–69.

McCune, Mary (2002). "Creating a Place for Women in a Socialist Brotherhood: Class and Gender Politics in the Workmen's Circle." *Feminist Studies* 28 (Fall): 585–685.

Majka, Lorraine and Brendan Mullan (2002). "Ethnic Communities and Ethnic Organizations Reconsidered: South-East Asians and Eastern Europeans in Chicago." *International Migration* 40: 71–92.

Mormino, Gary and George Pozzetta (1987). *The Immigrant World of Ybor City: Italians and Their Latin Neighbors in Tampa, 1885–1985*. Urbana: University of Illinois Press.

Nelli, Humbert (1970). *Italians in Chicago, 1880–1930: A Study in Ethnic Mobility*. New York: Oxford University Press.

Pienkos, Donald (1990). *A Centennial History of the Polish National Alliance of the United States of North America*. New York: Columbia University Press.

Puskas, Julianna (1996). "The Historical Model of a Hungarian Fraternal Association in the United States from the 1880s to the 1990s." In Matjaz Klemenčič, ed., *Ethnic Fraternalism in Immigrant Countries*. Maribor, Slovenia: University of Maribor, pp. 171–83.

Smith, Judith (1985). *Family Connections: A History of Italian and Jewish Immigrant Lives in Providence, Rhode Island, 1900–1940*. Albany, NY: State University of New York Press.

Soyer, Daniel (1997). *Jewish Immigrant Associations and American Identity in New York, 1880–1939*. Cambridge, MA: Harvard University Press.

Stolarik, M. Mark (1980). "A Place for Everyone: Slovak Fraternal-Benefit Societies." In Scott Cummings, ed., *Self-Help in Urban America: Patterns of Minority Business Enterprise*. Port Washington, NY: Kennikat Press.

—— (1996). "Slovak Fraternal-Benefit Societies in North America: An Overview (1883–1993)." In Matjaz Klemenčič, ed., *Ethnic Fraternalism in Immigrant Countries*. Maribor, Slovenia: University of Maribor, pp. 148–59.

Sulič, Nives (1996). "A Home Away from Home: Brothers in Distress." In Matjaz Klemenčič, ed., *Ethnic Fraternalism in Immigrant Countries*. Maribor, Slovenia: University of Maribor, pp. 45–52.

Taylor, Paul (1970; 1928). *Mexican Labor in the United States, 1928–1934* (reprint). New York: Arno.

Index

CPSIA information can be obtained
at www.ICGtesting.com
Printed in the USA
FSHW01n1532310818
51805FS